The Law of the Baltic States

Tanel Kerikmäe • Kristi Joamets
Jānis Pleps • Anita Rodiņa
Tomas Berkmanas • Edita Gruodytė
Editors

The Law of the Baltic States

Springer

Editors
Tanel Kerikmäe
Tallinn Law School
Tallinn University of Technology
Tallinn, Estonia

Kristi Joamets
Tallinn Law School
Tallinn University of Technology
Tallinn, Estonia

Jānis Pleps
Faculty of Law
University of Latvia
Riga, Latvia

Anita Rodiņa
Faculty of Law
University of Latvia
Riga, Latvia

Tomas Berkmanas
Law Faculty
Vytautas Magnus University
Kaunas, Lithuania

Edita Gruodytė
Law Faculty
Vytautas Magnus University
Kaunas, Lithuania

ISBN 978-3-319-54477-9 ISBN 978-3-319-54478-6 (eBook)
DOI 10.1007/978-3-319-54478-6

Library of Congress Control Number: 2017934084

Printed on acid-free paper

This Springer imprint is published by Springer Nature
The registered company is Springer International Publishing AG
The registered company address is: Gewerbestrasse 11, 6330 Cham, Switzerland

Preface

The current volume is a unique accomplishment from several aspects. To begin with, it is the first international collaboration project of Estonian, Lithuanian and Latvian legal scholars that provides comprehensive analytical overviews of the legal systems in the three countries. Moreover, it is a significant milestone marking the era of already mature states and their legal societies containing descriptions of historical development and explaining the achievements and challenges of lawmaking—it is a development story of states that are all having different languages but are sharing a lot in their political, economic and legal dynamics.

Baltic states cannot be crucial global players alone, taking into account their population (all together slightly over six million), but they can be a louder voice in international decision-making process as members of the European Union (EU) (all states joined 2004) and other international alliances. The trust of their own citizens and foreign partners, the key for better establishment and stability of all three relatively small states, is the rule of law as the main ground for statehood. This is also a primary soul of the project—the editors believe that there is a need for a systematic overview of legal systems in the Baltic region that has never been offered with sufficient depth.

We can assure that the text recites the perceptions of experienced and learned specialists in the field. This voluminous book is not only instructing a reader on domestic legal pecularities but gives also a solid discourse on the positioning of these legal orders to the international and EU legal space. Although the authors are all active in academic sphere, many of them are also related to legal practice both in the public and private sectors, which makes the text simultaneously theoretical and practice oriented, referring to the problematics and details that can be derived only from real life. It is also a doctrinal statement—the leading authors cannot avoid their own understandings and approaches that are, in the end, framing the main concept of the book. This compilation not only is based on legal text but also is using broader perspective in explaining the legal policies, guiding authorities in making crucial choices, tailoring the methodologies and intepretation approaches.

We hope that this excellent project is only a first stage in our joint cooperation. The process of writing and editing introduced relevant experts in the field to each other. Already during the drafting of the chapters, several authors from different countries had passionate discussions on how to structure and frame certain branches of law, how much to use extra-legal sources, etc. These conversations become a fertile soil for further, more specific joint ventures between legal scholars. The book is a collective effort of Baltic legal scholars to present an adequate scene of legal reality with the assumptions of further developments as the law and legal systems, accordingly, are living and constantly changing.

The thrust of the book is that we have to see a holistic picture of the whole legal system to be able to analyse a specific part of it. The volume is also carrying the role of comparing the three states with the purpose of learning from each other and finding the ways of using the best practices in the Baltic region. The book makes reasonable use of relevant legal materials to allow the reader to become familiar with the essential elements of the legislation. The most difficult for the authors, patriots of their legal field, was certainly to be limited with the pages and establish a structure focusing mainly on the core elements of the particular regulation area.

The parts of this book are divided by countries involved; however, the length and priorities vary by legal systems. Estonia is stressing its capacity and perspectives as an e-governed society; Latvia points out particularities of building up a modern legal system based on the rule of law, which roots to the constitution passed in 1922 and renewed in full amount after the restoration of independence in 1993; and Lithuania, starting from its rich legal tradition dating back to the three monumental Statutes of the Grand Dutchy, proceeds with the representation of the dynamic and fourth industrial-revolution-ready Lithuanian Rechtsstaat.

Tallinn, Estonia Tanel Kerikmäe

Contents

Contributors

Paulius Astromskis Faculty of Law, Vytautas Magnus University, Kaunas, Lithuania

Viliušis & Astromskis Law Firm, Kaunas, Lithuania

Māris Badovskis Labour Relations and Labour Protection Policy Department, Ministry of Welfare, Riga, Latvia

Marius Bartninkas Faculty of Law, Vytautas Magnus University, Kaunas, Lithuania

Kėdainiai District Court of the Republic of Lithuania, Kaunas, Lithuania

Tomas Berkmanas Faculty of Law, Vytautas Magnus University, Kaunas, Lithuania

Mindaugas Bilius Faculty of Law, Vytautas Magnus University, Kaunas, Lithuania

Jautrīte Briede Law Faculty, University of Latvia, Riga, Latvia

Arnis Buka Faculty of Law, University of Latvia, Riga, Latvia

Paulius Čerka Čerka & Partneriai Advocates Bureau, Kaunas, Lithuania

Linda Damane Faculty of Law, University of Latvia, Riga, Latvia

Edvīns Danovskis Law Faculty, University of Latvia, Riga, Latvia

Tomas Davulis Faculty of Law, Vilnius University, Vilnius, Lithuania

Kristīne Dupate Law Faculty, University of Latvia, Riga, Latvia

Tatjana Evas Tallinn Law School, Tallinn University of Technology, Tallinn, Estonia

Jurgita Grigienė Faculty of Law, Vytautas Magnus University, Kaunas, Lithuania

Čerka & Partneriai Advocates Bureau, Kaunas, Lithuania

Edgar Grünberg Tartu Notary, Tartu, Estonia

Edita Gruodytė Faculty of Law, Vytautas Magnus University, Kaunas, Lithuania

Marek Herm Tallinn Law School, Tallinn University of Technology, Tallinn, Estonia

Law Firm ATTELA, Tallinn, Estonia

Thomas Hoffmann Tallinn Law School, Tallinn University of Technology, Tallinn, Estonia

Kristi Joamets Tallinn Law School, Tallinn University of Technology, Tallinn, Estonia

Marius Jonaitis Faculty of Law, Vytautas Magnus University, Kaunas, Lithuania

Faculty of Law, Mykolas Romeris University, Vilnius, Lithuania

Marko Kairjak Faculty of Law, University of Tartu, Tartu, Estonia

Estonian Business School, Tallinn, Estonia

Aušra Kargaudienė Faculty of Law, Vytautas Magnus University, Kaunas, Lithuania

Law Firm "Miškinis & partners", Vilnius, Lithuania

Annija Kārkliņa Law Faculty, University of Latvia, Riga, Latvia

Jānis Kārkliņš Faculty of Law, University of Latvia, Riga, Latvia

Tanel Kerikmäe Tallinn Law School, Tallinn University of Technology, Tallinn, Estonia

Kārlis Ketners BA School for Business and Finance, Riga, Latvia

Julija Kiršienė Faculty of Law, Vytautas Magnus University, Kaunas, Lithuania

Helen Kranich Law Enforcement Affairs Department of the Chancellor of Justice, Tallinn, Estonia

Irēna Kucina Faculty of Law, University of Latvia, Riga, Latvia

Kaido Künnapas Tallinn Law School, Tallinn University of Technology, Tallinn, Estonia

Law Firm Sorainen, Advokaadibüroo Sorainen AS, Tallinn, Estonia

Rene Lauk Tallinn Law School, Tallinn University of Technology, Tallinn, Estonia

Jānis Lazdiņš Faculty of Law, University of Latvia, Riga, Latvia

Inese Lībiņa-Egner Faculty of Law, University of Latvia, Riga, Latvia

Valentija Liholaja Law Faculty, University of Latvia, Riga, Latvia

Ramon Loik Estonian Academy of Security Sciences, Tallinn, Estonia

University of Tartu, Tartu, Estonia

Johan Skytte Institute of Political Studies, University of Tartu, Tartu, Estonia

Vadims Mantrovs Faculty of Law, University of Latvia, Riga, Latvia

Maret Maripuu Labour Inspectorate, Tallinn, Estonia

Linas Meškys Faculty of Law, Vytautas Magnus University, Kaunas, Lithuania

KMM Law Firm, Kaunas, Lithuania

Monika Mikiver Law Enforcement Affairs Department of the Chancellor of Justice, Tallinn, Estonia

Saulė Milčiuvienė Faculty of Law, Vytautas Magnus University, Kaunas, Lithuania

Katrin Nyman-Metcalf Tallinn Law School, Tallinn University of Technology, Tallinn, Estonia

Daina Ose Faculty of Law, University of Latvia, Riga, Latvia

Martins Osis Faculty of Law, University of Latvia, Riga, Latvia

Priidu Pärna Faculty of Law, University of Tartu, Tartu, Estonia

Tallinn Notary Priidu Pärna, Tallinn, Estonia

Aušrinė Pasvenskienė Faculty of Law, Vytautas Magnus University, Kaunas, Lithuania

Margus Poola Tallinn Law School, Tallinn University of Technology, Tallinn, Estonia

Aleksandr Popov Tallinn Law School, Tallinn University of Technology, Tallinn, Estonia

Birutė Pranevičienė Faculty of Public Security, Mykolas Romeris University, Kaunas, Lithuania

Dainius Raižys Faculty of Law, Vytautas Magnus University, Kaunas, Lithuania

Supreme Administrative Court of the Republic of Lithuania, Kaunas, Lithuania

Evaldas Rapolas Faculty of Law, Vytautas Magnus University, Kaunas, Lithuania

Magnusson Law Firm, Kaunas, Lithuania

Daiga Rezevska Faculty of Law, University of Latvia, Riga, Latvia

Anita Rodiņa Law Faculty, University of Latvia, Riga, Latvia

Lehte Roots Tallinn Law School, Tallinn University of Technology, Tallinn, Estonia

Jānis Rozenfelds Faculty of Law, University of Latvia, Riga, Latvia

Addi Rull Tallinn Law School, Tallinn University of Technology, Tallinn, Estonia

Sandra Särav Tallinn Law School, Tallinn University of Technology, Tallinn, Estonia

Siuzana Ščerbina-Dalibagienė Faculty of Law, Vytautas Magnus University, Kaunas, Lithuania

Ministry of Finance of the Republic of Lithuania, Kaunas, Lithuania

Stasys Šedbaras Lithuanian Parliament (Seimas), Vilnius, Lithuania

Jurgita Spaičienė Faculty of Law, Vytautas Magnus University, Kaunas, Lithuania

Jurgita Spaičienė Advocates Bureau, Kaunas, Lithuania

Kristīne Strada-Rozenberga Law Faculty, University of Latvia, Riga, Latvia

Dmitri Teplõhh Tallinn Law School, Tallinn University of Technology, Tallinn, Estonia

Faculty of Law, University of Tartu, Tartu, Estonia

Kalvis Torgāns Faculty of Law, University of Latvia, Riga, Latvia

Violeta Vasiliauskienė Faculty of Public Security, Mykolas Romeris University, Kaunas, Lithuania

Tomas Veršinskas Faculty of Law, Vytautas Magnus University, Kaunas, Lithuania

Vigintas Višinskis Faculty of Law, Mykolas Romeris University, Vilnius, Lithuania

Court of Appeal of Lithuania, Vilnius, Lithuania

Kristīne Zīle Faculty of Law, University of Latvia, Riga, Latvia

Evelina Žurauskaitė Faculty of Law, Vytautas Magnus University, Kaunas, Lithuania

List of Abbreviations

AFSJ	Area of freedom, security and justice
AL	Trade Union Law
APA	Administrative Procedure Act
ASC	Appeals Selection Committee
BGB	Bürgerliches Gesetzbuch/German Civil Code
BPLC	Baltic Private Law Code
B2B	Business to business
CA	Commercial association
CAA	Constitutional Amendment Act
CC	Commercial Code
CCP	Code of Civil Procedure
Ch	Chapter
CCM	Civil crisis management
CCP	Code of Civil Procedure
CEPOL	European Police College
CFC	Controlled foreign company
CISG	Convention on Contracts for the International Sale of Goods
CIT	Estonian Corporate Income Tax
CJ	Chancellor of Justice
CL	Civil Law
Const	Estonian Constitution
CPL	Civil Procedure Law
CSDP	Common Security and Defence Policy
DAL	Work Safety Law
DCFR	Draft Common Frame of Reference
DL	Labour Law
DDOAL	Employer's Organizations and Their Associations Law
DSL	Labour Disputes Law
EC	European Commission
ECA	Employment Contracts Act
ECHR	European Court of Human Rights
EConvHR	Convention for the Protection of Human Rights and Fundamental Freedoms

EDF	Estonian Defence Forces
EJN	European Judicial Network
ESM	European Stability Mechanism
ESSR	Estonian Soviet Socialist Republic
EU	European Union
GP	General partnership
GPCCA	The General Part of the Civil Code Act
HNS	Host nation support
ICT	Information and communications technology
ID	Identification
IKL	Law on Informing and Consulting Employees of European Community Scale Undertakings and European Community Scale Groups of Undertakings
IT	Information technology
ITA	Income Tax Act
JHA	Justice and Home Affairs
KCL	Commercial Law
KL	Criminal Law
KPL	Criminal Procedure Law
LOA	Law of Obligations Act
LP	Limited partnership
LPA	Law of Property Act
LV	Official gazette 'Latvian Herald'
MoD	Ministry of Defence
NATO	North-Atlantic Treaty Organization
NBC	Nuclear, biological, chemical
NLMB	National Labour Market Board
OwiG	Gesetz über Ordnungswidrigkeiten/German Administrative Offences Act
PE	Permanent establishment
PECL	Principles of European Civil Law
PETL	Principles of European Tort Law
PICC	Principles of International Commercial Contracts
PNR	Passenger name record
Private LC	Private limited company
Public LC	Public limited company
SC	Supreme Court
SFSR	Soviet Federative Socialist Republic
SISG	Convention on Contracts for the International Sale of Goods
SL	Strike Law
SLA	Succession Law Act
SP	Sole proprietor
SSR	Soviet Socialist Republic
TFEU	Treaty on the Functioning of the European Union
UIF	Unemployment Insurance Fund

UN	United Nations
USSR	Union of Soviet Socialist Republic
VAT	Value Added Tax
VCLK	Codification of Local Laws
VIS	Visa Information System
WEU	Western European Union
WWII	World War 2

Part I

Estonian Law

General Frameworks

1

Tatjana Evas, Thomas Hoffmann, Kristi Joamets, Tanel Kerikmäe, Ramon Loik, Katrin Nyman-Metcalf, Aleksandr Popov, and Sandra Särav

Abstract

The current chapter gives a general overview of Estonian legal system by its historical development, describing the most relevant periods of the ancient Estonian legal society, influences to the local law by the foreign powers and the contemporary impact and position of EU and international law to the current Estonian legal system, and its judicial system. The legal policy of implementation and interpretation of international and supranational law have been explained through the approaches derived from evolving constitutional legal traditions. Estonia is famous for its e-governance and so-called e-law, which is often presented as characteristics of Estonian legal society where the most of the public services offered and used on-line. As the law of e-Governance is not framed as one branch of law, the chapter focuses on e-identity, data protection, ICT law and other relevant legal regulation fields and issues. The last part of the chapter is dedicated to the legal regulation of state security as a part of a legal system. In recent years Estonia has promoted the enhanced international cooperation in state security and the last section provides corresponding overview of the international and EU level legal instruments and their application in Estonia.

T. Evas • T. Hoffmann • K. Joamets • T. Kerikmäe (✉) • K. Nyman-Metcalf • A. Popov • S. Särav
Tallinn Law School, Tallinn University of Technology, Akadeemia tee 3, 12618 Tallinn, Estonia
e-mail: tatjana.evas@ttu.ee; thomas.hoffmann@ttu.ee; kristi.joamets@ttu.ee; tanel.kerikmae@ttu.ee; katrin.nyman@ttu.ee; aleksandr.popov@ttu.ee; sandra.sarav@ttu.ee

R. Loik
Estonian Academy of Security Sciences, Kase 61, 12012 Tallinn, Estonia

University of Tartu, Ülikooli 18, Tartu, Estonia
e-mail: ramon.loik@sisekaitse.ee; ramon.loik@ut.ee

T. Kerikmäe et al. (eds.), *The Law of the Baltic States*,
DOI 10.1007/978-3-319-54478-6_1

1.1 The Historical Development

Tanel Kerikmäe, Thomas Hoffmann, and Sandra Särav
Tallinn Law School, Tallinn University of Technology, Akadeemia tee 3, 12618 Tallinn, Estonia
e-mail: tanel.kerikmae@ttu.ee; thomas.hoffmann@ttu.ee; sandra.sarav@ttu.ee

1.1.1 Ancient Estonia

The first reference to Estonians belongs to Greek authors Hekateus (V–IV century B.C.) and Herodotos (IV century B.C.)[1]. However, these sources are not informative about legal norms but rather describing the administrative system of the nation. *Chronicon Henrici Livoniae*[2] (XIII century) describes well the surrender process of Estonians but also the capacities and jurisdictions of the local governments. It is relevant to mention that the counties, consisting the smaller units (*kihlakond*), were created according to the treaties (*conioratio*). Every county had a decision making body (*käräjä*) and execution power (council of elders) with defined competences. Most of the law existed in the form of customs, decision-making bodies had specific rules for trial. The evidences were often based on tryouts with fire or water but "divine truth" was also identified metaphysically by observing, for example, behaviour of animals, such as birds. Beside criminal law (where the talion principle was gradually replaced by redress ideology), private law was also developed and ancient Estonia recognised legal (administrative entities) and physical persons (except slaves who were objects not subjects of the rights). There are written sources about developed family law, ownership regulations, sales law and obligations law[3]. By Ilmar Arens, ancient Estonians clearly had a developed legal system, and the preserved folklore refers to the prioritising the justice in the society.[4]

[1]Uluots (1938), p. 33.
[2]Ibid, pp. 83–94.
[3]Ibid, pp. 93–105.
[4]Arens (1956), p. 32.

1.1.2 Estonian Law Until 1865

1.1.2.1 Early Period

Estonian history has many centuries been marked by foreign powers, in terms of law starting with the conquest of Livonia (and after 1346 also of the until then Danish-ruled Northern Estonian territories) by the German Order of the Brethren of the Sword (later joining the Teutonic order) in the early thirteenth century. The Order—just as German merchants and noblemen mainly from Westphalia and the Northern Rhine region settling soon after in the soon rapidly developing Hanseatic cities of Dorpat (Tartu), Reval (Tallinn), Pernau (Pärnu) and Narva—brought with them their local German laws, which were either based on/strongly influenced by Eike von Repgov's *Sachsenspiegel* (created between 1220 and 1235) or the City statutes of the respective home Hanseatic cities (mainly Bremen, Hamburg and Lübeck). They soon were transformed into regional versions, as e.g. the *Harrisch-Wierische Landrecht* or the City statutes of Dorpat or Reval. The entire Livonian confederation was until 1561 part of the Holy Roman Empire, represented with seats and votes on the Regensburg Everlasting Assembly (the *Immerwährender Reichstag*, the imperial parliament).

1.1.2.2 Changing Powers 1561–1710; The Early Russian Period

Being attacked by Moscow forces as early as the late 1550, the Livonian federation was unable to cope with the aggressors themselves and sought for help, which they found in the Polish Commonwealth (Rzeczpospolita), at that time reigned by King Sigismund the Great. Livonia thus subdued to Poland, while in terms of law the regional (German-law based) Livonian and Estonian law and legislation remained in force (a Polish-law influenced codification endeavour by David Hilchen in 1599 was never enacted)[5]. The Livonian/Estonian privileges (mainly rights for self-administration and proper jurisdiction) were confirmed[6] also during the subsequent Swedish period, just as well when the entire territory was ceded from Sweden to Russia in 1710[7] as a result of the Great Northern War, ultimately becoming the "Baltic Sea provinces".

This continuity—strongly stressed and supported by the German nobility which justified their privileges mainly by these sources—had the effect that until the 1860s basically medieval law (variations of the *Sachsenspiegel*, Hanseatic law, and various individual privileges as the *Privilegium Sigismundi*) formed the main body of law applicable in Estonia; as Luts-Sootak points out, Estonia was marked by "a conglomerate of legal sources of various origin and nature and the provisions contained therein".[8]

---

[5]For details see Hoffmann (2007).

[6]Schmidt (1894), p. 240.

[7]In fact, cession was formally performed only by the *Nystedt treaty of 1721*.

[8]Luts-Sootak (2000), p. 158.

1.1.3 The Baltic Private Law of 1865 and Other Codifications in the Nineteenth Century

Against this background, already in the early nineteenth century a thorough codification of the law applicable in Estonia, especially of its private law (parallel to discussions in Germany mainly initiated by Thibaut and Savigny) was claimed by various legal scholars and practitioners, among which Friedrich Georg von Bunge—professor for Baltic provincial law at the University of Tartu—soon became most influential. Bunge himself was considerably influenced by Savigny and his historical school, applying a clear pandectist approach to his work in both scholar and law-making matters.

As early as 1838, Bunge published one of the so far most comprehensive scholarly works in the field of law of the Baltic provinces, his *Liv- und esthländisches Privatrecht* (the Private Law of Livonia and Estonia). He soon presided a commission charged with drafting a comprehensive private law codification for the Baltic Sea provinces, which finally resulted in the *Baltisches Privatrecht*, the *Baltic private law code* (*BPLC*), entering into force upon confirmation of Emperor Alexander II on 1 January 1865.

Preparing this code, Bunge had collected within years of assiduous work all the particularities of the local law. Moreover, he managed to organise this mosaic of differences in an essentially satisfactory manner. By means of the table of contents and index, it was still possible to find a legal verdict from the casuistic BPLC.[9] This well-balanced amalgam of pandectist systematisation—at that period perfected in German jurisprudence –, local law and demands of practice made the *BPLC* a rather successful endeavour, which did not only survive the social and political upheavals of the early twentieth century, but remained in force even during the subsequent period of Estonian independence.

Public law found less intense codification initiatives; in contrast to private law, fields like administrative law, public security or criminal law were much stricter regulated directly by Russian legislation,[10] and Russian constitutional law would anyway directly apply in its provinces.

1.1.4 Transition Period After 1918

When Estonia gained independence from the corroding Russian empire in 1918, preparations for an Estonian civil code started as one of the major reform projects of the young Estonian State, which was in the field of private law lead by Jüri Uluots (the later Estonian prime minister). Estonia decided in favour of an update and simplification of the *BPLC* rather than for an entire new codification, and until 1927 "the relevant sections of the draft *Civil Code* were largely nothing but the

[9]Luts-Sootak (2000), pp. 157–167, p. 167.

[10]For details see Schmidt (1894), pp. 242–243.

translation of the *BPLC*"[11]. The preparations for this code took more than 15 years and finally resulted in the draft for an *Estonian Civil Code* consisting of five books which was presented to the public in 1939. Also being based on the *BPLC* in terms of structure and dogmatic approach, it was also directly influenced by several of the new major continental European private law codifications coming into force in the early twentieth century, among which the *German BGB*—which was a "dogmatic relative" of the *BPLC*—and the *Swiss civil code*[12] were of especial importance. But also further private law acts as the *Austrian Law of Obligations*, Scandinavian acts, the draft codes of Hungary, Czechoslovakia, and Poland had their impact on the genesis of the *Estonian Civil Code*[13]. The draft, anyway, could not be approved anymore by the Estonian parliament because Estonia was occupied by the Soviet Union in 1940.

1.1.5 Soviet Period (After 1940)

By June 1940, the Republic of Estonia had been newly independent for 20 years before it lost its *de facto* independence when it was occupied and annexed by the Russian Soviet Federative Socialist Republic (RSFSR) and subjected to the Soviet legal regime. Over the course of 3 months, the RSFSR gave the false impression that the laws of the Estonian state would continue to apply in the Estonian territory;[14] however, the sovietisation throughout the Baltics began with putting into effect[15] not only the Union of Soviet Socialist Republic (USSR or Soviet Union) monetary system, but also its penal, civil and litigation codes, and took full effect on the Estonian territory by the end of 1940. Amendments to such legal acts were made with the decision of the Estonian Presidium of the Supreme Soviet[16] and were made public to the wider audience in local newspapers, called the voice of the Executive Committees of the Soviets of Workers' Representatives', such as was at the time the still running newspaper "Postimees".[17]

To legalise the occupation and to indicate the lawfulness of the process, parliamentary elections were staged on 14–15 July 1940, and resulted in the election of the puppet parliament ("People's Parliament") loyal to the Soviet communist regime. Ignoring the still in force *Constitution of the Republic of Estonia*, the

[11]Luts-Sootak (2001), pp. 152–158, p. 157.

[12]Varul (2000), pp. 104–118.

[13]Kull (2008), pp. 122–129, p. 123.

[14]http://www.mnemosyne.ee/hc.ee/pdf/conclusions_en_1940-1941.pdf, p. XI.

[15]The term "put into effect" is the most accurate at this point because the states annexed by the USSR had no choice between legal order existing so far and the USSR legal regime.

[16]The Presidium was a Soviet governmental institution, a permanent body of the Supreme Soviets (parliaments) governing all the presidiums of the Soviet states.

[17]See for instance the 19 August 1945 Postimees, publishing an amendment to the *Civil Code*, http://dea.digar.ee/cgi-bin/dea?a=d&d=postimeesew19450819.2.5&l=en.

"People's Parliament", on 21 July 1940, then passed declarations according to which Estonia became a Soviet Socialist Republic (ESSR).[18] This, in return, resulted in the application for membership in the Soviet Union by the same puppet parliament, which was accepted by the Supreme Soviet of the Soviet Union on 6 August 1940, and incurred the constitutional regime to be applicable in Estonia. Therewith, the process of harmonisation of Estonian national laws with the Soviet legal regime began.[19] It has later been established that all the decision, and legal acts signed by the President during the occupation period were void as they were made under the violent pressure from the occupational powers.[20]

The formal membership in the USSR, entailed the passing of a new Constitution, approved by the Communist Party Politbureau in Moscow on 25 August 1940.[21] With that, the legal and political powers of the Republic of Estonia were completely abolished—the *ESSR Constitution* stated that outside of §14 of the *Soviet Constitution* (also known as the Stalin *Constitution*) ESSR exercises the state authority independently, fully preserving its sovereign rights.[22] However, §14 of the *Soviet Constitution* set forth the extensive limits of the Soviet Republics by granting the highest organs of state authority and organs of government of the Soviet Union jurisdiction in significant areas, including legislation on the judicial system and judicial procedure, criminal and civil codes.[23] Therefore, the *ESSR Constitution* stated that all the laws of the Soviet Union are binding also on the territory of ESSR.[24]

By the end of 1950s, the Republics of the USSR gained the right to create their "own" judicial systems that, however, had to be constructed based on the precept of the central government. Thus from 1960s–1970s, Soviet supranational and nationally created laws existed in parallel. In Estonia, all legal acts were available both in Estonian and Russian languages, and although the laws could only be created under specific set of rules set forth by Moscow, there were possibilities to exercise legislative discretion to certain extent. One such example is the *Estonian Criminal Code* that apparently had stood because of its legal-cultural quality level.[25]

The aforementioned regime in the three Baltic States, the Baltic SSRs, has been considered to be "puppet creations" given that the Soviet Union claimed the states not to have been annexed territories but represented the states as its constituent republics, autonomous bodies that had their own legal will.[26] This labelling rests on the non-recognition principle *ius ex iniuria non oritur* (a right does not arise from

[18]Declaration on the State Authority in Estonia, RT 1940, 733.

[19]Maruste (2004), p. 52.

[20]Sarv (1997), p. 61.

[21]Ibid.

[22]*ESSR Constitution* §13, 1940.

[23]*Soviet Constitution* §14(u), 1936.

[24]*ESSR Constitution* §17, 1940.

[25]Järvelaid (2002), Ch. 5: Reforms in Estonian legal system.

[26]Marek (1968), p. 396.

wrongdoing), supported by the Stimson theory[27], as invoked by the U.S. Undersecretary of State Sumner Welles's declaration, dating back to 23 July 1940, condemning the occupation and not *de jure* recognising the Soviet annexation until the regaining of independence of the Baltic States in 1991.[28]

Therefore, the Estonian Soviet Socialist Republic was formally a sovereign state, which, like the two other Baltic States annexed by the USSR, had *de facto* no independence under the Soviet regime. The second president (first after the regaining of independence), Lennart Meri, has stated that "The people of Estonia drew their faith in the uninterrupted continuity of their State from the underlying principles of international law," praising the non-recognition policy as basis for inspiration for struggling for the re-independence and offering the possibility to "restore the Republic of Estonia on the basis of legal continuity."[29] In 1988, the Estonian Supreme Soviet issued a declaration for independence[30], asserting the sovereignty of the Republic of Estonia and emphasised the primacy of Estonian laws over those imposed by the USSR.[31] Given document clearly stemmed from the presumption that the Republic of Estonia has been continuous subject of international law.[32] Indeed, on 20 August 1991, by the decision of the Supreme Council of the Republic of Estonia, that can be called a pre-constitutional act, the country was declared independent based on the continuity of Estonian status as a subject of international law and announced the restoration of the Republic of Estonia (*restitutio ad integrum*[33]), leading to a transition period that included drafting a new constitution for the Republic—Estonian Constitution (*Const*).[34]

1.1.6 Reforms After the Restoration of Independence in 1991

After regaining the independence, the USSR Constitution became obliterated; the 1937 Constitution was *de jure* still valid but could not be applied in a proper way.[35] One of the most important aspects of political and cultural development of a former USSR state like Estonian is to overcome the Soviet heritage by developing a

---

[27]Grant (2001), pp. 23–110.

[28]Statement by the Acting Secretary of State, the Honorable Sumner Welles. 23 July 1940. No. 354. See the copy: http://photos.state.gov/libraries/lithuania/331079/balciunasa/sumner-welles_1_500.jpg.

[29]Meri (2001) the former President of the Republic of Estonia.

[30]*Declaration on the Sovereignty of the Estonian SSR.*

[31]Walker (2003), p. 63.

[32]Mälksoo (2005a), p. 70.

[33]*Restitutio ad integrum* also resulted in the fact that the Republic of Estonia was not seen as a successor state of the Soviet Union and hence does not carry responsibility for rights and obligations of the USSR. See Salulaid (2001).

[34]*About Estonian national sovereignty (Eesti riiklikust iseseisvusest).* Decision of the Supreme Council on 20 August 1991. RT 1991, 25, 312.

[35]Hallaste (1996), p. 438.

national, independent legal system. A former minister of justice, acting lawyer and professor of law in Estonia has stated that: “A precondition for the survival and functioning of an independent state is the existence of an effective legal system.”[36] After 20 August 1991, Estonia was facing a transition period—the Soviet legal system was still in force, but because of the change in political regime, including change in state administration and economic principles, e.g. the question of land ownership, lack of competition regulation, etc., it could no longer be applied.[37] To exemplify, in the ESSR, the concept of a legal person did not exist, hence commercial relations were regulated in accordance with public-law-like rules, transactions between natural persons covered only objects of personal and family use; by the same token, there was no real property as all land belonged to the state.[38]

ESSR Super Soviet, therefore, when announcing *restitution ad integrum* on 30 March 1990, had declared the Soviet state powers unlawful and thus was ready to adopt a new *Const* for the Republic of Estonia. The new *Const* was adopted based on §1 of the *Const* which entered into force in 1938, and by a referendum held on 28 June 1992.[39] Herewith, the cornerstone for the new legal system of the Republic of Estonia was set, and with the adoption of the *Const*, the Implementation Act laid down that with its entry, the legal acts in force at the time of the adoption of the *Const* continue to have validity only if they are not in conflict with the *Const.*[40]

What concerns the private law, the need for a comprehensive modern civil code, was recognised. Thus, the reform of private law started already in the early 1990 as it was seen that the draft statutes dating back to the previous republic period could not have catered to the needs of the new republic.[41] *The Baltic Private Law Code* valid during the first independence could not be re-enforced, and hence the *ESSR 1965 Civil Code*[42] remained in force until new civil law was being gradually adopted on an act by act basis.[43] Because of the different legal regime, the old laws could not be followed, especially for example in the field of contract law and non-contractual obligations as regulated by the *Soviet Civil Code* from 1965.[44] Inspiration for reform in the area was thus drawn not only from Germany, but also Switzerland and the Netherlands.[45]

[36]Varul (2000), p. 104.
[37]Ibid.
[38]Kull (2008), p. 126.
[39]RT 1992, 26, 349.
[40]RT 1992, 26, 350.
[41]Kull (2008), p. 126.
[42]*ESSR Civil Code*. RT 1964, 25, 115.
[43]Käerdi (2001).
[44]Kull (2008), p. 126.
[45]Järvelaid (2002), Ch 5: Reforms in Estonian legal systems.

According to Varul, the drafting of the new private law can be divided into three conditional periods:

1. 1988–1991: preparatory period for the creation of Estonia's own legal system. The goal toward restoration of an independent state and law was set but restrictions had to be considered because of the fact that Estonia was still a Soviet Republic.
2. 1992–1993: period of decisions and choices. This was the most important period in choosing the private law system and model—legal policy decisions could be taken independently without potential interference by Moscow. The main choices were made in this period. The passing of the *Law of Property Act* and its entry into force on 1 December 1993 was the cornerstone.
3. 1994–2000: this is a period of implementation of earlier decisions and choices, during which the majority of private law legislation was drafted and passed.[46]

The profoundly outdated *ESSR Soviet Civil Code* remained in force until 2002 when the new *Law of Obligations Act* came into force, finalising the Estonian private law reform.[47] Nevertheless, the effect of the Soviet legal regime in the Republic of Estonia did not come to a halt until the legal draft proposal by the Ministry of Justice in 2013, to repeal the *ESSR Civil Code* in full. With the act of 26 March 2014, the *Estonian SSR Civil Code* and 50 others laws were declared invalid and as a result no laws of previous state authorities are applicable in the Republic of Estonia.

It has been claimed, "In speaking about the influences from the recent past, we should recognise that the main purpose of the reform was to make a break from the past and build a new legal system, one based on principles common to all European countries and legal systems."[48] The reforms of Estonian private law after regaining its independence have been called as revolutionary.[49] The changes in the legal environment, leaving behind the Soviet regime and taking the German legal system as a model, changed the civil law to become more modern, democratic and inverted the role of law and justice in Estonian legal space. For the first time in Estonian legal history, the country could codify its private law, free from absolutistic codification that, instead of empowering private autonomy, would contribute to endowing the state to exercise control in the areas which modern private law leaves for the free and equal subjects of law to shape.[50] There have been several major codification and restructuring stages in the field of criminal law, private law after regaining the independence. The major shift in legal society has been related to the accession to EU. Also the era of digitalisation imposes new legal questions and dilemmas on e-governance, e-citizenship and e-democracy.

[46] Varul (2000), pp. 104–118.

[47] *Law of Obligations Act*. RT I 2001, 81, 487.

[48] Kull (2008), p. 126.

[49] Ibid.

[50] Luts (2003), pp. 261–270.

1.2 The Structure of Judicial System

Kristi Joamets
Tallinn Law School, Tallinn University of Technology, Akadeemia tee 3, 12618 Tallinn, Estonia
e-mail: kristi.joamets@ttu.ee

On 24 February 1918 "The Manifesto to all Peoples of Estonia"[51] stated that: "All citizens of the Republic of Estonia irrespective of their religion, nationality and political views, shall enjoy equal protection before the laws and the court of the Republic" and required that the Provisional Government immediately sets up courts for the protection of security of the citizens. Although court system has been a part of Estonian legal system since the ancient times, a new era of so-called contemporary court system has been counted since 1918. Already in November 1918 was the first legal regulation of the Estonian courts passed[52]. The court system then had three instances but it had four links. The justices of the peace or the magistrates constituted first link of the court system. The appellation instances of the justices of the peace were the Commissions of the peace, later known as circuit courts. The third link was the national Court of Appeal—the *Kohtupalat*, later the *Kohtukoda*. The Supreme Court (SC) formed the fourth link. A peculiarity of the whole system was that all courts functioned as courts of first instance in regard to certain cases. In the summer of 1940 the power to appoint and release judges was taken from the President of the Republic and vested in the Council of People's Commissars. The new government actively started to release from office and arrest judges. On 16 November 1940 the Presidium of the Provisional Supreme Council of the Estonian SSR passed a decree on reorganisation of the judicial system[53]. In 1940 and 1941 the judges of lower instance courts were relocated, some were released from office forever. The magistrates and circuit courts were maintained. The SC of the Estonian SSR was formed based on the Court of Appeal; the SC of Estonia ceased to exist.[54]

On 16 May 1990 the Supreme Council of the Republic of Estonia adopted the *Principles of Temporary Procedure of Estonian Government Act,* putting an end to the subjection of the SC of Estonia to the SC of the USSR. The administration of justice on Estonian territory was separated from the judicial power of the USSR and given into the sole competence of Estonian courts.[55] In 1991 the *Republic of Estonia Courts Act*[56] and the *Status of Judges Act*[57] was passed providing a three-

[51]A document declaring the sovereignty of Estonia.

[52]See newspaper "Tallinna Teataja", no. 71, 23 Nov 1918, http://dea.digar.ee/cgi-bin/dea?a=d&d=tallinnateataja19181123.2.3.

[53]ENSV Teataja 1940 no 38.

[54]More specifically see http://www.nc.ee/?id=181.

[55]History of Estonian Court system http://www.nc.ee/?id=181.

[56]RT 1991, 38, 472.

[57]RT 1991, 38, 473.

level court system. The next important step was taken in the spring of 1992[58], when the Supreme Council passed a resolution on the judicial reform. According to the resolution the SC was to be re-established.

Pursuant to the *Const* Estonia has a three-level court system. On 2002[59] a new *Courts Act* was entered into force establishing the Council[60] for Administration of Courts. The aim of establishing the Council was to involve the judges of all court instances in making the decisions concerning the whole judicial system, as up to then it was only the Ministry of Justice who had governed the first and second court instances. On 2004 by acceding to the EU Estonian courts became the courts of the EU.

Estonian court system is often considered as one of the simplest in Europe and bases on shared responsibility model of judicial administration quite close to the German version[61]. System consists of three instances: county and administrative courts are the first instance courts; circuit courts are the courts of the second instance, and the SC is the third instance. SC functions as a court of cassation and a court of constitutional review. The formation of emergency courts is prohibited by the *Const.* The peculiarity of the system lies in the fact that the SC performs simultaneously the functions of the highest court of general jurisdiction, of the supreme administrative court as well as of the constitutional court.

County courts hear all civil, criminal and misdemeanour matters[62]. There are four county courts and they are divided into courthouses. In the composition of county courts are land registries, registry departments and probation supervision departments. Administrative courts[63] hear administrative matters i.e. complaints about the activities or inactivity of officials of the Estonian government and local governments, as well as other public disputes. There are two administrative courts in Estonia. Administrative courts are also divided into courthouses.

Circuit courts[64] are the courts of second instance. They review judgments of county and administrative courts based on appeals against judgments and rulings. A circuit court is divided into committees, which are specialised for different cases. At a meeting of a committee, at least three judges must participate in discussing appealed cases.

Although the *Const* provides for the possibility to create specialised courts[65] for the adjudication of matters relating to narrower fields of civil, criminal or

[58]On 28 June 1992 the *Const* was adopted.

[59]RT I 2002, 64, 390.

[60]The aim of establishing the Council was to involve the judges of all court instances in making the decisions concerning the whole judicial system, as up to then it was only the Ministry of Justice who had governed the first and second court instances.

[61]Ginter (2010), p. 111.

[62]*Courts Act* §9. RT I 2002, 64, 390.

[63]*Courts Act* §18. RT I 2002, 64, 390.

[64]There are two circuit courts in Estonia, in Tallinn and in Tartu. *Courts Act* §22. RT I 2002, 64, 390.

[65]§148.

administrative law, there can consider an administrative court as a specialised court. The creation of emergency courts[66] is prohibited.

The highest court is the SC, which reviews court decisions by way of cassation proceedings[67]. In addition to the latter function, the jurisdiction of the SC also includes the review of court decisions which have entered into force and the correction of court errors in court decisions which have entered into force[68]. At least three justices participate in the hearing of cases by way of cassation proceedings in the sessions of Chambers of the SC. Given the importance of the SC as the authority overseeing judicial practice in Estonia and ensuring the uniform application of law, the review of a case by the SC may require the participation of a greater number of justices to ensure harmony in the interpretation of legal acts by the SC. If fundamental differences of opinion arise in the Civil, Criminal or Administrative Law Chamber concerning the application of law, the matter shall be referred to the full panel of the respective Chamber for adjudication. If the full panel of the Civil, Criminal or Administrative Law Chamber offers an opinion different to the one expressed by another Chamber of the SC or Special Panel in its most recent judgement concerning the application of law, the panel shall refer the matter for hearing to a Special Panel consisting of members elected from two or three Chambers. The Special Panel shall contain two members from each Chamber which has a difference of opinion to be resolved by the Panel.[69]

Before a case is decided to approve for examination, a group of judges decides whether the action, protest or petition contains grounds for the grant of leave to appeal prescribed in legal acts concerning court procedure (incorrect application of a provision of substantive law or a material violation of a provision of court procedure by the circuit court) or not. The decision is prepared in writing as an unreasoned resolution. If at least one member of the group finds that the petition materials contain grounds for the grant of leave to appeal prescribed in legal acts concerning court procedure, leave to appeal is granted.[70]

Pursuant to the *Const* the SC is also the court of constitutional review. The composition of the SC includes the Constitutional Review Chamber[71]. The Constitutional Review Chamber of the SC consists of nine justices elected by the SC *en banc* for 5 years. Whereupon, members of the Chamber shall not be elected for longer than two terms of office. Estonian constitutional review system differs from the systems of other EU member state. Estonian system ensures the uniformity of

[66]Created for the adjudication of a certain specific case only.

[67]*Courts Act* §25. RT I 2002, 64, 390.

[68]*Courts Act* §26. RT I 2002, 64, 390.

[69]*Code of Civil Procedure* §18, 19 etc. RT I 2005, 26, 197; *Criminal Procedure Code* §20, Ch. 12 etc. RT I 2003, 27, 166; *Code of Administrative Court Procedure* §11, Ch. 20 etc. RT I, 23.02.2011, 3.

[70]Code of Civil Procedure §679; Criminal Procedure Code §349; Code of Administrative Court Procedure §219.

[71]*Courts Act* §29. RT I 2002, 64, 39.

judicial practice and excludes possible conflicts between the highest instance of the administrative and general court system and the constitutional court in the interpretation of law and the *Const*. This is because members of the Constitutional Review Chamber are, at the same time, members of other Chambers of the SC, a fact that ensures an integrated development of legal practice. The Estonian system also decreases the possibility of constitutional review becoming politicised: the instance of constitutional review belongs to the highest court of the state judicial system, the members thereof being appointed from among the justices by the highest court itself. One of the functions of constitutional review is to check that the decisions of the supreme political body of power in the state—the representative body of the people—are in compliance with the norms and principles established by the *Const*. Constitutional review in Estonia is therefore carried out both by way of *ex ante* review (the President of the Republic monitors legal acts which have not yet entered into force, the Chancellor of Justice monitors international agreements which have not yet entered into force) and *ex post* review (of acts and other legislation of general application which have already entered into force).

Pursuant to the *Const*, the SC has the right to declare invalid any legal act or other legislation, which is in conflict with the provisions or spirit of the *Const*.[72] The lower courts have no such right.

General principles of judicial proceedings are similar to other democratic states. Pursuant to the *Const*, everyone whose rights and freedoms are violated has the right of recourse to the courts and the right, while his or her case is before the court, to petition for any relevant legislation or procedure to be declared unconstitutional. The *Const* prohibits the transfer of a person, against his or her free will, from the jurisdiction of the court specified by law to the jurisdiction of another court. Everyone has the right to be tried in his or her presence and the right of appeal to a higher court against the judgment in his or her case pursuant to procedure provided by law. Court sessions are public. However, a court may, in certain cases and pursuant to procedure provided by law, declare that a session or a part thereof be held in camera, either to protect a state or business secret or the morals or private and family life of a person, or where the interests of a minor, a victim, or justice so require. Court judgments are made public unless the interests of a minor, a spouse or a victim require otherwise. No one has the duty to prove his or her innocence in criminal proceedings and no one shall be compelled to testify against himself or herself, or against those closest to him or her. Everyone is entitled to legal aid to protect his or her rights and freedoms at all stages of judicial proceedings. Suspects, accused and accused at trial shall be ensured the right of defence in criminal proceedings. Oral hearing of a case in a court session shall take place in a court of first instance. To ensure continuity in the hearing of a case, the case shall be heard by the same panel of a court from beginning to end; if a judge or a lay judge is replaced during the hearing of a case, that case shall be re-heard from the beginning. Judicial proceedings are conducted in Estonian, in another language

[72] *Const* §152.

only if the court and the persons concerned are proficient in the language. Persons concerned who do not understand the language of the judicial proceedings shall be ensured the right to examine the records of the case and participate in the judicial proceedings through an interpreter or translator.[73]

Despite the fact that courts are independent in their activities and administer justice in accordance with the *Const* and the laws, the administration of the courts in Estonia is not independent and separate from the executive power. The first and second instance courts are financed from the state budget through the budget of the Ministry of Justice[74]. Courts of the first instance and courts of appeal are administered in co-operation between the Ministry of Justice and the Council for Administration of Courts[75]. So far, Estonia does not have special state institution or administrative authority which would be responsible for the courts' administration as a whole. The SC, being an independent constitutional institution, administers itself and is financed directly from the state budget. The Chief Justice of the SC is appointed to office by the parliament (*Riigikogu*), on the proposal of the President of the Republic. Justices of the SC are appointed to office by the *Riigikogu*, on the proposal of the Chief Justice of the SC. Other judges are appointed to office by the President of the Republic, on the proposal of the SC.

Court procedure is one of the examples where digital procedure has been established to make it easier for a citizen to turn to the court and form the administrative part to save the costs of the court. It is possible to submit documents to court via e-mail (then the documents must be signed with digital signature, but there are some exceptions) or it is also possible to use web based portal—the "Public e-File". It is a portal which allows procedural parties and their representatives to electronically participate in proceedings of civil, administrative, criminal and misdemeanour cases. Also, it allows submitting digitally signed documents to the body conducting proceedings and monitoring the progress of the proceedings. Portal allows using pre-filled petitions for submission to courts; users can also supplement and amend unfinished petitions initiated by themselves. It is also possible to challenge decisions of bodies conducting proceedings and to file appeals on court judgements. The Public e-File is based on the e-File system which combines the information systems of the police, the Prosecutor's Office, the courts and other bodies conducting proceedings, ensuring central sharing of

---

[73]*Const* §§15–25.

[74]The Minister of Justice determines the territorial jurisdiction and location of courts of first instance and courts of appeal, as well as the total number of judges to be appointed to office at each of the above-mentioned courts, also appoints the chairmen of county and circuit courts with the approval of the Council for Administration of Courts.

[75]The Council for Administration of Courts is comprised of the Chief Justice of the SC, five judges elected by the Court *en banc* for 3 years, two members of the *Riigikogu*, a sworn advocate appointed by the Board of the Bar Association, the Chief Public Prosecutor or a public prosecutor appointed by him or her, the Legal Chancellor or a representative appointed by him or her, the Minister of Justice or a representative appointed by him or her shall participate in the Council with the right to speak.

proceedings information between parties and a quick and paperless data exchange. In the Public e-File, communication between parties takes place only via the x-road channel[76]. This ensures security of the data exchange. Digital developments are reflected also in the current development plans of Estonian court system[77]. Current developments in court system are mainly concerned with the economy of the procedure: fastening and simplifying the procedure, saving the time of the court officials, lessening the costs related to the procedure etc. This all means more trainings, more translators, better organisation of state legal aid, more secure databases, better connections to the Population Register and other registers to exchange the data, immediate translations of the adopted legal acts etc. Many of the tasks are related to the ICT and are not considerably difficult to perform.

1.3 The Impact and Position of International and EU Law

Tanel Kerikmäe, Tatjana Evas, and Aleksandr Popov
Tallinn Law School, Tallinn University of Technology, Akadeemia tee 3, 12618 Tallinn, Estonia
e-mail: tanel.kerikmae@ttu.ee; tatjana.evas@ttu.ee; aleksandr.popov@ttu.ee

1.3.1 Position of International Law in National Legal System

Estonian legal system is a monistic one. It views international legal obligations as the inseparable part of the national legal system,[78] therefore effectively creating the direct connection between *Const* of the state and states obligation to both people living on the territory of the state and other parties to international obligations binding on the state. In practical terms, monistic legal systems do not demand from the state to distinguish on the level of national legislation between the normative obligations created by the will of the sovereign—prohibition and approval of an action by the command of the state—and normative commands issued by the state because of its obligation under international law and therefore deriving not from will of the people expressed by the actions of the state but from the consensus reached between multiple sovereigns in regards to particular behavior. In accordance with the provisions of *Const*, for the purposes of the functioning of Estonian national legal system, all "general principles and norms of international law" are considered to be an inseparable part of the national legal system.[79]

[76]X-road is a secure data exchange infrastructure established and supported by the Republic of Estonia.

[77]See Development plan of the Ministry of Justice for the years 2015–2018, file:///C:/Users/Kristi/Downloads/justiitsministeeriumi_arengukava_aastateks_2015-2018.pdf.

[78]Ginsburg et al. (2008), p. 204.

[79]*Const* §3(1). RT 1992, 26, 349.

Authors of the Commentaries to the *Const* regard provisos of the §3 of the *Const* as giving a widespread acclaim to international law. In their opinion, *Const* does not only entail the treaty law of international community as giving rise to international obligations of the state and therefore becoming a constituent part of the national legal system. Any norm that can be because of its origins and nature constitute basis for international legal obligation is because of the constitutional provisions considered to be of a binding nature in the national legal order.[80] Sources of international law are enumerated e.g. in the Art. 38(1) of the *Statute of the International Court of Justice,* where it is stated that for the purposes of the functioning of the court, it will considered as sources of international law[81].

In accordance with the *Const*, any obligations that can be derived from the aforementioned sources becomes binding upon the state apparatus and people living on the territory of the state. Constitutional provision entail the easy access of people to the rights and obligations stemming from the international law and therefore leave the state with an obligation to consider its international agreements when modifying or amending its legislation. Supreme Court (SC) of the Republic of Estonia has found that states ought to follow the norms and customs of international law based on the fact of its supremacy to the national legal systems.[82] This decision created direct procedural linkage between the idea of the monistic incorporation of the norms and principles of international law and procedural regulations of national legal system. Furthermore, SC of the Republic of Estonia has found that seeking guidance in the "historically formed principles of laws" is one of the cornerstones for the legal systems of democratic nations.[83]

1.3.2 Treaties and National Legislation

In modern day and time, easiest way for determining whether or not the state is bound by any international legal obligation is to look at the amount for treaties that state has considered to enter in one way or another. For all practical purposes, treaties have become the driving force of international legal regimes and therefore constitute the majority of the consolidated textual expression of international legal obligation.[84]

[80] *Const* §3. Commentaries 2008.

[81]
1. international conventions, whether general or particular, establishing rules expressly recognized by the contesting states;
2. international custom, as evidence of a general practice accepted as law;
3. the general principles of law recognized by civilized nations;
4. judicial decisions and the teachings of the most highly qualified publicists of the various nations, as subsidiary means for the determination of rules of law.

[82] SC III-4/A-10/94.

[83] SC III-4/A-5/94.

[84] Baxter (1980), p. 549.

Birth of the Republic of Estonia itself has a direct connection to international treaty obligation. Estonian War of Independence with Soviet Russia was ended with the Tartu Peace Treaty on 2 February 1920. This treaty did not only end the bloody conflict between the two nations but is considered by both lawyers and historians to be the "birth certificate" of the Republic of Estonia and it is the first treaty in the history of international legal order to recognise secession as the exercise of the people's right to self determination.[85]

§123 of the *Const* specifies that state has no authorisation to enter into treaty obligations that are not in accordance with the constitutional provisions.[86] This part of the *Const* forms the basis for the previously mentioned monistic approach to the legal system—it gives the formula for solution to the problem of the conflict between the *Const* and the treaty obligations of the state.[87] General idea of these provisions is consistent with the underlying ideas of the 1969 *Vienna Convention on the Law of Treaties* that codifies the general principles of the international law in regards to the conclusion, application and termination of the treaties.[88] General idea behind the provision is in the fact that when entering into treaty obligation, the state is mandated to make sure that all necessary action demanded by the national legislation to make obligation applicable towards the state are followed when entering into treaty obligation. Theory behind the clause presumes, that agents of the state will only exercise they right to enter into treaty obligation, when there is sufficient grounds to warrant the necessity the undertaking the obligations and when they are satisfied that undertaking of the relevant obligation will not constitute a violation of national law. Importance of assurances about conformity between national legislation and international obligation are necessary to prevent the non-fulfilment of the treaty obligations by the states who attempt to hide behind national legislation. Such approach is not allowed under the provisions of the Vienna Conventions and do not provide for the possibility of negating international obligation as a necessity under national law.[89]

To prevent the state officials from entering into treaty agreements that can be viewed as unconstitutional, §121 of the *Const* provides for the necessity of referendums in case of treaty obligations that might: (1) change the borders of the state; (2) that create the need for a new legislation, legislative amendment or nullification of existing law(s); (3) agreements creating obligations stemming from the membership in international organisations or unions; (4) agreements that create military or monetary obligations; (5) agreements that provide for the ratification of the treaty.[90]

---

[85]Mälksoo (2005b), p. 147.

[86]*Const* §123(1). RT 1992, 26, 349.

[87]*Const* §123. Commentaries 2008.

[88]*Vienna Convention on the Law of Treaties*, 23.05.1969, 8 International Legal Materials 679.

[89]*Vienna Convention on the Law of Treaties* Art. 46, 23.05.1969, 8 International Legal Materials 679.

[90]*Const* § 121(1). RT 1992, 26, 349.

Stemming from the provisions of the previously mentioned Art., people were given a right to decide in the case of the joining the European Union (EU). Referendum on the accession to the EU was held in Estonia on 14 September 2003; whereas NATO was joined without the referendum, since the majority opinion among national political parties was that there is no need to have a referendum in this case, by reason of incorrect interpretation of the constitutional provisions.

§121 makes a special mention of the procedure known as "ratification". In legal practice, "ratification" points to the practice of approval by the parliament of the states accession to international treaties.[91] *Vienna Convention on the Law of Treaties* defines ratification as an act whereby "state establishes on the international plane its consent to be bound by a treaty."[92] Ratification is commonly misconceived as a constitutional process, whereas in reality the idea of the process of ratification is to give legislators time to do necessary changes in national legislation before the letter or ratification can be issued which is then presented to the holder of the treaty as a proof of intention to be bound by its entirety.[93]

As mentioned previously, Republic of Estonia operates on the monistic doctrine and therefore all of the treaties that have been entered into in accordance with provisional measures of the *Const* become binding upon the laws of the land. This makes these treaty norms "self-executing" in nature; the idea is that because of the Constitutional mechanism of non-separation of national and international obligation under national legal system, no separate legislation is needed to create the binding force of the treaty provisions for both material and procedural purposes.[94] Permanent Court of International Justice has seen fit to elaborate, that "the very object" of treaties is to create individual rights that can be directly enforced in national courts.[95] Under the provisions of the §3 of the *Const*, this becomes possible. For all relevant purposes of any judicial procedure, international legal obligations undertaken by the state, become accessible to both national and non-nationals alike. Therefore, the idea of monistic self-execution of norms and principles of international law is fully achieved by the constitutional mechanisms and provides its full-fledged protection to both physical persons and legal personalities existing on the territory of the state.

For the purposes of the functioning of the national legal system, any treaty obligation undertaken by the state has to be premised on the idea of *pacta sunt servanda*—promises are binding. The idea is in the creation of binding agreements that are binding in law as well as in word. Any legal person entering into binding

[91] Liivoja (2006), p. 44.

[92] *Vienna Convention on the Law of Treaties* Art. 2(b), 23.05.1969, 8 International Legal Materials 679.

[93] Aust (2000), p. 81.

[94] *Ibid*, p. 146.

[95] Advisory Opinion on Jurisdiction of the Courts of Danzig, 1928, PCIJ, set. B, No. 15 (Judgment of 3th March), para. 17–18.

agreement is presumed to honor it by living up to the expectations of the other parties by following the black-letter stipulations of the undertaken obligation.[96] For the purposes of international treaties, the idea is reflecting on the general obligation of member states to the treaty to not violate the treaties object and purpose. Under Art. 26 of the *Vienna Convention on the Law of Treaties*, idea of *pacta sunt servanda* is expressed via the connection to the idea of good faith providing, that parties are both bound by the treaty and expected to perform their obligations in good faith.[97] Under international law, this clause ought to be viewed as creating an obligation for fulfilment of the treaty until such time as the treaty has been dissolved in accordance with the relevant provisions of international legal order. The idea portrays the inviolability of treaties, not their unchangeability.[98] It is the burden of the principle to ensure that international law is actually viewed as a law.[99]

1.3.3 National Law and International Obligations

For the purposes of evaluation of the fulfilment of international obligations in national law, one of the starting points could be provided by the §5 of the *Const* that grants the right to a free trial.[100] That created the procedural nexus between the second chapter of the *Const*, that enumerates fundamental freedoms provided for anyone under the jurisdiction of the *Const* and states obligations towards people, stemming from the international agreements. This allows for non-nationals to receive equal protection under national legislation with that granted for nationals of the state. SC of the Republic of Estonia has seen fit to categorise *European Convention on Human Rights and Fundamental Freedoms* as serving in the capacity of "priority treaty" in regards to the national legislation.[101] This decision creates the situation, wherein norms of the convention acquire the *lex specialis* status in regards to the national legislative acts for the purposes of fundamental rights adjudication.

At the same time, one must not forget, that for the purposes of the functioning of such a relationship, day to day practice of law on the national level has to be administered from the viewpoint of the supremacy of the *Const* over all and any particular norm in question.[102] Although the treaty norms are an inseparable part of the legal regime, for the purposes of judicial administration of justice, supremacy over normative conflicts relies solely within the *Const* of the state on whose

[96]Hyland (1994), p. 406.

[97]Art. 26, Vienna Convention on the Law of Treaties, 23.05.1968, 8 International Legal Materials 679.

[98]Kunz (1945), p. 197.

[99]Lukashuk (1989), p. 513.

[100]*Const* §15. RT 1992, 26, 349.

[101]SC 3-1-3-13-03.

[102]Azoulai (2013), p. 110.

territory the judicial proceedings are being carried out. For the purposes of the judicial proceedings treaties can serve as the reasoning for the annulment of legislation,[103] therefore serving as an additional factual basis for meeting the burden of proof in the case of unconstitutionality of the legislation.

For the purposes of application of the Estonian law, all of these ideas are directly connected with the *Const* and relevant provisions deriving from the *Const*, that serve as the guiding light to find relevant answers to the proposed questions. Estonia is a constitutional democracy. Stemming from the wording and idea of the *Const*, highest power in the state is vested with the people.[104] Therefore, the legal system becomes the representation of the "unrestricted will"[105] of the citizens and therefore derives its power directly from the people.

1.3.4 Estonian Constitutional Law and European Union Law

The two main EU constitutional level principles regulating relationship between national and EU legal orders are the principle of primacy (supremacy) and principle of direct effect. In comparative terms Estonian legal system may be classified as one of the most liberal and open to the EU law.[106] This normative position of EU law in the national legal system was not self-evident considering the strict 'sovereignty' wording of the *Const*.[107] To the contrary, even the fact of accession of Estonia to the EU in 2004 was a complex legal challenge.[108] Based on the intensive political and academic debates to overcome possible negative public sentiment it was decided not to directly amend the text of the *Const*. In legal terms the accession of Estonia was enabled by way of adopting on the public referendum a separate legal act, the *Constitutional Amendment Act* (*CAA*).

The, *CAA* was a creative political solution to enable accession, however, in the legal doctrine this form of constitutional amendment and very concise wording of the *CAA* created few years of uncertainty for courts and practitioners. Two contesting opinions have emerged. According to one opinion: the *CAA* was merely permission for Estonia to accede to the EU. Accordingly, the EU law did not have any automatic primacy in the national legal system. Another opinion, later adopted and confirmed by the SC, suggested that *CAA* is not a mere permission to enter the EU but rather a fundamental change to the entirety of the Estonian constitutional

[103]SC 3-4-1-1-96.

[104]*Const* §1. RT 1992,26, 349.

[105]Habermas (2001), p. 766.

[106]Chalmers et al. (2010), pp. 188–197.

[107]§1 of the *Const* provides: "Estonia is an independent and sovereign democratic republic wherein the supreme power of state is vested in the people. The independence and sovereignty of Estonia are timeless and inalienable."

[108]On the challenges of the EU Membership for the Estonian constitutional doctrine see Kerikmäe (2001, 2009, 2010); Nyman-Metcalf (2006), pp. 110–120.

order. This means that the *Const* must be always interpreted and applied considering EU law. According to the widely cited position of the SC "... the text of the *Const* must always be read with the amendments and only that part of the constitutional text shall be applied which is not in conflict with the amendments. Thus, the *Const* must be read together with the *Const Amendment Act*, applying only the part of the *Const* that is not amended by the *CAA*."[109] The SC further explained that the EU law "became one of the grounds for the interpretation and application of the *Const*. In the substantive sense this amounted to a material amendment of the entirety of the *Const* to the extent that it is not compatible with the EU law."[110] This line of reasoning of the SC, developed in subsequent case law, is called 'the EU law integrated interpretation'. According to this doctrine, the normative conflict between EU law and national constitutional is excluded, as only EU law conforming application of the constitutional provisions are possible.[111]

This doctrine of the EU law integrated interpretation of the *Const* and unconditional primacy of EU law was challenged in the 2012 SC case concerning the European Stability Mechanism (ESM).[112] In this case the SC had to specifically address the legal question on the relationship between *CAA* §1 on the protection of fundamental principles of the Estonian *Const* and *CAA* §2 on the relationship between EU and national constitutional law. Prior to the ESM case, the SC primarily focused on the *CAA* §2 from which the court derived the unconditional primacy of EU law over national constitutional law and developed the doctrine of 'EU law integrated constitutional interpretation.[113] However, precisely the relationship between the fundamental principles protected by the *Const* and primacy of EU law have never been directly addressed by the court. This lack of engagement on the constitutional relationship and possible constitutional limiting conditions to the principle of primacy of EU law have been heavily criticised already in 2006 in the dissenting opinion by justice Kõve,[114] however it took the SC over 6 years to revisit this question and address the criticism and concerns.

In the reasoning of the ESM judgement the court started by reconfirming its earlier jurisprudence on primacy of EU law and the EU law integrated constitutional interpretation doctrine. However, partly reflecting on the criticism on lack of normative constitutional engagement on the issue of relationship between constitutional fundamental principles protected by the *Const* and primacy of EU law, the court has stated that "Estonia may belong to the EU, provided that the fundamental principles of the *Const* of Estonia are respected."[115] Therefore, the court has importantly stated (albeit with no detailed reasoning) that respect for fundamental

[109] SC 3-4-1-3-06, pp. 15–16.

[110] Ibid.

[111] For reasoning of the course, see for example SC 3-3-1-79-08.

[112] SC 3-4-1-6-12.

[113] SC 3-4-1-3-06.

[114] See dissenting opinion of justice Kõve to SC 3-4-1-3-06.

[115] SC 3-4-1-6-12, p. 222.

constitutional principles, as articulated in *CAA* §1 is a precondition for EU membership and application of EU law in the national legal system.

Against this background, the normative primacy of EU legal order is well-established in the Estonian constitutional doctrine and tested and upheld through numerous SC decisions. Contrary to the more contested constitutional struggles in other EU members, the Estonian constitutional legal system may be considered as one of the most open and liberal to the acceptance of EU law, however, arguably not unconditional but subject to the fundamental principles safeguard.

1.3.5 Application of EU Constitutional Principles of Primacy, Direct Effect and Harmonious Interpretation

In the context of the very open and liberal position of SC toward EU legal order, the interpretation and application of the two fundamental constitutional principles of EU law: principle of primacy and direct effect did not trigger any major inconsistencies or disputes in the national courts. The SC, already shortly after accession to the EU, has clearly formulated its position on primacy of EU law. The court has stated: "[...] within the spheres, which are within the exclusive competence of the EU or where there is a shared competence within the EU, the EU law shall apply in the case of a conflict between Estonian legislation, including the *Const*, with the EU law."[116] The court has further explained that conflicting national provisions must be inapplicable and suspended.[117] This applies also to the provisions of the *Const.*[118] The overview of jurisprudence of national courts of the first and second instances also suggests that courts of the lower level consistently and correctly apply the principle of primacy.[119]

The principle of direct effect has equally been well-understood and applied by national courts. The SC has explained with reference to the provisions of the *Treaty on Functioning of the European Union* and case law of the Court of Justice the direct effect of regulations[120] and in detail the conditions of the direct effect of the directive. The SC has stated that provision of the directive are directly effective if three conditions are fulfilled: (1) the directive is not implemented on time or transposed into national law incorrectly; (2) the provision of the directive is clear, precise and unconditional and does not require further measures at the national

[116] SC 3-4-1-3-06, p. 16.

[117] SC 3-3-1-84-12, p. 20; SC 3-3-1-36-10.

[118] SC 3-4-1-3-06, p. 16.

[119] See for example judgement of the Tallinn Administrative Court 3-2562/2004 of 28 December 2005, p. 9. For the detailed overview and analysis of the jurisprudence of national courts, including courts of first and second level see Evas (2012).

[120] SC 3-3-1-77-14.

level; (3) the directive although addressed to member states gives rights to citizens.[121]

The SC doctrine of EU law integrated interpretation, based on *CAA* §2, has also found its reflection in the legal reasoning of the courts of lower levels. For example, in the recent case one of the legal issues disputed by the parties was whether the *Directive 2010/24/EC* can be applied to the facts of the case and whether the provisions of the Directive are directly effective. The Tallinn Circuit Court (the court of appeal) found that although disputed provisions of the Directive are not directly effective, based on *CAA* §2 the court of the first instance has correctly referred to the provisions of the Directive as an interpretative tool for national law.[122]

1.3.6 The Case Law of National Courts

The very liberal and open approach of the SC had a positive impact on the overall engagement of the national courts on all levels with issues of EU law.[123] The first stage of development of national jurisprudence (approximately from 2004 to 2010) was characterised by two elements: first, there were great number of cases where applicants referred to the EU law. However, the majority of those cases did not engage with EU law, the EU law or Court of Justice jurisprudence was referred by the parties but the legal questions of EU law have been hardly addressed. Therefore, EU law was more of a supporting reference rather an argumentative substantive strategy of the parties. The exceptions here are series of four groups of cases: surplus stock (sugar case), structural funds cases, residence permit and pension rights cases that have intensively engaged with the questions of EU law. The second stage is more diverse. The parties and the courts engage with EU law in more detail, referring to the EU law and case law of the Court of Justice in the argumentative strategies and reasoning of the judgments. The SC has adjudicated over 300 cases related to EU law.

The SC has provided important guidance to the national courts of lower levels, not only through its jurisprudence but also through guidelines (i.e. on the requests for the preliminary ruling) and analytical materials on EU law and EU case law. The SC therefore played an important role in the national legal system facilitating the acceptance of EU law and adjudication of EU law related disputes in the Estonian legal system.

[121]SC 3-3-1-36-10; see also for example judgement of the Tallinn Administrative Court 3-11-2682/2013, p. 25.

[122]See Tallinn Circuit Court 2-13-54612, p. 35 and reasoning of the parties.

[123]From very first days after accession Estonian courts have actively engaged with EU law, for a detailed overview of case law of national courts see Evas (2012, 2016). As of October 2016, there are over 3800 judgments of national courts from all levels where EU law is invoked.

1.4 E-governance and Law

Katrin Nyman-Metcalf
Tallinn Law School, Tallinn University of Technology, Akadeemia tee 3, 12618 Tallinn, Estonia
e-mail: katrin.nyman@ttu.ee

Estonia is a world leader in e-governance. It is among the states with the most services offered and used on-line, significant use of digital signatures and several innovative uses of e-services, like on-line voting. The Estonian example is studied by many countries and used as a model. It is not unusual that people expect to find a large number of Estonian legal acts related to e-governance, which however is not the case. Estonia in fact has only very little legislation that can be seen as directly linked to e-governance.[124] This is not by accident, but a conscious choice, as it is important to be able to enjoy benefits of e-governance to see it as an integral part of the legal and administrative system of the country with e-services well-integrated into whatever legislation or systems there are for service delivery.[125] One of the aspects allowing Estonian e-government to be characterised as successful is that the electronic services offered are widely used. Many countries have introduced various e-services but find that people are not interested in using them—often because they are seen to be complicated or there is a need for a special procedure to have access. This leads to a vicious circle, as it means there is less of an impetus to provide additional services and thus people will think that there is no need to make the effort to access services. In Estonia, e-government services are accessed with the same ID-card and codes that people use for a variety of purposes.

Areas of law that are affected by e-governance includes among other administrative legislation, administrative and criminal procedural legislation, intellectual property law and consumer protection law. These areas of law will not be dealt with in any detail in this chapter. Some aspects are highlighted in other chapters of the book. Here only the most relevant points will be mentioned. Legislation on digital identities (signatures) as well as on data protection and public information are very important in the context of e-governance and these will be discussed further below. Also information and communication technology (ICT) law and competition law will be mentioned.

[124] Nyman-Metcalf (2014b), pp. 33–34.

[125] "Noting that e-governance is about democratic governance and not about purely technical issues, and convinced therefore that the full potential of e-governance will be harnessed only if ICTs are introduced alongside changes in the structures, processes and ways that the work of public authorities is organised", Preamble, Council of Europe Recommendation Rec(2004)15 adopted by the Committee of Ministers of the Council of Europe on 15 December 2004 and explanatory memorandum, www.coe.int.

1.4.1 Key Legal Issues of e-Governance

Legal issues of e-governance do not form a single, unified area of law. The term e-governance (or e-government) denotes use of ICT for governance but is not exactly defined in treaties, law or literature[126] and Estonian law does not contain a definition. In Estonia, as in any country, e-governance is generally dealt with so that legislators and regulators fit new phenomena into legal frameworks created in a different situation.[127] The key stipulations in Estonian law are that documents and signatures can be electronic as well as paper based, with electronic signatures having the same value as traditional ones, unless there is a specific exception to this in law.[128] Another important element is interoperability of databases. In Estonia a system called the X-road has been developed, an interface that allows different databases to communicate so that there can be direct access to data by various authorities. There is no need to create unified, centralised databases but it is possible to have automatic use of data without a need for requests for each access. This is what permits applying the principles that individuals do not have to provide data to authorities more than once. Estonia used to have a law on databases from 1997 until 2006, when it was repealed and the key provisions on databases (how to create or close them, basic requirements for data etc.) are instead found in the *Public Information Act.*[129] Interoperability requires a basic level of unified standards of data as well as cooperation between organs, but each body holding a database can still decide most issues about it itself. Basic provisions to enable the operation of the system are found in the X-road regulation, the Data Exchange Layer of Information Systems[130] as well as in the Government Regulation on System of security measures for information systems.[131] Details of data exchange are stipulated in service level agreements between concerned parties, i.e. authorities having data and those needing access to it.

1.4.2 On-Line Elections

So-called "e-elections"—remote internet voting with binding results[132] to parliamentary, local and European elections[133]—have been held in Estonia since 2005.[134] This

[126]Schneiberg and Bartley (2008).

[127]Brownsword and Goodwin (2012), pp. 19–21.

[128]*Digital Signature Act.* RT I 2000, 28, 150.

[129]RT I 2000, 92, 597.

[130]RT I 2008, 18, 129.

[131]*Regulation 252:2007*, RT I, 71, 440, established based on §43^9 (1) 4) of the *Public Information Act*. See also the *Regulation 251:2007 on the Address Data System*—an essential Regulation to ensure uniform use of address information.

[132]The term "e-voting" is used also for various kinds of machine voting, etc.

[133]http://vvk.ee/voting-methods-in-estonia/.

[134]Madise and Vinkel (2014).

aspect of e-democracy has attracted a lot of attention internationally as until now, Estonia is the only country to allow this method of national elections.[135]

The Estonian e-voting system was examined by the Supreme Court (SC)in 2005,[136] following a complaint by the President in his role of examining constitutionality of legislation. The case centred on the principle of one person—one vote. SC found that there was nothing in the system that compromised this principle and ruled that the system of e-voting appropriately balanced all electoral principles of the *Const.*[137] There have been some more legal challenges to e-voting since,[138] but it has not been found to violate any laws. A key to using such elections is the safe identification of persons. Preferably people should be used to such a system from other contexts—as is the case in Estonia—to be able to trust it for elections. On-line elections are thus suited for a society with a lot of e-services and not as the first major e-service.

1.4.3 e-Identification

One of the topics that needs specific regulation in a society using e-governance is electronic or digital identification systems. This is because of the importance of these, as the entry point to e-services, and because of the fact that several concepts of digital signatures are in need of clarification while for traditional signatures some elements are self-evident. Certain provisions are found in EU legislation, currently *Regulation 910/2014*[139] which is under implementation and which repeals *Directive 1999/93/EC*. The Regulation takes over several of the definitions of the Directive and these are also used in Estonian law.

A secure electronic signature should be a digital signature using different keys—a private and a public one. Certification authorities issue and control identification systems that ensure the validity of the signature.[140] The law needs to require such systems. In addition, an important role of the law is to ensure acceptance of e-signatures.[141] These must have the same force as regular signatures and such force shall be provided by law.

For the legal system, the question of approving a signature or other identification should not be related to the form but to whether it is capable of fulfilling its function

[135]There are other examples of local elections or special elections for different organs.

[136]SC 3-4-1-13-05, Petition of the President of the Republic in 2005. http://www.nc.ee/?id=823.

[137]Ibid.

[138]SC 3-4-1-16-11, case brought by Tallinn City Council in 2011.

[139]*Regulation 910/2014 of the European Parliament and of the Council of 23 July 2014 on electronic identification and trust services for electronic transactions in the internal market and repealing Directive 1999/93/CE.*

[140]Wang (2006), p. 254.

[141]Malkawi (2007), p. 163.

of authenticating something. Relevant in this context is whether the signature is susceptible to intervention, modification or technical compromise.[142]

1.4.4 Data Protection and Access to Information

The *Const* contains protection of privacy, in §26 on the inviolability of the family and private life as well as in §33 on the inviolability of the home. There are specific rules on secrecy of channels of communication (§43) and on access to information with data protection (§44). In addition, §42 stipulates the ban on collecting or processing information about the opinions of individuals.

As e-governance facilitates to access to information, the legislation on such access and, as a corollary, on privacy and data protection is essential in the context of e-governance. Not least for the perception of e-governance and the trust in it, there must be careful consideration of data protection. This is highlighted the in relation to interoperability of databases like the X-road, as any breaches of data protection in a situation of high interoperability could have widespread negative consequences. For a highly electronic society, there is a need for legal acts like on analysis of data that allow for a suitable and effective protection of it in practice. This is stipulated in a Government decree on determining the security class as well as potential damage arising from failed data protection.[143] There are also a number of other specific acts on aspects of data handling, mainly in the form of regulations or other sub-legal acts from the government of from specific ministries.[144]

As an EU member, Estonia implements EU law on data protection and will be affected by the currently ongoing changes in this area.[145] It is expected that a Regulation will be in force in 2018, setting up a detailed system for how data processors shall ensure for example the proper informed consent of data subjects.

[142]This aspect has been recognised by courts as a reason for not accepting electronic means of signing. See Wang (2006), p. 259 referring to German court cases.

[143]*Regulation on the security measures of information systems*, RT I, 2007, 71, 440.

[144]*Regulation 252: 2009 on the system of information systems security measures*; *Ministry of Defence regulations 34:2008 on computer system security requirements and 6:2009 on processing and protection of encryption materials; Ministry of Economics and Communication regulation 93: 2009 on the installation and use of technical means and processing of data; Ministry of Interior regulation 13:2013 on registration and processing of data collected by the information office for money laundering; Ministry of Justice regulation 10: 2013 with the basic charter and composition of the Data Inspection Authority* (amending the initial, 2007, regulation).

[145]The EU is in the process of reforming its existing data protection provisions (found in *Directive 95/46/EC of the European Parliament and of the Council of 24 October 1995 on the protection of individuals with regard to the processing of personal data and on the free movement of such data*), with a view to making the rules more suitable for modern ICTs as well as to avoid the rather significant differences in interpretation and application that have occurred between EU Member States (which is one reason a Regulation is proposed instead of a Directive). The text of a Regulation has been made and is in the process of adoption, estimated to be able to enter into force in 2018. See http://ec.europa.eu/justice/newsroom/data-protection/news/120125_en.htm.

EU Regulations are directly applicable in all member states. The terminology in the current Estonian legislation on data protection comes to a large extent from EU legislation as does the system of oversight, via the Data Protection Inspectorate. The main law in Estonia today is the *Personal Data Protection Act* adopted on 15 February 2007.[146] It is too early to say how this law will change once the Regulation enters into force.

The right to privacy is the fundamental right underlying data protection. *The Charter of Fundamental Rights of the EU* is the first major international convention to include a specific Art. on data protection, Art. 8,[147] while otherwise, provisions on protection of privacy are interpreted to include data protection[148]. By mentioning data protection specifically, the importance of it not least seen against an increased use of ICTs is underlined.[149] In Estonia, one key aspect that also illustrates well the necessary link between law and technology is that any access to personal data by any authority leaves a footprint, so the person can see that his or her data was accessed, by which authority and when.

1.4.5 ICT Law

Access to ICT is a prerequisite for using e-services. The more a state makes use of e-governance, the more essential it becomes that the physical and actual access of sufficient speed and quality is guaranteed. Question on providing real access are similar the question on universal service obligation—a well-known concept for utilities.[150] In Estonia the main law is the *Electronic Communications Act*.[151] This law sets out principles for licences and general authorisations for providing communications services. The general principles follow from EU law. There is an independent regulator to deal with such matters, the Technical Surveillance Authority,[152] which deals with a variety of infrastructure services.

ICT law is close to competition law and can be seen as *lex specialis* to general competition law. Aspects of competition law that are important in the communications field include undertakings given special rights (in the EU, Art. 106 of the *Treaty on the Functioning of the EU*): competition should be limited only to the extent this is needed given the special nature, like universal service obligation.[153] This obligation aims to ensure access for all at affordable prices and the

[146]RT 2007, 24, 127.

[147]This right includes the right to access and rectify data about oneself and the need for control by an independent authority.

[148]Charter includes also an Art. on protection of privacy, Art. 7.

[149]Nyman-Metcalf (2014a), pp. 28–30.

[150]De Muyter (2012), pp. 453–454; Nikolinakos (2006), p. 181.

[151]RT I 2004, 87, 593.

[152]www.tja.ee.

[153]ECJ C-320/91 *Corbeau* and ECJ C-280/00 *Altmark*.

quality and availability of the service at all times. It used to relate mainly to telephony but increasingly on-line access is seen as a universal service, whether by computer or lately largely by mobile phone. Basically, the technology does not matter as such but regulation should be technology neutral. Estonian law incorporates European and international best principles to create an environment that allows and facilitates e-governance.

1.5 State Security and Law

Ramon Loik
Estonian Academy of Security Sciences, Kase 61, 12012 Tallinn, Estonia

University of Tartu, Ülikooli 18, Tartu, Estonia
e-mail: ramon.loik@sisekaitse.ee; ramon.loik@ut.ee

Challenge to guarantee a peace and stability in Europe has been one of the most fundamental goals and central arguments of integration advancements after World War II. Through Common Security and Defense Policy (CSDP) and Schengen instruments, the European Union (EU) has been seeking for development of sustainable improvement and lasting peace not only within but also beyond its borders, especially in neighbourhood. Assignment of stability projection, and both *peace-making* or *peace-building*, as well as humanitarian and rescue tasks, peace-keeping and exercising of combat forces in crisis management with projection impacts to internal security and law enforcement cooperation has become the most challenging options of the EU's security activities and for its public service institutions during the last decade. In subsequent steps, the European Councils in Helsinki, Feira, Nice and Goteborg stated that the EU should develop and increase its ability and capabilities to undertake the full range of conflict prevention and crisis management responsibilities, defined as *Petersberg Tasks*[154] through the development of full range civil-military cooperation between the EU member states. Joining both with the EU in and NATO in 2004, Estonia (as well as other new member states) faced the challenging task to fit and contribute to the common civilian- and military cooperation mechanisms after transitional pre-accession period.

[154]The Petersberg Tasks were integral part of the European Security and Defense Policy (ESDP), which were explicitly included in the TEU (Art. 17) and covered humanitarian and rescue tasks, peace-keeping, tasks of combat forces in crisis management, including peace-making approach. The Tasks were set out in the Petersberg Declaration adopted at the Ministerial Council of the Western European Union (WEU) in June 1992 by which the WEU member states declared their readiness to make available for the WEU—but also for NATO and the EU—military units from the whole spectrum of their armed forces. To this purpose, *The Civilian Headline Goal* (CHG 2008, 15863/04), set by the Council of the European Union on 7 December 2004, confirmed the EU's ambitions to be active, capable, flexible and effective in Civil Crisis Management (CCM) cooperation.

Political and security environment around and within Estonia has been remarkably changed during the last long decade. These changes reflect also from the development dynamics of security-related legislation. The main framework for major normative transformations is constituted by the membership in EU and NATO from 2004. The EU promotes its 'constitutional' values and norms such as human rights, the rule of law and democracy in its internal and external relations[155], especially for associated and candidate countries during their pre-accession period in conditional way[156]. The NATO Alliance's impact is mainly directed to military management system with democratic control of armed forces. It also determines the formation and implementation of Host Nation Support (HNS) functions and legislation about the organisation of command and control. Hereby, to understand the main progress achieved in Estonian state security and law, we should evaluate surrounding international framework in combination with domestic sensitivity and responsive adaptation.

1.5.1 Military Defence Reforms

The military troops of Russian Federation left from Estonia in August 1994. Since then, the strategic priority of Estonia's foreign, security and defence policy has been to achieve an active NATO membership, which allows but also demands to participate in international security and defence cooperation as a capable ally. The mainstream belief of Estonian governmental establishment has been that membership in NATO Alliance guarantees sufficient level of political and military deterrence against potential aggression for a small country in hardly predictable eastern neighbourhood. Because of the membership obligations, one of the main transitions during the last decade has been the development of mobile expeditionary armed forces with high level of interoperability skills to contribute to Alliance's military operations abroad. The other important tasks have been related to the HNS building to guarantee some important logistical capabilities for swift hosting of allied forces in Estonia if needed.[157] From that perspective, the achievements of so-called independent defence capabilities have been developed in parallel with

[155] E.g. Balzacq (2009); Jones (2007); Schroeder (2011); Sjursen (2006); Loik (2016); Manners (2002), pp. 240–241.

[156] E.g. Schimmelfennig and Sedelmeier (2005); Veebel and Loik (2012).

[157] The 'Estonian Long Term Defence Development Plan 2009–2018' programming (2009: 6) resulted in three main categories of capability priorities to develop—(1) Capabilities that are necessary for national defence, but are too expensive and can be achieved only in cooperation with NATO and Allies (for example, fighter aircraft and attack helicopters, Strategic Airlift Capability—SAC); (2) Capabilities that are necessary for national defence, but are unreachable within the next decade (for example, multiple launch rocket systems with a range of up to 70 km and surface-to-surface missile systems for destroying surface naval targets); (3) Capabilities that are necessary for national defence and the development of which can be launched within the next decade (those form the basis of the Plan 2018).

alliance-focused approach. Estonia also allocates at least 2% of its GDP as defence spending among the few NATO countries.

As result of series legal reforming, the Estonian Defence Forces (EDF) is part of an executive national authority under the Minister of Defense (MoD) and government. The EDF are structured in accordance to the principles of professional interoperability and a total defence. This kind of mixed and comprehensive approach means that there are active professional units training together with conscript troops and the main part of the military are formed as readiness units in reserve. In situation of serious crises, the main tasks of the EDF in cooperation with other governmental agencies are—to increase readiness levels of its units; to prepare for transition to wartime structure and; to begin partial or total mobilisation if ordered; to integrate units from other ministries, and to prepare for assistance from and hosting of allied forces. If the crisis escalates into wartime then the EDF are obliged: (1) to defend the territorial integrity of the constitutional state, (2) to facilitate the arrival and deployment of allied forces (ref. HNS), (3) to maintain control over national airspace, and facilitate the air defence of strategic assets in cooperation with allied forces.[158]

Formally, the President of Republic is a Chief of the state defence but with very limited legal competences after the last constitutional amendments[159], which revised and abandoned the pre–WWII constitutional principle about the President as a Supreme head of all military forces. The constitutional amendment coursed the series of legislative revisions, shifting and concentrating the main state defence competencies, responsibilities and powers from the President's office to the government, especially around the Prime Minister[160]. Thus, the President of Republic could be characterised as a 'balancing' constitutional institution between the political government and the Parliament, without any 'direct' or executive powers with regard to Estonian military. The President still holds an exclusive right to impute military officer's ranks.

Another important transition has been a shift towards so-called *comprehensive approach*[161] in Estonia's security strategy thinking. This kind of defensive doctrine includes the aspects of psychological counter-warfare and enhanced inter-institutional cooperation to common operational activities. Thus, in peacetime, the main tasks of the EDF are as following—(1) to monitor and maintain control over Estonian airspace, (2) to maintain combat readiness, (3) to train conscripts and develop reserve units, (4) to participate in NATO and UN-led international missions, and

[158]Based on several materials published on official websites of the Estonian Ministry of Defence (MoD) and Estonian Defence Forces (EDF) in 12/2016.

[159]*Const* §78.

[160]See also *National Defence Act*, RT I, 12.03.2015 and *National Defence Forces Act*. RT I, 10.07.2012, 1.

[161]The 'comprehensive approach' means in general that all actors involved to state defence need to contribute in a well-coordinated manner, based on a shared competences of responsibilities, taking into account their respective functions, tasks, resources, strengths and legal mandates in respect with their decision-making autonomy.

(5) to provide assistance to civilian authorities in case of national emergency.[162] Latter refers to some important cooperation tasks, need for coherence between the military and civil services during cases of crises in accordance to state emergency norms, as *Extraordinary Situation Act*[163], and related implementation regulations.

1.5.2 Internal Security and Crises Management

Estonia is responsible to guard over 1100 km external borders of the *Schengen Area*. The border guard and –policing relies on the Schengen *acquis* and the principles and regulations of integrated border management, including border protection and immigration management tasks[164]. The important parts of the integrated border management are also border surveillance and risk analysis, checking of documents, cross-border crime investigation in cross-border international cooperation to fight against organised crime. According to several law enforcement legislations[165], the cross-border and transnational cooperation should aim to stop the infiltration of illegal immigrants and radicalised subjects, to ensure the implementation of international agreements, close off the financing of terrorism and smuggling of strategic goods or dual-use commodities.

Recent developments confirm that because of high mobility, Estonian residents have been and can continuously be the objects of terrorist attacks in abroad.[166] Hence, one of the crucial measures for combating terrorism is increasing the efficiency of international justice, home affairs and law enforcement cooperation. Pursuant to the *Prym Treaty/UN Security Council Resolution 2178* (2014) and in accordance with a *Security Authorities Act*[167], the responsible contact point of counter-terrorism combat in Estonia is the Estonian Internal Security Police Board.

The security of essential and vital infrastructure depends on contemporary technologies that enable protected exchange of sensitive information and intelligence cooperation. Since 1 January 2016, as one of the important anti-terrorism measures, the air carriers are going to exchange the gathered booking information to the Police and Border Guard Board services. The data will make up a single database, i.e. the booking information and exchange system. Another area of fast technology-related regulative development is cyber security domain, which is also

---

[162]Based on several materials published on official websites of the Estonian Ministry of Defence (MoD) and Estonian Defence Forces (EDF) in 12/2016.

[163]RT I 2009, 39, 262.

[164]See also *Police and Border Guard Act*. RT I 2009, 26, 159; *State Border Act*. RT I 1994, 54, 902.

[165]See *Anti-corruption Act*. RT I, 29.06.2012, 1; *International Sanctions Act*. RT I 2010, 26, 129; *Anti-money laundering and Terrorism Financing Act*. RT I 2008, 3, 21; *Customs Act*. RT I 2004, 28, 188; *Law Enforcement Act*. RT I 2005, 27, 198; *Strategic Goods Act*. RT I, 22.12.2011, 2.

[166]Two Estonian citizens were killed during the Nice's terrorist attack on 14 July 2016.

[167]RT I 2001, 7, 17.

mainly responsibility of the Police and Border Guard Board within the administrative area of the Estonian Ministry of the Interior.[168] In addition, the national cyber security policy is governed and coordinated by the Ministry of Economic Affairs and Communications while the advancement of the national information systems and response to cyber security incidents (alerts) are organised by the Estonian Information System Authority.

Reformed national crisis management system in Estonia involves the prevention and preparedness of emergencies, corresponding responsive action-plans and mitigation of consequences, as well as ensuring a sustainable supply of defined vital public services.[169] Thus, emergencies are dangerous event or a series of events that threaten lives or health of people, cause major resource damage, serious scale of environmental damage and large-scale disruption of vital services, interruption of which would endanger the life or health of people and/or paralyse the functioning of the state and/or significantly decrease the security perceptions in society as defined by the Estonian Ministry of the Interior.[170] Providers of such vital services have specific tasks to fulfil and ensure the functioning of services, as well as are obliged to prevent any major interruptions and ensure necessary service-restoration.

The declaration of the emergency situation gives the competent authorities some special rights, for instance the right to task for certain works, enter to the facilities and limit traffic at the critical sites. The government shall set out exact time of the start and close of the emergency period as legal competency. As an important part of the national risk management system, the correspondent analyses are presented every 2 years. Seven types of emergencies were indicated and assessed lately in 2013 as having a very high level of risk according to the Ministry of the Interior, including large-scale marine, coastal and environmental pollution, epidemics, pandemics and other large-scale events. The recent risk analysis also included a governmental action-plan for principal risk-reducing measures, which addresses responsibilities and tasks of specific ministries and other governmental agencies with regard to prevent emergencies and mitigate possible consequences of risk-realisation. The correspondent emergency plans in Estonia need to be approved by special governmental decisions.

[168]About the recent developments of defence-related cyber security domain, find also some strategic documents collected by NATO Cooperative Cyber Defense Centre of Excellence (CCDCOE, 2016) as an accredited research, development and training institution in Estonia.

[169]There are 45 services considered to be vital in Estonia, ensured by a total of 167 providers, including 131 public and private limited companies, 19 foundations, 16 state agencies and one municipal institution according the Ministry of the Interior. The *Emergency Act* regulates the services and lists the vital ones along with those responsible for their provision as from 2009.

[170]Based on several crises management materials published on official website of the Estonian Ministry of the Interior in 12/2016.

1.5.3 Enhanced International Cooperation

The EU, NATO and their member states also cooperate to prevent and resolve crises and armed conflicts within and outside of Europe. The closer cooperation between the two organisations has taken place since the Berlin Plus agreements (2003), which allow the EU's access to NATO's collective resources and capabilities for EU-led operations in certain cases.[171] NATO allows the EU to use resources that NATO itself is not using and can be recalled if needed in quite a short notice. It should be noted that the EU–NATO cooperation deploys the resources contributed by the member states, and it might be course of some limits for the small states' capabilities to frequently participate in such missions. The EU also develops criminal law and regulates the internal security and law enforcement cooperation between its member states from supranational level in certain aspects[172]. Thus, there are several legal initiatives of the European Union is to recently adopt the legal acts, which falling under the jurisdiction of the Estonian Ministry of the Interior to strengthen the security and law enforcement cooperation in the Schengen area. Both collective responsibilities demand for careful domestic attention, efficient coordination and appropriate resources delivery to meet the needs of enhanced international security cooperation.

At first, the safety of contemporary EU largely relies on security cooperation functioning of various ICT-solutions. Because of that, the formation of 'Entry–Exit' System and the Registered Traveller Program as legal instrument connected to so-called smart borders package is one of the Estonia's priorities in EU Justice and Home Affairs' (JHA) policy domain[173]. Taking the Schengen area, the main information system (SIS), visa information system (VIS) and the fingerprint database for asylum seekers (Eurodac) have been developed as necessary tools for the JHA cooperation in the Area of Freedom, Security and Justice (AFSJ). The aim to develop the large-scale IT solutions are to facilitate border crossing, better consolidate border-cross, and offer some additional technical support with regard of controls and identification of offenders. Estonia has been interested in implementation of the smart borders instrument as soon as available as an important 'compensation measure' assist to manage smoother border crossing and to curb cross-border illegal migration and serious organised crime activities. The smart borders initiative is also intended to provide some cost-effectiveness in EU's border management.

[171]The EU and NATO's first practical cooperation under the 'Berlin Plus' was the operation CONCORDIA from March–December 2003 in Macedonia.

[172]E.g. Herlin-Karnell (2012); Bergström and Cornell (2014); Loik et al. (2016).

[173]See the governmental framework document 'Estonia's European Union Policy 2015–2019', which sets Estonia's EU policy priorities. The national interests in the document are expressed by 69 operational aims, the implementation of which serves also as a preparation for the Estonian Presidency of the Council of the EU. Approved by the Estonian Government on 10 December 2015.

The second important initiative is the approval and ongoing implementation of the EU Passenger Name Record's (PNR) directive[174] as the airline passenger booking information system that facilitates countering organised crime. It is important to note that the PNR is the European development of the system implemented already in Australia, the U.S. and some other countries after the 9/11 terrorist attacks. Estonia expressed its support to implement this system also on domestic EU flights as an additional measure to fight against terrorism, especially to prevent the acts of terrorism via better monitoring of terrorism-related logistics. The third important enhanced transnational law enforcement cooperation matter is adoption and implementation of the European Police Office's Europol new regulation (directive). In this case, the Estonian Ministry of the Interior expects[175] that the new revision of the Europol's act would improve the analytical and criminal intelligence capacities of the agency to tackle with cross-border serious organised crime, including the widening mandate related to fight against cyber-crime with respect to more rigorous data protection regulations.

Analysed changes in political- and security environment around Estonia bring about normative and organisational transitions and adaptation into new cooperation structures both inter-governmentally and in supranational level. The prospect of quite unexpected threats from unpredictable sources is a growing matter of concern for both to the post-modern state and international organisations facing asymmetric challenges. Possibility to threats from non-state actors employing unconventional means to strike anywhere has been increased during the post-9/11 period. Threats for both internal and international security can also combine in new and multiple ways, as fundamentalists operating in war-torn states to produce NBC[176]—weapons, computer hackers cyber-attacking on international monetary systems, and criminal organisations capitalising on accidental catastrophes to extract profit and even territory, etc. This approach fits well with the widening conception of threats in the EU and NATO's member states, drawing attention towards governments' capabilities across an array of crisis prevention and crises management dimensions for preventing threats from materialising, preparing for potential transnational crises, coping with these when occur, and redressing the damages wrought by optional scenarios.

The changing face of contemporary globalised security arena stresses the increased need for more coherent and sustainable transnational cooperation between nation states and different international bodies of security and law

[174]*The Directive (EU) 2016/681 of the European Parliament and of the Council of 27 April 2016 on the use of Passenger Name Record (PNR) data for the prevention, detection, investigation and prosecution of terrorist offences and serious crime*. Under the directive, air carriers are obliged to provide the PNR data for flights entering or departing from the EU. It also allows member states to collect the PNR data of selected intra-EU flights. Each member state is required to set up a Passenger Information Unit, managing the PNR data collected under the directive.

[175]Based on several EU policy materials published on official website of the Estonian Ministry of the Interior in 12/2016.

[176]Nuclear, Biological and Chemical weapons.

enforcement. As we pointed out some major transitions of state security and law in Estonia, we followed the reflections from enhanced international security cooperation's influence to functional, normative and organisational domains of adaptations and change. Thus, majority of relevant legal acts have been revised and updated during the last decade, and even very recently for better fit of international security cooperation. It was also highlighted that multiple threats of international terrorism have centred discussions of more effective transnational crisis prevention and crisis management. However, at the same time other types of crisis and criminal activities have visited and visit Europe continuously, as public health scares, natural disasters, transport failures, smuggling of drugs, illegal weapons, NBC materials, illegal immigration and smuggling of human beings, etc. These and other challenges will test the European cooperation and give impulses for further integration or secessions.

The dynamics of future threats appears to continuously challenge the cross-border and transnational security cooperation. Nobody is living in 'isolated island' anymore, and this perspective demands number of new legislation and competencies of services responsible for security cooperation and stability in European as well as in national levels. One of the characterising trend is developments towards the comprehensive approach and interoperability between contemporary military and civilian security resources, which calls for integrative type of law and regulations to enable concerted civil-military actions. Described and other forthcoming legal initiatives from the supranational level demonstrate that further cooperative security integration measures are work in progress and that respective national laws are steadily under pressure for coherence and adaptation to enable more efficient transnational security cooperation.

References

Arens I (1956) Põhijooni Eesti õiguse ajaloost I. Stockholm: Eesti Teadusliku Instituudi Kirjastus. Republished in Ilus.P. (2008). Eesti õiguse ajalugu. Tallinn: Penikoorem

Aust A (2000) Modern treaty law and practice. Cambridge University Press, Cambridge

Azoulai L (2013) Forces and forms of European legal integration. Law Ukraine 3(2013):109–124

Balzacq T (ed) (2009) The external dimension of EU Justice and Home Affairs: governance, norms, security. Palgrave Macmillan, Basingstoke

Baxter RR (1980) International law in "Her Infinite Variety". Int Comp Law Rev 29 (1980):549–566

Bergström M, Cornell AJ (eds) (2014) European police and criminal law co-operation, Swedish Studies in European Law, vol 5. Hart Publishing, Oxford

Brownsword R, Goodwin M (2012) Law and the technologies of the twenty-first century. Cambridge University Press, Cambridge

Chalmers D, Davies G, Monti G (2010) European Union Law. Cambridge University Press, Cambridge

De Muyter L (2012) Regulatory asymmetry? The competition between telecommunication operators and other ICT players. J Eur Competition Law Pract 3(5):452–464

Evas T (2012) Judicial application of European Union Law in post-Communist countries: the cases of Estonia and Latvia. Ashgate, Farmham

Evas T (2016) Judicial reception of EU law in Estonia. In: de Witte B et al (eds) National courts and EU law. New issues, theories and methods. Edward Elgar Publishing Limited, Glos

Ginsburg T, Chernykh S, Elkins Z (2008) Commitment and diffusion: how and why national constitutions incorporate international law. Univ Illinois Law Rev 1(2008):201–238

Ginter J (2010) Judicial independence and/or(?) efficient judicial administration. Juridica International XVII/2010, 108–115

Grant TD (2001) United States practice relating to the Baltic States 1940–2000. Baltic Yearbook Int Law. 1., Editor-in-Chief Ineta Ziemele, 23–110

Habermas J (2001) Constitutional democracy, a paradoxical union of contradictory principles? Polit Theory 29(2001):766–781

Hallaste I (1996) Eesti Vabariigi põhiseaduse sünd. Juridica 1996(9):438

Herlin-Karnell E (2012) The constitutional dimension of European criminal law. Hart Publishing, Oxford

Hoffmann T (2007) Rechtshist. Reihe, Der Landrechtsentwurf David Hilchens von 1599. Peter Lang, Frankfurt, Main

Hyland R (1994) Pacta Sunt Servanda. A meditation. Virginia J Int Law 34(1994):405–434

Järvelaid P (2002) Õigus ja Poliitika Kultuuris. Chapter 5: Reformid Eesti õigussüsteemis. Akadeemia Nord, Tallinn

Jones SG (2007) The rise of European security cooperation. Cambridge University Press, Cambridge

Käerdi M (2001) Requlation of limitation periods in Estonian private law: historical overview and prospects. Juridica Int 8:2001

Kerikmäe T (2001) Estonian constitutional problems in accession to the EU. In: Kellermann AE, de Zwaan JW, Czuczai J (eds) EU enlargement. The constitutional impact at EU and national level. T.M.C Asser Press, The Hague, pp 291–300

Kerikmäe T (2009) Estonia as EU Member State in the context of deliberative supranationalism. www.tlulib.ee/files/arts/95/SOTS%20a3e6f5864bf7222495ac84feddc0c8d6.pdf

Kerikmäe T (2010) Estonia as an EU state: lack of proactive constitutional dialogue. In: Topidi K, Morawa AHE (eds) Constitutional evolution in Central and Eastern Europe expansion and integration in the EU. Ashgate Publishing, Farnham, pp 11–42

Kull I (2008) Reform of contract law in Estonia: influences of harmonisation of European private law. Juridica Int 14(2008):122–129

Kunz JL (1945) The meaning and the range of the norm pacta sunt servanda. Am J Int Law 39 (1945):180–197

Liivoja R (2006) Ratifitseerimise mõiste Eesti konstitutsiooniõiguses ja rahvusvahelises õiguses. Õiguskeel 2(2006):40–49

Loik R (2016) Integration trends of EU internal security and law enforcement: how legal, technological and operational advancements matter. Baltic J Eur Stud 6(2):3–27

Loik R, Hämäläinen E, Veebel V (2016) Internal security cooperation under functional expectations: initial law enforcement Europeanization – case of Finland and Estonia. Romanian J Eur Aff 16(1):5–23

Lukashuk II (1989) The principle pacta sunt servanda and the nature of obligation under international law. Am J Int Law 83(1989):513–518

Luts M (2003) Võtta kordki vabadust tõsiselt: Eesti eraõigusreform kui ajalooline ja humanitaristlik väljakutse. Juridica 4(2003):261–270

Luts-Sootak M (2000) Private law of the Baltic Provinces as a Patriotic Act. Juridica Int 5 (2000):157–167

Luts-Sootak M (2001) Textbook of pandects or new style of legislation in Estonia? Juridica Int 6 (2001):152–158

Madise Ü, Vinkel P (2014) Internet voting in Estonia: from constitutional debate to evaluation of experience over six elections. In: Kerikmäe T (ed) Regulating eTechnologies in the European Union. Springer, pp 53–73

Malkawi BH (2007) E-commerce in light of International Trade Agreements: the WTO and the United States-Jordan Trade Agreement. Int J Law Inf Technol 15(2):153–169

Mälksoo L (2005a) Nõukogude anneksioon ja riigi järjepidevus: Eesti, Läti ja Leedu staatus rahvusvahelises õiguses 1940.a – 1991.a ja pärast 1991. a. Tartu Ülikooli Kirjastus
Mälksoo L (2005b) Which continuity: the Tartu Peace Treaty of 2 February 1920, the Estonian-Russian border treaties of 18 May 2005, and the legal debate about Estonia's status in international law. Juridica 1(2005):144–149
Manners I (2002) Normative power Europe: a contradiction in terms? J Common Mark Stud 40 (2):235–258
Marek K (1968) [1954] Identity and continuity of states in public international law, 2n edn. Librairie Droz, Geneva
Maruste R (2004) Konstitutsionalis ning põhiõiguste ja –vabaduste kaitse. Juura, Tallinn
Meri L (2001) Baltic Yearbook of International Law, Vol 1
Nikolinakos NT (2006) EU competition law and regulation in the converging telecommunications, media and IT sectors. Kluwer Law International, Alphen aan den Rijn
Nyman-Metcalf K (2006) Common values as a basis for legal integration: is there an end to Europe? The Baltic States as a bridge between Europe and BEYOND. In: Kasekamp A, Pääbo H (eds) Promoting democratic values in the enlarging Europe. Tartu University Press, Tartu, pp 110–120
Nyman-Metcalf K (2014a) The future of universality of rights. In: Kerikmäe T (ed) Protecting human rights in the EU. Springer, Heidelberg, pp 21–35
Nyman-Metcalf K (2014b) E-Governance in law and by law. In: Kerikmäe T (ed) Regulating eTechnologies in the European Union. Springer, Heidelberg, pp 33–53
Salulaid J (2001) Restoration of the effect of Estonian international treaties. Baltic Yearbook Int Law 1, 2001, Editor-in-Chief Ineta Ziemele
Sarv E (1997) Õiguse vastu ei saa ükski, Eesti taotlused ja rahvusvaheline õigus. OÜ Greif, Tartu
Schimmelfennig F, Sedelmeier U (2005) The Europeanization of Central and Eastern Europe. Cornell University Press, Ithaca
Schmidt O (1894) Rechtsgeschichte Liv- Est- und Kurlands. Dorpat
Schneiberg M, Bartley T (2008) Organizations, regulation, and economic behavior: regulatory dynamics and forms from the nineteenth to twenty-first century. Annu Rev Law Soc Sci 4:31–61
Schroeder UC (2011) The organization of European security governance: internal and external security in transition. Routledge, London
Sjursen H (2006) The EU as a 'Normative' power: how can this be? J Eur Public Policy 13 (2):235–251
Uluots J (1938) Eestimaa õiguse ajalugu. Konspekt, compiled by V.E Muhel. In Ilus, P. Eesti õiguse ajalugu. Tallinn: Penikoorem. He also mentions other authors such as Tacitus, Plinius, Younger etc
Varul P (2000) Legal policy decisions and choices in the creation of new private law in Estonia. Juridica Int 5(2000):104–118
Veebel V, Loik R (2012) Estonia: life in post-Communist Eastern Europe after EU Membership. In: Beachain DO, Vera S, Stan S (eds) Life in post-Communist Eastern Europe after EU Membership – happy ever after? Taylor & Francis Group, London, pp 163–184
Walker EW (2003) Dissolution: sovereignty and the breakup of the Soviet Union. Rowman & Littlefield, p 63
Wang M (2006) The impact of information technology development on the legal concept – a particular examination on the legal concept of 'Signatures'. Int J Law Inf Technol 15 (3):253–274

Public Law

2

Marek Herm, Kristi Joamets, Marko Kairjak, Tanel Kerikmäe, Helen Kranich, Kaido Künnapas, Ramon Loik, Maret Maripuu, Monika Mikiver, Lehte Roots, and Dmitri Teplõhh

M. Herm
Tallinn Law School, Tallinn University of Technology, Akadeemia tee 3, 12618 Tallinn, Estonia

Law Firm ATTELA, Ahtri 6a, 10151 Tallinn, Estonia
e-mail: marek.herm@attela.ee

K. Joamets • T. Kerikmäe (✉) • L. Roots
Tallinn Law School, Tallinn University of Technology, Akadeemia tee 3, 12618 Tallinn, Estonia
e-mail: kristi.joamets@ttu.ee; tanel.kerikmae@ttu.ee; lehte.roots@ttu.ee

M. Kairjak
Faculty of Law, University of Tartu, Näituse, 18 Tartu, Estonia

Estonian Business School, Lauteri 3, Tallinn, Estonia
e-mail: marko.kairjak@ut.ee

H. Kranich • M. Mikiver
Law Enforcement Affairs Department of the Chancellor of Justice, Kohtu 8, 15193 Tallinn, Estonia
e-mail: helen.kraich@oiguskantsler.ee; monika.mikiver@oiguskantsler.ee

K. Künnapas
Tallinn Law School, Tallinn University of Technology, Akadeemia tee 3, 12618 Tallinn, Estonia

Law Firm Sorainen, Advokaadibüroo Sorainen AS, Pärnu mnt 15, 10141 Tallinn, Estonia
e-mail: kaidokynnapas@gmail.com

R. Loik
Johan Skytte Institute of Political Studies, University of Tartu, Lossi 36, 51003 Tartu, Estonia
e-mail: ramon.loik@ut.ee

M. Maripuu
Labour Inspectorate, Gonsiori 29, 10147 Tallinn, Estonia
e-mail: maret.maripuu@ti.ee

D. Teplõhh
Tallinn Law School, Tallinn University of Technology, Akadeemia tee 3, 12618 Tallinn, Estonia

Faculty of Law, University of Tartu, Näituse, 18 Tartu, Estonia
e-mail: dmitri.teplohh@varul.com

T. Kerikmäe et al. (eds.), *The Law of the Baltic States*,
DOI 10.1007/978-3-319-54478-6_2

Abstract
The chapter gives an overview of the main legal branches, concepts and institutions of Estonian public law. The authors are reflecting on the main principles of the Estonian constitutional law and its interpretation—on one hand quite liberal and in another hand rather dogmatic—considering the concept of relationship between Estonian constitution and EU law. The chapter is focusing to the administrative law and procedure and its current topical issues. The chapter discusses also both theoretical and practical aspects of Estonian penal law and criminal procedure (with some emphasis to surveillance, bankruptcy offences), financial law, civil law procedure (with illustrative charts) and labor law in the context of their unique character, solved dilemmas and existing challenges. The reform ideas, future outlooks and relevant case-law have been included.

2.1 Constitutional Law

Lehte Roots and Tanel Kerikmäe
Tallinn Law School, Tallinn University of Technology, Akadeemia tee 3, 12618 Tallinn, Estonia
e-mail: lehte.roots@ttu.ee; tanel.kerikmae@ttu.ee

Monika Mikiver and Helen Kranich
Law Enforcement Affairs Department of the Chancellor of Justice, Kohtu 8, 15193 Tallinn, Estonia
e-mail: monika.mikiver@oiguskantsler.ee; helen.kraich@oiguskantsler.ee

Ramon Loik
Johan Skytte Institute of Political Studies, University of Tartu, Lossi 36, 51003 Tartu, Estonia
e-mail: ramon.loik@ut.ee

2.1.1 Constitution of the Republic of Estonia and Its Amendments

In the referendum held on 28 June 1992, Estonian Constitution (*Const*) was adopted, which assured the legal continuity of the Republic of Estonia after half a century of soviet occupation. The implementation of the Stimson Doctrine by the Welles Declaration,[1] where a significant part of the international community

[1]A diplomatic statement issued on 23 July 1940 by the US Acting Secretary of State Sumner Welles, condemning the June 1940 occupation by the USSR of the three Baltic States and refusing to recognize their annexation. The Declaration was an application of the Stimson Doctrine of non-recognition of international territorial changes that were executed by force. The Declaration also enabled the Baltic States to maintain their independent diplomatic missions and financial assets (Executive Order 8484).

refused to deal out formal approval for the soviet annexation, the resistance by the occupied Baltic nations to the regime of the Soviet Union (USSR), and the continuous functioning of their governments and ambassadors in exile supported the legal application that sovereignty never passed to the USSR, and that occupation *sui generis* (in German: *Annexionsbesetzung* or 'annexation occupation') lasted until re-independence of the Baltic States as subjects of international law in 1991.[2] According to the preamble, the goals of *Const* are to strengthen and develop the state, which is founded on liberty, justice and the rule of law; internal and external peace, welfare for the present and future generations; preservation of the Estonian people, the Estonian language and the Estonian culture.[3] The state power is to secure the achievement of the goals.[4]

The *Const* of 2016 has been amended five times. In 2003—Local Government Council will be elected for a term of 4 years.[5] In 2004—Estonia may belong to the European Union, provided the fundamental principles of the *Const* are respected.[6] *The Amendments Act* is important link between the Estonian national legal order and the European Union (EU) law.[7] The approach on how to tackle the relationship of supranational law and domestic law was largely discussed before accessing the EU. The Government of Estonia appointed the special Commission for legal expertise on 14.05.1996 to review the need to amend the *Const* by looking at its whole. First conclusions of the legal specialists were quite dogmatic: The Commission found that the *Const* does not allow for accession considering the provisions of independence and sovereignty[8]. However, after latter discussions, the general question of accession and the amendment of the *Const* were decided by the referendum 14.09.2003 and the following constitutional law (so-called IIIrd Act) was adopted[9]: §1. Estonia may belong to the EU in accordance with the fundamental principles of the *Const*; §2. As of Estonia's accession to the EU, the *Const* applies taking account the rights and obligations arising from the *Accession Treaty*; §3. This Act may be amended only by a referendum; §4. This Act enters into force 3 months after the date of proclamation.

The EU law is one of the grounds for the interpretation and application of the *Const*. The effect of those provisions of the *Const* that are not compatible with the EU law and thus inapplicable is suspended.[10] In a court case of the European

[2]Hiden et al. (2008), Mälksoo (2003), Van Elsuwege (2003), Van Elsuwege (2008), and Ziemele (2005).

[3]*Const* (1992).

[4]SC 3-4-1-1-98.

[5]*The Const Amendment Act* RT 2003, 29, 174.

[6]*The Const Amendment Act* RT 2003, 64, 429.

[7]Narits (2009).

[8]Kerikmäe (2001), p. 295.

[9]*The Const Amendment Act* RT 2003, 29, 174. See also Kerikmäe (2010).

[10]SC 3-4-1-3-06. Laffranque (2007).

Stability Mechanism[11] the Supreme Court (SC) found, that the Treaty is in accordance with the *Const.*[12] *Amendment Act* allows Estonia to be a part of the changing EU. At the same time, the *Amendment Act* does not authorize the integration process of the EU to be legitimized or the competence of Estonia to be delegated to the EU to an unlimited extend.[13] The interpretations of IIIrd Act have been criticized as unused tool of constitutional dialogue between Estonia and the EU[14] as stated by several dissenting opinions of the SC judges[15].

In 2007 the state's objective of guaranteeing the preservation of the Estonian language through the ages was amended.[16] In 2011 the leadership appointment and release system of the armed forces was changed (to underlie it to the Government).[17] In 2015 the voting age to 16 years for Local Government Council Elections was reduced.[18]

Estonia has a liberal constitution. The constitutional governmental system is characterized by parliamentary democracy based on legitimacy, the principle of the rule of law, republicanism, and sovereignty of the people, unitary statehood is derived from and based on the *Const.*[19] State powers are distributed between the executive, legislative and judicial branches of the government. Such distribution is due to the needs of *small state* (limited scope of activity, multi-functionalism, reliance on informal structures, constraints on steering and control, and high personalist)[20] not absolute. For example, the court performs some executive functions (e.g. consent of a court for the parents to conclude transactions on behalf of a child,[21] a court's permission for the examination of premises[22]) which is not the judicial function in the formal and substantial senses. It has been warned that such solution may harm the achievement of reasonable time principle and the procedural economy.[23]

The core values are the fundamental principles of the *Const* which are universal in character and connected with the general principles of the EU law. The *Const* does not define the fundamental principles. Theoretical approaches derive the fundamental principles of the Const from its preamble, Ch. 2, "General Provisions" and §10 and 11 of Ch. 2, "Fundamental Rights, Freedoms and Duties". The

[11]The *Treaty Establishing The European Stability Mechanism* (*ESM*).

[12]Fabbrini (2016).

[13]SC 3-4-1-6-12.

[14]Kerikmäe (2011).

[15]For detailed analysis, see: Kerikmäe (2009).

[16]*The Const Amendment Act* RT I 2007, 33, 210. Laffranque (2007).

[17]*The Const Amendment Act* RT I 27.04.2011.

[18]*The Const Amendment Act* RT I 15.05.2015.

[19]Narits (2009); *Const.* Commentaries 2002.

[20]Sarapuu (2010).

[21]*Family Law Act.* §131.

[22]*Law Enforcement Act.* §51.

[23]Jäätma (2016).

fundamental principles should be defined in the form of an open catalogue, which covers, above all, the following principles: national sovereignty; the state's foundations of liberty, justice and law; protection of internal and external peace; preservation of the Estonian nation and culture through the ages; human dignity; social statehood; democracy; the rule of law; respect for fundamental rights and freedoms; proportionate exercise of the authority of the state.[24]

The most important fundamental principle of the *Const* is human dignity, which is a basis for all other principles and regulations in the *Const*, the basis of all individual basic rights, as well as the aim of the protection of all individual basic rights and liberties.[25] It is a core element of the state's policy and of the expression of human rights which is applicable in any single instance.[26] Human dignity is furthermore the complex of different basic rights, including dissimilar elements.[27] In the certain context there cannot be made any exceptions to ensure the criteria of human dignity, neither in the *Const* nor in the regulations of the international law.[28]

The Estonian public administration is strongly related to rule of law and legal acts. All state authority shall be exercised solely pursuant to the *Const* and laws which are in conformity therewith,[29] and for limiting the rights and freedoms, clear and concrete legal basis is needed. The whole state organization and its activities shall be in conformity with the *Const*. For example, because of the needs of *small state* it is possible to deliver the legislative power to the Government, minister or to legal person in public law[30], except the issues which are important in sense of the *Const*.[31] The principle of importance is one of the core constitutional rules which reserves certain decisions to direct state power (parliament, government, minister).[32] In accordance with the *Const*[33] and *Civil Service Act*[34] only an official shall be appointed to a post in an authority, which involves the exercise of official authority listed in the law[35].

---

[24]Laffranque (2007).

[25]SC 3-3-1-2-06.

[26]*Const*. Commentaries 2008.

[27]For example, the right to have equal rights, respecting and protecting for the physical integrity, the right to have personal identity, the right to the informational self-determination, proceeding for guaranteeing the person as a subject (SC 3-1-1-80-97, 3-3-1-27-02, 3-3-1-6-06; 3-3-1-53-06; 3-3-1-56-02).

[28]*Const*. Commentaries 2008.

[29]*Const* §3.

[30]E.g. Local Government or Estonian Bar Association.

[31]SC 3-2-1-40-15.

[32]SC 3-1-1-86-07; Parrest (2009).

[33]§§3, 30, Ch 2.

[34]*Civil Service Act*.

[35]E.g. the exercise of state and administrative supervision; the ensuring of the security and constitutional order of the state; the substantive preparation or implementation of the policy-making decisions; the activities which, in the interests of strengthening and developing the official authority.

According to the *Const* §14 the guarantee of rights and freedoms is the duty of the legislative, executive and judicial powers, and of local governments. This firstly carries both an organizational and a procedural dimension and secondly also implies that public authority is related to fundamental rights. The requirement to guarantee rights and freedoms does not consist only of the obligation to respect fundamental rights but also relates to their active formalization in societal structures.[36] The importance of the Section 14 has increased constantly. The SC concluded from the §14 the fundamental right to good administration which is one of the fundamental rights;[37] the fundamental right to fair and effective procedure and organization;[38] the state's obligation to guarantee the rights and freedoms which includes state's normative and actual activities.[39]

2.1.2 State Organization and Constitutional Institutions of the Republic of Estonia: The Small State Context

With only 1.3 million people and national budget of 8.8 trillion euros[40] Estonia can be characterized as a *small state*[41]. Upon performing its functions, the state has to be capable of acting like a state.[42] At the end of 2014 there was 136,800 workers employed in public sector, but only 29,361 of them were officials.[43]

According the *Const*, the legislative authority is vested in the unicameral *Riigikogu*, the Parliament. The legislative power has as well the people, the President, the Government, the minister, local government. It is possible to deliver the legislative power to legal person in public law, except the issues which are important in sense of *Const*.[44] The Riigikogu's 101 members are elected at general elections for a term of 4 years.[45] Republic of Estonia is divided into multi-member electoral districts, where the 101 Parliamentary seats are distributed in proportion to the number of citizens with the right to vote. The specific distribution of mandates in the electoral districts is determined by three rounds of counting. At first, a *simple quota* is calculated for each electoral district by dividing the number of valid votes cast in the district by the correspondent number of mandates. A candidate is elected

[36] Merusk (2004).

[37] SC 3-4-1-1-03.

[38] Auby (2013).

[39] SC 3-1-1-86-07.

[40] *State Budget Act* 2016 RT I 23.12.2015, 6.

[41] Limited scope of activity, multi-functionalism, reliance on informal structures, constraints on steering and control, and high personalism. Sarapuu (2010).

[42] Parrest (2009).

[43] 23,571 of them worked in the state and 5790 in the local government agencies; Personnel Policy of State.

[44] SC 3-2-1-40-15.

[45] Parliament of Estonia.

in favor of whom the number of votes exceeds (or equals) the simple quota. In the second round of counting, the candidates are ranked according to the number of votes received. The votes cast in favor of all candidates running on the same list are added up. A list receives as many mandates as the number of their votes exceeds the simple quota of electoral district. Thirdly, the mandates, which are not distributed in the electoral districts, are distributed as *compensation mandates* to the declared lists of political parties among the candidates of which received at least 5% of the votes nationally. A modified d'Hondt distribution method with the distribution series of $1, 2^{0.9}, 3^{0.9}$, etc., is used to deliver rest of the mandates.

The head of state of Estonia is the President of the Republic, who is elected by the Parliament (or by an electoral body) and has mainly representational and balancing functions between the other Constitutional institutions. The President has some specific responsibilities in regard to the *Riigikogu*, to the Government, to legislation[46], powers to appoint and release Constitutional public servants and powers to grant clemency.[47] More specifically, the *Const* § 78 states that the President shall (1) represent the Republic of Estonia in International relations; (2) appoint and recall diplomatic agents on the proposal of the Government, and receive the credentials of diplomatic agents accredited to Estonia; (3) declare elections to the Riigikogu; (4) proclaim laws and sign instruments of ratification; (5) initiate amendment of the Constitution; (6) designate the candidate for Prime Minister; (7) appoint to and release from office members of the Government; (8) make recommendations to the Riigikogu regarding appointments to the office of Chief Justice of the Supreme Court, Chairman of the Board of the Bank of Estonia, Auditor General and Chancellor of Justice; (9) on the proposal of the Board of the Bank of Estonia, appoint to office the President of the Bank of Estonia; (10) on the proposal of the Supreme Court, appoint judges; (11) confer state awards, military and diplomatic ranks; (12) make proposals to the Riigikogu to declare a state of war, to order mobilization and demobilization, and to declare a state of emergency; (13) in the case of aggression against Estonia, to declare a state of war and orders mobilization pursuant; (14) by way of clemency, release or grant commutation to convicts at their request and (15) initiate the bringing of criminal charges against the Chancellor of Justice. The President of the Republic shall be elected for a term of 5 years. No one shall be elected to the office of the President for more than two consecutive terms (*Const* § 80).

Executive power is vested in the Government, which has the main policy-making and administrative functions. The *Const* § 87 states that Government of the Republic shall (1) execute the domestic and foreign policies of the state; (2) direct and co-ordinate the activities of government agencies; (3) administer the implementation of laws, resolutions of the Parliament, and legislation of the President; (4) introduce bills, and submit international treaties to the Parliament for

---

[46]Shall proclaim the laws passed in the *Riigikogu* and proclaim the law or shall propose to the SC to declare the law unconstitutional.

[47]Powers and responsibilities of President.

ratification and denunciation; (5) prepare the draft state budget and submit it to the Parliament, administer the implementation of the state budget and present a report on the implementation of the budget to the Parliament; (6) issue regulations and orders on the basis of and for the implementation of law; (7) manage relations with other states, and (8) declare an emergency situation throughout the state or in a part thereof, in the case of a natural disaster or a catastrophe, or to prevent the spread of an infectious disease. The Government may also perform other executive duties given by the Constitution and the laws.

Implementing the policies of the state the public power can be applied only to governmental authorities, e.g. Ministries, the Estonian Defense Forces, the Government Office and the county governments as well as executive agencies and inspectorates and their local authorities with authority to exercise executive power.[48] According to *Administrative Co-operation Act*[49] it is possible to transfer some public administration duties to the private sector in purpose to achieve less costly public service with some higher quality, except non-transferable public functions which are 'the core functions of the state authority'.[50]

The Bank of Estonia (the *Eesti Pank*) is the central bank of the Republic of Estonia and a member of the European System of Central Banks. Estonia adopted the euro on 1 January 2011 and the *Eesti Pank* joined the euro system. The primary objective of the *Eesti Pank* is to contribute to price stability within the euro area. After 1 January 2011, the *Eesti Pank* lost its exclusive right to issue Estonian currency established by *Const* §111, but it shall annually report to the Parliament about its main activities and results to guarantee financial stability in Estonia as a member of Eurozone.

The State Audit Office as a Constitutional institution is an independent public body that carries out performance and financial audits concerning public spending and that is independent in discharging its duties. The main function of the State Audit Office is to conduct economic control how the state and local authorities have spent the taxpayer's money.[51] In more detailed way, the *Const* § 133 states that the State Audit Office shall control (1) the economic activities of state agencies, state enterprises and other state organizations; (2) the use and preservation of state assets; (3) the use and disposal of state assets, which have been transferred into the control of local governments, and (4) the economic activities of enterprises in which the state holds more than one-half of the votes by way of parts or shares, or whose loans or contractual obligations are guaranteed by the state. The State Audit Office shall be directed by the Auditor General who is appointed for 5 years to and released from office by the Parliament on the proposal of the President of the Republic (*Const* § 134). The Auditor General shall also present its annual report on the use and preservation of state assets during the preceding budgetary year at the same

[48] *Government of the Republic Act* RT I 1995, 94, 1628.

[49] *Administrative Co-operation Act* RT I 2003, 20, 17.

[50] Parrest (2009).

[51] National Audit Office of Estonia.

time as the report on the implementation of the state budget is debated in the Parliament (*Const* § 135).

The Chancellor of Justice (CJ) or the *Legal Chancellor* supervises the implementation and interpretation of the *Const*. The CJ is an independent official whose duties are to ensure that the legislation would be constitutional and that the fundamental rights and freedoms are protected. The *Const* § 139 states that the CJ shall analyze proposals concerning the amendment of laws, the passage of new laws, and the activities of state agencies, and shall present a report to the Parliament. If the CJ finds that legislation passed by the legislative or executive powers or by a local government is in conflict with the *Const* or law, he shall propose to the body which passed the legislation to bring the legislation into conformity with the *Const* or the law (*Const* § 142). If it is not implemented within 20 days, the CJ shall propose to the Supreme Court to declare the legislation invalid. In addition, the CJ shall make a proposal to the Parliament if criminal charges be brought against a member of the Parliament, the President of the Republic, a member of the Government, the Auditor General, and the Chief Justice of the Supreme Court or a justice of the Supreme Court. The Chancellor of Justice as Constitutional institution in Estonia combines the function of the general body of petition and the guardian of constitutionality by constitutional review, protection of fundamental rights and good administration principle in its broad sense, protection of the rights of a child, prevention of ill-treatment and other tasks. Such a combined competence of legislative supervision and ombudsman is quite unique internationally.[52]

According to the *Const*, the local self-government is an important constitutional institution. Local governments provide about 70% of all public services in Estonia.[53] *Const* § 154 states that all local issues shall be resolved and managed by local governments, which shall operate independently. Duties may be imposed on a local government only pursuant to law or by agreement with the local government. Expenditure related to duties of the state imposed by law on a local government shall be funded from the state budget. The entities of local self-government in Estonia are rural municipalities and cities (*Const* § 155); the representative body of a local authority is its council which is elected in a free election for a term of 4 years (*Const* § 156). A local government shall have an independent budget and has the right to levy and collect taxes, and to impose duties (*Const* § 157).

In 2016, there were 213 local government units in Estonia: 183 rural municipalities and 30 cities.[54] The experts had pointed out that Estonian local government law is in the need of further substantial development if the administrative capability of rural municipalities and cities is to be raised to the level required by the *Const*.[55] In 2016, the Parliament started to discuss *Administrative Reform Act*, which was enforced in June 2016. The main objective of the administrative

[52]Chancellor of Justice. Sustainable Governance Indicators (2014).

[53]National Audit Office of Estonia (2008).

[54]Local government.

[55]Olle and Merusk (2013).

reform is to form bigger local self-government units that would be able to offer better public services, ensure some higher level of competitiveness for regions, and independently fulfill the tasks set to them.[56] For that purpose, the optimal population of the local government is seen to be at 11,000, including 5000 inhabitants as a minimum size to form capable local government unit.

2.2 Administrative Law and Procedure

Lehte Roots
Tallinn Law School, Tallinn University of Technology, Akadeemia tee 3, 12618 Tallinn, Estonia
e-mail: lehte.roots@ttu.ee

Helen Kranich and Monika Mikiver
Law Enforcement Affairs Department of the Chancellor of Justice, Kohtu 8, 15193 Tallinn, Estonia
e-mail: helen.kraich@oiguskantsler.ee; monika.mikiver@oiguskantsler.ee

Estonian public administration is strongly based on law and legal principles. All state authority shall be exercised solely pursuant to the *Const* and laws which are in conformity therewith.[57] The whole administrative organization[58] and the activities shall be in conformity with the *Const*. The basis for the Administrative law is the Estonian *Const*. §14 of the *Const* firstly carries both an organizational and procedural dimensions but also suggests that public authority follows and respects the fundamental rights. The requirement to guarantee rights and freedoms does not consist only of the obligation to respect the fundamental rights but also relates to their active formalization in societal structures. Therefore §14 of the *Const* guarantees subjective rights, and its provision are implemented in conjunction with other material, addressing fundamental and subjective rights, and its provisions are implemented in conjunction with other material rights—addressing fundamental and subjective rights, as it lacks clearly defined and independent substantial elements of content.

The exercise of official authority is mainly the monopoly of officials named in the *Const*[59] and the *Civil Service Act*.[60] Delivering the official authority to legal

[56] *Administrative Reform Act* RT I, 21.06.2016, 1.
[57] *Const* §3.
[58] Taro and Parrest (2014).
[59] §3, 30, Ch II.
[60] *Civil Service Act*. §7(3) RT I, 06.07.2012, 1.

person in public or private law is regulated by the *Administrative Co-operation Act*[61].

The objective of §14 of the *Const* is to guarantee the rights and freedoms, state the duty of the legislative, executive and judicial powers, and of local governments.

The Estonian administrative law consists of general and special parts. General regulations, principles, terms, and legal institutions are important for all of the branches of administrative law. Administrative activities shall be efficient, purposeful[62] and human-friendly in its most general sense. Also, the principle of good administration is based on: legality, human dignity, legal certainty (a clarity and a legitimate expectation),[63] proportionality (interference-free or minimally infringing activities),[64] large discretion and flexibility, freedom of format, expediency and efficiency, the principle of investigation, publicity and transparency, cooperation between the law enforcement agencies. At the same time, the citizen's own duty of care[65] and responsibility[66] and the public interest must be considered.

The general part of administrative law of Estonia, consists of *Administrative Procedure Act, Administrative Co-operation Act, Substitutive Enforcement and Penalty Payment Act, State Liability Act, Law Enforcement Act.* Special part of the administrative law consists of more than 180 thematic laws. The general and special parts of Estonian administrative law is complete and should guarantee the protection of rights and public interest without any gap in the law.

The *Administrative Procedure Act*[67] contains two equal and important goals, which includes the guarantee of appropriate and lawful activity in reaching and taking administrative decisions and the guarantee of a respect of individuals' rights in administrative decision making procedure. Both the decision itself and the procedure are important. The equity of the procedure is based on human dignity[68]. The purpose of this act is to ensure the protection of the rights of persons by creation of a uniform procedure, which allows participation of persons and judicial control. The act provides that in administrative procedure, the fundamental rights and freedoms or other subjective rights of a person may be restricted only pursuant to rule of law. All administrative acts and measures shall be appropriate, purposefulness, necessary and proportionate to the stated objectives. The lawfulness of an act, in any single case should guarantee the comprehensive right of discretion[69]. Administrative procedure shall be purposeful, efficient and straightforward and

[61]Economically justified, quality of the performance, interests of public and people. *Administrative Co-operation Act.* §6 RT I 2003, 20, 17.

[62]SC 3-3-1-94-08.

[63]SC 3-4-1-14-06.

[64]SC 3-3-1-22-15.

[65]SC 3-3-1-25-09.

[66]SC 3-3-1-100-10.

[67]RT I 2001, 58, 354.

[68]Proceeding, without the person being heard, treats the person as an object not the subject.

[69]An authorization to consider making a resolution or choose between different resolutions).

conducted without undue delay, avoiding superfluous costs and inconveniences to persons. Good administration principle must be considered.

State Liability Act[70] provides the bases of and procedure for the protection and restoration of rights violated upon the exercise of powers of a public authority and performance of other public duties and deals with compensation for damage caused by the state action or inactivity. Firstly, a person may request that a public authority annul an administrative act, terminate continuing measures, refrain from issuing an administrative act or taking a measure, or issue an administrative act or take an action. Secondly, if damage could not be prevented and cannot be eliminated by the administrative measures, a person may request that a public authority compensate for the damage caused to him or her.

One of the key objectives of the Estonian administrative law is its proactive approach. The *Substitute Enforcement and Penalty Payment Act*[71] gives the public authorities the power to influence people to fulfill their obligations, warning people with a penalty payment or performance of a substitute enforcement. There is accumulated jurisprudence, which reveals different interpretations of the application of law.

Administrative Co-operation Act[72] concerns two independent objects of regulation—professional assistance and granting of authority to perform public administration duties. The professional assistance allows for improvement of co-operation between various administrative authorities and thereby increases the efficiency of administration. There should be no gap in administrative organization for protecting rights of individuals or the public interest. The Act enables the needs of small state, to deliver the authority to natural and legal persons, to perform public administration duties of the state and of local governments independently.

Law Enforcement Act[73] provides the general principles, the bases and the organization of the protection of public order. Law enforcement means, the prevention of a threat endangering public order[74], ascertainment of a threat in the case of a suspicion of a threat, countering of a threat and elimination of a breach of public order. The Law enforcement is the responsibility of a person liable for public order[75]. *The Law Enforcement Act* has a proactive approach. Unless the act contains a large catalog of general and special supervision measures, the main objective is to act interference-free or infringing minimally the rights.

[70]RT I 2001, 47, 260.

[71]RT I 2001, 50, 283.

[72]RT I 2003, 20, 17.

[73]RT I, 22.03.2011, 4.

[74]A state of society in which the adherence to legal provisions and the protection of legal rights and persons' subjective rights are guaranteed.

[75]Who has caused a suspicion of a threat or a threat, violates public order or has caused the possibility of the occurrence of a situation in the case of which there will be a threat or a suspicion of a threat.

2.2.1 Historical Developments Estonian Administrative Law and Procedure

The first Estonian *Administrative Procedure Act* entered into force on 1 April 1936.[76] The objective was to lay down general rules for settlement through adjudication of administrative matters, which was assigned among the powers of the state or local government agencies insofar as specific law did not provide otherwise. The adoption of the *Administrative Procedure Act* also confirms the fact that Estonia had managed to develop uniform administrative law theory and practice of 1930s, which was discontinued when Estonia was occupied by the Soviet Union.

Today the basis for administrative procedure can be found in the *Const*. With the respect to the law of administrative procedure, §14 of the *Const* plays an important role, according to which guaranteeing rights and freedoms is the duty of the legislative, executive and judicial powers and of local government. The first sentence of §15 of the *Const* is important from the sight of administrative procedure. It states that everyone whose rights and freedoms are violated has the right of recourse to the courts. This provision ensures the right to appeal. Additionally, §20 of the *Const* should be mentioned as according to the clauses of 4.5 and 6 of §20 (2) a person may be deprived of liberty only in cases specified by law and pursuant to the appropriate legal procedure.

§21 of the *Const* says that "everyone who is deprived of his or her liberty shall be informed promptly, in a language and manner that he or she understands, of the reason for the deprivation of liberty and of his or her rights, and shall be given the opportunity to notify those closes to him or her". §44(1) sets forth the general right to receive public information and the duty of a pubic authority to provide information about its activities to an Estonian citizen at his or her request.

After the *Const* was re-established in 1992 the reforms in administrative law could start. As Merusk in his analysis states, the government acknowledged that Estonia was part of continental European legal culture. He also claims that it was not an easy task to combine the European administrative systems to the Estonian reality. Some drafters of the administrative law got ideas from Germany, others from Scandinavia or England. It was suggested by the study done in 1993 that Estonian public administration law should be derived from Germany and Austria.[77] The acts of special parts were drafted by different ministries and it created a problem of uniformity. There was a pressing need to have universal rules and the decision was made that German administrative rules will be taken over and foreign experts started to draft the laws. This kind of automatic overtake of German legislation was criticized by professors and legal scholars. At the end of nineties, it was evident that the draft acts did not reflect the reality of Estonia and corresponded to the *Const*. There was an emerging need for the reform, so it was decided to found the organizational structure on the classical system.[78]

---

[76] *Administrative procedure Act* RT 1936, 4, 25.

[77] Merusk (2004), p. 53.

[78] Ibid.

After 1999 Estonia started to develop its public administration and several attempts to change the system and proposals were issued in 2001, 2003, 2007, 2009 and in 2013.

After 2000 many important acts related to public administration were adopted. *Administrative Procedure Act, State Liability Act, Substitutive Enforcement and Penalty Payment Act, Administrative Co-operation Act, Code of Administrative Court Procedure*. To ensure coherence between the general part and special part of administrative acts, the *Administrative Procedure Act Amendment and Implementation Act* was prepared and adopted by the Parliament, amending over 130 specific laws.

2.2.2 Current Issues

Administrative Procedure Act guarantees appropriate and lawful activity in research and administrative decisions making procedure and gives a guarantee to respect for rights of individuals' in administrative decision making process.[79]

The protection of rights of persons, which is supported also by §3(1) of the *Administrative Procedure Act*. The fundamental rights and freedoms of other subjective right of a person may be restricted only pursuant to the law. It also corresponds with the §11 of the *Const*, which requires that any activities of public authority restricting fundamental rights has to be in accordance with the provisions of the *Const*.

Another important principle underlying the *Administrative Procedure act* is lawfulness. It is also supported by §3(1) and §4 of the Act, which sets out both internal and external limits for exercising the right of discretion. This right entails a rather high degree of threat that administrative authority may act arbitrarily. It is limited by the law that, the right of discretion shall be exercised in accordance with the limits of authorization, the purpose of discretion, and the general principles of justice, taking into account relevant facts and considering legitimate interest.[80]

Next principle that has to be mentioned is the principle of proportionality. It is protected by the *Const* §11, according to which some restriction of rights and freedoms is necessary in a democratic society and shall not distort the nature of the rights and freedoms. *Administrative Procedure Act* states that administrative acts and measures shall be appropriate, necessary, and proportionate to the stated objectives.

Principle of good administration is reviewed also by the Estonian SC, which has stated that it is derived from §14 of the *Const* and is one of the fundamental rights.[81] The principle of good administration is also manifested in §5(2) of the *Administrative Procedure Act*—administrative procedure shall be purposeful, efficient and

[79] *Administrative Procedure Act*, RT I 2001, 58, 354.

[80] §4 (2).

[81] SC 3-4-1-1-03.

straightforward, and conducted without undue delay. The Administrative Law Chamber of the SC of Estonia has emphasized that on ground of human dignity, in a state based on the rule of law, efficient legal protection, and the principle of good administration, each individual must be involved in an administrative procedure even if in the case of a conscientious performance of administrative duties, the administrative act may be foreseen to limit his or her rights.[82]

Principle of good administration presumes that administrative proceedings are conducted in a fair and impartial manner. §10 of the Act grants the participants the right to submit a petition for removal of an official.

Administrative law reforms have been affected by practice of the courts, particularly—the SC of Estonia. SC has elaborated on several important principles of administration of the State.

Administrative reform is something that is an ongoing and never-ending process. In the past the discussions on constitutional and fundamental rights of the persons lead to the administrative law creation and political discussion. Estonian Administrative law is based on the principles of European Union and has taken over good practices of other democracies, having big impact from the German law as it served as a model for preparing the *Const* and Administrative system. The Acts that address the general part of administrative law including the principles stated there have an important impact on further laws dealing with special parts of administrative law. The special parts of the administrative law have to be interpreted in conjunction with the main principles and general part of administrative law.

As the last amendments in Estonian Administrative system were introduced in 2016,[83] The draft Act of the Public Administration Reform[84] §1 states that the aim of the act is to give the grounds for the amendment for an administrative—territorial organization and procedures including the territorial organization needed, deadlines for the decision-making procedures and deadlines for the reform of the local government units, criteria for the size based on the minimum number of inhabitants for the local municipality and exceptions, the rights and obligations of a local municipality in the process of the reform. The aim of this reform is to support the capacity of local governments to provide quality public services by using the prospects of development, increase the competitiveness and ensure more even development at local level. The local governments should be able to organize and manage the local life and to fulfill the statutory duties. The planned administrative reform will be implemented on bases and goals of public administration which is ensuring good quality public services and being contemporary cost effective. There should be established local governments with minimum of 11,000 inhabitants. Nevertheless, this number is considered to be recommendable. Future developments in the public administration are related to the development of the

---

[82]SC 3-3-1-56-02. (§11(1)3, participation).

[83]More about the reforms can be read https://valitsus.ee/en/state-reform, and https://valitsus.ee/en/news/government-approved-criteria-administrative-reform-concept.

[84]RT I, 21.06.2016, 1.

current public administration reform. There is a clear roadmap of different activities agreed upon.

The small counties in Estonia have to be united with bigger ones to save the public costs and increase the efficiency and effectiveness of the services that the local authorities and state should provide for its citizens and residents, it shows that reforms are part of the developing society and the same applies to the administration of the state.

The Estonian administrative law nevertheless stays under the control and strict observation of constitutional principles and fundamental rights, which have to be applied in any case.

2.3 Estonian Penal Law and Criminal Procedure

Marko Kairjak
Faculty of Law, University of Tartu, Näituse, 18 Tartu, Estonia

Estonian Business School, Lauteri 3, Tallinn, Estonia
e-mail: marko.kairjak@ut.ee

Dmitri Teplõhh
Tallinn Law School, Tallinn University of Technology, Akadeemia tee 3, 12618 Tallinn, Estonia

Faculty of Law, University of Tartu, Näituse, 18 Tartu, Estonia
e-mail: dmitri.teplohh@varul.com

The *Estonian Penal Code* entered into force on 1 July 2002. It is a modern penal code largely based on the theory of German penal law (though not the *German Penal Code*),[85] which introduced into the Estonian legal system a definitive three-step delictual structure,[86] a clear differentiation between the error in elements of the offence, the error concerning circumstance which precludes unlawfulness and the error as to unlawfulness of act,[87] as well as the penal liability of legal persons. The latter could not have been based on the example of German penal law—since German penal law does not recognize the criminal liability of legal persons—which is why the law relating to the issue is a particular mixture of common law and French and Finnish[88] penal laws.

During the last 14 years, the penal code has gone through two extensive reforms—the first considerable set of changes entered into force on 15 March 2007 and the second—significantly more substantial than the earlier reforms,

[85] See Sootak (2005).
[86] See Sootak (2001).
[87] As an introduction to post-penal code case law, see decision of Supreme Court (SC) 3-1-1-95-05.
[88] See Lahti (2003).

with the official title of "The Revision of Penal Law"[89]—came into effect on 1 January 2015. The revision of the penal law was mainly based on criminal-political considerations—legal literature observed both statistically and theoretically a clear over-criminalization in Estonia, the boundaries of the principle of *ultima ratio*[90] were blurred and issues were regulated with penal law, although their primary regulatory instrument could have been of a more lenient nature—either civil or administrative law.[91] The changes adopted within the framework of the revision affected both the general and the special part: an important change was the establishment of liability for attempted misdemeanor in exceptional circumstances, the liability of legal persons was expanded, several economic criminal offences were decriminalized and simplifications were made in relation to corruption and offences against the person.

Inherently, there is nothing distinguishing about Estonian penal law in the aforementioned considerations—in examining financial sector offences the revision of penal law also tangled with new European Union (EU) legislation, which in addition to norms of penal law, also obligates member states to foresee appropriate and effective measures of administrative enforcement without actually specifying their exact meaning.[92] Therefore, the issue of what really is and is not penal law remains not only active but also bound to attract further attention in the future, regardless of the case law of the European Court of Human Rights (ECHR)[93].

The following concentrates on a some of the main issues to illustrate the preceding considerations, which were, so to say, brought to the table in the context of the revision—the liability of legal persons and the criminalization of bankruptcy offenses. In connection with criminal procedure, the focus is on matters relating to the taking of evidence based on the example of surveillance activities.

2.3.1 Liability of Legal Persons

According to §14(1) of the *Penal Code*, the liability of a legal person is a derivative liability. This means that a legal person is held responsible for the acts of a natural person associated with it. Unlike civil law, which attributes to legal persons at least a formally equal legal capacity than to natural persons, under Estonian penal law a legal person's hands are tied with respect to penal liability.[94] The liability of legal persons is therefore based on two presumptions: the act committed by the governing

[89]See Sootak (2013). Siitam-Nyiri (2014), p. 577.

[90]For an introduction see: Jareborg (2004).

[91]See Sootak (2013). Reinthal (2010), pp. 740, 748. Siitam-Nyiri (2014), pp. 578 etc.

[92]See Kairjak (2015).

[93]See e.g. ECtHR 08.06.1976, 5101/71, 5354/72, 5102/71, 5370/72, *Engel and other v The Netherlands*, p. 12, 80 etc.; ECtHR 04.03.2014, 18640/10, *Grande Stevens v Italy*.

[94]See early case law: SC 3-1-1-82-04, newer case law: SC 3-1-1-66-4, SC 3-1-1-133-13.

body, a member thereof, a senior official or competent representative of the legal person is identified; the act is committed in the interests of the legal person.

Before moving on, it is important to note that the liability of legal persons only applies in circumstances provided for in the special part of the *Penal Code*. Until the changes, which entered into force on 1 January 2015, the liability of a legal person was rather exceptional, meaning that it was not foreseen in relation to most offences. The revision of penal law introduced the possibility of holding a legal person liable to most offences—for example, the fact that liability of a legal person was envisaged for also sexual delicts understandably caused some controversy in the press. In addition, liability of a legal person was envisaged for war crimes and most offences against the person (including manslaughter and causing serious bodily injury) and against the family. The principle that liability of a legal person does not apply to the state, local governments, international organizations and to legal persons in public law was left largely unchanged.[95]

The liability of a legal person does not exclude the liability of a natural person, nor vice versa[96], although presumably the natural person will be held accountable first and then the legal person, provided the conditions outlined in §14(1) of the *Penal Code* are satisfied. Case law has managed the fundamental questions since the enactment of the 2002 *Penal Code* rather (at least seemingly) well. The SC of Estonia saw no problems with the fact that in cases with a convicted legal and natural person, the sole shareholder and member of the board of the legal person is that same natural person, essentially in conflict with the principle of *ne bis in idem*.[97] In addition, the SC also gave sufficiently clear guidance on the enforcement of a legal person: in cases where the basis for the commission of an offence was a decision of a board consisting of several members, all members who voted in favour of the decision were held liable, and in cases where the decision was adopted by a secret vote, all members of the board who participated were held liable.[98] However, unfortunately the foregoing lacks—including to date—clarity. Even now the case law of the court of the highest instance—the SC—continues to deal with, at first sight, rather trivial questions, emphasizing that in cases involving an offender consisting of several persons, the contribution of all parties must be ascertained[99] or that the liability of a legal person is independent, meaning it is not the case of the so-called fourth characteristic of the elements of a crime[100].

As mentioned above, to attribute an act to a legal person, the person mentioned in §14(1) of the *Penal Code* must be identified—either a member of the governing body, a senior official or a competent representative. Despite the previously

[95]See more precisely the *Penal Code* §14 lg 3. RT I 2001, 61, 365.

[96]See more precisely the *Penal Code* §14 lg 1. RT I 2001, 61, 364.

[97]See also SC 3-1-17-04 and SC 3-1-1-53-12.

[98]See academic discussion regarding instrumental offences, Randma (2011). With regard to secret votes, see SC 3-1-1-137-04.

[99]SC 3-1-1-21-12.

[100]SC 3-1-1-30-11.

mentioned rather theoretical problems there have not been many issues in current practice regarding the implementation: essentially, a situation is possible where an offence is committed by one of the previously mentioned persons (for example a member of the governing body submits a false declaration or—since 1 January 2015 a completely feasible situation—commits rape in the interests of a legal person) or a lower level employee, who respectively acts on the orders of a member of the board or a mid-level manager. In such circumstances it is either an instrumental offence or joint criminal offence and the act of the person specified in §14 (1) of the *Penal Code* is attributed to the legal person.

At times seemingly insurmountable problems emerged in the case law when the act of the person specified in §14(1) of the *Penal Code* was not evidenced during the proceedings—meaning that the act was committed by a lower level employee of the legal person (respectively whether the person was identified or not). Such a situation raises the question of whether the action of a member of the governing body, a mid-level manager or a competent representative can be attributed to a member of the board when the action is an omission, meaning conducting sufficient supervision.[101] The case law has actually correctly indicated that the general part must be consulted—according to §13 of the *Penal Code* a person is responsible for an omission if the person was legally required to act. In legal literature and case law the prior duty to act has been described as a duty to act as guarantor, which may arise either on the basis of a law, a contract, earlier conduct, etc.[102] The basis for the corresponding action is simple in case of a legal person—it is either the duty of care of a member of the governing body under civil law[103] or arising out of the respective employment relationship with a legal person under private law.

The main problem has nevertheless become the question of how far one has to look when determining the extent of the duty to act under §14(1) of the *Penal Code*. According to the theory relating to §13(1) of the *Penal Code*, the required act and whether it was objectively foreseeable, must therefore be identified.[104] For example, the SC has found that in matters where serious bodily injury is caused by the provision of substandard healthcare services out of negligence and omission, it would also suffice, provided other prerequisites are satisfied, to hold a person responsible if the court ascertains that lawful alternative conduct, that is, the required act, would have decreased the risk and the harm to the victim.[105] By having a narrow approach towards the liability of legal persons, the case law of the SC has not provided any abstract guidelines on the matter. However, in two cases involving copyright infringement by playing music in a shop and a hotel restaurant

[101]Similar to the liability of the so-called violation of the obligatory supervision, arising from the §130 of the German OWiG (the Administrative Offences Act).

[102]SC 3-1-1-104-09, for newer case law see decision no. 3-1-1-33-14.

[103]General Part of the *Civil Code Act* §35 RT I 2003, 35, 2016. For an introduction in the context of penal law, see SC 3-1-1-61-09, 3-1-1-100-09 and 3-1-1-89-11.

[104]Sootak (2010), pp. 569–570, 573.

[105]SC 3-1-1-79-10, p. 26.

respectively, the SC adopted the view that merely enabling the playing of music (i.e. not preventing the potential copyright infringement) is not a required act. Unfortunately, there is no guidance on what the required and objectively foreseeable act of the person mentioned in the *Penal Code*[106] would have consisted of: should the manager have informed the staff that playing music publicly was prohibited, performing immediate checks (if yes, how frequently) or substantive prevention.[107]

Issues that *prima facie* seem rather trivial, in practice give rise to a considerably wider question in relation to the liability of legal persons, such as relating to the duties imposed on members of the governing body. Inherently, the content of the aforementioned duty of care of the governing body is still a question of obligations arising from the internal relationship between the member of the governing body and the association and is aimed at the governing body managing the association and making decisions which lead to the best possible benefits. The content of the aforesaid duty is not the establishment of a supervisory duty on members of the governing body over their subordinates. This issue was also discussed in the course of the revision. The only alternative for bringing possible clarity was to specify § 14 of the *Penal Code*—by stipulating what, for example, the required act of the member of the governing body in the present situation would be. This, however, would have caused the following two problems:

In practice, in some spheres of life, the respective overseeing and supervisory duties of members of the managing board clearly exist—for example, with regard to the financial sector, such duties are explicitly highlighted in the specific laws governing the sector. Therefore—though probably not intentionally, rather over time—the choice has been to include the respective special obligations in the sector-specific laws.

The regulation of liability of legal persons in the Estonian *Penal Code* is brief, abstract and specific. Although it has taken years of case law for an understandable system to emerge, the so-called important problems have been resolved. Thus, the creation of separate rules for only omissions is fundamentally at odds with the general approach of legal solutions. All the more so, since the previously mentioned and sometimes amusing examples regarding playing music publicly for example in a shop show that creating an effective and clear guiding set of rules which applies to every isolated occurrence in such abstract questions is a complicated, if not a hopeless, task.

In the context of the revision, the idea of giving specific guidance was abandoned, although with one—and in practice quite incomprehensible—exception. Namely, §37^1 was introduced into the *Penal Code* of 1 January 2015, which states that "Legal persons are deemed to have acted without guilt if an act committed by a competent representative thereof was inevitable for the legal person." This change

[106]Either the member of the governing body or the mid-level manager—the manager of a hotel restaurant of a specific shop.

[107]SC 3-1-1-137-04, SC 3-1-1-39-04, SC 3-1-1-72-09.

narrowly affects the potential exclusion from liability of the competent representative. As stated above, the liability for omissions of the person mentioned in §14 (1) of the *Penal Code* should in any event be excluded in case the required act is not objectively foreseeable—meaning that regardless of even the most fervent of efforts, the infringement is not avoidable since the employee commits the offence anyway.[108] Therefore, narrowly stipulating such a separate provision is incomprehensible and may cause confusion, since it is guilt which is excluded under the provision and not the objective elements.

2.3.2 Bankruptcy Offences

§385[1] of the *Penal Code*, which was in force until 1 January 2015, criminalized the failure to perform an obligation to submit a bankruptcy petition. The *Bankruptcy Act* regulated (and also currently regulates) both the questions of what bankruptcy and a bankruptcy petition are. According to §1(2) of the *Bankruptcy Act*, a debtor is insolvent if the debtor is unable to satisfy the claims of the creditors and such inability, due to the debtor's financial situation, is not temporary. According to §1 (3), a debtor, who is a legal person, is insolvent also if the assets of the debtor are insufficient for covering the obligations thereof and, due to the debtor's financial situation, such insufficiency is not temporary. According to §4(2), bankruptcy petitions shall be filed with a court pursuant to the general jurisdiction applicable to the debtor. It is presumed that the seat indicated in the register 1 year before filing of a bankruptcy petition is the seat of the debtor unless it is proved that the seat of the debtor is elsewhere. The foregoing is complemented by §36 of the General Part of the *Civil Code Act*, which stipulates that if a legal person is clearly permanently insolvent, the members of the management board or the body substituting for the management board shall submit a bankruptcy petition. The concepts of bankruptcy and bankruptcy petition are therefore regulated by civil law. Pursuant to the general guidelines of the SC, uniform concepts in penal and civil law should have been construed in the same way, except where it was necessary for attaining the specific objectives of penal law.[109] However, what exactly these objectives are or how they should be identified remain unspecified by case law.

Subsequently, an issue arose in the case law in 2010 on whether to interpret the question of when a person is insolvent, that is to say, when a bankruptcy petition must be submitted, in penal law in a similar way as in civil law. In addition, the necessity of criminalizing the given infringement was questioned in the context of the revision—the considerations on *ultima ratio* presented in the introduction of the present art. It is also worth noting that, according to Estonian law, if the court identifies a delay with the bankruptcy petition during the bankruptcy proceedings, a member of the board becomes directly liable before the creditors under civil law.

[108] Sootak (2010), pp. 569–570 and 573.

[109] SC 3-1-1-28-09, 3-1-1-46-09.

Considerations regarding the reasonableness of the corresponding elements were given an impetus by two decisions of the SC from 2011: 3-1-1-49-11 and 3-1-1-85-11, which firstly interpreted the concept of bankruptcy (and thereby also the formation of the obligation to submit a bankruptcy petition) and provided guidelines in relation to proving the corresponding elements. To ascertain whether a debtor company has become permanently insolvent at a particular moment, a complete evaluation has to be made of the debtor's financial situation and the likely future prospects of the debtor's economic activity. Therefore, within the meaning of the given elements, permanent insolvency is apparent if the data characterising the debtor's financial situation is such to give grounds for an objective and competent bystander to consider that the debtor is permanently insolvent. Such an evaluation must be based on information that was available at the time the insolvency allegedly appeared (so-called *ex ante* evaluation). For example, in retroactively evaluating the debtor's solvency, significant changes that have occurred in the development of technology or the price of raw material, which affected the realization of the debtor's business plan, but were not reasonably foreseeable at the time of the evaluation, cannot be taken into account. Furthermore, it is generally not possible to identify the debtor's permanent insolvency only on the basis of a few accounting indicators—including the status of net assets or the amount of losses. To ascertain, within the meaning of the elements of the offence, whether a company had become objectively permanently insolvent by a particular time, all relevant circumstances relating to the financial situation of the debtor must be evaluated, without solely focusing on one criteria or indicator. In addition to net assets, other accounting data must also be analyzed, and also from the perspective of the debtor's business plan.[110] As a rule, an examination has to be conducted to identify insolvency, merely interrogating the interim trustee and considering the interim trustee's report as documentary evidence is not sufficient.[111]

In practice, the guidance provided by the previously mentioned decisions, signified that in addition to the evidence submitted by the interim trustee, a very intricate and time-consuming examination had to be conducted in matters deemed even slightly more complicated[112]. The guidance of the SC also meant that the concept of bankruptcy would have one meaning under criminal law and a separate one under civil law. The foregoing was a clear sign to the legislator to contemplate whether the previous elements of the offence—especially considering that the prescribed punishment is maximum 1 year imprisonment—were appropriate and reasonable. It had to be taken into account that the legal right protected by the offence—similarly to German law, under Estonian penal law the elements also have to be legitimized by identifying the legal right protected by it—is clearly defined:

[110] SC 3-1-1-49-11, pp. 17-19, 21.

[111] SC 3-1-1-85-11, pp. 34–35.

[112] SC 3-1-1-52-14.

the elements of the offence protected the interests of the creditors whose proprietary rights were infringed by the delayed submission of the bankruptcy petition.

Based on the prior considerations, the offence of failing to submit a bankruptcy petition was repealed and since 1 January 2015 only knowingly causing insolvency[113] is punishable under bankruptcy regulations and the unequal treatment of creditors[114] as a new offence. According to the explanatory note of the draft law, in the light of judgments 3-1-1-85-11 and 3-1-1-49-11 of the SC, proving §385^1 in both pre-trial and court proceedings has become extremely complicated[115]. Established case law is an obvious example that by its nature the delayed submission of a bankruptcy petition does not have to be punishable, since in any event the delayed submission of a bankruptcy petition gives rise to a board member's direct liability. Therefore, the additional criminal liability is excessive. All the more so, as determining the moment when the insolvency occurred requires a much higher burden of proof in criminal proceedings than it does in bankruptcy proceedings, and in addition, the question of intent also arises (see again the abovementioned decisions of the SC, especially the implementation of the so-called micro-enterprise criteria, which may lead to completely unpredictable results in the future).[116]

This appears to be a permanent solution to one problem. Understandably, practitioners have argued after the revocation of the abovementioned elements of the offence that along with the revocation, the additional protection of penal law also disappears. It should be borne in mind that in itself the change made by the legislator only affects the so-called intentional delaying of a bankruptcy petition, and knowingly causing insolvency remains punishable. Further practice will clarify whether the protection of the legal rights mentioned above requires that the creation of additional elements of an offence is considered. It should, however, be noted that the scope of the offence of unequal treatment of creditors created simultaneously with the revocation of §385^1 is rather wide. The offence is currently established with the following wording: "Preferring of one creditor to another in a manner knowingly prejudicial to such creditor by a member of a management body of a debtor who is a legal person or a body substituting therefor upon performance of the obligations of the debtor, if the ability of the debtor to satisfy the claims of injured creditors decreased thereby by an amount corresponding to or exceeding major damage".[117]

According to the explanatory note of the draft law, §384^1(1) in force before 1 January 2015, made the unequal treatment of creditors punishable on the

[113] *Penal Code* §384. RT I 2001, 61, 354.

[114] *Penal Code* §384^1. RT I 2001, 61, 364.

[115] In the light of the referred guidance of the SC a complicated and time-consuming examination for determining the moment of insolvency should always be prescribed.

[116] *Draft Law on the Amendments to the Penal Code and Related Laws*. Draft no. 554SE. Explanatory Note. http://www.riigikogu.ee/tegevus/eelnoud/eelnou/78433b29-8b2f-4281-a582-0efb9631e2ad/Karistusseadustiku%20muutmise%20ja%20sellega%20seonduvalt%20teiste%20seaduste%20muutmise%20seadus/.

[117] *Penal Code* §384^1(1). RT I 2001, 61, 364.

condition that it caused a material decline in the debtor's solvency or the debtor's insolvency, which was an unsuccessful construction: the fact that a debtor fulfils an actual obligation which has fallen due before one creditor can almost never be the cause of the debtor's insolvency. Although the debtor's assets decrease when complying with an obligation, the debtor's obligations also decrease. Even if it were considered that the decrease in the number of claims by creditors caused by the debtor complying with one obligation could be treated as a decline in the solvency of the debtor within the meaning of §384, the unequal treatment of creditors is not inherently a suitable alternative for causing insolvency. The unequal treatment of creditors is punishable not because it causes the debtor's insolvency, but because in fulfilling the duties of the debtor in financial difficulties, the principles of distribution arising from §153 of the *Bankruptcy Act* are not adhered to.[118] Although the criminal-political object of the abovementioned offence is understandable, terms like "preferring in a manner knowingly prejudicial" and "ability" will presumably cause as much headache in practice as the terms "insolvency" and "the time of submission of the bankruptcy petition" did in the previously mentioned cases with regard to the repealed §385[1] of the *Penal Code*. Therefore—a new beginning, but the same problems.

2.3.3 Overview of the Regulation Relating to Surveillance Activities

Provided it is necessary to collect information about an offence in criminal proceedings, surveillance activities can only be employed in the context of certain criminal offences, i.e. a definitive list of crimes in relation to which surveillance activities may be employed established by the legislator. In creating the catalogue, determining the permissibility of surveillance activities has been primarily based on the principle of *ultima ratio*—whether collecting evidence through surveillance activities with regard to a specific type of crime is unavoidably necessary and whether the evidence could be gathered via other steps or whether it is hindered.

Surveillance activities, which severely infringe fundamental rights, that is, covertly examining postal items, covertly intercepting communications and performing imitations of the crime, are authorized by courts. For covert surveillance of a person, object or an area, covert collection of reference material and initial examination of material, covert examination and replacement of objects, an authorization from a prosecutor's office is required.

The court examining a request for authorization of surveillance activities proceeds on the facts that are available to them at the time of making the decision

[118] Draft Law on the Amendments to the Penal Code and Related Laws. Draft no. 554SE. Explanatory Note. http://www.riigikogu.ee/tegevus/eelnoud/eelnou/78433b29-8b2f-4281-a582-0efb9631e2ad/Karistusseadustiku%20muutmise%20ja%20sellega%20seonduvalt%20teiste%20seaduste%20muutmise%20seadus/.

(so-called *ex ante* approach) and the court cannot be reprimanded for not taking facts, which were not known at the time the decision was made, into account. When granting an authorization for surveillance activities, the principle of last resort or *ultima ratio* must be followed: the collection of evidence through other proceedings must be precluded or significantly hindered[119]. Even if the prerequisites for surveillance activities are met[120] in justifying the necessity of the surveillance activities, the court must not limit itself to declaratory justifications. The conclusions of the court must be connected with an existing evidentiary basis. Merely referring to the prosecutor's request and stating that the court holds the request to be reasonable is inadequate[121]. If these requirements are not fulfilled, the evidence becomes inadmissible in the court proceedings.

Estonian criminal procedure sets out a so-called two file system for storing collected information, where all the information collected through surveillance activities and all data recordings made in the course of surveillance activities are stored in the surveillance file. Only those photographs, films, audio or video recordings or other data recordings, or parts of it, collected in the course of surveillance activities, which are necessary for resolving the criminal case, are stored in the criminal file, and all other information is stored in the surveillance file. The body conducting the proceedings decides what information is stored in the criminal file and what information in the surveillance file. At the same time, every party to the court proceedings must have an opportunity to present their own version to the court on the same conditions as the opposing side. Therefore, the accused, his or her counsel and also other persons, whose identities have been ascertained and whose data has been collected in the course of surveillance activities are guaranteed the right to access the material collected in the course of the surveillance activities. In this context, the main weakness of the regulation is arguably the fact that the information collected in the course of surveillance activities is made accessible before all the material collected in the course of criminal proceedings is introduced. This means that when the counsel has an opportunity to access the material collected during the surveillance activities, the counsel will not have an overview of which information is already in the criminal file and what the prosecutor's office wants to use as evidence.

Regardless of the fact that the counsel and the accused have an opportunity to access the surveillance file, the law does not allow to make copies of the collected material, so the examination has to be conducted at the investigating authority. To exercise the right of defence, it is necessary to examine the material collected in the course of surveillance activities. In the absence of copies, the examination of the materials is extremely impracticable, if not precluded, and in the light of the time period given for the examination, a thorough analysis of the materials collected in

[119]SC 3-1-1-68-14.

[120]Including compliance with the principle of *ultima ratio*.

[121]SC 3-1-1-14-14.

the course of surveillance as well as drawing conclusions, which are important for the exercise of the right of defence, is impossible.

If the criminal matter has not yet been sent to the court for substantive deliberation, i.e. during pre-trial proceedings, it is not known whether the criminal matter will be sent to court and what evidence the parties wish to rely on. In such an event it is not clear whether the person subjected to surveillance activities will have an opportunity in the subsequent criminal proceedings to address the court to protect his or her rights. Therefore, it is possible to challenge the legality of an authorization for surveillance activities granted by a court during pre-trial proceedings by way of an appeal.[122]

During the substantive deliberation of a criminal matter it is not possible to challenge the authorization of the court for surveillance activities by way of an appeal[123]. Based on the principle of fair and just legal proceedings, courts have an obligation to verify the legality of surveillance activities since it is the only way to ensure equality between the parties to the legal proceedings[124].

An application during court proceedings for verifying the legality of surveillance activities is accompanied by a duty of the court to make sure that the authorization of the court or the prosecutor's office for conducting surveillance activities exists and that the information used as evidence has been gathered in the course of permissible activities and during the time period stated in the authorization[125]. Courts also have a similar duty if contradictions or deficiencies, which can only be eliminated by consulting the authorization granted by a court or the prosecutor's office, appear in the evidence received in the course of surveillance activities.

2.3.4 Overview of the Regulation Relating to Preventive Custody

Detention of a person is not a preventive measure and a person may be detained for up to 48 h without a court authorization. A person may be detained if he or she is apprehended in the act of committing a criminal offence or immediately thereafter, an eyewitness to a criminal offence or a victim indicates such person as the person who committed the criminal offence, or the evidentiary traces of a criminal offence indicate that he or she is the person who committed the criminal offence.

Detention in criminal proceedings is a measure that most intensively infringes the fundamental rights of the accused or the suspect, which is why it is essential to monitor, during the criminal proceedings, that persons are only detained if and for as long as it is indispensable to ensure the proceedings[126].

[122] SC 3-1-1-76-15.

[123] SC 3-1-1-48-15.

[124] SC 3-1-1-31-11, p. 27.

[125] SC 3-1-1-63-08.

[126] SC 3-1-1-80-07, p. 13.

A person's detention is lawful only if the arrest warrant clearly and unequivocally sets out, first of all, the existence of reasonable doubt that the person to be taken into custody has committed an act with the elements of a criminal offence, and secondly, the presence of a basis for detention[127]. Only two circumstances can form the basis for detention—a person may commit new criminal offences or there is a risk of escape. In all other cases detention is excluded[128].

An accused or a suspect may be taken into custody on the request of the prosecutor's office and on the basis of an order of a preliminary investigation judge or on the basis of a court ruling. According to the redaction in force until 31 August 2016, if a person is detained, he or she may be held in custody (provided a basis for detention exists) for up to 6 months. According to the amendment, which enters into force on 1 September 2016: in the course of pre-trial proceedings, an accused or suspect of a criminal offence in the first degree cannot be detained for longer than 6 months and an accused or suspect of a criminal offence in the second degree for no longer than 4 months; a minor, who is an accused or a suspect cannot be detained for longer than 2 months during pre-trial proceedings. Therefore, the amendment reduces the maximum duration of detention for criminal offences in the second degree from 6 months to 4 months, but makes the conditions for detention for criminal offences in the first degree more restrictive. In cases of particular complexity or extent of a criminal matter or in exceptional cases arising from international cooperation in criminal proceedings, a preliminary investigation judge may extend the term for holding a person in custody at the request of the Prosecutor General. According to the amendment coming into effect, upon detention, a preliminary investigation judge may permit that an accused or a suspect be held in custody for up to 2 months. A preliminary investigation judge may extend this deadline by a maximum of 2 months at a time at the reasonable request of the prosecutor's office.

Instead of custody, a court may impose bail or electronic surveillance. A court shall determine the amount of bail on the basis of the degree of the potential punishment, the extent of the damage caused by the criminal offence, and the financial situation of the suspect or accused. The minimum amount of bail is 500 days' wages[129]. At the request of an accused, a suspect or prosecutor, a preliminary investigation judge or court, with the consent of the person held in custody, may commute holding in custody to the obligation to submit to electronic surveillance. The time of electronic surveillance is not deemed to be custody pending trial or detention and it is not included in the term of punishment. In the event of electronic surveillance, the accused or suspect is confined to fixed locations and his or her movements are electronically monitored, which aims to avoid the risk of escape.

[127]SC 3-1-1-127-12.

[128]SC 3-1-1-32-12.

[129]Calculated on the basis of the suspect's income.

Although in national criminal proceedings a court may impose bail or electronic surveillance instead of custody, in extradition proceedings persons must be held in custody. In extradition proceedings, a person can be deprived of his or her liberty on separate conditions and grounds. The constitutional basis for the application of provisional custody is outlined in §20(1)(6) of the Estonian Constitution (*Const*), which permits the deprivation of a person's liberty in cases and pursuant to a procedure provided by law to prevent illegal settlement in Estonia and for removing a person from Estonia or for extraditing a person to a foreign state. In two cases: 3-1-1-101-13 and 3-1-1-102-13, the position of the SC was similar: "As regards the different opportunities of persons in custody to apply for a commutation of holding in custody in extradition proceedings and national criminal proceedings, the Supreme Court has repeatedly held, in determining the scope of protection afforded by the fundamental right to equality before the law, that according to §12(1) of the Const, equals must be treated equally and unequals unequally. Thereby, the question of equal or unequal treatment of two persons, a group of persons or a situation can only arise in circumstances where groups, which are treated differently, are comparable. Persons held in custody in the context of extradition proceedings and in the context of national criminal proceedings are in different legal situations, and are therefore not comparable. Accordingly, such different treatment is neither arbitrary nor unconstitutional."

The amendment to the *Code of Criminal Procedure*[130], which entered into force on 1 July 2014, allowed suspects to request access to any evidence which is essential to discuss whether an arrest warrant is justified and for contesting detention and taking into custody in court. A prosecutor's office decides whether to enable access to the evidence. A prosecutor's office may adopt a ruling to refuse to enable access to evidence if this may significantly damage the rights of another person or if this may damage the criminal proceedings. Before this amendment was adopted, the collected materials were presented to the suspect and his or her counsel at the end of the pre-trial proceedings. The respective amendment is related to *Directive 2012/13/EU of the European Parliament and the Council of 22th May 2012, which addresses the right to information in criminal proceedings*[131]. The legislator considered it necessary on a national level to guarantee the suspect the right to access evidence before being held in custody and also for contesting the custody.

According to the Directive (art 7(4)), member states shall ensure that, in accordance with procedures in national law, a decision to refuse access to certain materials in accordance with the art is taken by a judicial authority or is at least subject to judicial review. Thus, the Directive also emphasizes that a person must be guaranteed a real opportunity to challenge the prosecutor's refusal in a court. A question had been raised in case law, according to which Estonian legislation does not comply with the spirit of the Directive, and the right to appeal in cases where

[130] RT I 2003, 27, 166.

[131] OJ EU 6.11.2013 L294/1.

materials have not been presented may have been established in an illusory manner at the national level. Obviously the requirement of accessing materials is primarily based on the obligation to guarantee fair proceedings where a person has been taken into custody and for effectively challenging the taking into custody. At the same time, in the opinion of the author, this is rendered completely pointless by the national procedure for appeals and the extremely long deadlines for settling a complaint, given the speed of taking a person into custody. Namely, in a situation where a prosecutor's office has made a ruling refusing to introduce materials, such a ruling must be contested with a separate complaint, which at first goes to the Office of the Prosecutor General, who has 30 days to resolve the respective complaint, and only then may an application be made to a county court, which in turn also has 30 days to deal with the complaint. Practice clearly shows that such complaints are solved at the last moment, meaning that contesting the ruling of a prosecutor's office not to introduce materials takes longer than 2 months. By the time the challenge regarding access to the materials has been finalized, the person has already been taken into custody a long time ago and even the person's appeals regarding his or her detention have been addressed. The SC has held that "a court deliberating an arrest warrant is competent to assess the legality of the refusal to provide access to evidence, which have been presented to the court and form the basis of the arrest warrant. If a court does not agree with the justifications of the prosecutor's office on the refusal of access to evidence and finds that the suspect's right of access to evidence has been unduly interfered with, the court must exclude all such evidence when deliberating the question of taking into custody (so-called prohibition of assessment). A court can notify the prosecutor's office prior to the exclusion of evidence, thus giving the prosecutor's office an opportunity to consider whether to withdraw the submitted request, provide access to the evidence or present further evidence."[132]

The general right of the accused to access the materials collected in the course of criminal proceedings can be factually realized at the end of the pre-trial proceedings. If a prosecutor's office declares the pre-trial proceedings finished, the office presents the criminal file to the counsel, the victim and the civil defendant. Essentially, this is the first time when the accused has the opportunity to access the collected materials and submit requests for the collection of additional evidence.

The effects of European Union criminal law on Estonian penal law are felt, but barely. The *Penal Code* has been in force since 2002 and 14 years is evidently enough time to highlight several problems. Fourteen years has also been enough to substantially resolve some major problems—the most genuine overview of this is provided by the revision of penal law, which was at the centre of the present art and with amendments to the 1 January 2015 *Penal Code* reached a significant milestone in the development of Estonian penal law. It was a revision in the best sense of that word—although problems were identified in the course of the revision, this did not

[132] SC 3-1-1-110-15.

always entail immediate interference in the form of legislative amendments. Good examples of this are matters relating to the liability of legal persons. The foregoing also clearly demonstrates that the legislator has reached a mature analytical phase represented by the notion that every important problem cannot involve an immediate and imprudent interference by the legislator. Naturally, the reality that sometimes a need arises for such interference—the example of the liability of legal persons—cannot be excluded. However, it is important to highlight the resolution of several important problems in the context of the revision—be it the internal problems of the system of violent criminal offences (the imprecision of the elements of arbitrary action, lack of gradation in the internal elements of the offence of physical abuse) or settling the points of contact between penal law and other laws (*ultima ratio*) (the example of bankruptcy offences).

2.4 Financial Law

Marek Herm
Tallinn Law School, Tallinn University of Technology, Akadeemia tee 3, 12618 Tallinn, Estonia

Law Firm ATTELA, Ahtri 6a, 10151 Tallinn, Estonia
e-mail: marek.herm@attela.ee

Tax law is part of financial law. In addition to tax law, financial law encompasses circulation of money, composition of the states' and local governments' budgets and other laws which regulate the collection of governments' income (state fees, fines, etc.). Whereas the budgetary legislation is mainly internal legislation[133], tax law regulates the relationship between public authorities and natural/legal persons. Therefore, this legal area should protect the rights of the taxpayers as well as states' fiscal interests.[134] The purpose of this art is to give the reader an overview of the most interesting aspects of Estonian (corporate) tax law.

Estonia's independent tax system's history started with adoption of the *Taxation Act* in 28 December 1989 by the ESSR Supreme Council[135]. The *Taxation Act* listed all the taxes in Estonia and named the essential features, e.g. object of taxation and taxpayers. It was followed by development of fiscal legislation. Estonia's fiscal legislation came into force in the beginning of 1991. Those tax laws were relatively short (often under 10 paragraphs) and included only the most important regulations. Everything else was written in the implementation regulation written by the Ministry of Finance. Before the Estonian Constitution (*Const*) came into force, it was

[133]Legal norms regulate the relationship between government agencies.

[134]Lehis (2012) p. 21.

[135]ÜVT/89/41/648.

rather common that some of the taxes were enforced with government's regulations.[136]

§113 of the *Const* provides that all the state taxes, duties, fees, fines and compulsory insurance payments are introduced by the law. §106 and 110 of the *Const* preclude the introduction of taxes by the referendum or by the decree of the President. On the interpretation of §113 of the *Const*, the Constitutional Chamber of the Estonian Supreme Court (SC) confirmed that all the essential elements of the tax liability must be provided by the law, including the object of tax and the tax rate[137]. According to the court, delegation of such an important matter to the executive power would be in violation of the principle of separation and balance of the powers. The SC invalidates laws that conflict with the *Const* upon application of the President, Chancellor of Justice, municipal council or lower level court.[138]

Const §157 entitles also local municipalities to levy and collect taxes, but these may be levied by the regulations issued in accordance to the *Local Taxes Act*. In levying local taxes, the municipality's freedom is thus limited by the list of taxes and the rules set out in the law[139]. Those principles are further confirmed in §4(2) of the *Taxation Act*[140], which provides that the taxpayers are required to pay only the state and local taxes prescribed by the law and at the rates and pursuant to the procedure provided in the tax laws and regulations of the local municipalities.

In addition to the law reservation, the supremacy of law must also be taken into consideration. In collecting taxes, the text of the act must be strictly adhered to; taxpayers' freedoms may not be restricted and the act may not be construed in an arbitrary manner under any acts of the executive power or under unwritten law. Tax liability may not be increased under any provision inferior to the law[141].

It can be concluded, that the authority to introduce taxes in Estonia is the prerogative of the *Riigikogu* (the Estonian Parliament). None of the essential elements of the tax law relationship can be delegated to the government. Regulations issued by the government or the Ministers for the implementation of the tax laws are of an explanatory and assisting character only and there must be a relevant delegation in the law.[142] The SC has ruled that the issue of a delegation norm does not legalize any earlier regulations that have been issued without a legal basis as well as the delegation contained in a law constitutes not only an authorization to issue regulations, but is an obligation to the executive power to issue a regulation needed for the implementation of the law[143].

[136]Lehis (2012), p. 24.

[137]For more in-depth analysis, please see Lehis (2000a, b), pp. 537–544.

[138]Loor (2015), p. 323.

[139]Lehis (1999), p. 100.

[140]RT I 2002, 26, 150.

[141]Lehis (1999), p. 101.

[142]Albin et al. (2010), p. 188.

[143]SC 4-1-5-98.

According to §3(2) of the *Taxation Act* currently in force, the following state taxes exist in Estonia: (1) income tax, (2) social tax, (3) land tax, (4) gambling tax; (5) value added tax (VAT); (6) customs duty; (7) excise duties; (8) heavy goods vehicle tax. Local taxes can be imposed by a rural municipality or city council in compliance with the conditions provided by the *Local Taxes Act*[144]. Currently, the following local taxes can be introduced: (1) advertisement tax, (2) road and street closure tax, (3) motor vehicle tax, (4) animal tax, (5) entertainment tax, (6) parking charge. However, the importance of local taxes is very low.[145]

As regards the customs duties, Estonia is fully integrated into the European Union (EU) Customs system with effect from 1 May 2004. The same applies to excise duties and VAT.

The first VAT system was introduced in Estonia by Government Regulation 209 of 10 October 1990, which came into effect on 1 January 1991. The current *VAT Act* of 10 December 2003 entered into force on 1 May 2004, the date of Estonia's accession to the EU, and is based on the *Council Directive 2006/112/EC on the common system of value added tax*[146]. As most provisions of that Directive have "direct effect", taxable persons may rely on them if the provisions of the national VAT Law deviate from the provisions of Community law. The standard VAT rate is currently 20%.

The income tax was enforced in 1991. Until 1994 different income tax acts applied to natural persons and legal persons. The tax rates were different as well. For the natural persons the income tax was progressive (tax rates were 16%, 24% and 33%), after the monetary reform in 1992 the corporate income tax rate was 35%. Starting from 1994 the income tax rate has been the same for both natural and legal persons.[147] According to the current *Income Tax Act*[148] (*ITA*), Estonia operates a flat 20% tax rate system for both natural persons and legal persons. The author of this art has always seen that for foreign readers, the most notable and interesting aspect concerning Estonian fiscal law has always been the unique corporate income tax system. Therefore, this art is mainly dedicated to introducing the corporate income tax system which now has been in operation for more than 16 years, but still attracts a lot of attention.

2.4.1 Estonia's Unique Corporate Income Tax System

On 1 January 2000, Estonia radically changed its corporate income tax system. The most notable feature of this reform was the elimination of the traditional corporate income tax and the introduction of the so-called *distribution tax*.[149]

[144]RT I 1994, 68, 1169.

[145]Lehis (2016), p. 427.

[146]Former Sixth Directive 77/388/EC.

[147]Lehis (2012), p. 24.

[148]RT I 1999, 101, 903.

[149]For more in-depth overview of the new Estonian corporate income tax system, as well as for the reasons for its introduction, see Kurist and Uustalu (2003), pp. 333–350; Lehis (2000a, b), pp. 135–141; Lehis et al. (2008a), pp. 389–399; Lehis et al. (2008b), pp. 14–24.

Under the new system, corporate taxpayers are not subject to corporate income tax, as the rest of the world knows it. Instead, they are subject to a flat 20% distribution tax[150] on distributed profits (both monetary and in-kind), including transactions that are considered as hidden profit distributions. The taxable base for the distribution tax, therefore, comprises the following components: dividends; gifts, donations and entertainment expenses; fringe benefits; transfer pricing adjustments;[151] and non-business-related expenses.

Liquidation proceeds and payments upon the reduction of share capital or redemption of shares are also taxed as profit distributions to the extent that these payments exceed the contributions made to the equity capital of the company.

It can also be said that under the new corporate income tax system the tax object is reversed. Normally, corporate income tax is imposed on corporate net income and tax legislation disallows the deduction of certain expenditure. Under the new system, however, corporate income tax is imposed on such "non-deductible" expenses. Thus, only profits retained within the Estonian entity effectively remain tax exempt. Corporate income tax is no longer applied on the taxable base, i.e. taxable corporate income but on taxable transactions, i.e. any transaction qualified as direct or hidden profit distribution.[152]

As no tax is levied on any retained earnings of a company the moment of taxation is shifted to the indeterminable future. Therefore, it can even be said that Estonia has a voluntary corporate income tax system. It depends entirely on the management or shareholders of the company when and if at all they decide to distribute profits out of the company.[153] There are no forced distribution rules in Estonia.

Resident companies have unlimited tax liability and are subject to tax on their worldwide income and capital gains. A legal entity is resident in Estonia if it is incorporated under Estonian law. All persons that are not residents are considered to be non-residents. All resident legal entities are taxable persons in Estonia. Under domestic law, no differences exist in the tax treatment of domestic and foreign income. Thus, foreign income is fully taxable in Estonia at the time of a later distribution, unless a double taxation relief method applies. In general, there are no types of income which would not bear distribution tax upon distribution. The exceptions are dividends and payments made out of equity capital from substantial subsidiaries[154] and income attributed to resident companies' permanent establishments (PE) abroad. The latter three are exempt from distribution tax (i.e. subject to participation exemption) when distributed by the resident company.

---

[150]The rate is 20% on the gross amount (distribution + distribution tax) of the profit distribution, corresponding to 20/80 (25%) of the net amount of the distribution.

[151]For more in-depth overview of the transfer pricing rules, see Herm and Lind (2007), pp. 181–184; Raudsepp (2013), p. 284.

[152]Kurist and Uustalu (2003), pp. 334–335.

[153]Tulvik and Vahesaar (2014), p. 300.

[154]At least 10% of the capital or voting power.

As there is no tax on retained earnings and the distribution tax is applied only on actual profit distributions (including hidden profit distributions), it is not possible to make any deductions for tax purposes. Losses have also no significance for tax purposes. Profit distributions are subject to distribution tax even if the company has an accounting loss. Losses, however, generally reduce the accounting profit from which the taxable distributions are made.

For the absence of annual net taxation of corporate profits, the valuation of assets has no significance for tax purposes and no rules exist for tax depreciation and amortization. In addition, no reserves and provisions are applicable and no tax incentives[155] are offered. No types of income or capital gains are taxed separately. Any income or gain derived by companies remains exempt from tax until a distribution is made. All the above features make the system simple and transparent. There is even no need for separate accounting for tax purposes.

As the taxation of corporate profits takes place on a voluntary basis, the elimination of double taxation can, therefore, also be only voluntary (unless the state is willing to repay to its resident companies the taxes that were imposed by foreign countries). As Estonia only imposes distribution tax on voluntary distributions, it consequently follows that the avoidance of double taxation can only occur through the relief from such distribution tax. If the company does not effect taxable transactions, there would not be double taxation and relief would not need to be given.[156]

Until 2005, the double taxation on foreign dividends was eliminated through the credit method—the resident company could deduct the withholding tax and the underlying corporate income tax from its distribution tax liability when redistributing the received dividends. For the rest of the foreign income only the deduction method was available—foreign taxes reduced the accounting profit from which the taxable distributions were made, but not the tax payable on the distribution. However, when a company received income from a treaty country it was able to claim credit under a treaty.

According to the changes to the *EC Parent-Subsidiary Directive*[157] by *Directive 2003/123/EC*[158], EU member states using the credit method to avoid double taxation on dividends were obliged from 1 January 2005 to allow companies a credit for, in addition to the income tax paid by their directly-owned subsidiaries, the income tax paid by any lower-tier subsidiaries. By the extension of the credit system to lower-tier subsidiaries, the fraction of income tax paid by the subsidiary that corresponded to the participation of the parent company in its subsidiary would

[155]Künnapas (2015), p. 271.

[156]Herm (2011), p. 289.

[157]*Council Directive 90/435/EEC on the common system of taxation applicable in the case of parent companies and subsidiaries of different Member States* OJ L 345/8 29/12/2011.

[158]*Council Directive 2003/123/EC of 22 December 2003 amending Directive 90/435/EEC on the common system of taxation applicable in the case of parent companies and subsidiaries of different Member States* OJ L 007, 13/01/2004.

have had to be computed separately with respect to every subsidiary and lower-tier subsidiary.

According to the Estonian authorities, the administration and implementation of such a system would have been burdensome for both companies and the tax administration. The Estonian authorities considered that, in these circumstances, the costs related to the application of the credit system would be disproportionate with respect to the additional proceeds from its application. Therefore, it was decided to replace the credit system with the exemption system from 1 January 2005 to avoid double taxation on dividends from substantial shareholdings and on income attributed to a PE abroad. The rest of the foreign income continued to be relieved by the deduction method.

From 1 January 2009, an ordinary tax credit is granted for withholding and income tax levied abroad on any type of foreign-source income derived by a resident company or a PE of a non-resident company. The foreign tax credit is set off against the distribution tax liability arising at the moment of the profit distribution. Dividends from subsidiaries where the parent has at least 10% holding and income attributed to PE-s continue to be exempted when distributions are made out of such income. In addition, the exemption was extended to liquidation proceeds and capital reductions received from at least 10% subsidiaries. Dividends paid by an Estonian resident company to its shareholders are exempt from any further Estonian taxation.

In a more detail, the general rule is that all companies making dividend distributions subject to the distribution tax. However, where a resident parent company redistributes dividends that it has received from its subsidiaries (both resident and non-resident) from 1 January 2005, the further distribution by the resident parent company is exempt from distribution tax if the parent holds at least 10% of the capital or voting power of the subsidiary and one of the following conditions is met: (1) the subsidiary is resident in Estonia or another EEA country or Switzerland and is a taxable person there (it is not required that the income tax has actually been paid or assessed); or (2) the subsidiary is resident outside the EEA and Switzerland and either the subsidiary was subject to tax on its profits (the tax does not have to be actually paid, it is enough if tax has been assessed, though, not yet due), or the dividends received by the parent were subject to withholding tax.[159]

If these conditions are not met, or the subsidiary is resident in a low-tax territory[160], the further distribution will be subject to distribution tax. Ordinary

[159] *ITA* §50(1^1)(1) and (3).

[160] The term "low-tax territory" is defined in *ITA* §10 as a foreign state, or a territory with an independent tax jurisdiction in a foreign state, which does not impose a tax on the profits earned or distributed by a legal entity or imposes a tax which is less than one third of the income tax that an Estonian resident individual would have to pay on business income of the same amount, without taking into account the deductions (i.e. less than 7%). A legal entity is not considered to be situated in a low-tax territory if more than 50% of its financial year's income is derived from real economic activity or whose home country or territory provides to Estonian tax authority information on income of entities controlled by Estonian residents. The government has adopted a "white list" of territories which are automatically not regarded as low-tax territories.

credit for foreign withholding taxes paid will in that case be allowed for foreign dividends, whereas domestic dividends will suffer double taxation.

Liquidation proceeds and payments upon the reduction of share capital or redemption of shares are similarly to dividends taxed as profit distributions, at the level of the distributing company, to the extent that these payments exceed the contributions (monetary and in-kind) made to the equity capital of the company. Liquidation proceeds not exceeding the value of paid-in contributions are not subject to distribution tax.[161]

Liquidation proceeds and payments upon the reduction of share capital or redemption of shares, which would normally be taxable (i.e. exceeding the paid-in contributions), paid out of exempt dividends or out of liquidation proceeds and capital reductions which were taxed, or the underlying income of which was taxed, are exempt from distribution tax if the parent company held at least 10% of the capital or voting power of the subsidiary at the time of receiving the payment.[162]

In addition, a resident company is exempt from distribution tax upon the distribution of dividends out of profits attributable to its PE situated in an EEA country or Switzerland without any further conditions. If the dividends are distributed out of profits attributable to a resident company's PE situated in any other foreign country, the distribution is exempt from distribution tax if the PE's profits have been subject to income tax (the tax does not have to be actually paid, it is enough if tax has been assessed, though, not yet due).[163]

A PE of a foreign company in Estonia is treated as separate taxable person. For the calculation of the taxable income attributable to its PE in Estonia, the separate entity approach is applied. The income of a non-resident, derived through a PE in Estonia, is taxed in the same manner as income of a resident company, subject to minimal differences.

Besides fringe benefits, gifts, donations, entertainment expenses and non-business expenses, a non-resident company has to pay distribution tax on the profits attributed to the PE and taken out of the PE.[164]

However, a non-resident company is exempt from distribution tax on profits taken out of its PE if it makes those payments out of dividend income received through or on account of its Estonian PE, if it holds at least 10% of the capital or voting power of the subsidiary that paid the dividend and the same conditions are met as are required for the dividend to be exempt when received by a resident company.[165]

If those conditions are not met, or the subsidiary is resident in a low-tax territory, the distribution tax on profits taken out of the PE is reduced by any foreign withholding taxes paid on the dividend.

---

[161] *ITA* §50(2^1).

[162] *ITA* §50(1^1)(5).

[163] *ITA* §50(1^1)(2) and (4).

[164] *ITA* §53(4).

[165] *ITA* 53(4^1).

In addition, a non-resident company is also exempt from distribution tax on profits taken out of the PE if the profit is based on exempt liquidation proceeds or payments upon the reduction of share capital or redemption of shares that were received through or on account of its Estonian PE, if it held at least 10% of the capital or voting power of the subsidiary at the time of the payment.[166]

Although the application of the exemption through the above rules may seem to be complicated it is not really difficult for the companies or the tax authority to administer the system. As most of Estonia's international business is conducted through subsidiaries resident in EU member states it means that in most cases it is only necessary to report the reception of income from the subsidiary without the need to produce evidence of any taxes having been paid in the foreign country.

Estonian tax law contains relatively few anti-avoidance provisions with international scope.[167] There are no specific anti-avoidance rules incorporated in the credit system.

For the exemption to apply on dividends the subsidiary must not be located at a low-tax territory. If the subsidiary is located at a low-tax territory, the further distribution will be subject to distribution tax. Ordinary credit for foreign income tax paid or withheld will in that case be allowed for foreign dividends if the Estonian parent company holds a certificate proving the payment of the tax.

In addition, on 1 November 2016, amendments in the *ITA* came into force which implemented *Directives 2014/86/EU*[168] and *2015/121/EU*[169] aimed to eliminate double non-taxation and introduce a common minimum anti-abuse rule, respectively. First, a specific anti-abuse provision was introduced according to which the dividend received by an Estonian resident company will continue to enjoy tax exemption only if a transaction or a chain of transactions is genuine. A transaction is not considered as genuine if the main or one of the main objectives of the transaction is to obtain tax benefits. According to the explanatory notes of the amendments, it will no more be necessary for the tax authority to determine the real economic substance of the transaction(s). As soon as at least one of the main objectives of the transaction(s) is to obtain tax benefits the Estonian company is not allowed to apply the exemption method for the elimination of double taxation, i.e. distribution of profits will be taxable and foreign taxes will be allowed to be deducted). Until 1 November 2016, Estonia only had a general anti-abuse provision which required for the determination of the real economic substance to re-qualify a transaction. Second, the dividend exemption is now denied where the dividend distributing subsidiary had the right to deduct distributed profits from its taxable

[166] *ITA* §53(4^7).

[167] For more information on Estonian anti-avoidance provisions see Klauson (2010), pp. 281–299.

[168] *Council Directive 2014/86/EU of 8 July 2014 amending Directive 2011/96/EU on the common system of taxation applicable in the case of parent companies and subsidiaries of different Member States* OJ EU L219/40 25/7/2014.

[169] *Council Directive (EU) 2015/121 of 27 January 2015 amending Directive 2011/96/EU on the common system of taxation applicable in the case of parent companies and subsidiaries of different Member States* OJ EU L 21/1 28/1/2015.

profits. As the application of the *Parent-Subsidiary Directive* should not lead to situations of double non-taxation, the aim of this amendment is to avoid double non-taxation on interest gained from so-called hybrid loans.

Controlled foreign company (CFC) legislation applies in Estonia. However, as a consequence of retained earnings of resident companies being tax exempt, under the CFC rules the income of the CFC-s can only be attributed to resident individuals.[170]

As the Estonian corporate income tax system differs considerably from the systems in force in the rest of the world it has sometimes made it difficult to apply it in the context of the tax treaties and EU directives.

Sometimes it is difficult for the foreign investors to understand that the distribution tax is not a withholding tax, but is an integral part of the corporate tax system. The distribution tax is the equivalent of the traditional corporate income tax being the first taxation of profits earned. The taxpayer is the company that has generated the profit and not the company to whom the profits are subsequently distributed.[171] As such it is also not subject to a lower rate under tax treaties.

The distribution tax was also considered to be in breach of Art. 5 of the Parent-Subsidiary Directive,[172] as interpreted by the European Court of Justice (ECJ) in the *Athinaiki*[173] case. Therefore, during the negotiations preceding Estonia's accession to the EU it was agreed that the distribution tax, which Estonia applies to distributed profits, would need to be abolished. Estonia was granted a transitional period until 31 December 2008, during which it could continue to apply the distribution tax. Although the legislator did not consider that Estonia's income tax system contradicts EU law, it was nevertheless decided to amend the law to clarify that Estonia's distribution tax is not a withholding tax.

In March 2008, the Parliament adopted changes to the *ITA*. In fact, the essence of the tax system would still have remained the same, but the collection of the tax and filing of the tax return would have taken place on an annual basis and not any more on a monthly basis. The annual taxation was to be complemented by the introduction of a complicated system of advance payments of income tax three times a year. This was believed to convince the European Commission of being compliant with the case-law of the ECJ.[174]

On 26 June 2008, the ECJ released a judgment in the German *Burda*[175] case where it concluded that a tax similar to Estonian distribution tax, which taxes the income of the subsidiary at the moment of distribution, is not a withholding tax in the sense of the Parent-Subsidiary Directive.

[170]Uustalu (2004), pp. 173–189.

[171]Kaarma (2012), p. 254.

[172]See Lehis et al. (2008a), pp. 389–399; Lehis et al. (2008b), pp. 14–24; Uustalu (2003), p. 165; Zukowski (2006), p. 130.

[173]ECJ C-294/99.

[174]Lehis et al. (2008a), pp. 397–398.

[175]ECJ C-284/06.

As the *Athinaiki* case was the reason why Estonia was required to change its distribution tax system it was considered after *Burda* that there is no more any basis for such a change. The adopted amendments introducing the complicated advanced income tax system turned out to be obsolete. On 20 November 2008 the income tax reform was abolished before it could take effect on 1 January 2009.

However, on it is worth to mention that until 2009 there was an additional withholding tax on dividend distributions where the parent company did not have at least 15% holding in its subsidiary.[176] This was the tax meant to be caught by Art. 5(1) of the *Parent-Subsidiary directive*. For the purposes of this tax, the taxpayer was the parent company, but the tax was withheld by the paying company. As of 1 January 2009, such additional withholding tax on dividend payments to non-residents was completely eliminated.[177]

2.4.2 The Future Outlook

Estonian corporate tax system offers several tax planning opportunities for investors. First, as the retained earnings are not taxed, it is possible to establish group financing companies in Estonia. In this way the interest income is accumulating in Estonia and can continuously be lent to group companies without incurring any corporate income tax until a distribution is made from the Estonian financing company. In principle, taxation can be deferred indefinitely.

However, such a system has also brought along harmful practices where income generated in Estonia has been lent to foreign affiliated companies without the real intention of receiving it back, e.g. long repayment time limits, etc.. There are no specific anti-avoidance rules for these situations. It would be possible to apply the general anti-avoidance rule which provides that where from the content of a transaction it is evident that the transaction is performed for the purposes of tax evasion, the conditions that correspond to the actual economic content shall apply for tax purposes.[178]

In addition, from 1 May 2004, the withholding tax on interest paid to non-residents was abolished[179] and therefore, paying interest instead of dividends has become more attractive from a tax perspective. The Estonian authorities have, therefore, declared that they started to pay more attention to interest payments made to non-residents.[180] In practice, the extraction of profits through interest payments is still common.

[176]Uustalu (2011), p. 450.

[177]Kalamäe (2009), pp. 95–96.

[178]*Taxation Act* §84.

[179]Except on excessive interest. From 2014, the taxation of interest is only allowed in related-party transactions.

[180]Pahapill (2005), p. 383.

The introduction of the exemption system has made it possible to strip profits to countries with lower tax rate than in Estonia and then repatriating them free of Estonian distribution tax. Although the dividends from low-tax territories cannot enjoy the exemption method for relieving double taxation there are still a lot of white-listed countries, e.g. Malta, Cyprus, Singapore, etc., where the final tax rate is lower than the Estonian 20%.

The main objective of the 2000 tax reform was to provide businesses (both local and foreign) with a tax incentive to make investment into Estonia more attractive. The purpose of imposing tax on hidden profit distributions was to discourage shareholders from extracting profits from an Estonian company in any conceivable manner, e.g. making gifts to shareholders, incurring expenditure which benefits shareholders and not the company, etc., thus encouraging the accumulation and reinvestment of profits in the Estonian economy.[181]

As a result of the reform, the amount of reinvested profits has increased as well as the earned profits reported by the companies. The latter indicates that companies used to hide a considerable amount of profits before the reform. However, under the new system, companies provide more reliable data about their profits.[182]

The introduction of the exemption system for dividends and PE income enhanced considerably Estonia's international competitiveness. However, if dividends are exempted then capital gains from the sale of shares should also be exempted. As the income of a subsidiary has already been taxed the exemption on the dividends distributed by the subsidiary avoids the economic double taxation of the same income at the level of the shareholder. The situation is the same in respect of capital gains—the income of the subsidiary has been taxed. The taxation of the subsequent capital gain from the sale of shares and not the dividends received from the subsidiary puts these two types of income in an unequal situation. As dividends and capital gains are similar types of income they should be treated similarly and if it has been decided to avoid economic double taxation on dividends then the same treatment should be afforded to capital gains.

Avoidance of double taxation on capital gains is especially important if the tax system avoids double taxation on dividends. The more advantageous taxation of dividends creates a situation where the taxation starts to directly influence business decisions and the structures of groups of companies. It consequently affects the neutrality of the tax system. The double taxation of capital gains drives companies not to sell shares but to set up a business structure where instead of taxable capital gains it would be possible to receive exempt dividends.[183]

Therefore, currently the investors are inclined to establish holding companies in countries, e.g. The Netherlands, Luxembourg, Malta, Latvia, Lithuania, with the participation exemption available both for dividends and capital gains. At the holding company level it can then be decided whether to receive dividends or sell

[181]Kurist and Uustalu (2003), p. 334.

[182]Lehis et al. (2008a), p. 391.

[183]Uustalu (2008).

shares. The subsequent dividends from the holding company to Estonian shareholders are not taxed in Estonia. The dividends are tax free even in the hands of individual shareholders as they flow through the companies and do not constitute a taxable income for Estonian resident individuals.

Estonian corporate income tax (CIT) system sustains all the substantial elements of a traditional CIT system and at the same time minimizes the number of technicalities which are essential in a traditional CIT system. As a result, the Estonian CIT system is simple, transparent, fosters investments and mitigates companies' motivation to hide profits. By comparison with the traditional systems, one can observe that the Estonian CIT system is easier to comply with both for the taxpayer and tax administration.[184]

Every now and then there are arts published and opinions expressed that Estonia should return to the traditional CIT system.[185] It is, however, not realistic that in the next few years the tax system will be changed.

The application of the double taxation relief measures in the context of Estonian CIT system may at first seem complicated to apply but at a closer look the complexity is only perceptual. The elimination of double taxation is quite easy in most common transactions with the main trading partners.

Recently, there have been substantial changes in the ways that Estonia provides relief from double taxation. The introduction of the exemption system on certain types of qualifying income and granting of tax credit to any other type of foreign income has reduced the administrative burden and promotes Estonian companies to invest abroad.

Currently there is no active discussion on any substantial changes in the systems of avoiding double taxation. However, there have been proposals that Estonia should implement participation exemption for capital gains. Such a move would make Estonia even more attractive to foreign investments and would stimulate the establishment of Estonian holding companies. Until now, such an amendment is unfortunately not yet proposed by the government.

2.5 Estonian Civil Law Procedure

Kaido Künnapas
Tallinn Law School, Tallinn University of Technology, Akadeemia tee 3, 12618 Tallinn, Estonia

Law Firm Sorainen, Advokaadibüroo Sorainen AS, Pärnu mnt 15, 10141 Tallinn, Estonia
e-mail: kaidokynnapas@gmail.com

[184] Lehis et al. (2008a), p. 399.

[185] OECD Economic Surveys: Estonia, OECD, 2009, p. 136.

2.5.1 Current Status of Civil Law Procedure

Under section 2 of the *Estonian Code of Civil Procedure*[186] (*CCP*), the purpose of civil procedure is to guarantee adjudication of matters arising from private law relations by the court justly, within a reasonable period of time and at the minimum possible cost. Along with inherent characteristics both of adversarial and inquisitive type of procedure[187] and elements based on game theory reflecting court procedure as a game between equal opponents[188], these three objectives explain the essence of Estonian procedural law, both in existing law and in its developments through legal evolution and technological advance.

2.5.1.1 Genesis of Estonian Civil Procedure Law

Current *CCP* has been in force since year 2006. It replaced the *Code of Conducting of Civil Procedure*, the first Estonian civil court procedure regulation adopted in 1993 shortly after Estonia left the Soviet Union, and amended in 1998. The reform[189] of 1993 was aimed for establishing three-level court system[190]. The second main goal was to separate the court from the executive power in greater extent that it was during the Soviet times.[191]

This reform has proven to be successful. What is more, the reform has led to establishing several pre-court dispute settlement bodies[192], which provide rather quick and cheap procedure, in some cases enforceable ruling and which has reduced work load for courts significantly. No specialized civil courts exist in Estonian though.

2.5.1.2 Fundamental Principles of Civil Court Procedure

The driving principle behind the *CCP* is the principle of procedural efficiency.[193] It must be noted that as prior to enforcing *CCP*, the purpose of the procedure was to hear and solve the dispute *as fast as possible*.[194] New law brought a clear shift towards *reasonableness* of the period of procedure, placing greater emphasis on reducing the costs of the procedure as well as accenting the need to have just

[186]RT I 2005, 26, 197.

[187]Härmand (2003), p. 7.

[188]See further about game theory and civil process in: Neuhaus and Nel (2013), pp. 108–112.

[189]Design of the act of 1993 was influenced by Norwegian, Swedish and Finnish civil process regulations as well as, in some aspects, by Soviet regulation which was applicable in Estonia up to 1940 (e.g. delivering writ of summons by newspaper announcement—see Odar 1993, pp. 51–52), and by draft bill of civil procedure code prepared during the first republic of Estonia in 1930s (see Odar 1993, pp. 51–52).

[190]County courts as the first level courts, circuit courts as appellate courts, and Supreme Court (SC) at the final stage.

[191]Odar (1993), pp. 51–52.

[192]Such as Labour Dispute Committee.

[193]Kergandberg et al. (2008), p. 345.

[194]*Code of Conducting of Civil Procedure* (1993) §3(2).

Table 2.1 Successful cases based on violation of Art. 6 (1) of the EConvHR

Case	Content	Length of the procedure
Rummi v Estonia[a]	Seizure of property	5 years between quashing of the first judgment by an appeal court and the re-hearing of the case at the first level court
Missenjov v Estonia[b]	Debt claim	Court was passive almost 5 years
Saarekallas OÜ v Estonia[c]	Corporate law issues	Procedure took 8 years, many prolongations
Shchiglitsov v Estonia[d]	Division of property	New dates for prolonged court hearing were set by significant delay (6 months, 1 years and 2 months), 10 months between last preliminary hearing and hearing
Treial v Estonia[e]	Divorce	Court was passive almost 2 years

[a]*Rummi v. Estonia*, no. 63362/09
[b]*Missenjov v. Estonia*, no. 43276/06
[c]*Saarekallas OÜ v. Estonia*, no. 11548/04
[d]*Shchiglitsov v. Estonia*, no. 35062/03
[e]*Treial v. Estonia*, no. 48129/99

outcome. The efficiency of a court's work should not be reduced to mere quantitative indicators—performance and duration of proceedings.[195] Otherwise, we will create "a world of perverse values".[196]

This shift brought the *CCP* closer to reflecting the principle of reasonable time of procedure referred to in art 6 (1) of the *Convention for the Protection of Human Rights and Fundamental Freedoms*[197] (EConvHR), under which in the determination of his civil rights and obligations against him or her, everyone is entitled to a fair and public hearing within a reasonable time by an independent and impartial tribunal established by law. As the reasonableness of the length of proceedings must be assessed in the light of the circumstances of the case and with reference to set of criteria[198], specific time limits cannot be set for the reasonableness. However, several cases have been heard by *EConvHR* under which the Estonian applicant has relied on violation of Art. 6(1) of the *EConvHR* in civil case successfully (see Table 2.1).

It can be noticed that the successful complaints from Estonian applicants reached the European Court of Human Rights (ECHR) quite a few years ago. The reduced number of complaints may be explained by the efforts made to make the civil procedure faster.

Many changes to *CCP* were introduced in 2015, aimed at accelerating the procedure and preventing *mala fide* party to prolong the procedure above acceptable. For

[195]Pilving (2015), p. 7.

[196]Ibid.

[197]Signed on 4 November 1950 in Rome.

[198]The complexity of the case; the conduct of the applicant and the relevant authorities; what was at stake for the applicant in the dispute. See also *Frydlender v. France*, no. 30979/96, §43.

example, the right to submit application for expedition of court proceeding was added to *CCP* in 2011. For applying this instrument, the party may request the court to take steps needed, if the court has been conducting proceedings in a civil matter for at least 9 months and the court fails to perform a necessary procedural act (including to schedule a court hearing) without good reason in a timely manner to ensure the conduct of the court proceeding within a reasonable period of time.[199] This constitutes an effective remedy[200] for a party which was lacking before adopting such regulation. Secondly, the burden of bearing risk of not receiving documents sent by the court was shifted from the court to the person to whom the documents were sent—in case the party has notified court about its contact details or the document has been delivered to the party at some address, the document can be *deemed to be received* after 3 days has passed from *sending* the document.[201] Possible errors in delivery can give ground for restoration of term[202]. Thirdly, certain minimum period of time (7 days) was set which must be between presenting applications to the other party (and to the court as well) and preliminary hearing.[203]

Great effort has been made towards digitalizing the court procedure to enhance efficiency and reduce paperwork by professional players. Estonia has adopted the e-File system, which allows procedural parties and their representatives to electronically submit procedural documents to courts, pay state fees through integrated bank links and observe the progress of the proceedings related to them.[204] Many useful functions has been added to e-File from time to time, e.g. the system sends reminders on different deadlines applicable in specific case, it is possible to use e-office environment to share your cases with certain persons.[205] It is nevertheless not mandatory for the procedural parties to use the e-File system (except attorneys-at-law) and problems with delivering the initial document—action or petition—to defendant or to some other party remain. In addition, the judges have found that it most probably is and will be much easier to use a multi-volume paper file when adjudicating a case and to view and compare the documents submitted than use e-File digital document database for that.[206]

When it comes to efficiency of cross-border procedures and cooperation in civil matters within the EU, Estonian legal practitioners are using more and more actively possibilities provided by the European Judicial Network in civil and

[199] *CCP* §333^1.

[200] See art. 13 of the EConvHR about the state's obligation to provide individual with the effective remedy.

[201] *CCP* §314^1.

[202] Application of §67 of the *CCP* and restoration of a term requires a good reason, i.e. an objectively unforeseeable event which could not be prevented (see SC 3-2-1-40-11).

[203] *CCP* §329(2).

[204] Centre of Registers and Information Systems (2016).

[205] At the contest of Crystal Scales of Justice Awards, European Council and European Commission nominated e-File as one of the four best solutions assisting judicial system to perform its tasks. See: Centre of Registers and Information Systems (2016).

[206] Kõve (2014), p. 27.

commercial matters (EJN-civil). It mostly assists legal practitioners in questions related to application of European Union (EU) law as well as member State's law.[207] The latter one is especially time consuming without coordinated assistance, when it comes to applying foreign law in domestic courts.

The principle of autonomy[208] is the other leading principle behind the norms which regulate who and how should design the procedural strategy and questions to be solved. The court conducts proceedings only under an action submitted by a person[209], except in certain cases where the court can initiate the procedure under a petition or at its own initiative[210], e.g. expedited procedure in matters of payment order, imposition of a restraining order and other similar measures for the protection of personality rights, establishment of custody over property of an absent person.

Under the principle of autonomy, the parties determine the object of the dispute and the progression of the proceedings[211], choose which evidence they want to use for evidencing their claims and objections[212], can agree the burden of proof differently from the law[213], agree on applicable law during the process[214], etc.

As the purpose of administering justice is to support peace and not to work on an axe method, the parties may choose to terminate the procedure at any stage of the procedure by concluding a compromise agreement[215] which has the legal power of notarized agreement/application and execution document.[216] As court can reject the compromise agreement only in certain severe cases[217] or if it is not enforceable, one may argue that the principle of autonomy has greater importance in court procedure than reaching the legally sound solution for the dispute.

Principle of autonomy limits court's rights to give mandatory instructions to the parties as regard of choosing specific procedural steps and deciding which evidence to present to court. However, to ensure the efficiency of the procedure, the court has obligation of explanation. The purpose of such obligation is to find out the actual purpose of the procedure as well as channel and structure the procedure so that the parties can concentrate on arguing about matters which are actually important.[218] When it comes to the matter of the case, the court can direct parties to specify the claim, but not direct parties to change their claim or generate an intention to submit

[207] Koit (2015), p. 673.

[208] Kergandberg et al. (2008), p. 345.

[209] *CCP* §4(1).

[210] See the catalogue of such cases in *CCP* §475.

[211] *CCP* §4(2).

[212] *CCP* §230(1).

[213] Ibid.

[214] SC 3-2-1-165-04, 17.

[215] *CCP* §4(3).

[216] In some cases, it has been used as a tool to avoid high notary fees.

[217] If it is contrary to good morals or the law, or it violates significant public interest.

[218] Soots (2011), p. 324.

a totally new claim by defendant.[219] The similar rule applies in German law.[220] When the set of facts of the case is not complete, the court should draw party's attention to this, but again, court cannot ask the party to present new set of facts which would justify a new claim.[221] There has been some problems with implementing the obligation of explanation. For example, when applying it already before delivering the claim to the defendant, it has led to many amendments to the actions before having defendant standpoint on what was actually under dispute and which was not. This arises question, from which point it may not meet the standards of the principle of equality of arms.

2.5.1.3 Outline of the Structure of the Civil Procedure

The basic structure of the Estonian civil procedure law in action matters can be roughly divided in four stages—initiating the procedure, preliminary procedure, hearing of the case, making the judgment. The structure can be seen on the following block diagram below on Scheme 2.1, demonstrating some basic options for designing the process.

2.5.1.4 Main Challenges of Current Procedural System

The main challenges of civil procedure are quite the same in every jurisdiction—how to achieve higher speed and quality of the process and make it more cost-efficient both for the state and the parties? The solutions for such challenges mostly stumble into manpower and financial issues, and not into the legal issues. But some specific legal problems and challenges may be outlined which have got the spotlight.

In the recent SC practice, the most important issues relating to procedural law seem to concern the determination and distribution of procedural expenses.[222] In civil matter no 3-2-1-153-13, the case concerned the establishment of limits on the amount of a contractual representative's expenses that can be ordered to be paid by the other party to proceedings.[223] Such limits, set under the separate regulation, were directly related to the value of civil matter—the larger the value of the claim, the higher was the threshold for compensation. However, some claims are considered to be non-monetary with the presumed value of 3500 euros regardless of the actual value and possible complexity of the case. The SC *en banc* held that the establishment of limits on the compensation of a contractual representative's expenses infringes a number of fundamental rights. The SC declared the establishment of limits on the compensation of a contractual representative's expenses unconstitutional and invalid.[224]

[219] SC 3-2-1-66-09, p. 11.

[220] Van Rhee (2005), pp. 301–302.

[221] Soots (2011), p. 325.

[222] Aavik and Krillo (2015), p. 50.

[223] Ibid, p. 54.

[224] Ibid.

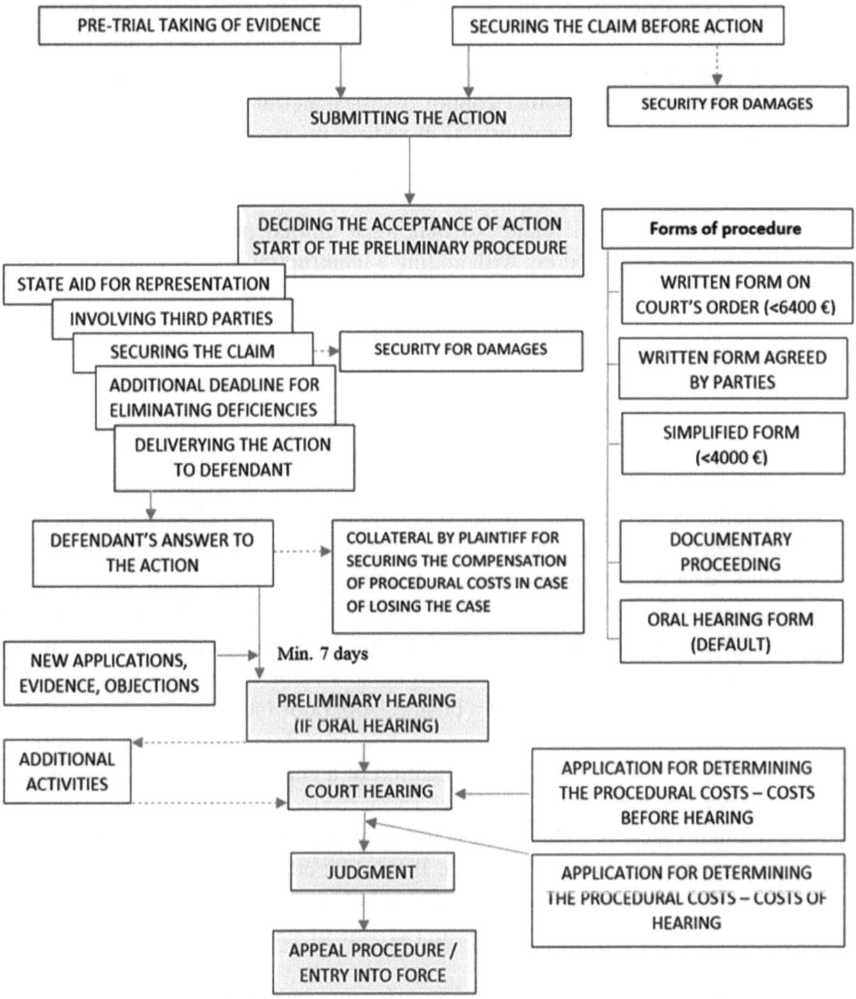

Scheme 2.1 Basic structure of Estonian civil court procedure

As a consequence of this decision, it has become much more unclear for the parties in what extent the costs for legal representation will be compensated in case of positive outcome of the dispute. The general rule applies, stating that the court orders payment of the costs to a reasoned and necessary extent.[225] This, however, damages the principle of legal certainty and makes it difficult for the plaintiff and other parties to predict possible procedural costs and risks related thereto.

The overall efficiency of the procedure is the most problematic in enforcement procedure stage—an extension of civil process. The Estonian enforcement

[225] *CCP* §175(1).

procedure is conducted by a separate enforcement body—the freelance bailiff.[226] *Mala fide* debtors can easily prolong the enforcement process for months and even years by disputing the claim which is enforced by the bailiff in court (under the principle of formality, the bailiff cannot assess material objections to the claim acknowledged by the court ruling[227]), disputing prices for auctions, by leaving Estonia *de facto* or *de jure* only, etc. As the common development for such cases is initiation of insolvency procedure, one solution for speeding up these two procedures in combination relates to making a unified procedure for execution and insolvency procedure, along with adding a bankruptcy administrator's function to the bailiff.

Another set of problems relate to design of insolvency procedures, especially when it comes to reorganization of debts procedure under the *Reorganisation Act*[228]. In 2015, 20 application for restructuring procedure was presented to the county courts.[229] Although having a really noble purpose—business operator faced with solvency problems includes the option of overcoming the financial difficulties and continuing to operate by restoring liquidity[230]—the procedure has been used for postponing the certain bankruptcy as the percentage of recovery is extremely low. It is argued that the problem is a fundamental one. Insolvency systems with proceedings strictly separated from each other, permitting initiation of either reorganization or liquidation proceedings on the basis of distinct applications and imposing different threshold requirements for the two types of proceedings, do not support consideration of the option to reorganize a viable business operator.[231] On the contrary, the system might push a business operator into applying for reorganization only when its solvency problem has become irreversible and liquidation is the only option left, or preclude reorganization of a viable business operator whose bankruptcy petition has been filed.[232]

Fundamental changes in the restructuring procedure is definitely one of the challenges the legislator must deal with. It must be added that as the restructuring process is not regulated under the new EU regulation no 2015/848 on insolvency proceedings[233], regulation for cross-border effects of such procedure require closer attention.

Current developments in the Estonian procedure law aims at quicker and more efficient civil procedure, digitalizing the process through e-File system and, from more practical side, dealing with the change of generation among the judiciary.

---

[226] Alekand (2008), p. 115.
[227] Alekand (2003), p. 331.
[228] RT I 2008, 53, 296.
[229] Courts' statistics of 2015 (2016), p. 1.
[230] Habakukk (2012), p. 101.
[231] Ibid, p. 106.
[232] Ibid, p. 106.
[233] See further: Jürgenson and Torga (2015), p. 626.

From the legal side, the enforcement procedure along with insolvency or insolvency-prevention procedures is expected to have more attention in the nearest future. The combination of these procedures has proven to be non-efficient and time-consuming, which in many cases does not provide creditors with effective remedy and procedural justice.

When it comes to compensating the damages caused by court procedures exceeding reasonable time, the remedy of compensation for proceedings that have lasted for unreasonable time has not yet been introduced into the *State Liability Act*.[234] The Strasbourg Court considered in its case law in respect of Estonia that the enactment of legislation clearly establishing grounds and speedy procedures for awarding compensation for excessively lengthy proceedings would contribute considerably to legal certainty in this field.[235] This would be definitely one of the developments one may expect eagerly. When to take a more general look to the development of the procedure, reflecting the human rights in the rules of conducting the civil process and guaranteeing the purposes of the procedure may be the next general goal for development.

2.6 Labor Law

Kristi Joamets
Tallinn Law School, Tallinn University of Technology, Akadeemia tee 3, 12618 Tallinn, Estonia
e-mail: kristi.joamets@ttu.ee

Maret Maripuu
Labour Inspectorate, Gonsiori 29, 10147 Tallinn, Estonia
e-mail: maret.maripuu@ti.ee

Historically, labor relations were regulated in Estonia by the *Baltic Private Law Code* (1864) and there existed a separate law for the employees in the industries. The first specific law regulating employment contract—*Labourer Employment Contract Act*[236], was adopted in 1936. This act did not regulate the employment in public service[237], creative work, work in the farms and forest, and sailor's work. At that time also collective agreements were known and regulated by separate legal act. Actually, the first unions of employees were founded in Estonia already in 1905. Classic trade unions developed by the end of the 1920s.

[234] Laffranque (2015), p. 10.

[235] Ibid.

[236] RT I 1936, 83, 663.

[237] In 1924 a special *Public Service Law Act* was adopted (RT 1921, no 113). Working in a public service was regulated already earlier but this was the first special law act for public servants.

Currently, Estonian labor law can be divided into the three periods: up to 1992—as soviet labor law (*Labour Code of Soviet Republic of Estonia*[238]); 1992–2009 when the first Estonian Employment Contracts Act was enforced[239] drafted in a hurry[240] and characterized as a relatively inflexible act for employers, but easily to follow; and 2009-until today—a new legal act[241] *Employment Contracts Act* (*ECA*) based on a concept of flexible and secure employment relations.

Considering that Estonia became a member state of European Union (EU) in 2004, the second half of the 1990 was harmonization of Estonian law with EU law, including labor law. Global crisis in 2007–2008[242] impacted the drafting of new rules as well. Development of Estonian labor law was influenced also by the EC Green Paper on Modernising Labour Law to Meet the Challenges of the 21st Century[243] which one aim was to "help to promote flexibility in conjunction with security, regardless of the type of employment contract" as a European social model[244].

Flexicurity[245] was also promoted by the European Employment Strategy[246], the revised Lisbon Strategy[247], in the Guidelines for the employment policies of the Member States[248] etc. TFEU does not reflect the flexibility and security but provides a minimum set of social policy objectives (art 153). Pillar of Social Rights initiative is taking into account the changing realities of Europe's world of work and seeking fairer balance between flexibility and security on the labor markets.[249] Next to Denmark and Netherlands Estonia was a third state in Europe to implement flexicurity into the labor law.[250]

[238]Adopted on 5 July 1972. Tallinn: Eesti Raamat.

[239]In 1996 a first *Public Service Law Act* was passed dividing servants in public service officials and employees. Employees labor relations were regulated by the *ECA*.

[240]See Muda (2009), p. 113.

[241]RT I 2009, 5, 35.

[242]Weisbrot and Jorgensen (2013), p. 8; World of Work Report 2014. Developing with jobs. ILO. ISSN 2049-9272 (web pdf), p. 20; Inventory of labor market policy measures in the EU 2008–13: The crisis and beyond. Synthesis Report. European Commission. ILO 2015. ISBN 978-92-2-130247-6 (web pdf).

[243]COM (2006) 708. http://eur-lex.europa.eu/legal-content/EN/TXT/?uri=URISERV%3Ac10312.

[244]There is no uniform and clear definition for this concept, most widely it is described as a simultaneous promotion of sustainable economic growth and social cohesion. See Jepsen and Pascual (2005).

[245]About flexicurity see Sultana (2013) and Heyes (2013).

[246]See http://ec.europa.eu/social/main.jsp?catId=101&langId=en.

[247]See www.europarl.europa.eu/document/.../20110718ATT24270EN.pdf.

[248]Council decision of 12 July 2005 on Guidelines for the employment policies of the Member States (2005/600/EC) art 21.

[249]See Employment and Social Developments in Europe 2015. European Commission, Directorate-General for Employment, Social Affairs and Inclusion Directorate A, 2016, p. 87.

[250]See also Muda (2010), p. 348.

Today the employment contract is regulated by the ECA and other labor relations by other acts. The former *Employment Contracts Act*, *Wages Act*, *Holidays Act*, and *Working and Rest Time Act* were all integrated into one act—*ECA*, which reduced the administrative burden and abolished several formal provisions in labor law, like the Labor/Employment Record Book, etc.

As mentioned above in 2009 a new law which is also currently in force, was adopted. 2009 can be described as a year of the beginning of the new labor market reform. The reform had two goals: firstly, to amend the *ECA* and secondly to introduce an institutional reform.

The main idea for the new law was to give more rights and freedoms to the parties involved in negotiating the labor contract so they could decide what the best solution is for them. Four pillars were built: (1) flexibility; (2) modern social security systems to guarantee sufficient income during the unemployed period; (3) effective working policy to make it easier and faster to change jobs; and (4) effective lifelong learning system to give employees the possibility to stay competitive in the labor market.

2.6.1 Flexicurity in Labor Relation

One of the main characteristics of Estonian labor (contract) law is flexibility and security following the policy of EU. Flexicurity, on the one side meaning the combination of the work and private responsibilities of employees, keeping their training up-to-date and giving flexible working hours (flexibility), and on the other side providing people with the training they need to keep their skills up-to-date and to develop their talent as well as providing them with adequate unemployment benefits if they were to lose their job for a period of time (security) should create labor relations which allow quickly react to the economic changes, i.e. law does not enforce employer by the high labor relation termination costs to keep the jobs in a difficult economic situation, when on the other side supports the employment capability during the employment relation and the income security after the termination of the contract.

In Estonian law the main tool attaining flexicurity in labor relations is an open agreement between employer and employee—law leaves too many working conditions open to decide by the parties through their mutual agreement. Unfortunately, as a status of an employee has not been changed notably in time, an employee is in most cases still a weaker party[251] of the employment contract, flexicurity favors more employer. From the history it is known that state intervenes the free labor market to protect the working people[252], today the law favors more an

[251]See Employment and Social Developments in Europe 2015. European Commission, Directorate-General for Employment, Social Affairs and Inclusion Directorate A, 2016, p. 79.

[252]See Rigaux (2014), p. 4.

employer. Normative foundations of labor law are efficiency and social justice.[253] Labor law is tensely related to the economy and certainly needs flexibility for both parties of employment contract. Another thing is whether a holder of certain right knows how to use it. In principle, in a labor contract an employee should be protected by the collective agreement but this agreement has never been very popular in Estonia, by the economic crises their conclusion further decreased, e.g. in 2011 only 4–7% of entities had collective agreements[254]. Even more, in Estonian practice collective agreements are concluded mostly in big entities[255] but ECA was created for small entities.

Estonia does not have a practice of strong trade unions comparing to other European countries and one can argue whether at all it is possible to create a trade union in a small entity. In principle, Estonia has a good consulting system—a lot has been done to promote the knowledge of employees and employers related to labor relations. But, as the legal regulation is too general assuming the mutual negotiations between the employer and employee then in reality the parties do not negotiate and the problems remains unsolved.

A study of *ECA* conducted in 2013 showed that 5–9% of employers considered their knowledge of labor law very good, 78–85% good and 4–8% poor.[256] From the employees considered their knowledge 7–10% very good, 55–60% good, 26–31% poor and 2–3% very poor.[257] According to this study 65–70% of workforce believes that they know where to find additional information about their rights in labor relation when needed. This means that the knowledge of almost one third of employees are low and therefore can lead to the problems in labor relations.[258]

Also, too general knowledge is not enough to manage with regulations of *ECA* as this act provides often exceptions from the general rules and usually employees (sometimes also employers) do not know those exceptions. However, *ECA* purposely does not provide very specific norm to facilitate parties of contract to reach to the mutual flexible agreement on conditions.[259] Furthermore, inherently to Estonian practice the interpretation of certain legal norms or rules change in time without changes in the formulation of the norm. Certainly, it is important to use a contemporary interpretation. But, it is not always possible to deliver immediately

[253]See Employment and Social Developments in Europe 2015. European Commission, Directorate-General for Employment, Social Affairs and Inclusion Directorate A, 2016, p. 79. The existence of labour legislation is related to society's goals of fairness and ensuring a fairer distribution of wealth, power and goods. According to ILO Social justice is based on equality of rights for all people and the possibility for all human being without discrimination to benefit from economic and social progress everywhere. See: http://www.ilo.org/wcmsp5/groups/public/---dgreports/dcomm/documents/publication/wcms_151740.pdf.

[254]Masso et al. (2013), p. 34.

[255]Põldis and Proos (2013), p. 4.

[256]Masso et al. (2013), p. 15.

[257]Ibid, p. 17.

[258]Ibid, p. 18.

[259]Explanatory note of ECA, 2008 (in Estonian).

the new interpretations in all the sources available for employees and employers. And, the court practice in different regions is sometimes not similar as well.

Flexicurity is ensured additionally by the legal certainty. But, when providing rules for flexible agreement a norm cannot be rigid, it should be "open" constituting only general rights and obligations. Based on the study of *ECA*—2–5% of employers and 27–32% of employees have had problems in applying *ECA*. Employees state that they would not do anything when employer violates their rights: 15–19% because of the fair to lose a job, 13–16% because of not to impair the relations with an employer, 10–13% because the dispute can cause additional costs for the litigation, 10–13 % because they do not believe that the situation would change, and 6–8% because they believe that nobody can help them.[260] This shows that employees are still in a weaker position in a labor relation which does not efficiently support the application of the principle of flexicurity in a labor relation.

2.6.2 Institutional Reform

The reform in 2009 included an institutional reform. This meant a merger of National Labour Market Board (NLMB) and Unemployment Insurance Fund (UIF). The aim was to provide the best social security for the unemployed and help them to get back to the labor market and stay competitive.

The research[261] conducted in 2012 shows that since the *ECA* came into force, the flows between labor market states have been increasing. It means that the law has had a positive impact on the market mobility. However, statistics also show that while looking at the flows between states, the impact on the probability of moving out from employment is more significant than moving into employment. The analysis also shows that *ECA* has had a statistically significant impact on the probability of moving from unemployment to inactivity. In addition, it appeared that the *ECA* has had a negative impact on the probability of job-to-job mobility. In this respect the expectations of a state as those of the liberal-market-professors were higher than the actual results.

The most important change brought about by the new *ECA* was *severance payment* and also the novelty that the *notice time* was reduced. According to the new Act, if the employment had lasted 5–10 years, the UIF would pay compensation of 1 month's wage and if the employment relationship had lasted for over 10 years, it would pay compensation of 2 months' wages. Before the change the employer had to pay 6 month wages for the employee who had worked for him 10 years and the notice period was 6 months. Now the employer has to pay in all

[260]Masso et al. (2013), p. 27.

[261]Employment and working life in Estonia 2012. http://www.sm.ee/sites/default/files/content-editors/Ministeerium_kontaktid/Uuringu_ja_analuusid/Toovaldkond/employment_and_working_life_in_estonia_2012.pdf.

cases only for *one* month. In addition, the advance notice of redundancy was shortened from 2–4/6 months to 15–90 days.

Another important clause in the new *ECA* establishes that if an employer cannot provide the employee with the agreed amount of work due to unforeseen economic circumstances beyond the employer's control the employer may reduce the employee's wages for up to 3 months over a 12-month period. The reduction can only be to a reasonable extent and only if the contractually agreed wage would be unreasonably burdensome for the employer. The lowered wage cannot be lower than the official minimum wage agreed by the social partners and approved by the government and reduction of the salary is possible only when the working time is reduced and this must be done proportionally.

Notably, all changes mentioned so far are unfavorable for workers and that is exactly what Estonian trade unions thought at first, too. But they reached a consensus when the economic crisis was clearly manifested that the minimization of the burdens of capital providers actually help to keep the jobs, cut their losses and help them to avoid bankruptcies that would produce additional unemployment.

The aim of the merger of NLMB and UIF was to reduce the administrative costs and to include more the social partners into solving the problems of the current labor market. The need to increase the unemployment insurance premium was explained as being necessary for the UIF to cover the growing costs caused by the continuing recession and by new redundancy regulations that raised unemployment levels and the number of benefit recipients. At the end of 2014 the Government approved the proposal made by the social partners for 3 years. The contributions were lowered from January 2015: now the employer pays 1.6% and the employee 0.8%.

Characterising the authority of the renewed UIF the following services can be emphasized: (1) Labor market training. The training can last for up to 1 year. People who take part in a training lasting for more than 40 h receive a grant as well as transport and accommodation allowances; (2) Career counseling. This is designed to help people make and carry out informed decisions about their career development; (3) Wage subsidy. This is a benefit paid to employers who hire an unemployed person. It is designed for high-risk groups such as people released from prison, the long-term unemployed and young unemployed people; (4) Business start-up subsidies. Unemployed who are at least 18 years old and have completed business training or have higher or vocational education qualifications in economics or business experience can apply for a subsidy to start their own business. This subsidy is paid out once and the maximum sum is 4474 EUR; (5) Adaptation of work premises and equipment. This is a service designed for unemployed people with disabilities.

Evaluating the expenditure on labor market policy there can be stated that passive labor market policy includes expenditure on unemployment allowance and special social tax. Benefits paid from unemployment insurance fund are not taken into account (unemployment insurance benefit, benefit upon insolvency of the employer, insurance benefit upon lay-off). Rapid increase in the number of unemployed persons due to the recession in 2009–2010 significantly increased the share of expenditure on passive labor market policy. The crisis was over in 2011 and the above-mentioned expenditures started to decrease. UIF offers active labor market measures that aim to increase the potential of unemployed persons in returning to the labor market. It contributes to improving the qualifications of the unemployed and offers them services to help them return to the labor market as soon as possible.

2.6.3 The Promises and Problems

Although the main features of the new legal regime in labor relations is in place, there are still some obligations that have not been met. For instance, to improve the labor flexibility Estonian law presumed that an employee leaving the job on his/her own initiative will get compensation. The idea was simple: to stimulate people to move forward and create an incentive to vacate the jobs that might be filled by less ambitious laborers. This clause actually did not work and Estonian government unilaterally backed away from it. The evident reason for it was that state simply did not have money for that in the budget. However, there were other features, too. For instance, it gave an opportunity to collect the unemployment money for people who left their work just for 1 year and then intended to come back.

Although the *ECA* is not really new anymore, it has been in effect for 7 years already, some memories are hard to die. Many employees still have an expectation that if the employer has illegally cancelled their contract, the labor dispute committee or court reinstates them to work. In fact, this does not happen. The *ECA* says clearly that there is only monetary compensation possible in such cases. It is like in a marriage—if one side does not want to be in a relationship, no one can force the other party to take the partner back.

One problem with the *ECA* is that state lost too much time while drafting and implementing the new law. It was a complicated reform as it touches the lives of everyone to smaller or larger extent. Also, to find a political will to start the reform, to develop new bill and negotiate and find consensus with the social partners took a considerable amount of time.

ECA originated in the pre-crisis time. The crisis is behind now, although in Europe there can still see the remnants of it. To put it briefly: Estonian labor contracts are still too costly to businesses. It is not only the share to be paid as social taxes (all in all 33%) but also meeting sometimes quite expensive labor standards related to the working time, labor safety, health insurance, employment risks etc.

As a result, on the one hand, Estonia may have the most progressive and up-to-date labor law in the EU based upon the fundamentals of free and competitive market economy. But on the other hand, this law is already outdated as in many cases the labor relations appear under the cover of standard private-legal ones. Instead of labor contract, there can see contracts of locatio-conductio, of mandamus, of performance, of agency and others where the guarantees and support provided by labor contracts are missing.

The rule here is the old one: if you regulate something more than is needed or you regulate it the way that is not reasonable, you have to face the consequence: this law will be avoided.

Estonia also experienced a problem with the new Act that is mostly philosophical, psychological, cultural, and historical or however it would be appropriate to call it. As mentioned early on, one of the main ideas and intentions was to provide flexibility and room for negotiation for both parties, for employer and the employee to find the best solution and write it down in the contract. In most cases, this new freedom has not been used. Practice of labor dispute committees often show that employees feel that they cannot ask for better conditions, often the employer is perceived as the one with whom nothing can be negotiated, why even bother. Still, practice shows that employers often try to find a solution with an employee instead of going to the labor dispute committee or court.

Another controversial issue is that of minimum wages[262]. It is even more important as it touches a chord of social consciousness and left-wing politics. On the one hand, the minimum salary requirement seems reasonable and fair, on the other hand, it has an economically negative consequence: if the minimum wage is above the productivity of the labor and it is paid by the company, employers will simply end their business or will not start it in the first place.

Wage flexibility declined during the boom time. Up to 2004 the wage increase followed closely productivity increase. From 2005 to 2007, the increase in real wages was largely in excess of labor productivity growth due to labor shortage resulting from rising demand and increasing labor emigration, mostly to Finland. As a result, employees' salaries consist of relatively low basic wages that are heavily taxed, and relatively high additional fees and bonuses. Approximately 80% of Estonian entities pay some kind of performance-related bonuses. The share of bonuses is around 20% of the total payment. The other interesting fact about pay systems is that 26% of Estonian entities remunerate employees on a piece-rate basis, about 30% pay hourly based wages. In the euro area, these two components of pay methods on average do not include more than 20% of total remuneration methods. Monthly based wage is largely dominating.

One potential way to adjust the labor market to the changing market conditions is to reduce working hours. The Estonian Labour Force survey enables to distinguish between "ordinary" part-time work and so-called "forced" part-time work. The first is the case when an employee want to work part-time, e.g. because of a small child or studying etc. The latter means that employees work part-time for economic reasons, for example, their company is not able to provide a full-time job because of a decline in demand or for other crisis-related reasons. In such cases, a worker is underemployed, or in other words, would like to work more but there are no job opportunities in their entity. So, due to the fact that the economic activity of

[262]In Estonia, there are exceptions in minimum wages for civil servants and some industries with strong unions (transportation sector) that are set on the national level, especially in the areas where there is a significant national fiscal cushion to back the level of wages.

many companies declined during the recession period, the working time of employed persons was reduced and full-time workers were given part-time work.

Looking for the future, it is visible that Estonian labor marker develops the same direction the other states do: employees have become more active in developing their skills and knowledge to be able to work in different jobs, technological progress allows more distant-work, and more often employees are their own employers through the companies they own. Young people coming to the labor market are more open to discuss working conditions with the employer and hence use the flexibility law offers in a greater extent the old ones do. As a final point, it is important to understand that in the twenty-first century an employee and an employer should be partners who care for each other, and then employment contracts can be judicious, viable and following the best practices.

References

Aavik M, Krillo K (2015) Overview of the case law of the SC in civil matters in 2014. In: Teeveer R et al (eds) Yearbook of Estonian Courts 2014. Riigikohus, Tartu

Albin T, Herm M, Klauson I, Uustalu E (2010) Estonia. In: Procedural rules in tax law in the context of European Union and domestic law. Kluwer Law International, The Netherlands, pp 187–213

Alekand A (2003) Formaliseerituse printsiibi sisu ja ulatus täitemenetluses. Juridica 5 (2003):330–337

Alekand A (2008) The Estonian universal enforcement procedure and the Bailiff as the taker of procedural decisions. Juridica Int 15(2008):115–124

Auby J-B (2013) Codification of administrative procedure. Primento

Fabbrini F (2016) Economic governance in Europe: comparative paradoxes and constitutional challenges. Oxford University Press, Oxford

Habakukk K (2012) The importance of the structure of the insolvency system for facilitation of business operators' reorganisation. Juridica Int 19(2012):99–106

Härmand K (2003) Tsiviilmenetlus. Sisekaitseakadeemia, Tallinn

Herm M (2011) Estonia. In: Cahiers de droit fiscal international. Key practical issues to eliminate double taxation of business income, vol 96b. Sdu, The Netherlands, pp 287–304

Herm M, Lind K (2007) Changes to transfer pricing legislation. Int Transfer Pricing J 14 (3):181–184. IBFD, The Netherlands

Heyes J (2013) Flexicurity in crisis. European labour market policies in a time of austerity. Eur J Indus Relat 19(1)

Hiden J, Made V, Smith DJ (2008) The Baltic question during the cold war. Routledge, London and New York

Jäätma J (2016) Kas õigusemõistmine on üksnes õiguse mõistmine? Juridica 2:2016

Jareborg N (2004) Criminalization as last resort (ultima ratio). Ohio State J Crim Law 2004:521–534

Jepsen M, Pascual AS (2005) The European social model: an exercise in deconstruction. J Eur Soc Policy 15(3):231–245

Jürgenson K, Torga M (2015) Maksejõuetusmenetluse (uuesti sõnastatud) määrus – samm tervendamise ja rahvusvahelise koostöö suunas. Juridica 9(2015):624–635

Kaarma R (2012) Estonia. In: Cahiers de droit fiscal international. The debt-equity conundrumm, vol 97b. Sdu, The Netherlands, pp 253–269

Kairjak M (2015) Blurring the boundaries between penal law and administrative law in the new sanctions system under the law of financial markets of the European Union. Juridica 5 (2015):351–359

Kalamäe P (2009) Estonia reduces withholding tax on non-resident income. In: European taxation, vol 49, no 2. IBFD, The Netherlands, pp 95–96

Kergandberg E et al (2008) Kohtumenetlus. Juura, Tallinn

Kerikmäe T (2001) Estonian constitutional problems in accession to the EU. In Kellermann AE (ed) EU enlargement: the constitutional impact at EU and national level. T.M.C. Asser Institute, The Hague, pp 291–293

Kerikmäe T (2009) Estonia in the European legal system: protection of the rule of law through constitutional dialogue. Tallinn University Dissertations on Social Sciences No 42

Kerikmäe T (2010) Euroopa Zeitgeist ja Eesti valikud Põhiseaduslikkuse mõtestamisel. In Kalmo H, Luts-Sootak M (eds) Igavene või iganenud? Tekste kaasaegsest suveräänsusest. Tartu ülikooli kirjastus, Tartu

Kerikmäe T (2011) Estonia as an EU state: lack of proactive constitutional dialogue. In: Topidi K, Morawa AHE (eds) Constitutional evolution in Central and Eastern Europe: expansionand integration in the EU. Ashgate, pp 11–42

Klauson I (2010) Estonia. In: Cahiers de droit fiscal international. Tax treaties and tax avoidance: application of anti-avoidance provisions, vol 95a. Sdu, The Netherlands, pp 281–299

Koit H (2015) EJN-civil ehk Euroopa õigusalase koostöö võrgustik tsiviil- ja kaubandusasjades. Juridica 9(2015):669–673

Kõve V (2014) The main problems of civil proceedings from the point of view of a justice of the SC and lecturer. In Teeveer R et al (eds) Yearbook of Estonian Courts 2013. Riigikohus, Tartu

Künnapas K (2015) Estonia. In: Cahiers de droit fiscal international. Tax incentives on Research and Development (R&D), vol 100a. Sdu, The Netherlands, pp 271–288

Kurist A, Uustalu E (2003) Estonia. In: Cahiers de droit fiscal international. Trends in company/shareholder taxation: single or double taxation, vol 88a. Sdu, The Netherlands, pp 333–350

Laffranque J (2007) A glance at the Estonian legal landscape in view of the Const Amendment Act. Juridica Int 12:2007

Laffranque J (2015) European human rights law and Estonia: one- or two-way street? Juridica Int 23:4–16

Lahti R (2003) Die jüngsten Entwicklungen im finnischen Strafrecht. Die Zeitschrift für die gesamte Strafrechtswissenschaft (ZStW) 2003 115, 142

Lehis L (1999) Means ensuring protection of taxpayers' rights in Estonian tax law. Juridica Int 1:100–107

Lehis L (2000a) Constitutional and statutory requirements for levying tax in Estonia. In: Bulletin for international taxation, vol 54, no 10. IBFD, The Netherlands, pp 537–544

Lehis L (2000b) Radical Income Tax Reform: Abolition of Corporate Income Tax on retained earnings. In: European Taxation, vol 40, no 4. IBFD, The Netherlands, pp 135–141

Lehis L (2012) Maksuõigus. Juura, Tallinn

Lehis L (2016) Eesti maksuseaduste kommentaarid 2016. Eesti Maksumaksjate Liit, Tartu

Lehis L, Uustalu E, Pahapill H, Klauson I (2008a) Compatibility of the Estonian Corporate Income Tax System with the community law. INTERTAX. 36(8/9):389–399

Lehis L, Uustalu E, Pahapill H, Klauson I (2008b) The compatibility of the Estonian Corporate Income Tax System with community law. Juridica Int 1:14–24

Loor K (2015) Estonia. In: Cahiers de droit fiscal international. The practical protection of taxpayers' fundamental rights. Vol. 100b. Sdu, The Netherlands, pp 317–324

Mälksoo L (2003) Illegal annexation and state continuity: the case of the incorporation of the Baltic States by the USSR. Martinus Nijhoff Publishers

Masso M et al (2013) Töölepingu seaduse uuring. Poliitikauuringute Keskus Praxis, Tallinn. ISBN 978-9949-507-05-4

Merusk K (2004) Administrative law reform in Estonia: legal policy choices and their implementation. Juridica Int 9:2004

Muda M (2009) The evolution of labour law in Estonia. In: The evolution of labour law in the EU-12. Office for Official Publications of the European Communities No 3, Luxembourg

Muda M (2010) Estonian labour law reform: the successful implementation of the idea of flexurity? Int J Comp Labour Law Indus Relat 26(3)

Narits R (2009) About the principles of the Const of the Republic of Estonia from the perspective of independent statehood in Estonia. Juridica Int 16:2009

Neuhaus T, Nel AL (2013) Modeling the civil litigation process in South Africa using game theory. Conference Paper. Johannesburg, International Conference on Education, Law and Humanities, 27.-28.11.2013. https://ujdigispace.uj.ac.za/handle/10210/12415

Odar J (1993) Uuest Tsiviilkohtupidamise seadustikust. Juridica 3(1993):51–52

Olle V, Merusk K (2013) Problems of Estonian local government in 2013 and co-operation as an instrument of their resolution. Juridica Int 20:2013

Pahapill H (2005) Estonia. In: European taxation. A comparative study of the thin capitalization rules in the member states of the European Union and certain other states, vol 45, no 9. IBFD, The Netherlands, pp 383–386

Parrest N (2009) Constitutional boundaries of transfer of public functions to private sector in Estonia. Juridica Int, 16

Pilving I (2015) A discussion on the economy of administrative court procedure. In: Teeveer R et al (eds) Yearbook of Estonian Courts 2014. Riigikohus, Tartu

Põldis E, Proos M (2013) Kollektiivlepingud Eestis. Sotsiaalministeeriumi toimetised, no. 1

Randma P (2011) Organisational governance of an act – the notion of the principal offender in theory and its application in practice. Doctoral Thesis, Tartu

Raudsepp P (2013) Estonia. In: Cahiers de droit fiscal international. The taxation of foreign passive income for groups of companies, vol 98a. Sdu, The Netherlands, pp 279–287

Reinthal T (2010) The direction of penal law – over-criminalisation? Juridica 2010(10):740–750

Rigaux M (2014) Labour law or social competition law? The right to dignity of working people questioned (once again). Observations on the future of labour law. In: Rigaux M, Buelens J, Latınne A (eds) Labour law to social competition law? Intersentia, Cambridge-Antwerp-Portland

Sarapuu K (2010) Comparative analysis of state administrations: the size of state as an independent variable. Halduskultuur 11(1):30–43

Siitam-Nyiri K (2014) The development of penal law from the revision until the harmonised penal law of the European Union. Juridica 2014(8):576–581

Sootak J (2001) The notion of offence in the penal code and delictual structure. Juridica 2001 (7):447–455

Sootak J (2005) Two years of penal code – new law and new problems? Juridica 2005(1):35–44

Sootak J (2010) et al Karistusõigus. Üldosa. Tallinn, Juura

Sootak J (2013) The revision of penal law verging on the limits of criminal, misdemeanour and administrative law. Juridica 2013(4):242–248

Soots I (2011) Kohtu selgitamiskohustus hagimenetluses. Juridica 2011(5):323–332

Sultana RG (2013) Flexibility and security? Flexicurity and its implications for lifelong guidance. Br J Guidance Couns 41(2)

Taro K, Parrest N (2014) Valikud Eesti haldusorganisatsiooni loomisel. Juridica 10:2014

Tulvik E, Vahesaar T (2014). Estonia. In: Cahiers de droit fiscal international. Qualification of taxable entities and treaty protection, vol 99b. Sdu, The Netherlands, pp 299–312

Uustalu E (2003) EU accession and the Estonian tax system. European taxation 43(5):162–166

Uustalu E (2004) National Report Estonia. In: CFC legislation. Domestic provisions, tax treaties and EC law. Kluwer Law International, The Netherlands, pp 173–189

Uustalu E (2008) Vabastame osaluste võõrandamise topeltmaksustamisest. In: MaksuMaksja. Vol. 4, April 2008. Available in Estonian at: http://www.maksumaksjad.ee/modules/smartsection/item.php?itemid=730

Uustalu E (2011) The compatibility of the Estonian tax treatment of real estate income with EU law. INTERTAX. 39(8/9):449–458

Van Elsuwege P (2003) State continuity and its consequences: the case of the Baltic States. Leiden J Int Law. Cambridge Journals 16:377–388. doi:10.1017/S0922156503001195

Van Elsuwege, P. (2008). From Soviet republics to EU member states: a legal and political assessment of the Baltic states' accession to the EU. BRILL.

Van Rhee CH (ed) (2005) European traditions in civil procedure. Antwerpen, Oxford

Weisbrot M, Jorgensen H (2013) Macroeconomic policy advise and the Art IV consultations. In "Comparative overview of European Union Member States". ILO Research Paper No 7. ISBN web/pdf: 2306-0875

Ziemele I (2005) State continuity and nationality: the Baltic States and Russia. Martinus Nijhoff Publishers

Zukowski R (2006) Estonian Corporate Income Tax and the European Union: the implications. In: European taxation, vol 46, no 3. IBFD, The Netherlands, pp 128–130

Private Law

3

Edgar Grünberg, Kristi Joamets, Rene Lauk, Priidu Pärna, Margus Poola, and Addi Rull

Abstract

The Chapter gives an overview of the main branches of private law: property law, obligation law, company law, insolvency law, family law and inheritance law. Estonian private law can be described as an European private law. There are significant similarities with German law. Currently the changes in development of certain law branches derive from the cross-border legal relations. Estonian civil law is constructed as a pandectic system. The General Part of the Civil Code Act includes the general provisions applicable to all sections of the civil law. It provides general provisions regarding persons, objects, transactions, terms, expressions of will, grounds of nullity and prescription. The catalogue of Estonian property law includes the right of ownership, the right of security, servitudes, real encumbrances, the right of superficies and the right of pre-emption. Law of obligations makes up the most extensive part of civil law regulating obligations arising out of contracts and non-contractual relationships. The business environment in Estonia is vibrant and liberal. The vast development of e-services has been one of the triggers of success in business law. Family and inheritance law develops according to the new family relations in society and spread of cross-border family relations.

E. Grünberg
Tartu Notary, Turu tn 2, 51014 Tartu, Estonia
e-mail: info@tartunotar.ee

K. Joamets (✉) • R. Lauk • M. Poola • A. Rull
Tallinn Law School, Tallinn University of Technology, Akadeemia tee 3, 12618 Tallinn, Estonia
e-mail: kristi.joamets@ttu.ee; renelauk@hotmail.com; margus.poola@ttu.ee; addi.rull@ttu.ee

P. Pärna
Faculty of Law, University of Tartu, Ülikooli 18, 50019 Tartu, Estonia

Tallinn Notary Priidu Pärna, Rävala pst 2, 10145 Tallinn, Estonia
e-mail: priidu.parna@notarmail.ee

T. Kerikmäe et al. (eds.), *The Law of the Baltic States*,
DOI 10.1007/978-3-319-54478-6_3

3.1 Property Law

Priidu Pärna
Faculty of Law, University of Tartu, Ülikooli 18, 50019 Tartu, Estonia

Tallinn Notary Priidu Pärna, Rävala pst 2, 10145 Tallinn, Estonia
e-mail: priidu.parna@notarmail.ee

3.1.1 The Evolution and Sources of Property Law

After the Estonian re-independence it was decided in 1992 that there is not enough time to deal with the compilation of a new civil code to create a legal basis for economic reforms and that instead it should be established in parts and codified sometime in the future.[1] Under the *Land Reform Act* adopted in 1991[2] the return of illegally disposed land and the privatisation of the solely state owned Land Fund began. The establishment of private ownership of land as well as the basis for further commerce were needed since the *Civil Code* of the Estonian SSR[3] only regulated movable assets and the commerce of buildings and the *Land Code* of the Estonian SSR[4] only the land use rights. The option of reintroducing the civil law in force before 1940 was considered, however the new *Civil Code* could not be adopted in Estonia before the occupation and the re-entering into force of the *Baltic Private Law Code* (*BPLC*)[5] of 1864 would have meant going too far back in time.

The 1940 draft section on the law of property of the *Civil Code* of the Republic of Estonia[6] was used as a basis in preparing the *Law of Property Act* (*LPA*).[7] The draft *Civil Code* had further developed the property law book of *BES* based on the new codifications from the beginning of the century, the *German Civil Code* (*BGB*)[8] and the *Swiss Civil Code*.[9] In compiling the *LPA*, these codes became the most important external sources. The influence of the *BGB* has been especially significant on Estonian property law since the principal adviser during the drafting was the Foundation for International Legal Cooperation created by the Ministry of Justice of the Federal Republic of Germany.

[1]Estonian civil law is not codified and the part on property law is established with the *Law of Property Act*.

[2]RT 1991, 34, 426.

[3]*The Civil Code of the Estonian SSR* 1965.

[4]*The Land Code of the Estonian SSR* 1971.

[5]*Privatrecht der Ostseeprovinzen Liv-, Est- und Curland*.

[6]*Civil Code of the Republic of Estonia* (draft proposal in special committee of the National Council 1940 redaction).

[7]RT I 1993, 39, 590.

[8]*Bürgerliches Gesetzbuch* 1896. *BGB*l.I S.441.

[9]*Schweizerisches Zivilgesetzbuch* (*ZGB*) 1907. BBl 1904 IV 1.

The *LPA* was the first part of the provisional new *Civil Code* which entered into force on 1 December 1993. Accordingly, the chapter concerning property law was repealed from the *USSR Civil Code*. One of the most notable shortcomings of establishing the civil code in parts was the fact that European property law had to be applied in conjunction with the Soviet law of obligations, which was only replaced with the *Law of Obligations Act* (*LOA*) in 2002.[10] The *LPA* is not the only legal act containing property law. In 1994 the *Apartment Ownership Act*[11] was adopted and in 1995 the *Commercial Pledges Act*.[12] The commerce of large seagoing vessels is separately prescribed by the *Law of Maritime Property Act*[13] and the *Law of Ship Flag* and *Ship Registers Act*.[14] To hold and maintain a land register a separate *Land Register Act* was adopted, which entered into force at the same time as the *LPA* on 1 December 1993.[15]

The *LPA* is comprised of a general part and a specialised part. The general part includes common rules for immovables and the principles for a strong land register as well as provisions outlining possession as factual control. The institution of possession is the basis for the commerce of movable property. The specialised part stipulates the creation, extinguishment and content of individual real rights.

3.1.2 General Provisions of Property Law

The catalogue of Estonian property law includes the right of ownership, the right of security, servitudes, real encumbrances, the right of superficies and the right of pre-emption. Real rights are characterised by the principle of *numerus clausus*—the types of real rights and the basis for their creation and extinguishment ensue from the law and the parties to the commerce cannot, by themselves, create more. The content of real rights can only be modified within the boundaries permitted by law. Another important principle is the separation of transactions, which requires that in the commerce of real rights, transactions constituting an obligation under the law of obligations be differentiated from dispositions under the law of property. This is accompanied by the abstraction principle[16]—the validity of a disposition is not contingent upon the validity of the transaction which requires the transfer of the right or obligation.

As a general rule, the objects of real rights are things. One of the principles of Estonian property law is the principle of legal certainty, meaning that real rights

[10] RT I 2001, 81, 487.
[11] RT I 1994, 28, 426.
[12] RT I 1996, 45, 848.
[13] RT I 1998, 30, 409.
[14] RT I 1998, 23, 321.
[15] RT I 1993, 65, 922.
[16] The abstraction principle was included in the *LPA* on the recommendations of German legal experts and the law in force before 1940 and Soviet law did not recognise the principle.

cannot apply to a collection of things and every thing must be separately disposed. Property as a set of rights and obligations belonging to a person is not the object of real rights. Objects are things, rights and other benefits, which may be objects of the law.[17] The commerce of things is thus differentiated from the commerce of rights and a thing is separated from a right by its corporeal nature. Things are classified as immovables (*res immobiles*) and movables (*res mobiles*).[18] The treatment of things is derived from Germanic law. The concept of immovables is defined by the law and all other corporeal objects are classified as movables. The law may also apply the provisions governing immovables to movables—an example of this are seagoing vessels over 12 metres long flying the national flag of Estonia.[19]

A movable is a delimited part of the ground, that is to say, a plot of land. Law of immovable property does not extend to general benefits such as ground-water, important mineral resources, air, etc. Permanently merged constructions are not considered as independent things but instead as substantial parts of immovables. Vegetation and related real rights also form a significant part of immovables. Constructions built on foreign land based on property law (for example servitude or right of superficies) as well as constructions temporarily joined to a plot of land or constructions owned based on the statutory obligation to tolerate are not important parts of immovables. Such a statutory obligation to tolerate is applicable to utility works built before 1999[20] and to other constructions that have been established contrary to the will of the owner on public interest grounds by way of an administrative act or a judicial decision. Nevertheless, there is a transitional provision in the commerce of constructions built during the Soviet era—until the entry of the land below the construction into the land register in the course of the land reforms, which started in the 1990s, such a construction was classified in commerce as movable property.[21] Since 2006, the expropriation of such constructions without land is limited—it is only possible in the course of general succession, e.g. by inheritance.

The central tenets of property law are possession and the land register. According to the *LPA*, possession (*possessio*) is actual control over a thing. Possession is thus not a legal but a factual relationship with a thing and the exercise of possession does not require a legal basis. Depending on the existence of a legal basis, possession is categorised as either in good faith or in bad faith. Such a differentiation has an important significance with respect to the acquisition in good faith of movables and prescription, as well as in case of a claim for reclamation, the position of the deliverer of a thing to make a counterclaim depends on the

[17]When the *LPA* entered into force in 1993, it included provisions on the classification of things. The regulation of things was transferred to the *General Part of the Civil Code Act* when it entered into force in 2002.

[18]*General Part of the Civil Code Act* §50. RT I 2002, 35, 216.

[19]*Law of Ship Flag and Ship Registers Act* §31. RT I 1998, 23, 321.

[20]*Law of Property Act Implementation Act* §15^2 RT I 1993, 72/73, 1021.

[21]*Law of Property Act Implementation Act* §13.

legal basis of possession. Possession is presumed to be in good faith. *LPA* differentiates between indirect and direct possession and the concept of serving a possession. In case of indirect possession the person has no actual control over the thing, only a right of reclamation against the actual person. A person serving a possession exercises possession over a thing according to the orders of another person. However, the measures for the protection of possession are applicable to both the indirect possessor and the person serving a possession. Possession is acquired by obtaining actual control and terminated if a possessor relinquishes actual control or loses it. The creation or termination of possession has a decisive meaning for the creation of movable property ownership and other movable property rights (above all right of security) where possession has an important signalling function. The possessor of movable property is presumed to also be the owner of the thing until contrary is proven.[22] With regard to immovables, possession has no significant meaning for the creation of ownership (except in the case of prescription). According to *LPA* §38, possession automatically transfers to a successor, meaning that the successor is the possessor of a thing even if the successor is not aware of his inheritance rights.[23]

Possession gives the possessor the position to protect the possession regardless of it being in good or bad faith.[24] Self-help, that is, the opportunity for the use of force, which is permitted within the limits of self-defence against the user of arbitrary action, including the right to regain control over the immovable, provided this is done immediately after losing possession, has its roots in the former so-called law of the fist.

The commerce of immovables is determined by the principles of a so-called strong land register. Maintaining land registers at the courts was restored simultaneously with the entry into force of the *LPA* on 1 December 1993. Formerly, the commerce only occurred with constructions and such transactions were registered in the building register maintained by administrative authorities. One of the goals of the property law reform was to create registration of immovable property rights independent from the executive. Land registers are maintained by first instance civil courts (county courts) and the power to make entries has been granted to independent assistant judges.[25]

The concept of a strong land register is similar to the Germanic system[26] and includes several basic principles. The most important one is the presumption that information entered in the land register is correct. Parties to the transaction are not

[22]*LPA* §90.

[23]In Estonia there is a system of automatic transfer of estate to the successor instead of a system of acceptance (*Succession Law Act* (*SLA*) §4. RT I 2008, 7, 52).

[24]*LPA* §§40–50.

[25]Initially, from 1 January 1993, the register was kept by judges. However, this excessively increased their workload and thus in 1996 the institution of assistant judges was created with the courts based on the examples of Austria and Germany.

[26]An example is the *German Grundbuchordnung* (*GBO*) 1897. *BGB*l. I S 114.

required to verify the documents which are the basis for the entry nor the validity of these transactions. The correctness of the land register must be guaranteed by double verification—the dispositions of immovables reaching the court conducting the registration must be notarially authenticated. The security of the commerce is guaranteed by the land register being public. Everyone has the right to examine information in the land register and to receive extracts therefrom. No one may be excused by ignorance of information in the land register. Since nowadays the maintenance of the land register is electronic, it is possible to access the register via electronic means by using electronic identity cards for identification. Access to the documents which form the basis of the entry is only allowed upon the existence of a legitimate interest.

The clarity of the land register is guaranteed by the principle that only information permitted by law can be entered into the register. Immovables and related real rights and notations permitted by law are entered in the land register. Maintaining the land register is based on the principle that an independent register part is opened for each immovable.[27] The technical data of an immovable (a plot of land) are reflected in the land cadastre, which is maintained by the Ministry of the Environment.[28] The rights being entered receive a ranking in the register and the earlier right has superiority over subsequent rights—this point generally becomes evident during enforcement proceedings conducted in relation to immovables. The rankings are mobile—upon the deletion of an earlier right, the rights move forward in the rankings.

The possibility of acquisition in good faith of immovable property rights is also based on the presumption that information entered in the land register is correct.[29] If a person acquires an immovable property right based on information in the land register, the acquisition is final, except in a situation where the acquirer should have known that the information entered in the land register was incorrect or an objection had been entered in the register.

The general part of the *LPA* also contains general provisions regarding transactions involving immovable property rights and the specialised part adds specific rules for every real right. *LPA* §64[1] outlines the universal principle according to which the transfer of immovable property ownership or encumbrance of an immovable with a real right as well as the transfer or the amendment of the content of such a real right require a notarially authenticated disposition (a real right contract) and a corresponding entry must also be made in the land register. Outside the land register immovable property rights may only be transferred in the course of general succession,[30] in which case the entry in the land register must be amended.

---

[27] Nevertheless, several cadastral units may be entered in a single part of the register.

[28] The maintenance of the land cadastre is regulated by *The Land Cadastre Act*. RT I 1994, 74, 1324.

[29] *LPA* §56[1].

[30] For example by succession or merger of a capital company.

The termination of a real right encumbering an immovable requires a simpler form—a notarially authenticated application by an entitled person is sufficient.[31]

Disposition is therefore the basis for entries in the land register and transactions constituting an obligation under the law of obligations do not need to be submitted to the register. Provided a transaction under the law of obligations is not valid, for example if it has been withdrawn from, then the transaction constituting an obligation continues to apply and the entry is correct. A redisposition obligation applies to a real right acquired based on an invalid transaction constituting an obligation.[32] When relying on such an entry during further acquisition, the new acquirer does not have to rely on acquisition in good faith since the real right was acquired from the current owner. These principles reflect the abstraction principle of Estonian civil law, which was introduced by the 1993 *LPA* on the recommendation of German legal experts and modelled on the dogmatic of the *BGB*.[33] Compared to the existing principle of consensus this was a crucial change and this arguably historical choice has shaped the rest of the modern private law system in Estonia.

3.1.3 Right of Ownership

The *LPA* construes right of ownership as full legal control by a person over a thing. Ownership is an absolute real right. Under Estonian law, ownership is also a constitutional right. §32 of the Estonian Constitution (*Const*) stipulates that property of every person is inviolable and may only be limited pursuant to a procedure provided by law and compulsory expropriation is only allowed in the public interest and for fair and immediate compensation.[34] Right of ownership may exist as sole ownership, common ownership or joint ownership. Common ownership is ownership in legal shares of a shared thing belonging to two or more persons concurrently. Joint ownership is ownership in undefined shares of a shared thing belonging to two or more persons concurrently and it arises only in specific cases established by the law. Joint ownership exists for example in the proprietary relations of spouses,[35] proprietary relations between successors[36] and partnerships.[37] While a co-owner may freely dispose his share of the thing, in case of joint ownership the thing may only be disposed by the joint owners acting together.

[31] *LPA* §64^2.

[32] A situation of unjust enrichment based on the *LOA* §1028.

[33] The principle of abstraction is established also in substantive law in the *General Part of the Civil Code Act* §6(4), according to which the validity of a disposition is not conditional upon the validity of the transaction for the transfer of the right and obligation.

[34] RT I 1993, 39, 590.

[35] *FLA*§25. RT I 2009, 60, 395.

[36] *SLA* §147.

[37] *LOA* §589.

A specific form of common ownership is apartment ownership. The *Apartment Ownership Act* was adopted in 1994, but a new *Apartment Ownership and Apartment Associations Act* will enter into force in 2018.[38] Apartment ownership constitutes a trinity for the physical share of a construction work in exclusive ownership, the immovable which is part of common ownership related to it and membership rights in an association formed by apartment owners.[39] Such a *sui generis* real right (apartment ownership right) is capable of commerce since it has been essentially equated with an immovable with ownership.[40] Apartment ownership may also exist as a right of superficies in apartments. When an immovable is divided into apartment ownerships an independent land register part is opened for every apartment ownership and the register part of the plot of land is closed. Apartment owners jointly administer the apartment building and appoint an administrator or establish an independent legal person, a competent apartment association. The administration of apartment associations will change from 2018—a compulsory association with automatic legal capacity will be created in every apartment building that does not yet have one. This aims to solve the current legal issues relating to the taking of obligations in the name of apartment owners or acquiring rights in buildings without apartment associations. The new act is based on the 2007 reforms of the *German Apartment Ownership Act*.[41]

The validity of ownership in relation to all persons reflects the absolute nature of ownership and to protect the right of ownership the owner may submit claims for the protection of possession and ownership. *LPA* §80 sets out the vindication claim—an owner has a right of claim against anyone who possesses a thing of the owner without legal basis and the claim is directed towards recognition of the right of ownership and reclamation of the thing from illegal possession into the owner's possession. The burden of proof is on the person filing the claim. In addition, the owner also has use of the negatory claim[42]—an owner has the right to demand elimination of any violation of the right of ownership even if the violation is not related to a loss of possession.

The basis for the creation of immovable property is an entry to the land register, also in relation to the parties of the transaction themselves. Outside the register, immovable property can only be transferred in the course of general succession. The disposition forming the basis for the entry (so-called real right contract) and the causal transaction under the law of obligations (for example a sale contract) must be notarially authenticated. In case these transactions are not completed simultaneously, the notary must verify the existence of the causal transaction which

[38]RT I 13.03.2014, 3.

[39]Estonian private law also allows for ownership of dwellings through building associations (*Building Association Act* RT 2004). In such circumstances the immovable belongs to the association and in commerce the possessor will have the membership rights of the association.

[40]*Apartment Ownership Act* §1. RT I 2000, 92, 601.

[41]*Gesetz über das Wohnungseigentum und das Dauerwohnrecht* 1951. *BGB*l. I S. 370.

[42]*LPA* §89.

forms the basis of the disposition. Nevertheless, the basis for the entry is still only the disposition. A real right contract may not be conditional. A notarially authenticated application by the owner addressed to the registrar of the land register is sufficient for the relinquishment of immovable property ownership.

In addition to acquisition through the land register, the *LPA* also recognises acquisition of immovables through prescription (*usucapio*).[43] If a person has been entered in the land register as an owner of an immovable without legal basis, the person becomes the owner of the immovable if the person possesses the immovable as an owner for 10 years without interruption. Prescription occurs in 30 years if a person has without interruption possessed an immovable, whose owner is not evident from the land register.[44]

Movable property ownership is created by delivery of a movable (*traditio*). A form free disposition has to be concluded for delivery and the possession of the movable must be transferred.[45] The delivery of possession can be replaced with a delivery of measures for the exercise of possession or assignment of the right of reclamation of the thing. In addition to the disposition, a transaction obligating the delivery of movable property must also be concluded. Likewise, the abstraction principle applies to the delivery of movable property. The disposition for the delivery of movable property may be conditional.

The possibility of acquisition in good faith protects the security of the commerce of movables.[46] A person acquires a movable by delivery in good faith even if the transferor was not entitled to transfer ownership. However, acquisition in good faith does not apply if the movable was dispossessed from the actual owner against the will of the owner (for example stolen). In such circumstances the acquirer in good faith only becomes the owner after 5 years through prescription. In addition to delivery and prescription, the *LPA* also recognises occupation, acquisition of finding and treasure, specification and accession, and acquisition of natural fruit as foundations for the creation of movable property, although they have very little significance in practice.[47]

3.1.4 Restricted Real Rights

Restricted real rights do not grant an equally broad set of rights over a thing like right of ownership does. Their content is more limited. According to *LPA* §64[1], a

[43]With regard to prescription, the basis of ownership has little meaning in commerce.

[44]*LPA* §123–124.

[45]The transfer of movable property centred on possession is inconsistent with the proposals made for the harmonisation of civil law at European Union level. The Principles, Definitions and Model Rules of European Private Law/Draft Common Frame of Reference (DCFR) published in 2009 recommend the adoption of the principle of consensus in transfering movable property.

[46]*LPA* §95.

[47]*LPA* §§96–115.

notarially authenticated disposition (a real right contract) and an entry in the land register in the part of the immovable being encumbered is required for the creation of a restricted right. Unlike with a disposition of ownership, the disposition of restricted real rights may be conditional. Likewise, there is no required standard format for the causal transaction which forms the basis for the disposition of restricted real rights.[48] For the termination of a restricted real right the presentation of a notarially authenticated application by an entitled person to the other party or the land register is sufficient. Under Estonian law, restricted real rights can only be established in relation to immovables.[49]

Estonian property law recognises restricted real rights for own things. Real rights are not terminated if the owner of the encumbered and servient immovable coincide as the same person (in the case of servitude and right of superficies) or the owner of an immovable encumbered with a mortgage acquires the mortgage (creating an owner mortgage). The owner may also initially encumber his immovable for his own benefit based on an application. Restricted real rights for own things allow for flexible commerce.

One of the most common restricted real rights is servitude.[50] A servitude between a servient and dominant immovable is a real servitude and a servitude for the benefit of a specific person is a personal servitude. Obligation to tolerate or obligation to refrain of the owner of the encumbered immovable forms the content of a servitude. According to the *LPA*, the different types of personal servitude are usufruct (*usus fructus*) and personal right of use. The former real right is often used as a long-term and inheritable right of use for indigenous land since the *LPA* does not establish indigenous rent as a separate real right. The differentiation between a contract of use under the law of obligations and under property law is made more complicated by §324 *LOA*, which also permits a notation regarding the lease contract of an immovable to be entered in the land register, in which case the lease contract gains, in relation to the new owner, an effect as a real right. Servitudes are not transferable without the consent of the owner of the immovable, an exception being the personal right of use set up for the construction of utility works.

Rights of pre-emption are divided into a right created pursuant to law and a transactional right of pre-emption, which is entered into the land register.[51] Right of pre-emption of an immovable created pursuant to law may have a public character (arising from the *Nature and Heritage Conservation Act*[52]) or private character (co-owner's right of pre-emption). In addition, the *LOA* establishes the possibility of agreeing on a single right of pre-emption under the law of obligations (*LOA* §244–253). The aforementioned *LOA* provisions have a significant impact since

[48]Except for the establishment of the right of superficies and the right of pre-emption.

[49]Only rights of security can be applied to movable property and rights.

[50]*LPA* §172 and etc.

[51]*LPA* §256.

[52]RT I 2002, 27, 153.

they also apply to the actual right of pre-emption under property law. In case of a right of pre-emption, the seller has an obligation to notify the owner of the right of the sales transaction and its terms after it has taken place. With immovables the deadline for exercising a right of pre-emption is 2 months since the notification. To exercise a right of pre-emption, the owner of the right must present the seller with a notarially authenticated application, which gives rise to a new sales transaction between the seller and the owner of the right of pre-emption.

Right of superficies (*superficies*) has an important significance with regard to constructions built on foreign land and therefore this restricted real right is also considered an immovable. Right of superficies is equal in commerce as a plot of land and an independent part in the land register is created for it. Erected constructions are important parts of the right of superficies and not of the plot of land. A right of superficies may only be established for a term no longer than 99 years and it may only be ranked first in the land register. Upon expiry of the right of superficies, the constructions become an important part of the plot of land unless they have been moved away. Payment of compensation depends on the agreement establishing the right of superficies.

A real encumbrance is the active obligation of an actual owner of the immovable to make periodic payments in money or in kind or perform particular acts. A real encumbrance may be established for the benefit of another immovable or a specific person and must always be entered in the land register. Payments for a right of superficies to the land owner are usually guaranteed by setting up a real encumbrance.

3.1.5 Securities Under Property Law

According to the *LPA*, right of security is also a restricted real right. Right of security is an encumbrance of a thing, which gives the pledgee the right of satisfaction of the claim secured by the pledge out of the pledged property. A pledge is a priority realisation right and the agreement for acquiring the object of the pledge to satisfy the claim can only be made by the pledger and the pledgee after the right of sale of the pledged thing has arisen. The *LPA* differentiates between a security over movables for movables and rights, and real security for immovables. Securities over movables are characterised by the fragmented and diverse regulation that governs them. The *LOA* also stipulates several statutory rights of security for movable property.[53] The *LPA* does not exclude the security acquisition of immovables and movables, although in accordance with the *numerous clausus* principle of real rights such security agreements cannot be labelled as rights of security.

The simplest type of security over movables is a possessory pledge.[54] To establish a pledge a disposition and a transfer of possession of the pledged movable

[53]For example, the landlord's right of security over the tenant's movables, *LOA* §305.

[54]*LPA* §281.

are required. An agreement for the establishment of a pledge must be in writing if the value of the object of the pledge exceeds 50 euros. Possessory pledges are most commonly used in pawnshops and thus lack notable economic significance. The acquisition of a possessory pledge in good faith is possible if the pledgee acts in good faith and the object of the pledge has not been dispossessed from the actual owner against the owner's will. A possessory pledge presumes the existence of a secured claim. In case of non-compliance with a claim secured with a pledge, the pledgee must sell the thing at a public auction and no recognition of the claim by a court is necessary.[55] The economic importance of the provisions governing possessory pledges is evidenced by the fact that the same provisions are also applied to the pledging of rights, including claims.[56] Rights[57] which are transferable can be pledged.

Estonian law recognises registered securities over movables as a type of securities over movables.[58] Such a right of security can exist in relation to registered movable property permitted by law like the different forms of intellectual property, motor vehicles and aircrafts.[59] A written disposition and an entry in the public state register for the respective object of property (patent register, aircraft register, etc.) is required for the establishment of a pledge. Registered security over movables is a right of security similar to a mortgage where the pledge enters into force with its entry in the register. Similarity with a mortgage also appears in that one object of property may be encumbered by many registered securities in the order of arrival of applications and a registered security does not presume the existence of a secured claim for it to be valid. Instead the provisions governing maritime mortgages are applied to such pledges.[60] Registered securities can be subjected to compulsory execution.

The *LPA* provisions on mortgages are shaped along the lines of German charges of land.[61] *LPA* recognises a non-appurtenant mortgage (*hypoteka*), which can be created for a plot of land, apartment ownership and a right of superficies.[62] In addition, a mortgage extends to the important parts and accessories of immovables.

---

[55]*LPA* §294.

[56]*LPA* §314.

[57]The chapter in the *LPA* on pledge of rights also includes provisions on financial collateral, which incorporates into Estonian law Directive 2002/47/EC of the European Parliament and of the Council of 6 June 2002 on financial collateral arrangements. (OJ L 168, 27.6.2002). Financial collateral cannot, however, be classified as a classical right of security.

[58]*LPA* §297.

[59]A special category of registered security over movables is commercial pledge, which based on its general character is more similar to a mortgage. Commercial pledge was introduced into Estonian property law in 1993 with the *LPA*, but in 1996, because of a necessity of more detailed regulation, a separate *Commercial Pledges Act* was adopted.

[60]*LMPA* §15–66.

[61]*BGB* §1191.

[62]Regulation imposed on seagoing vessels and maritime mortgages entered in the ship registry are based on the provisions governing mortgages. (*Law of Maritime Property Act* §15–66).

The establishment of a mortgage does not preclude the owner from continuing to dispose the immovable. The effectuation of a mortgage requires a notarially authenticated bilateral disposition and an entry in the land register and a system of covered bonds outside the land register does not exist. A security agreement, that is, an agreement specifying which claim is secured with a mortgage, must also be notarially authenticated. In practice, the conclusion of excessively wide-ranging security agreements is problematic. In most cases, the mortgage will be subjected to immediate compulsory execution and in such circumstances a court is not required to recognise the claim to initiate enforcement proceedings. One immovable may be encumbered with several mortgages in the order of arrival of applications. The strength of a mortgage is secured by §158 of the *Code of Enforcement Procedure*,[63] according to which the rights causing the claim for payment which have a lower ranking than the mortgage will be extinguished. Upon satisfaction of a claim secured with a mortgage the owner may demand that the security mortgage is entered in the name of the owner, although the *LPA* also allows for the entry of the owner mortgage as an original owner mortgage.[64] The *LPA* allows several immovables to be encumbered with a single right of security (combined mortgage, *LPA* §359). A judicial mortgage can be employed for securing a financial claim in action proceedings.[65] Mortgage is a pledgeable right. Regulation imposed on seagoing vessels and maritime mortgages entered in the ship registry are based on the provisions governing mortgages.[66]

3.2 Law of Obligations

Margus Poola
Tallinn Law School, Tallinn University of Technology, Akadeemia tee 3, 12618 Tallinn, Estonia
e-mail: margus.poola@ttu.ee

The process of developing a new system of Estonian civil law started as early as in 1989.[67] Estonia, unlike its neighbouring country Latvia,[68] took the view that in the process of departing from the soviet legal system a totally new civil code should be developed, although initially the main source of the new civil code was to be the *Estonian 1940 Draft Civil Code*[69] developed by a committee led by Mr. Jüri Uluots.[70] It was however realised that neither the *1940 Draft Civil Code* or the

[63] RT I 2005, 27, 198.
[64] *LPA* §328.
[65] *LPA* §363.
[66] *LMPA* §§15–66.
[67] Varul (1993), p. 120.
[68] Balodis (2013), p. 69.
[69] Varul (1993), p. 120.
[70] Varul et al. (2006), p. 2.

Baltic Private Law Code—that was still in force in Estonia in 1940—would serve as a suitable example for a new and modern civil law.[71]

Estonian law of obligations is mainly contained in the *Law of Obligations Act* (*LOA*) that came into force on 1 July 2002.[72] The main sources in the development of the *LOA* were the *German Civil Code* (*Bürgerliches Gesetzbuch*—*BGB*), Principles of European Private Law (PECL), Unidroit Principles of International Commercial Contracts (PICC) and 1980 United Nations Convention on Contracts for the International Sale of Goods (CISG). In addition to the above mentioned, the civil codes of the Netherlands, Switzerland, Austria, Finland, Sweden, Russia, Louisiana and Quebec have served as important sources for many provisions of the *LOA*.[73] The 1940 *Draft Civil Code* has also been mentioned as one of the sources.[74] In the development of the *LOA* the then in force consumer *acqui* of the European Union (EU) was taken into account to ensure *LOA*'s full compliance with it.[75]

Since the adoption of the *LOA* several changes have been made in the law of obligations. However, the main features and concepts of the law have not changed.

3.2.1 The Main Characteristics of Estonian Law of Obligations

Estonian civil law is constructed as a pandectic system. The General Part of the *Civil Code Act* (*GPCCA*) includes the general provisions applicable to all sections of the civil law. It provides general provisions regarding persons, objects, transactions, terms, expressions of will, grounds of nullity and prescription.[76] The *LOA*, which itself is divided into a general and a special part, provides more specific provisions applicable to legal relationships governed by rules of law of obligations.[77] With regard to its scope the law of obligations makes up the most extensive part of civil law.

In Estonia, the law of obligations is understood as the part of the law that regulates obligations arising out of contracts and non-contractual relationships. An obligation is defined in the *LOA* as a legal relationship which gives rise to the obligation of one person (obligated person or obligor) to perform an act or omission (perform an obligation) for the benefit of another person (entitled person or obligee), and to the right of the obligee to demand that the obligor perform the obligation.[78]

---

[71]Ibid.

[72]The original version of *Law of Obligations Act* had the title *Law of Contractual and Non-Contractual Obligations*.

[73]Explanatatory note of *Law of Obligation Act* (116 SE I); Varul (2006), p. 2.

[74]Explanatory note of *Law of Obligation Act*. (116 SE I).

[75]Ibid.

[76]See *GPCCA;* also Kull et al. (2004), p. 15.

[77]*LOA*.

[78]*LOA* §2(1).

The law of obligations and *LOA* in specific is structured in a way that it starts form definitions, rules and concepts common to the whole law of obligations and then proceeds to specific legal relationships. §§1–207 of the *LOA* make up the general part of law of obligations. §§208–1004 regulate specific types of contracts: contracts of sale, services, loan, gift, carriage, etc. The *LOA* only provides regulation for the most typical types of contracts. The parties' choice of a contract is not limited to the list found in *LOA* and the parties are free to conclude other types of contracts not regulated in any legal acts.[79] §§1005–1067 of *LOA* deal with different types of non-contractual relationships.

The general part of the *LOA* applies to all obligations whether they arise from contract or a non-contractual relationship.[80] However, there are chapters and individual provisions of the general part of the *LOA* that only apply to contractual relationships (e.g. the second chapter of the general part of the *LOA* that defines contracts and the formation of contracts).[81] The general part of *LOA* is also applied to employment contracts,[82] although an employment relationship is more specifically regulated by a separate *Employment Contracts Act* (*ECA*) (the provisions of which cannot be derogated from to the detriment of the employee[83]) and the *LOA* is only applicable as far as it does not conflict with the *ECA*.[84]

The fundamental principle of Estonian law of obligations is that upon agreement between the parties to an obligation or contract, the parties may derogate from the provisions of *LOA* unless *LOA* expressly provides or the nature of a provision indicates that derogation from *LOA* is not permitted, or unless derogation is contrary to public order or good morals or violates the fundamental rights of a person.[85]

The liability of a party according to Estonian law of obligations is generally based on strict liability (guarantee liability), which means that the obligee is liable regardless of why the breach of obligation occurred.[86] In case of strict liability the only possibility to be excused of liability is if the breach was caused by a detriment beyond the obligee's control and that the obligee could not have reasonably foreseen and taken into account at the time when the obligation arose and provided that the obligee cannot be expected to avoid or overcome the detriment.[87] In this regard the Estonian law is modelled on provisions of the PICC, PECL and CISG.[88] Strict liability is however not applied in tort or delict law, except for liability for

[79] Varul (2006), p. 4.
[80] *LOA* §1(1).
[81] *LOA* §§8–623.
[82] *LOA* §1(1).
[83] *ECA* §1(3).
[84] *ECA* §2.
[85] *LOA* §5.
[86] Varul (2006), p. 325.
[87] *LOA* §103.
[88] Varul (2006), p. 325.

damage caused by major source of danger and liability for defective product, and in the case of some types of contracts, e.g. contract for provision of health care services[89] and in some specific situations where liability arises out of contract, e.g. in gratuitous contracts[90] and contracts of loan for use[91] the donor/lender is only liable for a breach if it was committed intentionally or with gross negligence).[92] In these cases the obligee's liability depends on whether he/she is at fault or not. It is of course also possible for parties to agree on fault-based liability in a contract.[93]

One of the fundamental principles in Estonian civil law is the principle of good faith. Unlike the CISG,[94] Estonian civil law specifically provides a general obligation to act in good faith. This obligation is provided in §138 of the *GPCCA* and more specifically regarding the law of obligations in §6 of *LOA*. While the general obligation to observe the principle of good faith as provided in §6(1) of the *LOA* is an obligation commonly found in the civil codes of several countries,[95] Estonian law of obligation goes further. §6(2) provides for a possibility not to apply to a relationship what arises from law, a usage or a transaction if that would be contrary to the principle of good faith. Estonian Supreme Court (SC) has confirmed several times that §6(2) of *LOA* gives an objection to the obligee allowing to refuse to perform an obligation arising from law, contract or usage if it would be against the principle of good faith.[96]

In theory it is generally said that the good faith principle has three functions in Estonian law of obligations: supplementing obligations, limiting rights and changing the conditions of a contract. In several legal other systems another function of the principle is to assist in the interpretation of legal rules.[97] Although Estonian *LOA* does not specifically list interpretation as one of the functions of the principle of good faith, in legal practice the good faith principle has been used to develop legal dogmatic concerning the institutes of law to which a particular case belongs to.[98] Also given the fact that Estonian *LOA* has been greatly modelled on the CISG, PICC and PECL, it seems to be in line with these instruments to take good faith into account in the interpretation of the law or contractual provisions.[99]

During its 14-year history the provisions of Estonian law of obligations have been amended several times. Many of the amendments have been in connection

[89]*LOA* §770.

[90]*LOA* §242.

[91]*LOA* §390 (1).

[92]Varul (2006), p. 331.

[93]Ibid. p. 330.

[94]Schwenzer et al. (2010), pp. 122 and 127–130.

[95]Varul et al. (2006), p. 24; von Bar et al. (2008).

[96]SC 3-2-1-99-07, p. 15; SC 3-2-1-28-11, p. 16; SC 3-2-1-1-15, p. 19.

[97]von Bar et al. (2008).

[98]Varul et al. (2006), p. 26.

[99]See Schwenzer et al. (2010), pp. 122, 127–130, but also Art. 4.8 (2) c) of PICC and Art. 1:106 (1) of PECL.

with amendment of the consumer *acqui* of the EU, although several other amendments have also been implemented. However, the main principles of the law of obligations have remained the same.

3.2.2 Developments in Contract Law

In Estonian civil law a contract can be described as a set of interrelated acts by which one party or the parties intend to undertake a legally binding (and enforceable) obligation to perform an act or omission.[100] The free will of a party to assume an obligation is the main characteristic that distinguishes a contractual obligation from other obligations. However, Estonian civil law also includes a few other types of obligations, which are assumed by persons at their free will, but which are not considered to be contracts. These are so-called obligations of courtesy and imperfect obligations, e.g. moral obligations or obligations arising from gambling, also a promise to get married.[101] These obligations differ from contracts in that they do not constitute a binding (i.e. legally enforceable) obligation, although if the obligation is fulfilled by the debtor, there would be no grounds to claim back what was transferred as fulfilment of the obligation.[102]

Estonian contract law is based on the principles of freedom of contract and the binding effect of a contract (*pacta sunt servanda*).[103] It has taken most of its characteristics from the sources of Estonian law of obligations mentioned above. The PECL, PICC and the CISG have had an especially strong impact on the rules of Estonian contract law.

Over the 14 years that the *LOA* has been in force several amendments have been made to the part of *LOA* applicable to contracts. This art will not discuss all the amendments made, but will only look at the most important amendments made within the past 5 years.

The first area of law of obligations that has been amended several times over the past few years is the regulation concerning consumer credit. This has been a hot topic of much discussion in Estonia for years, mainly because of easy availability of instant credit in Estonia, a large number of instant loans taken and a very big number of defaulting debtors as a result. For example it has been estimated in 2014 that the number of people who have taken an instant loan is far more than 100,000 (some estimations are even as high has 190,000 people).[104] According to Estonian Chamber of Bailiffs and Trustees in Bankruptcy at the end of 2013 the number of involuntary enforcement proceedings connected with instant loans was 23,275 and

[100] *LOA* §8 and *GPCCA* §67. See also Torga et al. (2013), p. 63.

[101] Torga et al. (2013), pp. 63–64. See also *LOA* §4 and *FLA* §8.

[102] *LOA* §4.

[103] Varul (2006), pp. 36–37.

[104] Instant loan market—analysis and suggestions, https://www.mkm.ee/sites/default/files/kiirlanuturg_analyys_ja_ettepanekud.pdf, p. 8.

the number of debtors involved was 20,492 people. However, this does not reflect the total number of enforcement proceedings active at the end of 2013 against debtors who had taken instant loans—it comprises of data from the 10 largest instant credit providers only and includes claims that were not transferred to collection agencies.[105] Taking all this into account the estimation in 2014 was that the total number of enforcement proceedings regarding instant loans might have been as high has 65,344 or possibly even more. The total number of "unique" debtors involved is however unknown.[106] Several problems in the market of instant loans were identified in another study concluded in 2013.[107] This has been seen as a signal that there should be more restrictive rules concerning consumer credit and especially instant loans.

In the field of consumer credit, Estonia has made several amendments to the *LOA*, some of which derive from the incorporation of EU directives into Estonian law and some have been adopted for other reasons.

On 1 July 2011 several amendments of the *LOA* came into effect.[108] These amendments were made to incorporate *Directive of the European Parliament and of the Council No 2008/48/EC* (consumer credit directive) into Estonian law of obligations. The main amendments included a significant increase in the amount of pre-contractual information that has to be provided to a consumer, changes in the calculation of the annual percentage rate of charge, a clear obligation of the credit provider to assess the creditworthiness of the consumer and to apply the principle of responsible lending. Also the possibilities for consumers to terminate the consumer credit contract were extended.[109] As a result of the amendments, the 2nd division of Ch. 22 of *LOA* regulating consumer credit was pretty much re-written to ensure it complies with the consumer credit directive. But other provisions in the *LOA* concerning consumer credit were also heavily amended. The main purpose of these amendments was to ensure that consumers are better informed about the terms of the credit and to force credit providers to assess more carefully the creditworthiness of consumers applying for credit and to provide counselling to the consumers regarding the risks and terms of consumer credit.[110]

On 1 May 2013 another amendment came into force regarding the calculation of the annual percentage rate of charge.[111] This amendment was made to implement *Directive of the European Parliament and of the Council No 2011/90/EU*. Together with adopting the new directive also many changes were made in the wording of the provisions of consumer credit to make the provisions clearer and to deal with

[105]Ibid.

[106]Ibid.

[107]Ibid.

[108]*Amendment Act of obligations law and other laws*. RT I, 04.02.2011, 1.

[109]Explanatory note of obligations law and other laws, http://www.riigikogu.ee/download/f08d18c1-acda-3661-1941-f77f9226a3b7.

[110]Ibid.

[111]*Amendment Act of obligations law and advertisement law*. RT I, 11.06.2013, 3.

several issues that had arisen in practice in the implementation of the consumer credit provisions.[112]

Two significant changes in the field of consumer credit were enforced from 1 July 2015.[113] Firstly *LOA* now provides that a consumer credit contract is void, if the annual percentage rate of charge payable by the consumer exceeds at the time of granting the credit the past 6 months' average annual rate of charge of consumer credits granted by credit institutions to private individuals and last published by Bank of Estonia for more than three times.[114] At the end of May 2016 the average annual percentage rate of charge was 19.49%.[115] Thus a consumer credit contract with an annual percentage of charge of more than 58.47% would be void. The *LOA* also provides an exceptional rule concerning the consequences of a void consumer credit contract.[116] The general rule in Estonian civil law is that if a contract is void, then each party is under obligation to return what they have received under the provisions of unjust enrichment. The latter provide that if something was received under a void contract, it must be returned together with any gains derived from it. This means that according to the general rule, if a contract is void, the party who has received money under the contract is under obligation to return it immediately and pay average interest on the money received as well as penalty interest if money is not returned immediately. The above-mentioned special rule applicable to consumer credit contracts is however different in that the consumer has the obligation to return the money received only by the date by which the consumer had to repay the whole credit according to the void consumer credit contract and the interest rate shall be the statutory interest rate. Currently the statutory interest rate in Estonia is 0.05% per year.[117] The author believes that this solution should motivate consumer credit providers to stay within the allowed limits and avoid unreasonable interest and charges. Along the same lines as this amendment, a recent judgement by the Estonian SC confirmed that an unreasonably high penalty interest rate provided in standard terms is null and void.[118]

The second significant change that was made with the amendment that came into force on 1 July 2015 was that an arbitral agreement is void if its object is a consumer credit contract. With this change consumer credit contracts were excluded from the jurisdiction of arbitral tribunals. The reason for this change was that consumer's

[112]Explanatory note of *Amendments Act*, http://www.riigikogu.ee/download/9eed784d-db2e-48c8-9880-9daa23da2ac9/old.

[113]*Amendment Act of Civil Procedure Act and other Acts*. RT I, 21.05.2014, 1.

[114]*LOA* §406^2 (1) and (2).

[115]The average annual percent rate of charge for consumer credits provided to individuals by credit institutions, see: http://statistika.eestipank.ee/?lng=en#listMenu/2273/treeMenu/FINANTSSEKTOR/147/979.

[116]*LOA* §406^2(3).

[117]The statutory interest is regulated in §94(1) of *LOA* and the interest rate is published by Bank of Estonia twice a year on 1 January and 1 July. The current rate is 0.05% per year, see: https://ametlikudteadaanded.ee/avalik/teadaanne?teated_id=977856&sid=&pdf=1.

[118]SC 3-2-1-25-16, p. 13.

rights may not be protected in an arbitral tribunal since the consumer does not have access to legal aid in arbitration and some of the rules of some arbitral tribunals, e.g. the rules concerning the service of documents are not enough to ensure a fair process in case of a consumer dispute.[119]

Although this is not mentioned in the preparatory materials of the amendment of *LOA*, this change was probably at least somewhat inspired by a public discussion that arose at the end of 2014, when it appeared that a small group of people had been misusing Estonia's liberal approach to the enforcement of arbitral awards given by a permanent arbitral tribunal operating in Estonia.[120] The problem was as follows. *Estonian Code of Civil Procedure* (*CCP*) provides that arbitral awards given by a permanent arbitral tribunal operating in Estonia are enforced automatically.[121] At the same time, Estonia has no regulation how to establish whether an arbitral tribunal is permanent or not and there is no control over who and how can establish a permanent arbitral tribunal in Estonia. This situation was misused by a group of people who established an arbitral tribunal, calling it permanent. The arbitral tribunal produced arbitral awards without even notifying defendants of the proceedings and totally ignoring the right of defence. Awards of this tribunal were used to enforce claims that had little or no legal grounds. It was reported that this scheme had been used to institute at least 500 enforcement proceedings.[122] This sparked a public discussion and a promise by the state to take measures to exclude such misuses.[123]

One of these cases regarding the validity of enforcement proceedings based on an arbitral award reached the SC, who just recently gave a judgement concerning this case. The SC found that because Estonia has no criteria to establish whether an arbitral tribunal is permanent or not, the provision of the *CCP*[124] allowing automatic enforcement of arbitral awards of permanent arbitral tribunals situated in Estonia, cannot in fact be given effect.[125] Thus all arbitral awards will have to be declared enforceable by a court before they can be enforced. In the author's opinion, this judgement of the SC will significantly change the practice concerning arbitral awards since this far it has been general practice to assume that the awards

---

[119]Explanatory letter for the amendment of *Court Civil Procedure Act*, *Obligation Act*, *Application Act of Court Civil Procedure Act* and *Enforcement Proceedings Act* and *General Part of Civil Law Act*: http://www.riigikogu.ee/download/a76da880-c15a-4dab-85df-af0e32b234f4/old.

[120]About this discussion see for example "State wants to increase the control over the arbitration which misuses the system", http://uudised.err.ee/v/eesti/0eefb110-98f3-4f13-9b3a-e6863f19f065.

[121]*CCP* §735(1).

[122]Warning for the activity of permanent international and independent arbritation (Hoiatus alalise rahvusvahelise ja sõltumatu vahekohtu tegevuse eest), https://www.das.ee/hoiatus-alalise-rahvusvahelise-ja-soltumatu-vahekohtu-tegevuse-eest/.

[123]State wants to increase the control over the arbitration which misuses the system (Riik tahab süsteemi kuritarvitavate vahekohtute üle kontrolli suurendada), http://uudised.err.ee/v/eesti/0eefb110-98f3-4f13-9b3a-e6863f19f065.

[124]*CCP* §735(1).

[125]SC 3-2-1-142-15, p. 15–16.

of permanent arbitral tribunals established in Estonia are directly enforceable. It will probably also make arbitration in Estonia much less attractive.

On 1 October 2015 another amendment concerning consumer credit came into effect.[126] This amendment set maximum limits to all debt collections costs that are recoverable from a consumer. This was designed to deal with the problem that had emerged in practice that in case of indebtedness a consumer was under obligation to pay un-proportionally high charges for measures taken to collect the debt.[127] Another important change concerned that from then on all charges paid by the consumer that are designed to be a charge for allowing the use of credit are treated the same way as interest and thus it is prohibited to claim penalty interest on these charges (the same applies for interest).[128]

The most recent amendment of the *LOA* that came into force on 21 March 2016 (partially 1 July 2016) also concerns consumer credit. This amendment was made to implement *Directive 2014/17/EU of the European Parliament and of the Council on credit agreements for consumers relating to residential immovable property*[129] into Estonian law. The main amendments to *LOA* were the following. Several additional obligations to provide information (including pre-contractual information) were imposed on credit providers to allow consumers to make a better decision regarding credit. In addition to an obligation to passively provide information, an obligation to provide counselling to consumers was also imposed.[130] Amendments were made to the regulation concerning the application of the principle of responsible lending—an obligation was imposed on credit providers providing credit related to residential immovable to make sure that the consumer is in fact creditworthy. To make sure that credit providers follow this obligation, it was provided that the breach of this principle will result in that the rate of interest to be paid on the credit will automatically be lowered to the rate of statutory interest—at this moment it is 0.05% per year—which is much lower than the average rate of interest.[131] As a result of the amendments consumers receiving credit related to residential immovable now also enjoy a possibility to terminate the credit contract within 7 days. A right that was previously unknown in the field of credit related to residential immovable.[132]

[126]*Amendment Act of Obligation Law Act*, *Consumer Protection Law Act* and *Study Grants and Study Loan Law Act*, RT I, 11.03.2015.

[127]Ibid.

[128]Explanatory letter for the *Amendment Act of Obligation Law Act* and *Consumer Protection Law Act*, http://www.riigikogu.ee/download/f4527236-c986-460a-939f-ce4a598503fb.

[129]*Directive 2014/17/EU of the European Parliament and of the Council of 4 February 2014 on credit agreements for consumers relating to residential immovable property and amending Directives 2008/48/EC and 2013/36/EU and Regulation (EU) No 1093/2010 Text with EEA relevance*. OJ L60/34 28/2/2014.

[130]Explanatory letter for the *Amendment Act of the Obligation Law Act* and the *Amendment Act of Other Acts*, http://www.riigikogu.ee/download/25070d36-73ec-43cf-9e02-0eba67f2ec6e/old.

[131]Ibid.

[132]Ibid.

Significant changes in Estonian contract law were made in connection with the adoption of *Directive No 2011/83/EU of the European Parliament and of the Council on consumer rights.*[133] These changes came into effect on 13 June 2014.[134] The amendments mostly concerned contracts concluded outside business premises and mainly two areas were affected—additional obligations to inform were imposed on businesses and several changes were made concerning the right of the consumer to terminate the contract. With regard to the latter termination was made easier and clearer by adopting standard forms for termination and by specifying more clearly the consequences of termination. Another important amendment was that the right of termination of the consumers was somewhat limited, allowing businesses to exclude the termination right under some specific circumstances—the idea was to allow some more flexibility in consumer contracts. Also, businesses received a right under some circumstances to claim form consumers compensation of costs in case of return of goods sold.[135]

Other noteworthy amendments made in the *LOA* in recent years were connected with the adoption of *Directive No 2011/7/EU of the European Parliament and the Council on combating late payment in commercial transactions*. These amendments came into force on 15 April 2013.[136] The most important changes made by these were the adoption of a maximum payment deadline of 60 days in B2B contracts and 30 days in a business to public sector contract.[137] However it seems to the author that these changes had a much larger impact on contracts concluded in public procurement than in case of B2B contracts, since in Estonia the amount of transactions where payment deadline exceeds 60 days has always made up less than 4% of all transactions (this percentage has actually increased after this amendment).[138] Other amendments included the fixing of a default amount that that can be claimed in case of indebtedness in B2B contracts without the need to produce evidence of actual costs and the increase of statutory penalty interest rate by 1%.[139]

[133] *Directive 2011/83/EU of the European Parliament and of the Council of 25 October 2011 on consumer rights, amending Council Directive 93/13/EEC and Directive 1999/44/EC of the European Parliament and of the Council and repealing Council Directive 85/577/EEC and Directive 97/7/EC of the European Parliament and of the Council Text with EEA relevance* OJ L304/64 22/11/2011.

[134] *Amendment Act of Obligation Law Act and Consumer Protection Act.* RT I, 31.12.2013, 1.

[135] Explanatory note for the draft of *Amendment Act of Obligation Law Act* and *Consumer Protection Law Act*, http://www.riigikogu.ee/download/a47cd4af-91a9-4974-83a1-cdb442383efd.

[136] *Amendment Act of Obligation Law Act and CCP*. RT I, 05.04.2013, 1.

[137] Explanatory note for Amendment Act of Obligation Law Act and CCP. http://www.riigikogu.ee/download/2a335664-e42e-432f-b4ec-8bf105b6bd48/old.

[138] See Market Survey of the credit policy 2016 (Eesti ettevõtete krediidipoliitika turu-uuring 2016), http://www.krediidiinfo.ee/files/kredpoluuring2016.pdf.

[139] Ibid.

All in all it can be said that although several amendments to the *LOA* have been made in the recent years, these amendments have not fundamentally changed the principles applicable to contractual relations.

3.2.3 Developments in Non-Contractual Obligations

Non-contractual obligations are regulated in §§1005–1067 of the *LOA*. Estonian law of obligations recognises several different non-contractual obligations. In addition to the more widely known non-contractual obligations such as torts or delicts (§§1043–1067 of *LOA*), unjust enrichment (§§1027–1042 of *LOA*), *negotiorum gestio* (§§1018–1026 of *LOA*) and pre-contractual obligations or *culpa in contrahendo* (§14 of *LOA*), Estonian law of obligations also includes non-contractual obligations arising from a public promise to pay (§§1005–1008 of *LOA*), non-contractual obligations relating to a competition (§§1009–1013 of *LOA*) and non-contractual obligation to present a thing (§§1014–1017 of *LOA*).

Estonian regulation concerning non-contractual obligations has remained very stable. From the time when the *LOA* came into force (i.e. 1 July 2002) only one amendment was made in 2006 when the current *Code of Civil Procedure* was adopted to the provisions concerning torts[140] and in 2014 some additional obligations for businesses to provide pre-contractual information to consumers were added when *Directive No 2011/83/EU of the European Parliament and of the Council on consumer rights* was adopted in Estonian Law.[141] But neither of these amendments has had a wider effect on the regulation concerning non-contractual obligations.

Estonian regulation of torts is made up of three different sections—a general regulation of obligations arising out of unlawfully caused damage, regulation of liability for damage caused by major source of danger and regulation of liability for defective products. Tort claims fall under the general regulation as far as they are not covered by the two special sections. While the general regulation of torts is based on fault based liability with the assumption of fault,[142] the regulations concerning liability for damage caused by major source of danger and regulation of liability for defective products are mainly based on strict liability.[143] Estonian tort law does not have one particular source, although it has been much influenced

[140] *Code of Civil Procedure and Code of Enforcement Procedure Implementation Act.* RT I 2005, 39, 308.

[141] *Directive 2011/83/EU of the European Parliament and of the Council of 25 October 2011 on consumer rights, amending Council Directive 93/13/EEC and Directive 1999/44/EC of the European Parliament and of the Council and repealing Council Directive 85/577/EEC and Directive 97/7/EC of the European Parliament and of the Council Text with EEA relevance.* OJ L304/64 22/11/2011; *Amendment Act of Obligation Law Act and Consumer Protection Act.* RT I, 31.12.2013, 1.

[142] Varul et al. (2009), p. 622; *LOA* §1050; also Tampuu (2003), pp. 71–82.

[143] Varul et al. (2009), p. 622; see also Tampuu (2003), pp. 161–168.

by the *German BGB*, the proposals of Prof. Christian von Bar and Prof. Hein Kötz for the reform of the provisions of delict of the *BGB* and Swiss and Dutch Civil Codes.[144]

Estonian law on unjust enrichment is based on the proposals of Prof. Detlef König made in within the reform of German law of obligations and they are much influenced by the *BGB*.[145] Estonian regulations of *negotiorum gestio*, obligations arising out of a public promise to pay, competitions and non-contractual obligation to present a thing are based on *BGB*.[146]

It can be seen from the analysis above that in the past 5 years many amendments to the Estonian *LOA* have been made because of the adoption of the principles of EU directives. With the evolvement of EU law in the area of private law, it is probable that directives and regulations of the EU in private law area will continue to have a strong effect on Estonian law of obligations. However the author believes that despite these attempts to harmonise civil law, Estonia will be able to hold on to its own principles of private law—the changes in recent years have triggered many amendments, but have not changed the fundamental principles of law of obligations.

A need to seriously reconsider and amend the provisions of law of obligations might be triggered by the development of e-technologies and e-commerce. It is obvious that the fast development of information and communications technology will significantly change the ways that business is conducted and this will surely not leave the law of obligations, which is very much connected with business, unaffected.

In a more foreseeable future it is possible that amendments will be made to the regulation on lease contracts. Problems concerning lessees acting in bad faith have attracted much public attention in recent years and Estonian Ministry of Justice is planning to conduct an analysis of this area of law by the end of this year.[147] Whether any changes will emerge as a result, remains yet to be seen.

3.3 Company Law and Insolvency Law

Rene Lauk and Addi Rull
Tallinn Law School, Tallinn University of Technology, Akadeemia tee 3, 12618 Tallinn, Estonia
e-mail: renelauk@hotmail.com; addi.rull@ttu.ee

[144]Varul et al. (2009), pp. 625–626.

[145]Ibid., pp. 583–584.

[146]Ibid., pp. 546, 554–557, 559, 560, 562–564.

[147]Overview of the legislation plans of the ministries 2016 (Ministeeriumide õigusloomeplaanide ülevaade 2016), http://www.just.ee/sites/www.just.ee/files/2016_tooplaanide_ulevaade.pdf.

The business environment in Estonia is vibrant and liberal. The administration of business is easy and convenient, and Estonia has one of the most efficient and simple tax systems in the world. The vast development of e-services has been one of the triggers of success. This has also created the need to implement changes into commercial law to facilitate the development of innovative business-motivated-concepts based on the utilisation of different IT solutions. The trend that commercial law shall be changed because of the development of new e-services shall continue in coming years.

One of the forthcoming changes concerns the requirement for the domicile of board members of legal persons. Internally Estonia has followed the incorporation theory in commercial law.[148] Since legal persons are only registered (incorporated) if their domicile is in Estonia and based on §29(1) of the *General Part of the Civil Code Act* the domicile of a legal person is the place where the central management of a legal person is residing, then both a legal person and its board is required to be in Estonia. Now the draft law is in the proceedings to abolish such requirement for the board, meaning that the board of a legal person can reside outside Estonia. The rationale is based on the objectives devised in several action plans of the Government by which the successful implementation of e-residency project requires the possibility for e-residents to be able to register and manage legal persons without obligation to be in Estonia.[149]

The following gives a brief overview of the forms of business, the registration and taxation, the board member's liability and the main trends of insolvency law in Estonia.

3.3.1 Forms of Business

Estonian law recognises six different forms of business: Sole proprietor (SoP); Private limited company (Private LC); Public limited company (Public LC); General partnership (GP); Limited partnership (LP); Commercial association (CA).[150] The forms of business differ from each other primarily with regard to the principles, extent and share of shareholder liability; the company's management bodies and decision-making processes, right of representation; the amount of required share

[148]Nurmela et al. (2008), p. 108.

[149]The explanatory note to the draft of the *Commercial Code* (*CC*) SE 16-0445. The draft law has been criticised, in particular, in the light of Mossack Fonseca scandal, stipulating that it becomes difficult to hold a board liable for its decisions and actions if it does not locate in Estonia. Questions such as how to solve the delivery of official documents have risen. One of the solutions is to register a contact person in the Commercial Register to whom the delivery of documents at the Estonian address shall be made.

[150]*CC* §2 and 3; GP, LP and CA are not common forms of business, because they involve some or unlimited personal liability.

capital and means of contribution; the company's audit requirements; the simplicity of organising everyday activity (such as accounting).[151]

The simplest and therefore one of the most common forms of business in Estonia is SoP. The number of registered SoPs is changing and is in correlation with the highs and lows of economy. According to the latest data there are more than 32,000 SoPs in Estonia.[152]

SoP is a natural person who offers goods or services on his name and this activity is permanent. The sole proprietor is a form of business that is cheap to start and easy to manage. SoP does not have any reporting obligation except it is required to submit an income tax declaration. There is no minimum required startup capital and as the SoP is acting alone it does not need any management bodies either. A person acting as sole proprietor bears unlimited financial liability for its actions. Since 1 January 2009 all SoPs have to be registered to commercial register. The income tax rate for SoP is 20%[153] and the basic exemption is 170 euros per month and will rise year by year to 205 euros per month by 2019.

If a person wishes to end his activity as an SoP, he should notify the registrar of the commercial register of the suspension of the activities of his or her enterprise in advance specifying the period of time when the enterprise does not operate. An SoP, the activity of whose enterprise because of the nature of the area of activity is seasonal, may notify the registrar of the commercial register of the starting date and final date of the activity of the enterprise. The notification of the starting date and final date of the activity of the enterprise may also be provided in case of temporary activity.[154] The most popular form of business in Estonia is the Private LC. There were 157,303 registered private limited companies in Estonia in 2016.[155] That is more than 67% of all companies. A Private LC is relatively easy and cheap to establish and manage, as the minimum required number of founders is either a natural or a legal person,[156] Partners of private limited company are not personally liable for the obligations of the company. Absence of personal liability is one of the main reasons why private limited company and public limited company are preferred forms of business.

The cost of establishing a Private LC is low. Although the minimum required startup capital is 2500 euros,[157] it is not needed if the share capital is not bigger than 25,000 euros. In case of founding the Private LC without making contribution of 2500 euros the shareholder shall be personally liable to the company for the obligations of the Private LC in the amount of the outstanding contribution unless

[151] Estonian State Portal, https://www.eesti.ee/eng/topics/business/ettevotte_loomine/ettevotlusvormi_valik/ettevotlusvormide_vordlus.

[152] E-business Register, http://www2.rik.ee/rikstatfailid/failid/tabel.php?url=16_02mk.htm.

[153] *Income Tax Act* (*ITA*) §4(2) and §23.

[154] *CC* §3(3).

[155] E-business Register.

[156] *CC* §137.

[157] *CC* §136.

the obligation of the company can be performed on the account of the assets of the company.[158] The actual minimum cost for establishing a private limited company is a state fee of 145 euros or if you establish it electronically under expedited procedure, the state fee will be 190 euros. The state fee can later be recognised as a business expense as the costs of establishing the Private LC. If you are using a help from notary, the notary fees will be added. The precise amount depends on the size of share capital and the number of founders.[159]

The Private limited company is mostly meant for smaller and medium size business and therefore the management requirements are made as easy and flexible as possible. The obligatory management body of the private limited company is the management board and a supervisory board is mandatory only if specified in the arts of association.[160]

A Private LC is dissolved by the resolution of the shareholders or judicial decision. The basis of a voluntary dissolution is the shareholders' meeting where the resolution must be approved by at least 2/3 of the shareholders participating at the meeting. To dissolve the private limited company, the management board must submit a request to the Commercial Register (in writing or electronic form via the company registration portal), the shareholders' dissolution resolution and the minutes of the general meeting.[161]

The Public LC is a business form meant for bigger businesses. It is the third most popular form for making business after SoP and Private LC, but the number of registered Public LCs is remarkably smaller (3466 registered Public LCs in 01.02.2016) than Private LCs.[162] The reason for such a big difference is obvious—the minimum required startup capital is 25,000 euros and it must have a multi-tiered management structure. In addition, Public LC cannot be established using Company Registration Portal.[163] The minimum required number of founders is one and it can be either a natural or a legal person who is not personally liable for the public limited company's obligations. There is an option of listing the Public LC on the stock exchange and possibility of involving a wide number of shareholders and therefore it is more suitable for implementing major projects.

The Public LC has an obligatory multi-tiered management system. The supreme management body of the public limited company is the general meeting of shareholders who exercise their rights at the general meeting of shareholders. In practice, the most important right of shareholders' general meeting is the appointing supervisory board but it also makes all major strategical decisions like

[158]Ibid. §140[1](4). Until the complete payment of the contributions by all the shareholders, the Private LC shall not make any disbursements to the shareholders.

[159]Estonia State Portal, https://www.eesti.ee/eng/osauhing.

[160]*CC* §180 and 189.

[161]*CC* Ch. 22.

[162]E-business Register.

[163]Estonia State Portal, https://www.eesti.ee/eng/topics/business/ettevotte_loomine/ettevotlusvormi_valik/aktsiaselts.

amending the arts of association, increasing and reducing share capital etc. The supervisory board shall plan the activities of the public limited company, organise the management of the public limited company, supervise the activities of the management board and notify the general meeting of the results of a review. The supervisory board has to have at least three members if the arts of association do not establish a bigger number. The supervisory board appoints the management board. The management board is the managing body of the Public LC, which represents and manages the company. The management board shall, in managing, adhere to the lawful orders of the supervisory board. All transactions, which are beyond the scope of everyday economic activities, may only be concluded by the management board with the consent of the supervisory board.

The basis for voluntary dissolution of a public limited company is a resolution adopted by shareholders, which must be adopted by 2/3 of the shareholders who participate at the meeting. If a company has different types of shares, the adoption of a dissolution resolution requires additionally to that at least 2/3 of the votes represented by each type of share be in favour of the resolution. To dissolve a company, the management board must submit an application to the Commercial Register and the dissolution resolution of the shareholders along with the minutes of the general meeting. If the dissolution of the public limited company is decided by an extraordinary meeting, the management board shall submit the approved annual report for the last financial year and an overview of the economic activities of the public limited company in the current year. It must indicate the term during which the demands of creditors may be satisfied with the public limited company.[164]

As mentioned above, an obligatory contribution has to be made for establishing a Private LC, Public LC or CA. This contribution can be made as monetary payment to the company's bank account but it can also be made as a non-monetary contribution. A non-monetary contribution may be anything which is monetarily appraisable and transferable to the private limited company or a proprietary right which may be the object of a claim. Nevertheless, a non-monetary contribution shall not be service or work provided to the private limited company or the activities of the founders in the foundation of the private limited company.[165]

3.3.2 Company Registration and Taxation

Traditionally, a company registration is done through notary. The discomfort of this procedure is that all the founders of the company have to be physically present at notary's office to sign the documents. Another option is to register a company digitally. Undoubtedly, this is the fastest and most convenient way. One does not need to leave an office and usually it takes an hour or two (in 2009 Estonia received a Guinness World Record for "the fastest time to register a new legal entity"—

[164] *CC* Ch. 30.
[165] *CC* §142, 248.

18 min).[166] All the members of the management board, founding members, founders of supervisory board and other persons related to the establishment have to have an ID card or a mobile-ID to log in to the Company Registration Portal and sign the initial application and establishment documents digitally. Company Registration Portal can be used to register private limited companies, general partnerships, limited partnerships and non-profit associations and sole proprietor. Public limited companies and commercial associations have to be registered through notary. Also, if the contribution of the company's share capital is not monetary but rather a monetarily appraisable thing or proprietary right to be transferred to the company (such as equipment, software etc.), one cannot register a company via the e-commercial register's Company Registration Portal but you have to use the services of a notary.[167]

A major advantage when doing business in Estonia as an Estonian citizen is that it can all be done online. You can establish, run or dissolve a company online, all documents and contracts can be signed digitally and sent all over the world in minutes, reporting and communication with Tax and Customs Board are done online. It results in huge time saving and remarkable growth of freedom and convenience. To offer the same possibilities to foreigners, Estonia has introduced e-residency[168]—a transnational digital identity available to anyone in the world interested in administering a location-independent business online.[169]

E-residents can digitally sign documents and contracts, verify the authenticity of signed documents, encrypt and transmit documents securely, establish an Estonian company online, administer the company from anywhere in the world, conduct e-banking and remote money transfers, access online payment service providers, declare Estonian taxes online.[170]

The opportunity to become an e-resident is relatively new, only one and a half years, and therefore there are difficulties as well. The Estonian digital identity is not yet sufficiently regulated nor does Estonia have the institutional capacity for the purposes of effectuating the concept of a borderless digital citizen. However, the existing technical platform has a capability to serve as a key for a supranational identity management system within the meaning of eIDAS regulating on the EU level.[171] Recently Estonia got its 10,000th e-resident.[172]

---

[166]Official website of E-Estonia, https://e-estonia.com/e-residents/services-and-benefits/.

[167]Estonia State Portal, https://www.eesti.ee/eng/topics/business/ettevotte_loomine/ettevotte_asutamise_toimingud/ettevotte_registreerimine.

[168]See e.g. Särav and Kerikmäe (2016), pp. 57–81.

[169]Official website of E-Estonia, https://e-estonia.com/e-residents/about/.

[170]E-residency does not confer citizenship, tax residency, the residence or right of entry to Estonia or to the European Union. The e-resident smart ID card is not a physical identification or a travel document but only gives access to digital services.

[171]*The Regulation (EU) No. 910/2014 on electronic identification and trust services for electronic transactions in the internal market (eIDEAS Regulatio*n) OJ L 257, 28/8/2014.

[172]Official website of E-Estonia, https://e-estonia.com/e-residents/about/.

Taxation in Estonia is the same for all forms of business, except for sole proprietor who has to pay social tax from the income, because this form of business has the primary objective to sell the labour of a person.[173] A company has to pay income tax, value added tax and taxes connected with labour.[174] The uniqueness of the Estonian tax system is that the income tax is only paid on profit distributed as dividends or other profit distributions upon payment thereof in monetary or non-monetary form.[175] If the profit is reinvested into a company, then it is tax-free. Similarly to dividends, the income tax has to be paid for gifts, donations and costs of entertaining guests, and expenses and payments not related to the business and an objective specified in the arts of association made by a resident legal person and a profit-making state agency. The rate of income tax is 20%.

The value added tax of 20% applies to the sale of goods and services. A reduced rate applies to accommodation, books, certain periodicals, listed pharmaceutical products and medical devices. The VAT rate on the export of goods, intra-community supply of goods and certain services is 0% (i.e. exemption with credit).[176] If the taxable annual turnover of a company exceeds 16,000 euros[177] per calendar year, then a company is required to register with the Estonian Tax and Customs Board as a VAT payer. If the turnover is below that limit, registration is not obligatory.

3.3.3 Board Member's Liability

The general rule in private law is that the activities of a member of the board of the legal person do not create legal relations between the member of the board and third persons. Still, in some specific cases the member of the board might be personally liable for the obligations of the legal person.

The regulation of civil liability of a management board member in Estonia is rather precise and conservative. In the cases of causing damages, a board member is liable for non-performance only if he is culpable of the non-performance. The current legal system does not provide a possibility to limit the liability of a culpable board member because it establishes unlimited personal liability in cases of culpability. The types of culpability are carelessness (failure to exercise necessary care), gross negligence (failure to exercise necessary care to a material extent), and intent

[173]The social tax rate is 33% of taxable income. At the moment a draft law is in proceedings to reduce social tax rate to 32%. Information System for draft laws, available online: http://eelnoud.valitsus.ee/main#S5fsRlaG.

[174]Estonia State Portal, https://www.eesti.ee/eng/topics/business/maksud_ja_toll/ulevaade_eesti_maksususteemist_1.

[175]Lehis (2004), p. 217.

[176]*Council Directive 2006/112/EC of 28 November 2006 on the common system of value added tax* OJ L347/1 11/12/2006.

[177]The Estonian Government has decided to raise that limit to 40,000 euros, but the decision has to be approved by EU.

(the will to bring about an unlawful consequence). The law does provide possibility to agree on arts of association or in the decision of higher organ to limit the liability of a board member but the victim can still claim indemnifications from the board member responsible for causing damages. Complainant has to prove the existence of the obligation but the board member has the right to prove that he is not culpable of damages.[178]

Generally, a board member is not liable for damages caused by other board members without his knowledge or if he voted against the unlawful decision. If determining liability, the law primarily protects board members who have fulfilled their obligations correctly and have been loyal to the company. In the case of more than one board member, it is advisable to make sure that a board member has enough means to prove their innocence. Suitable means could be, for example, meeting protocols or agreements on shared responsibilities. If a board member shows that he specifically is not culpable of causing damages and it cannot be connected to his responsibilities or work line, he is not liable.[179]

Similarly to general rule, the member of board might be personally liable even for companies' tax arrears. In that case, the tax bearer has to ascertain the breach of duty by a member of the board arising from tax laws. The member of the board must have acted with culpability. If the legal person has more than one member of the board, everyone's culpability has to be ascertained separately.[180]

3.3.4 Insolvency Law

The first *BA* was enacted on 1 September 1992 in Estonia.[181] This Act was too biased towards protecting the interests of creditors.[182] It established so-called liquidating bankruptcy proceedings. The interests of creditors had to be protected at all costs. The liquidating system did not offer balanced possibilities for entrepreneurs to escape insolvency in circumstances where it was feasible to improve financial results of a company. The Act only recognised the equity insolvency definition of bankruptcy.[183] Over a decade of practice it became clear that the Act had to be renewed.[184]

The *BA*, adopted on 22 January 2003 and entered into force on 1 January 2004, used bankruptcy laws of Germany, Switzerland and Sweden as a model that provide

[178]SC 3-2-1-91-99.

[179]Tiivel (2001), pp. 723–732.

[180]Lopman and Lorents (2013), pp. 118–127.

[181]*BA* RT 1992, 31, 403.

[182]Varul (2013), p. 235.

[183]See Fletcher (1999), p. 3 ('equity' insolvency, 'cash-flow' insolvency definitions).

[184]The 1992 *BA* was supplemented and changed in 1996 (RT I 1997, 5, 32; 2002, 44, 284), but the changes in 2004 have greater impact on the protection of the debtor's interest.

options for debtors to recover from bankruptcy situations.[185] §1(2), (3) of the *BA* cover both equity and balance sheet definitions of bankruptcy now.[186] In general, this Act has been characterised by the following trends: (1) greater emphasis on the protection of debtors, e. g., a chapter on release of a debtor, who is a natural person, from the debts was included; (2) the principle of equal treatment is applied to creditors; (3) protection of the interests of pledgees has been prioritised over other creditors, for instance, a pledgee has the right to demand immediate sale of the pledged object.[187]

In Estonia, the law prescribes for the companies the obligation to file a bankruptcy petition. §36 of the *GPCCA* and §180 (5^1), §306(3^1) of the *CC* establish an obligation for the management board of an insolvent company to submit promptly, but not later than within 20 days after the date on which insolvency became evident, a bankruptcy petition to a court.[188] These provisions abstain a board member from making payments after insolvency has become apparent.[189] Board members are often accused for not making bankruptcy petitions in due course, but at the stage when avoiding insolvency is not possible and assets left do not enable to satisfy claims of creditors. According to the *BA*, a debtor is insolvent if the debtor is unable to satisfy the claims of the creditor and such inability, due to the debtor's financial situation, is not temporary. Therefore a board member must make a sound assessment whether the financial situation of a company is temporary or permanent.

The SC practice on the assessment of permanent insolvency has not been overly consistent. Based on the decision no. 3-1-1-49-11,[190] the determination of the objective insolvency of a debtor, which is an enterprise, requires a comprehensive assessment of its proprietary situation and the probable future prospects of its economic activities. The permanent insolvency of a debtor cannot generally be identified only based on negative net assets, as it is a factor to be considered amongst other factors that characterise the financial state of a company. On the other hand, the decision no. 3-2-1-188-12[191] purports that the state of net assets is a determining factor while assessing the solvency of an enterprise and only data which clearly indicates the improvement in the financial state of a company has a bearing on the determination of insolvency. In the decision no. 3-1-1-49-11 the Court has further noted "that permanent objective insolvency of a debtor is obvious if its financial situation is characterised by data, which would provide an objective and independent expert with sufficient grounds to regard the debtor as permanently insolvent. Such assessment should be based on information, which was available at

[185]*BA* RT I 2003, 17, 95.

[186]*BA* RT I 2003, 17, 95; 31.12.2017.

[187]Varul (2013), p. 235.

[188]*GPCCA* RT I 2002, 35, 216; CC RT I 1995, 26, 355.

[189]Toom (2014), pp. 487–488. See for the discussion on making payments by the board member in the state of insolvency.

[190]SC 3-1-1-49-11.

[191]SC 3-2-1-188-12.

the time of the alleged discovery of insolvency (*ex ante* assessment). For instance, an assessment of a debtor's solvency cannot post facto include any technological developments or significant raw material price movements, which affected implementation of the debtor's business plan but could not have been reasonably foreseen at the time, which is subject to assessment".[192] Furthermore, methods such as Atman Z-score formula used in the United States to determine solvency of an enterprise in bankruptcy cases are not necessarily applicable in Estonia as stated by the Court.[193]

Compromise, which means an agreement between a debtor and the creditors concerning payment of debts and involves reduction of the debts or extension of their terms of payment,[194] is possible pursuant to §178(3) of the *BA*. A compromise decision shall be made by a general meeting of creditors. The court shall decide on the approval of the compromise decision by a ruling. However, the compromise is not used often.[195]

Foremost, it is important to determine whether insolvency of an enterprise is caused by criminal act or by management error. In case, a management error is a grave error, which means intentionally or grossly negligent violation of the obligations of a debtor by a board member[196])), then this can be grounds for imposing a prohibition on business pursuant to §91(3) of the *BA*. Failure to submit a bankruptcy petition in due time can be the grounds for imposing a prohibition of business.[197] Tubin suggests that such punishments should be moved to §49[1] of the *Penal Code* under violation of prohibition to engage in enterprise.[198] The SC has deliberated in its decision no. 3-2-1-124-09 that a prohibition on business can only be applied to a person, who is justifiably suspected of committing a crime and would be likely to commit new similar crimes if the prohibition on business would not be applied.[199] This interpretation has been criticised, because it diminishes the possibility of applying a prohibition on business in instances of grave management errors or late submission of a petition.[200]

The bankruptcy regulation in Estonia has been criticised as inefficient because of the high number of abatements. Manavald concludes that the abatements of bankruptcy proceedings are generally caused by insufficient equity and assets of a debtor to be able to cover the cost of the proceedings, meaning also that claims of creditors

---

[192]SC 3-1-1-49-11.

[193]Ibid. p. 20.

[194]*BA* §178.

[195]E. g. a compromise was agreed only in five bankruptcy proceedings in 2006 and another five in 2007.

[196]*BA* §28(2).

[197]See e.g. Kairjak (2014), pp. 636–637. Discussion on decriminalising §385[1] on failure to perform obligation to submit petition in bankruptcy (*Penal Code*).

[198]Tubin (2012), p. 446.

[199]SC 3-2-1-124-09.

[200]Varul (2013), pp. 236–237.

are fully unsatisfied.[201] Lukason has conducted a comprehensive study on reasons of insolvency in the period of 2000–2009, analysing 1706 court decisions and financial data of 5000 enterprises that have become insolvent in this period.[202] This study provides data on abatements of bankruptcy proceedings without declaration of bankruptcy.[203] The number of abatements was 974 whereas the number of bankruptcies was 689 in the review period. The total number of abatements is even higher if abatements that occur after the declaration of bankruptcy are added, but this data is not available in the study. The study shows that mostly there are two causes for insolvency of a company. Broadly, these causes are categorised as following: (1) changed market situation (26%), (2) management mistakes (20%), (3) intensified competition (18%), (4) insolvency caused by some unexpected event (17%) and (5) cases involving instances of criminal behaviour (11%).[204]

In 2004 a supervisory institution was established in the Ministry of Justice. The role of this authority is to monitor the activities of bankruptcy governors,[205] but it does not engage in conducting studies about the causes of bankruptcies and abatements. Unlike Finland that has the Bankruptcy Ombudsman who analyses causes of insolvency systematically, the Estonian State does not have a comparable institution.[206] The Estonian Chamber of Bailiffs and Trustees in Bankruptcy is an occupational union which amongst other functions also engages in the development of insolvency law in Estonia.[207]

3.3.5 Reorganisation Act

The *BA* provides a possibility to rehabilitate an insolvent enterprise, e.g. through a compromise, but in Estonia these cases are very rare. This is because the bankruptcy regulation has been mainly designed for liquidating companies. The motivation behind establishing the reorganisation regulation in Estonia was to tackle the high number of abatements and bankruptcies by offering a possibility for enterprises to opt for reorganisation instead of bankruptcy proceedings. This proposition was mentioned by drafters of the 2004 *BA* in the explanatory memorandum to the draft of the *BA*.[208] Reorganisation laws of Switzerland, Finland, Poland and Ch. 11 of the United States *Bankruptcy Code* were used as a model for the Estonian

---

[201] Manavald (2008), p. 386.

[202] Lukason (2010).

[203] *BA* §29.

[204] Lukason (2010), p. 25.

[205] *BA* §70.

[206] Laki konkurssipesien hallinnon valvonnasta (*Finnish Act on the Supervision of the Administration of Bankrupt Estate*).

[207] The Estonian Chamber of Bailiffs and Trustees in Bankruptcy, http://www.kpkoda.ee/content/chamber.

[208] Niklus (2008), p. 369.

reorganisation regulation.[209] The first *Reorganisation Act* in Estonia was adopted on 4 December 2008.[210]

The study by Lukason ordered by the Estonian Ministry of Justice before the adoption of the *Reorganisation Act* contemplates that it must be possible to reduce the number of abatements and bankruptcies.[211] This conviction was based on the analyses of financial data of bankruptcies in between 2004–2006. All companies with positive net assets were qualified as suitable for reorganisation. Depending on a year, the percentage of suitable candidates ranges in between 12.5 and 18.3%.[212] Furthermore, the study presented an estimate of potential financial gain for a state from reorganisation proceedings, which results from saved businesses and preserved jobs that are the main source of income for a state. Nevertheless, the efficiency of the reorganisation regulation can be questioned, because in between 2008 and 2014 approximately 160 reorganisation applications were submitted and approximately 20 of these applications received a positive resolution. This is a relatively low number of saved enterprises in comparison to numbers of abatements and bankruptcies. Lukason points out that based on the data from German regulatory environment, the successful reorganisation of enterprises that otherwise have to undergo bankruptcy proceedings is only about 5%.[213] Further analyses is needed to understand where the shortcomings of the reorganisation regulation are and whether it is possible to make improvements that would result in more positive statistics than described above.

European Commission recommendation of 12 March 2014 on a new approach to business failure and insolvency includes several suggestions, if implemented, may improve insolvency proceedings in Estonia.[214] For instance, the reorganisation proceedings should involve more extrajudicial actions and the appointment of mediator by the court must not be mandatory. Overall, the court involvement should be decreased and the proceedings must be simplified.

Moreover, the Estonian business sector has changed considerably over the past decade. The new booming start-up sector is striven by IT innovation and research. Its difference from traditional sectors is the composition of resources without which this sector does not maintain momentum. Talented people are the primary resource, but also immaterial assets such as patents, copyright, licenses, know-how, trade secrets etc. are part of successful business strategies for many start-ups. The complex analyses of commercial, tax, accounting, insolvency and other laws that impact and address the needs of this sector are absent. This must be done before proceeding to new substantial reforms in insolvency or commercial laws.

---

[209] Ibid. p. 372.

[210] *Reorganisation Act* RT I 2008, 53, 296.

[211] Lukason (2008).

[212] Ibid. p. 38.

[213] Ibid. p. 4.

[214] European Commission recommendation of 12 March 2014 on a new approach to business failure and insolvency, http://ec.europa.eu/justice/civil/files/c_2014_1500_en.pdf.

3.4 Estonian Family and Inheritance Law

Kristi Joamets
Tallinn Law School, Tallinn University of Technology, Akadeemia tee 3, 12618 Tallinn, Estonia
e-mail: kristi.joamets@ttu.ee

Edgar Grünberg
Tartu Notary, Turu tn 2, 51014 Tartu, Estonia
e-mail: info@tartunotar.ee

3.4.1 Legal-Historical Development of Estonian Family and Inheritance Law

Historically, Estonian family and inheritance law has been influenced by many different developments of law brought here by the conquerors.[215] Still, local law in this area maintained to have a certain specialty and independence. From the earlier times Estonian family law can similarly to other European countries be described as patriarchal, marriages were contracted by robbery and buying. Later church had its power over customary law. Civil law was based on Roman law and was fragmented as in other parts of Europe until the codifications. Reformation undermined church.[216]

In family law marriage, divorce and marriage property was regulated, in inheritance law intestate and testamentary succession as well as succession contract had their norms. *Baltic Private Law Code* (1864) as a codification of Baltic law had norms of family law but not inheritance law. In 1918 when Estonian Republic was established, new legal acts regulating family and inheritance law were also passed and a new civil code was worked out,[217] but because of the occupation of Estonia in 1940 it was not passed. Similarly to other European countries Estonia adopted the institution of civil marriage.[218] In 1925 a *Civil Status Law Act* was enforced regulating specifically the registration of vital statistics events. Property relations were still regulated by the *Baltic Private Law Code*. In 1925 was also adopted the Social Welfare Law providing the clear rules for the social protection of children. In general, the following concepts were regulated: marriage, divorce, marital property, adoption, filiation, guardianship and custody.

In 1940 the *Code of Marriage, Family and Custody of Russian Soviet Republic* was applied to occupied Estonia. This was a complicated era for family matters

[215]In thirteenth century Germany, sixteenth century Poland and Denmark, in seventeenth century Sweden, in eighteenth century Russia etc. In this respect Kullerkupp states that the greater part of the Estonian family law has been imported (see Kullerkupp (2001), pp. 95–110, p. 95).

[216]See also Joamets (2012), pp. 97–115, p. 101–104.

[217]*Estonian Bill of Civil Code*, containing also a chapter of family law.

[218]By the *Marriage Law Act* in 1922. RT 1922, 138, 88.

because in a short time too many different rules were to be applied. New rules did not reach into every local government so quickly and led to the situation where Estonian, German and Russian rules were applied in mix. In 1969 a new code—the *Marriage and Family Code of the Estonian Soviet Republic*[219] was adopted. By this period the practice of family matters became more stable. After Estonia's restoration of independence, in 1992, again new legal acts were worked out, in private law with the view of codification (civil code) and based on the civil code of 1940. However, as family relations are vulnerable to the changes in society, new principles from time to time were added to the regulations as well. In 1995 a *Family Law Act*[220] entered into force and was replaced in 2010 by the new Family Law Act[221] (*FLA*) which is in force today. Specific for Estonian family law is that procedural rules for family events are provided by a separate legal act[222]—*Vital Statistics Registration Act*[223] enforced in 2010.

Estonian *Const* provides a protection for both, family and succession, but the rules are very general and were specified in aforementioned *Family Law Act* of 1995 and in 1997 in a new *Succession Law Act (SLA).* It has been said that new family law was more influenced by the soviet rules[224] than succession law.[225] This can be one reason why in succession law it was easier to follow the *Estonian Bill of Civil Code* of 1940. Liin describes the new succession law as a regulation where role of a state and local government in gaining the property "is reduced to minimum compared with the Soviet law". She explains this by the expansion of the intestate heirs and that the right to inherit of the bequeathers so-called dependent was recognised.[226] Thus, Estonia's succession law has remained, in specifying the circle of heirs, within the boundaries recognised for example in Austria, Liechtenstein, Switzerland and the Nordic countries.[227]

In the beginning of 1990 there was a clear plan to give succession cases to the court as it was before the Soviet occupation in 1940 but the task remained to the notary as it was in the time of Soviet Occupation. However, the decision was based on the suggestions and experience of German Succession Law. Since 1993 was restored the model of the Latin notaries' office. In 2002 notary became a holder of a public office.[228]

However, in 1997 it was stated that succession law has still too much characters of Soviet law and a new family law act was started to draft which was passed in

[219]ENSV Teataja 1969, 31.

[220]RT I 1994, 75, 1326.

[221]RT I 2009, 60, 395.

[222]As mentioned above in 1925 it was a *Civil Status Law Act.*

[223]RT I 2009, 30, 177.

[224]Author states that compared to other states in Europe, the family law in Soviet Union was more liberal and therefore did not need a considerable change.

[225]See Liin (1998), pp. 105–109.

[226]Ibid.

[227]Ibid.

[228]See Andresen (2009), pp. 157–167, p. 163.

2009 and brought along radical changes, e.g. transition from the heritage reception system to the renunciation system, the better status of the spouse in inheritance rights, supplement of the liability of the inheritor and joint co-heirs.

Estonian succession law can be characterised by the following main principles: private succession[229] and freedom of testament.

In Estonian legal system succession law and family law are treated as separate legal branches in Estonian civil law, hence they are regulated by separate legal acts. They are discussed separately, lawyers who have specialised on family matters often do not know much about succession law and vice versa. In the curriculum of universities they are two separate courses and lecturers are specialised only on one of them. When succession law is the responsibility field of Ministry of Justice then family law is divided between the Ministry of Justice, the Ministry of Internal Affairs and the Ministry of Social Affairs, however, in practice also the Ministry of Foreign Affairs acts an important role in solving the cross-border family cases and referring to the global developments.

3.4.2 Characteristics of Estonian Family Law

Today's Estonian family law has been described as a liberal law. One of the reasons for this in international context is probably an easy regulation of divorce—spouses can divorce by mutual consent in vital statistics offices—no grounds for divorce are asked, only the consent of both spouses is needed. By the law of 2010 this procedure was made even more convenient—divorce by the consent was separated from the disputes over the children's custody and matrimonial property.[230] This meant that spouses could divorce by consent and later turn to the court to solve disputes related to their children's custody and matrimonial property matters. In principle, the development of family law[231] considers a lot of the freedoms of an individual, the regulations are trying to cover as many aspects as possible creating the norms more comfortable for them. However, thinking about the debates over same-gender marriage regulation,[232] Estonia cannot be characterised as a progressive state.[233] A small group of conservative politicians have successfully slowing down the

[229]Estonian Constitution (*Const*) §32.

[230]Earlier it was so that even when spouses had agreement on divorce as such but there were disputes over the custody of their children or matrimonial property, they had to divorce in a court.

[231]See more Joamets and Kerikmäe (2014), pp. 70–92; Scherpe (2016); Joamets (2016), pp. 101–117, p. 101–105.

[232]In 2014 was adopted a *Registered Partnership Act* (RT I 16.10.2014, 1) and enforced in the beginning of 2016. However, as this act needed for the administrative deeds an application act which was supposed to be passed and enforced latest on the 1st Jan 2016, this act has not been passed because of the raised political disputes over the need of *Registered Partnership Act* at all. By this Estonia is in a situation where substantial law exists but administrative bodies have no clear rules for the procedure. Such situation is very regrettable from the point of human rights and legal certainty.

[233]About progressive and regressive states see Antokolskaia (2007), pp. 49–67.

legalisation process of same-sex marriages, unfortunately based not on a research-based and legal profound reasoning but more of populism.

FLA provides substantive law for marriage, divorce, including marital property, parentage, custody and guardianship. Procedural rules for family events are provided by the *Vital Statistics Registration Act*.[234] As in some deeds related to family events a court is evolved then also a *Code of Civil Procedure*[235] is applied. Private International law rules dealing with family matters are provided by the separate legal act—*Estonian Private International Law Act*.[236]

Marriage can be contracted between a man and a woman, adolescent can marry from the age of 15 by the consent of court. Marriage obstacles are kinship, adoption relationship and another valid marriage.[237] Marriage can be contracted by the vital statistics officials, notaries, and by the clergymen who have granted a right to contract civil marriages. A court can annul a marriage and marriage can be void. Spouses have equal rights and obligations with respect to each other and family. They organise together their marital cohabitation and satisfaction of the needs of their family considering the wellbeing of each other and their children and they shall each accept responsibilities relating to marriage with regard to the other. They participate in the organisation of shared household and earning of income to the best of their ability. In the process of marriage prospective spouses choose a proprietary relation—joint property, set-off of assets increment or separateness of property. Instead, they can make a marital property contract before the marriage as well but its consent must accord more or less to one of the aforementioned proprietary relation. Also, when spouses want to change the type of proprietary relations into another type this can be made by the marital property contract. Before 2010 the only proprietary relation was joint property and in case spouses needed "something specific" in their property relation they could agree this by the martial property contract. Today this contract is limited by the options of aforementioned three proprietary relations.

Marriage terminates if a spouse dies or the marriage is divorced. As discussed above if there is no dispute over the divorce itself then divorce can take place in a vital statistics office or at the notary. However, there is one exception when spouses have to go to the court though they have an agreement over their divorce—it is a case when only one spouse does not reside in Estonia. Whether this rule is justified or not needs a further analyse. It appears that this rule bases more of the literal interpretation of the norms in different legal acts, especially *Estonian Private International Law Act* when in a justified need. It is important to emphasise that in Estonia in the process of divorce an intention to divorce or dispute over divorce as such, dispute over marital property and custody are treated separately. Spouses can divorce by an agreement and then later turn to the court to solve a dispute over

[234]RT I 2009, 30, 177.

[235]RT I 2005, 26, 197.

[236]RT I 2002, 35, 217.

[237]See more about marriage impediments in Estonia Joamets (2012), pp. 97–115.

property or custody over children. On a small scale also maintenance over divorced spouse is provided.

The woman who gives birth to a child is the mother of the child. Being a father of the child there are several options with different legal meanings. The general principle is that a man by whom a child is conceived is the father of the child. However, it shall be deemed that a child is conceived by a man who is married to the mother of the child at the time of birth of the child, who has acknowledged his paternity or whose paternity has been established by the court. Until 2014 there was a rule that in case a man who is married to the mother of a child is not a biological father of the child the spouses had to submit a respective joint application to the vital statistics office in the process of registering a birth of the child. In 2014 a new rule was enforced providing that there is no consent of the mother's spouse needed when another man acknowledges his paternity in the process. This change in a law was grounded by the need to exclude the spouses of the cross-border marriages which are not terminated. Does this regulation support the general principle in family law that one (legal) relation should be terminated before starting a new one is arguable. Also, does this new regulation protect a child or make a life of a mother more convenient instead,[238] is doubtful as well. When a child does not have a father—parents are not married to each other and a mother is not married then a biological father becomes a legal father of the child by the acknowledgement of paternity. In this deed a man applies that he is a father of the child and a mother gives consent to this application. When there is no man acknowledging paternity, a born child will have no father at all, only a mother.

In Estonia adult ascendants and descendants related in the first and second degree are required to provide maintenance and persons entitled to receive maintenance are: a minor child; a child who is acquiring basic, secondary or higher education or formal vocational education as an adult but not more than until he or she attains 21 years of age; and other descendant or ascendant who needs assistance and is unable to maintain himself or herself.[239]

Custody[240] is a rather new concept in Estonian family law provided by the law in 2010. However, also before 2010 responsibility of parent and the possibility to restrict the rights of the parent were regulated.[241] Regulation of custody is more detailed and many obligations previously performed by the local governments are transferred to the court. In principle, custody, meaning that parents have the obligation and right to care for their minor child is divided into custody over person and custody over property and the right to decide on matters related to the child. In

[238]There is a regulation to contest the paternity (*FLA* §91).

[239]More specifically see *FLA Ch. 8 and 9.*

[240]See *FLA* Ch. 9.

[241]The term used at that time in a legal act was the same as today in *Council Regulation (EC) No 2201/2003 of 27 November 2003 concerning jurisdiction and the recognition and enforcement of judgments in matrimonial matters and the matters of parental responsibility, repealing Regulation (EC) No 1347/2000: parental responsibility*. OJ L 338 , 23/12/2003.

general, parents have equal rights and obligations but court can change the extent of it, assigning all or some of the custody to one parent. Maintenance and custody are not related in this respect that a parent who does not have custody over his or her child has still maintenance obligation over the child. Application of the regulation of custody was probably most complicated part of new *Family Law Act*. Though the idea of custody regulation was to provide a principle that parents who have joint custody must represent their child jointly, based on a former rule that only one parent was enough caused a lot of troubles and misunderstandings in the deeds related to the child (applications to schools, travelling, school excursion abroad, change of the name of the child etc.), now the regulations has been changed and a former principle has been put back to the law causing uncertainty in the representation of the child.[242]

Regulation of adoption[243] accords to the international principles. Adoption is permitted if it is necessary in the interests of the child and there is reason to believe that a parent-child relationship will be created between the adoptive parent and the child. Upon the selection of an adoptive parent, his or her personal characteristics, relationship with the child being adopted, his or her financial situation and ability to perform the obligations arising from the adoption relationship and, if possible, the presumed will of the parents of the child is taken into account. If available, upon making a decision of adoption the need for consistency of raising of the child and his or her national, religious, cultural and linguistic origin is considered. In Estonia, only minors may be adopted and if possible the separation of sisters and brothers is avoided. An adoptive parent must be attained at least 25 years of age, with court consent also at least 18 years of age person can adopt if he or she adopts his or her spouse's child or if there is any other good reason for adoption. In practice a married couple is preferred to be an adaptive parents, they can adopt a child jointly. A single person may adopt a child only alone. A child may be adopted also by only one spouse if he or she adopts the child of the other spouse or the other spouse cannot adopt because he or she has restricted active legal capacity. A child who is at least 10 years of age may be adopted only with his or her consent and in some cases court can also consider the consent of the child younger than 10 years. Child acquires the legal status of a child of an adoptive parent(s) and the family relationship of the child and his or her descendants with the former relatives and the rights and obligations arising from the family relationship terminate. Adoption is secrecy and only by a certain procedure and legal bases the data about adoption is possible to get and use. Also international adoption is decided by a court but with consent of the committee for international adoptions formed at the Ministry of Social Affairs. Adoption from Estonia to a foreign state may occur primarily if it is not possible to care for the child to the necessary extent in the Republic of Estonia. In practice such adoptions are very few.

---

[242]See *FLA* §120.

[243]*FLA* Ch. 11.

Guardianship[244] is regulated separately for minors and adults. If neither of the parents of a minor child has the right of representation or if it is not possible to ascertain the origin of a child, a guardian is appointed to the child by a court. If an adult person is permanently unable to understand or direct his or her actions because of mental illness, mental disability or other mental disorder, a court appoints a guardian to him or her based on an application of the person, his or her parent, spouse or adult child or rural municipality or city government or on its own initiative. A guardian has both, the right of custody over the person and his or her property. A guardian can be an adult natural person with full active legal capacity and only in specific cases a legal person. Until appointment of guardian, the duties of a guardian can be performed by the rural municipality or city government of the child's place of residence entered in the population register if the prerequisites for the establishment of guardianship have been complied with. Guardian is a legal representative of persons under guardianship having the rights and obligations to care for the person and property of the person under his or her guardianship within the limits of his or her duties—in certain cases a guardian needs court's permission in representing a child.

Cross-border family regulations are in the beginning of the development—a small state with no attractive social security system does not promote migration. On the other hand, considerable amount of young Estonians have moved abroad to learn or work. By this, step by step a number of cross-border family relations has raised and brought in Estonian legal system new relations and questions how to manage with them.

3.4.3 Characteristics of Estonian Succession Law

The main legal source regulating succession law in Estonia is *SLA* enforced in 2009,[245] consisting of all the general principles of succession inherent in Europe, e.g. private heirdom, full heirdom, the freedom to bequeath and family heirdom. Principle of private heirdom consist already in *Const* providing a general right to inherit. Specification of this right is in the *SLA* providing that the bases for succession are law (intestate succession), the testamentary intention of the bequeather expressed in a will (testate succession) or a succession contract (succession by succession contract). In case of intestate succession persons who have a right to inherit are above all the bequeather's spouse and the relatives, and only in specific cases local government or the state. The meaning of the full heirdom is that estate is the whole property of a bequether, which is transferred to the successor

[244] *FLA* part 3.

[245] Because the succession law as a branch of civil law is tensely related to other branches of private law also other legal acts consist the rules related to succession law, e.g. General Principles of Civil Law Act (GPCCA), Law of Obligation Act, *FLA*, *Commercial Code (CC)*, Civil Law Procedure Act (*CCP*), and regulations provided by those acts.

irrespective the bases for succession. The only exceptions from the estate are the rights and obligations which are inseparably bound to the person of the bequeather.[246]

In Estonia the settlement of succession is in the jurisdiction of notaries, hence all the legal acts regulating the authority of notary are the legal sources for succession as well, e.g. *Notaries Act,*[247] *Notarisation Act,*[248] *Notaries Fee Act*[249] etc. Cross-border succession is regulated by the *Private International Law Act,*[250] international agreements,[251] and conventions Estonia has acceded, e.g. *Convention of 5th October 1961 on the Conflicts of Laws Relating to the Form of Testamentary Dispositions,*[252] *Convention of the 1972 on the Establishment of a Scheme of Registration of Wills*[253] and so-called Succession Regulation.[254] As in settlement of succession is applied a law which was in force in a time succession opens also the *Baltic Private Law Code*, Russian and Soviet laws, and *Estonian SLA* from 1996 can be applied. Developments of civil law, including private international law in Europe allow to predict that also in Estonia soon the cross-border succession and its regulation and application become more important than today. Though Succession Regulation of EU provides rules only for the procedure and jurisdiction, leaving aside substantive law of member states the EU policy on enhanced cooperation will probably impact also Estonian substantive law of succession as well.

As already mentioned above Estonian succession law recognises two bases for succession—intestate succession and succession by the last will of the bequeather. The last one is divided into the testate succession and succession by the succession contract. According to the *SLA* the right of succession by succession contract is preferred to the right of succession by will, but both of these are preferred to the right of succession by law. This means that intestate succession takes place when the bequeather has not left a valid will or succession contract or arrangements in

---

[246]*SLA* §2.

[247]RT I 2000, 104, 684.

[248]RT I 2001, 93, 564.

[249]RT I 1996, 23, 456.

[250]RT I 2002, 35, 217.

[251]Estonia has several legal assistance treaties, e.g. with Russia, Latvia, Lithuania, Ukraine and Poland.

[252]Estonia acceded in 1998 and made a reservation to the art 10 of the convention stating that Estonia does not recognise testamentary dispositions made orally, save in exceptional circumstances, by an Estonian national possessing no other nationality.

[253]*Convention on the Establishment of a Scheme of Registration of Wills* 1972, enforced in Estonia 2001. ETS No.077.

[254]*Regulation (EU) No 650/2012 of the European Parliament and of the Council of 4 July 2012 on jurisdiction, applicable law, recognition and enforcement of decisions and acceptance and enforcement of authentic instruments in matters of succession and on the creation of a European Certificate of Succession*, enforced in Estonia 2015 (application acts for this Regulation are enforced in Estonia on 20 March 2016). OJ L 201, 27/7/2012.

both of them do not concern the whole estate of the bequeather. The remaining share is succeeded to the intestacy.

Succession capacity has every natural person who is alive at the time of death of the bequeather or a legal person who exists at that time. A child born alive after the opening of a succession has succession capacity if he or she was conceived before the opening of the succession. A person is unworthy to succeed if the person intentionally and unlawfully has caused or tried cause the death of the bequeather, or has put him or her in a situation where he or she is incapable of making or revoking a testamentary disposition until his or her death, or duress or deceit has hindered the bequeather from making or altering a testamentary disposition or in the same manner induced the bequeather to make or revoke a testamentary disposition if it is no longer possible for the bequeather to express his or her actual testamentary intention, or intentionally and unlawfully has removed or destroyed a will or succession contract, or has falsified the will made by the bequeather or the succession contract.

Intestate successors are the bequeather's spouse and the relatives specified by the law. Relatives succeed in three orders, and the second order successors succeed if there is no first order successors and third order successors when there are no first or second order successors. First order intestate successors are the descendants of the bequeather. However, if at the time of death of the bequeather a descendant of the bequeather is alive, the descendants of that relative who are related to the bequeather through him or her are not succeed. The principle is that the children of the bequeather succeed in equal shares. Third order intestate successors are the grandparents of the bequeather and their descendants. Grandparents also succeed in equal shares.[255]

Spouse of the bequeather does not belong in to the order of intestate successors. A spouse succeeds with the first and second order successors. He or she succeeds equally with the share of a child of the bequeather but not less than one-quarter of the estate. This means that when a bequeather has more children than three, their parts of the estate will be smaller. With second order intestate successors a spouse succeeds to one-half of the estate and when there are no relatives from the first or second orders, he or she succeeds to the entire estate, with third order intestate successors a spouse has no succession capacity. In addition to his or her share of estate a spouse may request establishment of real right on an immovable which was the matrimonial home of the spouses provided that the standard of life of the bequeather's spouse would deteriorate due to succession, and with second order successors a share of the estate the standard furnishings of the spouses' matrimonial home as a preferential share if the objects are not accessories of an immovable. For the preferential share provisions about bequest are applied.[256]

In case there are no successors (relatives or spouse), the intestate successor is the local government of the place of opening of the succession. When a succession is

[255] See more specifically *SLA* §§10–15.

[256] *SLA* §16.

opened in a foreign state and Estonian law applies to the succession, the Republic of Estonia is the intestate successor.[257]

A will can be notarial or domestic. Notarial will can be notarially authenticated will which has been made according to the intent of testator and signed by the testator in the presence of notary, or a will deposited with a notary in a sealed envelope. In the deposited will a notary does not participate in making the will and hence does not know the content of the will. Domestic will can be a will signed in the presence of witnesses or a holographic will. All wills must be signed by the testator. Will made in the presence of witnesses can be written also by someone else, but next to testator the will must be signed by the at least two unbound witnesses. In case of holographic will witnesses are not needed but the text of the will must be written by the testator by his or her own hand.[258] In principle, all the wills despite the type have an equal legal force. Testator can revoke a will or a part thereof at any time by a later will or succession contract and the preceding will is valid as much as it is not contrary to the later will or succession contract. The biggest difference between the notarial and domestic will is this that a domestic will becomes invalid if 6 month have elapsed from the date of its making and the testator is alive at the time.[259] In case testator has revoked his or her preceding notarial will by the domestic will and 6 months has been passed then again a preceding notarial will is valid.[260] For this it is important that in a domestic will there is always written the date it has been made. In case it is not possible to ascertain the exact time the domestic will has been made, it is void.[261]

Testator can make a disposition with different content in both—notarial and domestic will. Together with nominating the successor in Estonian succession law there can also be nominated an alternative successor, provisional successor and subsequent successor. Bequeather can make a conditional disposition, give a legacy and dispose a testamentary obligation or a testamentary direction, also, nominate the executor of will or demand a dispose division of the estate. Possible is also a reciprocal will of spouses[262] and make a succession contract.[263] Such dispositions must always be made into in a notarially authentic form and there are special rules for altering or annulling those dispositions.

Freedom to testate is rather wide in Estonian succession law. In principle, everyone can succeed his or her property to anyone and this right is practically not limited for the favour of intestate successors. Compulsory portion can be claimed only by those intestate successors who are subject to the maintenance obligation of bequeather but only in case they actually need a support. Support is

[257] *SLA* §18.

[258] *SLA* §§20–24.

[259] *SLA* §25(1).

[260] *SLA* §88(6).

[261] *SLA* §25(2).

[262] *SLA* §§89–94.

[263] *SLA* §§95–103.

assumed only related to the adolescent children, other persons must prove their need. Recipient of compulsory portion does not acquire a part of succession property but only a monetary claim against successor in a half of a estate he or she would have got in case of intestate succession.[264]

Upon the opening of a succession, the estate transfers to successor. No declarations of intention or legal deed should be done by the person entitled to succeed.[265] Person entitled to succeed can withdraw in 3 months from the death of the bequeather and from the awareness of his or her right of succession. He or she has to make an application of renunciation to the notary. Renunciation of succession is irrevocable and cannot be conditional. This means that it is not possible to renunciate for a certain person.

As in Estonia all the rights and obligations of the bequeather are transferred to the successor the primary question in the procedure of succession is specification of the successors. This means that nominating the successors is most important declaration in succession. Other beneficiaries, who will get only certain objects or rights, are not considered as successors, they have a right as a claim against the bequeather as an ordinary creditor.[266] When a person entitled to succeed has not renunciated the estate, he or she is considered to accept the estate and all the rights and obligations of the bequeather are transferred to the successor, including the responsibility of all the fixed arrangements.[267] Liability can be limited by the value of the estate only when bequeather demands an inventory and presents an application for this to the notary. In the case a successor does not demand the inventory of the estate, successor will respond by his or her personal assets. Obligations related to the estate must be fulfilled in turn.[268] Estate is considered to be joint successors and they are solidarily liable for the performance of an obligation which is part of the estate,[269] the same principle is applied also in case of co-successors.[270]

Cross-border family matters have internationalised also succession law. On 2 March 2016 the *Succession Regulation* has begun to be applied in practice in Estonia following the mutual recognition and cooperation principle of EU law[271] and providing more clarity in choosing the applicable norm.

---

[264]*SLA* §§104–105.

[265]*SLA* §4(1).

[266]See *SLA* §62(1), §104(4) and (5).

[267]See *SLA* §130(1).

[268]See *SLA* §142.

[269]*SLA* §151.

[270]*SLA* §152(2).

[271]See more about the regulation e.g. Requejo (2013), Devaux (2013); Commission staff working document accompanying the Proposal for a Regulation of the European Parliament and of the council on jurisdiction, applicable law, recognition and enforcement of decisions and authentic instruments in matters of successions and on the introduction of a European Certificate of Inheritance—Impact Assessment (SEC(2009) 411 final C7-0236/09), Brussels, 14.10.2009; Deville (2014).

Year after year Estonia learns to apply conventions regulating cross-border family relations and international family law has become more essential part of family law practice. In cross-border family relations Estonian Embassies act an important role in cooperation with other states. Ministry of Foreign Affairs has done an efficient work in preparing the contracts of several international agreements facilitating the recognition of family event's documents. There are preparations in joining the Rome III Regulation.[272] More and more the knowledge of international family law is needed in everyday practice of lawyers. One example was already mentioned above—an amendment in the Family Law Act providing the rule that in the registration of the birth of the child mother's husband can be dropped and register another man as a father of the child. This change in law was caused by the ostensible and other unfinished marriages abroad. However, there can be brought examples from the *Name Law Act,*[273] adoption, custody etc. where cross-border elements of family relations have strongly influenced the development of Estonian law to be more harmonised with the family laws of other EU member states.

References

Andresen E (2009) State tasks of the public Office of Notary – belonging to the domain of national or European Union law? Juridica Int 16:157–167, 163

Antokolskaia M (2007) Objectives and values of substantive family law. In: Meeusen J, Pertegàs-Sender M, Straetmans G, Swennen F (eds) International family law for the European Union. Intersentia, Antwerpen-Oxford, pp 49–67

Balodis K (2013) The Latvian law of obligations: the current situation and perspectives. Juridica Int 20:69–74

Devaux A (2013) The European regulations on succession of July 2012: a path towards the end of succession conflicts of law in Europe or not? Int Lawyer 47(2), (Fall 2013)

Deville R (Dr.) (2014) Brussels IV in a nutshell. In EJTN seminar on cross-border inheritance law, direct link: www.ejtn.eu/PageFiles/6333/Brussels_IV_nutshell.pdf

Fletcher IF (1999) Insolvency in private international law. Clarendon Press, Oxford

Joamets K (2012) Marriage capacity, social values and law-making process. Int Comp Law Rev 12 (1):97–115, 101–104

Joamets K, Kerikmäe T (2014) The new developments in family law – green paper 'less bureaucracy for citizens: promoting free movement of public documents and recognition of the effect of civil statud records', its applicability in marriage on the example of Estonia. Eur Stud Rev Eur Law Econ Polit 1:70–92

Joamets K (2016) Eastern partnership and family law. In: Kerikmäe T, Chochia A (eds) Political and legal perspectives of the EU eastern partnership policy. Springer, Cham, pp 101–117. ISBN 978-3-319-27381

Kairjak M (2014) Majanduskaristusõigus karistusõiguse revisjoni raames. Juridica 8:633–637

Kull I et al (2004) Võlaõigus I. Üldosa, Juura

Kullerkupp K (2001) Family law in Estonia. Int Surv Family Law 2001:95–110

[272] *Council Regulation (EU) No 1259/2010 of 20 December 2010 implementing enhanced cooperation in the area of the law applicable to divorce and legal separation.* OJ L 343/10, 29/12/2010.

[273] RT I 2005, 1, 1.

Lehis L (2004) Maksuõigus. Juura
Liin U (1998) On reform of succession law. Juridica Int 3:105–109. http://www.juridicainternational.eu/?id=12471
Lopman V, Lorents K (2013) Vastutusotsus. Äriühingu juhatuse liikme maksuõiguslik vastutus äriühingu maksuvõla eest Juridica 2:118–127
Lukason O (2008) Saneerimismenetluse majanduslikud mõjud ja nende hindamine Eestis. http://www.just.ee/sites/www.just.ee/files/elfinder/art_files/saneerimise_majanduslike_mojude_hinnang_2008_0.pdf
Lukason O (2010) Maksejõuetuse põhjuste analüüs, pp 1–38. http://www.just.ee/sites/www.just.ee/files/elfinder/art_files/maksejouetuse_pohjuste_analuus_2010_0.pdf
Manavald P (2008) Pilk eesti maksejõuetusõigusele läbi õigusökonoomika prisma. Juridica 6:383–389
Niklus I (2008) Saneerimisseaduse eelnõust. Juridica 6:369–376
Nurmela I et al (2008) Rahvusvaheline Eraõigus. Juura
Requejo M (2013) Regulation N° 650/2012: Some Open Issues. http://www.conflictoflaws.net/2013/regulation-no-6502012-some-open-issues/
Särav S, Kerikmäe T (2016) E-residency: a cyberdream embodied in a digital identity card? In: Kerikmäe T, Rull A (eds) The future of law and etechnologies. Springer, New York, pp 57–81
Scherpe JM (2016) The present and future of european family law. In: Scherpe JM (ed) European family law, vol IV. Edward Elgar Publishing, Cheltenham, Northampton
Schwenzer I et al (2010) Commentary on the UN convention on the international sale of goods (CISG). Oxford University Press, Oxford
Tampuu T (2003) Deliktiõigus võlaõigusseaduses. Üldprobleemid ja delikti üldkoosseisul põhinev vastutus Juridica 2:71–82
Tiivel T (2001) Aktsiaseltsi juhatuse vastutuse piiramine. Juridica 10:723–732
Toom T (2014) Äriühingu püsiv maksejõuetus ja edasiste maksete tegemine, Kus on piir keelatu ja lubatu vahel? Juridica 6:485–489
Torga M et al (2013) Fitting the estonian notions of contractual and non-contractual obligations under the european private international law instruments. Juridica Int 20:61–68
Tubin A (2012) Menetlusjärgne ärikeeld: kas pankrotiõiguslik prriang või karistusõiguslik lisakaristus? Juridica 6:442–449
Varul P (1993) Tsiviil- ja kaubandusseadusandluse arengust Eestis. Juridica 7:120–121
Varul P et al (2006) Võlaõigusseadus I. Kommenteeritud väljaanne, Juura
von Bar et al (2008) Principles, Definitions and Model Rules of European Private Law Draft Common Frame of Reference (DCFR). http://ec.europa.eu/justice/contract/files/european-private-law_en.pdf
Varul P et al (2009) Võlaõigusseadus III. Kommenteeritud väljaanne, Juura
Varul P (2013) Maksejõuetusõiguse areng eestis. Juridica 4:234–241

Part II

Latvian Law

General Frameworks

4

Arnis Buka, Irēna Kucina, Jānis Lazdiņš, and Daiga Rezevska

Abstract

The chapter deals with the overview of the historical development of the law in the territories historically inhabited by Latvians as well as the development of the legal arrangement starting with the German and Russian influence, proclamation of the Republic of Latvia in 1918, then the occupation by the USSR, and finally the restoration of Latvia's independence *de facto* in 1990. The chapter also gives brief information about Latvian judicial system, main institutions for implementation of justice and basic functions of judicial bodies and administrative authorities. It provides overview on the status and normative regulation for the application of the international law as well as the European Union law. Finally, the chapter stresses the future possible challenges for the legal arrangement for example, the enlargement of the EU and the protection of the inviolable core of the Constitution at the same time, the increasing role of the judiciary and the elevated required qualities for the judges in the contemporary legal arrangement, increasingly important role of the communication with the society through the mass media and the quality of its content, the influence of the terrorism on the human rights, and regulatory frameworks for the modern technologies.

4.1 The Historical Development

Jānis Lazdiņš
Faculty of Law, University of Latvia, Raina blvd. 19, Riga LV-1586, Latvia
e-mail: janis.lazdins@lu.lv

A. Buka (✉) • I. Kucina • J. Lazdiņš • D. Rezevska
Faculty of Law, University of Latvia, Raina blvd. 19, Riga LV-1586, Latvia
e-mail: arnis.buka@lu.lv; irena.kucina@lu.lv; janis.lazdins@lu.lv; daiga.rezevska@lu.lv

T. Kerikmäe et al. (eds.), *The Law of the Baltic States*,
DOI 10.1007/978-3-319-54478-6_4

4.1.1 History of Latvian Law Before the Proclamation of the State of Latvia

Before the thirteenth century the Balts (Latgalians, Curonians, Semigallians and Selonians) and the Liivs (hereafter—Latvians) had reached the highest degree of social cooperation as regards state organisation, with community members gathering around the most prominent tribal leaders. Historical sources refer to some outstanding tribal leaders as kings (*rex*).[1] It is not known that independent courts existed. In special cases justice was administered at gatherings. Murder and rape of a woman were seen as the most severe crimes. Blood feud was considered to be a lawful measure of self-defence.[2] Marriage was established violently (stealing/kidnapping of wives) or in a more civilised, contractual way.[3] Marriage transformed into a family after the birth of the first child. Protection of the family's interests in public relationships, including by blood feud, was considered a specifically male right and obligation. In the western lands inhabited by Latvians, the eldest son was usually given preference in terms of inheritance (primogeniture system), but in the eastern part—the youngest son (ultimo geniture system).[4] Daughters were excluded from inheritance by dowry. Entry into contracts was linked to symbolic actions. Thus, a legally protected contract required shaking right hands, since "left hand never me justice did".[5] Obligations could arise from both a contract and a delict.[6]

Within a hundred years of the Crusade, or the so-called expansion to the East (*Drang nach Osten*), beginning at the turn of the twelfth or thirteenth century, the lands inhabited by the Latvians were colonised by Catholic Christians (mainly from Germany). The majority of the local nobility perished in military clashes lasting for nearly a century. Those who remained either left their native land or assimilated into German culture. Latvian proto-national groups began to form, comprising farmers and lowest urban strata. At the Diet (*Landtag*) in 1435, the Livonian Union (hereafter—Livonia) was founded to ensure closer cooperation between dioceses, cities and the Livonian Order. Thus, a complex of dioceses and vassal states of the Order, dependent on the medieval German Empire, emerged. Livonia did not become a uniform state. Concurrent with the spread of the Roman Catholic faith and construction of towns, German medieval law as feudal law (*Ritterrecht/Lehnrecht*) and the Charters of Hanseatic towns modelled upon the cities of Lübeck and Hamburg, entered the lands inhabited by Latvians. Until the end of the fifteenth century, the reception of Roman law can be discussed only conditionally.[7] Canon

[1] Šterns (2002), pp. 109–111.
[2] Lazdiņš (2009), pp. 59–66.
[3] Švābe (1927), p. 3.
[4] Lazdiņš (2006), pp. 1–9.
[5] Kalniņš (1972), p. 27.
[6] Lazdiņš (2006), p. 8.
[7] Bunge (1862), pp. 3–4, 9–130; Meļķisis (1998), pp. 101–120, 178–181, 239–250.

law was an exception. During the Livonian War, brought by the Muscovites (1558–1583), Livonia ceased to exist on 28 November 1561.

After the Livonian War, all lands inhabited by the Latvians became part of the Polish-Lithuanian State (*Rzeczpospolita*) (hereafter—Poland) as the Duchy Beyond the Daugava (*Ducatus Transdunensis*)[8] and the Duchy of Courland and Semigallia (*Ducatus Curlandiae et Semigalliae*) (hereafter—Duchy of Courland).[9] This status did not last for long. During the Polish-Swedish War (1600–1629) the Duchy Beyond the Daugava ceased to exist. On 16 September 1629, Sweden obtained the so-called Swedish Livonia in the Truce of Altmark, and Poland retained only the eastern part of the Duchy Beyond the Daugava, or the so-called Polish Livonia (*Inflantkie*) or Latgale.[10] In 1677, the Lithuanian Charter was applied to Latgale.[11] This introduced the separation of Latgale law from the law of other territories inhabited by the Latvians until the State of Latvia was proclaimed (1918).

The Duchy of Courland (1561–1795) was a vassal state of Poland. On 18 March 1617, the Government Formula (*Formula Regiminis in Ducata Curlandiea et Semigalliae*) was proclaimed.[12] The Government Formula became the constitution of the Duchy of Courland. The constitutional law restricted the power of the duke and the Diet in the general interests of the Polish State. Freedom of faith was guaranteed in compliance with the Augsburg Confession of Faith, along with the inviolability of property to nobility and townsmen. Other rights in the Duchy were regulated by "The Statutes of Kurzeme and Zemgale" (*Statuta et leges Curlandiae et Semigalliae*) drafted concurrently with the Government Formula, but the rights in the Pilten autonomous district were prescribed by "The Laws and Statutes of Pilten District" (*Gesetze und Statuete des Piltenischen Kreises*) of 28 October 1611. The Statutes, *inter alia*, legalised serfdom (*Leibeigenschaft*).[13] Generally, law in the Duchy continued to develop in the spirit of German law.

In Swedish Livonia (1629–1721), German and Swedish law competed. The contribution of the Swedish enlightenment was predominance of the citizenship principle over that of class. Thus, all subjects of "His Majesty" were subjected to district courts (*Land-Gerichte*). Serfs only had the right to submit collective complaints about excessive oppression to the Provincial Supreme Court (*Hoff-Gericht*). The Riga Council Court retained autonomy in legal proceedings. Educational reform was initiated to eliminate illiteracy, and in 1632 the University of Tartu (*Dorpat*) was founded.[14]

On 30 August 1721, the Nystad Peace Treaty between Sweden and Russia ended the Northern War (1700–1721). Russia added Swedish Livonia to its empire as the

[8]Blūzma (2006), p. 49.

[9]Ziegenhorn (1772), pp. 51– 56.

[10]Dunsdorfs (1962), pp. 70, 127–131.

[11]Blūzma (2006), p. 113.

[12]Ziegenhorn (1772), pp. 129–134.

[13]Blūzma (2006), pp. 189–257; Kalniņš (1972), pp. 142–145.

[14]Švābe (1930), pp. 112–117; Dunsdorfs (1962), pp. 397–411.

Governorate of Livonia and the former Swedish Province of Estonia, along with Saaremaa and other islands, as the Governorate of Estonia. In 1795, during the third division of Poland, the Duchy of Courland and the autonomous district of Pilten came under the governance of the Russian Empire as the Courland Governorate. The classes of Baltic governorates retained their former rights, privileges, as well as class institutions and courts. Thus, the so-called autonomy of the law of the Baltic district evolved. Law in Latgale had a somewhat different fate. During the first division of Poland in 1772, Latgale was added to the Russian Empire. In 1831, the general law of the Russian Empire came into force in Latgale.[15]

During the rule of Alexander I Romanov (*Александр I Романов*) (1801–1825), serfdom was abolished in the Baltic Latvian lands—in the Governorates of Courland (1817) and of Livonia (1819). The Manifesto of 19 February 1861 abolished serfdom throughout the Russian Empire, including Latgale. In contrast to the Latgalians, in the Baltic region the serfs were given the status of free citizen without the right to own or to use the previously cultivated land ("bird's freedom").[16]

Starting with the 19thc, the Russian Empire began gradually replacing the Baltic law with unified laws of the state. On 1 May 1846, the unified "Regulation on Criminal Sanctions and Correctional Sanctions" (*Уложение о наказаниях уголовных и исправительных*) (hereafter—Regulation on Criminal Sanctions) entered into force. The Regulation on Criminal Sanctions revoked barbaric forms of execution (breaking wheel, quartering, burning, etc.). On 22 March 1903, the modern Penal Law (*Уголовное уложение*) (hereafter—Penal Law of 1903) was adopted.[17] On 20 November 1864, Court By-laws that met the modern requirements (*Учрежденія судебныхъ установленій*) were adopted in the Russian Empire. The aim was to separate the administrative, police and judicial power. Concurrent with the Court By-laws, the Regulation on Criminal Procedure (*Уставъ уголовнаго судопроизводства*) and Regulation on Civil Procedure (*Уставъ гражданскаго судопроизводства*) came into force. To centralise the state and implement the policy of Russification, Court By-laws and procedural law were applied to the Baltic Governorates on 9 July 1889.[18] Until the collapse of the Russian Empire, only the civil law continued developing in the spirit of Romano-Germanic law traditions. On 12 November 1864, during the reign of Alexander II Romanov (*Александр II Романов*) (1855–1881), Part III of the Collection of Local Laws of the Baltic Provinces, Civil Laws (*Сводъ местныхъ узаконеній губерній остзейскихъ. Часть третія. Законы гражданскіе*[19]) (hereafter—BVLK III),

[15] Blūzma (2006), pp. 113.

[16] Jundzis and Zemītis (2014), pp. 173–196.

[17] Kalniņš (1972), pp. 348–350; Lēbers (2000), pp. 41–59.

[18] Schäfer Frank and Schubert (2013), pp. 91–106.

[19] Part III of Collection of Local Laws of the Baltic Provinces, Civil Laws (Сводъ местныхъ узаконеній губерній остзейскихъ. Часть третія. Законы гражданскіе). 1864. Санктпетербург. Въ типографіи втораго отделенія собственной Е.И.В. канцеляріи.

elaborated by professor Friedrich Georg von Bunge, was approved and granted the force of law. BVLK III was drafted in the spirit of the Pandect doctrine of the German historical school. Historical sources of Germanic law were also retained, to the extent possible.[20]

The revolution of 1905 ushered in democratic changes across the Russian Empire. On 23 April 1906, "Basic Laws of the State" were promulgated (*Основные государственные законы*)[21] (hereafter—Basic Laws of the State). The emperor (czar), however, retained the supreme power of an autocrat (*верховная сомодержавная власть*). The basic rights and obligations of the subject, incorporated into the Basic Laws of the State, was a positive development. Following the collapse of the monarchy at the end of World War I, the Russian Empire was proclaimed a republic on 1 September 1917.

4.1.2 Latvian Law after Proclamation of the Republic of Latvia

On 18 November 1918, the Latvian People's Council (hereafter—the People's Council) proclaimed the Republic of Latvia, based on "The Political Platform" of the People's Council.[22] "The Political Platform" became the first provisional constitution of the Republic of Latvia,[23] but the People's Council was the first legislator of the Latvian State. The provision included in Para 1 of Article II of "The Political Platform", which states that Latvia is "a republic on democratic foundations", permeates the constitutional system of the Republic of Latvia even today.[24]

For a short period (December 1918–January 1920), the Republic of Latvia was partially occupied by the Red Army. The Latvian Socialist Soviet Republic was proclaimed. On 15 January 1919, the first Soviet constitution was adopted—"The Constitution of the Latvian Socialist Soviet Republic" (hereafter—Constitution of 1919). The structure of the Constitution was based on the principle of democratic centralism. A centralised bureaucratic-totalitarian state order was created with the principle of democratic centralism as its foundation.[25]

A law adopted on 5 December 1919 by the People's Council, "Law on Retaining the Former Laws of Russia Valid in Latvia," granted temporary validity to the former Russian laws which had been in force in the territory of Latvia until 24 October 1917, according to the old style calendar. The law came with a disclaimer—"insofar as these have not been replaced by new laws and are not contradictory to the order of the State of Latvia and the Platform of the People's

[20]Нольде АЭ., Баронъ (1914).
[21]Томсинов (2004), pp. 311–320.
[22]Political Platform. Pagaidu Valdības Vēstnesis, 1918, No. 1.
[23]Dišlers (1935), pp. 1, 35.
[24]Lazdiņš (2014), pp. 9–20.
[25]Lazdiņš (2013), pp. 10–12.

Council", thus strictly stating that the Soviet law of the Bolsheviks, who had come to power in the former Russia, dating from after 24 October 1917 (old-style), was not a source of law for the Republic of Latvia. On 11 August 1920, "Peace Treaty between Latvia and [Soviet] Russia" was concluded. Article II of the Treaty provides that "Russia recognizes without objection the independence and sovereignty of the Latvian State and forever renounces all sovereign rights held by Russia in relation to the Latvian nation and land". The first parliament elected by the people—the Constitutional Assembly—convened on 1 May 1920. On 27 May 1920 the law, "The Declaration on the State of Latvia" was adopted, and on 1 June 1920—the law "Provisional Regulation on the Order of the Latvian State". These two laws became the Second Provisional Constitution of the Republic of Latvia. The Second Provisional Constitution continued the law policy of "The Political Platform".[26]

On 15 February 1922, "The Satversme [Constitution] of the Republic of Latvia" was adopted[27] (hereafter—Satversme). The Satversme provides that "Latvia is an independent, democratic republic" (Art. 1). The structure of the Satversme is founded on the principle of parliamentary democracy. The people elect only the Saeima (parliament). The legislator holds the central place in the political system of the Latvian state. The check and balance principle of state powers is not implemented. Thus, the separation of state powers in accordance with classic theories of separation of powers can be discussed only conditionally.

On 15 May 1934, an anti-constitutional *coup-d'état* took place, led by the Prime Minister Kārlis Ulmanis. The democratic state order was abolished. Activities of the Saeima were not allowed. Public governance followed the principle of authoritarianism. On 11 April 1936, K. Ulmanis also assumed the duties of the State President. Formally, state power was passed to the Cabinet. In fact, until the Soviet occupation, the President of the State and Cabinet, K. Ulmanis, was the sole ruler in the state.

From 1919 to 1937, land reform was implemented. As part of this process, the land belonging to churches and large landowners (landed gentry) was nationalised. The rural landscape of Latvia consisted of farms not exceeding 100 hectares. The reform fulfilled the ancient dream of the majority of Latvians to have the chance to have their own "corner" of land, and also prevented against the threat of Communists coming into power. In economic terms, however, the land reform failed. Small farms were falling into disuse, unable to attract investment. Farmers were only able to participate in the market economy thanks to state aid.[28]

"The Penal Law" of the Republic of Latvia was drafted from the Penal Law of 1903, and was adopted on 24 April 1933 (hereafter—Penal Law of 1933). The Penal Law of 1933 was the first law in the Latvian lands that did not envisage capital

[26]Lazdiņš (2015c), pp. 50–58.

[27]The Constitution of the Republic of Latvia (Latvijas Republikas Satversme). Valdības Vēstnesis, 1922, No. 141, http://likumi.lv/doc.php?id=57980.

[28]Aizsilnieks (1968), pp. 242–246, 343–349, 711–722.

punishment. On 1 February 1921, the "Law on Marriage" was adopted, introducing the institution of secular, State-recognised marriages. The right to divorce in a State court, in turn, implemented the principle of spouse's freedom in private law relationships.[29] On 28 January 1937, "The Latvian Civil Law"[30] (hereafter—CL) was adopted. It came into force on 1 January 1938, starting the unification of Latvian civil law. BVLK III and the most recent civil law findings in continental Europe became the most significant sources of the CL.[31] Thus, the historical development of civil law in the traditions of Romano-Germanic law was not interrupted. Shortly before the beginning of World War II (1939), a number of laws linked to the CL were adopted, e.g., The Law on Land Registers of 22 December 1937, The Law on Cheques, The Law on Promissory Notes of 27 September 1938, etc. These, like the Civil Law, were reinstated after the independence of the Republic of Latvia was *de facto* restored in the 1990s.[32]

On 17 June 1940, the Union of Soviet Socialist Republics (hereafter—USSR or the Soviet Union) occupied the Republic of Latvia. On 21 June, the government of Prime Minister Augusts Kirhenšteins, subservient to the occupying power, set to work. On 14–15 July, the election of the so-called "People's Saeima" was held. On 21 July, K. Ulmanis resigned from the office of the State President. The same day, Latvia was proclaimed a Soviet Socialist Republic (hereafter—Latvian SSR), and a decision was adopted to request admittance of the Latvian SSR to the Soviet Union. On 5 August, the Supreme Soviet (hereafter—SS) of the USSR, by "satisfying" the request by the Latvian Saeima, "admitted" the Latvian SSR into the Soviet Union with the rights of a united republic. Thus, Latvia's *de facto* annexation was formally completed.[33] In fact, the Republic of Latvia, as an occupied state, continued to exist *de jure*.

Latvia was incorporated into the Soviet Union and concurrently the Soviet law was imposed within a surprisingly brief period of time. Before the annexation of Latvia was completed, preparation for nationalising the property of Latvia's inhabitants began, paving the way for further "socialist transformations".[34] On 25 August 1940, the Constitution of the Latvian SSR (hereafter—Constitution of 1940), modelled on the Constitution of the USSR of 5 December 1936 came into force, and on 26 November, the codification of law according to the most important fields of law of the Russian Soviet Federative Socialist Republic (hereafter—Russian SFSR) did likewise. Thus, formally, Latvia no longer differed, in terms of its law, from other Soviet republics.[35]

[29]Lēbers (2000), pp. 200–201, 245–253.

[30]Latvian Civil Law. Likumu un Ministru kabineta noteikumu krājums, 1937, (document) No. 29.

[31]Švarcs (2011), pp. 254–262.

[32]Lēbers (2000), pp. 274–276.

[33]Lazdiņš (2015c), pp. 168–186.

[34]Lazdiņš (2007), pp. 19–20.

[35]Lazdiņš (2015c), pp. 187–203.

From July 1941 until May 1945, Latvia was occupied by the Nazi German army. By the regulation of 13 June 1942, "On the Law Valid in Province General of Latvia and Handling of Judgements and Decisions", the occupational power formally reinstated the Latvian law. The restoration of the State of Latvia was not permitted. Germany implemented a policy of racial hatred in the occupied State of Latvia. Regretfully, because of this policy, crimes against humanity were committed on the territory of Latvia.[36]

After World War II, the USSR decided to grant greater legislative rights to the united republics. The supreme councils of the united republics had to draft republican codes for various fields of law, with legislation in these fields elaborated by the USSR and united republics as their basis. Thus, the SS of the Latvian SSR adopted the codification of "The Criminal Code of the Latvian SSR" and "The Criminal Procedure Code of the Latvian SSR" on 6 January 1961, and on 27 December 1963 "The Civil Code of the Latvian SSR", followed by "The Marriage and Family Code of the Latvian SSR" on 18 April 1969, etc. The laws and codes adopted by the Latvian SS gradually replaced the respective codifications of the Russian SFSR, which had been in force since 26 November 1940.

The constitutional structure of the USSR complied with the requirements of a federative state. The new Constitution of the USSR, adopted on 7 October 1977, and the Constitution of the Latvian SSR, based on the former and adopted on 18 April 1978 (hereafter—Constitution of Latvian SSR of 1978), changed nothing in this respect. The SS as the legislative body of the USSR consisted of two chambers—the Soviet of the Union and the Soviet of Nationalities; general governance of the state was ensured by the USSR Council of Ministers as the All-union government and the supreme courts. Moreover, if a conflict of law arose between a republican law and the united laws of the USSR, the law of the USSR prevailed; a citizen of the Latvian SSR was simultaneously also a citizen of the USSR, just like a citizen of any other united republic. Although the Constitution of 1940 and the Constitution of the Latvian SSR of 1978 formally defined the Latvian SSR as a sovereign state with the right to freely secede from the USSR, the actual situation revealed this to be an illusion, put in place to serve ideological considerations. The nature of the USSR as a totalitarian state was evident in the Communist Party's leading and guiding role in the state, defined by Article 6 of the Constitution of the USSR of 1977 and the Constitution of the Latvian SSR of 1978. Article 6 granted to the Communist Party of the USSR the legal right to interfere in the activities of the legislative, executive and judicial power, and to establish censorship to manage public affairs. Pursuant to the principle of democratic centralism referred to above, as a sole political power it could control the situation in the state. Thus, separation of the state powers was non-existent in the Soviet state, just as guaranteed fundamental rights based on human dignity.[37]

[36]Lēbers (2000), pp. 355–357.

[37]Lēbers (2000), pp. 373–415.

On 4 May 1990, the Supreme Soviet of the Latvian SSR adopted the historic "Declaration on the Restoration of Independence of the Republic of Latvia"[38] (hereafter—Declaration of Independence). "The Latvian people did not recognise the occupying regimes, resisted them and regained freedom, restoring the independence of the state on 4 May 1990 based on the continuity of the state [. . .] condemn communist and Nazi totalitarian regimes and their crimes."[39] Article 2 of the Satversme provides: "The sovereign power of the State of Latvia is vested in the people of Latvia". It gave the right "not to recognise the changes of the constitutional order that are incompatible with the Satversme and to restore the unlawfully interrupted statehood of Latvia".[40] "The doctrine of the continuity of the Republic of Latvia, on the basis of which *de facto* statehood of Latvia was restored, is first of all founded on the wish of the Latvian people to maintain their statehood and to continue to exist as an independent state."[41] The restored *de facto* Republic of Latvia, thus, is not a new state, but an internationally recognised continuation of the State of Latvia, which existed between the wars.[42]

The Soviet powers, guided by Marxist-Leninist ideology, had ignored the right of the Latvian State to exist. By nationalising the property of the citizens of the occupied state, the USSR had grossly violated one of the fundamental human rights—the right to the inviolability of property. After the State regained legal capacity, and a democratic state governed by the rule of law was reinstated, restoration of historical justice and legal property relations, i.e., the de-nationalisation of nationalised property was one of the most pressing tasks.

Several fundamental principles complying with the principle of justice were incorporated into the legal acts linked to the de-nationalisation of property:

1. de-nationalisation and privatisation of the same objects of property were not concurrent, to protect the interests of former owners and their heirs. I.e., de-nationalisation of property was a priority vis-à-vis general privatisation;
2. de-nationalisation of property is not linked to the citizenship or place of residence of the former owner or his heirs. I.e., neither the citizenship, nor the present place of residence of the former owner could become an obstacle to restoration of property rights.[43]

The policy of de-nationalisation was oriented towards restoring the right to immoveable property. Restoration of rights to moveable property or compensation for it was an exception to the general procedure. Monetary deposits were not

[38]Declaration on the Restoration of Independence of the Republic of Latvia. Latvijas Republikas Augstākās Padomes un Valdības Ziņotājs (1990), Nr. 20, http://likumi.lv/doc.php?id=75539.

[39]Amendment to the Latvian Constitution. http://likumi.lv/ta/id/267428-grozijums-latvijas-republikas-satversme.

[40]Balodis (2014), p. 255.

[41]Lazdiņš (2015c), pp. 206–207.

[42]Schöbener and Knauff (2013), pp. 107–108.

[43]Lazdiņš (2015a), pp. 357–360.

compensated at all. Regretfully, after more than 50 years of occupation, absolute restoration of historical justice in the field of property rights is not possible. Therefore, legal acts pertaining to de-nationalisation comprised the right of dissatisfied former owners and their heirs to receive equal property instead of the nationalised property or the right to receive compensation for irreclaimable property.

On 6 July 1993, the Satversme was reinstated in its full scope. Numerous laws that had not become morally outdated and complied with contemporary requirements were also reinstated.[44] Only the citizenship of former citizens and their successors was recognised. Other candidates for the citizenship of the Republic of Latvia must follow the procedure for naturalisation.[45] Thus, the State of Latvia has established a policy that complies with the doctrine of state continuity.

4.2 The Structure of the Judicial System

Irēna Kucina
Faculty of Law, University of Latvia, Raina blvd. 19, Riga LV-1586, Latvia
e-mail: irena.kucina@lu.lv

4.2.1 The Court System

The basic principles of the judiciary are laid down in the Constitution of Latvia (Satversme),[46] which regulates the independence of the judges, judge appointment procedure and the irrevocability of the judge. In accordance with the Satversme, court cases in Latvia shall be heard by district (city) courts, regional courts and the Supreme Court, but in the event of war or a state of emergency, also by military courts. However, the Constitutional Court reviews cases concerning the conformity of laws with the Constitution, as well as other cases conferred within the jurisdiction thereof by law (Satversme, Chapter VI). The Law on Judicial Power[47] regulates the judicial system in more detail, prescribing the principles of and guarantees for the independence of the judiciary, basic principles for adjudicating matters, judge

[44] Lazdiņš (2015b), pp. 43–67.

[45] Schöbener and Knauff (2013), p. 108.

[46] Constitution of the Republic of Latvia. http://www.vvc.gov.lv/export/sites/default/docs/LRTA/Likumi/Constitution.doc.

[47] Law on Judicial Power. http://www.vvc.gov.lv/export/sites/default/docs/LRTA/Likumi/Judicial_Power.pdf.

appointment procedure, etc. The procedural laws—CPL,[48] KPL[49] and the Administrative Procedure Law[50]—prescribe the procedure for hearing cases. The Law on the Constitutional Court[51] defines the institutional and legal framework regarding the Constitutional Court.

Latvia has a three-level court system, a so-called "clear" three-level court system: district (city) courts—first instance, regional courts—second instance and the Supreme Court—third instance. All matters in the 1st instance are adjudicated in district (city) courts. Regional courts act as the courts of appeal, and the Supreme Court reviews cases in cassation.

In accordance with procedural laws or orders regulated by special provisions of law in certain categories of cases, there are several exceptions when access to justice is granted in two, or more rarely in one instance. Civil cases where claims are submitted in accordance with small claims procedure and cases on invalidation of the decisions of capital companies' shareholders' meetings are settled in two instances. Matters related to administrative offences are also heard in two instances. There are certain categories of administrative case which are heard only in two instances, e.g., limitations and prohibitions laid down by the local government to organise meetings, processions, and pickets, refusals to provide information or to exercise a request of information, as well as the actual action expressed as non-provision or undue provision of the information, et. al. Parliamentary election violations can be settled in two instances or even in the first instance in cases when it is determined by law.

Courts of General Jurisdiction

Courts of general jurisdiction adjudicate civil matters, criminal matters and matters related to administrative offences. District (city) courts and regional courts examine the merits of cases. This means that they have the competence to evaluate evidence, hear witnesses, etc. While the Supreme Court is considered a court of cassation, it has a very limited competence for examination of cases on merits (e.g. ancillary complaints).

District (City) Courts

District (city) courts are courts of first instance for civil, criminal and administrative matters. District courts may have one or several court houses, which are located within the territory of operation of the relevant district (city) court. There are

[48]Civil Procedure Law. http://www.vvc.gov.lv/export/sites/default/docs/LRTA/Likumi/Civil_Procedure_Law.pdf.

[49]Criminal Procedure Law. http://www.vvc.gov.lv/export/sites/default/docs/LRTA/Likumi/Criminal_Procedure_Law.doc.

[50]Administrative Procedure Law. http://www.vvc.gov.lv/export/sites/default/docs/LRTA/Likumi/Administrative_Procedure_Law.doc.

[51]Constitutional Court Law. http://www.vvc.gov.lv/export/sites/default/docs/LRTA/Likumi/Constitutional_Court_Law.doc.

27 district courts of general jurisdiction.[52] District (city) courts examine cases by reviewing them on their merits.

There are several specialised district (city) courts designated for the hearing of certain categories of case. The Jelgava court is the only court with jurisdiction over civil cases on the invalidation of capital companies' shareholders' meetings. The city of Riga Vidzeme district court has jurisdiction as the court of first instance in civil cases which involve State secrets, cases on the protection of patent law, design law, topographies of semiconductor products, trademarks and indications of geographical origin. This court also has jurisdiction as court of first instance over criminal proceedings involving state secrets.

Regional Courts

Regional Courts are courts of appellate instance for civil and criminal matters as well as administrative offences. The decisions of the courts of first instance can be appealed. Cases in regional courts are reviewed on appeal (de novo). In Latvia, the procedure for hearing cases in the first and second instance has only some minor differences. In the last several years, there have been some changes in the admissibility of evidence submissions, but in general terms, the procedure in the first instance and appeal instance is the same. There are five regional courts of general jurisdiction corresponding to the regions of Latvia—Riga, Vidzeme, Kurzeme, Zemgale and Latgale.

The Supreme Court

The Supreme Court operates as the third, or the highest-level court, which hears cases in the cassation instance. The cassation instance at the Supreme Court has three Departments—the Department of Civil Cases, the Department of Criminal Cases and the Department of Administrative Cases. A cassation instance court examines only questions or issues regarding the correctness of applying the norms of substantive and procedural law. The principle of cassation is of a public law nature, since it is aimed at uniform application and interpretation of legal norms throughout the state. Accessible and understandable jurisprudence, analysis and interpretation of problematic issues provided by the cassation instance court are important tools for developing a uniform judicature, as well as ensuring the development of law. In the cassation institute that exists in Latvia, particularly within the framework of civil procedure, is that public law interests are of decisive importance, since the dispute between the parties is examined by reviewing the civil case on its merits in the first two instances.[53]

---

[52]Regulations of Cabinet of Ministers No. 412 "Terms of the district (city) courts, regional courts and the judicial activity areas", LV, 2015, No 147 (5465), 29.07.2015.

[53]Judgement of the Constitutional Court in case No. 2003-04-01, on 27 June 2003, para 2.1. the concluding part. http://www.satv.tiesa.gov.lv/wp-content/uploads/2003/02/2003-04-01_Spriedums_ENG-1.pdf; Judgement of the Constitutional Court in case No. 2007-22-01, on 2 June 2008, para 18.2. http://www.satv.tiesa.gov.lv/wp-content/uploads/2007/10/2007-22-01_Spriedums_ENG.pdf.

The Land Registry Office

Land Registry Offices have been incorporated into district courts of general jurisdiction since 2012. Judges of Land Registry Offices oversee Land Registers and examine applications for undisputed compulsory execution, the procedure for warning of undisputed compulsory execution of obligations and the confirmation of statements of auction (excepting approval of the statement of auction in cases regarding insolvency proceedings).

Administrative Courts

Administrative courts are specialised courts which constitute a part of the judiciary. Administrative courts have exclusive jurisdiction to review administrative acts, actions and omissions. The administrative courts began their work concurrent with the Administrative Procedure Law coming into force on 1 February 2004. Until this reform, administrative cases were adjudicated by courts of general jurisdiction. There are three levels of Administrative courts—The Administrative district court, with 5 court houses- in Rēzekne, Liepāja, Valmiera, Jelagava and Rīga, the Administrative regional court in Rīga, which acts as a court of appeal, and the Department of Administrative Cases in the Supreme Court, which acts as court of cassation.

The Constitutional Court

The Constitutional Court (Satversmes tiesa) is an independent judicial authority.

Notarial Proceedings

To prevent an overload of civil cases in the courts, parliament has expanded the functions of notaries. Therefore, certain categories of cases are now diverted from the courts to notaries in matters where there is no dispute between parties. Since 1 January 2003, inheritance matters have been conducted by notaries and since 1 January 2011, divorce matters have also been conducted by notaries. In accordance with the Notariate Law, a sworn notary has jurisdiction to: make notarial deeds; make certifications; accept money, securities and documents for bailment; accept subject matter of an obligation for bailment; conduct inheritance matters; draw up property division drafts in cases provided for by law; conduct divorce matters; perform other activities provided for by laws.[54] This list is not exhaustive, but it is limited by legal norms. The status of notaries in the Latvian legal system has been evaluated by ECJ, which supported the opinion of the Commission that the activities carried out by notaries in the Latvian legal order have no connection with the exercise of official authority within the meaning of the first paragraph of Article 51, TFEU (the Treaty on the Functioning of the European Union).[55]

[54]Notariate Law. http://vvc.gov.lv/export/sites/default/docs/LRTA/Likumi/Notariate_Law.doc.

[55]Judgment of the European Court of Justice in case No. C-151/14, on 10 September 2015, European Commission V Republic of Latvia. http://eur-lex.europa.eu/legal-content/EN/TXT/PDF/?uri=CELEX:62014CJ0151&from=EN.

4.2.2 The Office of a Judge and Court Hearings

Requirements for Applying to the Office of a Judge

Judge is the people's servant, who implements a justice in the name of public.[56] In selecting a candidate for the office of judge, only Latvian citizens, who are highly qualified and fair lawyers, may serve as judges. The selection of candidates for the office of judge shall take place in open competition. Pursuant to the recommendation of the Minister for Justice and the Chief Justice of the Supreme Court, the Board of Justice approves the competition by-law.

A candidate for the office of judge may not be a person: (1) who has been previously convicted of committing a criminal offence (irrespective of whether the conviction has been extinguished or set aside); (2) who has previously committed a criminal offence, but has been released from serving the sentence in connection with the expiration of a limitation period, amnesty, or clemency; (3) who has been subjected to criminal liability, although the criminal matter has been terminated based on non-rehabilitativeness; (4) against whom a criminal prosecution has been commenced; (5) who are or have been employed in staff positions or as super numeraries of the State Security Committee of the USSR or the Latvian S.S.R., the Ministry of Defence of the USSR, or the state security service, army intelligence service or counter-intelligence service of a foreign country, or as an agent, resident or safe house keeper of the aforementioned institutions; (6) who are or have been participants (members) of organisations which are prohibited by the laws of the Republic of Latvia, decisions of the Supreme Council, or adjudications of a court, after the prohibition of such organisations; (7) who have been removed from the office of judge, sworn bailiff, assistant of sworn bailiff, sworn notary, assistant of a sworn notary, excluded from the number of sworn advocates or assistants of sworn advocates or dismissed from the position of prosecutor based on a decision in a disciplinary matter, and 5 years have not passed from the coming into force of the decision taken in the disciplinary matter.

For the office of district (city) court judge, a person may be appointed who: (1) is a Latvian citizen; (2) is fluent in the official language at the highest level; (3) has attained at least 30 years of age; (4) has acquired a higher vocational or academic education (except the first level vocational education) and a lawyer qualification, as well as a Master's or Doctoral degree; (5) has at least 5 years length of service in a legal specialty after acquiring a lawyer qualification or has been working in the position of assistant to a Chief Judge or assistant to a judge for at least 5 years; (6) has passed the qualification examinations.

In the law On Judicial Power, higher standards are set for applying to the office of judge of the Regional Court or the Supreme Court. A minimum age requirement—at least 40 years—must be reached for a person to be considered for the office of judge of the Supreme Court or Constitutional Court. The maximum age for holding the office of judge is 70 years. In Latvia, it is prohibited for a judge to

[56]Osipova (2016), pp. 12–15.

become a member of a political party, which was formulated for the first time by the plenary session of the Supreme Court on 14 February 1990, and later also recognised by the Constitutional Court of Latvia on 23 May 2013.[57]

Hearings of Cases in Courts

Regardless of the type of case before a court of first instance, proceedings are heard by a single judge or a panel of three judges. In the court of appeal instance, proceedings are only heard by a panel of three judges. In the court of cassation, there is variation between Departments. In the Department of Criminal Cases of the Supreme Court, proceedings are always heard by a panel of three judges. In the Department of Civil Cases and Department of Administrative Cases, proceedings are heard mainly by a panel of three judges, but the case may also be referred to an expanded panel. In the Department of Administrative Cases, this means that all judges of the Department hear the case in joint meeting. In the Department of Civil Cases, there are more options—the case can be referred to an expanded panel consisting of an odd number of judges from 7 to 17.

The normal procedure for hearing civil and criminal cases in the first and appeal instance is an oral hearing, but in administrative cases—the procedure calls for written preparation of the case in conjunction with an oral hearing by the parties' request. However, the situation has been changing over the last several years, and written proceedings are becoming more common in civil cases as well (ancillary complaints, small claim procedure, etc.). In the Supreme Court as the cassation instance, the normal procedure for hearings in all Departments is written preparation of the case, and oral hearings are practiced only if deemed necessary by the panel.

4.2.3 Administration of Courts and Self-governance

Administration of Courts

The functioning of the judiciary and the administration of justice in Latvia are strictly separated. Adjudication of cases, of course, is a part of the judiciary, but for the functioning of the judiciary there are several other issues which are within the responsibility of the executive power, e.g. staff issues, court equipment and others.[58] In the judiciary system of Latvia, there are two institutions whose activities are associated with the implementation of judicial power—the Ministry of Justice and The Court Administration. The Ministry of Justice is the leading State administrative institution in the administration of courts. The Court Administration is a direct administrative institution, subordinate to the Minister of Justice, which

[57]Judgement of the Constitutional Court in Case No 2012-16-01, on 10 May 2013. http://www.satv.tiesa.gov.lv/wp-content/uploads/2012/07/2012-16-01_Spriedums_ENG.pdf.

[58]Levits (2014), pp. 21–24.

organises and ensures the administrative work of district (city) courts, regional courts and Land Registry Offices.

Since 2010, a Judicial Council has been established in Latvia with a view to balancing executive, judicial and legislative power by its investment with a significant role in matters concerning the judicial system. Such intersection of powers is considered to be more useful than undesirable.[59] The Judicial Council is a collegial body involved in the policymaking and strategy development of the judicial system, as well as improving the operation of the judicial system.[60] The Judicial Council is composed of fifteen members who are elected for a term of 4 years.

Self-Governance of Courts

The evaluation of the professional misconduct of judges is regulated by the Judicial Disciplinary Liability Law.[61] A disciplinary matter can be initiated by the Chief Justice of the Supreme Court, the Minister of Justice, the Chief Judges of regional courts, the Heads of Land Registry Offices and the Commission of Judicial Ethics based on and defined in the law. There is a two-level revision system for disciplinary matters that is formed of the Judicial Disciplinary Committee and the Disciplinary Court.

The Judicial Disciplinary Committee is a judicial self-governance body which reviews disciplinary and administrative offences committed by judges of district (city) courts, Land Registry Offices, regional courts, and the Supreme Court. The Judicial Disciplinary Committee consists exclusively of elected judges from all levels of courts. The members of the Committee are elected by the Judicial Conference by secret ballot for a 4-year term. The Judicial Disciplinary Committee, after examination of the case, may dismiss the matter, impose a disciplinary sanction (an annotation, a reprimand or a salary reduction) or recommend the removal of the judge. The sanction may be imposed on a judge not later than 3 months after the day of detection of the disciplinary or administrative offence, but not later than 2 years after the day the disciplinary or administrative offence was committed.

The Disciplinary Court is the appellate instance for the decisions of the Judicial Disciplinary Committee. The decisions of the Judicial Disciplinary Committee can be appealed by the judge who has been subjected to disciplinary liability. The Disciplinary Court is composed of six judges of the Departments of the Supreme Court: two judges from each Department.

The Commission on Judicial Ethics is a collegial, judicial self-governance body which issues opinions in instances of breaches of ethical norms, and interpreting and updating judicial ethical norms. The Commission on Judicial Ethics is composed of 10 members who are elected by the Judicial Conference by secret ballot.

---

[59] Balodis (2010).

[60] Krūmiņa (2013), p. 25.

[61] Judicial Disciplinary Liability Law. http://www.vvc.gov.lv/export/sites/default/docs/LRTA/Likumi/Judicial_Disciplinary_Liability.pdf.

The members are elected for a term of 4 years. Latvian Judicial Code of Ethics is adopted by Latvian Republic Judicial Conference on 20 April 1995 and since then has not been amended.[62]

The Judicial Qualification Board is a self-governing judicial institution elected by the Conference of Judges. The Judicial Qualification Board is composed of six judges and assesses the professional activity of judges.

4.2.4 Persons Belonging to the Court System

The Law on Judicial Power regulates the status of persons belonging to the court system—prosecutors, sworn advocates, sworn notaries and sworn bailiffs.

Prosecutors are officials belonging to the court system who participate in the adjudication of matters in a court and perform other duties in accordance with the law.[63] The Office of the Prosecutor shall supervise the work of investigative institutions and the investigatory operations of other institutions; organise, manage, and conduct pre-trial investigations; initiate and conduct criminal prosecution; maintain charges of the State; supervise the execution of sentences; protect the rights and lawful interests of persons and the State in accordance with the procedures prescribed by law; submit a complaint or a submission to a court in cases provided for by law; and take part in the adjudication of matters by a court in the cases provided for by law.

Sworn advocates are persons belonging to the court system who provide legal assistance and perform other duties in accordance with the law.[64] Sworn advocates are assigned to regional courts. They participate in the adjudication of matters as counsel or as a representative. Only members of the Sworn Advocates Collegium of the Republic of Latvia have the rights of a sworn advocate. The laws on civil procedure, criminal procedure and administrative procedure determine the rights and duties of a sworn advocate in a court. An advocate shall be an independent and professional lawyer who provides legal assistance in defending and representing the lawful interests of persons in court proceedings and pre-trial investigations, providing legal consultations, preparing legal documents and performing other legal activities.

Sworn notaries and sworn bailiffs are persons belonging to the court system and they are assigned to regional courts. Sworn notaries perform their duties as specified by law. A sworn notary has jurisdiction to make notarial deeds; make certifications; accept money, securities and documents for bailment; accept subject matter of an

[62]Kalniņš et al. (2008), http://providus.lv/article_files/1903/original/Zinojums_FINAL.pdf?1339440792.

[63]Office of the Prosecutor Law. http://www.vvc.gov.lv/export/sites/default/docs/LRTA/Likumi/Office_of_the_Prosecutor.doc.

[64]Advocacy Law of the Republic of Latvia. http://www.vvc.gov.lv/export/sites/default/docs/LRTA/Likumi/Advocacy_Law_of_the_Republic_of_Latvia.doc.

obligation for bailment; conduct inheritance matters; draw up property division drafts in cases provided for by law; conduct divorce matters; perform other activities provided for by laws.[65] The duties of sworn notaries have significantly increased during the last decade.[66] Sworn bailiffs perform the execution of adjudications of the court and other institutions, as well as other activities prescribed by law.[67] In respect of the work of their office, sworn notaries and sworn bailiffs are equivalent to State officials.

4.2.5 The Management of the Judiciary for Reduction of the Workload of Courts

The global financial crisis in 2008 had a remarkable impact on the judiciary of Latvia and led to a significant increase (by a factor of four) of the applications received by the courts and a backlog of pending civil cases. Various activities coordinated by the Judicial Council were expanded with the main goal of improving court management. As the result of recent reforms, 2012 was the first year since the crisis when the clearance rate (the ratio of the number of resolved cases over the number of incoming cases) showed that the incoming caseload is reducing. This positive trend can still be observed because of effective legislative solutions, the adoption of new tools and the activities of the courts.

Amendments to the Civil Procedure Rules

Since 1 January 2013, amendments to the CPL have provided such changes as restrictions in the presentation of new evidence at the court of appeal that the domicile of a natural person is linked to declared place of residence and that legal norms grant a wider basis for giving of default judgements. Since 22 May 2013, amendments to the CPL have introduced provisions on "particular civil proceeding" in matters concerning invalidation of the decisions of shareholders' meetings. The aim of the procedure is to re-establish an inner legal balance in case of internal disputes within the company. All such matters are adjudicated in one specialised court—the Jelgava court. Since 4 January 2014, amendments to the CPL provide for case file redistribution—introducing the possibility to redistribute case files (i.e. to transfer case files to another court) if the case has not been heard on the merits and the transfer of the case to another court can achieve a faster trial.

[65]Notariate Law. http://vvc.gov.lv/export/sites/default/docs/LRTA/Likumi/Notariate_Law.doc.

[66]Litvins (2016).

[67]Law on Bailiffs. http://www.vvc.gov.lv/export/sites/default/docs/LRTA/Likumi/Law_On_Bailiffs.doc.

Professional Evaluation of Judges

Amendments to the Law on Judicial Power establishing the principles and rules for the professional evaluation of judges came into force on September 1, 2013. The first evaluation process of all judges took place from 1 January 2013 to 1 January 2016. Evaluation of the professional work of a judge takes place every 5 years, in addition to extraordinary evaluation on special occasions (deciding on judges' transfer or substitution). The objective criteria for evaluating the professional work of a judge include, for example: the structure of adjudications; legal argumentation; application of material and procedural rules; conducting of hearings; organisation of case handling; participation in training activities and teaching and research; statistical data; etc. The professional evaluation process of judges is overseen by the Judicial Qualification Board (a self-governing judicial institution elected by the Conference of Judges).

Modernisation of the Judiciary (IT Tools)

Beginning in 2009, a project involving cooperation between the Republic of Latvia and Switzerland, "Modernization of the Judiciary in Latvia," was undertaken with the aim of improving the management and efficiency of the judiciary in Latvia. As part of the project, courts were equipped with videoconference systems. Courts are also obligated to make sound recordings of court hearings in accordance with the specifications set by procedural rules. Delivery and installation of videoconferencing and sound recording equipment was completed on 30 June 2012. During the project, other IT tools were developed such as: the ability to follow a case (trial data) via the Internet and view the case file electronically; accessible online electronic document templates; access to the lawyer's calendar. These tools help to reduce the number of suspensions of cases and to provide a faster trial process, including smoother cross-border processes. Since 1 September 2013, all court decisions that come into force are automatically published in anonymised form in a freely accessible database at https://manas.tiesas.lv/. Judgments on the internet are a new tool for the public power not to exclude, but to close society with the judiciary to promote dialogue and mutual trust.[68]

Other Legal Steps

Since 1 November 2013, amendments in the Notariate Law[69] have introduced a determination of the executive document force for contracts drafted in a certain form of notarial deed. Directly enforceable contracts drafted in the form of notarial deed include term contracts on cash payment or return of document or movable property, term real estate rental or lending contracts and arrangements for one-off or periodic sustenance payments.

---

[68]Kucina (2014).

[69]Notariate Law. http://vvc.gov.lv/export/sites/default/docs/LRTA/Likumi/Notariate_Law.doc.

4.2.6 Ongoing Judicial Reforms

In Latvia, gradual court reforms are being carried out in stages. The main activities are focused on implementation of the so-called "clear" three-level court system, strengthening the efficiency of justice and caseload reduction.

Organisational Improvements of the Court System in Latvia

Amendments to the Law on Judicial Power (September 1, 2013) come into force on 1 January 2017. These introduce the so-called "clear" three-level court system in Latvia. The amendments are aimed at creating a simple and transparent judicial structure, at preventing fragmentation of competences and using the available judicial resources as rationally, effectively and economically as possible.

Revision of Court Disposition, or So-called Revision of the Judicial Map

Review of the court disposition model, in view of population distribution and hubs of economic activity, was begun in 2014. Respective amendments to the Law on Judicial Power and CPL were adopted by parliament on 31 October 2014. The amendments came into force on 1 March 2015. The aim is to create greater courts—in particular, a mechanism to equalise court workload and to strengthen the principle of random attribution of cases and judge specialisation. The main gains of this reform are expected to be: district (city) court courthouses, maintaining judge and courthouse specialisations and ability to provide expertise, securing the principle of random attribution of cases and high quality of decisions; rotation of cases (judges) within courthouses; opportunity to use resources more effectively (e.g., written translation or archiving jobs to be allocated to courthouses that have less workload); review of court composition according to the number of cases.

4.2.7 Alternative Dispute Resolution Methods

During the last decade in Latvia, many legislative solutions have been adopted for improving dispute resolution. The most significant legislative activities have been in the sphere of mediation and arbitration. The Mediation Law was based on the idea of strengthening mediation as a state-recognised and recommend method of dispute resolution, and the Arbitration Law—on restoring the quality of operation and public confidence in courts of arbitration.

Mediation

Mediation is one of the alternative dispute resolution methods which can substitute litigation and conciliation.[70] During the last years in Latvia mediation was becoming more popular, despite the fact that the existing legislation did not regulate

[70]Pētersone (2013), p. 327.

mediation.[71] The Mediation Law[72] came into force on 18 June 2014. The law primarily governs dispute resolution through mediation in civil matters; however, it also addresses dispute resolution in other sectors of law, save to the extent in which the special legislation provides otherwise. The purpose of this law is to facilitate and promote the use of mediation, recognising its social role, to establish common basic principles (the standard procedure) of the mediation process, to provide a uniform interpretation of concepts related to the mediation process, as well as to contribute to the quality of the mediation process. In Latvia operates mediators and certified mediators, which can be recommended by court and chosen by parties from the certified mediators list.[73]

The Mediation Law, and its related amendments in the CPL, determines an obligation for a judge to suggest the parties use mediation to resolve a dispute: (1) after the initiation of proceedings,—by sending to the defendant the submitted statement of claim and notifying the plaintiff on sending of the statement of claim to the defendant, requesting to notify the court within the time limit provided for explanation, whether the person agrees to use mediation; (2) when preparing the matter for adjudication and in the preparatory sitting; (3) in the course of adjudication of the matter, until adjudication of the matter on its merits is completed.

In cases where the parties agree to mediation during adjudication of the matter, the CPL provides for the court an obligation to suspend adjudication of the matter.

When coming to an agreement resulting from court-suggested mediation, the parties may enter into a settlement, or the party may withdraw the claim, or admit the claim. The CPL provides that the State fee in the amount of 50% shall be repaid, if the legal basis for termination of the court proceedings is withdrawal of the claim brought by an agreement reached through mediation.

Arbitration

In Latvia there is widespread opinion that arbitration can settle disputes more quickly and also cheaper.[74] The Arbitration Law,[75] and related amendments to the CPL, has been in force since 1 January 2015. The main purpose of the Arbitration Law is to restore public confidence in the institution of courts of arbitration and to ensure the legitimacy of the activities of courts of arbitration; therewith, more stringent requirements are laid down for the founder of a permanent court of arbitration, by providing that a permanent court of arbitration may be established by an association, which is statutes have referred to the goal—operation of the court of arbitration, thus avoiding from the event when a permanent court of arbitration is established for the sake of derivation of profit. At the same time, a

[71]Rone (2008).

[72]Mediation Law. http://vvc.gov.lv/export/sites/default/docs/LRTA/Likumi/Mediation_Law.doc.

[73]Pētersone (2012).

[74]Lapsa (2014).

[75]The Arbitration Law. http://vvc.gov.lv/export/sites/default/docs/LRTA/Likumi/Arbitration_Law.pdf.

regulation has been kept, which also allows for the creation of a court of arbitration for resolution of a specific dispute—*ad hoc* arbitration. However an application for the issue of a writ of execution can be submitted only for a permanent court of arbitration judgments, but not *ad hoc* arbitration judgements. The only exception is when *ad hoc* arbitration has international elements.[76]

4.3 The Impact of the EU and International Law

Arnis Buka
Faculty of Law, University of Latvia, Raina blvd. 19, Riga LV-1586, Latvia
e-mail: arnis.buka@lu.lv

4.3.1 Overview of the Most Important Statutory Provisions

The Latvian Constitution is quite ambiguous on the status of international law and its correlation with domestic legislation. The main provision in the Latvian Constitution on international law is the first part of Art. 68, which briefly indicates that "international agreements require the approval of the Saeima (Parliament)".[77] Complementing this first part of Art. 68, there are several statutory instruments that stipulate various details with regard to international agreements. Most notable of these is the separate law "On International Treaties of the Republic of Latvia", which was already adopted in 1994, and mostly covers procedural aspects and the division of responsibilities of various state institutions.

The brevity of the Constitution on the matter of international law initially led academics to be uncertain as to whether Latvia is a monist or dualist country.[78] However, taking into account the above-mentioned provisions, modern academics have taken the uniform view that the Latvian legal system generally reflects a monist approach.[79]

The matter of the supremacy of international law is slightly more perplexing. Art. 13 of the law "On International Treaties of the Republic of Latvia" determines that "if international agreement affirmed by the Saeima provides for other provisions than those in the Republic of Latvia legislative acts, provisions of the international agreement shall be applied."[80] Additionally, Art. 16 of the

[76]Kačevska (2014).

[77]Constitution of the Republic of Latvia. http://www.vvc.gov.lv/export/sites/default/docs/LRTA/Likumi/Constitution.doc.

[78]Scheinin (1996), p. 14.

[79]See, e.g., Van Elsuwege (2008), pp. 157–161.

[80]On International Treaties of the Republic of Latvia. http://vvc.gov.lv/export/sites/default/docs/LRTA/Likumi/On_International_Treaties_of_the_Republic_of_Latvia.doc.

Constitutional Court Law specifies the jurisdiction of the Constitutional Court of Latvia to adjudicate cases on "the conformity of Latvian national legal norms with those international agreements entered into by Latvia that are not in conflict with the Constitution".[81] Although the above-mentioned provisions clearly point to the supremacy of international law over domestic law in general, some uncertainty remains in the nuances, especially in relation to those international agreements that have not been ratified by the Saeima. The approach of the Constitutional Court has been to make reference to Art. 15 of the Administrative Procedure Law, which lists the hierarchy of external normative acts,[82] and classify international agreements accordingly—those approved by the Saeima have higher legal force than Latvian statutes adopted by the Saeima, and those approved only by the government have higher force than other acts of the government but lower force than Latvian statutes adopted by the Saeima.[83] Such an approach is mistrusted by some Latvian academics, as it not only deviates from the underlying monism doctrine, but also fails to provide a clear status for other sources of international public law, especially international customary law.[84]

In addition to the general provision in part one of Art. 68 of the Latvian Constitution regarding international law, which has been a part of the Constitution from the very beginning, Latvia's accession to the European Union (EU) triggered discussions on whether the Latvian Constitution should be amended because of Latvia's EU membership. At the time, abstaining from constitutional amendments was considered because of the fact that brevity and a laconic style are essential features of the Latvian Constitution.[85]

Nevertheless, the decision to enact constitutional amendments reflecting EU accession was made—for legal reasons (to avoid overreliance on broad interpretation) as well as social reasons (recognising the importance of EU accession for Latvian society in general).[86] At the same time, the amendments were made in conformity with the preexisting style of the Latvian Constitution, and focused

[81]Constitutional Court Law. http://www.vvc.gov.lv/export/sites/default/docs/LRTA/Likumi/Constitutional_Court_Law.doc.

[82]Administrative Procedure Law. http://www.vvc.gov.lv/export/sites/default/docs/LRTA/Likumi/Administrative_Procedure_Law.doc.

[83]Judgment of the Constitutional Court in case No. 2004-01-06 on 7 July 2004, para 6. http://www.satv.tiesa.gov.lv/wp-content/uploads/2004/01/2004-01-06_Spriedums_ENG.pdf.

[84]Bērziņa-Andersone et al. (2009), p. 36.

[85]Kādēļ Latvijas konstitūcijā nepieciešami labojumi? Darba grupas Satversmes grozījumu izstrādāšanai piedāvātā projekta teorētiskais pamatojums (Why should the Latvian Constitution be amended? Theoretical Foundation of the Amendments to Satversme). (2001) Jurista Vārds. 14 (207), p. 3. This publication reflects the theoretical foundation of the amendments to the Latvian Constitution proposed by the working group of the Ministry of Justice that prepared those amendments.

[86]Kādēļ Latvijas konstitūcijā nepieciešami labojumi? Darba grupas Satversmes grozījumu izstrādāšanai piedāvātā projekta teorētiskais pamatojums (Why should the Latvian Constitution be amended? Theoretical Foundation of the Amendments to Satversme). (2001) Jurista Vārds. 14 (207), p. 3.

mostly on procedural aspects. Most importantly, Art. 68 of the Latvian Constitution was supplemented by adding the possibility "to delegate a part of its State institution competencies to international institutions". Also, the amendments made a distinction between two kinds of referendums in relation to the EU—the referendum on EU membership is obligatory, but a referendum on "substantial changes in the terms regarding the membership of Latvia in the EU" may happen only if half of the deputies in the Saeima initiate it.[87]

At the statutory level, accession to the EU also presented the Latvian legislator with the dilemma of how to ensure proper functioning of the main features of EU law, such as direct effect and preliminary rulings procedure, in Latvia. The first, simpler option would be to rely on the monism doctrine—in the context of Latvia's accession to the EU, this would mean that in principle there is no need for amendments to Latvian procedural laws, because from the moment of ratification of the Accession Treaty, all *acquis communautaire* becomes part of the Latvian legal order. Accordingly, any Latvian court should be able to apply EU law correctly without adding any norms to the texts of national laws.[88] Such an approach was used, for example, in the Netherlands in the context of administrative courts.[89]

The second option would be to add general provisions regarding the EU law to national legislation. Such an approach would recognise the impact of EU law, and would simultaneously provide some procedural guidelines within the texts of Latvian statutes. Thus, the legal basis for the use of the features of EU law in Latvian courts would still be EU law itself, while at the same time the national law would contain references to the essential legal instruments of EU law. This approach involves a certain degree of double coverage of legal issues at the level of EU law and the national law. However, it also encourages Latvian judges, who are accustomed to working almost exclusively with national law, to see clearly the main changes that EU law brings to the national law system, and to see the context of the national procedural law within which EU law should be applied.[90]

Among the different Member States, the second option is implemented mostly by providing space for at least a few general provisions in national procedural laws concerning the duties of national courts in the EU law context.[91] The Latvian legislator also opted in favor of this approach, and all three major Latvian procedural laws were amended by adding a general reference to the relevance of EU law and the case-law of the Court Of Justice of the EU in national court proceedings, and pointing out the possibility of making a reference for the preliminary rulings.

[87]Constitution of the Republic of Latvia, Art. 68. http://www.vvc.gov.lv/export/sites/default/docs/LRTA/Likumi/Constitution.doc.

[88]Buka (2014), p. 20.

[89]See Prechal and Widdershoven (2008), pp. 81–98.

[90]Buka (2014), p. 21.

[91]See Bobek (2008), pp. 1611–1643.

All those norms in Latvia were constructed as blanket norms with a direct reference to the EU law itself.[92]

4.3.2 Rulings of the Constitutional Court of Latvia

The two decades of jurisprudence of the Constitutional Court of Latvia contains several major contributions on international law and EU law issues. In all cases, the Constitutional Court firmly upheld its right to adjudicate on the compliance of Latvian laws with the international obligations of the Republic of Latvia.[93]

International law has influenced the jurisprudence of the Constitutional Court as a tool for interpretation as well, mostly in the field of human rights. In several judgments, the Constitutional Court has concluded that "the aim of the legislator has not been to contradistinguish the norms of fundamental rights, included in the Latvian Constitution, with the international human rights norms"[94] and that "the obligation to make use of international norms for interpretation of the protection of fundamental rights enshrined in the Latvian Constitution follows from Art. 89 of the Latvian Constitution, which determines that the State shall recognise and protect fundamental human rights in accordance with this Constitution, laws and international agreements binding on Latvia."[95]

As to their competence to evaluate the conformity of Latvian law with EU law requirements, the Constitutional Court is somewhat evasive, and there are no judgments that would directly declare the invalidity of Latvian law only because it is not compatible with the EU law. At the same time, there are some judgments where the Constitutional Court gave its opinion on the constitutionality of the EU law with the Latvian legal order. At least two of these are worth mentioning.

Firstly, the scope of the EU law supremacy doctrine was limited by the Latvian Constitutional Court. Although generally confirming that "Latvian law must be interpreted so as to avoid any conflicts with the obligations of Latvia towards the EU",[96] the Constitutional Court added a limitation to this obligation: "unless the fundamental principles incorporated in the Constitution of Latvia are affected"[97].

Secondly, the ratification of the Lisbon Treaty was challenged before the Constitutional Court of Latvia. The challenge was based on the alleged infringement of the applicant's right to participate in the work of the State and of local

[92]See, e.g., Art. 15 of the Latvian Administrative procedure law.

[93]See, e.g., judgment of the Constitutional Court in case No. 2004-01-06 on 7 July 2004. http://www.satv.tiesa.gov.lv/wp-content/uploads/2004/01/2004-01-06_Spriedums_ENG.pdf.

[94]Judgment of the Constitutional Court in case No. 2006-03-0106 on 23 November 2006, para 8.2. http://www.satv.tiesa.gov.lv/wp-content/uploads/2006/03/2006-03-0106_Spriedums_ENG.pdf.

[95]Ibid.

[96]Judgment of the Constitutional Court in case No. 2007-11-03 on 17 January 2008, para 25. http://www.satv.tiesa.gov.lv/wp-content/uploads/2007/05/2007-11-03_Spriedums_ENG.pdf.

[97]Ibid.

government, according to the procedures provided by law, because the Lisbon Treaty could have been adopted and confirmed only by a national referendum. The Constitutional Court agreed to review the case on substance, pointing out that failure to initiate the referendum could be regarded as a violation of the rights of the people to participate in the decision-making process of the state. Nonetheless, the on substance the claim was rejected.[98]

Finally, the Constitutional Court of Latvia has so far made no reference to the Court of Justice of the EU. Nonetheless, in one of its judgments it affirmed its readiness to do so. Even more, the Constitutional Court is one of the rare constitutional courts which has expressly stated that they consider themselves to be a "court or tribunal of a Member State against whose decisions there is no judicial remedy under national law" within the meaning of Art. 267 (3) of the Treaty on the Functioning of the EU and, therefore, are subject to the obligation to make a reference to the Court of Justice of the EU.[99]

4.3.3 Preliminary Rulings Procedure

Although most Member States have chosen to adopt some national legal background on the preliminary rulings procedure, the particularities of those provisions differ substantially from country to country. The range of such approaches includes, for example, reliance on legal precedents in the United Kingdom,[100] or the adoption of a separate and extensive Act on Reference for a Preliminary Ruling, in Sweden.[101] In Latvia, all three major Latvian procedural laws were amended with almost identical provisions which, firstly, indicated the possibility to make reference to the Court of Justice of the EU for a preliminary ruling and, secondly, mentioned such a reference as one of the grounds on which the adjudication of the case might be paused.[102]

An interesting feature regarding preliminary rulings procedure is contained in Art. 39 (3) of the Latvian Criminal Procedure Law. This provision allows the Prosecutor General, on the request of the prosecutors, to make a reference to the Court of Justice of the EU for the preliminary ruling.[103] However, in view of previous case law of the Court of Justice of the EU in similar cases, where that

[98]Judgment of the Constitutional Court in case No. 2008-35-01 on 7 April 2008. http://www.satv.tiesa.gov.lv/wp-content/uploads/2008/09/2008-35-01_Spriedums_ENG.pdf.

[99]Judgment of the Constitutional Court in case No. 2008-47-01 on 28 May 2009, para 15.2. http://www.satv.tiesa.gov.lv/wp-content/uploads/2008/11/2008-47-01_Spriedums_ENG.pdf.

[100]See Lenz and Grill (1995), pp. 844–865.

[101]Groussot et al. (2010), p. 36.

[102]See Arts. 5.1 and 214 of the Civil Procedure Law (Civilprocesa likums); Arts. 104.1 and 273 of the Administrative Procedure Law; Art. 478 of the Criminal Procedure Law. http://www.vvc.gov.lv/advantagecms/LV/tulkojumi/meklet_dokumentus.html.

[103]Criminal Procedure Law. http://www.vvc.gov.lv/export/sites/default/docs/LRTA/Likumi/Criminal_Procedure_Law.doc.

Court rejected requests for preliminary rulings from prosecutors,[104] Art. 39 (3) of the Latvian Criminal Procedure Law may be in conflict with Art. 267 of the Treaty on the Functioning of the EU. Yet, so far Latvian prosecutors have not used this option, and it is therefore not clear whether the Court of Justice of the EU would accept such a reference for the preliminary ruling.

As regards the particularities of the references, an overview of the case law in the post-2004 new Member States in relation to the preliminary rulings procedure reveals that, in the initial years after enlargement, the procedure has been used in relatively few cases—from 2004 to 2007, there were only 35 requests for preliminary rulings in total from the ten new Member States.[105] The Latvian courts were no exception in this regard, and requested their first preliminary ruling almost 4 years after Latvia's accession to the EU, at the end of 2007.[106] A large role in this initial lack of activity from national courts was played by the restrictive approach of the Court of Justice of the EU, which has changed its approach on the admissibility of requests for preliminary rulings in cases with factual circumstances before the state's accession to the EU—from a quite liberal approach during previous enlargements,[107] to a very restrictive one.[108]

However, after the initial period of inaction, Latvian courts have used preliminary rulings procedure on a regular basis. In total, Latvian courts by the end of the year 2014 had made 37 requests for preliminary rulings (2008 – 3, 2009 – 4, 2010 – 3, 2011 – 10, 2012 – 5, 2013 – 5 and 2014 – 7 requests),[109] surpassing the two other Baltic states in this regard. Mainly, these references were made by administrative courts (31 references out of a total 37) and in tax cases (16 of the 37 cases involved the State Revenue Service).

The vast majority of the requests for preliminary rulings from Latvian courts come from courts of last instance—32 out of the total 37 requests (the Court of Justice of the EU report provides incorrect data in this regard, most likely because of counting Latvijas Augstākā tiesas Senāts (Senate of the Supreme Court of Latvia) as one of the lower courts).[110] Such statistics are quite contrary to the general tendency of the courts of lower instance to be open-minded to the

[104]Judgment of the Court of Justice of the EU in joined cases C-74/95 and C-129/95 Criminal proceedings against X, 1996, ECR, p. I-6609.

[105]See Bobek (2008), pp. 1612–1613.

[106]As the case was registered in the Court of Justice of the EU in early January 2008, for statistical purposes usually it is attributed to the year 2008—see Ņesterova (2012), p. 6.

[107]Judgments of the Court of Justice of the EU in case C-43/95 Delecta Aktiebolag and Ronny Forsberg, 1996, ECR, p. I-466 (in the context of the accession of Sweden) and in case C-122/96 Saldanha and MTS Securities Corporation, 1997, ECR, p. I-532 (in the context of the accession of Austria).

[108]Judgment of the Court of Justice of the EU in case C-302/04 Ynos kft v. Janos Varga, 2006, ECR, p. I–371.

[109]See Court of Justice of the EU. Annual report 2014 (2015), p. 116.

[110]Court of Justice of the EU. Annual report 2014 (2015), Luxembourg, p. 118.

procedure.[111] In some other post-2004 Member States, courts of lower instance were much more active than their Latvian counterparts—e.g., in Poland, from the first seven references, none originated from the courts of last instance,[112] or in Hungary, where almost 4 out of 5 requests come from lower courts.[113] The fact that during the first decade of EU membership, only seven requests for preliminary rulings were made by courts other than the courts of last instance in Latvia signifies that Latvian courts of lower instance are skeptical of the preliminary rulings procedure and do not see the benefit in its use. Additionally, the disproportion in the numbers of references here may be influenced by the fact that the Latvian Supreme Administrative Court was created as a new, separate court at roughly the same time as Latvia's accession to the EU, and from the very beginning was composed of open-minded judges with sufficient knowledge of EU law.

4.3.4 Decisions of the ECHR

Already at the cradle of Latvia's regained independence on 4 May 1990, the Highest Council (Augstākā Padome, predecessor of the current Latvian parliament, the Saeima) declared that the legislation in Latvia should be compatible with international human rights standards.[114] Since then, the Latvian government has made several important steps in that regard, such as the ratification of the European Convention for the Protection of Human Rights and Fundamental Freedoms in 1997,[115] and including a human rights catalogue in the Constitution in 1998.[116] The Convention, and its interpretation by the ECHR, has had a major impact on human rights culture in Latvia.

According to the statistical data provided by the ECHR, that court has issued 107 judgments against Latvia. In 89 of these, at least one violation has been found.[117] The same table shows that most of these cases have concerned Art. 5 of the Convention—the right to liberty and security. The ECHR has also received a high number of applications regarding the rights enshrined in Art. 6 of the

[111] Broberg and Fenger (2010), p. 45.

[112] Miqsik (2008), p. 120.

[113] On Hungarian experience see Osztovits and Gobos (2014), pp. 223–240.

[114] Deklarācija "Par Latvijas Republikas pievienošanos starptautisko tiesību dokumentiem cilvēktiesību jautājumos" (Declaration on Latvia's accession to the international human rights documents). Ziņotājs, 21, 24.05.1990. http://likumi.lv/doc.php?id=75668.

[115] Latvijas Republikas likums "Par 1950.gada 4.novembra Eiropas Cilvēka tiesību un pamatbrīvību aizsardzības konvenciju un tās 1., 2., 4., 7. un 11.protokolu". LV, 143/144 (858/859), 13.06.1997. http://likumi.lv/ta/id/43857-par-1950-gada-4-novembra-eiropas-cilveka-tiesibu-un-pamatbrivibu-aizsardzibas-konvenciju-un-tas-1-2-4-7-un-11-protokolu.

[116] Grozījumi Latvijas Republikas Satversmē (Amendments to the Constitution of the Republic of Latvia). LV, 308/312(1369/1373), 23.10.1998. https://www.vestnesis.lv/ta/id/50292-grozijumi-latvijas-republikas-satversme.

[117] ECHR. Statistics on violations (2016), p. 1.

Convention, namely, the right to a fair trial and length of the proceedings, and Art. 8, the right to respect for private and family law.[118] If the first two types of complaints, and attendant violations, are amongst the most common types of complaint the ECHR receives in general,[119] the violations regarding Art. 8 of the Convention make up only approximately 4–5% of the violations found by the court overall since its founding.[120] The reasons for this situation may include an increase in the level of awareness of human rights among the general public and in law enforcement institutions, and the constant improvement of the conditions of the places of detention and prisons, as well as flaws in the laws regulating special operational activities and criminal proceedings.

Although the annotations of the amendments of laws are often silent regarding the matter, there are several examples of Latvian laws being amended after or at least in connection with a judgment of the ECHR. The most recent amendments include stricter rules for carrying out operational activities,[121] after a series of decisions on admissibility[122] and judgments[123] regarding the issue. The case-law of the ECHR[124] has helped to improve the Criminal Procedure Law, especially its regulation on involuntary placement and mental health care.[125] After several recommendations from the European Committee for the Prevention of Torture and Inhuman or Degrading Treatment or Punishment,[126] and several judgments of the ECHR,[127] the Sentence Execution Code was amended in 2015 and finally provides for a cell size compatible with European human rights standards.[128]

---

[118]See judgments of the ECHR in case Meimanis v Latvia on 21 July 2015, Šantare and Labazņikovs v. Latvia on 31 March 2016, A, B and C v. Latvia on 31 March 2016.

[119]More than 41% of the violations found by the Court have concerned Art. 6 of the Convention, whether on account of the fairness (17.63%) or the length of the proceedings (22.13%). The second violation most frequently found by the Court has concerned the right to liberty and security (Art. 5)—The ECHR. Overview 1959–2015 (2016), p. 6.

[120]The ECHR. Overview 1959–2015 (2016), p. 7.

[121]Grozījumi Operatīvās darbības likumā (Amendments in the Operational Activities Law). LV, 57(5629), 22.03.2016. http://likumi.lv/ta/id/281095-grozijumi-operativas-darbibas-likuma.

[122]Judgment of the ECHR in Zikovs v. Latvia, Kibermanis v. Latvia.

[123]For example, judgment of the ECHR in case Meimanis v. Latvia.

[124]Judgments of the ECHR in cases Beiere v. Latvia, Raudevs v. Latvia.

[125]See amendments in the Criminal Procedure Law, Arts. 283 and 595 –Grozījumi Kriminālprocesa likumā. LV, 113(5173), 11.06.2014. Availble at: http://likumi.lv/ta/id/266815-grozijumi-kriminalprocesa-likuma.

[126]For example, Report to the Latvian Government on the visit to Latvia carried out by the European Committee for the Prevention of Torture and Inhuman or Degrading Treatment or Punishment (CPT) from 12 to 17 September 2013 (2014), p. 5. Available at: http://www.cpt.coe.int/documents/lva/2014-05-inf-eng.pdf.

[127]Bazjaks v Latvia, Kadikis v Latvia.

[128]See amended Art. 77—Grozījumi Sodu izpildes kodeksā (Amendments in the Sentence Execution Code). LV, 124(5442), 30.06.2015. Available at: http://likumi.lv/ta/id/274970-grozijumi-latvijas-sodu-izpildes-kodeksa.

The Latvian courts have also recognised the importance of the case-law of the ECHR. As has been previously mentioned, the Constitutional Court of Latvia has constantly emphasised that the analysis of the case-law of the ECHR is a mandatory element of the application of the European Convention on Human Rights, and can also be used when interpreting the respective norms of the Constitution. Currently, the Constitutional Court quotes the ECHR in almost every case dealing with fundamental rights issues.[129]

Encouraged by the example of the Constitutional Court, the Administrative courts and courts of general jurisdiction also tend to compare national human rights instruments with international law. Although there are no statistics on how often the courts refer to the case law of the ECHR, it is evident that Administrative courts do so more often than courts hearing civil and criminal cases. For example, the Administrative courts in their case-law had already solved the problem with the regulations of the Sentence Execution Code incompatible with human rights standards by interpreting the national law in the light of international human rights law—the case law of the ECHR and the recommendations of the European Committee for the Prevention of Torture.[130]

4.4 Perspectives

Daiga Rezevska
Faculty of Law, University of Latvia, Raina blvd. 19, Riga LV-1586, Latvia
e-mail: daiga.rezevska@lu.lv

4.4.1 Development of the European Union and the Core of the Constitution

Questions on the sovereignty of nation-states within the perspective of the further enlargement of the EU are, of course, inevitable in every legal arrangement of the EU Member States. This issue in Latvia was first addressed by the Constitutional Court of the Republic of Latvia (the Constitutional Court) in its 7 April 2009 judgment in the case *"On Compliance of the Law "On the Lisbon Agreement Amending the Treaty on European Union and the Treaty Establishing the*

[129]See, e.g., judgment of the Latvian Constitutional Court in case 2015-01-01, http://www.satv.tiesa.gov.lv/wp-content/uploads/2016/02/2015-01-01_Spriedums.pdf.

[130]Judgments of the Latvian Supreme Administrative Court in case SKA-0436-13. https://www.tiesas.lv/Media/Default/Page/AL_2901_raj_A-00923-13_43.pdf.

European Community" with Article 101 of the Satversme (Constitution) of the Republic of Latvia" (the Lisbon case).[131]

The Constitution of the Republic of Latvia (*Satversme*) states that: "*The sovereign power of the State of Latvia is vested in the people of Latvia*".[132] This Article names the two main entities of sovereign power: the state of Latvia and the people. The notion of state sovereignty is one of the basic concepts of the theory of the state, and the principle of popular sovereignty is one of the basic principles of the democratic state.[133]

The Constitutional Court has interpreted this article in the Lisbon case judgement, and has stated that the principle of popular sovereignty is formulated in this article. Nevertheless, the Constitution distributes the power between the body of Latvian citizens and the *Saeima*. It, however, grants the people of Latvia the exclusive right to deal with the fundamental norms of the Constitution, i.e., to annul the Constitution or to set up a new constitutional system. First, according to Article 78 of the Constitution, the body of Latvian citizens can adopt amendments to the Constitution; second, in accordance with Article 77 of the Constitution, only the body of citizens can modify Articles 1, 2, 3, 4, 6 and 77 of the Constitution. These articles are regarded as the most important articles of the Constitution, the modification of which could alter the democratic state structure and the order of the republic. For this reason, these articles of the Constitution are protected by the people—they can be changed only through a compulsory referendum where the people may express their will.[134] Thus, the *Saeima* cannot ignore the people's right to participate in the decision-making process, which follows from Article 2 of the Constitution.

At the same time, the Constitutional Court has indicated that the transfer of separate competencies to the EU is regarded not as the weakening of popular sovereignty, but, to the contrary—as the use of popular sovereignty to achieve the goals set by the EU agreements. However, with the development of EU integration, it should be noted that Article 2 of the Constitution does not allow for the unlimited transfer of competencies, in which case we would not be able to continue to speak about Latvia as a sovereign state.[135]

The notion of limits on the transfer of competencies was further developed by the Constitutional Law Commission (the Commission), which was established by the former State President, Valdis Zatlers. The main aim of the Commission was to advise the State President on various topical constitutional issues, touching on the issues of sovereignty and EU enlargement as well. During its existence, the

[131] Judgement of the Constitutional Court in case No 2008-35-01 on 7 April 2009. http://www.satv.tiesa.gov.lv/wp-content/uploads/2008/09/2008-35-01_Spriedums_ENG.pdf.

[132] Art. 2 of the Constitution of the Republic of Latvia 1922. http://www.saeima.lv/en/legislation/constitution.

[133] Dišlers (2004), p. 13.

[134] Dišlers (1930), p. 110.

[135] See also: Iļjanova (2011), pp. 367–429.

Commission delivered several significant opinions, and among them an opinion on the constitutional foundations of the State of Latvia and the inviolable core of the Constitution.[136]

The Commission found that the core of the Constitution is only partially covered by the text of the Constitution itself, while other significant parts of it can be found in unwritten form, such as in the general principles of law for example.[137] The Commission concluded that the inviolable core of the Constitution covers the Latvian national constitutional identity, that is, the identity of statehood and the identity of the state's political system. The constitutional core does not allow for its "infringement". This means that it is not possible in a lawful and legitimate manner or procedure to change and thus destroy the Latvian national constitutional identity chosen by the Latvian nation. Threats or attempts to destroy this identity are illegal.[138]

The Commission determined the inviolable elements of both the statehood's identity and the identity of the political system. The inviolable elements of the statehood's identity are as follows: first, the character of the State of Latvia as the nation state of the Latvian nation is its unalienable basis, purpose and meaning. It also means that any change of the political system that would reverse the principle of the nation state would not only be contrary to the identity of the political system, but also in contradiction to the statehood's identity of Latvia. Second, the territory and territorial unity defined in Article 3 of the Constitution falls entirely within the core of the Constitution and cannot be changed by the refusal of any substantial part of the territory. Third, the Latvian nation, which is the so-called carrier of the state of Latvia, is entirely included in the core of the Constitution. The Latvian nation forms the core of the concept of the people of Latvia. The self-determination of the Latvian nation is the constant objective and aim of the state of Latvia. From that follows the state's obligation, the enforcement of which is carried out within the principle of the nation state, to protect the continuity and identity of the people of Latvia. Fourth, regarding the sovereign power of the constitutional legislator (the *Saeima* and the citizens in general)—it is not permitted to use its power to change the adopted constitutional framework that the sovereign power belongs to the people of Latvia. It also includes a prohibition against withdrawal from Latvian national independence and sovereignty by joining another country, or building a new state together with other countries within the meaning of the international law.[139]

---

[136]On the Constitutional Foundations of the State of Latvia and the Inviolable Core of the Constitution. Opinion of the Constitutional Law Commission. 17 September 2012. http://www.president.lv/images/modules/items/PDF/17092012_Viedoklis_2.pdf.

[137]On the nature of the general principles of law and their application methodology see: Rezevska (2015).

[138]On the Constitutional Foundations of the State of Latvia and the Inviolable Core of the Constitution. Opinion of the Constitutional Law Commission. 17 September 2012. http://www.president.lv/images/modules/items/PDF/17092012_Viedoklis_2.pdf, para. 385, 388.

[139]Ibid., para. 390.

Furthermore, the core of the Constitution should be ensured by effective procedural remedies in the form of the competence of public institutions to assess and not permit any proposed new law or amendment which could lead to its elimination. The courts have an important role in the associated monitoring.[140]

4.4.2 The Role of the Judiciary in the Contemporary Legal Arrangement

Contemporary legal arrangements are becoming more and more complicated. This is connected not only with the increase in the volume of legislative texts, but also with the more and more sophisticated legal issues which arise in the modern world.

There are several reasons for the changes in the role of the judiciary. First, the increased role played by the law in modern society. More and more, the law extends into every aspect of the life of society. More and more people find themselves enmeshed in the law as the result of some act or because of their relationship to the modern bureaucratic state. And more and more, people are taking up the law and using it. Secondly, the complexity of the modern legal arrangement—the issues modern courts are being called upon to resolve. Among them, for example: (1) rights issues: the interface between the individual and the state—the limits of freedom of speech and freedom of religion, the right to liberty in the face of state detention or coercion, rights to equality, conflicts between individual rights themselves or between individual rights and the collective good; (2) issues arising out of the increasingly multicultural character of societies: how to balance the need to respect the rights of minorities with a collective conception of society; (3) issues arising out of the threat of terrorism; (4) issues relating to biotechnology, the information revolution and emergent quantum physics and nanotechnology.[141]

Traditional judicial qualities, such as impartiality, independence and integrity, must be maintained, indeed strengthened. But new practices must supplement the traditional judicial virtues, such as, the responsive court, the court of integrity, the diverse court, the accessible court, the court that communicates, the educated court and above all—the court with conscience and courage.[142] Especially important, in the current Latvian situation, for the successful development of the judiciary is to resolve the issues regarding communication with society, and to improve the selection process of candidates for judges' positions with an adequate level of knowledge, integrity and courage to face the above-mentioned challenges of the modern legal arrangement.

---

[140]Ibid., para. 392.

[141]Compare: McLachli (2006).

[142]McLachli (2006).

4.4.3 Latvian Language, Culture and Mass Media

The above-mentioned Opinion of the Constitutional Law Commission, "On the Constitutional Foundations of the State of Latvia and the Inviolable Core of the Constitution", served as the basis and was considered when the Preamble of the Constitution was drafted. Among other things, the Preamble states: "[..] Since ancient times, the identity of Latvia in the European cultural space has been shaped by Latvian and Liv traditions, Latvian folk wisdom, the Latvian language, universal human and Christian values. Loyalty to Latvia, the Latvian language as the only official language, freedom, equality, solidarity, justice, honesty, work ethic and family are the foundations of a cohesive society. [..]"[143]

Latvia as a state was created by the Latvian nation; its founding spirit and purpose was to create a national framework for the Latvian nation, which as a political-legal entity would be able to democratic self-determination and self-governing. This desire to establish and maintain its own nation state is one of the features of the state identity of Latvia that sets it apart from any other country in the world.[144]

To popularise and to protect the above-mentioned values, especially in a new democracy like Latvia, is primarily the duty of the public mass media. Lately, discussion on the quality of the content of the mass media, including the public mass media, has become very topical.[145] Former Prime Minister Laimdota Straujuma, reporting to the Parliament on national security, stated that "information gathered by the Latvian security services and strategic communications researchers indicates that the Latvian media environment for many years has been used to distribute biased information about Latvia which is created in Russia or initiated by Russia. This purposeful misinformation splits the society and cultivates doubts about the sovereignty of the state."[146] Furthermore, the information that flows from European Union countries is much more difficult to obtain than that which is being prepared by Russia.

This demonstrates that one of the future challenges of the legal arrangement in Latvia will be to further integrate the topics of Latvian culture and identity into the programs offered by the mass media. Moreover, this is still more significant considering that many of those who master the Russian language still choose to

---

[143]Law on the Amendment to the Constitution. 19 June 2014. http://www.saeima.lv/en/legislation/constitution.

[144]On the Constitutional Foundations of the State of Latvia and the Inviolable Core of the Constitution. Opinion of the Constitutional Law Commission. 17 September 2012. http://www.president.lv/images/modules/items/PDF/17092012_Viedoklis_2.pdf.

[145]See, for example: *TV kanālu proporcija – pilnīgi ačgārna. Saruna ar Satversmes tiesas tiesnesi Inetu Ziemeli* (The Proportion of the TV Channels – Absolutely Amiss. Interview with the Justice of the Constitutional Court Ineta Ziemele). Latvijas Avīze 2016. http://www.la.lv/tv-kanalu-proporcija-pilnigi-acgarna/.

[146]Ibid.

obtain their information from programmes provided by countries other than Latvia or the other EU countries.

In the specific conditions of Latvia, it is the duty of the electronic mass media, especially the public electronic mass media, to promote public awareness of Latvia as a nation state, to promote Latvian identity, the Latvian language, culture, art, traditions, promote democratic patriotism, social integration based on the Latvian language, to deepen the understanding of national values, the Latvian state and Latvian history. Thus, it is extremely important to significantly improve the quality and amount of Latvian language and to promote the Latvian environment in the information and cultural space of Latvia.[147]

4.4.4 Terrorism and Human Rights

There is no need to prove or convince anybody that terrorism has a direct impact on the enjoyment of human rights, and that states have a duty to take effective counter-terrorism measures. While the complexity and magnitude of the challenges facing states in their efforts to combat terrorism can be significant, international human rights law is flexible enough to address them effectively. So, on the one hand states have an obligation to ensure that all counter-terrorism measures comply with human rights standards, and on the other hand to ascertain the flexibility built into human rights law to deal with exceptional circumstances.[148]

The Security Council, at its meeting at the level of Ministers of Foreign Affairs on 20 January 2003, stated that "States must ensure that any measure taken to combat terrorism comply with all their obligations under international law, and should adopt such measures in accordance with international law, in particular international human rights, refugee, and humanitarian law."[149]

Effective counter-terrorism measures and the protection of human rights are complementary and mutually reinforcing objectives which must be pursued together as part of a state's duty to protect individuals within its jurisdiction. Most countries, when meeting their obligations to counter terrorism by rushing through legislative and practical measures, have created negative consequences for civil liberties and fundamental human rights.[150] The most relevant human rights

[147]Compare: On the Legal Framework of the Public Electronic Mass Media in a Democratic State. Opinion of the Constitutional Law Commission. 24 May 2010. http://www.president.lv/images/modules/items/Viedoklis_KTK_sab_mediji_240510(1).pdf.

[148]Compare: Human Rights, Terrorism and Counter-terrorism. Office of the United Nations High Commissioner for Human Rights. Fact Sheet No. 32. http://www.ohchr.org/Documents/Publications/Factsheet32EN.pdf.

[149]Security Council Resolution 1456 (2003) on combating terrorism. http://www.refworld.org/docid/3f45dbdb0.html.

[150]See, for example: Judgement of the European Court of Human Rights on 12 January 2016 (Application No 37138/14). http://hudoc.echr.coe.int/eng-press?i=001-160020#{"itemid":["001-160020"]}.

concern, which all states should take seriously, is to ensure that any measure taken to combat terrorism complies with its obligations under human rights law.[151]

The promotion and protection of human rights while countering terrorism is an obligation of states and an integral part of the fight against terrorism. National counter-terrorism strategies should, above all, seek to prevent acts of terrorism, prosecute those responsible for such criminal acts, and promote and protect human rights and the Rule of Law. The vast majority of counter-terrorism measures are adopted based on ordinary legislation. In a limited set of exceptional, national circumstances, some restrictions on the enjoyment of certain human rights may be permissible. Ensuring both the promotion and protection of human rights and effective counter-terrorism measures nonetheless raises serious practical challenges for states. One such example is the dilemma faced by states in protecting intelligence sources, which may require limiting the disclosure of evidence at hearings related to terrorism, while at the same time respecting the right to a fair trial and the right to a fair hearing for the individual.[152]

4.4.5 Regulation and Modern Technologies

The legal arrangement must confront issues concerning the regulation and adjudication of cases regarding new technologies more and more every day. The rapid development of modern technologies makes the task of the legislator to foresee future legal issues and the necessary regulatory framework almost impossible. Who would have imagined several decades, or even years ago that we would need to develop a strategy for cyber security, define the Rule of Law in cyberspace or work to curb cybercrime.[153]

The Rule of Law in cyberspace should be understood as a condition where the state guarantees the protection of the legal interests of its citizens in cyberspace to the same degree as in the real environment. This is a very ambitious goal, since it would seem that no state in the world could ensure such a condition. One of the instruments toward achieving this goal is the development and strengthening of the principle of functional equivalence within national legal systems.[154]

---

[151]Compare: Human Rights, Terrorism and Counter-terrorism. Office of the United Nations High Commissioner for Human Rights. Fact Sheet No. 32. http://www.ohchr.org/Documents/Publications/Factsheet32EN.pdf.

[152]Compare: Human Rights, Terrorism and Counter-terrorism. Office of the United Nations High Commissioner for Human Rights. Fact Sheet No. 32. http://www.ohchr.org/Documents/Publications/Factsheet32EN.pdf.

[153]On Guidelines "Latvian Cybersecurity Strategy for 2014–2018" (Par pamatnostādnēm "Latvijas kiberdrošības stratēgija 2014.–2018. gadam") The decision of the Cabinet of Ministers. 21 January 2014. LV 2014, No 16. http://likumi.lv/doc.php?id=263912. Extensively on the issue: Ķinis (2015).

[154]Ķinis (2015), p. 487.

The recent court practice of the Court of Justice of the European Union (ECJ), as in its judgment in Case C-264/14,[155] shows no less surprising modern trends in dealing with virtual currency. The case is related to the VAT Directive,[156] which provides that the supply of goods and services for consideration within the territory of a Member State by a taxable person acting as such be subject to VAT. However, Member States must exempt, inter alia, transactions relating to “currency, bank notes and coins used as legal tender”.

A Swedish national wanted to provide services consisting of the exchange of traditional currency for the “Bitcoin”[157] virtual currency and vice versa. Bitcoin is a virtual currency used for payments between private individuals over the Internet, and in certain online shops that accept it; users purchase and sell the currency based on an exchange rate. The ECJ concluded that transactions to exchange traditional currencies for units of the “Bitcoin” virtual currency (and vice versa) constitute the supply of services for consideration within the meaning of the Directive, and indicated that these transactions are also exempt from VAT under the provision concerning transactions relating to “currency, bank notes and coins used as legal tender”.

In conclusion, it must be noted that the legal arrangement of Latvia will have to face the developments and challenges of the modern world, and hopefully will find the right contemporary approaches for dealing with the legal issues in a democratic, based on the Rule of Law way.

References

Aizsilnieks A (1968) Latvijas saimniecības vēsture (Economic History of Latvia), 1914–1945. Daugava, Sundbyberg

Balodis R (ed) (2014) Latvijas Republikas Satversmes komentari. Ievads. I nodaļa. Vispārējie noteikumi (Commentaries on the Constitution of Latvia. Introduction. Chapter I. General Provisions). Latvijas Vēstnesis, Rīga

[155] Judgment of the Court of Justice of the European Union in case No C-264/14 on 22 October 2015. http://curia.europa.eu/juris/liste.jsf?num=C-264/14.

[156] Directive 2006/112/CE du Conseil, du 28 novembre 2006, relative au système commun de taxe sur la valeur ajoutée (JO L347, p. 1). http://eur-lex.europa.eu/LexUriServ/LexUriServ.do?uri=OJ:L:2006:347:0001:0118:fr:PDF.

[157] *Bitcoin* is a digital asset and a payment system. The system is peer-to-peer and transactions take place between users directly, without an intermediary. Bitcoin is often called the first cryptocurrency, and it is more correctly described as the first decentralised digital currency. Bitcoin is the largest of its kind in terms of total market value. Bitcoins are created as a reward for payment processing work in which users offer their computing power to verify and record payments into the public ledger. This activity is called *mining* and miners are rewarded with transaction fees and newly created bitcoins. Besides being obtained by mining, bitcoins can be exchanged for other currencies, products, and services. When sending bitcoins, users can pay an optional transaction fee to the miners. See more specific in: Espinoza (2014) Time to Bet on the Bitcoin? The Wall Street Journal, 22 September 2014. https://faculty.fuqua.duke.edu/~charvey/Media/2014/bitcoin.pdf.

Balodis R (2010) Tieslietu padomes nozīme laika dimensijā (Council of Justice and its role in the time dimension). Jurista Vārds, 25 January, No 4. Available: http://www.juristavards.lv/doc/204080-tieslietu-padomes-nozime-laika-dimensija/

Bērziņa-Andersone I, Repšs A, Paparinskis M (2009) Analītisks darbs par starptautiskajām līgumtiesībām un šo tiesību mijiedarbību ar Eiropas Savienības un tās dalībvalstu tiesībām. Tieslietu ministrija, Rīga, p 322

Blūzma V (ed) (2006) Latvijas tiesību avoti. Teksti un komentāri. 2. sējums. Poļu un zviedru laiku tiesību avoti (Sources of the Latvian Law. Texts and Commentaries. Vol. 2. Legal Sources of the Epoch of the Polish and Swedish Domination) (1561–1795). Autori: Romāns Apsītis, Valdis Blūzma, Jānis Lazdiņš. Rīga. Latvijas vēstures institūta apgāds

Bobek M (2008) Learning to talk: preliminary rulings, the courts of the new member states and the Court of Justice. Common Mark Law Rev 45:1611–1643

Broberg M, Fenger N (2010) Preliminary references to the European Court of Justice. Oxford University Press, Oxford, p 576

Buka A (2014) Requests for the preliminary rulings from Latvian courts: 10 years of the EU membership. In: Jundzis T (ed) The Baltic States in the EU: ten years as Member States. Proceedings of the international conference, Riga, pp 18–25

Bunge Fr G van (1862) Geschichte des Liv-, Est- und Curländishen Privatrechts. In der Buchdruckerei der Zweiten Abtheilung Sr. Kaiserl. Majestät Eigener Canzlei, St. Petersburg

Court of Justice of the EU. Annual report 2014. (2015) Luxembourg, p 156. Available at: http://curia.europa.eu/jcms/upload/docs/application/pdf/2015-03/en_ra14.pdf

Dišlers K (1935) *Negotiorum gestio publisko tiesību novadā* (Negotiorum gestio in the Area of Public Law). Tieslietu Ministrijas Vēstnesis, Nr. 1

Dunsdorfs E (1962) Latvijas vēsture (History of Latvia). 1600–1710. Daugava, Uppsala

Dišlers K (2004) Latvijas valsts varas orgāni un viņu funkcijas (The organs of the State Power of Latvia and their functions). Tiesu namu agentūra, Rīga, 204 lpp

Dišlers K (1930) Ievads Latvijas valststiesību zinātnē (Introduction to Latvian Administrative Science). A.Gulbis, Rīga, 211 lpp

ECHR Statistics on violations. (2016) p. 2. Available at: http://www.echr.coe.int/Documents/Stats_violation_1959_2015_ENG.pdf

Espinoza J (2014) Time to Bet on the Bitcoin? The Wall Street Journal. 22 September 2014. https://faculty.fuqua.duke.edu/~charvey/Media/2014/bitcoin.pdf

Groussot X., Wong C, Inghammar A, Bruzelius A (2010) Empowering national courts in EU law. Svenska institutet för europapolitiska studier, Stockholm, p 143. Available at: http://www.sieps.se/sites/default/files/541-2009-3-rapport.pdf

Iļjanova D (2011) The governmental system of the Republic of Latvia. In: Chronowski N, Drinoczi T, Takacs T (eds) The governmental systems of the Central and Eastern European states. Wolters Kluwer Polska, Warszawa, 62 pp

Jundzis T, Zemītis G (ed) (2014) Latvieši un Latvija. II sējums. Valstiskums Latvijā un Latvijas valsts – izcīnītā un zaudētā (Latvians and Latvia. Vol. II. Statehood in Latvia and the Latvian State – established and lost). Rīga. Latvijas Zinātņu akadēmija

Kalniņš V (1972) Latvijas PSR valsts un tiesību vēsture (History of the State and Law of the Latvian SSR). I. Rīga, Zvaigzne

Kalniņš V, Kažoka I, Litvins G (2008) Tiesnešu ētika, kvalifikācija un atbildība Latvijā: kā neapstāties pie sasniegtā? (Judges ethics, qualifications and responsibilities in Latvia: how not to rest on their laurels?). Pētījuma ziņojums. Sabiedriskās politikas centrs Providus. Rīga. http://providus.lv/article_files/1903/original/Zinojums_FINAL.pdf?1339440792

Kačevska I (2014) Ir normāla situācija, un ir Latvijas situācija. (A normal situation, and then the situation of Latvia) Jurista Vārds, 3 June, No. 22. Available: http://www.juristavards.lv/doc/264565-ir-normala-situacija-un-ir-latvijas-situacija/

Krūmiņa V (2013) Latvijas Republikas Satversmes komentāri. VI nodaļa. Tiesa. VII nodaļa. Valsts kontrole. (The Constitution of the Republic of Latvia comments. Chapter VI. The court. Chapter VII. State control.) Autoru kolektīvs prof. R.Baloža zinātniskā vadībā. LV, Rīga

Kucina I (2014) Tiesu prakses publicēšana kā viens no tiesas atvērtības instrumentiem. (Publication of judicial practice as one of the instruments of judicial openness) Jurista Vārds, 1 July, No. 25

Ķinis U (2015) Kibernoziedzība, kibernoziegumi un jurisdikcija (Cybercriminality, cibercrimes and jurisdiction). Jumava, Rīga, 518 lpp

Lapsa J (2014) Šķīrējtiesu regulējuma novitātes. (Arbitration regulation innovation) Jurista Vārds, 3 June, No. 22. Available: http://www.juristavards.lv/doc/264560-kirejtiesu-regulejuma-novitates/

Lazdiņš J (2006) Baltu un līvu privāttiesību paražas (Customary private law of the Balts and Livs). Jurista Vārds, No. 32 (435)

Lazdiņš J (2007) Experience of Nationalisation and Denationalisation of Land Ownership in Latvia (19-th and 20-th centuries). Journal of the University of Latvia. Law and Justice, 2007 (Selected Articles of 2004–2005)

Lazdiņš J (2009) Lībiešu krimināltiesiskās (soda) apziņas īpatnības 12. gadsimtā un 13. gadsimta sākumā (Peculiarities in the Awareness of Criminal Justice (Punishment) among Livs in the 12th Century and Early 13th Century). Pa somugru pēdām Baltijas jūras krastā. Starptautiskās zinātniskās konferences materiāli, 2009. gada 23. aprīlī. Turaida. Zinātne

Lazdiņš J (2013) Konstitucionālisma pirmsākumi un nerealizētie valstiskumi Latvijā (The Origins of Constitutionalism and Unrealized Statehood in Latvia). Jurista Vārds, Nr. 23(774)

Lazdiņš J (2014) Rechtspolitische Besonderheiten bei der Entstehung des lettischen Staates und seiner Verfassung. Latvijas Universitātes Žurnāls. Juridiskā zinātne, No. 7

Lazdiņš J (2015a) Īpašums kā vērtība. Īpašuma denacionalizācija (Property as Value. Denationalisation of Property). Tiesību efektivitāte postmodernā sabiedrībā. Latvijas Univeritātes 73. Zinātniskās konferences rakstu krājums. LU akadēmiskais apgāds

Lazdiņš J (2015b) Tendencies in the Development of Laws in the Republic of Latvia after the Renewal of Independence in 1990–1991. Journal of The University of Latvia. Law, Nr. 8

Lazdiņš J (ed) (2015c) Latvijas tiesību avoti. Valsts dibināšana – neatkarības atjaunošana (Legal sources of the Latvian state. Documents and commentaries). Dokumenti un komentāri. Tiesu Namu Agentūra

Lēbers A (ed) (2000) Latvijas tiesību vēsture (Legal History of Latvia) (1914–1940). Autoru kolektīvs: Romāns Apsītis, Valdis Blūzma, Tālavs Jundzis, Jānis Lazdiņš, Egils Levits. Fonds Latvijas Vēsture, Rīga

Levits E (2014) Valsts varas dalīšana un varas atzaru mijiedarbība tiesiskā valstī. Augstākās tiesas biļetens. 9:21–24. Available: http://at.gov.lv/files/uploads/files/2_Par_Augstako_tiesu/Informativie_materiali/ATBiletens9.pdf

Litvins G (2016) Notāra uzdevums tiesiskas valsts nodrošināšanā (The task of the notary ensuring the legal state). Jurista Vārds, 19 July, No. 29. Available: http://www.juristavards.lv/doc/268966-notara-uzdevums-tiesiskas-valsts-nodrosinasana/

Lenz CO, Grill G (1995) The preliminary ruling procedure and United Kingdom. Fordham Int Law J 19(3):844–865

McLachli B (2006) The 21st century courts: old challenges and new. Australian Institute of Judicial Administration Incorporated, Melbourne. http://www.aija.org.au/online/Pub%20no81.pdf

Miqsik D (2008) European Law and the General Courts of the Transition Countries. In: Europarecht un die Gerichte der Transformationsstaaten, Baden-Baden, pp 97–125

Meļķisis E (ed) (1998) Latvijas tiesību avoti. Teksti un komentāri. I. sējums. Seno paražu un Livonijas tiesību avoti 10. gs. – 16. gs. (Sources of the Latvian Law. Texts and Commentaries. Vol. 1. Sources of Ancient Customary Laws and the Livonian Law. 10th century –16th century). Autori: Jānis Lazdiņš, Valdis Blūzma, Sanita Osipova. Rīga. LU žurnāla “Latvijas Vēsture” fonds

Ņesterova I (2012) Eiropas Savienības Tiesa: svarīgākie nolēmumi. Latvijai aktuālie prejudiciālie nolēmumi. Jurista Vārds 47(746):4–6

On the Legal Framework of the Public Electronic Mass Media in a Democratic State. Opinion of the Constitutional Law Commission. 24 May 2010. http://www.president.lv/images/modules/items/Viedoklis_KTK_sab_mediji_240510(1).pdf

On the Constitutional Foundations of the State of Latvia and the Inviolable Core of the Constitution. Opinion of the Constitutional Law Commission. 17 September 2012. http://www.president.lv/images/modules/items/PDF/17092012_Viedoklis_2.pdf

Osipova S (2016) Tiesiska valsts vai "tiesnešu valsts". (A State or "judges country".) Jurista Vārds, 5 July. No. 27. Available: http://www.juristavards.lv/doc/268917-tiesiska-valsts-vai-tiesnesu-valsts/

Osztovits A, Gobos K (2014) Preliminary references and Hungarian courts: procedural context, trends and quality. In: Varju M, Varnay E (eds) The law of the EU in hungary: institutions, processes and the law. Hvg-orac Publishing, Budapest, pp 223–240

Pētersone Z (2012) Tiesas atvasinātā Mediācijas modeļa ieviešana civiltiesisku strīdu risināšanā Latvijā. Latvijas Republikas Augstākās tiesas Biļetens 4:12–15. http://at.gov.lv/files/uploads/files/docs/at_biletens4_web.pdf

Pētersone Z (2013) Mediācijas izmantošana komercstrīdu risināšanā. (The use of mediation in resolving commercial disputes) Grām: Komerctiesību aktuālie jautājumi Latvijā un Eiropā: Komercdarījumi. Atbildība. Komercstrīdi. – Rīga, Tiesu namu agentūra

Prechal S, Widdershoven T (2008) The dutch general administrative law act: Europe-proof? Eur Public Law 14:81–98

Rezevska D (2015) Vispārējo tiesību principu nozīme un piemērošana (Meaning and application of the general principles of law). D.Rezevskas izd., Rīga, 176 lpp

Rone D (2008) Darba tiesisko strīdu risināšana ar mediācijas metodēm. (Solving the legal dispute with mediation techniques) "Bilance". Nr. 13(193), 1 July

Scheinin M (1996) General introduction. In: Scheinin M (ed) International human rights norms in Nordic and Baltic countries. Kluwer Law International, The Hague, pp 11–26

Schäfer Frank L, Schubert W (ed) (2013) Justiz und Justizverfassung. Siebter Rechtshistorikertag im Ostseeraum, 3.–5. Mai 2012 Schleswig-Holstein. Frankfurt am Main. Peter Lang GmbH, PL Academic Reserch

Schöbener B, Knauff M (2013) Allgemeine Staatslehre. 2. Auflage. Verlag C. H. Beck, München

Šterns I (2002) Latvijas vēsture. 1180–1290. Krustakari (History of Latvia 1180–1290. The Crusades). Latvijas vēstures institūta apgāds, Rīga

Švābe A (1927) Vecākās zemnieku tiesības (Older rights of Peasants). Latvijas Skolotāju Savienība, Rīgā

Švābe A (1930) Zemes attiecību un zemes reformu vēsture Latvijā (Land relations and land reform in the history of Latvia). Latv. zemn. sav. spiest, Rīgā

Švarcs F (2011) Latvijas 1937. gada 28. janvāra Civillikums un tā rašanās vēsture (Latvian civil law of 28 January 1937 and the history of its Nascency). Tiesu Namu Agentūra

TV kanālu proporcija – pilnīgi ačgārna. Saruna ar Satversmes tiesas tiesnesi Inetu Ziemeli (The Proportion of the TV Channels – Absolutely Amiss. Interview with the Justice of the Constitutional Court Ineta Ziemele). Latvijas Avīze 2016. http://www.la.lv/tv-kanalu-proporcija-pilnigi-acgarna/

The ECHR. Overview 1959–2015 (2016), p 14. Available at: http://www.echr.coe.int/Documents/Overview_19592015_ENG.pdf

Van Elsuwege P (2008) From Soviet Republics to EU Member States. Leiden-Boston: Martinus Nijhoff Publishers, p. 584

Ziegenhorn Ch G (1772) Staatsrecht der Herzogthümer Curland und Semgallen. Königsberg

Нольде АЭ, Баронъ (1914) Очерки по исторіи кодификаціи местныхъ гражданскихъ законовъ при графе Сперанскомъ (Essays on the History of the Codification of Local Civil Law under Earl Speranski). Выпускъ II (Issue II). Кодификація местнаго права Прибалтійскихъ губерній (The Codification of the Local Rights of the Baltic Governorates). С.–Петербургъ: Сенатская типографія

Томсинов ВА (ed) (2004) *Хрестоматия по истории отечественного государства и права. X век – 1917 год*. (Readings on the History of Russian State and Law. X century–1917). ЗЕРЦАЛО-М, Москва

Public Law 5

Māris Badovskis, Jautrīte Briede, Edvīns Danovskis, Kristīne Dupate, Annija Kārkliņa, Kārlis Ketners, Valentija Liholaja, Anita Rodiņa, and Kristīne Strada-Rozenberga

Abstract

The chapter gives an overview of the main institutes of public law. It describes constitutional institutions in Latvia which realises public power, pointing out importance of the Constitutional Court within the system of division of powers. The chapter also explains structure and content of the administrative law which consists of four large groups: law of administrative structure, administrative procedure law, material administrative law and law on administrative offences. The chapter focuses on the theory and rules of criminal law which are regulated by the Criminal Law, as well as practical and theoretical aspects of criminal procedure which are codified in the Criminal Procedure Law. It also explicates basics of Latvian financial regulation, budget and tax law. Finally, the chapter discusses about main topics of labour law—individual employment relations, collective labour relations, health and safety protection, dispute resolution and other labour rights enforcement mechanisms, as well as importance of national regular courts, the Constitutional Court and the European Court of Justice.

M. Badovskis (✉)
Labour Relations and Labour Protection Policy Department, Ministry of Welfare, Riga, Latvia
e-mail: maris.badovskis@lm.gov.lv

J. Briede • E. Danovskis • K. Dupate • A. Kārkliņa • V. Liholaja • A. Rodiņa •
K. Strada-Rozenberga
Law Faculty, University of Latvia, Raiņa bulv, 19 Riga, Latvia
e-mail: jautrite.briede@lu.lv; edvins.danovskis@lu.lv; kristine.dupate@lu.lv; annija.karklina@lu.lv; Valentija.Liholaja@lu.lv; anita.rodina@lu.lv; Kristine.Strada-Rozenberga@lu.lv

K. Ketners
BA School for Business and Finance, K. Valdemāra iela 161, Riga, Latvia
e-mail: karlis.ketners@ba.lv

T. Kerikmäe et al. (eds.), *The Law of the Baltic States*,
DOI 10.1007/978-3-319-54478-6_5

5.1 Constitutional Law and Constitutional Review

Anita Rodiņa and Annija Kārkliņa
Law Faculty, University of Latvia, Raiņa bulv, 19 Riga, Latvia
e-mail: anita.rodina@lu.lv

5.1.1 Introduction: Characteristics of the State System and Constitution

The basis of the Latvian constitutional system is the Constitution of the Republic of Latvia (hereinafter—the Satversme).[1] The Satversme was developed by a Constitutional Assembly that was elected in 1920 in equal and free elections where both genders took part. The granting of voting rights to women was a progressive achievement in relation to other countries in those times. The Satversme was developed largely based on the constitutional experience of Germany, France, Switzerland, Britain, Finland, and the USA.[2]

The Satversme was adopted on 15 February 1922, and came into force on 7 November 1922. The Constitution successfully fulfilled the function of the fundamental law up until 15 May 1934, when it was terminated by an authoritarian regime. Subsequently, the occupation of Latvia and its illegitimate inclusion in the USSR followed.

On 4 May 1990, the declaration "On the Restoration of Independence of the Republic of Latvia" was adopted. The declaration determined the restoration of the Satversme of 1922. Of course, it was not possible to immediately restore the complete operation of the Satversme; therefore, the operation of the Satversme was partially restored and a period of transition was determined. The Constitution was restored in its full scope on 6 July 1993. By restoring the State of Latvia, the principle of continuity was observed, i.e., that it is the same state which was proclaimed on 18 November 1918.[3] The Satversme is one of the oldest constitutions still in force in Europe.

The first Article of the Constitution determines that Latvia is an independent, democratic republic. From this concept emerges the responsibility of the state to follow democratic, state-recognised constitutional basic principles in the operation of the state and its relations with its inhabitants.[4] Although it is not *expressis verbis* stated in the constitution, Latvia is a unitary and parliamentary republic.

---

[1]The Constitution of the Republic of Latvia (Latvijas Republikas Satversme). http://www.saeima.lv/en/legislation/constitution. The Satversme consists of the following eight Chapters: Chapter I—General Provisions; II—The Saeima (The Parliament); III—The President; IV—The Cabinet; V—Legislation; VI—Courts; VII—The State Audit Office; VIII—Fundamental Human Rights.

[2]Balodis and Lazdiņš (2014), pp. 43–79, 342–346.

[3]Balodis et al. (2013a), pp. 44–120; Lazdiņš (2015), pp. 43–67.

[4]Rezevska (2014), pp. 346–350.

The Constitution of Latvia can be classified as a laconic constitution, which consists of 116 articles divided into eight chapters. When the Satversme was adopted, in 1922, it was even more laconic—the Constitution did not have a preamble (only one short introductory sentence), and it consisted of 7 chapters. The Constitution was amended several times. Amendments affected almost all institutions indicated in the Constitution (except for the higher auditing institution—the State Audit Office). These amendments have not significantly altered the state system. The most significant amendments affecting the structure of the Satversme included adding a new chapter—the 8th chapter, "Fundamental Rights", in 1998—and a preamble in 2014. The Preamble addresses the proclamation of the State in 1918, historical twists that have affected the destiny of the State, as well as determines the values of the State and the people of Latvia.

The Satversme does not greatly differ from the constitutions of other countries—it regulates general provisions of the State, fundamental provisions and functions of the Parliament, State President, Cabinet of Ministers, court and Constitutional Court, and the State Audit Office. The Satversme also includes regulation on fundamental rights and regulation of the rights of the nation (entirety of citizens).[5] In contrast to the constitutions of many other countries, the Satversme does not include regulation about the Ombudsman, National Bank (Bank of Latvia) and Prosecutor's Office—these institutions are regulated on the level of laws.

The Satversme can be amended by Parliament (Saeima). Amendments are passed in three readings. Two-thirds of the members of Parliament must attend the Saeima meeting that decides on amendments to the Constitution, and at least two-thirds of the attending deputies must vote on the amendments. After their adoption in the Saeima, amendments to some articles must also be approved via referendum (Art. 77). A referendum is needed to approve amendments to Arts.1, 2, 3, 4, 6 and 77 of the Constitution—these articles determine the conceptual basis of the State, i.e., that Latvia is an independent, democratic republic with sovereign power belonging to the people of Latvia,[6] state borders, the status of the Latvian language as the only official language of the State,[7] the colours of the national flag of the State and principles regarding elections to Parliament.

5.1.2 Fundamental Rights

Until 1998, the Satversme did not include a chapter on human rights. In 1922, when the Constitution was developed, it was planned that the Satversme would consist of two parts—part I regulating the state system and constitutional institutions, and part II—regulating human rights. Part I of the Satversme was adopted on 15 February

[5] See also: Iljanova (2006), pp. V3–V65; Balodis (2006), pp. S.269–S.278.

[6] Rodiņa and Pleps (2013), p. 431.

[7] Druviete et al. (2014), pp. 295–331, 358–361.

1922, but the second part lacked sufficient votes because of various political disagreements and was not adopted.

On 15 October 1998, Parliament amended the Satversme, adding to the Constitution the new Chapter 8, "Fundamental Rights". The Satversme includes human rights of all three generations—civil and political rights, social, economic and cultural rights—as well as rights of solidarity (rights to live in a benevolent environment). An aspect that differs from the constitutions of other countries is that regulations on the limitation of fundamental rights are indicated not after each fundamental right, but in a special, dedicated article—Art. 116 defines fundamental rights that can be limited and prescribes the legitimate aims of this limitation.

If a person considers his/her fundamental rights to have been violated, that person has extensive options as to the protection of his/her rights—by approaching various law enforcement institutions, including the court, as well as the institution of Ombudsman.[8] Violated fundamental rights can also be considered in the Constitutional Court.[9] In cases where it is necessary to determine the content of the legal regulation of fundamental rights included in the Satversme, this legal regulation should be translated in compliance with the interpretation used in the practice of implementing international human rights legislation.[10]

5.1.3 Rights of the Entirety of Citizens

Art. 2 of the Constitution determines that the sovereign power of the State of Latvia is vested in the people of Latvia, i.e. to the entirety of its citizens. Latvian citizens are the second legislator, alongside the Saeima (Art. 64).

Lawful citizens who have reached 18 years of age are entitled to participate in referenda, elections and entitled to submit legislative initiatives of the electorate.

The Constitution determines seven cases which are to be resolved in referenda.[11] Cases calling for a referendum include issues around the dismissal of Parliament, Latvia's membership in the European Union and significant changes in the membership provisions, and the approval of the people to amend certain articles of the Constitution. In addition, a law adopted by the Saeima can be cancelled by the people in a referendum (if the State President has decided not to announce it in compliance with Art. 72).

All referenda in Latvia are legally binding; there are no consultative referenda in Latvia. Art. 73 of the Constitution determines issues which cannot be decided in

[8]Ombudsman Law. http://www.vvc.gov.lv/export/sites/default/docs/LRTA/Likumi/Ombudsman_Law.pdf., see also Rodiņa (2012), pp. 384–396.

[9]Constitutional Court Law. http://www.satv.tiesa.gov.lv/en/2016/02/04/constitutional-court-law. More about this topic in the chapter: Constitutional Court of the Republic of Latvia.

[10]Judgement of the Constitutional Court in case No.2000-03-01, on 30 August 2000, para. 5. http://www.satv.tiesa.gov.lv/en/cases/.

[11]See Art. 14, 48, 68, 72, 77, 78 of Satversme.

referenda—laws concerning loans, taxes, the state budget, declaration and commencement of war, peace treaties, declaration of a state of emergency, mobilisation and demobilisation, as well as agreements with other states, etc.

Legislative initiatives of the electorate are expressed when one-tenth of the electorate submits a completely developed draft law to the Saeima.[12] The Saeima has an obligation to review the submitted draft law. If the Saeima rejects or amends it, a referendum is organised, and all people with the right to vote have a chance to decide if they support the adoption of the draft law submitted by the one-tenth of the electorate (Art. 78).[13] Both during the pre-war period and after the restoration of independence, the mechanisms of referendum and legislation initiatives of the electorate have been applied many times in practice.

5.1.4 Parliament

The Latvian Parliament (Saeima) is a unicameral parliament consisting of 100 representatives. Parliament is elected for 4 years in general, equal, direct, closed and proportional elections. Elections of the Saeima take place on the first Saturday of October. In Latvia, there is a 5% threshold in Saeima elections.

All lawful citizens of Latvia who have reached 18 years of age are entitled to elect the Saeima. Any citizen of Latvia, who enjoys the full rights of citizenship and is more than 21 years of age on the first day of elections, may be elected to the Saeima.[14] A mandatory precondition for obtaining the mandate of a deputy is the giving of an oath (solemn affirmation) at a sitting of the Saeima. Members of the Saeima may neither be arrested, nor may their premises be searched or their personal liberty be restricted in any way without the consent of the Saeima. Members of Parliament have a free mandate, which means that voters can't recall any individual member of the Saeima.

In addition to the Satversme, the Rules of Procedure of the Saeima regulate the activities of the Parliament and legislation process.[15] Saeima sittings are open (in cases stipulated by law and in compliance with a specific procedure, the Saeima can decide to organise a closed sitting). Sittings of the Saeima are also broadcast to inform the public and make the work of the Saeima transparent.

As the representative organ elected by the people, Parliament has broad competence which includes various functions in relation to other state institutions. Analogous to the parliaments of other countries, the primary function of the Saeima is its legislative function. The Saeima also approves international treaties (Art. 68),

[12]Law On National Referendum, Legislative Initiative and European Citizens Initiative. www.vvc.gov.lv/.../On_National_Referendumx_Legislative_Initiative_.

[13]Karklina (2014), pp. 60–72.

[14]The Saeima Election Law. http://www.saeima.lv/en/about-saeima/saeimas-velesanas-1/saeimas-velesanu-likums-1.

[15]Rules of Procedure of the Saeima. http://saeima.lv/en/legislation/rules-of-procedure.

decides on amnesty (Art. 45), makes proclamations of the state of emergency and war (Art. 2, 43), and determines the size of the state armed forces during periods of peace (Art. 67).

There are also broad parliamentary functions as to the approval and dismissal of various state officials. For example, the Saeima elects the State President (Art. 35), approves the Cabinet of Ministers (Art. 59), approves judges at all levels of court and judges of the Constitutional Court (Art. 84, 85), Auditors General of the State Audit Office (Art. 88), General Prosecutor, Ombudsman, etc.

The Saeima controls the operation of the executive power. For example, the Saeima is entitled to submit requests and questions to the Prime Minister or other ministers; the work of the government depends on the confidence of the Saeima (Art. 27, 59). Annually, before the commencement of each financial year, the Saeima determines the state revenues and expenditures budget (Art. 66). In certain cases, it appoints a parliamentary investigation commission (in practice this form of parliamentary control is applied quite regularly).

The Satversme prescribes two cases in which the authorities of the Parliament may be terminated before the end of their term. First, the State President is entitled to propose the *dismissal* of the Saeima (Art. 48). It should be emphasised that the President is only entitled to propose dismissal, and if the President has proposed it, a referendum is carried out afterward. If more than half of voters approve the dismissal of the Saeima in the referendum, the Saeima is considered dismissed and new parliamentary elections must be announced. But if in the referendum more than half of the votes are cast against the dissolution of the Saeima, the State President must be considered removed from office, and the Saeima elects a new President to serve out the remaining term of office of the President so removed (Art. 50).

This construction is unique among the constitutions of other countries, as this kind of regulation cannot be found elsewhere. In practice, this procedure has been applied only once—on 28 May 2011, when the State President V. Zatlers issued the regulation "About the Proposal to Dismiss the Saeima". On 23 July 2011, a referendum was held, where 94.3% of participating voters voted for the dismissal of the Saeima.[16] This is the only type of referendum in Latvia that does not require a minimum quorum of voters—even if a relatively small number of voters participated in the referendum, their vote would decide whether to dismiss the Saeima. The Constitution does not prescribe any limitation on when the State President would not be entitled to propose the dismissal of the Saeima.

Second, since the year 2010, voters (i.e., at least one-tenth of eligible voters) have the right to propose a *recall* of the Saeima (Art. 14.). In contrast to the right of the State President to propose *dismissal* of the Saeima, the right of voters to propose the *recall* of the Saeima cannot be applied at any given moment (for example, these rights cannot be applied 1 year after a new Saeima convenes, the year before the end

[16]Referendum on 23 July 2011 about the dismissal of the 10th Saeima. http://web.cvk.lv/pub/public/29957.html.

of the term of the Saeima, during the last 6 months of the mandate of the State President, and no earlier than 6 months after the previous referendum regarding the recall of the Saeima). If a majority of voters, and at least two-thirds of the number of the voters who participated in the most recent Saeima elections, vote in the referendum regarding the recalling of the Saeima, the Saeima is deemed recalled.

5.1.5 President

The Saeima elects the State President for 4 years in a secret ballot. The State President must be elected by a majority of the votes of not less than 51 members of the Saeima.

Frequently, at various times in history, there were proposals to change the presidential election procedure (by entrusting it to the people), but none of these initiations have been realised by the adoption of constitutional amendments.

Every lawful citizen of Latvia who has reached the age of 40 is eligible to become the State President. Alongside the Constitution, the Law on Presidential Elections also regulates the election of the President.[17] The same person cannot hold office as President for more than eight consecutive years.

The office of the President cannot be held concurrently with any other office. The President, upon taking up the duties of office, takes a solemn oath at a sitting of the Saeima (Art. 40).

Although the functions of the State President in a parliamentary state are comparatively limited, the role of the President of Latvia expands in situations of crisis.[18] The rights and responsibilities of the State President are quite broad in the legislative area, including all stages of the legislative process. For example, the President is entitled to propose a law (including amendments to the law and the Satversme), and in this case the President does not need to develop a draft law—he/she may propose only an idea or recommendation (Art. 47). Also, if review of a draft law takes place in Parliament, the State President is entitled to submit proposals to the law. When the draft law is adopted in a final reading, it is sent to the State President for promulgation. At this stage, the President may act in several ways—to promulgate the law, or if the President objects to the contents of the law, he/she is entitled to return it to Parliament for reconsideration (to be done within 10 days, Art. 71). In this case, the President needs to justify his/her decision, indicating to the Saeima why the law has been returned for reconsideration. If the Saeima does not amend the law, the President may not raise objections a second time. In addition to these rights, the President has one more mechanism for objecting to the contents of a law adopted by the Saeima—i.e., the President is entitled to suspend publication of the law for a period of 2 months (Art. 72). If the President suspends publication of the law, voters may gather signatures to put the

[17]Law on Presidential Elections. LV No. 79 (3655), 17.05.2007.

[18]Balodis et al. (2013b), p. 53.

issue of the suspended law to a referendum. If, within 2 months, the signatures of 1/10 of the electorate have been collected, a referendum is organised by which voters may cancel the law adopted by Parliament. The right of the President to return the law for repeated revision and suspend publication of the law are called the *suspensive veto*, and these mechanisms have been applied in practice. If the State President is convinced that any law or regulation does not comply with a regulatory act of higher rank, he/she has the right to submit an application to the Constitutional Court.

The State President has a significant role in a representative capacity—the President represents his/her state internationally, appoints Latvian diplomats, receives representatives of diplomatic services from other countries, and fulfils the Saeima's decisions on the ratification of international treaties. The President also has a defence function—he/she is the Commander in Chief of the National Armed Forces, appoints the Commander in Chief during periods of war, and is entitled to take the necessary military defence steps if another state has declared war on Latvia or attacks Latvia, etc.[19]

The President also nominates the candidates for the post of Prime Minister, is entitled to request and host extraordinary meetings of the Cabinet of Ministers and has the right to pardon prisoners.

If the electorate has voted by referendum for dismissal or recall of the Saeima, the President also leads the work of the Parliament until the convening of the newly elected Saeima (Art. 49).

The Satversme determines that all ordinances of the President should be co-signed by the Prime Minister or Minister of the respective field, who therefore takes full responsibility for these regulations (except regulations regarding the proposed dismissal of the Saeima and nominating candidates for Prime Minister).

The State President may lose his/her position before the term ends in two cases. First, the Saeima is entitled to remove the President. Art. 51 of the Constitution determines that if at least half of the members of the Saeima propose removal of the President, the Saeima can remove the President in a closed meeting with no less than a majority consisting of 2/3 of the votes of all members of the Saeima. Therefore, regardless of the fact that Art. 53 of the Satversme determines that the President bears no political responsibility for the fulfilment of his/her presidential duties, the President is politically responsible before Parliament. The Satversme does not determine the preconditions under which the President may be dismissed from the position, and this is the most significant difference from the regulation in countries with an established impeachment procedure (where there are specific, established legal findings, criteria, and a procedure for the removal of the President). Secondly, as previously mentioned, the State President may also lose his/her position if he/she proposes the dismissal of the Saeima and the electorate reject this proposal (Art. 48, 50).[20]

[19] See. Dišlers (2004), pp. 114–137.

[20] Karklina (2013), pp. 1213–1229.

If, due to circumstances, the State President is incapable of fulfilling his/her duties (for example, is ill or outside the state), the Chairperson of the Saeima may replace him/her. Likewise, in cases where the position of the State President has become vacant following the dismissal, death or resignation of the President, the Chairperson of the Saeima fulfils the obligations of the President until the election of a new Saeima, as the Chairperson of the Saeima is second in rank in the hierarchy of positions, after the State President.

5.1.6 Cabinet of Ministers

The Cabinet of Ministers is the highest executive body of the Republic of Latvia.[21] The Cabinet is composed of the Prime Minister and the Ministers chosen by the Prime Minister. The Cabinet is formed by persons who have been nominated by the President.

As the Cabinet of Ministers is responsible to Parliament, the Cabinet begins to fulfil its duties after it has received the support of the Saeima in a vote of confidence. The Saeima can express no confidence in the complete Cabinet of Ministers by adopting a respective decision or rejecting the annual state budget draft prepared and submitted to the Saeima by the Cabinet. Additionally, if the Saeima expresses no confidence in the Prime Minister, the entire Cabinet must resign as well (Art. 59). Public institutions are subject to the authority of the Cabinet.

The Cabinet of Ministers has legislative rights and the right to appoint a broad range of civil servants or approve their status. The Cabinet discusses or decides on all issues within its scope of competence pursuant to the Satversme and other laws.[22] It can issue legislative enactments—Regulations of the Cabinet of Ministers (if the legislator has delegated such a right, and if the issue in question has not been regulated by law). The Cabinet of Ministers adopts decisions by a majority vote of members present at the Cabinet meeting.[23]

5.1.7 The State Audit Office

The State Audit Office is one of the constitutional institutions mentioned in the Satversme. The regulation concerning this institution in the Satversme is quite laconic—Chapter 7 is devoted to it and consists of two articles determining that the State Audit Office is an independent collegial institution, the supreme audit institution in the Republic of Latvia. Auditors General are to be appointed to their office pursuant to the same procedure as judges, although only for a fixed period,

[21] See also. Pleps (2013b), pp. 121–139.

[22] Law on the Structure of Cabinet Law. http://www.mk.gov.lv/en/content/cabinet-ministers.

[23] Pleps (2013a), pp. 106–132; Balodis et al. (2013a), pp. 44–120.

during which they may be removed from office only by a judgement of the Court. The organisation and responsibilities of the institution are provided by specific law.[24]

5.1.8 Court System

Alongside legislative and executive power, there is also an independent judicial power in Latvia. There are three court levels in Latvia—district (town) courts, regional courts and the Supreme Court. District (town) courts review cases as the first instance court; district courts are the appeal institution (*de novo* review), but cassation complaints are reviewed in the Supreme Court.

Courts of general jurisdiction in Latvia hear civil, administrative and criminal cases. Latvia does not have specialised courts, for instance family courts, or judges who specialise in particular legal issues.

The Satversme determines that in the event of war or a state of emergency, military courts may be established. Judges are independent and subject only to the law. Judges are appointed by the Saeima (in open voting) and their appointments are irrevocable. Judges can be removed from office against their will only by the Saeima in cases provided for by law, based on a decision of the Judicial Disciplinary Board or a judgement of the court in a criminal case.[25] The maximum age for the fulfilment of the duties of a judge is 70 years.[26]

5.1.9 Constitutional Court of the Republic of Latvia

Constitutional Status

The Constitutional Court of the Republic of Latvia is an institution of judicial power which realises its exclusive function as safeguard of the Constitution by ensuring the rule (priority) of the Constitution—the Satversme—and constitutional justice.[27] The constitutional status of the Constitutional Court is defined in one article of the Satversme—Art. 85.[28] All material and procedural regulations are

[24]State Audit Office Law. www.vvc.gov.lv/export/sites/default/.../State_Audit_Office_Law.doc.

[25]Karklina (2012), pp. 273–287.

[26]Law on Judicial Power. http://vvc.gov.lv/export/sites/default/docs/LRTA/Likumi/Judicial_Power.pdf.

[27]Judgement of the Constitutional Court in case No. 2009-11-01 on 18 January 2010, para 5. http://www.satv.tiesa.gov.lv/upload/judg_2009_11.htm.

[28]Art. 85 provides: In Latvia, there shall be a Constitutional Court, which, within its jurisdiction as provided for by law, shall review cases concerning the compliance of laws with the Constitution, as well as other matters regarding which jurisdiction is conferred upon it by law. The Constitutional Court shall have the right to declare laws or other enactments or parts thereof invalid. The Saeima shall confirm the appointment of judges to the Constitutional Court for the term provided for by law, by secret ballot with a majority of the votes of not less than fifty-one members of the Saeima.

explained in more detail in the Constitutional Court Law.[29] The Constitutional Court of Latvia has features typical of the European model of constitutional control: centralisation, implementation of abstract constitutional control, as well as the possibility of preventive (*a priori*) control alongside repressive *(a posteriori)* control, and *erga omnes* effect of its judgments.[30] The Constitutional Court cannot bring a case of its own initiative: a procedure may begin after an application is submitted by a subject whose right to stand before the Constitutional Court is granted by the law. Cases at the Constitutional Court are heard pursuant to the special constitutional court procedure, which is regulated by the Constitutional Court Law, as well as the Rules of Procedure of the Constitutional Court.[31] Procedural issues which are not normatively regulated are decided by the Constitutional Court.[32]

Judges of the Constitutional Court

The establishment of the corps of the Constitutional Court judges is different to that of judges of the general court system. At the Constitutional Court, there are seven judges from whom three candidates must be proposed by at least ten Members of the Saeima; two—by the Cabinet of Ministers; two by the Plenary Session of the Supreme Court, which may select candidates from among the judges of the Republic of Latvia. The requirements set for candidates to the office of Constitutional Court justice are very similar to those set for constitutional court justices in other countries and for Supreme Court judges.[33] In Latvia, only a citizen with an impeccable reputation may become a judge. Candidates for the office of Constitutional Court justice must have a higher professional or academic education in legal science and a master's degree or a doctorate, must have reached the age of 40 as well as have at least 10 years of work experience in legal science. Judges are appointed to the office by the Saeima for 10 years. The Constitutional Court judge assumes his/her duties, or comes into office, only after giving an oath (solemn promise), as stipulated in the law "On Judicial Power", to the President of the State.

Competence of the Constitutional Court

The essence of the administration of justice at the Constitutional Court is to solve special or specific disputes regarding the compatibility of legal provisions with provisions of higher legal force.[34] The aim of the legislator, in establishing the Constitutional Court, was to create an effective mechanism for safeguarding the

---

[29]Constitutional Court Law. http://www.satv.tiesa.gov.lv/?lang=2&mid=9.

[30]Rodiņa (2009), pp. 44–47.

[31]Rules of Procedure of the Constitutional Court. http://www.satv.tiesa.gov.lv/en/2016/02/04/hello-world.

[32]Rodiņa and Amoliņa (2014), pp. 128–129.

[33]Rodiņa and Spale (2013), pp. 145–152.

[34]Judgement of the Constitutional Court in case No. 2006-12-01 on 20 December 2006, para 9.2. http://www.satv.tiesa.gov.lv/upload/judg_2006-12-01.htm.

priority of constitutional provisions.[35] The Constitutional Court, within the jurisdiction specified in the Satversme (Art. 85) and in the Constitutional Court Law, adjudicates matters regarding (1) compliance of laws with the Constitution; (2) compliance of international agreements signed or entered into by Latvia with the Constitution (also until the confirmation of the relevant agreements in the Saeima); (3) compliance of other regulatory enactments or parts thereof with norms (acts) of higher legal force; (4) compliance of other acts of the Saeima, the Cabinet of Ministers, the President of the Republic of Latvia, the Speaker of the Saeima and the Prime Minister, except for administrative acts, with law; (5) compliance with law of such an order with which a Minister authorised by the Cabinet has suspended a decision taken by a local government council; and (6) compliance of Latvian national legal norms with those international agreements entered into by Latvia that are not in conflict with the Constitution.

All subjects which can apply before the Constitutional Court are included in the Constitutional Court Law (Art. 17), and these are first of all the so-called subjects of abstract constitutional control (the President of the State, the Saeima, at least 20 members of the Saeima, the Cabinet of Ministers, the Prosecutor General, the Council of the State Audit Office, as well as two subjects which have to abide by specific procedural restrictions,—the Judicial Council [it can stand before the court if the legal question is connected with the judges and courts or is within its competence] and the Ombudsman [if the authority or official who has issued the disputed act has not rectified the established deficiencies within the time period specified by the Ombudsman[36]] can submit an application to the Constitutional Court to safeguard general or public interests.[37] Local government councils can submit an application if an act being disputed infringes the rights of the relevant local government. Only the relevant council has the right to submit a request for the initiation of a case regarding the compliance with law of an order in which a minister, authorised by the Cabinet, has suspended a decision taken by the local government council.

The subjects of concrete control—courts (also, judges of the Land Registry Offices) have the right to challenge a law's compliance with the Satversme, if, during adjudication of a concrete case, doubts arise about the compatibility of the proposed provision with the Satversme. This means that the application submitted by a court can only be concrete—related to the adjudication of a case.[38]

[35]Judgement of the Constitutional Court in case No.2008-35-01, on 7 April 2009, para 10.4. http://www.satv.tiesa.gov.lv/upload/judg_2008_35.htm.

[36]Rodiņa (2012), pp. 384–395.

[37]Judgement of the Constitutional Court of the Republic of Latvia in case No 2013-15-01 on 23 April 2014, para 7. http://www.satv.tiesa.gov.lv/wp-content/uploads/2013/10/2013-15-01_2_Spriedums_ENG.pdf; Judgement of the Constitutional Court of the Republic of Latvia in case No 2010-51-01 on 14 March 2011, para 10.2. http://www.satv.tiesa.gov.lv/upload/Judgment_2010-51-01_ENG.htm; Judgement of the Constitutional Court in case No.2010-60-01 on 30 March 2011, para 9. http://www.satv.tiesa.gov.lv/upload/spriedums_2010-60-01.htm.

[38]Decision of the Constitutional Court on termination of the procedure in case No 2010-09-01 on 13 October 2010, para 12. http://www.satv.tiesa.gov.lv/upload/lem_izb_2010-09-01.htm.

The Constitutional Court is also open to individuals (persons), who can submit a special type of application—a constitutional complaint—directly to the Court. In contrast to other subjects, a person (physical or legal person of private law) may not contest the compliance of a law with any provision of the Satversme at the Constitutional Court, but only compliance with the fundamental human rights established in the Satversme if those rights are violated by the legal norm.[39] As the *action popularis* is not allowed in Latvia, the applicant (a person) has to abide by specific requirements which are also typical of constitutional complaints in other countries. First, there must be a violation of the constitutionally guaranteed fundamental rights which must either exist in the present, or in specific cases, as possible in the future and in very exceptional cases, potential.[40] Second, before submitting the constitutional complaint, a person must have exhausted other legal means which are real and effective, not theoretically possible, or observe and respect the principle of subsidiarity.[41] Third, a constitutional complaint can be submitted within a 6 month period which should be calculated from the moment the last ruling of the court comes into force or from the moment the violation occurred.[42]

A legal procedure begun at the Constitutional Court can be terminated in two ways: by passing a judgment or by passing a decision on termination of the procedure. The right to declare laws invalid, and other enactments or parts thereof, can be realised only by adopting a judgment. The legal nature of a Constitutional Court judgment is characterised by the following features: (1) universally binding force *(erga omnes)*; (2) final (cannot be appealed); (3) public; (4) directly applicable; (5) unsurpassable.[43] A legal provision (act) which has been declared unconstitutional shall be regarded as not in effect from the day of publication of the Constitutional Court judgment, unless the Constitutional Court has determined otherwise. The jurisprudence of the Constitutional Court shows that a provision can also become invalid from the day it was adopted or another date in the past (*ex tunc*); or on a date determined by the Court in the future (*pro futuro*). Retroactive judgments should be regarded as the exception.[44] However, the retroactive force of a judgment is of special importance within the constitutional complaint, since this may be the only means of safeguarding persons' fundamental rights.[45] Therefore, the Constitutional Court quite frequently, on declaring a contested provision incompatible with the Satversme and invalid, sets a special condition that, with

---

[39] Rodiņa (2009), pp. 20–25.

[40] Judgement of the Constitutional Court in case No 2012-16-01 on 10 May 2013, para 21. http://www.satv.tiesa.gov.lv/wp-content/uploads/2012/07/2012-16-01_Spriedums_ENG.pdf.

[41] Judgement of the Constitutional Court in case No 2012-23-01 on 24 October 2012, para 14. http://www.satv.tiesa.gov.lv/wp-content/uploads/2012/12/2012-23-01_Spriedums_ENG.pdf; see also Rodiņa (2014a), pp. 1636–1640.

[42] Rodiņa (2014c), pp. 319–335.

[43] Rodiņa and Spale (2013), p. 140.

[44] Rodiņa (2009), p. 146.

[45] Rodiņa (2015), pp. 139–146.

regard to the applicant, the provision becomes invalid as of the day of its adoption (*ex tunc*).[46] In some cases, retroactive force is also applied to other persons (groups of persons) which are under similar actual and legal conditions as the applicant.

5.2 Administrative Law and Procedure

Jautrīte Briede and Edvīns Danovskis
Law Faculty, University of Latvia, Raiņa bulv, 19 Riga, Latvia
e-mail: jautrite.briede@lu.lv

5.2.1 Introduction

The basic structure, concepts and methodology of application of Latvian administrative law is similar to other German-based administrative law systems. This is characterised in several features of the Latvian administrative law. First, the system of sources of law is similar to the German system. There are basic sources (normative enactments [the Constitution,[47] laws, regulations and bylaws], general principles of law and customary law) and secondary sources of law (jurisprudence, legal thesis in court rulings, etc.). Second, some of the basic concepts of administrative law are clearly derived from the German administrative law. This can be clearly seen in administrative procedure, where a German concept such as the Administrative Act (*Verwaltungsakt*) is introduced in the Latvian Administrative Procedure Law. Third, it is well known that several parts of the Administrative Procedure Law (general provisions and administrative procedure within institutions) were drafted under the influence of the German Administrative Procedure Law (*Verwaltungsverfarengesetz*) and Portuguese Administrative Procedure Law, which is also influenced by the German law.[48] Fourth, the doctrinal understanding of the structure of administrative law is also rather similar to in Germany. However, there are also many differences and national peculiarities.

The branch of administrative law comprises four large segments of law: (1) the law of administrative structure (on the status of government institutions and their officials), (2) administrative procedure law, (3) material administrative law (specific regulations of government activity, such as social security law, tax law, environmental law, education law, planning and building law, etc.), (4) law on

[46]Rodiņa (2014b), pp. 273–300.

[47]The Constitution of the Republic of Latvia. http://www.vvc.gov.lv/export/sites/default/docs/LRTA/Likumi/Constitution.doc.

[48]Administratīvā procesa izveide Latvijā: no idejas līdz likumam un administratīvajām tiesām (2009).

administrative offences. This chapter further outlines three of these branches; material administrative law is not further dealt with because of its volume and complexity.

In Latvia, administrative law is considered a very new branch of law, since many fundamental provisions regulating administrative law were adopted in the mid-1990s or at the beginning of the twenty-first century. Continuity with the legal regulation (direct renewal of legal provisions) of the period of first independence (1918–1940) was impossible, as the socioeconomic conditions and government institutions were completely different. Most of the legal provisions adopted during the period of Soviet occupation were also unenforceable after the adoption of the Declaration of Independence on 4 May 1990. Therefore, the structure of administration and the entire legal regulation of its activities were drafted anew. However, this process had its own hazards, and among them were a lack of proper understanding of legal principles (such principles as the rule of law, proportionality, fair and equal treatment were unknown to most Latvian lawyers), lack of knowledge on the methodology of application of law and other manifestations of "administrative weakness",[49] like corruption and lack of sound procedures in many activities of administrative institutions. These problems have been gradually overcome. A major factor accelerating the transition from the Soviet legal system to a continental European legal system was the doctrinal and practical contribution of Latvian lawyer and politician Egils Levits (b. 1955). Levits obtained his qualification as a lawyer in Germany and became a prominent figure in Latvian legal and political circles during the process of restoration of independence in 1990. From 1993–1994, he served as Minister of Justice and initiated several major reforms in administration, among them reforms of the civil service, adoption of the law of local governments, and initiation of the drafting of the Administrative Procedure Law. He is most notable for his influential publications on administrative and constitutional law, which were mainly based on German administrative law. He actively participated in drafting several major administrative laws—the Administrative Procedure Law (2001)[50] and State Administrative Structure Law (2002).[51] Since these laws came into force, administrative law has evolved from a rudimentary and obscure legal branch into a sound, effective and well-developed set of legal provisions in most of its sub-branches.

[49]The term "administrative weakness" was used in the Conception of the State Administrative Structure Law as characterising the state of Latvian public administration in the end of 1990. See Levits (2002).

[50]Administrative Procedure Law. http://www.vvc.gov.lv/export/sites/default/docs/LRTA/Likumi/Administrative_Procedure_Law.doc.

[51]State Administrative Structure Law. http://www.vvc.gov.lv/export/sites/default/docs/LRTA/Likumi/State_Administration_Structure_Law.doc.. See further on development of Latvian administrative law: Balodis et al. (2013b), pp. 57–63.

5.2.2 State Administrative Structure and the Public Service

5.2.2.1 State Administrative Structure

Article 58 of the Constitution states that administrative institutions shall be under the authority of the Cabinet of Ministers. This means that all institutions performing executive functions are hierarchically subordinated to the Cabinet of Ministers. This Article also comprises the principle of unity of executive power, i.e., that no government institution may operate outside this hierarchical structure. Article 57 of the Constitution provides that the number of ministries, their scope of activities and relations between state institutions shall be prescribed by law. This broad delegation entitles the Parliament to significant discretion in regulating the powers of the executive branch.

The Law of the Structure of the Cabinet of Ministers (2008)[52] inter alia prescribes the number of ministries and entitles the Cabinet of Ministers to adopt Regulations of the Cabinet of Ministers. The Cabinet of Ministers is entitled to adopt Regulations only (1) if a particular law contains authorisation to do so and only to implement the provisions of the law, (2) when the Cabinet of Ministers is entitled to ratify international agreements and (3) when it is necessary to implement the normative enactments of the European Union and if the law does not regulate the matter at issue. Therefore, the right to issue Regulations of the Cabinet of Ministers is performed within the executive (not legislative) function to execute the political will contained in the law.[53]

The structure and internal relations within the executive branch are prescribed by the State Administrative Structure Law. The basis for the legal structure of the state administration is the concept of "public legal entity". These legal entities are the State and legal entities derived from the State. The State is the original public legal entity. In the sphere of the executive branch, it operates through its institutions—the Cabinet of Ministers, ministries and other state institutions (for example, the State Revenue Service, State Police, Centre of Protection of Consumer Rights, state museums, professional education institutions, etc.). There are around 140 state institutions. Most of these are subordinated to the Cabinet of Ministers through the respective ministry, and several are directly subordinated either to the respective minister or the president of ministers. It is important to note that these institutions do not have their own legal capacity, i.e., they are not legal entities. The legal entity is the State. Therefore, legal disputes between two state institutions are impossible since they are part of one public legal entity. All such disputes are resolved hierarchically.

Besides the State, there are other public legal entities, which are called "derived public legal entities". If the State institutions do not have their own legal capacity, then public legal entities have legal capacity, i.e., they have their own budget, they

[52]Law on the Structure of Cabinet of Ministers. LV, 2008, no 82.

[53]Judgment of the Constitutional Court of 9 October 2007 in case No.2007-04-03. http://www.satv.tiesa.gov.lv/wp-content/uploads/2007/01/2007-04-02_Spriedums_ENG.pdf.

are entitled to own property, etc. The status of derived public legal entities is provided in particular laws on an *ad hoc* basis. Notable examples of derived public legal entities are local municipalities, state-owned institutions of higher education, the Bank of Latvia, the Financial and Capital Markets Commission, etc. These legal entities also may establish their own institutions which, like state institutions, lack legal capacity. For example, local municipalities may establish schools, municipal police, social security services, but these institutions only act on behalf of the municipality.

Local municipalities are a specific type of derived legal entity regulated by the Law on Municipalities (1994)[54] and the Law on Administrative Territories and Populated Areas (2008).[55] In 2015, there were 119 local municipalities. There is only one level of local municipalities; however, there are two types of local municipality—cities of the republic (9) and district municipalities[56] (110). In some regards (for instance, electoral matters), the legal regulation of these local municipalities is different. The Law on Municipalities prescribes the autonomous functions of local municipalities, their administrative structure and operation. The Cabinet of Ministers is entitled to execute supervision only in cases provided in the Law on Municipalities. For instance, the Minister for Regional Development is entitled to suspend the bylaws of local municipalities if they are unlawful. The local municipalities must send draft bylaws to the Ministry for Regional Development for inspection of their legality, and the Minister for Regional Development is entitled to suspend from office the Chairman of the Council of a local municipality, if the Chairman has acted unlawfully or has failed to fulfill his duties.

There are a few administrative institutions which are not subordinated to the Cabinet of Ministers. In Latvian legal terminology, these are called "self-dependent" institutions. These institutions are the Bank of Latvia, the Financial and Capital Markets Commission, the Public Utilities Commission, the National Electronic Mass Media Council, the Office of the Ombudsman, the Central Election Committee and the Central Land Committee. The leaders of nearly all these institutions are approved by Parliament. The "self-dependence" of these institutions is not provided in the Constitution *expressis verbis*. However, the Constitutional Court has ruled that such a status is compatible with the Constitution as far as such functions cannot be effectively carried out under the supervision of the Cabinet of Ministers and as far as there are provided other effective means to execute supervision.[57] Some of these institutions are authorised by law to enact regulations binding to private persons. The Constitutional Court has ruled that, in the case of regulations

[54]Law on Municipalities. http://www.vvc.gov.lv/export/sites/default/docs/LRTA/Likumi/On_Local_Governments.doc.

[55]Law on Administrative Territories and Populated Areas http://www.vvc.gov.lv/export/sites/default/docs/LRTA/Likumi/Law_On_Administrative_Territories_and_Populated_Areas.doc.

[56]In Latvian terminology the term is "novads".

[57]Judgment of the Constitutional Court of 16 October 2006 in case No.2006-05-01. http://www.satv.tiesa.gov.lv/wp-content/uploads/2006/04/2006-05-01_Spriedums_ENG.pdf.

enacted by the Bank of Latvia, these regulations as such do not contradict the Constitution, as far as they are enacted within the framework of the legal provisions which authorise their enactment.[58]

Limited liability companies and joint stock companies which are owned by public legal entities are outside the scope of the state administrative structure. They are private legal entities (i.e., subjects of private law), although in some instances (public procurement, law on squandering of financial resources and property of public legal entities) they equate to public legal entities. In many cases, public legal entities have authorised their company to carry out its own administrative tasks. Notable examples include the joint stock company "Latvijas Valsts Ceļi" (Latvian State Roads), which carries out the administrative task—the maintenance of state owned roads, and limited liability company "Ceļu satiksmes drošības direkcija" (Road Traffic Safety Directorate), which is authorised to issue driving licenses and register road vehicles.

The State Administrative Structure Law provides rather broad regulation for delegation of administrative tasks to private persons, as well as for other forms of involvement of the community in the fulfillment of administrative tasks. Delegation of administrative tasks to private persons is provided in many normative enactments, for example, the private association "Latvijas Ārstu biedrība" (Association of Latvian Physicians) is authorised to issue licenses for physicians. The public legal entity is liable for third persons with regards to the fulfillment of delegated administrative tasks.

5.2.2.2 The Public Service

The concept of "public service" in Latvia refers to particular employment relationships (relationships of public law) in various State institutions where the master (the State) has broad rights to determine the duties of the servants, including unilateral transfer to other positions. There are four major groups of public service employees: (1) civil servants (~11,500), (2) police officers, firefighters, border guards, and officers employed in Custody Authority (~ 12,000), (3) military officers (~5000) and (4) prosecutors. This list is not exhaustive; however, the remaining servants in several particular authorities (like Corruption Prevention and Combating Bureau) are small in number. These groups; however, are not regulated by uniform legal provisions; each group has its own law regulating the service. All the above-mentioned groups, except civil servants, are in a career service, i.e., they are divided into ranks. Positions of higher rank can be filled only by those who have served for some time in lower ranks. The civil service (except civil servants employed in diplomatic and consular service, which is a career service), on the contrary, is based on the position model. This means that even the highest positions in the civil service (e.g., state secretary of the ministry) can be filled by persons who

[58]See Judgment of the Constitutional Court of 2 March 2016 in case No.2015-11-03. http://www.satv.tiesa.gov.lv/wp-content/uploads/2015/04/2015-11-03_Spriedums_ENG.pdf.

have participated in an open competition and without prior experience in the civil service.

The civil service, as the most prominent branch of the public service, is regulated by the Civil Service Law (2000).[59] The law clearly defines the concept of a civil servant. The definition of a civil servant has two compulsory elements: institutional and functional. The institutional element states that a civil servant can be employed only in state institutions. Therefore, civil servants can be employed in ministries and other state institutions (there are some institutions, like the state police, which do not employ civil servants), but not derived public entities. Therefore, for example, employees of local municipalities, the Bank of Latvia and of state-owned universities are all employed under the general regulation of the Labour Law within private legal relationships. The functional criterion states that only those are civil servants who carry out tasks related to administration of public funds, coordinate the activities of government policy, or draft legal enactments and other binding legal acts. In practice, the application of this definition does not cause any fundamental problems.

Until 2008, the civil service system was centralised. However, in 2008 the Civil Service Authority, which supervised appointments, transfers and dismissals in the civil service, was liquidated. Since then, the civil service system has been decentralised, i.e., each institution makes its own appointments, transfers and dismissals. These decisions are only supervised by the respective ministry.

Vacancies in the civil service can be filled either by organising an open competition or by a transfer. The manager of the authority may choose between these two options at his own discretion. In practice, lower positions are filled by open competition and transfers are more common for senior positions.

In 2014, a draft law on the public service was submitted to Parliament.[60] The draft is an elaborated version of the Civil Service Law and concerns only those who are employed in state institutions—civil servants and employees. The main concept of the draft is to change the status of all employees (those who are currently employed under the Labour law) to servants employed in public legal relationships. This means, for example, that an IT employee who is employed in a ministry under an employment agreement will be transferred into a servant position. This means that the effected persons can be transferred to other posts without their consent and that all employment disputes will be handled in administrative courts. This concept has been criticised by labour unions, mainly because the State will no longer be obliged to ask the approval of the labour union before terminating an employment relationship with an employee who is a member of a labour union (this provision is not applied to persons employed in public service). The draft law was adopted in the

[59]Civil Service Law http://www.vvc.gov.lv/export/sites/default/docs/LRTA/Likumi/State_Civil_Service_Law.doc.

[60]Draft Administrative Offences Procedure Law (Administratīvo pārkāpumu procesa likums). http://titania.saeima.lv/LIVS12/saeimalivs12.nsf/0/8F85FC1AE272C759C2257D8E004788AD?OpenDocument. Accessed on 19 May 2016.

Parliament in the first reading; however, there is insufficient political will to prepare it for further readings.

Another concept peculiar to Latvian administrative law is the concept of the "public official" (valsts amatpersona). This concept is used in the Law on Prevention of Conflict of Interest in Activities of Public Officials[61] to describe the subjects of this law. The concept of "public official" is much broader than the concept of "civil servant" and comprises both clearly defined officials (member of Parliament, ministers, judges, members of the board of state-owned joint stock companies, councilors of local municipalities, etc.) and all other persons exercising state power (adopting administrative acts, making decisions regarding public funds or property, etc.). The law provides rather detailed, even casuistic obligations, limitations and prohibitions for public officials.

5.2.3 Administrative Procedure

The Administrative Procedure Law deals with the activities of administrative authorities as well as the administrative courts. Hence, administrative procedure means both an activity of administrative authority aimed at adopting an administrative act, making a physical act[62] or concluding an agreement under public law,[63] as well as activities of administrative courts aimed at controlling the exercise of executive power relating to specific public legal relations between the State and private persons.

5.2.3.1 Administrative Act

The most important form of action of the public administration in the execution of laws is an administrative act. The concept of administrative acts is similar to the German *Verwaltungsakt*. The main elements of an administrative act are: it must be a decision having external legal effect, issued by an administrative authority in the area of public law, with regard to an individually indicated private (natural or legal) person. Administrative acts are also decisions regarding the establishment, alteration or termination of the legal status of civil servants and disciplinary punishment. Administrative acts also include decisions regarding persons especially subordinate to the administrative authority (such as students, prisoners, mental patients in special hospitals, etc.) and civil servants, if they significantly limit the human rights of those persons. Other internal decisions regarding these persons, or decisions which affect only an administrative authority itself or bodies subordinate to it, are not administrative acts but "internal decisions." Likewise, political decisions

[61]On Prevention of Conflict of Interest in Activities of Public Officials. http://www.vvc.gov.lv/export/sites/default/docs/LRTA/Likumi/On_Prevention_of_Conflict_of_Interest_in_Activities_of_Public_Officials.pdf.

[62]On physical acts or actual actions see further Briede (2006), pp. 529–533.

[63]On administrative contracts see further Briede (2014), pp. 210–220.

(political announcements, declarations, invitations, election of officials, and similar) by the *Saeima* (the Parliament), the President, the Cabinet, or councils of local municipalities, as well as decisions regarding criminal proceedings and court adjudications are not administrative acts.[64]

The law also recognises the concept of the general administrative act. This concept is similar to the German general order (*Allgemeinverfügung)*. Such acts are decisions which are issued regarding indeterminate persons; however, addressees are determinable by common characteristics. General administrative acts include, for example, decisions on the closure of a public road or bridge, detailed plans of a part of a local government territory developed to lay down the requirements for the use of specific land units and building parameters.[65] At the same time, local government spatial plans and local plans (local government long-term spatial development planning documents, developed for a part of the territory) cannot be considered general administrative acts, but normative acts of local municipalities. These, therefore, are subject to judicial review by the Constitutional Court and not in administrative courts.

5.2.3.2 Statement Regarding Rights

The Administrative Procedure Law provides the right for a private person to receive a statement (*uzziņa*) regarding his or her rights in a specific legal situation from an administrative authority within whose competence it lies to decide the issue on merits. The aim of the statement is to help the private person to understand the legal rules applicable in a particular case, to exercise his or her rights and not to violate the law. A statement shall not be binding on its addressee. At the same time, if the addressee of a statement has acted in conformity with the issued statement, the administrative act issued later by the authority concerning the question regarding which the statement was given may not be more unfavorable to the addressee, even if the authority subsequently determines that the statement was not correct.

5.2.3.3 Principles of Administrative Procedure

The Administrative Procedure Law includes a set of principles of good administration laid down and developed in documents of the Council of Europe, the jurisprudence of the European Court of Human Rights and European Court of Justice. The principles are not only incorporated into the articles of the Law, but also listed and defined in the beginning of the Law. The aim of the listing and definitions is to highlight the role of the principles for those officials who do not understand that the public administration must act in the public interest and not just for the protection of the interests of a narrow group of people (as in the Soviet period).

These principles include, for example, the principle of observance of the rights of private persons, the principle of equality, the principle of the rule of law, the

[64]See Article 1 of the Administrative Procedure Law.

[65]Spatial Development Planning Law. http://www.vvc.gov.lv/export/sites/default/docs/LRTA/Likumi/Spatial_Development_Planning_Law.doc.

principle of reasonable application of the norms of law, the principle of disallowing arbitrariness, the principle of protection of legitimate trust and vested rights, the principle of lawfulness, the principle of proportionality, the principle of priority of laws, the principle of impartiality, the principle of right to be heard and procedural equity.

These principles shall be applied if the relevant issue is not governed by an external regulatory enactment, as well as to interpret regulatory enactments.

5.2.3.4 Administrative Procedure Before an Administrative Authority

An administrative procedure shall be initiated based on the application of a private person or on the initiative of an administrative authority. Applications may be submitted orally or in writing. The authority shall immediately formalise an oral application in writing and the applicant shall sign it. The Law provides that an authority shall, insofar as possible, provide an applicant with the necessary information or other form of assistance for successfully resolving the matter in accordance with the interests of the applicant.

After initiation of an administrative procedure, an authority shall acquire such information as, in accordance with the legal provisions, is necessary for an appropriate decision to be taken. In acquiring information, an authority may use all legal methods, and obtain information from participants in the administrative proceeding and from other administrative authorities, as well as by means of the assistance of witnesses, experts, inspections, documents, or other types of evidence. If the information needed by an authority is not at the disposal of participants but is at the disposal of another authority, the authority shall acquire the information itself rather than requiring it from participants. The participants have an obligation to submit all the evidence and information at their disposal. A participant in an administrative proceeding has the right, in principle, to become acquainted with the matter and express his or her opinion at any stage of the proceedings.

Before deciding on the issuing of an unfavorable administrative act, an authority shall clarify and assess the opinions and arguments of the addressee and third party, except in cases of urgency or inadequacy.

If an administrative procedure is initiated by an application, an authority shall take a decision within a month from the day the application is submitted, provided that a shorter term is not prescribed in a regulatory enactment. The Law allows an extension of this deadline.

When deciding on the issuing of an administrative act or deciding on its contents, an authority should consider: (1) the necessity of the administrative act for the achieving of a legal (legitimate) objective, (2) the suitability of the administrative act for the attaining of the relevant objective, (3) the need for the administrative act, that is, whether it is possible to attain such objective by means which are less restrictive of the rights and legal interests of the participants; and (4) the conformity of the administrative act, comparing the infringement of the rights of a private person and the benefit for the public interest, as well as taking into account that substantial restriction of the rights of a private person may only be justified by a significant benefit to the public.

An administrative act issued in writing shall include the basis for the administrative act, including, in particular, the above-mentioned considerations. An administrative act shall include information on remedies which are available against it.

An administrative act shall come into effect at the time the addressee is notified of it. The manner in which the addressee is notified of the administrative act—in writing, orally or otherwise—shall not affect its coming into effect. Notification procedure is regulated by the Law on Notification.[66] An administrative act can be notified on site at the authority or by delivery with the intermediation of an employee or courier appointed thereby, using postal services, using electronic communications and publicly.

If the addressee or the third person is not satisfied with the decision, it may be challenged before a higher authority within 1 month or 1 year (depending on whether an administrative act contains information on remedies). A higher authority deciding on an appeal can act to worsen the legal situation of the appellant, in principle, only when mandatory rules are applicable.

The Administrative Procedure Law provides the possibility for an administrative authority, under certain conditions, to annul an administrative act. However, in certain cases, if the administrative act is annulled, the addressee has a right to reimbursement for losses and personal harm caused him or her as a result of annulment of the administrative act. At the same time, if the addressee has achieved the issue of the administrative act by knowingly providing false information, by bribery, duress, threats or other illegal actions, the addressee has a duty to reimburse the relevant public legal entity for everything such addressee has obtained from the administrative act.

If an administrative act has become non-disputable, in certain cases an administrative proceeding regarding the same matter may be initiated *de novo* based on the submission of the addressee or the third party. This could be the case, for example, if the actual circumstances of the matter, which were the basis for taking the decision, have changed or the legal circumstances of the matter have changed in favor of the addressee.

An administrative authority may, instead of issuing an administrative act, conclude an agreement under public law with the person to whom it would otherwise direct the administrative act in three situations: (1) if it is expressly authorised by law, (2) to terminate a legal dispute, especially a judicial procedure; (3) if the applicable law confers discretion to the public administration with respect to the content of an administrative act.

An administrative act, a physical act and an agreement under public law are subject to judicial review by administrative courts.

[66] Law on Notification. http://www.vvc.gov.lv/export/sites/default/docs/LRTA/Likumi/On_Notification.doc.

5.2.3.5 Administrative Courts

After the restoration of independence of the Republic of Latvia, the administrative courts system was established in 2004. Since 1 February 2004 (the date the Administrative Procedure Law came into force), the decisions and acts of administrative authorities have been reviewed by the Administrative District Court, the Administrative Regional Court and the Department of Administrative Cases of the Supreme Court.

Before this, there was a great amount of work involved in selecting and training administrative judges. Candidates had to take exams on both constitutional and administrative law; they had to respond to the most important questions in the field of legal theory, moreover, they also had to pass exams in psychology, where their logical thinking was tested. After their selection, the studies began, wherein the candidates gained knowledge of the deeper and more complex questions of administrative law, administrative procedural law, drafting of judgments, etc.

Since, at the beginning of the functioning of administrative courts in Latvia, a great number of administrative acts were annulled because of infringement of essential procedural requirements, administrative authorities started to pay greater attention to the rules of the Administrative Procedure Law and its principles.

The substance of administrative procedure in court is court control of the legality and validity of administrative acts issued by institutions or physical acts of administrative authorities, as well as the determination of public legal duties or rights of private persons and the adjudication of disputes arising from agreements under public law.

While performing its duties in the course of administrative proceedings, a court must (*ex officio*) objectively determine the circumstances of a matter and provide a legal assessment, adjudicating the matter within a reasonable time.

In the course of an administrative proceeding, the court must determine: (1) whether the administrative act and the physical act of the administrative authority complies with the provisions of the Administrative Procedure Law and other norms of law; (2) whether the norms of law or agreements under public law give specific rights to, or impose duties on the participants in an administrative proceeding; and (3) the compliance of the agreement under public law with the norms of law, the fact of its being in force and the correctness of fulfilment.

In examining the legality of an administrative act or physical act, and in ascertaining public legal duties or rights of private persons, in case of doubt the court must verify whether the norm of law applied by the authority or to be applied in the administrative court proceeding conforms to the norms of law of higher legal force. If a court acknowledges that a norm of law does not conform to the Constitution or norms (acts) of international law, it will suspend court proceedings in the matter and send a substantiated application to the Constitutional Court. However, if a court acknowledges that the binding regulations of a local government do not conform to Cabinet regulations or the law, or that Cabinet regulations do not conform to the law, it will not apply the relevant legal norm.

In general, an application regarding the issue, setting aside, or validity of an administrative act may be submitted within 1 month from the day when the administrative act comes into effect. If it is not set out in the administrative act, where and within what time period it may be appealed, the application may be submitted in respective cases within a year from the day the administrative act comes into effect.

Submission of an application to the court regarding the setting aside of an administrative act or declaring it invalid, in general, results in automatic suspension of the administrative act from the day the application is submitted. There are exceptions to this rule, for example, in cases of urgency. If the applicant is not the addressee of the suspended administrative act, the addressee can ask the court to renew operation of the administrative act.

During the court procedure, the applicant may request the court take measures of provisional protection. Measures of provisional protection may be granted in particular if the administrative act or lack thereof may cause severe damage which could only be made good with difficulty and if there is a *prima facie* case against the validity of the act.

5.2.3.6 Execution

The Administrative Procedure Law provides regulation for the execution of administrative acts as well as decisions and judgments of administrative courts.

An administrative act shall be carried out on a compulsory basis, where the following aggregate circumstances exist: (1) the administrative act has come into effect; (2) the administrative act has become non-disputable; and (3) until the commencement of compulsory execution, the administrative act has not been executed voluntarily.

A private person against whom compulsory execution is directed may submit a complaint if the actions of an executive institution which are directed towards compulsory execution of an administrative act do not comply with the provisions of the Law. A complaint may be submitted within 7 days from the day the private person comes to know of the actions of the executive institution.

An administrative act imposing a duty on the addressee to carry out a specific action or prohibiting the carrying out of a specific action shall be executed on a compulsory basis by means of substitute execution, pecuniary penalty or direct force.

If a court decision or judgment imposes a duty on an administrative authority to perform a specific action or refrain from a specific action and the authority does not fulfil such duty, a pecuniary penalty may be imposed on the head or another official of the authority.

5.2.3.7 Compensation

Everyone is entitled to claim due compensation for financial loss or personal harm, including moral harm, which has been caused him or her by an administrative act or a physical act of an administrative authority. The procedure for compensation is regulated by the Law on Compensation for Damages Caused by Administrative

Authorities.[67] Disputes concerning compensation are subject to judicial review by administrative courts together with an administrative act, or separately after a court procedure in which the administrative act has been declared unlawful or invalid.[68]

In determining the pre-conditions of the financial loss and personal harm and the amount of compensation, the principles of civil law shall be applied if the law does not specify otherwise.

5.2.4 Administrative Offences

Administrative offences are offences listed in the Code of Administrative Offences[69] and the bylaws of local municipalities. Sometimes these are called "small crimes" because the general principles regulating administrative offences are derived from criminal law. Punishment for administrative offences is an important function of many administrative institutions.

The Code of Administrative Offences was adopted in 1984 within the framework of the Soviet legal reform on administrative offences. The law is still in force, although it has been amended more than 130 times and there have been several attempts to draft new law.

The Code provides that the subjects of administrative offences are physical persons and legal entities. Legal entities are the subjects of administrative offences only if it is clearly provided in the sanction of the respective offence. Only private legal entities are the subjects of administrative offences—public legal entities and their institutions cannot be punished. Instead, the managers of public legal entities and their institutions are to be punished for the illegal activities of public legal entities.

The punishment for an administrative offence is prescribed for each administrative offence. Generally, the punishment can be a warning, fine, termination of several rights (for instance, termination of a driving license) and even administrative arrest for up to 15 days. The largest part of the Code consists of a list of administrative offences (grouped in chapters) for many administrative offences in employment relations, labour safety, traffic safety, environmental, commercial activities, public order, etc. The Code also provides procedure for imposing punishment and appeals to higher institutions and courts.

Recently, a new draft Administrative Offences Procedure Law[70] has been submitted to Parliament. The draft law introduces major changes in the system of administrative liability law, mainly, it provides the uncodifying of administrative

[67]Law on Compensation for Damages Caused by Administrative Authorities. LV, 2005, no 96.

[68]See further on remedies in administrative procedure Danovskis (2014), pp. 230–240.

[69]Code of Administrative Offences. http://www.vvc.gov.lv/export/sites/default/docs/LRTA/Likumi/Latvian_Administrative_Violations_Code.doc.

[70]Draft Administrative Offences Procedure Law. http://titania.saeima.lv/LIVS12/saeimalivs12.nsf/0/8F85FC1AE272C759C2257D8E004788AD?OpenDocument.

offences. The present Code of Administrative Offences lists all administrative offences in the "Special Part" of the Code. The draft law provides only general provisions on all administrative offences and procedure for their adoption and judicial review. This means that administrative offences would be listed not in one law, but in each law's regulatory subject matter (for instance, administrative liability for breaches of consumer protection provisions would be provided in the respective law regulating consumer protection).

5.3 Criminal Law and Procedure

Valentija Liholaja and Kristīne Strada-Rozenberga
Law Faculty, University of Latvia, Raiņa bulv, 19 Riga, Latvia
e-mail: Valentija.Liholaja@lu.lv

5.3.1 Criminal Law

5.3.1.1 Introduction

The development of criminal law was influenced by the historical situation in Latvia, under which the criminal law framework in the twentieth century in the territory of Latvia originally comprised the Penal Codes[71] of the Russian Empire in 1903, which were replaced by the first criminal law—the Penal Law[72] of independent Latvia on 1 August 1933. This codification was in force until 25 November 1940, when because of the occupation and annexation of Latvia to the Soviet Union, the occupying authority introduced in Latvia the Criminal Code[73] of 1926 of the RSFSR, which was in force until 31 March 1961, except during the period of German occupation. From 1 April 1961 to 31 March 1999, the Latvian SSR (Criminal Code of Latvia)[74] was in force, which was replaced by the Criminal Law (hereinafter KL),[75] adopted on 17 June 1998.

5.3.1.2 The Structure of the Criminal Law

The structure of the Criminal Law in Latvia, like in the Republic of Lithuania and the Republic of Estonia, consists of a General and Special Part. The content of the Criminal Law includes four institutes—"criminal law", "criminal offence", "punishment", "release from criminal liability and punishment", which are systematised

[71]Penal Code of 22 March 1903. Rīga: Valsts tipogrāfija, 1925.

[72]Penal Code (Sodu likums). Rīga: Valsts tipogrāfija, 1936.

[73]Criminal Code of RSFSR. Maskava: PSRS Tieslietu Tautas komisariāta Juridiskā izdevniecība, 1944.

[74]Criminal Code of Latvia SSR. Rīga: Latvijas Valsts izdevniecība, 1962.

[75]Criminal Law. http://www.vvc.gov.lv.

in the General Part and Special Part of the Criminal Law and subdivided into lesser institutes and incorporated norms.

5.3.1.3 Criminal Law Functions and Principles

Criminal law functions and tasks, unlike in previous codifications and in other countries (such as the Lithuanian Criminal Code), are not defined in the Criminal Law of our country except based on the criminal law theory verities; one of the main criminal law action lines constitutes a protective function in the form of the protection of state, social, groups' or individuals' interests from criminal offences with those peculiar means—criminal punishments and other coercive measures.[76]

The deterrent or warning function of the criminal law must be stressed, because the legislature, criminalising and penalising offences, warns any person of the possible punishment in the case of committing a criminal offence, while one of the punishment target components is to make convicts and other persons comply with the law and refrain from committing criminal offences (KL Art. 35, Paragraph two).

At the same time, the legislature provides a person the possibility of not being punished, by voluntarily withdrawing from the commission of a criminal offence, that is, the complete discontinuance by a person, pursuant to his or her own will, of a criminal offence commenced by such person while knowing that the possibility exists to complete the commission of the criminal offence (KL Art. 16, Paragraph one) and voluntarily fulfilling the activities indicated in the Special Part of the Criminal Law (Art. 199^1, 221^4, 235, 254, $288.^5$), which is also regarded as an effective preventive measure.

Criminal law can implement its protective and preventive function only through strict adherence to the inherent legal principles, namely, to the leading ideas which are binding to the legislature, the institutions applying the law and every person.

The basic principles of criminal law in the Criminal Law of our country are not independently defined, but are referenced in certain sections of the General Part. In view of the Constitution of the Republic of Latvia,[77] binding international laws, the norms of the Criminal Law, as well as theoretical verities, the following principles of criminal law can be divided: the principle of legality, the principle of equality, the principle of guilt, the principle of justice and the humanitarian principle.

The principle of legality means that the criminality of the offence, convictions and other criminal consequences, as stated in the Criminal Law. The legality principle consists of a number of legislative regulations. First, a law must comply with the Constitution of the Republic of Latvia and be in accordance with Art. 85, which states that cases on the conformity of laws with the Constitution shall be heard in the Constitutional Court. Secondly, Latvian national laws must comply with international laws, recognising the supremacy of international law under the

[76]In greater detail see: Krastiņš and Liholaja (2015), pp. 57–58.

[77]The Constitution of Republic of Latvia. http://www.vvc.gov.lv/export/sites/default/docs/LRTA/Likumi/Constitution.doc.

common law (*lex internacionalis derogate legi nacionali*). And, thirdly, a person can only be held criminally liable for offences provided in the Criminal Law (*nullum crimen, nulla poena sine lege*), which also includes a prohibition to criminalise an offence, applying the law by analogy, that is directly specified in the fourth paragraph of Art. 1 of the Criminal Law.

The principle of equality is under international law and is enshrined in Art. 91 of the Constitution of the Republic of Latvia, stating that all people in Latvia shall be equal before the law and the courts. The equality of persons before the law also defines the general principles for the determination of punishment in Art. 46 of the Criminal Law, stating in the first paragraph that a punishment shall be determined to the extent provided for the committed criminal offence by the sanction of the relevant Art. of the Special Part of the Criminal Law, conforming to the provisions of the General Part of the Criminal Law.

The principle of guilt is contained in the first paragraph of Art. 1 of the Criminal Law, indicating that only a person who is guilty of committing a criminal offence, that is, one who deliberately (intentionally) or through negligence has committed an offence which is set out in the Criminal Law, may be held criminally liable and punished. Guilt detection is the basis of the concept of a criminal offence (KL Art. 6). Such an indication by the legislature embodies the ancient Roman law postulate—*nullum crimen, nulla poena sine culpa*, excluding criminal liability without guilt, the so-called objective capacity.

The principle of equity is mainly reflected by the punishment individualisation arising directly from the second and the third part of Art. 46 of the Criminal Law; in determining the type of punishment, it shall be taken into account the character of the offence committed and harm caused, as well as the personality of the offender. While determining the degree of punishment, mitigating and aggravating circumstances shall be taken into account.

The court, in considering various mitigating circumstances and the personality of the offender, in accordance with the first part of Art. 49 of the Criminal Law, may determine a punishment which is lesser than the minimum limit for the relevant criminal offence provided for by the Law. If the court, in consideration of the character of the offence committed and the harm caused by the offender's personality and other circumstances of the case, becomes convinced that the guilty, without serving sentence, will not commit violations of the law in the future, it may punish the offender with a suspended sentence (KL Art. 55, Paragraph one).

The principle of justice is also reflected in the inadmissibility of double punishment (*ne bis in idem*), which is notified in the fifth paragraph of Art. 1 of the Criminal Law, stating that "nobody shall be tried or punished again for an offence, for which he or she has already been acquitted or punished by an adjudication rendered in accordance with the procedures laid down in law and in effect in a criminal case or a case of administrative violation".

The humanitarian principle in criminal law, first of all, takes the form of a person: his or her life, health, fundamental rights and freedoms, and protection from criminal offence. The legislature not only provides for criminal liability for the threat to these interests, but also gives legal opportunities for the person itself, and to protect their and the interests of other persons, the necessary defence recognising circumstances that exclude criminal liability (KL Art. 29, 30).

As for the humanitarian principle—from the point of view of the subject of the criminal offence, it expresses the possibility of releasing a person from criminal liability, from punishment and from serving a sentence, a punishment reduction option in exceptional cases, and the minor criminal liability feature determined in the Special Chapter.

5.3.1.4 Actual Codification of Criminal Law Provisions (Criminal Law of 17 June 1998)

Criminal law in a narrower sense is a uniform set of rules that determines the basis and principles of criminal liability, recognised criminal offences and penalties for their commission, governs the principles of punishment, as well as the conditions for release from criminal liability and punishment.

In Latvia, these provisions are codified, and traditionally criminal law (Penal Code) is the only formal criminal law source, unlike in a number of other national criminal law systems in the continental European legal family, such as Belgium, the Netherlands, Spain and Germany, where in addition to criminal codes, there are also included a number of uncodified criminal law provisions adopted as separate laws, or found in the acts of other laws.

In the Criminal Law, codified provisions are divided into the General and the Special Part. The chapters of the General Part regulate issues such as general provisions; criminal offence; circumstances excluding criminal liability; punishment; determination of a punishment; release from criminal liability and punishment; characteristics of minor criminal liability; compulsory measures of a medical nature; application of coercive measures to legal persons.

The Special Part system is modelled after the group object features, and its 17 chapters describe specific criminal offences and specify the types of punishment and measures which a court may adjudge for their commission, or in the cases provided by law, to determine the prosecutor's injunction on the punishment. The Special Part begins with the chapter "Crimes Against Humanity, Peace, War Crimes, Genocide", followed by crimes against the State, crimes against the environment, and homicide. In the following order, individual chapters include offences against a person's health, fundamental rights and freedoms of a person, against personal liberty, honour and dignity, against morals, and sexual inviolability, against the family and minors, against property, criminal offences of an economic nature, crimes against general security and public order, criminal offences against traffic safety, against administrative order, against administration of justice, criminal offences committed in the state authority service and criminal offences in military service.

The following discussion will address separate General Part issues of the Criminal Law.

5.3.1.5 The Basis of Criminal Liability

Per the first paragraph of Art. 1 of the Criminal Law, a person shall be criminally liable if: (1) the person has committed a harmful offence (action or inaction), the liability for which is provided in the Criminal Law; (2) the offence has all the constituent elements of a criminal offence; (3) the person is guilty of an offence; (4) the offence is punishable by criminal punishment.[78]

A court may find a person guilty of committing a criminal offence and impose criminal punishment in accordance with the law, but in certain cases provided in the law, a person is found guilty of a criminal offence and the punishment is determined by a public prosecutor drawing up a penal order (KL Art. 1, Paragraphs two and three).

5.3.1.6 The Concept of a Criminal Offence

Latvian criminal law for a criminal offence recognises harmful acts (action or inaction) committed through intention (intentionally) or through negligence, provided for in the Criminal Law and for the commission of which criminal punishment is set out (KL Art. 6 Paragraph one).

When the constituent elements of an offence involve circumstances which exclude criminal liability, the offence is not considered criminal as provided in the Criminal Law. Circumstances which exclude criminal liability are: (1) necessary self-defence; (2) detention of the person causing harm; (3) extreme necessity: (4) justified professional risk; (5) execution of a criminal command or a criminal order. If a person has breached the limits of necessary self-defence or the conditions of their detention, and caused harm to life or health by serious or moderate bodily injuries, this forms the favoured composition of a criminal offence (KL Art. 121, 122, 128, 129). An exception occurs in the case of causing bodily injuries breaching the limits of necessary self-defence, if a person has defended him or herself against a risk to life or against rape, when the offence is not criminally punishable.

5.3.1.7 Criminal Offence Classification

According to the person, or the public interest nature of the risks and harm, criminal offences are divided into criminal violations and crimes, while crimes are divided into less serious, serious, and especially serious crimes (KL Art. 7).

Criminal violations are criminal offences for which the Law provides for short-term deprivation of liberty (for a period of 15 days, but not longer than 3 months) or a type of lesser punishment. Examples of criminal violations include: causing intentional bodily injury, violating the limits of necessary self-defence (KL Art. 128), abuse of the rights of legal guardianship (KL Art. 171), violation of safety provisions regarding information systems (KL Art. 245), etc.

The division between less serious and serious crimes affects both the type of guilt as well as the punishment provided. A less serious crime is considered an

[78] In greater detail see: Krastiņš et al. (2008), pp. 61–65.

intentional offence for which the term of deprivation of liberty exceeds 3 months but does not exceed 3 years, as well as an offence which was committed through negligence, and for which is provided deprivation of liberty for a term not exceeding 8 years. Such an intentional crime, for example, includes fraud without aggravating circumstances (KL Art. 177 Paragraph one), or the destruction of property and damage through negligence, if it has resulted in the death of two or several persons (KL Art. 186 Paragraph three).

A serious crime is an intentional offence for which deprivation of liberty is provided for a term exceeding 3 years but not exceeding 8 years, as well as an offence which was committed recklessly and for which is provided deprivation of liberty for a period exceeding 8 years. Cruelty and violence against an underage person is classified as a serious crime (KL Art. 174 Paragraph two), as is robbery without aggravating circumstances (KL Art. 176 Paragraph one), etc.

An especially serious crime is an intentional offence for which is provided deprivation of liberty exceeding 8 years, or life imprisonment—murder (KL Art. 116 to 118), qualified content of rape (KL Art. 159 Paragraphs two and three).

5.3.1.8 A Criminal Offence Subject

In Latvian criminal law, a criminal offence subject is a natural, physically responsible person who, by the date of committing a criminal offence, has attained 14 years of age (KL Art. 11). A person who, at the time of the commission of the offence, was in a state of mental incapacity, that is, because of a mental disorder or mental disability was not able to understand his or her acts or control them, or was underage, i.e., a person who has not reached 14 years of age, may not be held criminally liable.

In some cases, regarding a criminal offence subject without the basic features—responsibility and the age of criminal liability—there must be the presence of other stated characteristics of the person, specified in the disposition of the Criminal Law Art., as mandatory features of a specific criminal offence subject. These are the so-called special subjects, such as a medical practitioner, a public official, a soldier, a captain, etc. Legal persons—institutions, enterprises and organisations cannot be a criminal offence subject, because, in the Latvian criminal law, the main condition of criminal liability has always been a guilt, "which is the manifestation of a human subjective attitude towards their committed unlawful acts or omissions".[79] According to Art. 12 of the Criminal Law, a natural person who has committed a criminal offence while acting in the interests of a legal person governed by private law, for the benefit of the person or as a result of insufficient supervision or control thereof, shall be held criminally liable.

The following coercive measures may be applied to a legal person: (1) liquidation; (2) restriction of rights; (3) confiscation of property; (4) monetary levy (KL Art. 70^2).

[79]See: Krastiņš et al. (2008), pp. 140; Krastiņš (2009), pp. 200–205.

5.3.1.9 Subjective Side of Criminal Offence

There are two forms of guilt in the Criminal Law—intent and negligence.

A criminal offence is considered to have been committed intentionally (deliberately) if a person has committed it with direct or indirect intent. The second paragraph of Art. 9 of the Criminal Law provides that a criminal offence is considered to have been committed with direct intent if a person has been aware of the harm caused by his or her act or failure to act and has knowingly committed it or permitted (in criminal offences of formal composition), or has also been aware of the harm caused by his or her act or failure to act, foreseen the harmful consequences of the offence, and has desired them (in criminal offences of material composition).

Likewise, an intellectual moment of indirect intent involves the same mental activity criteria—awareness that the action or inaction is harmful and foreseeing damaging effects (only criminal offences of the material composition). The moment of will of indirect intention is different, because the person does not desire harmful effects, but knowingly allows them or is indifferent to them (Art. 9 Paragraph three).

Negligence as a form of guilt, which is specific to criminal offences of the material composition, is of two types—criminal self-reliance or criminal neglect (KL Art. 10).

In the case of criminal self-reliance, the person has foreseen the possibility of the harmful consequences of his act or omission, but carelessly relied on these being prevented, while in the case of criminal neglect, the person did not foresee the possibility of the consequences resulting from his or her act or failure to act, namely the possibility, although according to the actual circumstances of the offence he or she should have and could have foreseen the referred to the harmful consequences.

If the person did not foresee and should not and could not have foreseen the possibility that harmful consequences of his or her act or failure to act would result, it is provided in the Criminal Law that the offence shall not be criminally punishable.

5.3.1.10 Completed and Uncompleted Criminal Offence (KL Art. 15)

In the provisions of the Special Part of the Criminal Law, criminal offence compositions are formulated in such a way that the features they contain are characterised by a completed offence. Depending on the nature of the criminal activities of a criminal offence, and the actual degree of realisation, criminal law distinguishes between two types of incomplete crime—preparation for a crime and attempted crime, when a crime is not committed or carried out to the end beyond the independent reasons of the guilty will.

Criminal liability shall result only from preparation for serious or especially serious crimes; a person is not criminally liable for an attempt to commit a criminal violation.

5.3.1.11 Participation of Several Persons in a Criminal Offence

The participation by two or more persons knowingly in joint commission of a criminal offence is referred to as participation or joint participation (KL Art. 18).

In the case of participation by two or more persons, that is, the group carries out a deliberate action, direct participation in the commitment of an intentional (intentionally) criminal offence realising a specific criminal offence. Each of these persons is a participant (joint participant) in a criminal offence and their jointly committed offence is qualified only in accordance with the Art. or Paragraph of the Special Part of the Criminal Law, which refers to a group of people.

Considering the joint perpetrators degree of harmonisation and organisation of the criminal acts, the Criminal Law delineates the following forms of participation: (1) a group of persons without prior agreement; (2) a group of persons pursuant to prior agreement; (3) an organised group; (4) a gang; (5) a criminal organisation.

A group of persons without prior agreement and a group of persons pursuant to prior agreement consist of at least two persons, who, while being present in the same place and time of the criminal offence, through common actions, directly implement an intentional criminal offence. These forms of participation have only one distinctive feature—in a group with prior agreement between the members of the group before the realisation of the criminal offence, there has been any kind of agreement on the joint criminal offence to be committed. So, in a murder by a group of persons (KL Art. 117 Paragraph 10), it must be stated that at least two persons with a common intention have participated directly in the process of the murder. If a theft committed by a group of persons by prior agreement (KL Art. 175 Paragraph two) is imputable, it need only be stated that members of the group commonly agreed on the offence to be committed before the act, which is directly targeted at the property of another person.

An organised group is also a criminal group by prior agreement, although it differs from the above-mentioned types of participation in numerical composition and higher degree of organisation (KL Art. 21). For example, a murder is committed by an organised group (KL Art. 118 Paragraph 5), if it is carried out by at least three persons who have set up an association with the purpose of committing one or more crimes, and if the members, in accordance with the previous agreement, have divided responsibilities. Irrespective of the role of the person in the organised group, every one of them is a perpetrator (joint perpetrator) in the group.

All features of an organised group also apply to a gang (KL Art. 224), the difference lies in the fact that a gang is armed with a weapon.

Criminal organisation (KL Art. 89^1), as a type of participation, in contrast to the types discussed above, is characterised by the fact that the association is composed of at least five persons and is established for a specific purpose—to commit extremely serious crimes against humanity or peace, war crimes, genocide or to commit especially serious crimes against the State. The participation of several persons in the commission of a criminal offence may be joint participation that is a deliberate act or of omission, by which the person (joint participant), together with another person (perpetrator), has participated in an intentional criminal offence, but has not themselves been the direct perpetrator (KL Art. 20 Paragraph one). Depending on their task in a jointly feasible offence, criminal offence joint participants include organisers, instigators, and abettors.

5.3.1.12 The Concept, Aim and Types of Punishment

Defining the concept of criminal punishment, the first paragraph of Art. 35 of the Criminal Law provides that punishment is a compulsory measure which a court, within the limits of the Criminal Law, adjudges on behalf of the State against a person guilty of the commission of a criminal offence, or in the cases provided for by law, determined by a public prosecutor by drawing up a penal order.

Under the Criminal Law system of penalties, punishments are divided into basic punishments, additional punishments, and punishments which can be applied as a basic as well as an additional punishment. Basic punishments include deprivation of liberty, community service and a fine; additional punishments—confiscation of property, deportation from the Republic of Latvia, community service, a fine, restriction of rights and probationary supervision, which was introduced instead of police control. Thus, community service and fines may be applied as a basic as well as an additional punishment. When a person has committed a criminal violation or a less serious crime, the public prosecutor, drawing up a penal order, may impose a fine or community service, as well as additional punishments—restriction of rights and probationary supervision.

5.3.1.13 The Implementation of the Criminal Punishment Policy Concept[80]

With the law of 13 December 2012,[81] criminal punishment policy reform was carried out which significantly affected both the regulatory part of the punishment, the determination and release from punishment in the General Part, as well as sanctions in sections of the Special Part of the Criminal Law.[82]

In discussing the amendments made to the General Part of the Criminal Law, it must first of all be noted that the aim of punishment was specified within the Law, which now consists of the following components: (1) to protect public safety; (2) restore justice; (3) to punish the offender for a committed criminal offence; (4) to re-socialise the punished person; (5) to ensure that the convicted person and other persons comply with the law and refrain from committing criminal offences (KL Art. 35 Paragraph two).

Secondly, it clarified the circumstances to be considered in determining the type and limits, that is, in determining the punishment, it is taken into account the nature of the criminal offence and the harm caused as well as the personality of the

[80]The Concept of Criminal Penalty Policy. httr://www.likumi.lv/doc.php?id=186355.

[81]On Amendments in the Criminal Law. httr://www.likumi.lv/ta/id/253698-grozijumi-kriminallikuma.

[82]In greater detail see Liholaja (2013), pp. 4–21; Zahars (2014), pp. 10–21.

offender, but in determining the punishment—liability mitigating and aggravating circumstances.

Thirdly, the conditions were reviewed to determine the punishment for several types of criminal offences and judgments, conditional release prior to completion of punishment, specified criminal liability limitation, limitation period on the execution of a judgment of conviction, as well as the extinguishment and setting aside of criminal record deadlines.

Radical changes have affected most of the sections of the Special Part sanctions by reducing the extent of minimum and maximum sentences, as well as expanding the possibility for the application of alternative punishments. As a result, in the sanction sections for crimes, including serious crimes which provide for deprivation of liberty for a term not exceeding 5 years, all other basic punishments were also included with the deprivation of liberty—temporary deprivation of liberty, community service and a fine. For the effectiveness of this change and achieving the intended results, a detailed punishment application practice analysis may be called for, which is also being planned for the near future.

5.3.1.14 Special Nature of Criminal Liability of Minors

In the Criminal Law, a separate chapter is devoted to minors; a minor is defined as a person who has not attained 18 years of age as of the commission of the criminal offence. Regulating the imposition of punishments for minors, Art. 65 of the Criminal Law stipulates that the period of deprivation of liberty may not exceed: 10 years for especially serious crimes; 5 years—for serious crimes, which are associated with violence or the threat of violence, or have given rise to serious consequences; 2 years for other serious crimes. For criminal violations and less serious offences, the punishment of deprivation of liberty shall not be applied.

The total time of deprivation of liberty for several criminal offences of such a person shall not exceed 12 years and 6 months, but after a series of judgments—15 years, which is half of the adult convicts' total allowable punishment time. Conditional release from a punishment before serving the term, in relation to a person who has committed any criminal offence before reaching 18 years of age, may be proposed if he/she has served at least half of the sentence, and the release of the sentence under electronic monitoring determination—if he/she has served not less than one-third of the imposed punishment.

Within the specific circumstances of the committed criminal offence, and any information obtained on the personality of the offender softening his liability, the court may exempt the minor from the imposed punishment by applying the statutory coercive educational measures prescribed by the law[83]—a warning; to impose a duty to apologise to the victims if they agree to meet with the perpetrator; determine behavioural constraints; to impose a duty to perform community service for a period of 10–40 h; for a minor who has attained 15 years of age, to oblige them

[83]Law on Application of Compulsory Measures of Correctional Nature to Children http://www.vvc.gov.lv/export/sites/default/docs/LRTA/likumi?Compulsory-Measures-of-a-Nature-to-Children.

with their work to eliminate the consequences of harm, and if he or she has an income—to pay damages. The law likewise provides for the possibility to place the minor in a social correction educational institution for a period of 1 to 3 years, but not longer than until they come of age.

In conclusion, it should be noted that work on the improvement of legislation in criminal law matters is still in progress, determined by both international law and the European Union legal document instructions, as well as practical needs. However, the fact that in the Criminal Law, during the 16 years of its operation, 55 amendments have been made which have affected practically all its provisions, some even repeatedly, raises concerns about the legality of criminal law as guarantor of stability and the role of criminal law relations in a fair settlement.

5.3.2 Criminal Procedure

5.3.2.1 Introduction

Currently, the legal regulation of criminal procedure is essentially included in a codified regulatory enactment—the Criminal Procedure Law[84] (hereinafter—the KPL). Compared to other laws in Latvia of equal significance, it must be recognised as one of the most recent, since it was adopted and came into force only in 2005. To provide a general insight, the development of criminal procedure legal norms in Latvia over more than five decades should be characterised; this period can be divided into three periods: 1961–1990, 1990–2005 and 2005–2016.[85]

The first period is characterised by the validity of the so-called legal norms of the Soviet age. On 6 January 1961, the Supreme Soviet of the Latvian SSR approved the Criminal Procedure Code of the Latvian SSR[86] (hereinafter—the LSSR CPC), ruling that it came into force in April of the same year. It is typical of the LSSR CPC that it was drafted in accordance with the foundations of criminal legal proceedings that were uniform for the whole USSR, therefore it differed little from the criminal procedure codes of other republics of the USSR.

The second period began with the restoration of Latvia's independence and concluded in 2005. On 4 May 1990, the declaration "On Joining by the Republic of Latvia International Legal Documents on Human Rights" was adopted, with which Latvia acceded to 51 international legal acts in the area of human rights.[87] This created a need also to elaborate a new criminal procedure legal act. In October

[84]Criminal Procedure Law The current version of the law available from http://likumi.lv/doc.php?id=107820 Unofficial translation of this Law into English is available from the link "Tulkojums" (Translation), however, not all amendments made to KPL have been incorporated into the translation.

[85]In greater detail about the development of criminal procedural provisions see Meikalisa (2012), pp. 326–338.

[86]Criminal Procedure Code of Latvia SSR: http://www.likumi.lv/doc.php?id=90971.

[87]On Accession by the Republic of Latvia International Human Rights Documents. Latvia SSR Supreme Council Declaration. Available at http://www.likumi.lv/doc.php?id=75668&from=off.

1990, the Presidium of the Supreme Council of the Republic of Latvia passed a decision "On setting up a working group for elaboration of the draft of the criminal code, criminal procedure code, penal execution code, administrative violations code of the Republic of Latvia and the draft law on the judiciary of the Republic of Latvia"[88] However, this work proceeded neither as swiftly, nor as easily as intended. Several variants of the future criminal procedure code were drafted, working groups and conceptions were replaced before the new law was adopted in 2005. The entire period is characterised not only by the elaboration of a new legal document, but also by very intensive work on introducing amendments to the existing code. At the beginning of this period, the title of the legal document was still Criminal Procedure Code of the Latvian SSR. This was changed only with the law of 21 August 1991, which prescribed that until the adoption of the Criminal Procedure Code of the Republic of Latvia, the Criminal Procedure Code of the Latvian SSR was to be considered as the Criminal Procedure Code of Latvia (hereinafter—the CPC).[89] Since 4 May 1990, until it became invalid on 1 October 2005 (approximately 15 years), this legal document was amended altogether 39 times. The following may be mentioned as the most significant changes: changes in terminology; amendments associated with the harmonisation of CPC provisions with the provisions of other laws, introduction of several essential basic principles (such fundamental principles of criminal proceeding as presumption of innocence were introduced to the CPC in 1993); revision of compulsory measures and creation of additional guarantees to persons against whom they are applied; changes of competence of different law-enforcement agencies involved in criminal proceedings; introduction of other procedural guarantees; changes in types of proceedings; inclusion of international cooperation into CPC.

The third period began in 2005, and is ongoing. The KPL was adopted on 21 April 2005, and came into force on 1 October 2005. This law was the basis for important changes in the legal regulation of criminal procedure. However, this did not conclude the reform in the legal regulation of criminal procedure—numerous and essential amendments to the provisions of criminal procedure law continue to be introduced, to which I shall return at the very end of this subsection.

5.3.2.2 Aims and Basic Principles of Criminal Procedure

Art. 1 of the KPL defines the purpose of criminal procedure as (1) effective application of the norms of Criminal Law, and (2) fair regulation of criminal legal relations without unjustified intervention in the life of a person.

Thus, punishing every person who has committed a criminal offence is no longer indicated as the purpose of the criminal procedure, as it was until 2005. This has

[88]On setting up a working group for elaboration of the draft of criminal code, criminal procedure code, penal execution code, administrative violations code of the Republic of Latvia and the draft law on judiciary of the Republic of Latvia http://www.likumi.lv/doc.php?id=72748.

[89]On amendments and addenda in the Criminal Code of Latvia SSR and in Criminal Procedure Code of Latvia SSR. Available at: http://www.likumi.lv/doc.php?id=68680.

been replaced by fair regulation of criminal legal relations. This fair regulation does not always prescribe punishing a person. It may be manifested in different ways—releasing a person from liability, conditional termination of criminal procedure, etc. Likewise, "fair regulation of criminal legal relations" does not comprise only the actions by the State with respect to the person who has committed a criminal offence; it also includes the treatment of the crime victim. Establishing the institution of compensation, expanding possibilities for reconciliation, *inter alia,* envisaging the institution of mediation, expanding the circle of those criminal proceedings that are to be initiated only if the victim wishes so, etc. can be mentioned as examples in this respect. The fact that the KPL directly points out that in reaching the aim of criminal procedure, unjustified intervention in the life of a person is inadmissible, deserves a special mention. This is a general position, which is not only formal by nature, but must be complied with throughout the course of criminal procedure. Obviously, during the course of criminal proceedings, the need to intervene in the life of various persons may and does occur, including restrictions on their human rights; however, such actions need to be particularly well-considered. One of the most essential criteria in assessing the legal validity of intervention and restrictions is exactly their justifiability (to characterise it simply—whether it is necessary at all and whether it is necessary in the particular scope/degree/intensity).

It is impossible to characterise criminal procedure without dwelling on the principles of criminal proceedings. Prior to 2005, studies of these principles and clarification of their content was left in the care of researchers and persons applying law; at present; however, the legislator has at least partially done this work by including into the KPL a separate chapter "Basic Principles of Criminal Proceedings". Currently, the following basic principles of criminal proceedings have been included in this chapter: the mandatory nature of criminal proceedings (Art. 6); public and private prosecution (Art. 7); equality (Art. 8); criminal procedural duty (Art. 9), immunity from criminal proceedings (Art. 10); language to be used in criminal proceedings (Art. 11); guaranteeing of human rights (Art. 12); prohibition of torture and debasement (Art. 13); right to the completion of criminal proceedings in a reasonable term (Art. 14); rights to the adjudication of a case in court (Art. 15); right to the objective course of criminal proceedings (Art. 16); separation of procedural functions (Art. 17); equivalence of procedural authorisations (Art. 8); presumption of innocence (Art. 19); right to assistance of counsel (Art. 20); right to co-operation (Art. 21); right to compensation for inflicted harm (Art. 22); court adjudication (Art. 23); defence of a person and property in the case of a threat (Art. 24); and inadmissibility of double jeopardy (Art. 25).[90]

Part of the enumerated principles should be recognised as principles for organising a system, but part is to be linked to human rights principles, which have gained more detailed expression in criminal procedure. The majority of human rights principles in Latvia do not differ significantly from other

[90] In greater detail see Meikalša and Strada-Rozenberga (2006a), pp. 43–68.

democracies; understanding and limits of application thereof have been influenced to a large extent by the European Convention on Human Rights and the case law of the European Court of Human Rights. Therefore, in the context of comparing states, a few words should be dedicated to the principles for organising systems. It is essential to note that currently in Latvia the mandatory nature of criminal proceedings has been enshrined as the leading position, which means that every time a cause and grounds for initiating criminal proceedings has been identified, criminal proceedings must be initiated and must be conducted until a fair resolution of criminal legal relations is achieved. Thus, essentially, the principle of mandatory nature and not the expedience of criminal proceedings is recognised. However, it must be noted that the Latvian criminal procedure recognises the existence of some features of expedience. Thus, for instance, at present it is possible to refuse initiating proceedings or to terminate these, if "harm that would warrant the application of criminal punishment" has not been caused (see KPL Art. 373, 379).[91] The discussion on whether the expediency approach should not be implemented more extensively is intensifying. For example, a proposal of this nature has been made with regard to criminal proceedings against legal persons.[92] It must be noted; however, that in Latvia the principle of the mandatory nature of criminal proceedings is restricted by another basic principle recognised in Latvia,—prosecution in criminal proceedings, according to which all criminal offences can be split into two large groups—those, with respect to which criminal proceedings are initiated only if the victim wishes so, and those, with respect to which criminal proceedings are initiated irrespective of the victim's will. The first group comprises such somewhat widespread criminal offences as petty theft, road traffic accidents with minor consequences, intentional infliction of mild bodily injuries, etc. In the case of such offences as these, the victim's will is decisive not only in initiating the proceedings, but also in continuing them, since reconciliation is envisaged as an obstacle for conducting the proceedings. Thus, in the case of specific criminal offences, the victim has a large influence on the existence of proceedings. Occasionally, this has been a cause for reflections and criticism.[93]

It must be noted that, at present, only public prosecution is known in Latvian criminal procedure, which is maintained by the prosecutor on behalf of the state. Private prosecution, upheld by the victim, was totally renounced in 2011.

5.3.2.3 Participants of Criminal Procedure

Pursuant to the KPL, participants of criminal procedure are split into four large groups; officials who have been authorised to conduct criminal proceedings;

[91]In greater detail see Strada-Rozenberga (2011a), pp. 185–191.

[92]Strada-Rozenberga (2015), pp. 636–637.

[93]Strada-Rozenberga (2007), pp. 637–660; Meikališa and Strada-Rozenberga (2012), pp. 245–260.

persons implementing defence; the victim and his representation, and other participants of the proceedings.[94]

The range of officials authorised to conduct criminal proceedings on behalf of the state comprises persons in charge of proceedings, as well as a list of other officials authorised to conduct proceedings, including the investigating judge, persons performing procedural tasks, members of an investigation team, an expert, an auditor, etc.[95] Admittedly, the range of these officials is very broad, their statuses are numerous and very fragmented. Thus, for example, a prosecutor may become involved in the proceedings in seven different procedural statuses. Therefore, in Latvia, each procedural status requires meticulous assessment, to verify the scope of a concrete official's authorisation at a particular moment in the proceedings. It must be noted that if an action has been performed by a person who had no right to perform it, then the obtained information is to be considered disallowed as evidence (absolutely inadmissible). The fact that criminal prosecution is an exclusive competence of the prosecutor should be seen as a feature typical of the current Latvian criminal procedure, likewise, the fact that the investigating judge is not actively involved in conducting the procedure. The function of control over human rights is typical of the judge; this is implemented in cases that have been precisely referred to (application and control of detention, adopting a decision on conducting certain investigative activities, etc.), and that punishment of a person falls within the competence of both the court and the prosecutor (in applying the prosecutor's penal order).

The circle of persons who implement the defence comprises those persons who have the right to a counsel's assistance, counsels and representatives of persons who enjoy the right to the assistance of a counsel (minors). Persons with the right to a counsel's assistance may have a number of possible statuses. This depends on the degree of validity (proof) of the assumption that a person has committed a criminal offence. Thus, in the proceedings that are conducted in general procedure, a person with the right to a counsel's assistance may be (1) a person, against whom proceedings have been initiated, (2) the detained person, (3) the suspect, (4) the accused, and (5) the sentenced person. The respective persons have specific statuses in the so-called special types of proceedings. Likewise, a legal person has the right to a counsel's assistance, if criminal proceedings regarding application of coercive measures to a legal person are conducted. In recent years, the development of the legal status of such persons has been influenced by the implementation of various EU legal acts, although the rights envisaged by the EU legal acts, undeniably, were previously known.

Only advocates (of Latvia, other EU Member States, as well as of other countries, if international treaties provide for it) may act as counsels in Latvia. Essentially, persons themselves make the arrangements for a counsel's assistance; however, if this has not happened and the person wishes to have an advocate's

[94]In greater detail see Meikališa and Strada-Rozenberga (2006b), pp. 68–71.

[95]In greater detail see Meikališa and Strada-Rozenberga (2006b), pp. 71–84.

participation, this is ensured by the State. It must be noted that the KPL provides for criminal proceedings with the mandatory participation of an advocate (for example, regarding a minor, a person who, because of physical or mental disabilities, is unable to exercise his own rights, etc.) Likewise, an advocate's participation in some activities (regarding a detained person) is envisaged, unless the person has declined it. It must be highlighted that the KPL points out that the counsel only provides defence and does not replace the defendant, i.e., only the defendant himself expresses his subjective opinion about admission of guilt, choosing simplified procedures and testifying.[96]

In Latvia, both natural and legal persons who have incurred harm because of an offence (material loss, bodily harm, or moral damages) may be victims. It is especially important to note that there is a difference between the actual victim and the legal victim as participant in proceedings. A person is recognised as being a victim as the participant of proceedings only if he wishes so (except for persons who, because of physical or mental disabilities, are unable to exercise their own rights). If a person does not want to be recognised as a victim, he is involved, if necessary, in the proceedings with the status of a witness. A person's choice to become or not to become a victim depends on the person's wish to influence the proceedings, to be informed about their course, to appeal against rulings and perform other activities. Only a person having the procedural status of a victim has these possibilities. If the actual victim is deceased, one of his relatives may be recognised as being the victim.[97] Implementation of EU provisions has had a significant impact on the legal status of victims.[98]

The circle of "other" participants of proceedings includes, for example, witnesses, experts, interpreters, etc. The owner of the property that has been infringed upon must be singled out as an important participant; this is a participant of the criminal proceedings whose disposition of property have been restricted, but is not a person with the right to legal counsel.[99]

Each participant in criminal proceedings has rights and obligations, regulated in great detail, the performance of which may be ensured by application of compulsory measures.

5.3.2.4 Procedural Compulsory Measures and Issues of Property in Criminal Procedure

Pursuant to the KPL, all preventive procedural compulsory measures are divided into two large groups: those that are linked to deprivation of liberty and those that are not linked to deprivation of liberty. The following fall into the group of

[96] In greater detail see Meikališa and Strada-Rozenberga (2006b), pp. 87–100.

[97] Strada-Rozenberga (2008a), pp. 352–371; Meikališa and Strada-Rozenberga (2006b), pp. 100–103; Meikališa and Strada-Rozenberga (2012), pp. 245–260; Strada-Rozenberga (2014), pp. 51–90.

[98] In greater detail see Meikališa (2014), pp. 4–19.

[99] In greater detail see Meikališa (2015a), pp. 360–377.

compulsory measures involving deprivation of liberty: detention, arrest, house arrest, placing minors in a social correctional institution and placement in a medical treatment facility for conducting expert-examination. Only the investigating judge or the court have the right to apply these coercive means, except detention, and strict terms of their application have been set, which are essentially linked to the degree of harm caused by the criminal offence.

The majority of compulsory measures can be applied only to the suspect and the accused person. A comparatively broad range of security measures has been established in Latvia, *inter alia*, arrest, house arrest, bail, personal guarantee, placement under police supervision, etc.[100]

According to the terminology used in the KPL, "property issues" include compensation, criminally acquired property, procedural costs and seizure of property.

Compensation is an institution that entered Latvian criminal procedure law in 2005, when "the civil claim" in criminal proceedings was, in turn, excluded. Currently, compensation in Latvia is understood as recompense expressed in monetary terms, which the guilty party pays to the victim voluntarily or as the result of a court ruling. Compensation can be claimed both for material loss and physical suffering or moral damages. It is particularly important to note that compensation should be regarded as regulation of criminal legal relations and it is not to be linked with the civil law regulation of the particular issue. The victim is obliged to substantiate the amount of compensation in the part regarding material losses, whereas in the other part he must only indicate the sum that he considers to be appropriate. If the guilty party is unable to reach an agreement with the victim about the amount of compensation, it is set by the court.

The institution of criminally acquired property in Latvia currently envisages that the following property is regarded as being criminally acquired: (1) property, which has come into a person's possession as the result of a criminal offence (proof of its criminal origin exists), (2) property, which is presumed to be criminally acquired, unless the opposite has been proven. At present presumptions are applicable only to a range of cases that have been precisely defined, i.e., only in cases, when charges of a particular criminal offence have been brought (terrorism and supporting terrorism, trafficking in human beings, etc.), property of persons, who have committed the offence, and of persons sharing a household with them can be recognised as criminally acquired, unless these persons prove legal origin of this property (see Art. 355 of the KPL). Significant changes may be expected soon in the solution to this issue, as the Ministry of Justice has proposed amendments to the relevant legal provisions. In Latvia, property may be recognised as being criminally acquired both by the final ruling in the proceedings (conviction-based confiscation), as well as during the pre-trial proceedings in the special procedure of proceedings (non-conviction-based confiscation). After a property has been recognised as

[100] In greater detail see Meikališa (2006b), pp. 428–455; Meikališa (2006a), pp. 428–455; Meikališa (2008), pp. 456–480; Strada-Rozenberga (2008b), pp. 501–527.

being criminally acquired, there are two options for resolving the matter—it can be returned to the legal owner or seized on behalf of the state.[101]

The category of procedural costs comprises the costs of proceedings, which are clearly referred to in the KPL provisions. It is typical of Latvian legal procedure that, during proceedings, none of the involved persons is imposed with the duty to cover these—the costs are covered by the State. Only after the proceedings have been completed, and a person has been recognised as being guilty, this person may be imposed with the obligation to cover the costs of the proceedings. Likewise, the person in charge of proceedings may release the person from covering the costs, if special circumstances have been identified.

Currently, the only security measure in property issues in Latvia is seizing property; a number of deficiencies and problems can be discerned in establishing the content and application thereof. To a certain extent, this is linked to the fact that the legal regulation of this legal institution has changed comparatively little over the last decades, whereas other fields of life have developed rapidly. Hence, this institution is no longer a modern, effective security measure and needs to be improved, which is being done at present.

5.3.2.5 Proving and Investigatory Activities

The analysis of legal regulation on proving points to five essential questions, the answers to which reveal the model of legal regulation on proving contained in the law. These questions arc as follows: (1) what is understood by the term "proving", (2) what must be proven or what is the object of proving, (3) which participants of proceedings conduct proving or are the subjects of proving, *inter alia*, who has the burden of proof, (4) what must be proven, (5) what can be used as evidence and what should evidence be like.[102]

Art. 123 of the KPL defines proving as "an activity of a person involved in criminal proceedings that is expressed as the justification, using evidence, of the existence or non-existence of facts included in an object of evidence."

Three groups of facts must be included in the object of evidence: circumstances (facts) to be proven in criminal proceedings, related facts, and auxiliary facts. Art. 124(2) of the KPL indicates that the circumstances to be proven in criminal proceedings are the elements of crime and other conditions provided for in the CL or KPL, upon which the outcome of proceedings depends. In practice, at present, identification of the range of conditions on which the final outcome of the proceedings (whether a person is or is not to be recognised as guilty, to be or not be punished, etc.) depends, is most important, thus, apart from the elements of a criminal offence referred to above, also circumstances excluding criminal liability, circumstances that are the basis for releasing a person from criminal liability, personality of the offender, and aggravating and mitigating circumstances are included in the conditions to be proven in criminal proceedings.

[101] In greater detail see Strada-Rozenberga (2011b), pp. 591–602.

[102] In greater detail see Strada-Rozenberga (2002), Strada-Rozenberga (2010), pp. 383–400.

The KPL defines related facts as facts that "are not conditions to be proven in criminal proceedings, but are connected thereto, and provide grounds for drawing a conclusion regarding the conditions to be proven." These facts are proven by indirect evidence. These are facts that *per se* are not decisive for the final outcome of proceedings, but allow for drawing conclusions regarding facts that are of decisive importance. Thus, for example, in a murder case, the presence of the accused person's fingerprints on the murder weapon, etc. is to be recognised as a related fact. Auxiliary facts are understood as facts that are needed in the proceedings only because they allow for assessing the possibility or non-possibility of using evidence. Thus, for example, a witness's ability/inability to adequately perceive, memorise or reproduce facts that he is testifying to; the competence of the source of evidence is to be seen as an auxiliary fact. Likewise, the conflicts of interests with respect to officials who have been authorised to conduct proceedings, as well as facts regarding deficiencies in the procedural form and other facts that allow assessing the possibility of procedural use of evidence fall within the category of auxiliary facts.

The issue of facts that should not be proven in proceedings is closely linked to the issue of the object of evidence. The existence of such facts obviously influences defining the object and limits of evidence. A reference to the existence of such facts was not included in the KPL, although practice and research, undeniably, recognise their existence. Such facts are included in the KPL (see in greater detail KPL Art. 125, Art. 355).

In the meaning of the KPL, all those persons who are involved in criminal proceedings, upon whom the duty has been imposed or the rights have been conferred to perform proving, are to be considered as the subjects of evidence (KPL Art. 126). In accordance with the principle of the presumption of innocence, the basic burden of proof lies on the person in charge of the proceedings in the pre-trial procedure, and on the person maintaining prosecution in the trial stage. The court's role in proving should be assessed as being limited, since the possibilities for the court to obtain and verify evidence on its own initiative depend upon certain prerequisites, i.e., the court may take this action, if there are doubts in favour of the defence and a person implements his own defence. The court has no right to intervene in the implementation of defence and prosecution, give concrete instructions, etc.

The KPL provides for some exemptions, when the burden of proof is partially "transferred" to other persons. The most striking one—a person must point to (but not prove!) his alibi and circumstances excluding criminal liability; the victim must substantiate the amount of compensation in the part regarding material losses, and in certain cases a person must prove legal origin of property.

The general standard of evidence that follows directly from the presumption of innocence has been consolidated in criminal proceedings—beyond reasonable doubt, which is basically applicable to those participants of proceedings who carry the main burden of proof. Currently, the possibility of introducing a "balance of probabilities" standard with regard to property issues is being actively discussed in Latvia.

The so-called strict system of evidence is known in Latvia; types of evidence are exhaustively listed and their procedural form is, more or less, strictly defined. At present, testimonies, conclusions by experts and auditors, minutes of investigative activities, material evidence, electronic evidence, documents, as well information obtained and technically recorded through investigative measures that can be verified in criminal procedural order may be used as evidence in criminal proceedings. To use this evidence in proving, it must be attributable, admissible and reliable.

Since admissibility is one of the mandatory features of evidence, the procedural order and form must be strictly observed in obtaining evidence. Essentially, information that is necessary for proving is acquired through investigative activities, the types of which are exhaustively listed in the KPL. The investigative activities that the KPL currently envisages can be divided into two large groups—the so-called classical, overt activities and special (covert) investigative activities. Those belonging to the first group, *inter alia*, interrogation, search, expert-examination, inspection, etc., are to be conducted in investigating any criminal offence. In some cases (for example, search), these are subject to control by the investigating judge. Special investigative actions are to be performed only in investigating crimes, but not criminal offences, and only if the necessary information cannot be obtained by other means.

Any violation committed while performing investigative activities allows contesting the possibility of using the obtained information in criminal proceedings, causing the so-called absolute inadmissibility or limited admissibility of evidence.

5.3.2.6 Types and Stages of Criminal Proceedings

Criminal proceedings can be conditionally split into three groups: (1) criminal proceedings conducted in general procedure, (2) simplified criminal proceedings, and (3) special criminal proceedings.

The establishment of the group of simplified proceedings is based on the purpose of introducing and conducting the respective proceedings—speeding up, simplifying criminal proceedings, which can be manifested as the significant simplification of procedural process, omitting a certain stage, etc. Although the person in charge of the proceedings is the one who, in each particular case, chooses whether to apply a simplified form of proceedings, it must be borne in mind that KPL Art. 14 imposes an obligation on the person in charge of proceedings to conduct it in as simple a form as possible. The simplified forms of proceedings may be divided into models for out-of-court settlement of criminal legal relations and models that comprise examination of the case in court. The following can be included in the first group: (1) releasing a person from criminal liability unconditionally (KPL Art. 379(1)); (2) conditional termination of criminal proceedings (KPL Chapter 34); (3) prosecutor's penal order (KPL Chapter 35). The second group comprises (1) agreement procedure (KPL Chapter 38,49, 50) and (2) adjudication of the case in court without conducting examination of evidence (KPL Art.

499). The proceedings, from the very beginning until completion (pre-trial or trial stage), may also be conducted in urgent (KPL Chapter 36) or summary procedure (Chapter 37). It must be noted that the court may also release a person from criminal liability unconditionally.

Special proceedings are such proceedings that are conducted in the presence of such circumstances that do not allow (envisage) the possibility of conducting the proceedings in the so-called general procedure. Currently, the KPL provides for several types of such proceedings, *inter alia*: proceedings in determining compulsory measures of a medical nature (KPL Chapter 55); proceedings in cases regarding exoneration of a deceased person (KPL Chapter 56); proceedings regarding criminally acquired property (KPL Chapter 59), etc.

In accordance with the regulation on the structure of proceedings included in the KPL, which can be deduced from the structure of the KPL, three mandatory stages of criminal proceedings can be singled out: (1) pre-trial proceedings (investigation [KPL Chapter 32]; criminal prosecution [KPL Chapter 33]); (2) adjudication of a case in a court of first instance (preparing the case for trial [KPL Chapter 45]; trial [KPL Chapter 46]; rendering and pronouncement of the judgement, issuance of a copy [KPL Chapter 47]); (3) entering into effect of the judgement and examination of issues related to rulings (transfer of judgements and decisions for execution [Chapter 60]); adjudication of matters that have arisen in the course of executing judgements and decisions (Chapter 61). Examination of a case at appellate and cassation instance, as well as renewal of criminal proceedings due to newly disclosed circumstances or substantial violations, are envisaged as optional.

5.3.2.7 Prospects of Development in Criminal Procedure

As noted above, in 2005, when the KPL was adopted, the reform of criminal procedure was not concluded. The numerous and sizeable amendments to the KPL that have been introduced thus far, and are still intended, is a proof of this. Thus, until spring of 2016, the KPL had been amended 29 times, and more than a half of its norms are no longer found in their initial wording. Three circumstances are recognised as grounds for introducing amendments: (1) implementing EU norms,[103] (2) rectifying inaccuracies, contradictions and deficiencies; and (3) responding to topicalities identified in the practice of applying law. It has also been forecast that, regrettably, a significant decrease in the flood of amendments to criminal procedure norms cannot be expected,[104] which causes concern regarding forthcoming stabilisation of criminal procedural order.

[103]See, for example, Baumanis (2015), pp. 108–127; Feldmane (2015), pp. 128–140; Ņesterova (2015), pp. 140–157; Strada-Rozenberga (2012), pp. 423–435.

[104]In greater detail see Meikališa (2015b), pp. 95–150.

5.4 Tax and Public Finance Law in Latvia

Kārlis Ketners
BA School for Business and Finance, K. Valdemāra iela 161, Riga, Latvia
e-mail: karlis.ketners@ba.lv

5.4.1 Introduction

Latvian financial law regulation is represented by three groups of laws—budgetary laws, tax laws and financial market regulation. As financial market legislation such as system monitoring (Law "On the Latvian Bank", The Financial and Capital Market Commission Law), financial system regulation (Financial Security Act, Law on Credit Institutions, Insurance and Reinsurance Act Law, the Financial Instruments Market Law, etc.) generally follows common European regulations and legislation, this paper is focused on public finance regulation in Latvia. The basis for the financial law system is the Constitution (*Satversme*) of the Republic of Latvia, which has only a few provisions covering financial law issues. Thus, Article 66 states that "annually, before the commencement of each financial year, the Saeima shall determine the State Revenues and Expenditures Budget, the draft of which shall be submitted to the Saeima by the Cabinet. If the Saeima makes a decision that involves expenditures not included in the Budget, this decision must also allocate funds to cover such expenditures. After the end of the budgetary year, the Cabinet shall submit an accounting of budgetary expenditures for the approval of the Saeima." Article 73 states that the Budget and laws concerning loans, taxes, customs duties, railroad tariffs, military conscription, declaration and commencement of war, peace treaties, declaration of a state of emergency and its termination, mobilisation and demobilisation, as well as agreements with other nations may not be submitted to national referendum. The Latvian tax system and tax laws have a very short history; initially introduced in 1990, the current tax legislation is mainly based on the continuation of the tax policy followed since the tax reform of 1995. Tax policy did initially target the relatively high profit and property taxes, in combination with high penalties and high overdue tax debt interest ratios, changing the focus on indirect taxation, influenced by the accession to the EU and EU tax regulations. The taxes and fees system in Latvia consists of state taxes, the object and rate of which shall be set by the Saeima; state fees which shall be applicable according to the Law "On Taxes and Fees", specific other laws and regulations of the Cabinet of Ministers; local government fees which shall be applicable according to the Law "On Taxes and Fees", binding regulations issued by the council of local government; directly applicable taxes and other obligatory payments set in the European Union regulatory enactments. While the Latvian tax system is very young, Latvia has succeeded in creating a viable and effective tax system in a comparatively short period of time, in which the main fiscal aims (ensuring state budget revenue), are balanced with the use of taxes as an instrument of economic policy.[105] Latvia has succeeded in doing so because, during the reorganisation of the tax system in the mid-90s, new tax laws were developed according to the experience of developed democratic countries, and taking into consideration advice from experts representing a number of international organisations. From this point of view, it could be argued that Latvia, creating its tax system from the start, has had certain advantages over "old" tax systems. The current Latvian tax policy is mainly based on the continuation of the tax policy followed since the tax reform of 1995; generally, the system's goal has been to ensure capital inflow and capital market activities, with the aim of increasing foreign direct investment and promoting the development of the national economy.[106] As remarked on by *Ketners, K., Petersone, M.,*[107] current Latvian tax policy relies on shifting the tax burden from the labour force and capital to consumption. The strong decline in the tax to GDP ratio over the past years has been largely owing to two major factors. Firstly, the cut in social contributions; secondly, the cut in the corporate income tax rate from 25% to 15%. The recent developments in the tax system have been mainly targeted at abolishing discriminatory and restrictive provisions by extending the relevant exemptions. The authors agree with the comparative analysis approach that, in classification of the tax law families, the tax laws of transition countries should be separated.[108] Following this classification, the Latvian system is a part of the transition countries' tax law group. For the most part, the tax legislation of these countries has been revised relatively recently, and in some cases, is still undergoing substantial revision, usually with the benefit of outside advice. In most cases, the result is fairly eclectic. However, in the case of the Baltic States, it seems to be appropriate to mark the influence of the German-speaking countries' and the Nordic countries' tax laws, as well as European Union legislation. Like other countries in the Northern European family, Latvia has separate taxes on individuals and on legal persons. In the case of Latvian tax law, noteworthy elements include division into personal income tax and corporate income tax and some income tax features. Under the income tax legislation, the definition of income for individuals was global in concept. Per Article 3 of the law "On Personal Income Tax",[109] residents are taxed on their worldwide income, non-residents only on their domestic-source income. The Latvian law "On Personal Income Tax" provides; however, the schedular definition of income and is based on six categories of income with a different calculation and assessment. Also similar to other transition countries, a wide variety of exemptions apply, covering many types of payments and benefits, including both items received from the State, and also many benefits offered by employers (social benefits, scholarships, interest on state bonds, lottery winnings, to mention only a

[105]Robezniece et al. (2003), p. 117.

[106]Ketners and Titova (2009), p. 59.

[107]Ketners and Pētersone (2014), p. 15.

[108]Thuronyi (2003), p. 33.

[109]Law "On Personal Income Tax" http://www.vvc.gov.lv/export/sites/default/docs/LRTA/Likumi/On_Personal_Income_Tax.doc.

few of the long list of exemptions). Before the financial crisis in 2008–2009, interest on deposits and capital gains were also exempted from personal income tax. The general orientation of the personal income tax regulation is focused on collecting tax from withholding in all possible cases, even for business income. The Latvian corporate income tax law has been designed with the influence of OECD countries, having adjustments according to tax accounting rules, as well as provisions targeted at eliminating traditional corporate tax avoidance methods—there are provisions in the law regarding withholding taxes, incomplete (thin) capitalisation, transfer pricing, withholding tax in respect of payments within transactions with low-tax and zero-tax states and jurisdictions ("blacklist" countries). The requirements of European Union directives were gradually incorporated into corporate income tax legislation in respect of taxation of dividends, interests, royalties, and the application of income taxes laws within corporate reorganisation. However, during the last decade, some additional exemptions were introduced, such as exemption from corporate income tax for capital gains (adjustments on income and losses from alienation of stock, from securities of public circulation of the European Union and European Economic Area other than stock), exemption for dividends received by domestic companies and abolition of any withholding taxes on dividends, interests and royalties paid to non-residents (extending directives to all cases excluding only low-tax jurisdictions). In the field of indirect tax legislation, value added tax and excise taxes in Latvia are based on EU secondary legislation. The Latvian law is generally in conformity with EU requirements with some EU accession derogations.

5.4.2 Tax Legislation

Latvian tax system regulation can be divided into two main parts—regulation on general matters represented by the law "On Taxes and Fees"[110] and the Law "On State Revenue Service",[111] and regulation on specific tax and fees levied in accordance with the provisions of this Law, other laws and Cabinet regulations.

The Law "On Taxes and Fees" (1995) lays down the types of taxes and fees and governs the procedures for assessment of taxes and duties, collection and recovery thereof, the rights, duties and liability of the payers of taxes and fees (taxpayers) and the rights, duties and liability of tax and fee administration (tax administration) as well as the procedures for the challenging and appealing of decisions taken regarding tax and fee matters. The Law On Taxes and Fees (1995) is based on its predecessor law, "On Taxes and Fees in the Republic of Latvia"[112] (1990), and

[110]Law "On Taxes and Fees". http://www.vvc.gov.lv/export/sites/default/docs/LRTA/Likumi/On_Taxes_and_Fees.doc.

[111]Law "On State Revenue Service". http://www.vvc.gov.lv/export/sites/default/docs/LRTA/Likumi/On_the_State_Revenue_Service.doc.

[112]Law "On Taxes and Fees in the Republic of Latvia" "Ziņotājs", 3/4, 31.01.1991., "Diena", 35, 21.02.1991.

represents a general tax law for a tax system similar to its analogues in other transition countries before codification, and contains more or less complete rules for tax procedure. The Law On Taxes and Fees in its general provisions defines the terms used in tax laws. According to the definition given in Article 1, tax is a mandatory periodic or one-off payment prescribed by law for ensuring the revenues of the State Budget or local government budgets (general budget or special budget) and the funding of the functions of the State and local governments. The payment of taxes does not imply any compensation to the taxpayer directly. The abovementioned term shall also apply to state social insurance mandatory contributions as well as customs duty and other equivalent payments laid down in the directly applicable legal acts of the European Union regarding customs matters. Article 1 also provides a distinction between state fee and local government fee. According to the Law, a state fee is a mandatory payment into the State Budget or, in the cases prescribed by this Law, into the local government budget for the functions to be performed by the State or local government institutions pursuant to the prescribed functions of the respective institution. State fees are intended for regulating (controlling, promoting or imposing restrictions) the activities of persons. The amount of a state fee is not directly related to the covering of the costs of the functions performed by the institution. However, a local government fee is a mandatory payment into the general or special budget of the local government imposed by the local government council in the cases laid down in this Law. The amount of a local government fee is not directly related to the covering of the costs of the functions performed by the institution. For tax procedures, the Law delineates the definitions of taxpayers, tax (fee) administration, tax administration control procedures (observation, audit [revision], thematic inspection, data conformity audit). Article 1 also provides the definition of tax evasion—the deliberate provision of false information in tax declarations, failure to submit tax declarations, informative declarations or requested information for the administration and monitoring of taxes, unlawful application of tax deductions, advantages and reliefs or any other deliberate (fraud) act or omission leading to a non-payment of taxes and duties in whole or in part. The Law On Taxes and Fees applies to all taxes and fees unless a specific tax law does not provide for other procedures according to the nature of the particular tax or fee, which may not conflict with this Law. If international agreements (treaty) ratified by the Saeima provide for a different tax assessment or payment procedure than the tax laws of the Republic of Latvia, the provisions of such international agreements shall apply. The Cabinet may issue regulations regarding the procedures for applying tax reliefs laid down in international agreements ratified by the Saeima. Chapters 2 and 3 of the Law on Taxes and Fees defines the system of taxes, fees, list of state taxes, list of fee objects and general issues on budget affairs. Chapter 4 provides a classification of taxpayers (residents and non-residents) and residency criteria (declared place of residence and 183 day stay period for natural persons, registration for legal persons). The Law On Taxes and Fees also provides some traditional general tax law provisions such as autonomy of the Tax Administration, confidentiality of tax information; a noteworthy feature is limitation of tax re-assessment and imposition of tax penalties within

3 years of the statutory payment term laid down in the laws and regulations. If a tax review (audit) has been performed in respect of a specific tax, tax declaration item, fee or other statutory payment for the relevant taxation period, the opinion thereof shall be final and may be reviewed only in criminal proceedings in respect of fraud, falsification of documents, tax evasion and similar non-payment or criminal offences which may affect the determination of the amount of a tax liability. However, in verifying the transfer price for the conformity with the arm's length principle, the tax administration shall, within the scope of a tax review (audit), assess or adjust the amounts to be indicated in the relevant captions of tax and informative declarations, taxable income (tax losses), tax (duty) assessments in accordance with the provisions of the laws and regulations governing taxes, impose penalties within 5 years of the statutory payment term laid down in the laws and regulations. The Law On Taxes and Fees also states the limitation for decision-making, e.g., the tax administration shall take a decision on the findings of a tax review (audit) not later than within a period of 90 days from the day of the commencement of the tax review (audit), except in cases where the chief officer of the tax administration extends the term for taking the decision in accordance with the procedures laid down in Article 23. Article 23 also provides regulation for indirect tax calculation (the right to assess taxes by reference to the increase in the existing property of the taxpayer or capital gains or other information at the disposal of the tax administration), as well as the right to assess the amount of the tax liability from observation carried out in the relevant taxation period and the taxpayer's business performance indicators determined as a result thereof, taking into account the nature and regularity of the taxpayer's activities. If, during the tax year, based on the results of observation the non-conformity between the taxpayer's business performance indicators indicated in its returns and actual indicators is identified repeatedly, the findings resulting from the observation shall be extrapolated to all tax liabilities for the whole tax year, taking into account the nature and regularity of the taxpayer's activities. Chapter 7 of the Law On Taxes and Fees defines some tax penalties and liabilities of taxpayers, such as a late payment charge (interest of 0.05% of the outstanding principal debt for each outstanding day), reporting obligation and restrictions on the use of cash (for taxpayers, except natural persons which are not individual merchants, if the amount of cash transactions with their counterparties [irrespective of whether the transaction involves a single operation or several operations] exceeds specific limits) and tax penalties for tax infringements (Articles 32., 32.4 and 34 state different percentage amounts subject to the conditions of the Law). For tax procedure purposes, the Law describes the obligation of cooperation with the State Revenue Service. Within a specified term, the taxpayer shall provide the informative declarations prescribed in this Law or required under the provisions of the specific tax laws or additional information (documents supporting business revenues and expenditures, accounting records as well as other information describing the activities which affected or could have affected the calculation and payment of tax) on request of the tax administration officer, by not receiving which the determination of the tax amount due into the budget or a refund is not possible or made difficult. The

provision of evidence is also determined as the taxpayer's obligation to provide evidence (burden of proof—if the taxpayer disagrees with the amount of the tax payments assessed by the tax administration, it shall provide evidence regarding the amount of tax liabilities). According to the procedures for challenging and appealing decisions taken by the State Revenue Service, regarding tax issues, in Latvia have a one-stage before-court (pre-trial) appeal procedure. The taxpayer who has been notified of the decision of the official of the State Revenue Service based on the results of the control procedure (a review or audit) or the decision to refund overpaid taxes, has the right to challenge it to the Director General of the State Revenue Service within 1 month of its entering into force. Where the taxpayer disagrees with the decision of the Director General of the State Revenue Service, it has the right to appeal such decision to a court. Upon receiving an application challenging the decision taken as a result of the control procedure (a review or audit) carried out by the tax authorities, the execution of the decision of the tax administration official shall be suspended for the term of the pre-trial examination of the application. Article 41 of the Law On Taxes and Fees also provides the possibility of agreement between the State Revenue Service and the taxpayer. If the State Revenue Service has assessed additional payments payable to the budget as the result of the tax review (audit), the taxpayer has the right to propose the conclusion of a settlement agreement to the Director General of the State Revenue Service. The terms of the settlement agreement shall specify that the taxpayer agrees to the amount of the additionally assessed tax payment, and that 50% of the assessed penalties and late payment charges assessed for the period during which the tax payments were outstanding from the due date for the payment of the particular tax up to the date on which the tax review (audit) was started, are cancellable. The Law on Taxes and Fees also regulates the exchange of information in accordance with the EU administrative cooperation directive.

The Law "On State Revenue Service" (1993) is very similar to those laws which regulated tax administration organisation in the 1990s in transition country systems. Despite the fact that, after 2000, a new Administrative Procedure Law and State Administration Structure Law was adopted, the Law "On State Revenue Service" continues to be part of the tax regulation system. The Law defines the State Revenue Service, its tasks, structure, and principles of operation. According to Article 1, the State Revenue Service is a direct administration authority under the supervision of the Minister of Finance, which ensures the accounting of tax payments and taxpayers, the collection of state taxes, fees and other mandatory payments determined by the State in the territory of the Republic of Latvia, as well as collects taxes, fees and other mandatory payments for the budget of the European Union, implements customs policy and organises customs matters. The Law On State Revenue Service defines the rights of the Director General of the State Revenue Service, as well as tasks in the field of tax and customs administration. Article 10 of the Law On State Revenue Service states the rights of civil servants in tax administration during the performance of service duties, such as the right to obtain information and visit the territories and premises in the ownership or use of legal or natural persons, where economic activities are performed, perform tax assessments and audits of tax payments, within the competence and in accordance with the procedures laid down in law to impose administrative penalties and to seize the objects and instruments for the committing of administrative violations or to summon a taxpayer to the State Revenue Service. Since the State Revenue Service is a joint tax and customs administration authority, the tasks of the State Revenue Service and rights of civil servants (employees) in implementation of customs policy are of a similar nature. In performing their service duties, the civil servants of customs authorities have the right, upon presentation of a service identification document and the authorisation of a higher civil servant, to enter the territory or the premises of merchants, institutions, and special and open economic zones in which the goods and other objects subject to customs control are located. Civil servants (employees) of customs authorities, when performing their service duties, also have the right, if necessary, in accordance with the procedures laid down in laws and regulations, to carry and use firearms, special means of protection, as well as special means for stopping transport on the customs border. Civil servants of customs authorities have the right and duty, independently or together with the employees of the border guard, immigration and public order service, to arrest violators of the state border of the Republic of Latvia in accordance with the procedures laid down in the laws and regulations. Civil servants of customs authorities have the rights determined in the customs laws and regulations, but in performing an investigation in matters regarding criminal offences in the field of customs matters, they have the authorisation of an investigator as determined in the Criminal Procedure Code. Civil servants (employees) of customs authorities specially authorised by the Director General of the State Revenue Service or the deputy of the Director General have the right, in accordance with the procedures laid down in law, to perform investigatory operations activities to detect and prevent criminal offences regarding matters within the competence of the customs authorities. As Finance Police and Customs Police are structural units of the State Revenue Service, the law defines the rights of civil servants engaged in investigation activities. Civil servants of the State Revenue Service police units have the right, in accordance with the procedures laid down in law, to perform investigatory operations regarding matters within the competence of the State Revenue Service. Civil servants of the Finance Police are entitled to perform investigatory operations activities according to the special method in accordance with the procedures laid down in law and in accordance with the relevant authorisation of the head of the Finance Police. The State Revenue Service Finance Police and Customs Police shall perform an investigation of criminal offences in accordance with the procedures laid down in the Criminal Procedure Law. Civil servants (employees) of the State Revenue Service Finance Police and Customs Police have the right to use physical force, special fighting techniques, handcuffs, means of tying, batons, and tear-eliciting substances as well as the right of civil servants (employees) of the State Revenue Service Finance Police to use firearms. The law also delineates the status and liability of civil servants and employees of the State Revenue Service, dispute and appeal procedures for their decisions, funding, symbols, and the seal of the State Revenue Service. The Law On the Prevention of Money Laundering and Terrorism

Financing[113] (2008) comprises supplementary financial control legislation which follows Directive 2005/60/EC.[114]

Specific tax and fees regulation generally follows EU regulations such as Council Directive (EU) 2006/112/EC[115] and Council Implementing Regulation (EU) No 282/2011 in the field of value added tax[116] and Council Directive 2008/118/EC for excises,[117] as well as OECD countries practices. Excise regulation is implemented in natural resource tax, excise tax and electricity tax. However, there are some peculiarities of specific taxes to be mentioned.

Companies and other entities (except partnerships) carrying on a business are subject to corporate income tax with a tax rate of 15%. Partnerships are transparent for tax purposes, their income being taxable only in the hands of the partners. An entity is considered to be resident in Latvia if it is established and registered, or is required to be established under Latvian law. The starting point for determining taxable income is the profit and loss statement prepared in accordance with commercial accounting law, including accounting standards. In general, all income is taxable. Adjustments are made for exempt income, certain non-deductible items of expenditure and depreciation. Domestic dividends are exempt in the hands of the recipient company. Foreign dividends, except those originating from tax havens (as defined in a "blacklist"), are exempt. In general, a company may deduct substantiated expenses directly related to the production of taxable income. However, certain expenses are expressly mentioned as non-deductible. These include: expenses not directly connected with the economic activity of the company; expenses incurred for the establishment of the company's social infrastructure; penalties and fines; amounts paid to non-residents if the company has failed to withhold tax where required to do so; expenditure on the leasing, use and maintenance of a luxury car and interest payable on a loan to acquire or lease such a car (except for those taxpayers whose business consists to the extent of 90% or more in the leasing or hiring-out of luxury cars); and 60% of entertainment expenses. For the purposes of computing taxable income, expenses not directly connected with the economic activity of the company or connected with the maintenance of social

[113]Law On the Prevention of Money Laundering and Terrorism Financing.. http://www.vvc.gov.lv/export/sites/default/docs/LRTA/Likumi/Prevention_of_Money_Laundering_and_Terrorism_Financing.doc.

[114]Directive 2005/60/EC of the European Parliament and of the Council of 26 October 2005 on the prevention of the use of the financial system for the purpose of money laundering and terrorist financing. http://eur-lex.europa.eu/legal-content/EN/TXT/?uri=CELEX:32005L0060.

[115]Council Directive (EU) 2006/112/EC of 28 November 2006 on the common system of value added tax. http://eur-lex.europa.eu/legal-content/EN/TXT/HTML/?uri=CELEX:32006L0112&from=LV.

[116]Council Implementing Regulation (EU) No 282/2011 of 15 March 2011 laying down implementing measures for Directive 2006/112/EC on the common system of value added tax. http://eur-lex.europa.eu/legal-content/EN/TXT/HTML/?uri=CELEX:32011R0282&from=LV.

[117]Council Directive 2008/118/EC of 16 December 2008 concerning the general arrangements for excise duty and repealing Directive 92/12/EEC. http://eur-lex.europa.eu/legal-content/EN/TXT/?uri=CELEX:32008L0118.

infrastructure are increased by the coefficient 1.5. There is also a restriction on the deduction of interest expenses in two forms. The first is a thin capitalisation rule. The second is a general restriction on excess interest: interest paid is disallowed to the extent that it exceeds the amount of the relevant loan multiplied by 1.57 times the average short-term interest rate for the last month of the taxable period, as determined by the Central Statistics Board. There are a number of exemptions from both the thin capitalisation restriction and the general excess interest restriction. Depreciation, as provided in the company's financial statements, is not an allowable expense. However, tax depreciation at rates provided in the Law On Corporate Income Tax[118] may be deducted in respect of tangible assets and certain intangible assets. Depreciation is computed under the declining-balance method. It is calculated by applying the depreciation rates (10–70%) to the balance for each category or each separate asset. Tax depreciation is not allowed for luxury cars (light motor vehicles designed to carry no more than eight passengers) with a value exceeding EUR 50,000. The costs of acquiring or developing intangible assets such as concessions, patents, licences and trademarks are amortised for tax purposes under the straight-line method. The costs of concessions are written off over 10 years, while the costs of patents, licences and trademarks are written off over 5 years. Research and development costs related to the economic activity of the taxpayer may be written off in the year in which they are incurred; a deduction of three times the amount of certain kinds of R&D expenditures may be claimed when computing taxable income. Companies may not make contributions to tax-free reserves. However, credit institutions may deduct contributions to provisions for doubtful debts, and insurance companies may deduct allocations to special technical reserves. Capital gains are, in general, taxable as ordinary income. However, gains from the disposal of shares are exempt for corporate income tax purposes, except for the shares of companies resident in tax havens. Losses incurred in taxable periods beginning in 2008 and thereafter may be carried forward indefinitely. Carry-back of losses is not permitted. In the case of a change of control of a company with brought-forward losses, those losses become disallowable. An exception applies where there is no change in the nature of the basic trade or business (as carried on by the company in the two taxable periods immediately preceding the change of control) for at least the first five taxable periods after the change of control. Donations to charitable, religious or state bodies resident in Latvia or another EEA country with which Latvia has a double tax treaty in force give rise to a tax credit equal to 85% of the amounts donated. However, the total tax credit for charitable donations may not exceed 20% of the amount of corporate income tax before the credit is granted. Another tax incentive to be mentioned is the special tonnage tax regime, as an alternative to normal corporate income tax, which is available to resident shipping companies in respect of their income from the operation of ships in international traffic. Taxable income under the tonnage tax

[118] Law "On Corporate income tax". http://www.vvc.gov.lv/export/sites/default/docs/LRTA/Likumi/Enterprise_Income_Tax.doc.

regime is computed by multiplying the net tonnage of each qualifying ship by the number of days in the tax year on which the ship was put to use in international transport or other qualifying activities and income coefficient ranging from 0.0022 to 0.0007 in inverse proportion to the ship's tonnage.

Individuals are subject to personal income tax. Personal income tax is levied in the form of withholding tax (salary tax) on salaries, wages and other income from employment (the amount of tax is normally adjusted by assessment); withholding tax on income from capital, including dividends and interest; self-assessed tax on income from business activities, which is levied on business income not subject to corporate income tax and self-assessed tax on other incomes. Personal income tax could be replaced with an elective "licence fee" (*patentmaksa*), payable instead of standard income tax by certain small traders or by the abovementioned micro-enterprise tax payable by micro-enterprises, their employees, and shareholders instead of the general income tax. A special feature, starting from 1 June 2014, is income tax on the earnings of seasonal agricultural workers employed for no more than 65 days in the period from 1 April to 30 November. All income received by the taxpayer in cash or in kind is subject to income tax. Net taxable income is annual income, less deductible expenses and allowances. Among the types of income exempt from income tax in the hands of resident taxpayers are insurance payments; income from bonds issued by the Latvian or another EEA country's government or local authority; income from inheritances (except inherited copyrights); gifts from closely related individuals or gifts up to EUR 1425 from other individuals. Certain other payments can also be received tax free if the payment does not exceed the limits determined by the government. The general tax rate is 23%. Domestic and foreign dividends are subject to income tax at a special rate of 10%. Gains on the sale of property manufactured or acquired for the purpose of sale are subject to income tax at a special rate of 15%. There is an allowance, referred to as "the non-taxable minimum amount", which is EUR 75 per month (EUR 900 per year). There is also an allowance for dependants, which is EUR 165 per month (EUR 1980 in a full year) for each dependant. Individuals may carry forward losses from business activities for 3 years. Otherwise, carry-forward or carry back of losses is not allowed. As a special tax regime, a micro-enterprise[119] may opt for the micro-enterprise tax regime starting from the beginning of the next taxable period, subject to certain conditions. The micro-enterprise tax is levied at the following rates: 9% on the first EUR 7000; 11% on the part of the turnover exceeding EUR 7000 but not exceeding EUR 100,000 (rising to 13% in 2016 and to 15% from 2017); and 20% on the part of the turnover exceeding EUR 100,000. The tax replaces personal income tax, corporate income tax and social security contributions payable by employers for their employees. The State Social Security system (special budget)

[119] A limited-liability company (SIA) qualifies as a microenterprise, provided that it meets the following criteria: the shareholders of the company are all individuals, who at the same time are members of the management board; the annual turnover of the company does not exceed EUR 100,000 (before 1 January 2014: LVL 70,000); and the total number of employees does not exceed five.

provides benefits for loss of income through illness, disability, maternity, unemployment, old age, industrial injury and occupational disease. Resident employers must pay contributions for employees of at least 15 years of age. The taxable base for employer contributions is the employee's gross income subject to individual income tax before the personal allowance, allowable deductions and other reliefs. Private pension contributions and life insurance premiums paid by the employer on the employee's behalf are, however, not included in the taxable base. With effect from 1 January 2015, the maximum annual taxable base for social security contributions is set at EUR 48,600 (EUR 46,400 in 2014). Starting from 1 January 2016 the object of mandatory contributions exceeding the maximum amount of the object of mandatory contributions is an object of solidarity tax, and mandatory contributions made of this object are assigned to the solidarity tax. According to the Solidarity Tax Law[120] solidarity tax applies to all socially insured individuals—employees, the self-employed, the income of whom over a calendar year exceeds the maximum amount of mandatory contribution of the statutory social insurance. Also, with effect from 1 January 2014, social security contributions must be paid for company directors performing their duties without remuneration (under conditions). The rate of contributions payable by employers for full coverage is 23.59% (same as in 2014 and 2015). The rate of social security contributions of employees is 10.5% (same as in 2014 and 2015).

Real estate tax is levied by local authorities on immovable property, such as land and buildings. Exempt immovable property includes land on which economic activity is prohibited by law; immovable property that is recognised as a national cultural monument and is maintained as required; recreation centres, sports stadiums, grounds and halls; constructions; and land covered by newly planted forests (less than 40 years old). From 1 January 2013, the basic rate of immovable property tax is 1.5% of the cadastral value of the land or building. The rates of tax on private residences are progressive (0.2–0.6%), depending on cadastral value. Local authorities may vary the rate from 0.2% to (in the case of real estate not properly maintained) 3%. Local authorities are entitled to grant tax reductions of 25%, 50%, 70% or 90%, subject to state aid limitations. Also, in direct taxation regulation, Latvia has an "excessive profit" tax—subsidised electricity tax and fringe benefit tax—Company Car Tax, levied on cars used for commercial and personal use under specific conditions.

5.4.3 Budgetary Legislation

Latvian budgetary law is represented by the organic Law On Budget and Financial management[121] (1994). The Law On Budget and Financial Management

[120]Solidarity Tax Law. LV, 248 (5566), 18.12.2015.

[121]Law On Budget and Financial Management http://www.vvc.gov.lv/export/sites/default/docs/LRTA/Likumi/Budget_and_Financial_Management.pdf.

determines the procedures for the formulation, approval and implementation of the State Budget and local government budgets, as well as responsibility in the budget process. Financial management within the meaning of this Law applies to the funds of the State Budget and local government budgets. The provisions of this Law apply to the financial activities of merchants and organisations if they have been allocated funds of the State Budget or local government budgets, a share of capital has been invested in them by the State or local governments, or it is specially so determined by a law or Cabinet regulations. The provisions of this Law shall also apply to the State and local government agencies and to public foundations. The Law "On Local Governments' Budgets"[122] determines some specific procedures for local government budget approval and execution, whereas the Local Government Finance Equalization Law[123] is devoted to local government financial transfers (horizontal equalisation similar to German *Länder* financial equalisation rules). According to OECD research, budget formulation in Latvia can best be described as "continuous".[124] During years of high economic growth, the approach to budgeting involved a pattern of in-year adjustments with at least one supplementary budget and additional expenditures each year. In contrast, a series of substantial expenditure cuts had to be made to the 2009 budget to adjust to the unfolding crisis and to maintain external financial support. In the process of fiscal adjustment, the regular budget formulation schedule has been suspended and budgeting has lost the character of an annual process. The budget formulation process was reformed in 2007 by introducing a formal medium-term budget framework. According to the Law on Budget and Financial Management, medium-term state budget planning is a process in which the resources accessible for the medium-term are determined, and the use of these resources is ensured in conformity with the priorities determined by the government. Medium-term is a 3-year period formed by the financial year for which the state budget is planned and the subsequent two financial years. Amendments to the Law on Budget and Financial Management, which entered into force on 1 January 2012, provided that a Framework, approved by the Cabinet of Ministers, shall be developed in the form of a law as the Medium-Term Budget Framework Law (Framework Law), to be approved by the Saeima, thus ensuring that financial indicators included in the Framework Law and to be achieved are legally binding and that they should underpin the annual State Budget Law. The first Framework Law was prepared in 2012 and was submitted to the Saeima in one legislative package with the State Budget Law for 2013. The Framework Law is linked to development planning documents, thus ensuring allocation of available financial resources in accordance with government policy priorities for the medium-term.

[122]Law "On Local Government Budgets". LV, 59 (342), 18.04.1995.

[123]The Local Government Finance Equalization Law LV, 118 (5436), 18.06.2015.

[124]Kraan et al. (2010).

In the field of budget regulatory legislation, in addition to Regulation (EU) No 1175/2011,[125] Latvia also adopted the Fiscal Discipline Law[126] in January 2013, which formulates national numerical fiscal rules, provides the principles of linking the annual budget to medium term budgetary plans, allows for justified escape clauses, and foresees long term stabilisation mechanisms for budget balance. The purpose of the Fiscal Discipline Law is to prescribe such fiscal policy principles and conditions which ensure a balanced budget in an economic cycle and thus facilitate sustainable state development, macroeconomic stability and reduce the negative impact of external factors on the national economy. The Fiscal Discipline Law also provided for the creation of the National Fiscal Council, an independent fiscal policy supervision institution functioning from 1 January 2014, and whose main task is to monitor compliance to set fiscal rules, to provide evaluation of budgetary elements at different stages of budget processes, and to warn the respective institutions in case of incompliance. The Fiscal Discipline Law also lays down numerical fiscal rules that act to constrain the budget. Firstly, a balance rule requires that the general government budget structural balance for every particular year of a Medium-Term Budgetary Framework Draft Law shall not be lower than −0.5% of GDP (if the target is not attained, specified annual budgetary corrections are imposed until the deficit is back within this limit). Secondly, an expenditure growth rule limits medium-term expenditure growth (net of the GDP deflator), as set out in the Medium-Term Budgetary Framework Draft Law, to within the average potential GDP growth for the period. Thirdly, a binding expenditure ceiling for the central Government is fixed in the Medium-Term Budgetary Framework Draft Law for every particular year, in compliance also with the limits arising under the previous two rules. A noteworthy feature of the fiscal rules is the inclusion of an automatic correction mechanism; any deviations of the structural balance from its planned targets are logged, and additional fiscal efforts must be made to ensure that the cumulative deviation–once it exceeds 0.5% of GDP–will be progressively corrected. The analysis of past development of fiscal discipline measures in Latvia, expressed in terms of the existence of fiscal rules and medium-term expenditure planning, makes it possible to conclude that the legislative framework on these issues has existed more for formal purposes than for real enforcement of fiscal discipline. The creation of the Long-term Stability Reserve and Fiscal Discipline Law can be viewed, rather, as a late response to crisis, than as the timely implementation of sound instruments of fiscal sustainability.

The main actors in the annual budget planning process are the Cabinet of Ministers, the Ministry of Finance and line ministries; the Bank of Latvia has an advisory role in the process. The abovementioned constitutional provision for the

[125]Regulation (EU) No 1175/2011 of the European Parliament and of the Council of 16 November 2011 amending Council Regulation (EC) No 1466/97 on the strengthening of the surveillance of budgetary positions and the surveillance and coordination of economic policies. http://eur-lex.europa.eu/legal-content/EN/TXT/?uri=CELEX:32011R1175.

[126]Fiscal Discipline Law. http://vvc.gov.lv/export/sites/default/docs/LRTA/Likumi/Fiscal_Discipline_Law.doc.

submission of the Draft Budget Law to Parliament is elaborated in the Law on Budget and Financial Management. It requires that the Cabinet submit the Draft Budget Law to the Saeima not later than 1 October (Article 21 of the LBFM). During the economic crisis, external actors—in particular the IMF and the European Commission—also exerted substantial influence on budgetary decisions. If the annual draft budget submitted by the Cabinet is rejected by the Saeima at the first or second reading, it is regarded as a vote of no confidence in the Cabinet (Article 30 of the Rules of Parliamentary Procedure). Since 1991, the government has had to resign for this reason only once. The Saeima is authorised to amend the draft budget proposed by the Cabinet. However, the Constitution restricts the amendment powers of Parliament by the following provision: "If the Saeima makes a decision that involves expenditures not included in the budget, then this decision must also allocate funds to cover such expenditures." The restriction is further elaborated in Article 10.[1]the Law on Budget and Financial Management: "In the decisions of the Saeima, the adoption of which relates to expenditures not provided for by the budget, provision shall also be made for funds by which such expenditures shall be covered. In cases provided for by law, the Minister of Finance shall submit an opinion in regard to submitted draft laws not later than within a two-week period from the date of receipt of the relevant draft law." In practice, an amendment increasing expenditures is possible by either correcting the revenue estimation or changing a tax rate for certain taxes. Both are difficult to realise; thus, the total amendment power of Parliament remains limited. The budget adopted by Parliament enters into force at the beginning of the budget year. But if an annual state budget has not come into force in time, the Minister of Finance approves the state budgetary expenditures, provided that the monthly expenditures cannot exceed one-twelfth of the appropriations of the previous year (the deadline is usually respected, although delays have occurred in some parliamentary election years). Separation of powers is also ensured by the financial independence of the Saeima. After its budget request has been examined by the committees and approved by the Presidium, it is submitted to the Minister of Finance, who incorporates it without any amendments into the Draft Budget Law. Issues related to the financial management of the Parliament are decided by the Presidium. Bookkeeping records, the legitimacy and usefulness of expenditures, and the annual report of the Parliament are audited by the Public Expenditure and Audit Committee (Chapter VII of the Rules of Parliamentary Procedure). The Law On Budget and Financial Management enumerates a set of documents that have to be submitted in conjunction with the annual budget bill: proposals for amendments to substantive laws so that they conform to the draft budget law (so-called "budget-related draft laws"), explanations of the draft budget law.

Budget execution in Latvia starts on 1 January, with the coming into force of the Annual State Budget Law. The organisation responsible for budget execution is the State Treasury *(Valsts Kase),* since 1997 an independent agency financed by the Ministry of Finance. According to Article 23 of the LBFM and subsequent regulation, the Treasury is an institution of direct administration subordinated to the Ministry of Finance assigning and making payments from the State Budget for specific purposes, performing functions for the implementation and accounting of the State Budget and for the management of the national debt, and the functions of the Paying Authority for the European Union policy instruments determined in the laws and regulations, as well as other functions determined in the laws and regulations. Latvia has a single treasury account that is held at the central bank, but for the purpose of transactions in foreign currency, the State Treasury holds several accounts with commercial banks. While budget holders in the central government are not allowed to open accounts in banks, but only with the State Treasury, local governments are not required to use the State Treasury accounts, except for the use of resources which they receive from the State Budget. Responsibility for the execution of the budget, including management of accounts and reporting, rests ultimately with the heads of the approximately 7000 spending units or budget holders (including public agencies, their local branches, prisons, schools and budget holders of ministries and independent agencies, but not municipalities or hospitals). The state secretary of each line ministry is formally responsible for the sector budget and accounts, including the budget and accounts of the budget holders signed over by the ministry. The budget is implemented after approval by Parliament based on a resource and expenditure plan based on the budget that is drawn up centrally at the Ministry of Finance. The line ministries then decide, by means of a regulation, which programme will be executed by which budget holder, and what amount will be transferred to that budget holder. The budget holders in turn draw up financial plans—that is, quarterly cash-flow surveys, which are consolidated at line ministry level, approved by the state secretary, and sent to the Treasury for approval. All budget holders prepare their own financial plans for each of their programmes separately. The Treasury conducts cash planning in the light of the cash plans as well as historical spending patterns. There are no incentives for budget holders to gradually improve spending plans. The financial accounts are a responsibility of the State Treasury. The State Treasury ensures the registration of central government budget execution and the aggregation of local government budget execution, and draws up operative and official reports of the State Treasury. The State Treasury also ensures a unified methodology for the registration of the central government and local governmental budget execution and releases regulations concerning accounting practices. Accounting data established by accounting units of line ministries at the central government level are introduced into a centralised electronic system. Based on the collected accounts, according to the Law on Budget and Financial Management, the State Treasury compiles two kinds of financial reports: monthly and annual. Monthly reports are cash-based and cover both the central government and the local levels. Reports are publically available and are disseminated on the State Treasury's website 15 days after the reporting month. The State Treasury also issues monthly reports on debt and guarantees, also available on the State Treasury's website. The annual consolidated report uses State Treasury data which are checked and reconciled with the budget holders' accounts by the State Treasury and its regional branches. Ministries and local governments are to submit annual accounts to the Treasury by 1 May of the financial year following the reporting year. The annual report is regulated in Article 30 of the LBFM. The report is fully accruals-based, but includes additional information on cash-based execution data. The Ministry of Finance uses the accounts to prepare a consolidated annual financial report. The consolidated annual financial report is thereafter submitted to the State Audit Office, and by 1 September, the State Audit Office provides its opinion on the report. The Treasury reports to the Cabinet in the middle of September and the Cabinet submits the report to the Saeima by the middle of October. Therefore, the annual consolidated report can be published in October, *i.e.* 10 months after the end of the reporting year. The annual reports provide both accrual and cash information and are available on the State Treasury's website. Financial reporting in Latvia is accurate and timely and in accordance with international accounting and transparency standards. All important data are released on the website of the Treasury after only a short delay.

Financial control procedure consists of external and internal revision provisions. Internal audit procedures within budget execution and public management in Latvia were initially introduced in 1999. According to the Internal Audit Law[127] and the regulation on the internal audit of the Cabinet of Ministers, state secretaries and heads of independent public agencies are responsible for the establishment of a comprehensive and efficient internal control system, as well as for its permanent improvement and supervision. The Ministry of Finance is responsible for overall co-ordination. The Cabinet has specified procedures for the certification of internal auditors, approved the methodology for internal audits, and determined procedures for peer review. The role of the Ministry of Finance includes the development of methodology, the coordination of training and professional development, consultative assistance and peer reviews every 2 years, as well as the preparation of an annual report, which is submitted to the Cabinet of Ministers and the State Audit Office on 1 June. In spite of these coordination efforts, the quality of internal audit in the ministries varies, depending on whether the units have experienced and qualified staff. The instrument of peer review is very helpful. It entails that the Internal Audit Department of the Ministry of Finance assesses the degree of independence, the application of legal acts and methodology, and the quality of reports, and recommends measures for improvement to the state secretaries. However, given the capacity constraints of the Internal Audit Department, it is planned to extend the period during which all units are reviewed from 2 to 5 years, except for those that need special attention. Another instrument to promote the introduction and development of a common policy and methodology in ministries and institutions is the Internal Audit Council. It is a consultative forum with five members of high professional standing and expertise that has an important role in the drafting of the annual report. The ministries must submit their contributions for

[127]Internal Audit Law. http://www.vvc.gov.lv/export/sites/default/docs/LRTA/Likumi/Internal_Audit_Law.doc.

the annual report to the Ministry of Finance by 30 January. The Council reviews and comments on all ministerial contributions and gives written opinions and recommendations. The Internal Audit Department consolidates the comments and sends the annual report to the State Audit Office and the Cabinet of Ministers by 1 June.

The internal audit units are directly subordinated to the state secretaries, to whom they report and who appoint the auditors. The units produce strategic audit plans before the beginning of the budget year. The Internal Audit Department receives the strategic plans at the beginning of the year but cannot change them. The Department similarly receives the compilation of the main audit results in the annual reports of the units, but not the detailed recommendations. This makes it hard for the Internal Audit Department to judge the effectiveness of the internal audits as regards relevance of findings and recommendations. The Internal Audit Department observes the largest problems in the area of performance indicators that are poorly developed, and the multiplicity of different IT systems in use that often cannot communicate with each other. There are monthly meetings between the Internal Audit Department and the heads of the internal audit units at ministry level to share views on these and related issues. The Internal Audit Law applies only to the central government. Local governments are regulated by the Law on Local Government, which only requires external audit but not internal audit. On a voluntary basis, the largest municipalities use the methodology of the Ministry of Finance and also participate in training.

An opinion of the State Audit Office (SAO) or, for local governments, of a sworn auditor, regarding the correctness of the annual accounts must be attached to the abovementioned annual financial report prepared by the Treasury. External audit in Latvia is performed by the SAO which is, per the Constitution, Latvia's independent and collegial supreme audit institution. The Auditor General and the members of the SAO Council are elected by Parliament pursuant to the same procedure as judges. As the Law on the State Audit Office specifies, its tasks are to perform financial and performance audits in conformity with international audit standards; ensure the lawful, correct, economical and effective utilisation of public funds—that is, central and local resources (revenues, expenditures, property) as well as EU funds; assist in developing a fair and transparent decision-making process. The Auditor General has the authority to determine the internal structure of the SAO, to approve procedures and instructions, and to maintain relations with the Parliament, in particular the Public Expenditure and Audit Committee. The SAO decides completely independently on its work plan by first determining audit priorities such as public services, investment, use of state property, or collection of revenues. The departments then develop a concrete work plan based on the findings from financial audits, press reports, or citizen complaints. In the last step, the audit teams are selected and concrete questions are proposed, together with a timeline, and approved by the SAO Council.

5.5 Labour Law

Kristīne Dupate
Law Faculty, University of Latvia, Raiņa bulv, 19 Riga, Latvia
e-mail: kristine.dupate@lu.lv

Māris Badovskis
Labour Relations and Labour Protection Policy Department, Ministry of Welfare, Riga, Latvia
e-mail: maris.badovskis@lm.gov.lv

5.5.1 Introduction

This chapter provides an overview of Latvian labour law. It describes the historical develoments and roots of labour law in Latvia. Further, the chapter describes the general sources of labour law currently, and explains the basic concepts under it. It covers both individual and collective legal regulation starting from the conclusion of an employment contract, health and safety, and ending with collective disputes as well as mechanisms for the enforcment of such rights. The chapter not only describes the normative regulation, but also reflects on the impact of EU law as well as the judicial practice of both national courts and the CJEU.

5.5.2 Historical Development of Latvian Labour Law

The history of Latvian labour law can be divided into three periods—the period from 1918 until 1940, from 1940 until 1990 and from 1991 up to now. During the period from 1918 until 1940, the legal regulation of the labour law had mixed legal sources—Tsarist Russian legislation and legal acts adopted by Latvian authorities.[128] The main legal acts which regulated the relations between an employer and employee were the Codification of Local Laws (1864) and Law on Industrial Work (1913).

During the period from 1940 until 1990, the sources of labour law were Soviet legal acts, since Latvia had a Soviet legal system during the Soviet occupation. The most important legal acts were the Labour Code of the Latvian SSR (1972) and Standard Statute for Kolkhoz (1969).

[128] In 1922 the Law on Working Time was adopted. The Civil Law of Latvia, which also contained provisions regulating legal employment relations, was adopted on 1937. As regards collective labour law, the legal regulation was introduced in 1923 by the Law on Associations, Unions and Political Organizations and Regulations on Collective Agreements (1927). The law regulating collective bargaining and the conclusion of collective agreements was adopted in 1940.

During both periods, a specific feature of labour legislation was that employees were divided into two separate groups—rural employees and those who were employed at industrial plants and service provider enterprises. In contrast, current legal regulation applies equally to all employees irrespective of the sector or type of work. The development of labour law during the period from 1991 and up to the present has been very dynamic. The labour law during this period was particularly influenced by EU law, owing to the obligation to transpose EU law into the national legal system. In 2001, a new Labour Law (DL) was adopted by the *Saeima* (Parliament), introducing comparatively new regulation of legal employment relations.[129] Other important labour rights are provided by the Constitution of the Republic of Latvia,[130] the Civil Law (CL),[131] the Labour Dispute Law (DSL),[132] the Strike Law (SL),[133] the Work Safety Law (DAL)[134] and other laws and regulations of the Cabinet of Ministers. Apart from normative acts, the case-law of both the national courts, especially the Supreme Court of Latvia and the CJEU, have become more and more important sources of law in defining different concepts of the DL.

5.5.3 Basic Concepts

There are legal definitions for several central concepts of employment law. Articles 3 of the DL defines an employee *(darbinieks)* as a natural person who, from an employment contract for agreed work remuneration, performs specific work under the guidance of an employer. As regards the other party in employment relationships, Article 4 of the DL stipulates that an employer *(darba devējs)* is a natural or legal person or a partnership with legal capacity that, from an employment contract, employs at least one employee. Notwithstanding this, some other terms are also used in Latvian legislation to describe persons who perform work; however, such terms are used in relation to other legal relationships. For example, social insurance law[135] uses the term *darba ņēmējs* (English—a job taker) and health and safety law uses the term *nodarbinātais*[136] (English—an employed person). These concepts are more extensive, and also include persons who are not

[129]The Labour Law, LV No.105, 6 July 2001.
[130]The Constitution of Latvia, LV No.43, 1 July 1993.
[131]Civil Law, LV No.41, 20 February 1937.
[132]Labour Disputes Law, LV No.149, 16 October 2002.
[133]Strike Law, LV No.130/131, 12 May 1998.
[134]Work Safety Law, LV No.105, 6 July 2001.
[135]The Law on State Social Security, LV No.274/276, 21 October 1997.
[136]Work Safety Law, LV No.105, 6 July 2001.

employees in the direct sense (or within the meaning of the DL), for example civil servants.[137] The same applies to the term *strādājošais*[138] (English—a worker).

For different purposes (collective redundancies, information, and communication, etc.), labour law defines the concept of an undertaking (*uzņēmums*). An undertaking shall mean any organisational unit in which an employer employs his or her employees.[139] Latvian labour law does not define other concepts which may be related to organisational units, such as establishments.[140]

The definitions provided by the normative acts are, however, not determinative in practice. So, in the case *Danosa*, originating from Latvia, the CJEU repeated that the autonomous concept of an 'employee' as defined by EU law is applicable in situations covered by the relevant EU law.[141] Also, the Supreme Court has used the CJEU interpretation of the concept of 'pay' to interpret the 'pay' concept under national law in general,[142] irrespective of the fact that the respective interpretation of the concept of 'pay' was given by the CJEU within the meaning of equal pay.[143] Such examples demonstrate the close relationship between national and EU labour law and the impact of the cooperation between national courts and the CJEU on the development of labour law.

5.5.4 Employment Contract: Individual Labour Law

5.5.4.1 The Concept of Employment Contract

According to the DL, an employer and an employee shall establish mutual employment legal relationships by an employment[144] contract. The definition of employment contract provided by the DL stipulates that, by an employment contract, the employee undertakes to perform specific work, subject to specified working procedures and orders of the employer, while the employer undertakes to pay the agreed work remuneration and to ensure fair and safe working conditions that are not harmful to the health (Art. 28). Thus, the definition includes a reference to both

[137] The decision of 7 November 2013 of the Constitutional Court of Latvia in case No.2012-24-03, paragraph 16.2.1.

[138] The Constitution of the Republic of Latvia Art. 108.

[139] DL Art.5.

[140] Directive 2002/14/EC of the European Parliament and of the Council of 11 March 2002 establishing a general framework for informing and consulting employees in the European Community contains both terms—undertaking and establishment, *OJ L 80, 23.3.2002, p. 29–34.*

[141] The decision of the CJEU in case C-232/09 Dita Danosa v LKB Līzings SIA, OJ C 220, 12.9.2009, p. 11.

[142] Decision of Civil Cases Department of the Senate of the Supreme Court (27 March 2014) in case no.SKC-1683/2014.

[143] The decision of the CJEU in case C-262/88, Douglas Harvey Barber v Guardian Royal Exchange Assurance Group, European Court reports 1990 Page I-018899.

[144] For the purposes of this article, the term "employment contract" will be used instead of term "labour contract" as an official translation of the term "darba līgums".

parties of the employment contract as well as to the essential elements of the employment contract—agreed work, remuneration for such work, and subordination. Additionally, the written form of the employment contract shall be deemed as an essential element of this type of contract. The respective obligations provide a higher standard than required by the EU Labour Law, in particular, Directive 91/533/EC.[145] As regards the object of an employment contract if the purpose of the contract is not work itself, but rather a specific result of work, then a contract for such shall not be considered to be an employment contract, but rather a work-performance contract.[146]

In addition, the Latvian law recognises the substance of an agreement, not a title. The Supreme Court of Latvia has stressed the importance of assessing the substance of a contract in possible employment relationships since the employee is a weaker party.[147] Consequently, an employment contract may exist even under a differently titled contract or contract in unwritten form if a court established the factual existence of an agreement on work, remuneration and subordination.

5.5.4.2 Conclusion and Amendments to an Employment Contract

Everyone has the right to choose freely his/her employment and workplace,[148] as well as freely enter into legal employment relations or to refrain from it. These rights are closely connected with the prohibition of discrimination, which is explicitly and in detail regulated by the DL.

The DL provides for the following compulsory requirements in the conclusion of an employment contract. Firstly, an employment contract shall be concluded in written form. Secondly, it must be concluded prior to commencement of work. Thirdly, an employment contract shall include certain information such as the names of the parties, expected duration of the employment contract, starting date, workplace, amount of remuneration, agreed working time, etc.[149]

Although an employment contract must be concluded in writing, the DL stipulates the consequences of failure to comply with the written form of employment contract. In such a case, an employee has the right to request that the employment contract be expressed in writing, because it is an obligation imposed on the employer to conclude the contract in written form. Moreover, to protect the employee from any malignity, the law states that if both parties, or at least one of the parties, has started to perform the duties contracted for without a written contract, it must have the same legal consequences as a written employment

[145]Council Directive 91/533/EEC of 14 October 1991 on an employer's obligation to inform employees of the conditions applicable to the contract or employment relationship, *OJ L 288, 18.10.1991, pp. 32–35.*

[146]CL Art. 2179.

[147]The decision of the Supreme Court in case No.437/2008 (26 November 2008) available in Latvian at : http://at.gov.lv/lv/judikatura/judikaturas-nolemumu-arhivs/senata-civillietu-departaments/hronologiska-seciba_1/2008/.

[148]Balodis (2011), pp. 479–502.

[149]See. DL Art. 40.

contract. During the last years, the principle of presumption was introduced; this means that, in case of any doubt regarding the duration of a de facto employment relationship, it shall be considered that it has lasted for at least 3 months under normal working time with a minimum monthly salary. Such a presumption applies where it is possible to prove the existence of the employment relationship, although none of the parties are able to prove the duration of the relationship and employment conditions.

One of the essential issues in relation to an employment contract is its duration. Employment contracts can be concluded for an indefinite term or fixed-term. Employment contracts of an indefinite term are the general and most common form of employment relations in Latvia. In this regard, the legal provisions of the DL clearly state that an employment contract shall be entered into for an indefinite period, except in limited and strictly defined cases. In other words, a fixed-term employment contract may be concluded in cases defined by law, and includes specific types of work or sectors of employment, for example, seasonal work, or cases of replacement.[150]

The length of employment contracts concluded for a fixed-term may differ. For seasonal work, the duration of a contract (including extensions of the term) may not exceed 10 months within 1 year. Any other fixed-term employment contracts may not exceed 5 years (including extensions). The duration of fixed-term contracts was extended from 3 to 5 years in 2014. At the same time, to prevent abuse of fixed-term contracts, the DL (Art. 45) stipulates that the entering into of a new employment contract within 60 days after termination or expiry of a previous employment contract with the same employer shall also be regarded as an extension of the term of the employment contract. Such regulation fully complies with the requirements under Directive 1999/70/EC.[151]

The DL allows a probation period when concluding an employment contract. This must be specified in the employment contract, otherwise the employment shall be regarded as entered into without a probation period. The probationary period may not exceed three months in duration. During the probationary period, either party may terminate the employment contract by giving notice 3 days prior to termination. In such a case, neither the employee nor the employer has an obligation to indicate the ground for termination.

As a general rule, an employee and an employer may amend an employment contract by mutual agreement. Any amendments to an employment contract shall be in writing. The DL (Art. 98) provides specific regulation for amendments to an employment contract. An employer has the right to give written notice of termination of an employment contract not later than 1 month in advance under the condition that employment relationships will be terminated if the employee does not agree to amendments to the employment contract proposed by the employer.

[150]See. DL Art 44.

[151]Council Directive 1999/70/EC of 28 June 1999 concerning the framework agreement on fixed-term work concluded by ETUC, UNICE and CEEP, *OJ L 175, 10.7.1999, p. 43–48.*

However, in case of termination of a contract, it must be in compliance with the provisions regulating termination of an employment contract by notice of the employer.

5.5.4.3 Obligations Arising from an Employment Contract

Employers and employees are bound by the obligations arising from an employment contract. Traditionally, an employee is obliged to work (principal obligation of an employee), and the employer is obliged to pay remuneration (principal obligation of employer) for work. According to the CL (Art. 1812), the performance of these obligations is valid only if it has been performed and received by the proper person, at the proper place, at the proper time, and in due time. As regards the principal obligation of an employee, the work must be performed by the employee himself. This obligation cannot be transferred to another person. The DL (Art. 49) states that the type, amount, time and place of performance of the employee's obligations shall be determined in an employment contract by an employer, insofar as they are not in contradiction with prescriptive or prohibitive norms in regulatory enactments, the collective agreement or internal procedure regulations. In addition, an employee has the duty to perform work with such care as, in conformity with the nature of the work and requisite competence and suitability of the employee for the performance of such work, would be reasonable to expect from him or her. The DL provides more detailed regulation on the type and volume of work to be performed, as well as the time and place of performance of work.[152]

The obligation of an employer to pay remuneration for work is regulated by the DL. The legal definition of remuneration provided the by the DL (Art. 59) stipulates that remuneration is the regular pay for work payable to an employee, and includes a salary and supplements specified by the regulatory enactments, a collective agreement, or an employment contract, as well as bonuses and other kinds of payments related to work. Thus, the definition embraces both pay for work and pay related to work. Pay related to work is essentially important when dealing with the concept of equal pay, explicitly stated by the DL as the result of the implementation of the EU gender equality and non-discrimination law.[153] The concept of pay under Article 59 is a national law concept, while the same concept under Article 60 of the DL is a concept under the principle of equal pay deriving from EU law. Nevertheless, the Supreme Court of Latvia tends to interpret both terms uniformly, which allows for avoiding misapplication of EU labour law.[154] Latvian law defines the statutory minimum salary. According to the DL (Art. 61), the minimum monthly salary within the scope of regular working time, as well as the calculation

[152]See. DL Art. 51–53.

[153]See. DL Art. 60.

[154]Decision of Civil Cases Department of the Senate of the Supreme Court (27 March 2014) in case no. SKC-1683/2014.

of the minimum hourly wage, shall be determined by the Cabinet of Ministers.[155] The procedures for the specification and review of the minimum monthly wage shall also be determined by the Cabinet of Ministers.

In relation to the organisation of pay systems, there is the possibility for an employer to introduce the time salary[156] or piecework[157] system. Pay systems as well as systems of bonuses and supplements are usually subject to information and consultation procedures with the employees and their representatives.

An employer is obliged to pay remuneration in due time (two times per month unless an employee and an employer have agreed on payment of remuneration once a month). As regards the type of payment, the DL (Art. 70) states that remuneration shall be paid in cash, but non-cash payments are allowed only where the employee and the employer have agreed to it. Notwithstanding this, non-cash payment is nowadays the most common method of payment.

Payment of remuneration is subject to very detailed legal regulation: the DL regulates payment of remuneration in case of improper performance, for paid annual paid leave and supplementary leave, and payment of remuneration in cases where the employee does not perform the work for justifiable reasons. It also regulates the calculation of average earnings, which must be considered in various cases, expenses, losses, and deductions from remuneration.

Apart from the principal obligations arising from an employment contract, an employee and an employer have secondary (additional) obligations which are regulated by law. In this respect, the DL regulates, for example, with regard to an employee, the duty to undergo medical examination, obligation of confidentiality, prohibition of competition, civil liability and, with regard to an employer—to employ or provide work, to protect the employee's health and safety, personal belongings, and privacy.

5.5.4.4 Termination of an Employment Contract

Termination of an employment contract may be initiated by either party in an employment relationship. The most common procedure applied for the termination of an employment contract is a notice of termination given either by an employee or by an employer. A notice of termination is a statement by one of the parties (employee or employer) regarding an employment contract. The notice of termination becomes effective irrespective of the acceptance by the other party following receipt.[158] A notice of termination must be submitted in written form. According to the DL (Art. 112^1), notice of termination may be notified to the other party in

---

[155] See. The Cabinet of Ministers Regulation No.656 The Regulations on the amount of monthly salary for normal working time and calculation of minimum hourly pay, LV No.232, 26 November 2015.

[156] A time salary shall be calculated in conformity with the actual time worked irrespective of the amount of work done.

[157] A piecework salary shall be calculated in conformity with the amount of work done irrespective of the time within which it was done. The working time regulation is applicable.

[158] The Supreme Court (2010/2011), 22 1 pp.

person, or delivered by a courier, including a sworn bailiff, as well as by using postal services. Notice of termination may also be notified to the other party via electronic mail using a secure electronic signature, if this is provided for in the employment contract or the collective agreement. As a general rule[159], an employee has the right to give notice of termination of an employment contract 1 month in advance, unless a shorter time for the giving of notice of termination is provided for by the employment contract or the collective agreement. There is no obligation for an employee to indicate the reason for a notice of termination; however, an employee is obliged to observe the time limits for giving a notice and to continue working during the notice period. At the same time, the legislator has introduced exceptions. According to the DL (Art. 100), an employee has the right to give notice of the termination of an employment contract without complying with the time limit specified in law (1 month) if the employee has good cause.[160]

To protect workers against unfair dismissal, an employer may give notice of termination to an employee only in cases strictly defined by the DL. An employer has the right to give notice of termination of an employment contract only based on circumstances related to the conduct of the employee, his or her abilities, or of economic, organisational, technological measures or measures of a similar nature in the undertaking.[161] In addition, an employer has an obligation to state the legal basis and reasons for dismissal in the notice.

Moreover, the employer is obliged to observe not only the substantial but also the procedural requirements of the termination of an employment contract.[162] Incompliance provides reasonable grounds for the recognition of a notice as void and reinstatement of an employee to previous work.[163]

In exceptional cases, an employer has the right within 1 month to bring an action before a court for the termination of an employment relationship in cases not referred to by the DL, if the employer has good cause.[164]

In cases of notice of termination by an employer, the DL (Art. 103) provides different statutory periods for giving notice depending on the grounds for termination. There are three statutory periods for giving a notice of termination—immediately, 10 days, and 1 month, depending on the basis for notice.

There are also restrictions and prohibitions for giving a notice of termination in relation to the most vulnerable groups of employees—for example, pregnant women, as well as women following the period after birth of a child up to 1 year,

[159]DL Art. 100.

[160]Each condition based on considerations of morality and fairness that does not allow the continuation of employment legal relationships shall be regarded as such a cause. The issue whether there is good cause shall be settled by a court at its discretion.

[161]DL Art. 101.

[162]DL Art. 101 (2) (3) (4).

[163]See. The Supreme Court (2010/2011), pp. 12–14.

[164]Any condition which does not allow the continuation of employment legal relationships on the basis of considerations of morality and fairness shall be regarded as such a cause. The issue of whether there is good cause shall be settled by a court at its discretion. DL Art. 101(5).

or for the entire period of breastfeeding (maternity period), and disabled employees. There are also restrictions on dismissal in relation to certain situations. Giving of notice of dismissal is prohibited during temporary incapacity for work, or when an employee is on leave or is not performing the work for other justifiable reasons.[165] Additionally, the DL (Art. 110) stipulates that an employer is prohibited from giving notice of termination of an employment contract to an employee who is a member of a trade union without the prior consent of the relevant trade union, except in certain cases set out in the DL. If the trade union does not agree, an employer may bring an action before a court for termination of the employment contract. This issue is one of the most controversial in relation to termination of employment contracts, and remains one of the hottest topics of discussion among social partners. The provision provides very strict protection for any employee who is a member of a trade union, and not only to those who are trade union representatives, as is the case in many other countries.

Notice of termination obliges an employer to pay severance pay if the ground for notice is not related to the behaviour of the employee.[166] An employer has a duty to provide severance pay to an employee in the amount specified by law (if a collective agreement or the employment contract does not specify a larger amount), which is based on the duration of the employment relations and average earnings of the employee.[167]

However, there may be cases where an employment contract can be terminated without giving notice. According to the DL (Art. 116), the death of an employer constitutes a basis for the termination of employment relationship, if the performance of the employee's obligations is related only and exclusively to the employer personally. The death of an employee terminates the employment contract per se. Expiration of the term of a contract is a basis for the automatic termination of a fixed-term contract.[168] An employee and employer may terminate an employment relationship by mutual agreement (written form is necessary).[169] In addition, the DL (Art. 115) recognises certain reasons for termination of an employment contract without notice. Such cases include requests by third parties (in case of employment of persons under age of 18), decisions by the courts (if an employee has been sentenced to deprivation of liberty or custody lasting longer than 30 days) and non-compliance with the law requirements on prohibition of employment of certain categories of persons.

The legal protection of employees against unfair dismissal includes regulation relating to the bringing of an action before a court. It regulates declaration of a notice of dismissal as void, reinstatement of an employee, burden of proof, and right

[165] DL Art 109.

[166] An employer is obliged to pay severance pay in cases set out in Art. 101, Para. One, Clause 6, 7, 8, 9, 10, 11 as well as in Art. 100, Para five.

[167] DL Art.112.

[168] DL Art 113.

[169] DL Art. 114.

to compensation and execution of a court decision. According to the DL (Art. 122.), an employee may bring an action before a court for the invalidation of a notice of termination. This must be done within 1 month from the date of the receipt of the notice of dismissal. Such a time limit is preclusive.[170] The 1 month period for bringing an action in court is also applicable in other cases when the right of an employee to continue an employment relationship has been violated, for example, if an employment contract was concluded for a fixed-term contrary to the law.

In the latter cases, the time-limit commences from the day of the actual dismissal. If an employee fails to comply with the time-limits for bringing an action, this right may be renewed by a court in light of justifying reasons.[171] In case of a claim of unfair notice, it is the employer's duty to prove that a notice of dismissal has legal basis and complies with the specified procedural requirements. In other cases, when an employee has brought an action in court for reinstatement to work, the employer has a duty to prove that, when dismissing the employee, the employer has not violated the right of the employee to continue the employment relationship.[172] If a court declares the notice of termination to be void, an employee is reinstated to previous work. According to the DL (Art. 126), an employee who has been reinstated to previous work based on a court decision must be paid the average earnings for the entire period of idle time. This obligation also applies in cases where an employee requests for the court to terminate the employment relationship instead of reinstatement. Compensation for the entire period of forced absence from work shall also be paid in cases where a court terminates employment legal relationships by a court judgment upon request of the employee, although there exists the basis for the reinstatement of an employee to previous work.

5.5.5 Collective Labour Law

The Constitution of the Republic of Latvia (Art. 108) provides that employed persons have the right to a collective agreement and the right to strike. The State shall protect the freedom of the trade unions.[173] General principles and rights are stipulated by the Constitution, while more detailed regulation is provided by the Trade Union Law (AL),[174] the Employers' Organisations and their Associations Law (DDOAL),[175] the Law on Informing and Consulting Employees of European

[170]Preclusive term is the period after which a right can no longer be executed. According to the case law of the Supreme Court, the courts have to take into account the end of the preclusive term by their own initiative. See. The Supreme Court (2004), pp. 16–20; Kalniņš (2004).

[171]DL Art. 123.

[172]DL Art. 125.

[173]See. Balodis (2011), pp. 527–548.

[174]Trade Union Law (*Arodbiedrību likums*), LV No.60, 25 March 2014.

[175]Employers' Organisations and their Associations Law, LV No.161/162, 19 May 1999.

Community-scale Undertakings and European Community-scale Groups of Undertakings (IKL)[176] as well as the DL.

The AL regulates the foundation of trade unions, joining trade unions, general rules of trade union activities and the principles which must be observed in relations with employers' organisations, state and municipal institutions. On the other hand, the DDOAL prescribes the legal status and system of employers' organisations, as well as the rights and duties thereof in relations with trade unions and state and municipal institutions. The IKL regulates the specific information and consultation process to ensure the right to information and consulting of employees of European Union-scale undertakings or European Union-scale groups of undertakings.[177]

The DL regulates the process of collective bargaining, exchange of information and consultation procedures and issues relating to collective agreements. The DL (Art. 17) determines the scope of collective agreements, stating that the parties to a collective agreement shall reach agreement on the provisions regulating the content of employment relationships, especially the remuneration and organisation of health and safety, establishment and termination of employment relationships, vocational training, working procedures, social security of employees and other issues related to employment relationships, and shall determine mutual rights and duties. Like employment contracts, a collective agreement shall take a written form. When concluding a collective agreement, the parties shall refrain from any measures which are directed at unilateral amendments to its provisions, unless otherwise provided for by regulatory enactments or by the collective agreement, and ensure that the provisions of the collective agreement are complied with and fulfilled by both parties—the employer and the employees. According to the DL (Art. 17), these obligations are applicable without special arrangements.

Traditionally, in an undertaking a collective agreement is concluded between a trade union and employer. At the same time, the DL (Art. 18) provides that collective agreement at the level of a single undertaking can be concluded by authorised employee representatives[178] instead of a trade union; however, this is possible only if the employees have not formed a trade union. Collective agreements concluded in an undertaking form the majority of the collective agreements concluded in Latvia.

[176] Law on Informing and Consulting Employees of European Community-scale Undertakings and European Community-scale Groups of Undertakings, LV No.82, 27 May 2011.

[177] This law transposes Directive 2009/38/EC of the European Parliament and of the Council of 6 May 2009 on the establishment of a European Works Council or a procedure in Community-scale undertakings and Community-scale groups of undertakings for the purposes of informing and consulting employees, *OJ L 122, 16.5.2009, p. 28–44.*

[178] According to the DL (Art.10), authorised employee representatives are one of the possible forms of employee representation. Authorised employee representatives may be elected if an undertaking employs five or more employees. Authorised employee representatives shall be elected for a specified term of office by a simple majority vote at a meeting in which at least half the employees employed by an undertaking of the relevant employer participate. The course of the meeting shall be recorded in minutes and decisions taken shall be entered in the minutes. Authorised employee representatives shall express a united view with respect to the employer.

Collective agreements can be concluded at the sectoral (territorial)[179] level between an employer, a group of employers, an organisation of employers or an association of organisations of employers, and trade union or an association (union) of trade unions if the parties to an agreement have the relevant authorisation or if the right to enter into a general agreement is provided for by the articles of association of such associations (unions). Sectoral collective agreements shall be binding on members of organisations and associations of employers who have concluded the collective agreement. At the same time, the DL (Art. 18) regulates the situation when a sectoral collective agreement can become universally applicable. Collective agreements (at any level) shall be entered into for a specified period of time or for a period of time required for the performance of specific work. If the collective agreement does not specify its effect in time, the collective agreement shall be deemed to have effect for 1 year.

As regards the personal scope of a collective agreement according to the DL (Art. 20), it shall be binding on the parties and its provisions shall apply to all employees who are employed by the relevant employer or in a relevant undertaking of the employer, unless provided for otherwise by such collective agreement. As the general principle, the derogations from the provisions of a collective agreement are possible only if the provisions of the employment contract are more favourable to the employee.[180]

The DL contains regulation of conclusion procedures, procedure for amendment of and information of a collective agreement. Additionally, the DL (Art. 22) regulates the approval of a collective agreement to validate it. The collective agreement in an undertaking shall be approved at a general meeting (conference) of the employees, except in cases of collective agreements concluded by an employer and employees' trade union which represent at least 50% of the employees of an undertaking. The collective agreement shall be approved by a simple majority vote at a general meeting[181] at which at least half the employees of the relevant undertaking are present.

A collective agreement may be terminated before the expiry of its term by the agreement of the parties, or if it has been agreed on in the collective agreement by notice of termination by one of the parties.

[179]Collective agreements at sectoral (territorial) level are called general agreements to differentiate them from agreements in an undertaking.

[180]According to the DL (Art.6), provisions of a collective agreement, working procedure regulations, as well as the provisions of an employment contract and orders of an employer which, contrary to regulatory enactments, erode the legal status of an employee, shall not be valid. Provisions of an employment contract which, contrary to a collective agreement, erode the legal status of an employee shall not be valid.

[181]If it is impossible to convene a general meeting of employees due to the large number of employees employed by an undertaking, or due to the nature of work organisation, the collective agreement shall be approved by a simple majority vote at a conference of employee representatives at which at least half of the employee representatives participate.

Although Latvian law provides quite detailed regulation of collective labour law, in practice it is not frequently used, as Latvia is among the few countries in the EU where the coverage of collective agreements is exceptionally low (below 20% of employees are covered).[182]

5.5.6 Labour Disputes

Labour disputes and their settlement are regulated mainly by the Labour Dispute Law (DSL), with the aim of ensuring the fair and rapid settlement of labour disputes. The DSL determines the labour dispute settlement bodies and the procedures for settlement of labour disputes. The settlement of labour disputes is also regulated by the Strike Law (SL), Civil Procedure Law (CPL)[183] and the DL. The settlement of labour disputes is based on the typology of labour disputes; therefore, the DSL contains legal definitions of labour disputes and the different types of labour disputes (individual disputes regarding rights, collective disputes regarding rights and collective disputes regarding interests).[184]

According to the general principle stipulated by the DL and DSL, individual disputes regarding rights in an undertaking shall be settled, as far as possible, in negotiations between an employee and an employer. In this respect, the DL (Art. 94) regulates the grievance procedure. At the same time, an employer and a representative of the employees may agree on the establishment of a labour dispute commission in the undertaking of the settlement of individual disputes regarding rights in relation to which an agreement has not yet been reached through negotiations between the employer and employees. The DSL allows using other procedures of dispute settlement if the employer and employee representatives agree to this; for example, the parties may agree on mediation. The establishment of a Labour Dispute Committee is not frequently used in practice. In case of an individual dispute, employees and employers usually apply to a court to protect their rights. In such cases, the CPL rules regulate the procedure for dispute settlement.

Collective rights disputes must be resolved in a conciliation commission (a commission established by the parties of a dispute). If the dispute is not settled in a committee, the parties have the right to apply to a court or arbitration, if so agreed.

According to the DSL (Art. 15), collective disputes regarding interests also must be settled in a conciliation commission. If a collective dispute regarding interests is not settled in a conciliation commission, and the parties do not agree on the settlement of the collective dispute regarding interests by a mediation or arbitration

[182]Eurofund (2015).

[183]The Civil Procedure Law (, OG No.326/330, 3 November 1998).

[184]DSL Art. 4, 9, 13.

method,[185] they have the right to protect their interests by a collective action strike or lockout. The right to strike is regulated[186] by the SL, which defines a strike as a method of resolving a collective interest dispute that manifests itself in such a way that employees or a group of employees of a branch of an undertaking voluntarily, completely or in part, discontinue working to attain the fulfilment of the demands. According to the SL (Art. 3), the right to strike shall be exercised as a last resort if no agreement or reconciliation has been reached in a collective interest dispute. At the same time, the DSL (Art. 21) provides regulation of lockouts, stating that, if for the settlement of a collective dispute regarding interests, the representative of employees or the employees (a group of employees) use a strike as a final means for the settlement of the dispute, the employer, employers (a group of employers) or an organisation of employers, or an association of such organisations have the right to a response action for the protection of their economic interests, namely, to a lockout. The DSL defines a lockout as a refusal by the employer, employers (a group of employers) or an organisation of employers, or an association of such organisations to employ employees and to pay work remuneration if a strike significantly affects the economic activity of the undertaking. The number of employees against whom the lockout has been directed may not exceed the number of employees on strike. Thus, the law only allows a defensive lockout.

5.5.7 Social Insurance

There is three-tier scheme of social insurance in Latvia. The first and second tier is statutory, while the third is private. The first tier is a pay-as-you-go-scheme providing earnings-related allowances depending on contributions and the duration of affiliation. The first tier covers the social risks of old-age, disability, maternity, paternity, parenting, sickness, unemployment, accidents at work and professional disease risks.[187] The second tier covers the old-age pensions funding (run by the State) scheme providing benefits linked to accrued pension capital.[188] The first and second tiers are mandatory and cover all economically active persons—employees, state officials as well as self-employed.[189] The third tier is the occupational social

[185]DSL regulates voluntary mediation and arbitration as dispute settlement methods.

[186]SL regulates general principles, declaration of strike, restrictions of right to strike, supervision of strike procedures and other issues related to strike.

[187]The Law on State Social Insurance, LV No.274/276, 21 October 1997. Self-employed persons are protected against the risks of old-age, disability, sickness, maternity, paternity and parenting.

[188]The State Funded Pension Law, LV No.78/87, 6 April 2000.

[189]Self-employed persons are subject to mandatory statutory social insurance if their annual income attains a certain level (Article 6(3) of the Law on Statutory Social Security, LV No.274/276, 21 October 1997). Usually, and also currently, this annual income level must exceed 12 monthly statutory minimum salaries (The Cabinet of Ministers Regulation No.1478 ‘Regulations on minimum and maximum amount of mandatory statutory social insurance contribution object’, LV No.250, 20 December 2013).

security scheme. It covers social security benefits provided by the employer.[190] However, this scheme is not in widespread application. In addition, for certain categories of employees (civil servants and officials), there are long-term service schemes provided by the State.[191] Long-term service pensions are granted with the aim to bridge early retirement and/or mitigate specific working conditions.

It follows that the Latvian social security system for economically active persons is predominantly based on the statutory social insurance system.

5.5.8 Health and Safety at Work

Health and safety at work is regulated by the Work Safety Law[192] (DAL) and a number of Regulations of the Cabinet of Ministers. The purpose of the DAL is to guarantee and improve the safety and health protection of employees at work by determining obligations, rights and mutual relations regarding labour protection between employers, employees and their representatives, as well as state institutions. The DAL is applicable to all fields of employment and obliges an employer to introduce labour protection measures in accordance with the general principles of labour protection. Legal acts regulating health and safety in principle follow EU law in this area, since EU legal regulation with regard to health and safety is very detailed and comprehensive, and Latvia, as an EU Member State, was required to implement it.[193]

In addition to the DAL and other normative acts, health and safety issues in relation to working time are regulated by the DL. The DL (Art. 130–157) provides detailed regulation on working time and rest time, defining the concept of working time and rest time, regulating maximum working time, different types of working time as well as the organisation of working time, minimum rest time and different types of rest time. Again, this regulation to a great extent implements the EU Working Time Directive.[194]

[190]Third tier pension schemes are regulated by the Law on Private Pension Funds (likums "Par privātajiem pensiju fondiem), LV No.150/151, 20 June 1997.

[191]The Law on Pensions for the Military, LV No. 86, 1 April 1998; Law on Pensions for Employees of the System of the Ministry of Interior Affairs with Special Ranks, LV No. 100/101, 16 April 1998; Law on Pensions for Prosecutors, LV No. 181, 3 June 1999; Law on Long-Term Service Pensions for Judges LV No. 7 July 2006; Law on Pension for Artists of State and Municipal Orchestras, Choirs, Concert Organisations, Theatres, and Circuses, LV No. 106, 7 July 2004.

[192]Darba aizsardzības likums, LV No.105, 6 July 2001.

[193]Council Directive 89/391/EEC of 12 June 1989 on the introduction of measures to encourage improvements in the safety and health of workers at work, *OJ L 183, 29.6.1989, p. 1–8.*

[194]Directive 2003/88/EC of the European Parliament and of the Council of 4 November 2003 concerning certain aspects of the organisation of working time *OJ L 299, 18.11.2003, p. 9–19.*

5.5.9 Law Enforcement

There are several enforcement mechanisms of the labour law. The administrative enforcement mechanism is provided by the State Labour Inspectorate,[195] which is the institution in charge of the supervision of compliance with individual and collective labour law. In cases of violation, it has a competence to apply administrative sanctions.[196] Criminal liability may be invoked in certain cases, for example, in the case of breach of employment law leading to considerable harm and breach of health and safety rules resulting in bodily injuries.[197]

Under civil law, employment and labour disputes fall within the competence of the regular court. Any person who considers his/her rights to have been breached, including labour rights, may bring a claim before a court under the civil procedure.[198] The civil procedure law provides certain procedural advantages for labour disputes. Among the most important, firstly, is that an employee may choose the competent court in a territorial sense—either according to the place of residence of the employee or the place of establishment of the employer.[199] Second, the claimants in labour disputes are exempted from the obligation to pay litigation duties to the State.[200] Employment disputes must be reviewed by the court as priority cases, i.e., a court must assign a sitting within 15 days of reception of the written observations of a respondent.[201]

The Ombudsperson of Republic of Latvia may have a competence in certain cases of the violation of labour rights.[202] Persons in Latvia have the right to bring a constitutional complaint before the Constitutional Court if they consider that a legal norm does not comply with the Constitution or, via Article 89 of the Constitution—with ratified international agreements.[203]

5.5.10 Conclusion

Historically, labour law in Latvia has been regulated to a great extent by legal sources coming from other countries. During the period from 1918 until 1940, the legal regulation of the labour law had mixed legal sources—the legislation of Tsarist Russia and some Latvian legal acts—and from 1940 until 1991, from the legal acts of the Soviet occupation power. Only in 2001 was the first Latvian Labour

---

[195]The State Labour Inspectorate Law, LV No.104, 9 July 2008.

[196]Latvian Administrative Violations Code, LV No.51, 20 December 1984.

[197]The Criminal Law, LV No.199/200, 8 July 1997.

[198]The Civil Procedure Law, LV 326/330, 3 November 1998.

[199]CPL Art. 28(9).

[200]CPL Art. 43(1)(1).

[201]CPL Art. 149(8).

[202]The Ombudsperson Law, LV No.65, 25 April 2006.

[203]The Law on the Constitutional Court, LV No.103, 14 June 1996.

Law adopted. Along with national employment law, it implemented provisions of the EU labour and non-discrimination law directives.

Normative regulation covers all aspects of labour law—individual employment relations, collective labour relations, health and safety protection, dispute resolution and other labour rights enforcement mechanisms.

Normative acts also provide definitions of the basic concepts; however, in practical application, an important role is played by the case law of various courts—national regular courts, the Constitutional Court and the CJEU. The case law of the national courts and the CJEU demonstrates mutual cooperation and the tendency of the national courts to interpret national law concepts in uniformity with the concepts under EU law.

The legal regulation of collective labour law is detailed; however, it is not very frequently enforced in practice because of low employee participation and coverage of the collective agreements.

Employees have various mechanisms for the enforcement of their rights.

References

Administratīvā procesa izveide Latvijā: no idejas līdz likumam un administratīvajām tiesām (Establishment of the administrative procedure in Latvia: from idea to the law and administrative courts) (2009). Jurista Vārds 807:7–14

Balodis R (2006) Evolution of Constitutionality of the Republic of Latvia: from 1918–2006. Jahrbuch des öffentlichen Rechts der gegenwart. Neue Folge/Band 56:S.269—S.278

Balodis R (ed) (2011) Latvijas Republikas Satversmes komentāri. VIII nodaļa. Cilvēka pamattiesības (Commentaries to the constitution of the Republic of Latvia. Chapter VIII. The human rights). Latvijas Vēstnesis, Rīga, p 863

Balodis R, Kārkliņa A, Danovskis E (2013a) The development of constitutional and administrative law in Latvia after the restoration of independence. J Univ Latvia Law 5:44–120

Balodis R, Kārkliņa A, Danovskis E (2013b) The development of constitutional and administrative law in Latvia after the restoration of independence. J Univ Latvia Law 5:44–119

Balodis R Lazdiņš J (2014) Satversmes vēsturiskā attīstība (The historical development of the constitution). In: LR Satversmes komentāri. Ievads. I nodaļa. Autoru kolektīvs prof. R.Baloža zinātniskā vadībā. Latvijas Vēstnesis, Rīga, pp 43–79, 342–346

Baumanis J (2015) Eiropas Savienības direktīvas Kriminālprocesa likuma grozījumu kontekstā (The European Union directives in the context of amendments to the criminal procedure law). In:Kriminālprocesa likumam – 10. Pagātnes mācības un nākotnes izaicinājumi. Latvijas Vēstnesis, Rīga, pp 108–127

Briede J (2006) Concept of actual action and its development in the perio od of transformation of law in the Baltic states and separation of actual action from an administrative act. In: International scientific conference harmonization of law in the Baltic sea region in the turn of the 20th and 21st centuries. Latvijas Universitātes Juridiskā fakutāte, Riga, pp 525–533

Briede J (2014) Problematic aspects of concluding an administrative contract. In: Jurisprudence and culture: past lessons and future challanges. University of Latvia, Riga, pp 210–220

Danovskis E (2014) The understanding of effective remedy in administrative law. In: Jurisprudence and culture: past lessons and future challanges. University of Latvia, Riga, pp 230–240

Dišlers K (2004) Latvijas valsts varas orgāni un viņu funkcijas. (State Organs of the Republic of Latvia and their functions). TNA, Rīga, pp 114–137

Druviete I, Kārkliņa A, Kusiņš G, Pastars E, Pleps J (2014) Satversmes 4.panta komentārs (Commentary of Article 4 of the Satversme) In: LR Satversmes komentāri. Ievads. I nodaļa.

Autoru kolektīvs prof. R.Baloža zinātniskā vadībā. Latvijas Vēstnesis, Rīga, pp 295–331, 358–361

Eurofund (2015) Collective bargaining in Europe in 21st century, Eurofound, Publications office of the European Union, available in English at http://www.eurofound.europa.eu/sites/default/files/ef_publication/field_ef_document/ef1548en.pdf

Feldmane E (2015) Eiropas Savienības regulējuma krimināltiesībās ietekme uz Kriminālprocesa likuma regulējuma attīstību) The impact of the European Union criminal law regulation upon the development of regulation established by the criminal procedure law). In: Kriminālprocesa likumam – 10. Pagātnes mācības un nākotnes izaicinājumi. Latvijas Vēstnesis, Rīga, pp 128–140

Iljanova D (2006) The constitutional law of the Republic of Latvia. In: Kortmann C, Fleuren J, Voermans W (eds) Constitutional Law of 10 EU member states. The 2004 Enlargement. Kluwer Law International, pp V3–V65

Kalniņš E (2004) Prasība par atjaunošanu darbā (The reinstatement claim). Jurista Vārds, Riga, No.13

Karklina A (2012) The creative function of the Saeima in the judicial branch. In: 4th International Scientific Conference "The Quality of Legal Acts and its Importance in Contemporary Legal Space", University of Latvia Press, Riga, pp 273–287

Karklina A (2013) Dissolution of parliament in Latvia: legal regulation and practice. Jurisprudence 20(3):1213–1229. Available: https://www.mruni.eu/upload/iblock/4ad/JUR-13-20-3-18.pdf

Karklina A (2014) Rights of the entirety of citizens in the legislative process in Latvia. Curentul-Juridic 57(2):60–72. Available: http://www.upm.ro/facultati_departamente/ehea/RePEc/curentul_juridic/rcj14/recjurid142_6F.pdf

Ketners K, Pētersone M (2014) Corporate income tax reform possibilities for Latvia. Econ Rural Dev 10(1):14–22. doi:10.15544/erd.2014.002

Ketners K, Titova S (2009) Nodokļu politika Eiropas Savienības vidē (Tax policy in the European Union environment). Banku augstskola, Biznesa un finanšu pētniecības centrs, p 244

Kraan D-J et al (2010) Budgeting in Latvia. OECD J Budgeting, vol 9/3. doi:10.1787/budget-9-5kmh6dmr9zvk

Krastiņš U (2009) Konceptuāli par juridisko personu kriminālatbildību (Conceptually on the criminal liability of legal persons). In: Krastiņš U (eds) Krimināltiesību teorija un prakse: Viedokļi, problēmas un risinājumi 1998–2008. Larvijas Vēstnesis, Rīga, pp 200–205

Krastiņš U, Liholaja V (2015) Krimināllikuma komentāri pirmā daļa (I-VIII[1] nodaļa) (Commentary on criminal law. First part) (pp 57–58). Tiesu namu agentūra, Rīga, p 320

Krastiņš U, Liholaja V, Niedre A (2008) Krimināltiesības. Vispārīgā daļa. Trešais papildinātais izdevums (Criminal Law. The General Part. Third Expanded Edition). Tiesu namu agentūra, Rīga, pp 504, 61–65

Lazdiņš J (2015) Tendencies in the development of laws in the Republic of Latvia after the renewal of independence in 1990–1991. Juridiskā zinātne/Law, No. 8, 2015. Available: http://www.lu.lv/fileadmin/user_upload/lu_portal/apgads/PDF/Jurid-zin-8.pdf

Levits E (2002) Valsts pārvaldes iekārtas likuma koncepcija (Conception of the state administrative structure law). Available at: https://www.vestnesis.lv/ta/id/63685

Liholaja V (2013) Concept of criminal penalty policy and the resulting criminal law amendments. Journal of the University of Latvia. 5 Law. University of Latvia Press, Riga, pp 4–21

Meikališa Ā (2006a) Apcietinājuma tiesiskās reglamentācijas reforma (Reform in the legal regulation on taking into custody). In: Meikališa Ā, Strada-Rozenberga K (eds) (2010) Kriminālprocess. Raksti 2005–2010. Latvijas Vēstnesis, Rīga, pp 528–543

Meikališa Ā (2006b) Kriminālprocesuālo piespiedu līdzekļu piemērošanas mehānisms kriminālprocesā (The mechanism of applying criminal procedural coercive measures). In: Meikališa Ā, Strada-Rozenberga K (eds) (2010) Kriminālprocess. Raksti 2005–2010. Latvijas Vēstnesis, Rīga, pp 428–455

Meikališa Ā (2008) Kriminālprocesuālās aizturēšanas tiesiskās reglamentācijas vēsturiskā attīstība Latvijā (1961.gada aprīlis līdz mūsdienām (Historical development of legal regulation on criminal procedural detention in Latvia (April 1961 until the present). In: Meikališa Ā, Strada-Rozenberga K (eds) (2010) Kriminālprocess. Raksti 2005–2010. Latvijas Vēstnesis, Rīga, pp 456–480

Meikalisa A (2012) 50 Years of Criminal Procedure Legislation in Latvia – Trends, Results, Prospects//Collection of International legal conference " The Quality of Legal Acts and its Importance in Contemporary Legal Space" research papers. University of Latvia Press, Riga, pp 326–338

Meikališa A (2014) Victims in criminal procedure: a review of Latvian criminal procedure norms through the prism of minimal EU standards. Journal of the University of Latvia Law. University of Latvia, Riga, pp 4–19

Meikališa Ā (2015a) Kriminālprocesā aizskartā mantas īpašnieka statuss un tā aktuālā problemātika (The status of an owner of property encroached in criminal procedure and relevant issues related to it) In: Meikališa Ā, Strada-Rozenberga K (eds) (2015) Kriminālprocess. Raksti 2010 2015. Latvijas Vēstnesis, Rīga, pp 3560–3378

Meikališa Ā (2015b) Kriminālprocesa likumam 10-fakti, vērtējumi, prognozes (The 10th anniversary of the criminal law – facts, assessments, forecasts). In: Meikališa Ā, Strada-Rozenberga K (eds) (2015) Kriminālprocess. Raksti 2010–2015. Latvijas Vēstnesis, Rīga, pp 95–150

Meikališa Ā, Strada-Rozenberga K (2006a) Kriminālprocesa veidi, uzbūves raksturojums un pamatprincipi (Types of criminal proceedings, characteristics of structure and basic principles). In: Meikališa Ā, Strada-Rozenberga K (eds) (2010) Kriminālprocess. Raksti 2005–2010. Latvijas Vēstnesis, Rīga, pp 43–67

Meikališa Ā, Strada-Rozenberga K (2006b) Kriminālprocesa dalībnieki (Participants of criminal proceedings). In: Meikališa Ā, Strada-Rozenberga K (eds) (2010) Kriminālprocess. Raksti 2005–2010. Latvijas Vēstnesis, Rīga, pp 68–111

Meikališa A Strada-Rozenberga K (2012) The victim — a passive observer or an active participant in criminal proceedings. General observations following from the assessment of Latvia's experience. In: Criminal justice and security – contemporary criminal justice practice and research: conference proceedings. Ljubljana University Press, Ljubljana, pp 245–260

Ņesterova I (2015) ES Pamatiesību Hartas Ietekme uz ES Krimināltiesību attīstību (Impact of the EU charter on fundamental rights upon development of the EU criminal law). In: Kriminālprocesa likumam – 10. Pagātnes mācības un nākotnes izaicinājumi. Latvijas Vēstnesis, Rīga, pp 140–157

Pleps J (2013a) Latvijas valsts konstitucionālie pamati. (Constitutional fundamentals of the Republic of Latvia) In: Latvieši un Latvija. III sējums. Atjaunotā Latvijas valsts. Latvijas Zinātņu akadēmija, Rīga, pp 106–132

Pleps J (2013b) Organisation of executive power in a democratic state. Конституционное Правосудие 4(62):121–139

Rezevska D (2014) Article 1 of the Constitution. In LR Satversmes komentāri. Ievads. I nodaļa. Autoru kolektīvs prof. R. Baloža zinātniskā vadībā. Latvijas Vēstnesis, Rīga, pp 346–350

Robezniece D et al (2003) Tax policy in Latvia on the Eve of enlargement. Baltic J Econ 4 (1):116–120. doi:10.1080/1406099X.2003.10840403

Rodiņa A (2009) Konstitucionālās sūdzības teorija un prakse Latvijā (Constitutional complaint: theory and practice). Latvijas Vēstnesis, Rīga

Rodiņa A (2012) The Ombudsman and the Saeima: cooperation and conflicts, solutions to them for ensuring the quality of legal acts. In: The quality of legal acts and its importance in contemporary legal space. 4–5 October, 2012. University of Latvia Press, Riga, pp 384–396

Rodiņa A (2014a) The constitutional court as the guardian of the constitutional order of the Republic of Latvia: some important decisions in 2013. Eur Rev Public Law 26 (4) 1627–1668 (Winter, 2014)

Rodiņa A (2014b) Constitutional court of the Republic of Latvia: constitutional regulation, competence and content of the petitions. Political science studies. Problems of Constitutionalism and Judicial Protection in Eastern Europe 32:273–300

Rodiņa A (2014c) Termiņš pieteikuma iesniegšanai Satversmes tiesā: aktuālākie jautājumi (Term of submitting an application to the constitutional court: recent actualities) In: Tiesību efektīvas piemērošanas problemātika. LU 72. Zinātniskās konferences rakstu krājums. LU Akadēmiskais apgāds, Rīga, pp 319–335

Rodiņa A (2015) The legal person before the constitutional court. Central Eastern Eur Legal Stud 1:105–147

Rodiņa A, Amoliņa D (2014) The procedure of the constitutional court: issues to be decided at the stage of initiation of a case. J Univ Latvia 6:126–151

Rodiņa A, Pleps J (2013) Constitutionalism in Latvia: reality and developments. New Millennium Constitutionalism: Paradigms of Reality and Challenges. pp 431–472. Available: http://www.venice.coe.int/CoCentre/Harutyunyan_newmillenium.pdf

Rodiņa A, Spale A (2013) Satversmes 85. panta komentārs (Commentary of the Art. 85 of the Satversme). In: LR Satversmes komentāri. VI nodaļa. Tiesa. VII nodaļa Valsts kontrole. Autoru kolektīvs prof. R.Baloža zinātniskā vadībā. Latvijas Vēstnesis, Rīga, pp 119–152

Strada-Rozenberga K (2002) Pierādīšanas teorija kriminālprocesā. Vispārīgā daļa (Theory of Proff. GeneralPart). Biznesa augstskola Turība, Rīga, p 250

Strada-Rozenberga K (2007) Personas, kurai ar noziedzīgu nodarījumu radīts kaitējums, loma kriminālprocesa uzsākšanā (The role of a person, to whom harm has been caused by a criminal offence, in initiating criminal proceedings). In: Meikališa Ā, Strada-Rozenberga K (eds) (2010) Kriminālprocess. Raksti 2005–2010. Latvijas Vēstnesis, Rīga, 637–660

Strada-Rozenberga K (2008a) Cietušais un tā tiesības kriminālprocesā (The victim and his rights in criminal proceedings). In: Meikališa Ā, Strada-Rozenberga K (eds) (2010) Kriminālprocess. Raksti 2005–2010. Latvijas Vēstnesis, Rīga, pp 352–371)

Strada-Rozenberga K (2008b) Kriminālprocesuālās aizturēšanas kā kriminālprocesuālā piespiedu līdzekļa būtība – nacionālie un starptautiskie aspekti (The nature of detention in criminal procedure as a criminal law coercive measure – national and international aspects). In: Meikališa Ā, Strada-Rozenberga K (eds) (2010) Kriminālprocess. Raksti 2005–2010. Latvijas Vēstnesis, Rīga, pp 501–527

Strada-Rozenberga K (2010) Pierādīšana kriminālprocesā- aktualitātes Latvijas likumā, teorijā un praksē (Proof in criminal proceedings – topical issues in latvian law, theory and practice). In: Meikališa Ā, Strada-Rozenberga K (eds) (2010) Kriminālprocess. Raksti 2005–2010. Latvijas Vēstnesis, Rīga, pp 383–400

Strada-Rozenberga K (2011a) Publisko un privāto interešu kolīzija kriminālprocesā (Collision of public and private interests in criminal proceedings). In: Meikališa Ā, Strada-Rozenberga K (eds) (2015) Kriminālprocess. Raksti 2010–2015. Latvijas Vēstnesis, Rīga, pp 185–191

Strada-Rozenberga K (2011b) Rīcība ar noziedzīgi iegūtu mantu kriminālprocesā (Handling criminally acquired property in criminal proceedings). In: Meikališa Ā, Strada-Rozenberga K (eds) (2015) Kriminālprocess. Raksti 2010–2015. Latvijas Vēstnesis, Rīga, pp 591–602)

Strada-Rozenberga K (2012) EU criminal justice – development trends and impact in Latvia. Collection of research papers in conjunction with the international scientific conference the quality of legal acts and its importance in contemporary legal space. University of Latvia, Riga, pp 423–435

Strada-Rozenberga K (2014) Victims and their criminal procedure status and law enforcement practices in Latvia. Journal of the University of Latvia. Law. University of Latvia, Riga, pp 51–90

Strada-Rozenberga K (2015) Piespiedu ietekmēšanas līdzekļu juridiskajām personām piemērošanas process un tā aktuālās problēmas Latvijas kriminālprocesā (The process of applying Coercive measures to legal persons and relevant related issues in the Latvian criminal procedure). In: Meikališa Ā, Strada-Rozenberga K (eds) (2015) Kriminālprocess. Raksti 2010–2015. Latvijas Vēstnesis, Rīga, pp 630–654)

The Supreme Court (2004) Par likuma piemērošanu, izšķirot tiesās strīdus, kas saistīti ar darba līguma izbeigšanos vai grozīšanu (On the application of the law in resolution of employment disputes concerned with termination or amendments of an employment agreement). http://www.lm.gov.lv/upload/darba_tirgus/darba_attiecibas_socialais_dialogs/quest_at.pdf
The Supreme Court (2010/2011) Tiesu prakse lietās par individuālajiem darba strīdiem, (The Court practice on individual employment disputes). http://at.gov.lv/files/uploads/files/docs/petijumi/darba%20stridi.pdf
Thuronyi V (2003) Comparative tax law. Kluwer Law International, The Hague, p 379
Zahars V (2014) Kriminālpolitika: mūsdienu tendencies un procesi (Criminal policy: contemporary trends and processes). Daugavpils Universitātes Akadēmiskais apgāds “Saule”, Daugavpils, p 143

Private Law

6

Linda Damane, Jānis Kārkliņš, Inese Lībiņa-Egner, Vadims Mantrovs, Daina Ose, Martins Osis, Jānis Rozenfelds, Kalvis Torgāns, and Kristīne Zīle

Abstract

The present chapter discusses the regulation of private law in Latvia from the point of view of main private law branches. The chapter commences with the discussion of property law by characterising historical background of its regulation, main institutes, regulatory approaches and recent developments. The next section provides an overview of the regulation of the law of obligations by distinguishing contract law and non-contractual obligations. Special attention is paid to the modernisation of that regulation, which took place in recent years. Furthermore, the commercial law section explores company law by analysing specific institutes such as commercial register or special authorisations, types of merchants, their reorganisation and insolvency and provides an overview of the regulation of commercial transactions, their basic principles and main institutes, considering that Latvian law exploits a dual concept of private law. The family law part covers marriage, rights and duties between parents and children, and guardianship and trusteeship. The inheritance law part discusses different inheritance models and procedure for conducting inheritance cases in Latvia. The last section provides an overview of the regulation of civil procedure, which has experienced more than 50 amendments since 2001.

L. Damane (✉) • J. Kārkliņš • I. Lībiņa-Egner • V. Mantrovs • D. Ose • M. Osis • J. Rozenfelds • K. Torgāns • K. Zīle
Faculty of Law, University of Latvia, Raina blvd. 19, Riga LV-1586, Latvia
e-mail: linda.damane@lu.lv; janis.karklins@lu.lv; inese.libina.egnere@lu.lv; vadims.mantrovs@lu.lv; daina.ose@lu.lv; martins.osis@lu.lv; janis.rozenfelds@lu.lv; kalvis.torgans@lu.lv; kristine.zile@lu.lv

T. Kerikmäe et al. (eds.), *The Law of the Baltic States*,
DOI 10.1007/978-3-319-54478-6_6

6.1 Property Law

Jānis Rozenfelds
Faculty of Law, University of Latvia, Raina blvd. 19, Riga LV-1586, Latvia
e-mail: janis.rozenfelds@lu.lv

6.1.1 Historical Background

Adopted in 1922, the Constitution of the Republic of Latvia (Satversme) became fully applicable again in 1993. It did not yet include a charter of fundamental rights. Property rights were not protected by the Constitution. These rights were regulated by a separate instrument—the Constitutional Law of 10 December 1991 on the Rights and Obligations of Persons and Citizens.[1] According to the Amendments to the Constitution of the Republic of Latvia adopted on 23 October 1998, amendments were introduced to the Constitution incorporating fundamental rights. Inter alia, Article 105 states: 'Everyone has the right to own property.' Property rights can be restricted by law. There are numerous case law examples regarding the application of this article by the Constitutional Court of the Republic of Latvia.[2]

The Civil Law (CL)[3] of the Republic of Latvia was originally drafted in 1937. However, most of the content of the CL is borrowed almost unchanged from the previous legal code—the so-called Baltic Civil Codification or Local Civil Laws or VCLK.

This code was called 'local' because at the time it was drafted in 1864, Latvia was still a part of the Russian Empire. The old VCLK was re-drafted in 1937 and enacted on 1 January 1938 as a brand new code that incorporated a significant portion of the previous law with some minor changes.[4] It was abandoned during the Soviet occupation (formally—from 26 November 1940, when it was replaced by Soviet law) and reinstated on 1 September 1992 by the Law on Time and Procedures for Coming into Force of Introduction, Inheritance and Property Law Part of the Renewed Civil Law of the Republic of Latvia of 1937.[5]

[1]The Constitutional Law On the Rights and Obligations of Persons and Citizens. Riga, "Ziņotājs", 4, 30.01.1992. Lost its force on November 6, 1998.

[2]Judgment of the Constitutional Court in case No. 09-02(98) on April 30, 1998. http://www.satv.tiesa.gov.lv/wp-content/uploads/1998/01/09-0298_Spriedums_ENG.pdf; Judgment of the Constitutional Court in case No. 2005-12-0103 on December 16, 2005. http://www.satv.tiesa.gov.lv/wp-content/uploads/2005/05/2005-12-0103_Spriedums_ENG.pdf.

[3]Civil Law. http://www.vvc.gov.lv/export/sites/default/docs/LRTA/Likumi/The_Civil_Law.doc.

[4]Schwartz (2008).

[5]Law On Time and Procedures for Coming into Force of Introduction, Inheritance and Property Law Part of the Renewed Civil Law of the Republic of Latvia of 1937. Riga, "Ziņotājs", 29, 30.07.1992.

The most significant amendment to the CL was the acknowledgment that rights to constructions that were 'legally' built during the period of the Soviet occupation belong to the persons that erected them.[6] As this was regarded as an exception to *superficies solo cedit maxim* (Article 968 of the CL),[7] this amendment led to what became known as 'dual property' or 'divided property' rights,[8] i.e., one person holds property rights in land but another in the building. There were several groundbreaking laws introduced shortly after regaining independence that are known in history as laws on property reform.[9] Based on these laws, restitution of dwellings,[10] land in rural areas[11] and in cities[12] was carried out. Large enterprises were not, as a rule, returned to the previous owners but privatised,[13] as well as dwellings erected during the occupation.[14]

Notwithstanding numerous attempts to reform current regulation on property law,[15] this regulation has remained essentially unchanged.[16]

Property rights in land and in cities can generally be acquired by Latvian and EU citizens.[17] Other persons can acquire property in land and in cities under certain specific restrictions.[18] Any person that wishes to acquire property in land for agricultural purposes should meet certain requirements that are similar for both citizens of Latvia and for any other physical person or legal entity. They must show their ability to run an agricultural business.[19] Restrictions on EU and EEA citizens and those of the Swiss Confederation to acquire property rights in land in Latvia were almost entirely removed in 2014. From 1 August 2014 onwards, the above-mentioned groups of persons can acquire land in rural areas, including agricultural land, in Latvia directly as well as through legal entities.[20] The maximum area for each person is restricted and should not exceed 20 million square metres.[21] They

[6] Art. 14 of the Law On Time and Procedure for Coming into Force of Introduction, Inheritance and Property Law Part of the Renewed Civil Law of the Republic of Latvia of 1937.

[7] Rozenfelds (2013b), pp. 120–136.

[8] Rozenfelds (2014a), pp. 43–50.

[9] Grūtups and Krastiņš (1995).

[10] Law On Denationalisation of Building Properties in the Republic of Latvia. http://www.vvc.gov.lv/export/sites/default/docs/LRTA/Likumi/Denationalisation_of_Building_Properties.doc.

[11] Law On Land Privatisation in Rural Areas. http://www.vvc.gov.lv/export/sites/default/docs/LRTA/Likumi/On_Land_Privatisation_in_Rural_Areas.pdf.

[12] Latvian Cities Land Reform Act. "Ziņotājs", 49, 19.12.1991.

[13] Law On Privatisation of State and Municipal Property Objects. Riga, LV, 27 (158), 03.03.1994.

[14] Law On Privatisation of State and Local Government Residential Houses. http://www.vvc.gov.lv/export/sites/default/docs/LRTA/Likumi/Privatisation_of_State_and_Local_Government_Residential_Houses.doc.

[15] Rozenfelds (2013a), pp. 30–46.

[16] Rozenfelds (2014a), pp. 43–50.

[17] Art. 20 of the Latvian Cities Land Reform Act.

[18] Art. 21 of the Latvian Cities Land Reform Act.

[19] Art. 28^1 of the Law On Land Privatisation in Rural Areas.

[20] Art. 28. of the Law On Land Privatisation in Rural Areas.

[21] Art. 29 (4) of the Law On Land Privatisation in Rural Areas.

can acquire agricultural land only by permission of the local municipality.[22] However, certain restrictions remain regarding foreigners from third countries, i.e., non-EU citizens, EEA or Swiss Confederation citizens.[23]

There is a special regulation regarding taxation of land and buildings provided by the State Land Service (the Cadastre) and correspondent laws—the Immovable Property State Cadastre Law[24] and Law on Information Systems of Encumbered Territories.[25]

6.1.2 Scope of Property Law

Property law includes the regulation of various things: possession, property, servitudes, pledges, real charges, right of pre-emption and, since 2017, also superficies.

6.1.3 Various Types of Things as Subject of Property Law

Various types of things are included in Part III (Property Law) of the CL; it is provided that all types of things—tangible or intangible, as well as an aggregation of property—should be regarded as subject to property law. Whether this implies intangibles that are not expressly mentioned by the CL, like intellectual property, is questioned by some scientists who insist (contrary to the plain meaning of Article 929 of the CL) that only tangible, i.e., corporeal things, can be regarded as the subject of property law.[26] Tangible things are either movable or immovable.

Property in assets, like shares in limited liability companies, is regulated by the Commercial Law.[27] The interests of creditors in the assets of bankrupt companies are protected by the Insolvency Law.[28]

---

[22] Art. 301 of the Law On Land Privatisation in Rural Areas.

[23] Art. 29 (2) and 30 of the Law On Land Privatisation in Rural Areas and Art. 21 (2) and 22 of the Latvian Cities Land Reform Act.

[24] Immovable Property State Cadastre Law. http://likumi.lv/wwwraksti/VVC_TULKOJUMI/LRTA/LIKUMI/IMMOVABLE_PROPERTY_STATE_CADASTRE_LAW.DOC.

[25] Law on Information Systems of Encumbered Territories. http://likumi.lv/wwwraksti/VVC_TULKOJUMI/LRTA/LIKUMI/LAW_ON_THE_INFORMATION_SYSTEM_OF_RESTRICTED_TERRITORIES.DOC.

[26] Grūtups and Kalniņš (2002), p. 27.

[27] Commercial Law. http://www.vvc.gov.lv/export/sites/default/docs/LRTA/Likumi/The_Commercial_Law.doc.

[28] Insolvency Law. http://www.vvc.gov.lv/export/sites/default/docs/LRTA/Likumi/Insolvency_Law.doc.

6.1.4 Possession Apart from Property

Possession as actual control over property is protected against intrusion by force or by stealth. An action can be brought against an intruder within a 1-year period from the time when the possessor becomes aware of the taking away of the possession (Articles 912–926 of the CL). This action is available for any person who is in actual control over a property, even if this person acknowledges another person as the owner (lessee, tenant, borrower and the like).[29]

A possessor in good faith, if he has administered the property of another as if it were his own, is entitled to reimbursement of useful expenditures to the extent that they have increased the value of the property, whereas a possessor in bad faith, although protected against intrusion by force or by stealth, may not request that useful expenditures be reimbursed in regard to the property of another person but may remove their improvements if this is advantageous to them and if it can be done without the principal property being damaged (Article 867 of the CL).

Possession in good faith is a precondition for acquiring a property through prescription (Article 1013 of the CL).

6.1.5 Contents of Property Rights

Property shall not be used contrary to the interests of the public (Article 105 of the Constitution). Owners have the right to self-defence.

The standards of liability for an owner who has overstepped the boundaries of self-defence have deviated in case law from those found in the CL, and for this reason the latter cannot be taken at face value. On the one hand, owners are entitled, in order to protect their own property, to destroy the property of other persons, due to which they should fear losing their own, if it is not possible for them to otherwise avert the threatened loss (Article 1040 of the CL). On the other hand, owners are usually liable for damage caused by their property—if there is fault. This is the liability of owners for not maintaining their structure in such a condition that harm cannot result from it to neighbours, passers-by or users of it (Article 1084 of the CL). There is strict liability for owners in specific cases: a person whose activity is associated with increased risk to other persons (transport, undertakings, construction, dangerous substances, etc.) shall compensate for losses caused by the source of increased risk, unless he or she proves that the damages have occurred due to *force majeure* or through the victim's own intentional act or gross negligence (Article 2347 of the CL). Similarly, the keeper of a domestic or wild animal shall be liable for losses caused by such animal unless the keeper can prove that he or she took all safety measures required by the circumstances or that the damages would have occurred notwithstanding all safety measures (Article 2363 of the CL).

[29] Rozenfelds (2008), pp. 42–60.

Ownership is regarded as the full right of control over property, i.e., the right to possess and use it, obtain all possible benefits from it, dispose of it and, in accordance with prescribed procedures, claim its return from any third person by way of an ownership action. Each of the above-mentioned rights is also limited to a certain degree.

Owners (proprietors) of land own not only the surface thereof but also the airspace above it, as well as the land strata below it and all minerals that are found in it (Article 1042 of the CL). This seemingly unlimited *ad caelum* power is, however, fairly restricted by special regulations. A proprietor must seek permission if interested in extending more than 20 metres beyond the surface.[30] Although treasures found buried in the ground belong to the owner of the land if immured or in any other way hidden, once discovered on one's own land they accrue to the finder (Articles 951 and 952 of the CL); the owners must nevertheless report to the relevant institutions regarding the artefacts (archaeological heritage) found buried in private land.[31]

6.1.5.1 Joint Ownership

Joint ownership under the CL is constructed as a kind of limitation of the disposal of one's property right. The consent of all the joint owners is required in order to act with the subject matter of the joint ownership.

No individual joint owner may, without the consent of the others, encumber the subject matter of joint ownership with property rights or alienate it in whole or in part or alter it in any way. Therefore, every joint owner has the right to protest such actions by one or by all the other joint owners, and this right may not be revoked by a majority vote (Article 1068 of the CL).

All the joint owners, proportionately to their share, shall receive all the benefits provided by the joint property and, in the same proportion, also bear the losses arising from it (Article 1069 of the CL). Charges on the joint property, encumbrances and expenditures necessary for the maintenance of the property shall be borne by the joint owners in proportion to their shares (Article 1071 of the CL).

Each joint owner's undivided share of a joint property belongs exclusively to that joint owner. Therefore, the joint owner is allowed to act with it in any way that conforms to its substance, as long as this action does not apply to the shares of the other joint owners. On this basis, each joint owner also has the right to alienate or pledge the share of the common property belonging to that joint owner (Article 1072 of the CL).

Each co-owner enjoys unlimited right of disposal of his or her share in joint ownership. This right is only restricted by the other joint owners' right of first

[30]Art. 11 of the Law On Subterranean Depths. http://www.vvc.gov.lv/export/sites/default/docs/LRTA/Likumi/Law_On_Subterranean_Depths.doc.

[31]Art. 2 and Art. 17 of the Law On Protection of Cultural Monuments. http://www.vvc.gov.lv/export/sites/default/docs/LRTA/Likumi/On_Protection_of_Cultural_Monuments.doc.

refusal for a period of 2 months, calculated from the date that a copy of the purchase agreement is received, but in cases where it has not been possible to exercise the right of first refusal due to the fault of the alienor, a right of pre-emption applies (Articles 1073, 1381 of the CL). The right of first refusal does not apply to alienation carried out through a transaction other than purchase (barter, donation, etc.).

None of the joint owners may be forced to remain in jointly owned property. In reviewing such a claim, a court, considering the characteristics of the subject matter to be divided and the circumstances regarding the property, shall adjudge to each of the joint owners actual shares, imposing certain servitudes, where necessary, on one share for the benefit of another share; give the whole property to one joint owner, with a duty to pay the others for their shares in money; determine that the property be sold and the moneys received be divided among the joint owners; or decide the issue by drawing lots, especially where it must be decided which of the joint owners is to keep their property themselves and which of them is to be satisfied monetarily (Article 1074 of the CL).

There are some specific kinds of co-ownership that differ from the above-mentioned regulation—for an apartment owner,[32] spouses (Articles 89–91, 124–139 of the CL), co-heirs in land of an agricultural nature that is outside the administrative boundaries of cities (Articles 741–751 of the CL), partners in joint ownership of the members of the partnership (Article 2244 of the CL).

6.1.5.2 Restrictions on the Right to Alienate Ownership

An owner's rights of alienation may be restricted by a prohibition provided for by law, court decision, will or contract (Article 1076 of the CL).

Such restrictions, if imposed by court decision, will or contract, are valid as against third parties only when recorded in the Land Register (Article 1081 of the CL).

The most common restrictions on the right to alienate ownership are court decisions regarding security for a claim.[33] An insolvency notation should be an obstacle to any corroboration (registration of the transfer of property rights). In other cases, a notation shall not be an obstacle to further corroboration but shall confer an advantage on the right ensured by the notation, beginning with the day the notation was entered in the Land Register.[34]

No person has the right to install on their land such industrial or trade institutions as may encumber or endanger public safety or people's health through danger of

[32] Art. 4 (2) of the Law On Residential Properties. http://www.vvc.gov.lv/export/sites/default/docs/LRTA/Likumi/Law_On_Residential_Properties.doc.

[33] Art. 138 (1) Clause 3 of the Civil Procedure Law. http://www.vvc.gov.lv/export/sites/default/docs/LRTA/Likumi/Civil_Procedure_Law.pdf.

[34] Art. 45 of the Land Register Law. http://www.vvc.gov.lv/export/sites/default/docs/LRTA/Likumi/Land_Register_Law.doc.

fire, noise, smell, excessive quantities of smoke and the like (Article 1087 of the CL). 'Excessive quantities' are determined by the Cabinet Regulations.[35]

Local governments have the right of first refusal, if immovable property in the local government's administrative territory is being alienated and such is necessary to perform the local government's functions prescribed by law, by taking into account the use of the territory permitted (planned) in the territorial planning, laws and regulations, development planning documents and other documents that substantiate the necessity of the relevant immovable property for the implementation of the local government's functions.

The right of first refusal shall not apply to

1. immovable property acquired by the state;
2. immovable property acquired by foreign states for the needs of their diplomatic or consular institutions;
3. property to be privatised by the state and local governments;
4. production facilities with all their equipment;
5. immovable property that is transferred from one person to another without remuneration or by way of exchange;
6. immovable property from which a part has been alienated and which property remains under joint ownership of the seller and purchaser;
7. immovable property that is being sold by voluntary or mandatory auction;
8. immovable property in relation to which third persons have the right of first refusal or pre-emption based on law, contract or will;
9. residential property, including a flat, the ownership of which has been acquired up to the privatisation of the residential building.

A local government that has acquired immovable property on the basis of first refusal may, within a period of 5 years, sell it only by open auction.[36]

6.1.5.3 Restrictions on the Right of Use of Installations and Gardens

These kinds of restrictions apply mainly to neighbouring land plots and are supplemented by special laws.[37]

---

[35]Cabinet Regulations No. 724 of 25.11.2014. Regarding the Methods for Determination of the Odours Caused by Polluting Activity, as well as the Procedures for Restricting the Spread of such Odours. http://vvc.gov.lv/export/sites/default/docs/LRTA/MK_Noteikumi/Cab._Reg._No._724_-_Determination_of_the_Odours_Caused_by_Polluting_Activity.doc.

[36]Art. 78 of the Law On Local Governments. http://www.vvc.gov.lv/export/sites/default/docs/LRTA/Likumi/On_Local_Governments.doc.

[37]Amelioration Law. http://vvc.gov.lv/export/sites/default/docs/LRTA/Likumi/Amelioration_Law.pdf; Protection Zone Law. http://www.vvc.gov.lv/export/sites/default/docs/LRTA/Likumi/Protection_Zone_Law_.doc ; Immovable Property State Cadastre Law; Construction Law. http://vvc.gov.lv/export/sites/default/docs/LRTA/Likumi/Construction_Law.doc.

6.1.5.4 Restrictions on the Right of Use of Water

The littoral zone, as well as the lakes and rivers listed in the Annex to the CL (Annex 1), are included in public waters. All other waters are private.

Public waters are the property of the state insofar as ownership rights of a private person do not exist in regard to them. The littoral zone shall belong to the state to that point that the highest breakers of the sea reach (Article 1104 of the CL).

Every person shall be permitted the everyday use of the water of public rivers insofar as this is not harmful to the public and does not infringe on the rights of landowners (Article 1110 of the CL).

A person who owns fishing rights[38] may use a towpath for fishing needs. More detailed provisions regarding towpaths shall be set out in a special law[39]; where the width of a towpath is not set out, it shall be four metres (Article 1118 of the CL).

6.1.5.5 Restrictions on the Right to Use of Forests

Although the CL states that the owners of private forests are unrestricted as to actions regarding their forests (Article 1128 of the CL), these actions are restricted by special laws.[40] Hunting is also regulated by special law.[41]

6.1.5.6 Other Laws and Restrictions

There are other laws that impose different restrictions to property and the owner. Such laws include the Protection Zone Law,[42] Energy Law,[43] Electronic Communications Law,[44] etc.

Restrictions on the right to use property that are not imposed by law are enforceable against third persons only if these restrictions are registered in the Land Book. There are, however, some exceptions. Tenants are not only entitled themselves to use a dwelling space, but this right is also enjoyed by members of their families and their heirs.

6.1.6 Acquisition of Ownership

The CL distinguishes between two types of acquisition: (1) property acquired independently from a previous owner if there was one, like acquisition by appropriation, and (2) property acquired pursuant to delivery. The former is presumed to

---

[38]Fishery Law. http://www.vvc.gov.lv/export/sites/default/docs/LRTA/Likumi/Fishery_Law.doc.

[39]Art. 36 of the Protection Zone Law; Art. 9 of the Fishery Law.

[40]Law on Forests. http://www.vvc.gov.lv/export/sites/default/docs/LRTA/Likumi/Law_on_Forests.doc.

[41]Hunting Law. http://vvc.gov.lv/export/sites/default/docs/LRTA/Likumi/Hunting_Law.doc.

[42]Protection Zone Law.

[43]Energy Law. http://www.vvc.gov.lv/export/sites/default/docs/LRTA/Likumi/Energy_Law.doc.

[44]Electronic Communications Law. http://www.vvc.gov.lv/export/sites/default/docs/LRTA/Likumi/Electronic_Communications_Law.doc.

be unrestricted (Article 928 of the CL); the latter is subordinated to the principle of causation, i.e., no one can transfer to the transferee more rights than that belonging to the transferor.

6.1.7 Property Acquired by Appropriation

Ownership may be acquired by appropriation only of ownerless property (Articles 930–986 of the CL). The CL perceives property as 'ownerless', not only regarding newly acquired things like fruits, newly erected buildings and wild animals but also regarding property that, due to certain activities—like finding of property, sowing and planting, joining and processing—or natural processes such as joining of one parcel of land to another by forces of nature or both, have lost connection with the previous owner.

However, acquisition by appropriation is only possible through specifically regulated, usually, licensed activities (erection of buildings, sowing and planting, catching of animals) or with permission from the authorities. For instance, a finder must first report his finding to the police. The police then puts an advertisement in the newspaper, and only if no one emerges seeking the lost property can it at last be acquired by the finder.

Acquiring ownership of the fruits of property applies not only to fruits grown naturally but also in relation to so-called civil fruits like interest, rent payments and the like (Article 855 of the CL).

The CL includes various detailed regulations regarding the acquisition of property through different natural causes (joining of one parcel of land to another).

6.1.8 Acquisition of Ownership Pursuant to Delivery

Two acts are necessary to acquire property:

1. alienation (sale, donation, etc.);
2. transfer of title.

Under Latvian legislation, property is acquired only when both of the above-mentioned acts are legally effective. The principle of Roman law—*Nemo plus iuris transfere (ad alium) potest quam ipse habet*—is generally applicable (principle of causation). There is no expressly stated protection of the acquirer of property in good faith.

However, there are some specific exceptions expressly stated in the law (Articles 122, 971, 977, 983, 985 and 1065 of the CL).

All but one (Article 122 of the CL) of the above-mentioned exceptions clearly state that, in relevant specific situations, a person who has acquired property in good faith can keep it as far as he or she compensates the previous owner for losses. Only Article 122 of the CL does not provide a clear answer, such that the situation can be solved in both ways—either a third person will keep the property rights acquired in good faith or otherwise. However, although Article 122 of the CL is devoted to a specific kind of common property owned by spouses, it is the only article containing a description of acquisition in good faith: 'If one spouse disposes of or pledges the movable property of the other spouse, the person who has received such shall be acknowledged as having acquired that property or pledge in good faith, if he or she did not know or ought not to have known that the property was that of the other spouse, or of both spouses, and that it had been disposed of or pledged contrary to the volition of the other spouse.' This description corresponds to what is in most cases understood by acquisition in good faith in Latvian case law.

Apart from these specific cases, there are only two ways for an acquirer in good faith to have his acquisition become irreversible in the CL: (1) prescription, i.e., adverse possession (Articles 998–1029 of the CL), and (2) corroboration: 'Corroboration shall be considered as completed, and the certified transaction shall not be disputed after the court has printed an announcement in the newspaper Valdības Vēstnesis that persons with objections should come forward within 6 months time.' The latter procedure is extremely rarely, if ever, used in practice although theoretically available.[45]

In practice, if internal defects of the transfer of title are found, a court can decide both ways: to protect the owner of the legal title or to declare it void and return it to the previous owner.

6.1.9 Acquisition of Property Through Prescription

Acquisition of property through prescription (Articles 998–1031 of the CL) stands out as a special kind of acquisition. There is no conveyance or legal succession of right if property is acquired by adverse possession.

Immovable property (land plot) that already registered in the Land Book (Land Register) in the name of any person cannot be acquired by another person via prescription (adverse possession). This option was accepted during the inter-war period,[46] according to legislation and practice, when acquisition was regarded as if it happened *ipso iure* (by prescription of law). Current law does not allow such acquisition,[47] although this conclusion was once wrongly disputed.[48]

The term of prescription for the acquisition of moveable property shall be considered completed after the lapse of 1 year (Article 1023 of the CL). A person who has possessed an immovable property for a 10-year period in accordance with the provisions on prescription (Articles 1000–1022 of the CL), and who has not registered such property in his or her name in the Land Register, shall be recognised

[45]Davidovičs (2012), pp. 318–330.

[46]Konradi and Walter (1935), pp. 141–142.

[47]Rozenfelds (2011), p. 10.

[48]Grūtups and Kalniņš (2002), p. 158.

as a person who has acquired such immovable property through prescription (Article 1024 of the CL).

6.1.10 Termination of Ownership

Confiscation to the benefit of the state without any compensation to the owner can be applied as a kind of punishment in criminal and administrative procedures. The alienation of ownership by the state for public needs, by procedures provided for by law (Article 1033 of the CL), is regulated by special laws.[49]

6.1.11 Protection of Property Rights

Owners have the right to self-defence. Apart from the above-mentioned protection against intrusion by force or by stealth, which is rarely seen in practice, the most effective tool available to the owner is an ownership claim. The CL sets forth excessively strict criteria for proving the plaintiff's ownership rights. The judicial practice mostly ignores them. The difference between a vindication (*rei vindicatio*) and a negatory claim has a solely historical meaning; therefore, legal norms regulating ownership claims shall be attributed in both cases.[50]

6.1.12 Encumbrances

Property rights can currently be encumbered by servitudes, real charges, pledge rights and right of pre-emption and, as of 1 January 2017, also by superficies. Each of the above-mentioned encumbrances is treated as a right in rem and, if applied to a land plot, registered in the Land Register as an encumbrance to the land plot. None of the above-mentioned rights, except the right of superficies, can be alienated to third persons, but only to the proprietor of the encumbered property.

Real servitudes can be established with regard to buildings (Articles 1172–1189 of the CL) or with regard to so-called rural servitudes (Articles 1155–1171 of the CL), whereas the difference between the two depends not on where the encumbered land plot is located but on the type of encumbrance.

Personal servitudes are usufructuary rights (Articles 1190–1226 of the CL) and rights of dwelling (Articles 1227–1230 of the CL).

Although under Latvian legislation a tenant is protected against eviction even more strongly than a subject of the right of dwelling as a specific type of personal

---

[49]Expropriation Law for Immovable Property due to Public Interest. LV, 174 (4366), 03.11.2010.; Law on Renewal and Regulation of Activities carried out by Credit Institutions and Investment Brokers Companies. LV, 127 (5445), 02.07.2015.

[50]Rozenfelds (2014b), p. 100.

servitude (contrary to the latter, the former rights can pass to members of the family on the condition that they are occupying the same apartment), tenancy is not regarded as a kind of encumbrance by the CL. In practice, it has become far more significant than the right of dwelling regulated by the CL,[51] such that there have been attempts to attack this law in the Constitutional Court (unsuccessfully) as unconstitutional.[52] Usufructuary rights can be established on behalf of physical persons, as well as legal entities.

A real charge is a permanent duty attached to immovable property to repeatedly provide specified performance of money, in kind or by corvee (Article 1260 of the CL). Real charge as such is hardly practised. Still, one can find a regular charge established by law that almost fits the definition in the CL—one who owns a building as a property apart from land can be compelled to pay rent to the owner of the land (if this is a person other than the owner of the building), which should not exceed six percent of the cadastral value of the land plot.[53]

A pledge right with regard to movable property is called a possessory pledge if, upon such property being pledged, possession of it is transferred to the creditor. Pledging of immovable property (or a ship)[54] without transfer of possession is called a mortgage.

Another type of pledge is a usufructuary pledge; if movable or immovable property bearing fruits is pledged such that the creditor possesses and derives fruits from it, such a pledge is called a usufructuary pledge (Article 1279 of the CL).

A usufructuary pledge is also applicable to interest in property—movable as well as immovable—because income that the property bears in connection with special legal relationships is regarded as a kind of fruits (Article 855 of the CL). However, interest in land, like rent charge due to case law,[55] cannot be registered in the Land Register as a mortgage, although this is not *expressis verbis* prohibited by law. Usufructuary pledges are not common. It is also impossible to mortgage and register encumbrances because they can only be alienated to the owner of the encumbered land plot (the exception will be superficies, which is now alienable to any third person after the relevant amendments to the CL introducing this kind of right came into force on 1 January 2017).

Commercial pledges (Article 1279 of the CL) are treated by special law.[56] These can also include assets of a company. Assets subject to registration must be

[51]Law On Residential Tenancy. http://www.vvc.gov.lv/export/sites/default/docs/LRTA/Likumi/On_Residential_Tenancy.doc.

[52]Judgment of the Constitutional Court in case Nr. 2013 -17-01 on July 7, 2014. http://www.satv.tiesa.gov.lv/wp-content/uploads/2013/10/2013-17-01_Spriedums_ENG.pdf.

[53]Art. 12 (1) 2) Note No. 2 of the Latvian Cities Land Reform Act. Riga, "Ziņotājs", 49, 19.12.1991.

[54]Art. 30-32 of the Maritime Code. http://vvc.gov.lv/export/sites/default/docs/LRTA/Likumi/Maritime_Code.doc.

[55]Judgment of the Civil Case department for the Senate of the Supreme Court of the Republic of Latvia in case Nr. SKC – 575/2004 on September 8, 2004.

[56]Law on Commercial Pledge. LV, 337/338 (1398/1399), 11.11.1998.

specified in a registration application; otherwise, they will be treated as if the intention of the pledgor was not to pledge those items.[57] Recently,[58] intellectual property was added to the list of items subject to registration as a type of commercial pledge (European Community trademarks and designs registered in accordance with Council Regulation (EC) No. 207/2009 of 26 February 2009 on the Community trademark, trademarks registered with the Patent Office of the Republic of Latvia,[59] patents registered under the regime of national registration or in regard to the European Patent Treaty, provided that Latvia is one of the Member States to which the registered patent applies[60]).

Financial collateral[61] was introduced in 2005 as part of the implementation of Directive 2002/47/EC (Directive).

However, regarding the subjects of financial collateral, Latvia did not take the option to exclude persons pointed to under Article 1, 2(e) of the Directive—a person other than a natural person, including unincorporated firms and partnerships.[62]

A pledge right, as an ancillary right, is, in regard to its effect, dependent on the effect of the claim (Article 1283 of the CL).

A simplified method of debt collection—undisputed compulsory enforcement of obligations—pursuant to agreements regarding obligations that are secured with a public mortgage or a commercial pledge, can be applied.[63]

Trusts are regulated by the Credit Institutions Law.[64]

A right of superficies can only be established by an agreement between the owner of the encumbered land plot and the person entitled to the right of superficies. The right of superficies can only be established under the condition that the construction erected in connection with this right will be used as a commercial building. The minimum term for such an agreement is 10 years. No maximum time limits are set forth. The agreement can be interrupted prematurely if it is violated by one of the parties. A right of superficies can be mortgaged. The mortgage term cannot exceed the term of the agreement on the right of superficies.

---

[57] Rozenfelds (2014c), pp. 13–23.

[58] Amendments to the Law on Commercial Pledge of 12.06.2014. LV, 123 (5183), 27.06.2014.

[59] Art. 25.[1] of the Law On Trade Marks and Indications of Geographical Origin. http://vvc.gov.lv/export/sites/default/docs/LRTA/Likumi/Trademarks.doc; *Art. 41 (4), of the Law* On Designs. http://vvc.gov.lv/export/sites/default/docs/LRTA/Likumi/Law_On_Designs.doc.

[60] Art. 50 (5) of the Patent Law. http://www.vvc.gov.lv/export/sites/default/docs/LRTA/Likumi/Patent_Law.doc.

[61] Financial Collateral Law. http://www.vvc.gov.lv/export/sites/default/docs/LRTA/Likumi/Financial_Collateral_Law.doc.

[62] Art. 3 (2) of the Financial Collateral Law.

[63] Art. 400 of the CPL.

[64] Credit Institutions Law. http://www.vvc.gov.lv/export/sites/default/docs/LRTA/Likumi/Credit_institutions.doc.

6.2 Contract Law and Non-contractual Obligations

Kalvis Torgāns and Jānis Kārkliņš
Faculty of Law, University of Latvia, Raina blvd. 19, Riga LV-1586, Latvia
e-mail: kalvis.torgans@lu.lv; janis.karklins@lu.lv

6.2.1 Contract Law

6.2.1.1 Introduction

The CL was elaborated based on the so-called Baltic Civil Codification (Codification of Local Laws, 1864) of tsarist Russia, as Latvia was at that time a province of the Russian Empire. Friedrich Georg von Bunge, a lawyer of German origin, drafted the relevant rules using Roman sources of law—Corpus Iuris Civilis, the Digest of Justinian and the Institutions of Justinian[65]—when elaborating this codification act. Thus, the Latvian CL was drafted under the great influence of Roman law, as well as German law.

Part IV of the CL regulates the relations of contractual obligations and obligations outside the scope of contractual relations under a common title, Obligations Law. Like in other states, the classification of obligations takes into consideration that, apart from obligations stemming from contracts and torts, there are also relations that derive from quasi-contracts and quasi-torts, including unjust enrichment and unauthorised management; therefore, the title of the review does not state 'Tort Law' but uses a wider designation, 'Non-contractual Obligations'.

Although the CL was created as a codification act, it was already indicated in 1937 that several fields of obligations law would be regulated by other laws. It had already been decided to develop a separate Trade Law, and the CL stipulates that transport relations are regulated by special laws as well. Chapters on insurance were not included in the CL; residential tenancy rights had not yet been delineated as the specific rent relations that are currently regulated by the Law on Residential Tenancy. After restoring the CL into force, the number of such laws has greatly increased.

In addition to laws, there are also legal principles that are recognised as a source of law, as well as customs, case law and scientific conclusions recognised as auxiliary sources of law.[66] The rules of law that are included in Articles 1–25 of the Introduction of the CL apply to all fields of private law, and special emphasis should be put on Article 3, which states that every civil legal relation shall be adjudged in accordance with the laws that are in force when such legal relations are created, varied or terminated. Certainly, the ECHR and knowledge of the judgments of the European Court of Justice have a great significance in the application of law.

[65]Rozenfelds (2013c), pp. 30–31; see also Schwartz (2008).

[66]See e.g.: Torgāns (2000), Torgāns (2014a), Torgāns (2013), etc.

Law unification projects such as PECL,[67] PETL,[68] DCFR[69] and the UNIDROIT principles of international commercial contracts are duly studied,[70] although only a few of their rules have been introduced by amendments to Latvian laws.

A peculiarity of the system of the CL, which makes it different from that of Germany[71] and several other European states (where a chapter on torts follows the chapters on contracts), as well as from the DCFR, is that in regard to violations of obligation and liability, part of the fundamental norms is summarised in a single chapter that refers both to contracts and damage outside the scope of contracts, respectively on the concept of a prohibited action, degrees of fault, etc.—Part IV (Chapter 3, Obligations and Claims arising from Wrongful Acts (Articles 1635–1668), as well as regarding compensation for losses in Chapter 8, Losses and their Compensation (Articles 1770–1792).

Contract law in the CL is regulated in Chapter 4 under the title Obligations Law. The CL of Latvia does not strictly separate the general part of contract law that refers to any contract and the special part that would describe special types of contracts. However, although the CL is not composed of two such parts, the regulation of contract law in the CL begins with general issues and then turns to special ones, foreseeing modified regulation specific to each contract.

All obligation rights (contractual, delictual) that have not been expressly exempted from the impact of prescription and the use of which is not by law subject to shorter terms shall terminate if the party entitled to them does not use them within a 10-year period (Article 1895). A shorter term, 2 years, is provided by the Law on Liability for Defective Goods and Deficient Services and Consumer Rights Protection Law and by special rules of the CL. The interruption and suspension of the limitation period is mentioned in the CL (Articles 1902–1906, 1898).

6.2.1.2 Contract Law. Concept of Contract

According to Article 1511 of the CL, a contract within the widest meaning of the word is any mutual agreement between two or more persons on entering into, altering or ending lawful relations. A contract in the narrower sense is a mutual expression of intent made by two or more persons based on an agreement, with the purpose of establishing obligations and rights. The CL separates the concept of a legal transaction from the concept of a contract since legal transaction is a broader concept—it includes transactions whose validity is possible after an expression of

---

[67]Principles of European Contract Law. Parts I and II. Combined and revised. Prepared by The Commission of Contract Law Chairman: Professor Ole Lando. Edited by Ole Lando and Hugh Beale. Kluwer Law International. The Hague, London, Boston.

[68]Principles of European Tort Law. European Group on Tort Law. Text and Commentary. Vienna/New York: Springer 2005.282 p. http://civil.udg.edu/php/biblioteca/items/283/PETL.pdf.

[69]*Draft Common Frame of Reference (DCFR).* Outline Edition. Prepared by the Study Group on a European Civil Code and the Research Group on EC Private Law. ec.europa.eu/justice/policies/civil/docs/**dcfr**_outline_edition_en.pdf.

[70]Kārkliņš (2003), Torgans (2008), Kārkliņš (2013).

[71]BGB Book 2, compare Title 1 and Title 27. http://www.gesetze-im-internet.de/englisch_bgb/.

intent by just a single person. Thus, the CL, according to its structure, initially regulates the concept and content of the legal transaction while indicating further regarding the regulation of contracts that everything the law assigns the participants of a legal transaction (capacity to act, legal capacity, expression of intent, etc.), the object of a transaction (an item, as well as an action), transaction form, transaction components, terms and interpretation of a transaction, applies to contracts as well.

The CL separates consensual contracts and real contracts, differentiating the provisions for the contract's coming into force. The most common are consensual contracts, which enter into force upon an agreement by the contractual parties on the key components of the contract. Real contracts, such as loan contracts, lending contracts and deposit contracts, in turn come into force only upon the transfer of an item. A real contract, which is concluded in the form of a consensual contract, i.e., only a promise to give an item, not that the item itself is given, does not establish a concluded final contract, establishing an obligation of concluding the contract. When a person refuses to transfer the item, it compensates the resulting losses since an obligation to give the item is effective. The CL allows separate contracts, such as lease agreements, to be concluded as consensual or real contracts depending on the preference of the contracting parties.

6.2.1.3 Binding Force of a Contract and Exceptions

The principle of *pacta sunt servanda* is anchored in the CL, and it foresees very few cases when a contract may be not executed. According to Article 1587, a contract legally entered into shall impose a duty on the contracting party to perform that which was promised, and neither the exceptional difficulty of the transaction nor difficulties in performance arising later shall give the right to one party to withdraw from the contract, even if the other party is compensated for losses. In Latvian contract law, there is the principle that a violation by the other contracting party does not provide the right to withdraw from a contract (Article 1588: one party may not withdraw from a contract without the consent of the other party, even if the latter fails to perform it, and due to the failure to perform it). The key remedy in the case of violating the binding force of a contract is specific performance, which is included in Article 1590, and a claim for the compensation of losses (Articles 1635, 1779). The CL takes the classical continental European approach as regards the binding force of a contract, granting rights to a contracting party to request execution of the contract. The CL does not foresee the application of this remedy if the specific performance of the contract is too cumbersome or economically unreasoned. Also, the condition that a victim may receive the contract's execution object from another source in just as simple a manner is not recognised as an exception for the application of this remedy. Thus, the Latvian CL takes the strict positions regarding the binding force of a contract that were a characteristic feature of Roman law.

Contractual obligations may be transferred to heirs (or successors of rights), except in cases where the obligation is restricted, pursuant to the contract, to the contracting person or when the subject matter of the contract is such an action for which the particular personal abilities and relations of the obligor are of importance.

The CL does not foresee a separate (common) remedy, which is the obligations' detainer rights. Still, in certain cases, such rights are foreseen as an exception. One such case is Article 1591, which regulates the rights to objections for non-performance of a contract, giving rights to the contracting parties to detain the execution of their rights until the other party has executed its obligations. The obligations' detainer rights are also foreseen in Article 2036, which states that when a sold property is in danger of replevin, the purchaser has the right to withhold the purchase price if the seller is not able to or does not wish to offer sufficient security against the replevin.

However, there are also exceptions to the binding force of a contract. The binding force of a contract is lost and its existence is terminated when the subject matter of the contract as an action has objectively become impossible or illegal (such as prohibited by law) or the object has been taken out of civil law circulation. A subjectively caused impossibility does not affect the contract's effect. *Force majeure* is not a reason to terminate the contractual relations since, according to the CL, in the case of *force majeure*, only civil liability does not occur, while obligations are still binding. The CL does not prohibit the use of other remedies in the case of *force majeure*, such as obligation execution or a property's detainer rights or withdrawal from the contract, if there are such rights. The CL does not regulate the concept of *force majeure*; thus, its content depends on doctrine and the contracting parties.

A specific exception of the binding force of the contract can be found in Article 1657. According to this article, a court may also release the debtor from consequential losses due to default in other cases where the debtor cannot be considered at fault due to lack of care, recklessness or negligence or if the performance did not occur due to *force majeure*. According to this article, a court may release the debtor from negative consequences but not from the contract as a whole.

The principle of *pacta sunt servanda*, which is anchored in Article 1587 of the CL, refers only to legally concluded contracts but not in cases where a contract has legal defects. Invalidity of a contract due to lack of mandatory elements is an exception of the binding force of the contract. There must be five elements in each contract (Article 1404): (a) the contracting parties should have the capacity to act, (b) expression of intent should be without deficiencies, (c) an agreement on significant components should be reached, (d) the form of the contract should be taken into account and (e) the subject matter of the contract should be in compliance with the law. If any of these elements is not met, the contract in most cases is invalid (for example, Article 2010: when the property of another person has been sold without the knowledge and consent of its owner and both parties had knowledge thereof, then the contract shall be void). Still, in certain cases, this can be contested, for instance, in the case of a mistake, which means that a court judgment is required in order to recognise that such contract is void.

The CL does not prohibit the contracting parties from reducing the binding force of a contract if it includes such an agreement. Thus, when contracts are concluded in Latvia, they often contain modified law regulation regarding the binding force of the contract, foreseeing it as being much more flexible than stipulated in the CL.

Contracts that contradict the public order (Article 1415) are absolutely void. Likewise, no contract that encourages anything illegal, immoral or dishonest shall be binding (Article 1592). An agreement reached on the opposite is not valid. Also, fictitious transactions that are concluded for appearances only are void (Article 1438). Regarding simulative transactions, the CL stipulates the following: when the transaction is with serious intent but is concealed by another transaction, the former shall be in effect, unless there has been an intention to deceive a third person thereby or to do something illegal in general (Article 1439).

6.2.1.4 Termination of a Contract

As already mentioned, one party may not withdraw from a contract without the consent of the other party, even if the latter fails to perform it, and due to the failure to perform it. However, this principle is not absolute and has exceptions. These exceptions, or cases when the parties may terminate their contractual relations, can be divided into three groups—unilateral withdrawal from the contract is allowed when this is foreseen by (a) law, (b) the contract or (c) the nature of the contract. The regulation of the CL very rarely allows immediate unilateral withdrawal from a contract unless this is specially defined therein. The CL emphasises the right to request termination of a contract, which means that a contracting party must file a claim at a court on such termination if the other party refuses the termination of the contract. The contract remains valid until the court adopts a final judgment in this regard. There are a number of cases where the contracting parties may unilaterally step back from a contract without involving a court, for example, a contract for work performance (in specific cases), employment contract, authorisation contract or maintenance contract. However, there are also other contracts that may be terminated prior to the term in specific cases set by law, for example, termination of a contract of bailment (Article 1951), a commission contract (Article 2323), etc.

The CL mainly foresees the termination of a contract through a court, i.e., filing an application. Such rights are foreseen to a great extent, and the application thereof is controlled by the court, except when the contracting parties have agreed in the contract that it may be terminated without court involvement. A general reason to request termination of the contract is mentioned in Article 1663, which states that in the case that the creditor is not interested in the performance of the contract due to the debtor's default, he or she may request its revocation. Delay as such is not a reason to request termination of the contract, and loss of interest should be proven.

If the contract is terminated, the CL does not foresee a separate restitution regulation; however, this can be assessed systematically from the structure of the CL. For instance, in the case of non-compliance with the form of a contract, Article 1488 of the CL stipulates: if one of the participants voluntarily performs the contract but the other accepts the performance in full or in part, then the former shall no longer have the right to reclaim what he or she has performed, unless the other is on his or her part willing to perform such as he or she must perform, but if the latter avoids the performance of his or her obligation, then the former, although he or she may not require the performance of the contract, shall have the right to reclaim what has been performed or to claim compensation. Also, reclaim without a lawful basis is mentioned in Article 2389 of the CL—if a person, without any basis therefor, is in possession of some item of another person's property, it may be reclaimed from the first-mentioned person. The above article refers to unjust enrichment, but in practice it is applied when a property is reclaimed in relation to a condition that contractual relations between the parties have terminated and it is not legally justified that the person should have the property (e.g., a person concludes a purchase contract that later loses its force in relation to a mistake in substance; also in this case, Article 2389 will be a basis of restitution).

6.2.1.5 Unjust Enrichment and Unauthorised Management

In situations where there are neither valid contractual nor delictual relations, Articles 2369–2392 stipulate how to reach a fair balance when the benefit to a person is legally unreasoned or the initial basis has become void. The CL divides such cases into four specific types, and also provides a general norm: "No one has the right to unjustly enrich himself or herself, causing harm and at the expense of another person. If a person has suffered losses therefrom, he or she may demand the return of that which was received and the amount the other person has been enriched by" (Article 2391).

Unauthorised management (Articles 2325–2342) corresponds to well-known regulation in Europe that is described using the term benevolent intervention in another's affairs (DCFR V – 1:101: Intervention to benefit another).

6.2.1.6 Modernisation of Contract Law

Following the renewal of the CL in 1993, its significant modernisation was initiated only in the twenty-first century. The main amendment to the CL in the field of contract law in Latvia took place in 2009,[72] namely, (a) the principle of a post-box was introduced when a contract is entered into between absent parties (Article 1537), (b) a debtor is now entitled to request the reduction of a contractual penalty (Article 1724^1), c) the principle of foreseeing losses in contract law has been introduced (Article 1779^1), as well as less important amendments. The package of amendments to the CL in 2009 also contained other modern concepts of contract law (such as hardship); however, due to the global financial crisis, the above amendments were not adopted out of fear of negative impact. The other fundamental amendment to the CL in relation to contract law took place in 2013,[73] when the application of contractual penalties was sharply restricted. According to the new regulation, a contractual penalty for a delay of the term of obligation execution is limited to up to 10% of the amount of the non-executed obligation. Thus, the lawmaker has indicated that the main remedy in the case of a delay of execution of contractual obligations is a claim for compensation of losses or, if the delay is a delay of money payment, the main remedy is interest compensation that is in proportion limited to an amount equal to 100% of the delayed debt. At the same

[72] Amendments to the Civil Law act. LV, 17.06.2009, No 94 (4080).

[73] Amendments to the Civil Law Act, LV 04.07.2013, No. 128 (4934).

time, to prevent avoidance of the limit of the contractual penalty, the Latvian Parliament adopted amendments to Article 1764, foreseeing that interest that is non-commensurate and non-conforming to fair dealing practice shall be regarded as unlawful. Thus, the amendments of 2013 in the field of contractual law were directed towards balancing the interests of creditor and debtor, avoiding a situation where the creditor may use the disadvantageous and materially dependent condition of the debtor. Although the above amendments caused sharp objections from banks, non-bank institutions and entrepreneurs, current court practice still does not demonstrate that the amendments would have caused any negative consequence to the economy of the country. Work on the Latvian CL continues, and the latest regulations are to a great extent introduced based on the theoretical knowledge of contractual law that can be found in the DCFR. The latest scientific articles are based on newer theoretical knowledge of contractual law, with an aim of introducing such regulation as soon as possible. Thus, Latvian contractual law is under continuous improvement.[74]

6.2.1.7 Institutions of Contractual Law That Are Not Regulated in the Latvian CL

Considering that the Latvian CL is to a great extent based on the principles of Roman law, and some legal norms are precisely taken from the sources of Roman law, the CL does not contain several currently recognised regulations of contract law. Their introduction is a question for the future.

The CL does not mention a number of contract law remedies that are recognised elsewhere. The general contractual obligations in Latvia do not foresee withdrawal from the contract in the case of a serious violation or of devastation of the purpose of the contract. Thus, there are no remedy rights stipulated in the CL that provide an additional term to execute the obligations in order to obtain the right to step back from the contract if the violation has still not been prevented. The CL does not provide the remedy of a price reduction to an injured party if it accepts performance of the other party that does not correspond to the content of the obligation that was initially agreed upon. The only case where the contracting party is entitled to request a price reduction in the case of violating the contract is related to defects of goods; however, the purpose of an action for property price reduction is to reduce the price or any other performance received equally to a lesser price or performance that would have been received for the property if its defects had been known (Article 1625). The CL does not foresee general detainer rights of obligation performance in the case of violating the contract or when it is known that the contract is not being executed. Finally, the CL does not foresee rights to request amendments to the content of the contract if conditions change, giving preference to the absolute binding force of the contract.

[74] *See*: Latvian scientific articles regarding contract law in Latvia (in English): Kārkliņš (2012a), Torgāns (2008), Karklins (2005), Kārkliņš (2003), Torgāns and Bushaw (2002).

As regards pre-contractual liability, the CL does not foresee a duty not to disclose information that is obtained from the other party during pre-contractual relations. Therefore, confidentiality contracts are popular in practice, and they protect a person against the undesirable transfer of information to the public space. Pre-contractual liability according to Article 1539 of the CL occurs only in one situation, namely, if the offer is revoked but the person to whom it has been made is not aware and cannot be aware of such revocation and also is not culpable for any delay, then the offeror shall pay this person for losses arising from the belief that the offer is still in effect.

The opinion that further modernisation of the CL is unavoidable, and work on this is continuous, dominates in the field of Latvian law. The latest initiative by the Ministry of Justice of the Republic of Latvia is the introduction of regulation for a clause on changing conditions in contractual law in the CL, thus making the principle of *pacta sunt servanda* more flexible and more appropriate to modern, changing conditions.

6.2.1.8 Special Laws and Regulations in Contractual Law

Apart from the CL, there are many special laws and regulations in Latvia that regulate special contractual law. In addition to common conventions joined by Latvia (UN Convention on the International Sales of Goods [the Vienna Convention] of 1980, CMR Convention, CVR Convention, COTIF Convention, etc.), there are many laws that stipulate specific exceptions from the regulation of contractual law in the CLA. These are the main laws and regulations: Law on Carriage by Road, Maritime Code, Carriage by Rail Law, Law on Aviation, Law on Insurance Contracts, etc. There is also special regulation concerning consumer rights, where the key source of law is Consumer Rights Protection Law, the Law on Liability for Defective Goods and Deficient Services, etc. Since Latvia is a Member State of the European Union, there are directives introduced or regulations directly applied in all fields that are related to contract law; thus, there are minimal differences from the other states of the European Union, and the overall understanding in Latvia about the principles of contractual law is identical to that of other Member States of the European Union.

6.2.2 Non-contractual Obligations

6.2.2.1 Introduction

The hearing of civil disputes deriving from torts forms a major part of the work of Latvian courts, along with disputes related to contract violations. These are related to road accidents, medical malpractice, violations of personal human rights, property damage and also damage to the environment. Along with claims on the compensation of pecuniary losses, in recent years the number of claims on the compensation of non-financial (non-pecuniary) damage has significantly increased. This has been caused by several tragedies with human victims that took place in Latvia that in turn encouraged the making of claims on compensation for non-financial (non-pecuniary) damage in other torts as well. In the original wording of the Civil Law in 1937, there was no concept of 'non-pecuniary damage'. Still, there were norms that foresaw that a court may award damage compensation at its discretion, for instance, for mutilation or disfigurement. Liability for such violations also includes compensation for non-pecuniary damage. Supplementing the CL with norms on liability for injury of reputation and dignity (Article 2352^1) and for deprivation of personal freedom (Article 2352), the term 'non-pecuniary damage' was introduced in 1992. In 2006, amendments to the general norms on torts (Article 1635) were introduced, providing the opportunity to claim non-pecuniary damage in all situations where a plaintiff can prove it or when the law presumes the occurrence thereof. In 2014, the Supreme Court summarised its research of court practice on non-pecuniary damage covering more than 1000 cases and provided recommendations on the grounds and scope of liability and on the request to define entitled persons.[75] All three Baltic states participate in a fundamental study organised by the Research Unit for European Tort Law of the Austrian Academy of Sciences and, as a result, are represented by three volumes in the series Digest of European Tort Law[76]; court judgments published in this series reflect the huge diversity of issues, and likewise the issue that there are differences among the states in certain questions regarding the basics of torts and liability.

The general ground of liability for a tort corresponds to the laws of other European states; therefore, this overview underlines the main peculiarities thereof in Latvia.

6.2.2.2 General Provisions

The right to life, liberty, human honour and dignity, inviolability of private life, the right to own property and other fundamental human rights are values that are protected by regulation anchored in Chapter VIII, Fundamental Human Rights, of the Constitution of the Republic of Latvia. This chapter was incorporated in the Constitution by the amendments of 15 October 1998. Both civil law and criminal and administrative law protect these rights.

Application of remedies is provided by the norms of the Civil Law, including the already mentioned remedies that refer to torts overall (in contracts and torts), as well as those that are included in a special chapter (Chapter 19) of Part IV of the CL, which comprises sub-chapters such as Compensation for Bodily Injuries; Right to Compensation for Offences against Personal Freedom, Reputation, Dignity and Chastity; Claims Due to Unlawful Damage of Property and Compensation for Losses Caused by Throwing, Pouring or Falling and Caused by Animals. The sub-chapter on unjust enrichment is included as well.

Several liability-related questions are also regulated in other laws, such as the Environmental Protection Law,[77] Carriage by Rail Law,[78] Law on Carriage by

[75]Supreme Court of Republic of Latvia. *Compensation of moral injury in civil cases.* Summarized research of Court Decisions. 2014. http://at.gov.lv/lv/judikatura/tiesu-es-apkopojumi/civiltiesibas/.

[76]Digest (2007, 2011, 2016).

[77]Environment Protection Law. LV,15.11.2006. No 183 (3551).

[78]Carriage by Rail Law. LV 05.01.2001. No 3(2390).

Road,[79] etc. Special emphasis should be put on amendments to the laws that refer to protection of intellectual and industrial property[80] and include several detailed explanations on liability, as well as the term 'non-pecuniary harm', which has now been included in Latvian laws instead of 'moral damage'.

In Latvia, there is a peculiarity—loss that derives from the unlawful action of administration, enquiry and investigation institutions is examined under administrative procedure, meaning that it is heard before an administrative court, not a court of general jurisdiction. Such relations that truly are administrative are regulated by a special law[81] and the Administrative Procedure Law.[82]

6.2.2.3 Preconditions of Liability

Article 1635, Paragraph 1 of the CL provides that every breach of right, that is, every illegal act *per se*, shall give the victim who has suffered harm therefrom the right to claim a remedy (including compensation for non-pecuniary damage) from the transgressor, insofar as he or she may be held at fault for such act. The wording in brackets about non-pecuniary damage was included into the article by amendments as of 26 January 2006, together with two new paragraphs about non-pecuniary damage.[83]

Tortious liability emerges from a breach of the provisions of law in the broadest sense; not only the provisions set by statutory law but also the principles of law, practice of Latvian courts and the ECHR are taken into consideration. In tort cases, where no strict rule or norm set by the authorities exists, the criteria of a reasonable person and details of the circumstances are considered.

The main objective when seeking a remedy is, first, to ascertain whether the conduct causes harm to another person and, second, whether the act or omission causing the harm is contrary to the law and there is no justification for such conduct.[84] The term 'illegal act' is used as an equivalent to 'wrongful act'. Harm may be pecuniary or non-pecuniary (moral). The third objective is a causal link between the illegal act and harm.

[79]Law on Carriage by Road. LV 12.09.1995. No 138(421).

[80]Amendments to the Patent Law. LV 08.12.2015. No. 240; Law On Industrial Property Institutions and Procedures LV 02.07.2015. No 127; Amendments to the Law on Trademarks and Geographical Indications LV 08.12.2015. No. 240; Amendments to the Law on Designs. LV 08.12.2015. No. 240.

[81]On Compensation of Loss as a Result of Unlawful or Unreasoned Action by an Enquiry Institution, Prosecutor's Office, or Court. LV 16.06.1998. No. 176/178 (1237/1239).

[82]Administrative Procedure Law LV 14.11.2011. No 164 (2551).

[83]The term "moral damage" does not fit well in Latvian understanding; still it corresponds to the French term "dommage morale". In the latest laws, there is a tendency to introduce the terms "non-pecuniary damage" and "moral harm". See: Amendments to the Patent Law. LV 08.12.2015. No. 240 (5558).

[84]Kubilis (2016a), p. 139.

The notion of an illegal act as a precondition for tortious liability includes culpability as well ('insofar as the person may be held liable for such act'). A person is liable for an intentional or negligent wrongful act (except strict liability).

Evaluation of the illegality of conduct includes an evaluation of whether the person may be held at fault (culpable) for such act.[85] The CL contains definitions of gross and ordinary negligence.[86] However, in court practice on torts, the degree of negligence is of small importance as the principle of full compensation for damage is common in all cases and a person is liable for all degrees of negligence.

A person may be exempted from liability for abnormally dangerous activity if the victim (not wrongdoer) has acted willfully or with gross negligence and in the case of *force majeure*.[87] The degree of negligence is relevant in cases of contributory negligence as well.

The legal capacity to be liable for a tort (at least 7 years of age or having the mental or physical ability to understand or control his or her conduct) is of importance. Liability limits for persons under 18, supervised persons and persons younger than 7 years of age are specially regulated. Latvian law recognises non-contractual liability for one's own conduct and liability for others (minors, employees and representatives—Articles 1638–1639, 1780–1782).

There are various terms in Latvian law: (1) loss or damages—for monetary, financial damage (damages include both *damnum emergens* and *lucrum cessans*); (2) moral (non-pecuniary) damage—compensation for bodily and other personal injury, reputation and dignity; and (3) remedy as the most general term.

The notion of loss is given in Article 1770 of the CL: a loss shall be understood to mean any deprivation that can be assessed financially.

There are several requirements for damage to be recoverable. Damage must be certain in terms of money and have already occurred. Anticipated losses give rise to a right to security (Article 1771). In evaluating a particular property, one shall consider not only its normal value but also its special value to the injured party. Value based only on personal inclinations need not be considered.

The burden of proof is on the aggrieved party. For calculating lost profits, it must be proven, at least to a level that would be credible as legal evidence, that such detriment resulted, directly or indirectly, from the act or failure to act (Article 1787). In some cases, compensation is determined pursuant to the discretion of a court, for example, potential lost income (Article 2347) or bodily injury by mutilation or disfigurement (Article 2349). The particular volume of damages must be proved on the basis of actual figures. Latvian law does not use the term *ex aequo et bono*, although 'pursuant to the discretion of a court' (Article 2347) corresponds to its idea.

The CL contains defences based on justifications similar to the ones provided by Article 7:101 of the PETL.

---

[85]Torgāns (2003), p. 96; Karklins (2006), Torgāns (2014b), p. 171.

[86]Art.1645 and 1646 of the CL.

[87]Kubilis (2014), pp. 199–207.

Damages should be compensated in full, except special cases based on law or international conventions. Caps on damages are recognised when implementing international conventions (Maritime Code, conventions on air carriage, etc.) Punitive or exemplary damages are not recognised in Latvian law.

6.2.2.4 Main Kinds of Delicts

Bodily Injuries If a person inflicts a bodily injury on another person, the first-mentioned person shall compensate the other person for the costs of medical treatment and, apart therefrom and pursuant to the discretion of a court, also potential lost income and compensation for non-pecuniary damage (Article 2347, Paragraph 1)[88]. There is a specific norm on liability for mutilation or disfigurement that is an expression of bodily injury. Regarding such a violation, the law stipulates the rights of the injured person to receive compensation at the discretion of a court in addition to the above compensation for medical treatment and lost income. Such compensation should be considered adequate to the provision for compensation for non-pecuniary damage that existed before the amendments of the CL and thus before the norm on the compensation of non-pecuniary damage was incorporated into the law. The Supreme Court has explained that double collection of non-pecuniary damage, pursuant to both Articles 2349 and 1635 of the CL, is not allowed.

If someone is at fault for the death of a person, he or she shall compensate the heirs of the deceased for medical treatment and burial expenses (Article 2350), as well as for non-pecuniary damage.

The volume of financial loss judged by a court according to that proven is relatively small when compared to compensation for non-pecuniary damage in the case of both bodily injury and death. Thus, for example, in the case of a tragedy that occurred at a firefighters' festival where people, including children, fell from a great height while being lifted in the basket of a truck to view the surrounding landscape, the compensation for non-pecuniary damage judged from the defendant varied, depending on the particular circumstances, amounting to LVL[89] 20,000; LVL 25,000; LVL 50,000; and LVL 100,000.[90]

Offences Against Personal Freedom, Honour, Dignity, Chastity, Privacy A duty to compensate non-pecuniary damage and in certain cases to return freedom, recall false information or apologise may be imposed on an infringer. If false and disreputable information has been published in mass media (press), the infringer can also be forced to recall the information, as well as compensate for financial and non-financial injuries. It should be noted that privacy violations are not directly

[88]Kubilis (2016b), pp. 20–26.

[89]1 LVL (Latvian lats) = about 1.4 EUR. *Euro* was introduced in Latvia in 2014.

[90]Torgāns (2014b), p. 133; See also judgments of the Supreme Court of Latvia in cases No. SKC-56/2011, SKC-319/2011, SKC-627/2011, SKC-588/2011, SKC-530/2013.

mentioned in the CL; still, the liability duty is justified by the Constitution and the European Convention for the Protection of Human Rights and Fundamental Freedoms. When hearing claims in relation to injury to reputation and dignity, courts carefully separate information from opinion.[91] Key officials and other public and well-known persons should be prepared to hear sharper critical assessments. The guidelines defined in judgments of the ECHR are widely used in hearing such cases.[92.]

Illegal Damage of Property Illegal damage of property imposes a duty to compensate financial losses or give an equal property. If a property has been taken arbitrarily, the victim may claim the highest price that the property attained from the time of the arbitrary taking and judgment of a court.

6.2.2.5 Specific Cases of Liability

Product Liability Liability that qualifies as strict liability takes several forms in Latvian law, the main forms being product liability and liability for damage caused by abnormally dangerous activity. Liability for animals and for throwing, pouring or falling is also a strict liability. It has been stated that this liability should not be thought of as the opposite of the so-called fault-based liability. In both cases, presenting justification is of importance, while there is a difference in that justifications regarding strict liability are indicated in the law (numerus clausus).[93]

There is strict liability for damage caused by defective products. The Product Liability Directive (85/374/EEC) was implemented by two laws: 'On Liability for Defects in a Product or Service' (20.06.2000) and 'Products and Services Safety Law' (07.04.2004); thus, the liability corresponds to the overall understanding in the European Union. In practice, active use of rights to bring proceedings against the manufacturer or distributor of a defective good is not observed, and purchasers prefer resolving disputes with the seller.

Liability for Damage Caused by a Source of Increased Risk (Dangerous Substances) A person whose activity is related to increased risk for other persons (transport, enterprise, construction, dangerous substances, etc.) shall compensate for losses caused by the source of increased risk, unless he or she proves that damages have occurred due to *force majeure* or through the victim's own intentional act or gross negligence. If a source of increased risk has gone out of the

[91] Supreme Court of Republic of Latvia. Compensation of moral injury in civil cases. Summarized research of Court Decisions. 2014. http://at.gov.lv/lv/judikatura/tiesu-es-apkopojumi/civiltiesibas/.

[92] See, e.g., judgments of the Supreme Court in case No. SKC-5/2010. *Judgment of the ECHR of 8 July 1986 in the case Lingens v. Austria, Article 42.*

[93] Torgāns and Kārkliņš (2015), pp. 14–26.

possession of an owner, holder or user without contributory fault of the latter but as a result of the unlawful actions of another person, such other person shall be liable for the losses caused. If the possessor (owner, holder, user) has also acted unjustifiably, both may be held liable for the losses caused, taking into account the extent of each person's fault.[94] Thus, not only the owner but also the holder or user of the property may be held responsible for damage caused by an increased-risk source if the holder or user has obtained control over the property on the grounds of rent, lease or others. If the driver of a vehicle (user, holder) is not established in the case of road accidents, liability can be imposed on the owner. There is the assumption that cars, which are equipped with modern control and braking devices, are still considered to be increased-risk sources, and it is stated that both qualifications—increased-risk sources or not—are possible. The question of what an increased-risk source is cannot be solved *in abstracto* [95] as it should be assessed in the context of the particular circumstances.

Compensation for losses caused by animals and caused by throwing, pouring and falling (Articles 2358–2368) correspond to a concept of obligations from *quasi delict*, which includes the principle that liability is not imposed on the owner of an animal or relevant building but on the person who is the holder, and thus he or she must take appropriate safety measures. However, this does not exclude the liability of the owner in specific situations.

6.3 Company Law and Insolvency Law

Jānis Kārkliņš and Vadims Mantrovs
Faculty of Law, University of Latvia, Raina blvd. 19, Riga LV-1586, Latvia
e-mail: janis.karklins@lu.lv; vadims.mantrovs@lu.lv

6.3.1 Introduction

6.3.1.1 Historical Background

After the collapse of the Soviet Union and the renewal of independence of the Republic of Latvia in 1991, the force of the Civil Law of the Republic of Latvia of 1937 (CL), which initially came into force on 1 January 1938, was restored in 1992–1993. The fourth part of the CL covers the regulation of the law of obligations, but it does not deal with commercial law matters.[96] This situation arose because, at the time the CL entered into force (on 1 January 1938), regulation

[94] Art. 2347, para. two of the CL.

[95] Kubilis (2014), pp. 202–203.

[96] For an overview of the fourth part of the CL and Latvian law of obligations, see Chapter on law of obligations above.

of these matters was subject to separate legal acts.[97] Therefore, after restoration of the force of the CL, the acute necessity arose to adopt regulation of commercial law as such, including company law and commercial transactions. The first legal acts on company law were adopted already at the beginning of the 1990s, concerning general regulation of commercial law and separate types of capital companies, such as limited liability companies (LLC) and joint stock companies (JSC). However, this regulation was provided on an incomplete and fragmentary basis, containing mutual discrepancies, suffering from lack of adjustment with other legal acts and ignoring modern trends in the regulation of commercial law.[98]

The work of drafting a commercial act began in 1992, when a working group was established.[99] The initial draft of the Commercial Act included not only company law but also regulation of commercial transactions.[100] However, during the discussion of the draft in the Parliament, the part concerning commercial transactions, as well as regulation of some other commercial institutes, was excluded.[101] This draft was inspired by the example of the German Commercial Act (HGB)[102] as it is noted in Latvian legal literature,[103] similar to in the period before 1940 when the HGB served as a source of inspiration for the drafting of the Trade Code in the 1930s,[104] which, however, was never adopted.[105]

The currently effective Latvian Commercial Act (KCL)[106] was adopted on 13 April 2000 and came into force on 1 January 2002. Initially, the KCL contained general regulation of commercial law, basic types of merchants and reorganisation of commercial companies. Later, the KCL was supplemented with regulation of commercial transactions, which took place with amendments adopted on 18 December 2008 and entered into force as of 1 January 2010. As noted in legal literature in this regard, the entry into force of the part on commercial transactions 'has reduced the need to amend the provisions of the commercial-law part of the law of obligations'.[107]

---

[97]Balodis (2003), pp. 111–113; Annotation to Draft Act *Amendments into Commercial Law*.

[98]For a discussion of necessity for adoption of a separate commercial act, see Lošmanis (2002), pp. 308–309.

[99]Annotation to Draft Act *Amendments into Commercial Law*.

[100]ibid.; Balodis (2003), pp. 110–111.

[101]ibid.

[102]German Commercial Act (Handelsgesetzbuch, HGB). http://www.gesetze-im-internet.de/hgb/BJNR002190897.html.

[103]Balodis (2003), p. 113.

[104]Annotation to Draft Act 'Amendments into Commercial Law'; see also Balodis (2003), p. 113.

[105]Annotation to Draft Act 'Amendments into Commercial Law'.

[106]Commercial Law. http://www.vvc.gov.lv/export/sites/default/docs/LRTA/Likumi/The_Commercial_Law.doc.

[107]Balodis (2013), p. 72.

6.3.1.2 Overview of the Current Commercial Law Regulation

Latvian law recognises the conception of dualism of private law in the regulation of commercial law. In accordance with that conception, regulation of commercial law is separated from regulation of civil law relationships and is solely applicable to merchants as commercial law subjects. This idea is *expressis verbis* reflected in the KCL, whose Article 3(2) provides that the CL shall apply to commercial activities only insofar as the KCL or other acts that regulate commercial activities do not specify otherwise. This provision also demonstrates that commercial law matters may be regulated under separate legal acts in addition to the KCL.

KCL Regulation included in the KCL has been influenced my two main sources: one is European Union (EU) company law, and the other is the HGB, which, to a large extent, influenced both the structure and separate institutes of the KCL. Yet certain substantive differences may be established between the HGB and KCL, for instance, there are differences concerning the legal definition of the concept of 'merchant', as discussed below; the HGB does not provide general regulation of capital companies, but the KCL does; the KCL does not provide regulation for maritime law, but the HGB does; the list of commercial transactions regulated within the part of commercial transactions, as discussed below, is different; and there are other differences being either of substantive or minor character.

The fact that different concepts and commercial law institutes were borrowed from the HGB in conjunction with introducing completely new regulation of commercial law alongside, with its specific approaches previously not applicable in Latvian law, caused problems in Latvian court practice for the application of the KCL. One may mention, among the topical, existing problems, the issue of whether partnerships may be viewed as legal persons, as Latvian courts would be unlikely to share the German approach that they are not legal persons since they fulfil the elements put forward for legal persons, requirements for the liability of members of a board in the case of capital companies, the scope of regulation of trade secrets, etc.

The KCL is divided into four parts: Part A envisages general rules for regulation of commercial activity; Part B provides regulation of company law, i.e., merchants (yet separate kinds of merchants, like commercial agents and brokers, are regulated in Part A); Part C refers to reorganisation matters of commercial companies; and, finally, Part D regulates commercial transactions.

Specific Legal Acts Relating to Commercial Law Matters In accordance with Article 3(2) of the KCL, specific legal acts may supplement the regulation of the KCL as *lex specialis*. These specific legal acts may cover different aspects of commercial law.

First, these special legal acts may relate to specific types of merchants, as Article 1(4) of the KCL provides that the status of a merchant may also be granted by law to other persons. Such merchants as cooperative societies regulated under the

Cooperative Societies Act,[108] as well as specific cooperative societies like savings and loan associations, are also regulated on the basis of separate legal acts.[109] Likewise, EU level legal entities such as European Company (SE), European Cooperative Society (SCE) and European Economic Interest Grouping (EEIG) are regulated on the basis of specific legal acts within the framework of EU company law.[110]

As well, Article 4(3) of the KCL provides that separate types of commercial activities may be specified by law, for the performance of which a permit (authorisation) is necessary, like in the case of sale of tobacco or alcohol products, providing credit services for consumers[111] or providing certain financial services, for instance, in the case of investment companies[112] or participants in the financial instruments market.[113] Similarly, specific activities of merchants based on these authorisations, for instance, insurance companies,[114] reinsurance companies[115] or credit institutions,[116] may be subject to special legal acts.

In addition, special provisions are provided in a special legal act applying to a capital company whose shares are fully or partially owned by a public person or a derived public person.[117]

Furthermore, special legal acts may cover specific aspects common to all merchants, like the Concern Act[118] in relation to concerns (groups of companies), or competence of maintenance of the commercial register by the Enterprise

[108]Cooperative Societies Law. http://www.vvc.gov.lv/export/sites/default/docs/LRTA/Likumi/Co-operative_Societies_Law.doc.

[109]Savings and Loan Associations Law. http://www.vvc.gov.lv/export/sites/default/docs/LRTA/Likumi/Law_On_Savings_and_Loan_Associations.doc.

[110]European Companies Law. http://www.vvc.gov.lv/export/sites/default/docs/LRTA/Likumi/On_European_Companies.doc; European Cooperative Societies Act. http://www.vvc.gov.lv/export/sites/default/docs/LRTA/Likumi/On_European_Cooperative_Societies.doc; European Economic Interest Grouping Act. http://www.vvc.gov.lv/export/sites/default/docs/LRTA/Likumi/European_Economic_Interest_Grouping_Law.doc.

[111]Consumer Rights Protection Law. http://vvc.gov.lv/export/sites/default/docs/LRTA/Likumi/Consumer_Rights_Protection_Law.doc.

[112]Investment Companies Law. http://www.vvc.gov.lv/export/sites/default/docs/LRTA/Likumi/On_Investment_Management_Companies.doc.

[113]Financial Instrument Market Law. http://www.vvc.gov.lv/export/sites/default/docs/LRTA/Likumi/Financial_Instrument_Market_Law.doc.

[114]Insurance and Reinsurance Act (Apdrošināšanas un pārapdrošināšanas likums). Latvijas Vēstnesis, no 124, 30.06.2015.

[115]Ibid.

[116]Credit Institutions Law. http://www.vvc.gov.lv/export/sites/default/docs/LRTA/Likumi/Credit_institutions.doc.

[117]Law On Governance of Capital Shares of a Public Person and Capital Companies. http://www.vvc.gov.lv/export/sites/default/docs/LRTA/Likumi/Governance_of_Capital_Shares_of_a_Public_Person_and_Capital_Companies.pdf.

[118]Concern Law. http://www.vvc.gov.lv/export/sites/default/docs/LRTA/Likumi/Group_of_Companies_Law.doc.

Register of the Republic of Latvia.[119] A good example is that commercial pledges were initially included in the draft Commercial Law, but excluded during review of this draft at Parliament, and are now based on a specific legal act.[120]

Insolvency of legal persons (discussed later in the Sect. 6.5 on insolvency in greater detail) was traditionally governed by a separate legal act (the first was adopted in 1996) providing substantive insolvency norms in conjuncture with the Civil Procedure Law[121] regulating procedural issues. The currently effective Insolvency Law,[122] adopted on 26 July 2010 and entered into force on 1 November 2010, provides the regulation of insolvency of both natural (merchants and other persons) and legal persons.[123] Specific legal acts apply in relation to insolvency of special subjects, which either excludes the application of the Insolvency Law, as in the case of credit institutions,[124] or provides special legal norms, as in the case of insurance companies.[125]

Dispute Resolution in Relation to Commercial Law Matters The procedure for dispute resolution over commercial law matters in Latvia may be characterised as dual, as disputes concerning these matters may be reviewed in courts of general jurisdiction (civil courts) and administrative courts. On the one hand, actions for the annulment of the decisions of shareholder (stockholder) meetings of capital companies may be brought in a specially designed first instance court of general jurisdiction (Jelgava city court).[126] Likewise, disputes in relation to commercial transactions may be brought before courts of general jurisdiction based on procedural rules of general jurisdiction, in a similar way as disputes relating to other legal transactions. On the other hand, decisions of state notaries of the Enterprise Register of the Republic of Latvia in relation to entries into a commercial register may be appealed to the chief state notary of the institution whose decisions may be appealed to administrative courts. Due to the dual character of reviewing disputes, there is discussion in Latvian legal literature as to whether disputes for revocation of chief state notary decisions should be transferred to the jurisdiction of civil courts.

---

[119]Law *On the Enterprise Register of the Republic of Latvia*. http://www.vvc.gov.lv/export/sites/default/docs/LRTA/Likumi/On_the_Enterprise_Register_of_the_Republic_of_Latvia.doc.

[120]Commercial Pledge Law. LV, No 337/338, 11.11.1998.

[121]Civil Procedure Law. http://www.vvc.gov.lv/export/sites/default/docs/LRTA/Likumi/Civil_Procedure_Law.pdf.

[122]Insolvency Law. http://www.vvc.gov.lv/export/sites/default/docs/LRTA/Likumi/Insolvency_Law.doc.

[123]As the currently effective Insolvency Law is largely based on regulation of the previous Insolvency Law of 2007 (Insolvency Law.). LV, No 188, 22.11.2007.), for discussion of the latter, see Mantrovs (2010), pp. 345–372.

[124]Credit Institutions Law.

[125]Insurance and Reinsurance Law.

[126]Latvian Civil Procedure Law art 30.4.

6.3.1.3 General Regulation of Commercial Law

The KCL may be considered an 'umbrella' act for Latvian commercial law regulation. This act provides general regulation of commercial activity and merchants, regulation in respect of basic types of merchants, reorganisation measures in respect of commercial companies and commercial transactions, to be discussed in this and the next chapters.

Part A of the KCL, which will be discussed within this chapter, provides general regulation of commercial law (except two types of individual merchants discussed in Sect. 6.3 below) whose essential elements relate to the main concepts (like merchants and commercial activity); commercial law subjects, i.e., merchants and the scope of the KCL; the functioning of the commercial register; rules in relation to property of merchants (the concept of enterprise, trade secrets and branches); firm names entered with the commercial register and used by merchants in commercial activities; and special types of authorisations, like a commercial power of attorney, a procuration (procura) as a special type of a commercial power of attorney in relation to the commercial activity of a merchant (including rights, as established by the Supreme Court, to unilaterally withdraw from a labour contract[127]) and an implied authorisation.

In contrast to the HGB,[128] the KCL links the status of merchants with the principle of registration (i.e., the fact of registration within the commercial register) but not with the principle of performance of commercial activity.[129] Therefore, Article 2 of the KCL states that the activity of merchants, i.e., persons registered as merchants within the commercial register, shall be classified as commercial activity without any exceptions. At the same time, the duty for registration within the commercial register is explicitly provided only for natural persons who comply with certain statistic conditions,[130] as discussed below in Sect. 6.3.1. So-called civil law partnerships are not subject to mandatory registration and, alternatively, may be regulated under the law of obligations based on the contract of society completely outside the framework of commercial law (i.e., without legal personality and other characteristics attributed to merchants).

The general principles of the regulation of commercial law include the good faith principle encapsulated in Article 1 of the CL and the underlying regulation of the KCL especially concerning commercial transactions, internationalism, the principle of protection of third parties, the principle of remuneration and the principle of speeding up of civil circulation.[131]

[127]Judgment of the Civil Case Department of the Senate for the Supreme Court in Case SKC-30 on 23 January 2008 (Volvo Truck Latvia). http://www.at.gov.lv/files/uploads/files/archive/department1/2008/30-08.doc (in Latvian).

[128]For its general overview in English, see, for instance, Köndgen and Borges (2005).

[129]KCL art 1 (1).

[130]KCL art 75 (1).

[131]Lošmanis (2002), pp. 314–317.

As regards the principle of protection of third parties, two other principles should be mentioned. The first one relates to the principle of public credibility of the commercial register, which means that third parties may rely on entries entered into the commercial register, except if they know entries entered into that register to be incorrect.[132] In this regard, the KCL distinguishes between positive publicity and negative publicity of the commercial register.[133] The commercial register is maintained by the Enterprise Register of the Republic of Latvia (Enterprise Register),[134] being an administrative institution that records entries into the commercial register and keeps the documents of merchants required by the KCL. The principle of public credibility is also extended to entries recorded in documents kept by the Enterprise Register in certain cases. So Article 181^1 of the KCL provides that an acquirer of shares may rely on entries about shareholders entered into the register of shareholders, which is attached to the registration file of the company kept by the Enterprise Register as the commercial register institution (except if the acquirer was aware of the incorrectness of these entries).

Another one relates to standardised institutes of commercial law being imperative norms, except if the KCL or other specific commercial law legal act explicitly provides otherwise.

6.3.1.4 Company Law/Merchants

General regulation of company law is included in the KCL and covers only persons recognised by the KCL as merchants. The KCL distinguishes two types of merchants: individual merchants, being only natural persons, and commercial companies divided into capital companies and partnerships.[135] As already mentioned above, the KCL envisages that a merchant is only such a person that is registered as such within the commercial register.[136] In this regard, the Supreme Court has held that 'considering that all commercial companies shall be registered within the commercial register (otherwise they do not acquire legal subjectivity), it is meaningless who owns capital shares (stocks)—a state, a derived public person or any other person'.[137]

Part B of the KCL provides regulation for basic types of merchants such as individual merchants and commercial companies—in the case of the latter, separately for partnerships and capital companies. This regulation will be discussed in further sections of this chapter.

[132] KCL art 12 (1) first sentence.

[133] KCL art 12 (2) and (3).

[134] KCL art 6 (2).

[135] KCL art 1 (1).

[136] KCL art 1 (1); see also KCL art 14 concerning termination of the status of a merchant.

[137] Judgment of the Civil Case Department of the Senate for the Supreme Court in Case SPC-46/2013 on 29 October 2013. http://at.gov.lv/files/uploads/files/archive/department1/2013/46-spc-2013.doc (in Latvian).

At the same time, other legal acts may provide special regulation for specific merchants as already indicated above, for instance, in relation to cooperative societies, by recognising them as merchants[138] (i.e., one of types of commercial companies) or EU level legal entities.

Likewise, Part A of the KCL, by lack of consequence, provides regulation for two specific types of merchants (irrespective of whether individual merchants or commercial companies), namely, a commercial agent and a broker.

A commercial agent is a merchant who has been authorised to permanently conclude transactions with third parties in the name and to the benefit of another person (principal), or else to prepare transactions for concluding. The KCL provides rules for contracts concluded by commercial agents, legal relationships existing between commercial agents and principals, and relations with third parties.[139]

A broker is a merchant who engages in intermediation for concluding transactions for the benefit of another person, not being permanently associated with such person through contractual relations. Similarly, as in the case of commercial agents, the KCL provides rules for contracts concluded by brokers and parties to a contract and their legal relationships, but, in contrast to commercial agents, it also regulates mandatory record keeping to be carried out by brokers.[140] Special rules on brokers in specific activities are provided in specific legal acts, as in the case of insurance and reinsurance intermediaries.[141]

Individual Merchants Regulation of individual merchants may not be considered comprehensive as it contains just the essential elements for basic regulation of the functioning of individual merchants. The following essential elements of regulation of individual merchants may be mentioned: the legal definition of the concept of an individual merchant, registration requirements and liability aspects.

An individual merchant is a natural person who is registered as a merchant within the commercial register.[142] The KCL provides mandatory and voluntary registration of individual merchants. A person is subject to mandatory registration as an individual merchant if he or she satisfies certain static conditions, either in relation to annual turnover (exceeding 284,600 euro), a combination of annual turnover (exceeding 28,500 euro) and employment simultaneously of more than five employees, or performs the activities of either a commercial agent or a broker, as discussed above.[143] Voluntary registration as an individual merchant may be carried out by natural persons involved in commercial activities at their choice.[144]

---

[138]Cooperative Societies Law art 6 (with certain exceptions laid down by this article).

[139]KCL Chapter VI.

[140]KCL Chapter VII.

[141]Activities of Insurance and Reinsurance Intermediaries Act. http://www.vvc.gov.lv/export/sites/default/docs/LRTA/Likumi/Activities_of_Insurance_and_Reinsurance_Intermediaries_Law.doc.

[142]KCL art 74.

[143]KCL art 75 (1).

[144]KCL art 75 (2).

An individual merchant is liable for his or her obligations with the whole of his or her property, yet claims against individual merchants are subject to special limitation periods.[145]

Capital Companies The KCL distinguishes two types of capital companies: LLC and JSC,[146] depending on the specifics of the formation of equity capital and administration.

The KCL provides two sets of rules for each type of capital company: a general regulation common for both capital companies (such as general rules on legal status, establishment of capital companies, formation of their equity capital, liability, drafting annual reports and distribution of profits, as well as termination of activity and liquidation) and a specific regulation for each of these capital companies. Both types of capital company are legal persons and acquire the status of legal person as of the date when an entry on registration is entered in the commercial register,[147] retaining this status until their exclusion from the commercial register.[148]

6.3.1.5 Limited Liability Company

An LLC is a capital company the shares of which are not publicly tradeable objects. The minimum amount of equity capital of an LLC shall be not less than 2800 euro. Though shares are not publicly tradeable, an LLC has the duty to keep a register of shareholders. Regulation of an LLC focuses on equity capital, changes in equity capital and administration.

The main essence for regulation of equity capital is focused on alienation of shares by providing rules on recording entries into a register of shareholders[149]; protection of existing shareholders by providing them the right of first refusal in relation to purchase of shares, though not in relation to other types of alienation, such as donation or exchange; and prohibition of acquisition of own shares except in specific cases listed as *numerus clausus*.[150]

Changes in equity capital relate to regulation of the increase and reduction of equity capital, which shall be based on the decision of a meeting of shareholders and registered in the commercial register.

Another aspect of the regulation of an LLC is its administration. Two mandatory administrative bodies may be distinguished: a meeting of shareholders and a board. In contrast to a JSC, a council is a voluntary body for an LLC. A meeting of shareholders is the highest body for administration of an LLC consisting of

---

[145]KCL art 76.

[146]Sometimes incorrectly referred to as 'public limited liability companies' (Brizgo et al. (2011), p. 64).

[147]KCL art 135 (2).

[148]KCL art 14.

[149]For discussion of alienation of shares of LLC, see Kārkliņš (2012b).

[150]KCL art 192.

shareholders. The KCL takes a dispositive approach to the regulation of the competence of a meeting of shareholders. Though the KCL provides a list of competence areas in respect of meetings of shareholders, it is not exhaustive as additional competence areas may be assigned to meetings of shareholders in statutes. In addition, a meeting of shareholders may decide on any issue relating to an LLC, including those issues falling within the competence of either a board or a council (if any).[151] A board consists of one or several board members, and its aim is the operation of daily activities and representation of an LLC in relation to third parties. Board members are liable for damage they have caused to a company on the basis of the presumption of their fault, i.e., board members have *onus probandi* to prove that their activity is not culpable, as consistently upheld by the Supreme Court.[152]

6.3.1.6 Joint Stock Company

A JSC is a capital company the stocks of which may be publicly tradable objects. The minimum amount of equity capital of a JSC shall be not less than 35,000 euro. Similar to the case of an LLC, the regulation of a JSC focuses on three issues, but considering the particulars of JSCs: capital and securities, changes in equity capital and administration.

The capital of a JSC consists of stocks, which can be in either a paper or dematerialised form (except bearer stocks, which may be only in dematerialised form), and be of different types, such as registered, bearer and preference stocks. In addition, a JSC may issue obligations, this being one of the possibilities for attracting investments. In contrast to LLCs, a JSC is an open company as its stocks may be publicly traded,[153] yet the KCL allows introducing restrictions on the sale of registered stock in the articles of association.[154]

Regulation of changes in equity capital is more specific and detailed than in the case of LLCs, by reflecting regulation of different types of stocks. In addition, a special regulation of securities is envisaged by providing rules for their emission, their registration and transactions with them.

Another significant difference from the regulation of LLCs relates to the administration of JSCs, as a JSC shall be mandatorily administered by a meeting of stockholders, a council and a board. A meeting of stockholders is entitled to elect or revoke council members, but a council elects, revokes and supervises a board that is responsible for the daily management of a JSC and its representation in legal relationships with third persons. Also, in contrast to LLCs, the KCL provides an exhaustive list of competence areas in respect of meetings of shareholders.[155] The

[151]KCL art 210.

[152]For the recent judgment in this regard, see Judgment of the Civil Case Department of the Supreme Court in Case SKC-7/2016 on 07 June 2016 (Euro Investment). http://at.gov.lv/files/uploads/files/archive/department1/2016/SKC-7-2016.doc (in Latvian).

[153]KCL art 134 (4).

[154]KCL art 238 (2).

[155]KCL art 268.

board of a JSC consists of one or several board members. A council is a supervisory body overseeing activities of a board and composed of three (five if the stock of the company is in public turnover) to 20 council members.[156]

Partnerships The KCL distinguishes two kinds of partnerships, namely, a general partnership and a limited partnership.[157] The main difference between these types of partnership lies in the distribution of liability among their members. If in the case of a general partnership the members have not limited their liability against the partnership's creditors, in the case of a limited partnership, the liability of at least one of the members in relation to the partnership's creditors is limited to the amount of their contribution.

Though partnerships have certain features of legal persons, the KCL does not clearly state whether partnerships are legal persons. However, the HGB, which was a source of inspiration for the KCL, including regulation of partnerships, does not recognise partnerships as legal persons. A similar approach could underline the regulation of partnerships in the KCL, yet this approach might not be shared by Latvian courts, as can be seen from existing court practice.[158]

Reorganisation Measures Part C of the KCL provides regulation for reorganisation measures of commercial companies, which covers organisational changes in respect of commercial companies and is not related to insolvency procedures. The following types of reorganisation are distinguished by the KCL: merging, division or restructuring.[159] Mergers can take the form of either acquisition or consolidation.[160] The regulation of mergers covers cross-border mergers as defined by Article 335.[1] of the KCL, which are regulated under this article and in a set of special provisions in a special division of the KCL.[161]

The main aim of regulation of reorganisation relates to the protection of the interests of the current shareholders (stockholders or shareholders depending on the type of commercial company) and creditors. For the fulfilment of this aim, regulation on reorganisation measures provides procedure, entry into force of reorganisation and legal effect concerning each type of reorganisation, as well as special provisions for both reorganisation measures and different commercial companies. In addition, reorganisation measures may be subject to special rules included in other legal acts, such as the regulation of mergers in Latvian

[156] KCL art 295 (4) and (5).

[157] For a discussion of commercial partnerships in general, see Balodis (2005), pp. 79–84.

[158] Judgment of the Civil Case Department of the Senate for the Supreme Court in Case SKC-7/2013 on 24 January 2013 (BMGS). http://www.at.gov.lv/files/uploads/files/archive/department1/2013/7-skc-2013.doc (in Latvian).

[159] KCL art 334 (1).

[160] KCL art 335 (1).

[161] Division XIX KCL (Articles 380–387 KCL). For a discussion of cross-border merger regulation in Latvia, see Brizgo et al. (2011).

competition law[162] or the consequences of reorganisation in relation to employees in Latvian labour law.[163]

6.3.2 Commercial Transactions

With regard to the fact that there is a dual concept of private law in Latvia,[164] the CL does not regulate specific contracts of commercial law, leaving them to the KCL Although the CL is still applicable as a legal act concerning general rules of transactions and contracts, the main source of law in Latvia regulating specific commercial transactions is the KCL. The provisions of the CL shall apply to commercial activities only insofar as the KCL or other laws that regulate commercial activities do not specify otherwise (Article 3(2) of the KCL). In such a way, regulation of commercial transactions included in the KCL is based on the *subjective criterion.*[165] However, the rules of the CL can be equally applied to merchants as general rules of law.

Part D, Commercial Transactions (Articles 388–480) of the KCL came into force on 1 January 2010, although the KCL that regulated company law was adopted in 2000. By 2010, the general rules for transaction law in the CL were applied to commercial transactions. According to the essence of the commercial law as special private law, the KCL does not regulate commercial transactions comprehensively; rather, it modifies, supplements and specifies the framework of the CL.

6.3.2.1 Meaning of Commercial Transactions

According to Article 388 of the KCL, commercial transactions shall be lawful transactions of a merchant that are connected with commercial activities. Thus, the concept of a commercial transaction in Latvian law is at first related to a merchant as a transaction subject pursuant to the *subjective system*, which is a basis of the Commercial Act (as an opposite of the objective system, where a legal transaction is a commercial transaction if it has any feature that is an objective characteristic of the scope of commercial rights).[166] Moreover, commercial transactions are only those transactions that are related to a commercial activity. Depending on the link between a merchant's transaction and commercial activity, commercial transactions are divided into (a) key transactions, (b) ancillary transactions and

[162]Competition Law arts 15–17 (Competition Law. http://www.vvc.gov.lv/export/sites/default/docs/LRTA/Likumi/Competition_Law.doc.).

[163]Labour Law arts 117–121 (Labour Law. http://www.vvc.gov.lv/export/sites/default/docs/LRTA/Likumi/Labour_Law.doc).

[164]For details, see Sect. 6.1.2. above.

[165]For discussion of the objective and subjective criterions in European commercial law, see, for instance, Kozolchyk (1979), pp. 3–5.

[166]For discussion of the objective and subjective systems of commercial transactions from the perspective of Latvian commercial law, see Lošmanis (2002), pp. 313–314.

(c) side transactions. Key transactions are typical and regular transactions concluded by a particular merchant. Ancillary transactions are transactions to support the commercial activity concluded by a merchant for launching, continuing or terminating commercial activity, and side transactions are exceptional, commercial transactions and related indirectly to the merchant's commercial activity. According to the theory of the Latvian commercial law, private transactions of a merchant are also possible; they are not commercial transactions, but in case of doubt it can be presumed that the merchant's transaction is related to commercial activity.

Not only a *bilateral commercial transaction*, where all participants are merchants, but also a *unilateral commercial transaction*, where only one of the participants is a merchant, is recognised as a commercial transaction pursuant to the KCL. Thus, the merchant is not released from the application of Part D of the KCL just because one participant of the transaction is not a merchant but, for instance, a consumer. However, there are norms that prohibit applying certain legal provisions of a commercial transaction to a non-merchant as this could be too cumbersome (such as Article 399(1) and Article 411(5)).

The CL also regulates the key aspects for the conclusion of commercial transactions, for example, (a) provisions on expression of intent (from Article 1427 of the CL); (b) provisions on elements of a lawful transaction (from Article 1404 of the CL); (c) provisions on the agreement of contractors (from Article 1533 of the CL), including division of contracts, agreement among non-present contractors; (d) provisions on the form of a lawful transaction (from Article 1473 of the CL); (e) general legal consequences in case of non-execution of a contract (Article 1587 of the CL); etc.

6.3.2.2 General Provisions of Commercial Transactions

According to Article 393 of the KCL, in the relations of commercial transactions, a merchant has a duty to act with the diligence of a respectable and accurate merchant, thus foreseeing responsibility for allowing even small negligence. Additionally, if several merchants jointly undertake to fulfil a divisible obligation, they shall be solidarily liable for this obligation in case of doubt (Article 394), which means that responsibility can occur also without one's own negligence but solidarily due to the negligence of a related person.

The KCL foresees a general right to retainer for a merchant in execution of commercial transactions. A merchant is entitled to retain movable property and securities owned by another merchant and possessed by him or her, which, pursuant to the will of the other merchant, have come into the possession of the retainer on the basis of a commercial transaction, and not to release this property and securities as long as the money claim of the retainer, arising from the commercial transaction entered into between them against another merchant, is not satisfied. In order to achieve the satisfaction of such a claim, the merchant may also retain such objects as he or she has obtained in the ownership from another merchant or a third party, however, in favour of the other merchant, and which the retainer has a duty to hand over in the ownership of the other merchant.

The KCL also regulates the question of good faith regarding acquisition of property in one's possession. Article 401 stipulates that even if a merchant alienates a property in favour of another person on the basis of a commercial transaction, the acquirer obtains the property rights with respect to this property, except in a case where he or she was not acting in good faith at the time of transfer. The acquirer is not acting in good faith if he or she knows that the property is not owned by the alienor or the alienor is not entitled to handle this property or the acquirer is not aware thereof due to gross negligence. If the alienated property is burdened by the rights of a third party, these rights shall expire with the transfer of the property rights to the acquirer of good faith, except in a case where he or she did not know about the referred to rights at the time of transfer or was not aware thereof due to gross negligence.

According to Article 406 of the KCL, claims arising from a commercial transaction are subject to a limitation period of 3 years, unless another limitation period is specified by the law. In separate cases, the limitation period is shorter; for instance, claims against a forwarder regarding damages, perishing, shortfall, destruction or loss of freight transferred for forwarding and delivery of the freight shall expire within 1 year (Article 445). Claims arising from tort law expire within 10 years.

The general provisions of the KCL also regulate the following questions: lawful right of possessory pledge, bill of lading, consignment note and warehouse receipt as instruments to order.

6.3.2.3 Special Provisions of Commercial Transactions

Division XXI of the KCL regulates several types of commercial transactions, and its provisions apply in addition to the general regulation of contractual law in the CL. The content of the KCL is rather similar to the HGB, but there are also some differences, such as that the KCL regulates lease and franchise contracts as well.

The KCL regulates the following types of commercial transactions: commercial purchase contracts (Articles 407–414), commercial commission contracts (Articles 415–429), forwarding agreements (Articles 430–446), commercial storage agreements (Articles 447–462), lease contracts (Articles 463–467), factoring contracts (Articles 468–473) and franchise contracts (Articles 474–480).

The KCL does not regulate such contract types as commercial rent contracts, insurance contracts,[167] banking contracts and licence contracts. Provisions on these specific contracts can be found in special acts, either solely relating to the regulation of such a contract, as in the case of insurance contracts,[168] or within the framework of a particular area, as in the case of banking contacts[169] or licence and assignment

[167]For a discussion of regulation of insurance contracts in Latvia, see Mantrovs (2012).

[168]Law 'On Insurance Contracts'. http://www.vvc.gov.lv/export/sites/default/docs/LRTA/Likumi/On_Insurance_Contracts.doc; Compulsory Civil Liability Insurance of Owners of Motor Vehicles Law. http://www.vvc.gov.lv/export/sites/default/docs/LRTA/Likumi/Compulsory_Civil_Liability_Insurance.doc.

[169]Credit Institutions Law.

contracts in *sui generis* intellectual property acts.[170] Likewise, rules on the protection of consumers in legal relationships with merchants and other persons selling goods or providing services in the course of their trade or profession are included in a special act.[171]

In addition, regulation of maritime trade cannot be found in the KCL, since this is regulated in a separate act—the Maritime Code[172]—as well as freight business, which is regulated in other specific laws.[173]

The KCL does not regulate the insolvency issues of merchants, and there is a separate law for that—the Insolvency Act, discussed in greater detail below.

6.3.3 Insolvency

The insolvency issues of merchants are regulated by the Insolvency Act, in conjuncture with the Civil Procedure Law regulating procedural issues. According to this Act, insolvency proceedings may be initiated by both merchants and other legal persons, as well as by physical persons. The purpose of the Insolvency Act is to promote the honouring of obligations by a debtor in financial difficulties and, where possible, the renewal of solvency, applying the principles and lawful solutions specified in that Act.

6.3.3.1 Insolvency Proceedings

Insolvency proceedings of a legal person are applied to a merchant if there are any of the features of insolvency proceedings of the legal person. The main features are the following: (a) it has not been possible to execute court adjudication regarding the recovery of debt from the merchant; (b) the merchant has not honoured one or more debt obligations, from which the basic debt amounts separately or in total exceeds 4268 euro, and whose deadline has expired, and the merchant has not paid its debt or raised justified objections to the claim within 3 weeks following the handover of the warning to the postal merchant; (c) the merchant has not paid an employee work remuneration in full, such as compensation for damages in connection with an accident at work or an occupational disease, or has not carried out mandatory social insurance payments within 2 months following the day specified for payment. In some cases defined by the law, insolvency proceedings can be initiated by the merchant itself.

---

[170] For instance, Copyright Law. http://www.vvc.gov.lv/export/sites/default/docs/LRTA/Likumi/Copyright_law.doc.

[171] Consumer Rights Protection Law. http://vvc.gov.lv/export/sites/default/docs/LRTA/Likumi/Consumer_Rights_Protection_Law.doc.

[172] Maritime Code. http://vvc.gov.lv/export/sites/default/docs/LRTA/Likumi/Maritime_Code.doc.

[173] Act on Carriage by Road. http://www.vvc.gov.lv/export/sites/default/docs/LRTA/Likumi/Law_on_Carriage_by_Road.doc; Carriage by Rail Law. http://www.vvc.gov.lv/export/sites/default/docs/LRTA/Likumi/Carriage_by_Rail.pdf; Law on Aviation. http://www.vvc.gov.lv/export/sites/default/docs/LRTA/Likumi/On_Aviation.doc.

Insolvency proceedings are conducted by an appointed administrator, who identifies a merchant's property and liabilities; accepts, registers and examines the claims of creditors; and organises the execution of a sales plan for the debtor's property within the proceedings. The administrator also has the duty of evaluating the debtor's transactions and bringing an action to court regarding the recognition of the respective transaction as invalid, regardless of the type of transaction, if it has been concluded (a) following the day of the proclamation of insolvency proceedings or 4 months prior to the day of proclamation and thereby losses have been caused to the merchant regardless of whether the person with whom or for whose benefit the transaction has been concluded knew or did not know of the losses caused to the creditors; (b) within 3 years prior to the day of the proclamation of the insolvency proceedings and thereby losses have been caused to the merchant; moreover, the person with whom or for whose benefit the transaction has been concluded knew or should have known of the cause of such losses.

There can be two solutions for insolvency proceedings: (a) liquidation of a merchant in relation to inability to pay the amount due to creditors or (b) renewal of the merchant's solvency, which takes place by transfer from the merchant's insolvency proceedings to legal protection proceedings with an aim to renew the usual commercial activity at the end of executing the proceedings.

The Insolvency Law foresees specific provisions of the insolvency proceedings for individual merchants and producers of agricultural products.

For the purpose of public awareness of insolvency proceedings, there is a special Insolvency Register with entries that are publicly reliable.

6.3.3.2 Legal Protection Proceedings

Legal protection proceedings (LPP) are an aggregate of measures of a legal nature whose purpose is to renew the ability of a debtor to settle their debt obligations if a debtor has come into financial difficulties or expects to do so. LPP shall be applicable to legal persons, partnerships, individual merchants or persons registered in a foreign country who perform permanent economic activity in Latvia and to the producers of agricultural products.

LPP are approved by a court, and the term for the implementation of these proceedings does not exceed 2 years after the day when a court adjudication on the implementation of the legal protection proceedings has entered into force. A merchant may ask to apply LPP itself before the merchant has actually become insolvent, thus avoiding insolvency proceedings.

LPP shall not apply to the following financial and capital market participants: insurers, insurance broker companies, exchanges, broker companies, depositaries, investment companies, savings and loan companies, credit institutions and private pension funds.

The court decision regarding the initiation of a matter of LPP has the following effects: (a) a stay of the enforcement of judgments in matters regarding that adjudged and the recovery of the amount not yet recovered, (b) a prohibition for the secured creditor to request the sale of the pledged property of the debtor, (c) a prohibition against the creditor submitting an application for the insolvency proceedings of a legal person, (d) a prohibition against performing the liquidation of a debtor, (e) the suspension of the penalty increment, (f) the suspension of such an interest increment that exceeds the lawful interest, (g) the suspension of the late charge increment (including when this is specified as a penalty), (h) the suspension of calculation of the late charges of tax claims.

LPP are implemented upon coordination of a plan of action with the creditors (the plan should be supported by at least 51% of non-secured creditors and at least 2/3 of secured creditors, if any). Implementation of the LPP plan may foresee different methods of renewing solvency of the merchant: (a) the postponement of the honouring of payment obligations, (b) the alienation of movable property or immovable property or encumbrance with rights in rem in order to achieve extension of the time period for meeting the creditors' claims or satisfaction of the creditors' claims, (c) the increase of the basic capital of the merchant (including the investing of the right of the creditors to claim against the debtor in equity capital), (d) reorganisation of the merchant, repaying a part of the creditors' claims or investing them into the equity capital of the merchant receiving shares or stocks in return. If execution of the coordinated plan and solvency renewal are impossible when implementing the LPP, the administrator has a duty to submit an application to court for the insolvency proceedings of the merchant.

Legal protection proceedings cannot be initiated if (a) the merchant's legal protection proceedings have been implemented and terminated during the last 5 years or (b) the merchant's legal protection proceedings have been initiated and terminated during the last 4 months.

6.4 Family and Inheritance Law

Inese Lībiņa-Egner, Linda Damane, and Kristīne Zīle
Faculty of Law, University of Latvia, Raina blvd. 19, Riga LV-1586, Latvia
e-mail: inese.libina.egnere@lu.lv; linda.damane@lu.lv; kristine.zile@lu.lv

6.4.1 Family Law

6.4.1.1 Introduction

The Civil Law of Latvia (CL),[174] 'Family Law' and other laws[175] regulate the entering into marriage and termination of marriage; personal and property relations of spouses; rights and duties between parents and children, including determination of filiation of children, termination of adoption and custody rights, matters of kinship and affinity, as well as guardianship and trusteeship.

6.4.1.2 Marriage

According to Latvian national laws, marriage is an opposite-sex union of two persons to be registered in accordance with the procedures laid down in law for the purpose of founding a family, thereby creating a series of reciprocal rights and obligations.

Entering into Marriage and Termination of Marriage (Civil Law Articles 32–83)
In the CL, compulsory rules for entering into marriage have been established, and if these rules are not observed, a marriage may be declared annulled.

Marriage between persons of the same sex is prohibited.

A marriage shall be solemnised in the General Registry office or by a pastor or priest from the Evangelical Lutheran, Roman Catholic, Orthodox, Old Believers, Methodist, Baptist, Seventh Day Adventist or believers in Moses (Judaism) church.

One can enter into marriage when he or she has attained 18 years of age. By way of exception, a person who has attained 16 years of age may marry with the consent of his or her parents or guardians with an obligatory requirement if he or she marries a person of age of majority.

A marriage shall be declared annulled in which, at the time of its being entered, one of the spouses was in such condition that such spouse was not able to understand the meaning of his or her actions or able to control them, if the marriage has been entered into between close relatives, if at the time the marriage is entered into one of the spouses is in another marriage.

---

[174]The main legislative act regulating family and inheritance law in Latvia is the Civil Law of Latvia. http://vvc.gov.lv/export/sites/default/docs/LRTA/Likumi/The_Civil_Law.doc), adopted as an act of codification in 1937 and restored into force in 1992/1993 after Latvia regained independence.

[175]Law On Orphan's Courts. http://vvc.gov.lv/export/sites/default/docs/LRTA/Likumi/Law_On_Orphanxs_Courts.doc; Law on the Change of a Given Name, Surname and Nationality Record. http://vvc.gov.lv/export/sites/default/docs/LRTA/Likumi/On_the_Change_of_a_Given_Namex_Surname_and_Nationality_Record.doc; On Registration of Civil Status Documents. http://vvc.gov.lv/export/sites/default/docs/LRTA/Likumi/On_Registration_of_Civil_Status_Documents.doc; Civil Procedure Law. http://vvc.gov.lv/export/sites/default/docs/LRTA/Likumi/Civil_Procedure_Law.pdf; Notariate Law. http://vvc.gov.lv/export/sites/default/docs/LRTA/Likumi/Notariate_Law.doc; The Constitution of the Republic of Latvia http://vvc.gov.lv/export/sites/default/docs/LRTA/Likumi/Constitution.doc.

A marriage shall be declared annulled if it has been entered into as a sham marriage, i.e., without the intent to create a family. If a court recognises a marriage as annulled, the marriage shall be considered annulled from the moment it was entered into.

A spouse may contest a marriage if the spouse entered into the marriage under the influence of criminal threats.

Dissolution of Marriage by Divorce (CL Articles 69–78) The second means of termination of marriage is the dissolution of marriage by divorce. Only a court or sworn notary may dissolve a marriage by divorce. Unlike a declaration of annulment, a marriage is considered terminated by divorce as of the day the court judgment concerning the divorce of the marriage comes into legal effect or as of the day a notary has drawn up a marriage divorce certificate.

A notary may dissolve a marriage if both spouses agree on the dissolution of the marriage and only in cases where the spouses do not have a joint minor child and joint property or, if the spouses have a joint minor child or joint property, they have entered into a written agreement regarding custody of the joint minor child, rights of access, the child's means of support and division of the joint property.

A court may dissolve a marriage by divorce based upon the application of one of the spouses. A marriage shall be deemed to have broken down if the spouses no longer cohabit and there is no longer any prospect that the spouses shall renew cohabitation. Additionally, the marriage is presumed to be broken down if the spouses have lived apart for at least 3 years.

If the spouses have lived separately for less than 3 years, the marriage may be dissolved by divorce by the court only if the reason for the breaking down of marriage is the physical, sexual, psychological or economical violation of the spouse against the other spouse who has requested the dissolution of the marriage or against his or her child or joint child of the spouses; one spouse consents to the request of the other spouse for the dissolution of the marriage; one of the spouses has commenced cohabitation with another person and in such cohabitation a child has been born or the birth of a child is expected.

If the spouses have not agreed on the custody, access rights of the minor child born in the marriage, maintenance for the children, the division of common property or relevant claims have not been resolved prior to the dissolution of the marriage and are not raised together with the request for the dissolution of the marriage.

Property Relations of the Spouses Set by Law (CL Articles 89–110) The main principles of the property relations of spouses state that everything acquired during the marriage by the spouses together or by one of them but from the resources of both spouses or with the assistance of the actions of the other spouse is the joint property of both spouses; in case of uncertainty, it shall be presumed that such property belongs equally to both spouses. At the same time, each spouse retains property that belonged to him or her before the marriage, as well as the property he or she acquires during the marriage as a separate property.

The separate property of each spouse especially is property owned by a spouse before the marriage or property that the spouses have, by contract, designated as separate property; articles that are suitable only for the personal use of one spouse or are required for his or her independent work; property that was acquired free of charge during the marriage by one of the spouses; income from the separate property of a spouse that is not assigned to the needs of the family and joint household finances; and property that replaces the property referred to previously.

With the words ‘that the separate property of each spouse especially is’, provision of the law was made open. This means that in practice, the most common types of individual property of the spouse are listed, not excluding the possibility of the spouse to prove in court that, additionally to his or her listed individual property, some unspecified property must be added.

In any case, the law defines that the burden of establishing that certain property is separate shall lie upon the spouse who asserts such. The fact that immovable property is the separate property of one spouse shall be recorded in the Land Register.

Each spouse has the right to administer and use all of his or her own property that he or she owned before the marriage throughout the time the marriage persists. While both spouses shall jointly administer and act in regard to joint property, on the agreement of both spouses, it may also be administered by one of them. Any acts regarding such property by one of the spouses shall require the consent of the other spouse.

Contractual Property Relations of Spouses (CL Articles 114–139) The spouses may establish, alter or terminate their property rights in a marriage contract before marrying, as well as during marriage. The parties entering into a marriage contract may, in place of lawful property relations of the spouses, stipulate separate ownership or joint ownership of all property of the spouses. Such contracts shall be entered into in accordance with notarisation procedures, in the personal presence at the same time of both persons to be married or of both spouses. Additionally, for marriage contracts to have binding effect as against third parties, they shall be registered in the Spousal Property Relations Register, and in respect of immovable property, also in the Land Register.

If a marriage contract provides for the separate ownership of all the property of the spouses, each of the spouses not only retains the property that belonged to him or her prior to the marriage but also during the time of the marriage may independently acquire, use and act in regard to property independently of the other spouse. If the marriage contract provides for joint ownership of the property of the spouses, the property that had belonged to them prior to marriage, as well as the property that has been acquired during the marriage, except for their separate property, which the spouses have specified in a marriage contract as the separate property of each spouse, shall be combined in one joint, indivisible whole, which, during the duration of the marriage, shall not belong to either of the spouses as separate parts. In the marriage contract, when providing for the joint ownership of their property, the spouses shall agree which of them shall be the administrator of the property in joint ownership (the husband, the wife or both jointly).

6.4.1.3 Rights and Duties, as Between Parents and Children

Determination of Filiation of Children (CL Articles 146–161) The Civil Law of Latvia distinguishes three methods of determining paternity: paternity presumption, voluntary acknowledgement of paternity or determination of paternity by the court. It is essential to comply with the order of the legal basis of paternity and to take into account that these three pleas cannot co-exist.

Paternity presumption means that the father of a child who is born to a woman during marriage or not later than 306 days after the marriage has ended due to the death of the husband, the dissolution of the marriage or the declaration of the marriage as annulled shall be considered to be the husband of the mother of the child. But a child who is born to a woman not later than 306 days after termination of a marriage shall, if the woman has already remarried, be considered born of the new marriage. In such cases, the former husband or his parents have the right to contest the filiation of the child. The mother of the child and husband of the mother of the child may contest the paternity presumption within a 2-year period from the day when he found out that he is not the natural father of the child. Also, the parents of a husband may contest the paternity presumption within a 2-year period if the husband until the moment of his death did not know of the birth of the child. The child himself or herself may contest the paternity presumption within 2 years after reaching the age of majority.

A person who considers himself as the natural father of the child, except in a case where the child is conceived as a result of a criminal offence against morality and sexual offence, has the right to contest the paternity presumption within 2 years from the day of the birth of the child if the mother of the child is dead during childbirth or if the mother of the child and husband of the mother of the child had been living separately at least 306 days before the birth of the child. Before this adjustment, the rights of the natural father to contest the paternity presumption arose solely from case law.

If the filiation of a child from the father cannot be determined in conformity with the paternity presumption or a court has acknowledged that the child has not been born of his or her mother's husband, the filiation of the child from the father shall be based upon the voluntary acknowledgement of paternity or by the determination thereof by a court proceeding.

Acknowledgement of paternity shall occur when the father and mother of a child personally submit a joint application. An acknowledgement of paternity shall be officially registered by an entry in the Birth Register. Paternity may be acknowledged also in cases where the mother of the child, husband of the mother of the child or former husband of the mother of the child and natural father of the child submit a joint application, when paternity presumption is not applicable. An application for recognition of paternity may be submitted when the birth of a child is registered, as well as after the registration of the birth of the child, or already prior to the birth of the child. However, the recognition of paternity requires the consent of the child if he or she has attained 12 years of age.

Before the acknowledgement of paternity, the law does not require an obligation for a man to actually prove that the child is biologically descended from him. The actual assumption is based on the idea that the man who acknowledges paternity of the child is the natural father. Similarly, the CL does not provide restrictive rules when persons cannot agree for voluntary acknowledgement of paternity. Therefore, both the mother of the child and the child itself, if he or she has reached 12 years of age, have the right not to agree on acknowledgement of paternity for any reason. Thereby, the provision of the law makes it possible to create obstacles to voluntary acknowledgement of paternity if the contestant holds the view that a person who wants to recognise the child as his is not the natural father of the child, as well as in other cases.[176] A court may declare an acknowledgement of paternity null and void only if a person who has acknowledged that a child is his cannot be the natural father of the child, and he has recognised the child as his as the result of a mistake, fraud or duress.

If paternity has not been determined by paternity presumption or voluntarily or the court has recognised that the husband of the mother is not the father of the child, a court shall determine paternity. A claim for the determination of paternity by a court may be submitted by the mother of the child or the guardian of the child or the children themselves after reaching the age of majority, as well as by a person who considers himself the natural father of the child. It is important to note that paternity that has been determined by a court judgment that has come into legal effect may not be disputed. Procedural proceedings for this kind of case are laid down in Chapter 30 of the Civil Procedure Law—Matters Regarding Determination of the Parentage of Children.

Adoption (CL Articles 162–176) According to Latvian national laws,[177] it is only permitted to adopt a child who, by the moment of adoption, has not reached the age of majority and if it is in the interests of the child. For the adoption of a child, a decision by an Orphans' Court that such an adoption is in the interests of the child is required. The Orphans' Court, in taking such a decision, shall ascertain the views of the adoptee, if he or she is able to formulate such, as well as shall take into account information regarding the adopter, including his or her personality, religious faith if there is such, material circumstances, household circumstances, capacity to raise a child, as well as information regarding the adoptee, including his or her personality, religious faith if there is such, health and ancestry.

[176] Judgment of Constitutional Court of the Republic of Latvia in case No. 2004-02-0106 on 11 October 2004. http://www.satv.tiesa.gov.lv/wp-content/uploads/2004/02/2004-02-0106_Spriedums_ENG.pdf.

[177] Regulations of the Cabinet of Ministers No 111, dated 11 March 2003: Procedures for Adoption. http://vvc.gov.lv/export/sites/default/docs/LRTA/MK_Noteikumi/Cab._Reg._No._111_-_Procedures_for_Adoption.doc.

A minor child may be adopted if prior to the approval of the adoption he or she has been in the care and supervision of the adopter, and the mutual suitability of the child and adopter has been determined and a true child and parent relationship has been established as the result of adoption.

For the safety of the child, the CL provides a number of obstacles that can prevent a person from becoming an adopter. For example, a person cannot become an adopter if he or she has been punished for criminal offences against morality and for sexual offences or has had custody rights removed by a court judgment.

A single adopter can adopt without being married, but if the adopter is married, it has been set in law that spouses shall adopt a child jointly, except in cases where the children of the other spouse are adopted or the spouse has been declared missing.

For the adoption of a child, it is necessary to receive confirmation from the adopter; the adoptee child, if he or she has reached the age of 12 years; the parents of the adoptee, if they have not had custody rights removed; and the guardian. Parties to the adoption may revoke their consent to the adoption until the time when the child is given to the care of the adopters.

The adoption procedure is held by the Orphans' Court. The adoption shall be considered as effected as soon as the court has approved such.

The adoptee shall become a member of his or her adoptive family, and the adopter shall acquire the right to implement custody. In relation to the adopter and his or her kin, the adopted child and his or her descendants shall acquire the legal status of a child born of a marriage in regard to personal as well as property relations. With adoption, the kinship relations and related personal and property rights and duties of the child with regard to his or her natural parents and their kin shall be terminated.

An adoption may be revoked by a court if an adoptee of age of majority has agreed with the adopter regarding the revocation of the adoption. An adoption may be revoked in an exceptional case also when such an agreement does not exist but the adoptee of age of majority proves that as a result of adoption a true parent and child relationship has not been established between the adopter and adoptee. When an adoption is revoked, the adoption terminates as of the day that the court judgment regarding the revocation of the adoption comes into effect. The legal kinship relations between the adoptee, their descendants and the natural parents of the adoptee and their kin are renewed by the revocation of the adoption.

Information regarding the adoption shall not be divulged without the consent of the adopters until the child reaches the age of majority. Questions about the confidentiality of adoption are covered in the KCL, the CL and the Law on Registration of Civil Status Documents.

Custody (CL Articles 177–205) The CL determines that until reaching the age of majority, a child is under the custody of his or her parents. Custody is the rights and duties of parents to care for the child and his or her property and to represent the child in his or her personal and property relations. Care for a child means his or her care, supervision and the right to determine his or her place of residence.

Parents, commensurate to their abilities and financial state, have a duty to maintain the child. Such duty lies upon the father and the mother until the time the child is able to provide for himself or herself. The duty to provide for the maintenance of the child shall not terminate if the child is separated from the family or does not live together with one of the parents or with both parents. The minimal amount of means of maintenance, which is the duty of each of the parents to ensure for the child irrespective of his or her ability to maintain the child and financial state, shall be determined by the Cabinet, taking into account the minimum monthly salary and the age of the child.

Parents living together shall exercise custody jointly—if a common household and home is existent, joint custody of the child is implemented. If the parents are living separately, the joint custody of the parents continues. However, the term 'daily custody' is used to refer to the parent with which the child lives and who provides child care and supervision.

One of the parents solely shall represent a child in his or her personal and property relations if the other parent has not reached the age of majority, except in the case when he or she has entered into marriage; the other parent has died; or with an agreement or a court judgment, separate custody of one parent may be established, except in cases where, in accordance with law, the personal relations of the child are represented by both parents.

The joint custody of the parents shall terminate upon the establishment, based on an agreement between the parents or a court adjudication, of the separate custody of one parent. The parent with whom the child is located in separate custody has all the rights and duties arising from custody, but the other parent has access rights. This means that the parent with the custody rights has the right to decide about essential issues in the child's life without asking the opinion of the other parent with the access rights. This covers issues such as education, questions related to health, change of residence, etc.

The law does not define the priority of one parent over the other when the separate custody of the child is determined. Only by evaluating the child's psychological and emotional relationship with each parent and each parent's ability and willingness to provide appropriate conditions for the child's interests and upbringing is it possible to come to an acceptable decision on the separate custody of one parent.[178] Case law recognises that if one parent is resident abroad, the parent who provides the daily care of the child must be determined to have separate custody of the child, while the other parent retains access rights.[179]

The access rights hold that the child has the right to maintain personal relations and direct contact with any of the parents. Each of the parents has a duty and the

---

[178] The Department of Civil Cases of the Supreme Court. On case-law in resolving disputes about rights of charge (joint, separate, daily) and communication and sustenance for children. 2012. http://at.gov.lv/en/court-proceedings-in-the-supreme-court/compilations-of-court-decisions/civil_law/.

[179] Ibid.

right to maintain personal relations and direct contact with the child. This provision shall also be applicable if the child is separated from the family or does not live together with one of the parents or both of the parents. The parent who does not live with the child has the right to receive information regarding him or her, especially information regarding his or her development, health, educational progress, interests and domestic circumstances.

The enforcement of access rights—time, place, duration—is set by the mutual agreement of both parents. In case of dispute, the procedures by which access rights may be utilised shall be determined by a court, requesting an opinion from the Orphans' Court. The decision of the court has legal force and is binding to all parties. A person who avoids complying with an adjudication of the court or Orphans' Court that arises from child custody rights, care rights or access rights can be held criminally liable. A court may restrict access rights, and, if necessary, it may be determined that the person be permitted to meet with the child only in the presence of third persons or at a specific place, insofar as this conforms to the interests of the child. The court can also impose an obligation to come to the Orphans' Court at a certain time. Furthermore, a court may temporarily revoke access rights if the access is harmful to the interests of the child and the harm cannot be otherwise prevented.

Termination and Restriction of Custody Rights (CL Articles 198–205) A parent may have custody removed by a court judgment if, due to his or her fault (due to an intentional act or negligence), the health or life of the child is endangered or the parent misuses his or her rights or does not care for the child or does not ensure the supervision of the child and it may endanger the physical, mental or moral development of the child. In removing custody rights from one parent, a court shall place the child under the separate custody of the other parent. If the custody that can be exercised by the other parent does not adequately protect the child from endangerment or custody rights are removed from both parents, a court shall assign to the Orphans' Court out-of-family care for the child.

For example, custody rights shall be terminated for a parent if an Orphans' Court finds that there are factual impediments that prevent the parent from the possibility of caring for the child, the parent misuses his or her rights or does not ensure the care and supervision of the child, violence against the child by the parent has been established or there is good cause for suspicion regarding violence against the child by the parent. In such cases, care shall be implemented by the other parent; however, if there are impediments to this as well, the Orphans' Court shall ensure out-of-family care for the child.

The custody rights of a parent can also be terminated in cases where a parent is using his rights in bad faith by failing to fulfil the judgment of the court in a case arising from custody or access rights, if it causes significant harm to the child and there are no obstacles for the other parent to implement child care. Terminated custody rights shall be renewed for a parent when an Orphans' Court finds that the circumstances for the termination of the custody rights no longer apply. If within a period of 1 year from the termination of custody rights it is not possible to renew them, the Orphans' Court shall decide regarding bringing an action to a court for removal of custody rights, except in cases where the custody rights cannot be renewed due to circumstances independent of the parent.

In cases where custody rights for parents have been terminated, they can be renewed not only by assessing the non-existence of previously listed barriers that were relevant to the termination of the custody rights but also by an assessment of the strength of the mutual ties of the child and the other participants in this process; the age of the child, when the child was placed under another person's care; the length of the termination of custody rights; as well as by assessing other conditions that ensure primary compliance with the rights and interests of the child.[180]

6.4.1.4 Guardianship and Trusteeship

Guardianship (CL Articles 219–354) Guardianship is established over minors. A father and mother already are, on the basis of custody rights, the natural guardians of their minor children.

Parents who have lost custody rights cannot also be guardians of a child. If both of the parents have lost custody rights over the child after a court judgment or for some other reason independent of their will, a guardianship shall be established over the child or the Orphans' Court shall assign out-of-family care for the child. But if it is lost by only one parent, guardianship shall be established or the Orphans' Court shall assign out-of-family care for the child in cases where it is necessary and in the interests of the child. Guardians shall assume the place of parents for their wards.

Guardianship over minors, if parents have not appointed guardians in their will for their children, in the first instance, devolves to their nearest kin, but for this the confirmation of an Orphans' Court is necessary. The nearest kin of minors shall be regarded as those who, upon the death of such minors, would be their heirs by intestacy. An Orphans' Court shall select as guardians the most suitable from equally near kin, but if the nearest kin should appear to be unsuitable, from more distant kin. However, if among the kin of a minor no one capable is to be found or those who are capable are unable to assume guardianship or they are discharged or repealed from the position of guardianship for legal cause or if the minor does not have any kin, the Orphans' Court shall appoint guardians from among other persons, and the court shall act on its own accord as soon as it is informed that there are such complete orphans.

Guardians shall be appointed by a decision of an Orphans' Court based on the application of a person, after they have examined the person to be confirmed or appointed to ensure he or she has the abilities and qualities necessary for the performance of such duty.

[180]The Department of Civil Cases of the Supreme Court. On case-law in resolving disputes about rights of charge (joint, separate, daily) and communication and sustenance for children. 2012. http://at.gov.lv/en/court-proceedings-in-the-supreme-court/compilations-of-court-decisions/civil_law/.

Trusteeship (CL Articles 355–381) Trusteeship is established over persons with health disorders of a mental nature, or other health disorders, whose capacity to act is restricted by a court; over persons with health disorders of a mental nature, or other, in urgent cases without restriction of capacity to act; over persons due to their living dissolutely or wastefully or over persons who, due to excessive use of alcohol or other narcotics, threatens to drive themselves or their family into privation or poverty and whose capacity to act has been restricted by a court; over the property of absent and missing persons and over the entirety of property of an estate.

Trustees of adults shall be appointed pursuant to the judgment of a court, by the appropriate Orphans' Court, which shall ascertain the opinion of the person regarding a trustee to be appointed, provided that such person is able to formulate it. The Orphans' Court may appoint as trustee a trustee selected by the person, the spouse of the person to be placed under trusteeship or one of the nearest kin. Likewise, the Orphans' Court shall observe the last will instructions of such person who has left him or her an estate.

The concept of total legal incapacity has been substituted with the concept of restricted legal capacity, which states that the individual's non-economic rights cannot be restricted. It also cancels the recovery criterion in the process of legal capacity restoration and provides an individual with the right to the regular reassessment of the status of restricted legal capacity, as well as provides him or her with the greater legal procedural protection.[181]

6.4.2 Inheritance Law

6.4.2.1 General

Under the Latvian law, the concept of 'the estate' is meant as an aggregate of articles consisting of all real property and movables, as well as the rights and obligations that are transferable to third parties, owned by the deceased. All such rights and obligations that were owned exclusively by the deceased (personal rights and obligations) are not transferable to heirs and terminate with the death of the deceased. Accordingly, the heir, by accepting the aggregate of articles of the deceased, inherits those rights and obligations that are transferable to third parties. The estate is a legal entity; it may acquire rights and undertake obligations.[182] The estate acquires the status of legal entity as of the moment of death of the deceased. The estate may enter legal transactions and may be a respondent or claimant in litigation proceedings; thus, the aggregate of assets of the deceased does not cease to be engaged in the legal environment of civil law relationships. However, the administrative process is an exception. It has been determined in the case law that an estate, existing as a private law legal entity, does not possess the legal authority

[181] Lībiņa-Egner (2013), pp. 24–29.

[182] Article 383 of the CL.

to act in administrative proceedings.[183] For the representation of an estate as a legal entity, a guardianship shall be established and a guardian shall be appointed for the estate.

Both individuals and legal entities can inherit. The ability to inherit is also possessed by an unborn child if incepted, although not yet born, at the time when the inheritance is opened; however, he or she becomes an heir only if born alive not later than after the 306th day from the date of death of the deceased.[184]

Invitation to inherit takes place by the opening of the inheritance with the death of the deceased or by the date he is declared dead by the respective court ruling. The basis for the invitation to inherit is either the will legally expressed by the deceased (the last will) or the law. The person leaving the estate may express his or her will by means of a testament or an inheritance contract.

6.4.2.2 Intestate Inheritance

Inheritance by law takes place in cases where there is no last will or if the last will is invalid or if the last will relates only to part of the estate. Based on law or intestate procedure, the persons invited to inherit are the spouse, relatives and adopted persons. Affinity (*svainība*) does not create a basis for the right to inherit based on the law. A living spouse inherits from the deceased irrespective of the type of economic relationship between the spouses during their marriage. It is essential, however, that the marriage be effective at the time when the inheritance opens, as well as at the time when the inheritance certificate is issued.

The spouse may inherit jointly with the descendants (children, grandchildren, great-grandchildren, etc.) based on Article 393 of the CL or jointly with the laterals of the deceased based on Article 396 of the CL.

The spouse is entitled to receive the same portion of the estate as the child (or the same portion of the estate as each of the children) if the number of children who have expressed a will to inherit is less than four or, if the number of children willing to inherit is four or more, one fourth of the estate.[185] If the deceased spouse leaves no descendants and no adoptees or if such persons renounce, the living spouse receives half of the estate and the furnishing of the apartment. If the deceased spouse has no descendants or adoptees, ascendants, full brothers or sisters or their children or if such persons renounce, the living spouse inherits the whole estate.[186] Accordingly, the living spouse may inherit jointly with the first or the second or the third category of relatives but not jointly with the fourth category of relatives (please see below regarding the split of relatives in kinship categories) because if

[183] Decision of the Administrative Law Department of the Senate of Supreme Court of the Republic of Latvia in case No 594/2009 on 24 July 2009. http://at.gov.lv/lv/judikatura/judikaturas-nolemumu-arhivs/senata-administrativo-lietu-departaments/hronologiska-seciba/2009-hronologiska-seciba/.

[184] Krauze and Gencs (1997), p. 19.

[185] Article 393 of CL.

[186] Article 396 of CL.

there is a spouse and the fourth category heirs, the entire estate shall be received by the spouse.

The intestate inheritance right is based only on such kinship that stems either from a birth during a valid marriage or such marriage that is later declared invalid or not later than the 306th day after such marriage is terminated or by the admission of paternity or the determination of paternity via litigation proceedings.

The rights of adopted children to inherit are determined in Article 401 of the CL, which has been in force in the current wording only since 1 July 2014 and which determines that the adoptee and his descendants inherit from the deceased and his relatives, whereas persons inheriting from the adopted child are his or her descendants, as well as the adopter and his or her relatives. Before these amendments, the inheritance regulation for adopted persons was different and was based on the respective historic regulation in the CL.[187]

The sequence of inheritance by relatives is based on certain categories and steps of kinship. Article 404 of the CL determines four categories of relatives:

1. in the first category inherit, without differentiating closeness by step of kinship, all those descendants of the deceased who do not have another descendant entitled to inherit in the kinship line between them and the deceased;
2. in the second category inherit ascendants who are closest by the step of kinship, as well as full brothers and full sisters of the deceased and the children of those who have deceased before the respective person leaving the estate;
3. in the third category inherit stepbrothers and stepsisters of the deceased and the children of those who have deceased before the respective person leaving the estate;
4. in the fourth category inherit all other relatives of lateral line of the deceased closest by the step of kinship, without differentiating between full and partial kinship.

The substitution right has a significant role in intestate inheritance—when descendants inherit from the ascendant, more distant descendants step in for their parent who deceased before the respective person leaving the estate based on the substitution right, without restrictions regarding closeness by step of kinship. According to the substitution right, the descendants are entitled to receive such a part of the estate that would have been received by their parent if he had lived longer than the deceased and had inherited from this person. Further, if the person invited to inherit passes away before he expresses the will to inherit within the term set forth by the law, the transmission of inheritance rights takes place—his heirs are entitled to the same terms for expressing their will to inherit regarding both his estate as well as the estate he was entitled to, although not yet accepted.[188]

[187] See Zīle (2012), pp. 117–123.

[188] Article 695 of CL.

6.4.2.3 Inheritance Based on Testament

Any unilateral order given for the case of ones' own death is called a testament. The testator is entitled to cancel, amend or supplement the testament at any time. By a testament, one may give orders regarding the whole estate, part thereof or any individual items of the estate (if there is an order for a specific item in the estate rather than the whole estate or certain part of the estate, such an order is called a legate (*legāts*) and the person entitled thereto is called a legatee (*legatārs*)).

A testament can be made by any person, except minors, either in public (before a notary public or the Orphans' Court) or in private (by handwriting the whole testament and signing it). However, until 1 July 2014, it was legally permissible to make different types of private testaments; therefore, a private testament shall be deemed legally valid if it complies with the requirements of the CL in force at the time when the respective testament was made.[189]

The testament shall be declared valid by the notary public when the latter issues an inheritance certificate. The testament can be challenged by submitting a respective claim to the court.

6.4.2.4 Inheritance Contract

An inheritance right on the basis of an agreement is created by a contract whereby one of the parties grants to the other party, or whereby several parties grant to each other, the right to the respective estate or a part thereof, or to the legate. The inheritance contract, in itself, creates an inheritance right.

An inheritance contract must be made in the form of a notarial deed. If the contract concerns real estate owned by the person leaving the estate, it should be registered in the Land Register for the contract to be binding on third parties. The appointment of the contractual heir cannot be unilaterally withdrawn, and the contractual heir may not unilaterally withdraw from the contract.

By the death of the person leaving the estate, the contractual heir becomes entitled to inherit and obtains the respective right to receive the estate. However, if the contractual heir passes away before the person leaving the estate, the former's right to inherit terminates and is not transferable to his or her heirs.

6.4.2.5 Preferential Share and Persons Entitled to a Preferential Share

The person leaving the estate may not infringe upon the interests of the persons entitled to a preferential share by the testament or the inheritance contract. If any of the persons entitled to a preferential share is omitted in the testament or in the inheritance contract or if without proper legal grounds is deprived of the estate, he is entitled to request allocation of his preferential share or, if according to the last will he receives less than the preferential share, he is entitled to request that his share is supplemented accordingly.

[189] The Law on Procedure for Application and Time of Coming into force of parts—Introduction, Inheritance Law, and Property Law—of the renewed 1937 Civil Law of the Republic of Latvia. Law of the Republic of Latvia: 07.07.1992. – ZIŅOTĀJS, 29., 30.07.1992.

Since 1 July 2014, in the CL, as well as in other laws, the concept of 'forced heirs' (*neatraidāmie mantinieki*) has been replaced by the concept of 'persons entitled to preferential share' (*neatraidāmās daļas tiesīgie*). Since the very beginning (1937[190]), the concept of 'forced heir' did not correspond to the material system for the protection of relatives introduced in the CL and to their respective rights to request the preferential share rather than the estate. Also, during the last several years, incongruity between the concept of 'forced heir' and the material system for the protection of forced heirs provided for in the CL[191] was repeatedly criticised in the legal literature. However, the concept of 'persons entitled to preferential share', introduced as of 1 July 2014, now clearly indicates the rights of certain persons to receive the preferential share rather than be approved as entitled to inherit part of the estate and to become heirs.

According to Article 423 of the CL, the persons entitled to a preferential share are the spouse and the descendants, but if there are no descendants, the spouse and next of kin ascendants. The persons entitled to a preferential share are only entitled to request allocation of the preferential share in cash, which is determined from the net assets of the testator after deduction of all his or her debts. However, there is no basis for the assumption that the persons entitled to a preferential share may not agree with the testamentary or contractual heirs for the distribution of the preferential share in kind within the scope of inheritance cases handled by notaries public, as well as within the scope of settlements in civil litigation initiated as the result of a claim for the allocation of the preferential share. The first sentence of Paragraph 2 of Article 423 of the CL stipulates the right to claim but does not preclude the parties from agreeing to settle the case in a manner where the person entitled to the preferential share would receive it in kind rather than in cash.

The right to preferential share can be inherited and transferred further. This is a significant novelty, introduced on 1 July 2014. Before that, in the case law, as well as in the legal doctrine regarding the applicability of transfer of the preferential share through transmission, it was determined that the rights of the forced heirs are their personal rights.[192]

The person entitled to a preferential share should apply for the preferential share until the expiry of the term set forth by the notary public in the invitation to inherit; otherwise, it shall be deemed that he has waived the right to the preferential share.

The preferential share will be determined based on the number of heirs as at the date of the testator's death, including his spouse and the heirs who have been excluded by the last will; however, a renounced heir (*atteikušais mantotājs*) will not count.

[190]See Lange (1937), p. 19.

[191]Damane and Zīle (2009), pp. 7–13. See also: Damane (2012). See also: Krūmiņa (2008), pp. 1–7.

[192]On the Application of Law in Inheritance Cases. Decision No 1 of the Summit of Supreme Court as of 27 March 1995. LV, 21 April 1995, No. 62, Paragraph 2 of Article 41. See also: Krauze and Gencs (1997), p. 52.

The amount of the preferential share is half of the value of the respective part of the estate that the person entitled to the preferential share would have inherited based on the law. This share shall be determined based on the composition and value of assets as on the date the deceased passed away. The preferential share may not be restricted by conditions or terms, and it may not be encumbered by legates or other encumbrances.

The persons entitled to a preferential share may be deprived of their right to inherit by the testator only for causes specifically provided for in the law that have been expressly indicated in the last will and that are true.

6.4.2.6 Acceptance and Waiver of the Estate, Loss of the Rights to Inherit

In order to acquire an estate, each of the respective intestate, testamentary and contractual heirs must be alive at the time the inheritance is opened and (simultaneously) the heirs are invited to inherit, whereas in respect of the heir who has been conditionally appointed as an heir, the respective condition should also be met. However, the invitation to inherit establishes only the possibility of becoming an heir. In order to acquire the estate, the person invited to inherit must also express his will to accept the estate he has become entitled to. Therefore, for the acquisition of an estate, it is of importance that the estate is accepted in due time and by due procedure. As soon as the person invited to inherit has accepted the estate, he may no longer waive it, and as soon as he waives the estate he may not accept it later on.

Article 689 of the CL grants to the persons entitled to inherit the right to choose whether to accept or to waive the inheritance, except for a contractual heir, unless he has expressly contracted the right to waive the estate. The will to accept the estate can be expressed either personally or via representative. Representation is mandatory where the person invited to inherit is a person with limited legal capacity (*persona ar rīcības spējas ierobežojumiem*) or a minor. The guardian of a person with legal capacity limitations and the custodian of a minor may accept or waive the estate only subject to the permit of the Orphans' Court.

The estate can be accepted either by a respective statement of will recorded by a notary public as a notarial deed or by taking actual possession of the estate with the purpose to manage and use it as one's own.

If the person leaving the estate has set a certain term for the acceptance of the estate, the appointed heir must comply with this term. If no such term has been set and the notary public has initiated the inheritance case and the heirs have been invited to inherit, the person invited to inherit must express his or her will to accept the estate before the expiry of the term set in the respective announcement. If no announcement took place, the heir must express his will to accept the inheritance within 1 year, which begins from the date the inheritance opens, if the estate is in his actual possession, or—in other cases—within 1 year of the date he was informed about the opening of the inheritance.

The term set forth in the announcement is binding on the heirs, legatees and the persons entitled to preferential share, as well as on creditors. The debt commitments to creditors that do not apply before the expiry of the term set in the invitation (an announcement regarding the opening of the inheritance) shall be discharged by the issuance of the inheritance certificate or the European inheritance certificate or by the deed on the termination of the inheritance case.[193]

According to Articles 709 and 711 of the CL, a person invited to inherit may limit his liability for the debts of the deceased by the amount of estate received if, within 2 months from the date the inheritance opens or the date he was informed about the opening of the inheritance, he accepts the estate subject to inventory right. When the estate is accepted subject to inventory right, the heir will not be liable for the commitments of the deceased with his own assets, and his liability will be limited by the amount of assets inherited.

It is possible to waive the estate even before the invitation to inherit by means of a written waiver agreement whereby one of the parties waives the right to inherit what he or she would have had following the death of the other party. After such an agreement is entered, the person who waived his or her right to inherit becomes a renounced heir (*mantotājs*), who will not be considered in the calculation of the shares of the other heirs and the preferential shares of the persons so entitled. Thereby, all inheritance rights of such person are terminated. Such an agreement also cancels the renounced heir's rights to the preferential share from the estate of the deceased. A renounced heir's waiver agreement can only be terminated by mutual written agreement.

6.4.2.7 Actual Division of the Estate

If an estate is acquired by several persons jointly, they are entitled either to manage it collectively or to request the actual division of the estate. The division of the estate is the last stage of an inheritance case.

Before the division process can be commenced, it should be determined what assets are subject to division or what the actual composition of the estate is.

The division of the estate can be either voluntary (by reciprocal private agreement or at a notary public or the Orphans' Court) or through court procedure if the co-heirs fail to reach an agreement. If among the co-heirs there are persons subject to custody or guardianship, any deed of division of the estate agreed among co-heirs shall be subject to approval of the Orphans' Court.

6.4.2.8 Escheat

If after the death of a person there are no heirs or if no heirs have applied after the opening of the inheritance or if they have failed to prove their inheritance right, the estate shall be declared escheat and shall be transferred to the state. The state, in this case, shall not be considered an heir. The state is liable for the debts on the estate only to the extent of the assets that the state acquires as a result of escheat. The state recognises those debts that have been secured by mortgage or commercial pledge, as well as the debts that have been reported to the notary public as claims of creditors before the expiry of the term set in the invitation (announcement regarding

[193]Paragraph 2 of Article 705 of CL.

opening of the inheritance) provided they follow from public deed or from a commitment that is recognised by a valid and enforceable court ruling. As of the date of the notarial deed on the termination of the inheritance case and recognition of the estate as escheat, accrual of interest, late penalties and other side claims stop.

The escheat is sold by the court bailiff.

6.4.2.9 The Procedure for Conducting Inheritance Cases

In Latvia, as of 1 January 2003, inheritance cases for intestate, testamentary and contractual inheritance are conducted by notaries public.[194] The territorial allocation of inheritance cases takes place based on the last place of residence of the deceased and, if this is unknown, based on the place where the estate, or the majority of its assets, is situated.

Inheritance cases are initiated based on the inheritance application of heirs, legatees, primary heirs (*pirmmantinieki*), secondary heirs (*pēcmantinieki*), substitutes, creditors of the deceased, persons entitled to preferential share, the living spouse of the deceased, the executor of the testament or the management of the employer of the deceased.

Each inheritance case is registered with the inheritance registry, which is owned by the Latvian state and managed and held by the Public Notaries Council of Latvia. The inheritance registry contains information on the deceased and the notary public who conducts the respective inheritance case. After the inheritance case is initiated, the notary public must verify with the registry of public testaments, which is managed and held by the Public Notaries Council of Latvia. The registry of public testaments comprises information on documents containing last will deeds, as well as documents regarding the withdrawal, amendment, supplement or cancellation of last will deeds.

In cases where the estate needs protection or guardianship until the issuance of the inheritance certificate, it must be procured by the notary public who handles the respective inheritance case. He shall request the court bailiff to take all necessary actions for the protection of the estate, indicating which particular estate protection measures shall be applied: sealing the real estate, seizure of the real estate or movables, seizure of cash. Where until the issuance of the inheritance certificate guardianship must be established over the estate, the notary public shall issue a notarial deed on guardianship over the estate and send it to the Orphans' Court for the appointment of a guardian.

According to the Notary Act, an inheritance case shall be suspended only if the notary public receives notice from a court that a claim challenging the last will has been filed. In such circumstances, the inheritance case shall be suspended until the dispute is resolved in the court.

[194] See Notariate Act. http://vvc.gov.lv/export/sites/default/docs/LRTA/Likumi/Notariate_Law.doc. See also Regulations of the Cabinet of Ministers No 618, dated 4 August 2008: Procedure for Handling Inheritance Registry and Inheritance Cases (Par mantojuma registra un mantojuma lietu vešanu). LV, 22 August 2008, No. 130 (3914).

If no heirs apply in the initiated inheritance case or if they waive the estate, the notary public shall issue a notarial deed on the termination of the insurance case and shall declare the estate as an escheat that shall be acquired by the state. If heirs, primary heirs, secondary heirs, substitutes, legatees accept the estate/legate and the notary public considers the respective inheritance application substantiated, the notary public shall issue an inheritance certificate certifying the respective rights to the estate based on the law or certifying the validity of the last will deed.

The inheritance certificate issued by the notary public is a document certifying the inheritance rights of the heir or the legatee's rights to the legate, but it does not certify the heir's title to the assets indicated in the inheritance certificate. The composition of such assets is indicated based on the list submitted by the heir himself.

By the issuance of an inheritance certificate, the claims of creditors that have not been reported before the expiry of the term set in the announcement of the notary public shall be discharged. The respective announcement is the publication on the opening of inheritance in the official media whereby the notary public invites to apply all persons who as heirs, creditors or otherwise have any rights to the respective estate. The term of the invitation shall be determined by the notary public based on an assessment of the information available in the inheritance case; however, the term of the announcement may not be shorter than 3 months.

6.5 Civil Law Procedure

Daina Ose and Martins Osis
Faculty of Law, University of Latvia, Raina blvd. 19, Riga LV-1586, Latvia
e-mail: daina.ose@lu.lv; martins.osis@lu.lv

6.5.1 Introduction

The Latvian Civil Procedure Law[195] (hereinafter CPL) took force on 1 March 1999 and is continuously being improved with amendments establishing new categories and updating existing regulations. Latvia's civil procedure system belongs to the Romano-Germanic legal family, and the process of updating the system takes its cues from civil procedure development trends in the European Union Member States, especially Germany and Austria. When drafting amendments to Latvia's CPL, the civil procedure regulations in Lithuania and Estonia are also taken into account.

[195] Civil Procedure Law. http://www.vvc.gov.lv/export/sites/default/docs/LRTA/Likumi/Civil_Procedure_Law.pdf.

6.5.2 Fundamental Principles of Civil Court Procedure

Latvia's CPL is the primary source for civil procedure; however, procedural regulations are also laid down in several substantive laws. For example, the Labour Law contains provisions on deadlines for submitting claims in court and the reverse burden of proof in some labour disputes. Relations between the court and the participants of the case are based upon adherence to specific principles of civil procedure.

The *principle of legality* is stipulated in Article 1(2) of the CPL, stating that a person who has applied to a court has the right to have his or her case adjudicated by the court in accordance with the procedures laid down by law.

The *hearing of both parties principle* is stipulated in Article 9 of the CPL. The court shall ensure that the parties have equal opportunity to exercise their rights in order to protect their interests. Latvian law experts have indicated that in the proceedings, parties take up equal procedural status and only the court, upon deciding the case on merits, may establish what the mutual rights and obligations of the parties are and that during the course of the dispute, the parties shall be provided with equal chances to enjoy the protection granted by the court. The equality of the parties does not mean that all procedural rights and obligations of the parties shall be absolutely equal. Equality is said to admit a differentiated approach to persons' rights if it is justified in a democratic society. Digressions from the equality of parties in the CPL are said to be objectively and reasonably grounded. Since the parties usually have different, mostly opposite legal interests, it is not always possible to balance the rights of the parties. However, in all cases when one party is granted more rights or imposed with less duties, the opposite party should be provided with the respective procedural means.[196]

The *principle of territorial jurisdiction of courts* provides that the court of first instance for all cases shall be the district (city) court, in the territory of which the defendant's residence or legal address is registered. The Land Registry Office of a district (city) court shall examine applications regarding undisputed compulsory execution and compulsory execution of obligations in accordance with the warning procedures, as well as approval of statements of auction. For some categories of cases, the specific court of first instance is determined based on subject matter jurisdiction. For example, the Riga City Vidzeme District has jurisdiction as the court of first instance over proceedings pertaining to matters of state secrecy, patent rights, topography of semiconductor products, design, trademarks and protected geographical indications. Jelgava City Court has jurisdiction over cases pertaining to invalidating decisions taken at shareholders' meetings of capital companies. The Riga City Northern District Court has jurisdiction over cases pertaining to unlawful

[196]Opinion of Prof., Dr. iur. J. Rozenbergs; Judgment of the Constitutional Court in case No 2009-85-01 on 30 March 2010. http://www.satv.tiesa.gov.lv/wp-content/uploads/2009/09/2009-85-01_Spriedums_ENG.pdf, see: Rozenfelds et al. (2015), p. 21.

movement of a child across the border or detention in another country, if the child's place of residence is in Latvia or abroad.

The *principle of individual and collegial adjudication* provides that a civil case is heard by an individual judge in the court of first instance, whereas in the court of appeal or cassation the case is adjudicated collegially by three judges.

The *principle of the official language* is set forth in Article 13 of the CPL, which stipulates that court proceedings shall take place in the official state language, which is Latvian. The participants in the proceedings shall submit foreign language documents accompanied with a translation thereof into Latvian. The court shall ensure the right of participants in the proceedings who are receiving state-ensured legal aid or have been exempted from paying court costs, and who do not have command of the language used in the court proceedings, to examine the materials of the case and participate in procedural actions utilising the aid of an interpreter. All other participants of the proceedings shall be personally responsible for ensuring themselves with interpretation of the proceedings should it be necessary. Costs for interpreting services may be recovered from the losing party. The Law on Judicial Power[197] of the Republic of Latvia Article 25 prescribes that in the course of the adjudication of a matter, the parties shall exercise their procedural rights in the form of an adversary proceeding.

The *adversarial principle*, as one of the main principles in civil procedure, is laid down in Article 10 of the CPL, which stipulates that adversarial proceedings shall take place through the parties providing explanations; submitting evidence and applications addressed to the court; participating in the examination of witnesses and experts, in the examination and assessment of other evidence and in court argument; and performing other procedural actions. The normative regulations fail to give a comprehensive enumeration of procedural activities but state only the most important one, allowing the court and participants in the matter to interpret compliance with the adversarial principle during a proceeding. Latvian civil procedure provides a passive role for a judge in collecting evidence but imposes an obligation upon the parties to assess and choose what evidence to submit to the court and in what way to prove the truth of their claims. In this way, the civil procedure diminishes the role of the principle of objective examination, although without fully excluding it from the civil procedure.[198] Compliance with the adversarial principle during civil procedure is a fundamental principle for adopting a fair judgment. All subjects involved in the matter comply with CPL norms and fulfil them according to their status in the procedure. Not only the parties, but also the court that is obliged to advance the procedure according to the law, is interested in compliance with the adversarial principle and advancing of the procedure. The Constitutional Court of the Republic of Latvia[199] has admitted in its judgment in the

---

[197]On Judicial Power. http://www.vvc.gov.lv/export/sites/default/docs/LRTA/Likumi/Judicial_Power.pdf.

[198]Rozenfelds et al. (2015), p. 7.

[199]Judgment of the Constitutional Court in case no. 2012-05-01 on 29 October, http://www.satv.tiesa.gov.lv/wp-content/uploads/2012/02/2012-05-01_Spriedums_ENG.pdf.

matter No.2012-05-01 that both parties have equal possibilities to prepare their opinion to the sitting of the court and justify it with arguments in the sitting of the court.

The *dispositive principle* results from civil procedure; it is the freedom of the parties to act upon their subjective rights and the procedural measures to protect those rights. This principle provides that the court shall not determine the subject of the claim or its basis; these are determined solely by the plaintiff. Still, the autonomy of the parties may not be arbitrary. Restrictions are provided both by law and by the court. The free choice of parties in the dispute is expressed as applying or failure to apply the rights set forth by law. By choosing certain rights, the party shall observe the procedure for exercise of the respective norm. The court shall make a judgment within the limits of the claim (Article 192 of the CPL). In assessing claims, the court shall only refer to facts and conditions indicated in the claim. Understanding of the principle of disposition is also contained in another legal acknowledgment given by the Civil Case Department of the Senate for the Supreme Court of the Republic of Latvia in judgment No. SKC-1627/2012, adopted on 17 October 2012, stating that 'a party itself shall choose either to apply to the court and itself shall set the limits of its claim and procedural means to use. The principle of disposition also refers to the appeal procedure, namely – a party shall choose either to appeal against the judgment and to what extent. According to Paragraph 2 Art. 203 of the CPL, if a part of a judgment is appealed, the judgment shall come into effect regarding the part which has not been appealed, after expiration of the time period for appeal thereof.' [200]

The principle of *unchangeability of a court panel* is enshrined within Article 14 of the CPL, which provides that replacement of a judge during the course of the adjudication of a case shall only be permitted if he or she cannot complete adjudication of the case due to taking up a different position, illness or another objective reason. As a result, if a judge is replaced by another judge during the course of the adjudication of a case, the adjudication of the case shall be commenced anew.

The *openness principle* provides that any person having reached the age of 15 has the right to be a listener or a participant of court proceedings, provided that the case is being adjudicated in a verbal process and at open court. The court has an obligation to hear specific categories of cases stipulated by law at closed court sittings, where only persons who are participants in the case and an interpreter (if a party of the case needs interpretation to be provided) may be present. Based on a reasoned request by a participant in the case or at the discretion of the court, the court sitting or part thereof may be declared as closed in order to safeguard the private life of a person, official secrets, commercial secrets, confidentiality of correspondence or if it is in the interests of court adjudication. The website of the

[200] Judgment of the Department of Civil cases of the Senate of the Supreme Court in case No SKC-1627/2012 on 17 October 2012, http://at.gov.lv/en/court-proceedings-in-the-supreme-court/archive-of-case-law-decisions/senate/chronological-order/2012/.

Court Administration contains anonymised data on court judgments that have taken effect and have decided a matter in substance at open court or by written procedure.

6.5.3 Informing a Person of Initiated Court Proceedings

A crucial element in the civil procedure by which to safeguard the right to a fair trial is informing a person of initiated court proceedings. The CPL of Latvia regulates in detail the method and procedure of sending court documents and notifications. A person has the right to inform the court of the method and address where he or she prefers to receive court documents and notifications. It is possible to deliver correspondence by postal service to a person's declared place of residence or another indicated address or a legal address or electronically to a person's indicated e-mail address, and, as an exception, it is also possible to have a sworn bailiff deliver documents to the recipient. All documents and notifications sent by mail are considered as having been served on the seventh day after they were sent out, while documents sent electronically are considered as having been served on the third day after sending. Concurrently, documents and notifications are also considered as having been served if the recipient has refused to accept them. If the defendant does not have a declared place of residence in Latvia and the plaintiff does not know the defendant's address, the defendant shall be summoned to court through publication in the official gazette *Latvijas Vēstnesis*. A court may adjudicate a matter without the participation of the defendant if not less than 1 month has passed since the day the summons was published in the official gazette. The condition that, regarding a person's legal relationship with the state and local government, they must be reachable at their declared place of residence reduces the number of postponed cases as it allows the court to adjudicate the matter without the person present provided that the notification about the court sitting has been sent to the person's declared place of residence.

6.5.4 Costs of Adjudication

The type and amount of costs of adjudication are set out in the CPL. All costs of adjudication are split into two groups: (1) court costs, including state fees that must be paid when submitting to the court an original claim or a counterclaim, and office fees, which must be paid for summoning witnesses, issuing certificates and reissuing court documents. This group also includes costs related to adjudication of a case, meaning amounts that must be paid to witnesses and experts; costs related to execution of court judgments; costs related to the delivery, service and translation of court summonses and other judicial documents; costs related to security for a claim; costs related to searching for defendants; and costs related to publication of notices in newspapers. Persons submitting court claims in specific categories, such as claims pertaining to child or parent support, employees submitting claims regarding recovery of remuneration and other employee claims arising from legal employment relations or related to such, as well as other persons listed in Article 43 of the CPL, including persons who are receiving state ensured legal aid, are exempt from paying court costs. Based on a reasoned request, the court may decide to exempt from covering court costs persons whose financial situation does not allow them to cover such costs and therefore hinders their access to court. In such cases, court costs are covered by the state. (2) costs related to conduction of a matter, including costs for the assistance of an advocate, travel and accommodation costs related to attendance at a court sitting; costs related to taking documentary evidence; costs for state-ensured legal aid; and costs for interpretation services at court sittings. These costs are to be recovered from the losing party to the party in whose favour the court has adjudicated. The court does not have the right to release a participant in a case from covering these costs. All costs of adjudication are to be considered procedural costs and may not be the subject of a separate claim for recovery of damages.

6.5.5 Representation of Natural and Legal Persons

Civil procedure in Latvia permits that the participants in a case—the plaintiff, the defendant, third parties with independent claims and third parties without independent claims—attend the adjudication in person or through an authorised representative. Any natural person, of legal age and with the capacity to act, may be an authorised representative in the civil procedure, provided that his or her right to represent another person has not been revoked by a court judgment. The CPL does not directly require that the representative be a lawyer. Representation by a sworn attorney is also currently not stipulated as compulsory when hearing a case in substance at the first instance or appellate court; however, at the cassation court, a person may only be represented by a sworn attorney. However, in some categories of cases, representation by a sworn attorney tends to be requested as compulsory. However, work on this concept is ongoing, and relevant amendments to the CPL are expected in the future. A natural person may represent another natural person in court only based upon an authorisation certified by a notary; however, Article 85 (1) of the CPL permits that authorisation of a representative may be expressed by way of an oral submission in court by the person to be represented and shall be recorded in the minutes of the court sitting. In both of the above-mentioned situations, the participant in the matter relinquishes to their authorised representative the right to act on their behalf and fully represent the participant in all procedural actions. Only a sworn attorney has the right to provide legal assistance during the hearing of a matter in parallel to the participant themselves taking active part in the proceedings, providing explanations about crucial conditions surrounding the matter and exercising other rights afforded to the participants in the matter. Legal persons are represented at court by their officials, who act within their authorisation as stipulated by law, statutes or regulations, or other representatives authorised by the legal person. Representation of legal persons shall be formalised with a written authorisation or documents attesting to the right of an official to represent the legal person without special authorisation. The members of the board of a legal person are considered to be such officials. Article 34(1) of the Commercial Law stipulates that the procuration holder has the right to implement all procedural activities within court proceedings. A special authorisation is necessary for the representative to fully or partially withdraw an action, change the subject matter of an action, raise a counterclaim, fully or partially admit a claim, enter into a settlement, transfer a matter to an arbitration court, appeal court adjudications in accordance with appellate or cassation procedure, submit execution documents for recovery, receive property or money adjudged and terminate execution proceedings. If the matter of a natural person is directed through the intermediation of an authorised representative, court notifications and documents shall be sent only to the representative.

6.5.6 Evidence and Providing Evidence

Article 92 of the CPL stipulates that evidence is information on the basis of which a court determines the existence or non-existence of such facts that are significant in the adjudicating of the matter. Evidence in a matter is submitted by the parties and other participants in the matter, but this information can be recognised as evidence only by the court, having heard the opinions of all of the participants in the matter. As regards the admissibility of kinds of evidence, the CPL of Latvia allows for the use of all of the kinds of evidence that are stipulated within the CPL, unless a particular kind of evidence is explicitly required. The evidence that is necessary is usually derived from substantive law. For example, sale of immovable property cannot be proved with witness testimony because Article 1483 of the Civil Law[201] requires a written form of transaction with the transaction being entered into land registers, while Article 1477 of the Civil Law stipulates that corroboration shall be required in those cases when the transaction grants property rights to immovable property.

There are strict requirements in place regarding providing evidence. When submitting the statement of the claim, the plaintiff shall also provide documents or indicate other evidence that substantiates the circumstances referred to in the claim statement. In turn, the defendant shall submit evidence to the court together with explanations and objections regarding the well foundedness of the circumstances indicated in the claim. Article 93 of the CPL states that each party shall prove the facts upon which they base their claims or objections. Plaintiffs shall prove that their claims are well founded. Defendants shall prove that their objections are well founded. The CPL of Latvia contains an obligation for all parties, third persons and representatives thereof to supply the court with only the truth regarding the facts and circumstances of a matter. Abuse of one's rights and

[201] Civil Law. http://www.vvc.gov.lv/export/sites/default/docs/LRTA/Likumi/The_Civil_Law.doc.

misleading the court is subject to procedural sanctions—a fine, which the court may levy immediately upon finding such a violation to have occurred. Honest actions on the part of the parties of the matter are constituted by providing the court with evidence in a timely manner, thus allowing the opposing party to examine the evidence prior to the court sitting. Therefore, Article 93 of the CPL stipulates that evidence shall be submitted to the court not later than 14 days before a court sitting. Evidence may be submitted during the court sitting only in exceptional cases; however, doing so may result in the sitting being postponed in order to allow the opposing party to exercise the principle of adversarial proceedings by submitting their own evidence and contestation. All evidence in a matter must be submitted to the court of first instance. Submission of new evidence to the appellate instance is possible only by exception—if a participant of the matter submits or requests examination of evidence that he or she could not submit while the matter was being heard in the first instance. In all other cases, when the submission of evidence has depended on the person's own will, the appellate instance does not accept new evidence. The CPL of Latvia allows the court to be involved in collection of evidence only in strictly regulated cases and in specific categories of matters:

1. in matters arising from trusteeship and access rights;
2. in matters regarding dissolution or annulment of a marriage, if a child's interests are at stake;
3. in matters regarding the unlawful movement of a child across the border to a foreign state or Latvia or detention in a foreign state or Latvia;
4. in matters regarding restricting the capacity to act of a person due to mental disorders or other health disorders.

During the exercise of the adversarial principle, the court may not interfere in the collecting of evidence as carried out by the parties, but the court has the right to control the sufficiency of evidence and indicate to the parties that evidence has not been submitted for particular facts. However, the choice of means of evidence will always be the right of the participant, and the court may not interfere in the exercise of the adversarial principle by pointing to the particular means of proof as to how the evidence should be presented.[202]

6.5.7 Specifics of Evidentiary Means

All permitted evidentiary means are listed within the CPL, allowing the participants in a matter to choose, within adherence to the adversarial principle, the means by which to defend their interests in court. Article 104(1) of the CPL stipulates explanations by parties and third persons as an evidentiary means. However, information (both written and verbal) submitted by the parties and third persons

[202]Rozenfelds et al. (2015), p. 7.

shall be admitted as evidence only if corroborated by other evidence verified and assessed at a court sitting. Therefore, it is important that the court distinguish which explanations supplied by parties and third persons are to be considered as relevant to the matter and which are to be admitted as evidence. Article 93(4) of the CPL states that if the court admits that, in respect of any of the facts on which the claims or objectives of the party are based, no evidence is submitted, it shall notify the parties thereof and, if necessary, set a time period within which evidence is to be submitted. Witness testimony may be used as evidence only in oral procedure. The court may summon as a witness only persons who have direct knowledge of facts related to the matter. The CPL of Latvia does not permit second-hand (hearsay) testimony or written testimony. Witnesses are examined at a court sitting. By exception, in order to secure evidence, it is possible to examine a witness outside a court sitting by documenting his or her testimony in the minutes of a meeting, which are read before the court at a court sitting. Such an exception may be made if the witness is seriously ill or if there are other objective reasons that cause the court to believe that at a later time it will not be able to obtain the witness's testimony at all. In the interests of procedural economy, a witness may be questioned in a video conference at the court nearest to the place of residence of the witness. Documentary evidence is information regarding facts relevant to the matter that are recorded by letters, figures or other written symbols or use of technical means in documents, in other written or printed manner or in other recording media, including audio and video recordings, photographs and electronically recorded data. The requirements regarding the preparation and formatting of electronic documents are contained in the Electronic Documents Law. Audio or video recordings or photographs shall be made only in accordance with the Personal Data Protection Law. Documentary evidence shall be submitted by way of original or true copy, copy or extract certified in accordance with the specified procedures. The requirements for certifying true copies, copies and extracts are contained in the Law on Legal Force of Documents. In assessing copies of documents, the court has the right to request that the original documents be presented for comparison. Due to its specifics, physical (real) evidence is rather rare in civil matters. Real evidence consists of tangible things that may, due to their properties, characteristics or very existence, be useful in clarifying facts, which are significant in a matter. In some cases, the inspection and examination of real evidence may be performed at the location where the evidence is kept; the examination is then performed by a sworn bailiff who officially registers this action. A court shall order expert examination in a matter, pursuant to the request of a party, where clarification of facts relevant to the matter requires specific knowledge in science, technology, art or another field. The Law on Forensic Experts regulates the professional activity of forensic experts, stipulating that there are state forensic experts and private forensic experts who perform examinations professionally and pursuant to their competence. Certified forensic experts are listed on the Register of Forensic Experts. Parties in a matter shall choose only forensic experts listed on the Register of Forensic Experts. Expert opinions submitted to the court by a party in the matter, and if there has not been a previous court decision regarding the expert examination, are examined and assessed as documentary evidence.

6.5.8 Types of Court Proceedings and the Specifics Thereof

Similar to its neighbouring countries, Latvia makes use of three types of legal proceedings: legal proceedings by way of action, special adjudication procedure and performance of obligations through the court. In line with the necessity of improving the types of legal proceedings, the CPL is being amended to introduce written procedure in certain categories of matters, and the opportunities to make use of procedural protection measures are being improved, e.g., securing claims in disputes of a financial nature or interim injunctions in certain categories of matters pertaining to protection of intellectual copyrights, invalidation of decisions taken at shareholders' meetings of commercial companies, in matters pertaining to provisional protection against violence and revocation of creditors' rights to vote in insolvency matters. In certain categories of matters pertaining to the interests of a child, the court has the right to issue provisional orders of a specific nature; for example, in matters determining parentage of a child, the court may issue an order prohibiting moving the child out of the country until a judgment is made regarding the parentage of the child. The measure of securing the claim in matters of a financial nature is imposed as an exception—only in cases when the potential plaintiff or the plaintiff submits a reasoned application and evidence that the execution of the court judgment in the matter may become problematic or impossible. Such an application may be submitted to the court prior to the submission of a claim, as well as at any time during the legal proceedings until the judgment takes effect. The court is obliged to decide on the request for securing a claim on the next day following the receipt of such an application. In deciding on the need for securing the claim and imposing upon the defendant's property one of the means of securing claims listed in Article 138 of the CPL, the court takes into account the *prima facie* formal legal argumentation and proportionality among the legal interests of all parties. The defendant has the right to submit to the court a reasoned application on revoking the securing of the claim, indicating losses that have arisen due to the securing of the claim being in place or that may arise if the securing of the claim is not revoked. Retaining the securing of the claim in place, the court has the right to have the plaintiff transfer into the account of a sworn bailiff an amount equal to the losses potentially incurred by the defendant, which may not exceed the amount of the claim itself. In rendering the judgment by which the action brought is refused, the court may concurrently decide on compensation of losses to the defendant from the amount paid into the bailiff's account. When applying to the court with a monetary claim, a person has the right to choose the procedure in which to protect these rights and interests. The possible choices are limited by the existing prerequisites. For example, if the person has at their disposal all evidence pertaining to the payment obligation and the amount claimed does not exceed 15,000 EUR, and if the registered place of residence or the legal address of the debtor is in the Republic of Latvia, an application on recovery of payment may be submitted for compulsory execution of obligations in accordance with the warning procedures, in which it is possible to obtain an unappealable court decision that is simultaneously also an enforcement document. In such matters, the application shall be examined in a written procedure with the applicant submitting a certain form. A matter falls under the jurisdiction of the land register of the district (city) court covering the territory where the debtor's registered place of residence or legal address is located. In this category of matters, a crucial requirement is the obligation of the plaintiff and debtor to include in their procedural documents (the plaintiff's claim and the debtor's answer) a written confirmation that the relevant party has submitted only true facts to the court and that the party or its representative, if the answer is being submitted by the representative, is informed that providing false answers carries criminal liability (stipulated in the Criminal Law). In turn, in choosing to apply to the court for legal proceedings by way of action, the person must assess whether the principal debt is up to 2100 EUR, as such monetary claims are examined as small claims in a written procedure, and only by exception and based on a reasoned request from a party may the court decide to examine the matter in an oral procedure. For a small claim procedure, a form of a specific template must also be submitted. The court judgment may be appealed in the procedure set out regarding small claims, and the appellate court is the final instance of appeal. Claims where the principal debt exceeds 2100 EUR, as well as claims where protection of a person's violated rights or interests is sought, are examined in an oral procedure. Judgments in matters examined in such a procedure may be appealed, and the judgment of the appellate court may be appealed again in cassation court. The categories of matters to be examined in the special adjudication procedure are exhaustively listed in Article 251 of the CPL. The special adjudication procedure always entails an oral procedure, and the court's judgment may be appealed in appellate court, and, in turn, the judgment thereof may be appealed once more in cassation court. An exception to the rule are adjudications in insolvency matters of natural and legal persons, as well as in legal protection proceedings, which may be appealed in appellate court in the case of a negative adjudication. A judgment recognising a strike or application to strike as unlawful and a judgment recognising a lock-out or an application to lock-out as unlawful may not be appealed.

6.5.9 Appeal of Court Judgments and Decisions

The procedural rules regarding the Appeal of Court Decisions and Judgments are separately provided in Part C of the CPL. Part C regulates the appeal of decisions of first instance and appellate courts, appeal of judgments of first instance courts, cassation procedure and re-adjudication matters regarding which a judgment or a decision has entered into lawful effect.

Appeal of court decisions is a procedural guarantee to ensure control of legality and justice of the first instance and appellate court decisions[203] by the submission of

[203]Torgāns (2012), p. 731.

an ancillary complaint or ancillary protest by a public prosecutor. These rights can be exercised only

1. in cases directly provided by the CPL,
2. if the court decision hinders the court proceeding.

The criteria 'hinders the court proceeding' urges the court to use the method of further development of the law by advisedly specifying it.[204] Case law applies this criteria to those court decisions that could irreparably terminate the whole court proceeding.[205] As a separate appellate procedure (Chapter 55), appeal of court decisions is intended for the settlement of the issues that are related to substantive or procedural norms of law due to the claim in the case.[206] An ancillary complaint and its true copies corresponding to the number of participants in the matter may be submitted within 10 or 15 days (Section 448) to the court that made the decision and must be addressed to the court that will adjudicate it. The court, when adjudicating an ancillary complaint by written procedure, has the competence to

1. dismiss the complaint by leaving the decision unamended,
2. set aside the decision in full or in part by referring the matter for re-adjudication or deciding the issue on the merits by its own decision,
3. amend the decision.

Appellate proceedings guarantee the right of the participants and public prosecutor in the case to submit an appellate complaint or an appellate protest regarding the judgment (supplementary judgment) of a first instance court. This proceeding is mainly characterised by adjudicating

1. a case on the merits,
2. a case to the extent it is petitioned for in appellate or appellate cross-complaints,
3. only according to the participants' initiative,
4. the same claims adjudicated in the first instance,
5. collegially by a panel comprising three regional court judges,[207]
6. according to the general provisions for trial of civil claims in the court of first instance with some exceptions directly provided by the law.

[204] Pleps (2005).

[205] Decision of the Department of Civil cases of the Senate of the Supreme Court No SPC –28 on 27 January 2010, http://at.gov.lv/en/court-proceedings-in-the-supreme-court/archive-of-case-law-decisions/senate/chronological-order/2010/.

[206] Torgāns (2012), p. 731.

[207] On Judicial Power. http://www.vvc.gov.lv/export/sites/default/docs/LRTA/Likumi/Judicial_Power.pdf (Art. 38.).

It should be mentioned that, by way of exception, some judgments of a first instance court are final and may not be appealed (e.g., a judgment regarding the liquidation of a credit institution, Section 377(1)). All other judgments may be appealed by submitting an appellate complaint (protest) within a period of 20 days. The law provides specific requirements for the contents and limits of an appellate complaint (protest). An appellate complaint (protest) generally contains similar elements to most other procedural documents; nevertheless, it should include references identifying the appealed judgment and the extent to which it is being appealed. An essential element is motivation on failures on the part of the court of first instance regarding the application of legal norms, fact finding and examination of evidence. Procedural provisions (Section 418(1)) set out limits regarding appellate complaints (protest) that restrict amending the action by including new claims or claims with an increased amount, different bases or a different subject matter. These limits are not violated if there are changes made directly specified by the CPL (e.g., correction of obvious errors, Section 418(2)). In Latvian civil procedure, the particularities of appellate proceedings, when compared with the general rules, are evident in the differing regulation of examination and submission of evidence. The court has been granted the authority to decide which evidence is to be examined at a court sitting (Section 430(1)). The legislator has set restrictions for the submission or request for examination of evidence in the appellate instance by providing the criteria of 'justifying reasons' for not submitting the evidence to the first instance court if there was such an opportunity. The participant is obliged to contest facts as there is no requirement for the appellate instance court to *ex officio* examine the facts that have been established by the first instance court. The CPL provides some particularities in appellate proceedings regarding certain categories of cases (e.g., cases of claims for a small amount, cases of disputes dealt with in the Board of Appeal of the Patent Office). Namely, in the cases mentioned above, an appellate complaint (protest) can be submitted if a court of first instance

1. has incorrectly applied the norm of substantive or procedural law, and this has led to an erroneous examination of the case;
2. has incorrectly assessed evidence, determined the facts or incorrectly legally assessed them, and this has led to an erroneous examination of the case.

These cases are essentially examined by written procedure, but at the discretion of the court—by court hearing. Judgments are final (Section 440^{12}). It should be noted that appellate proceeding generally means (*see above*) adjudicating a case on the merits, and this is the duty of the appellate instance court (Section 426(3)). Taking into account this duty, there are significant exceptions where the judgment of a first instance court shall be revoked by an appellate instance court's decision, and the case shall be sent to be re-examined in the first instance court.

The CPL (Section 427) provides that the appellate instance court, irrespective of the grounds for the notice of appeal, decides if it will determine that there has been a violation of procedural law regarding

1. the case examination by a lawfully constituted court,
2. the court's obligation to notify participants in the case of the time and place of the court hearing,
3. the language of the court proceedings,
4. the necessity of minutes or a full judgment,
5. the obligation that a court judgment confers rights or imposes obligations only upon the participants in a case but not upon a person who has not been summoned to the case as a participant.

6.5.10 Cassation Procedure

Cassation procedure is provided to secure uniform application of material and procedural law, and that is why this procedure is not provided for adjudicating on the merits of the case but examines only *quaestiones iuris*. The CPL grants the participants in the case the right to submit a cassation complaint within 30 days from the day a judgment of an appellate instance is declared. The legal basis of submitting a cassation complaint (protest) is incorrect application of norms of substantive law (Section 451) and breach of norms of procedural law (Section 452) by an appellate instance court. The contents of a cassation complaint are generally similar to all other complaints, but the CPL provides some specific elements (e.g., a petition for the Senate assignments hearing to refer examination in accordance with cassation procedures; an essential element is motivation on failures on the part of an appellate court regarding the application of legal norms). A cassation complaint shall be submitted to the court that gave the judgment, addressed to the Civil Law Department of the Supreme Court. The CPL obliges the payment of a security deposit in the amount of 300,000 euros. The law also grants the right to submit a cross-complaint or to join in a cassation complaint. A significant peculiarity of the cassation procedure is the assignments hearing. This hearing is obliged to refuse initiating a cassation court proceeding if it determines that the cassation complaint meets the CPL but

1. there is absence of doubt regarding the legality of the judgment,
2. examination of the case has no meaning in establishing of case law,
3. judgment of an appellate instance complies with the case law established by the Supreme Court.[208]

This decision is final. The CPL generally provides for the examination of a case in the Supreme Court by written procedure and grants the rights to

[208]Judgment of the Constitutional Court in case No 2013-02-01 on 29 October 2012. http://www.satv.tiesa.gov.lv/wp-content/uploads/2013/01/2013-02-01_Spriedums_ENG.pdf.

1. leave the decision unamended,
2. to revoke the whole judgment or a part thereof and transfer the case for re-examination to an appellate or first instance court,
3. amend the judgment regarding the extent of the claim, if it has been determined incorrectly.[209]

The CPL also provides specific rules for re-adjudication matters regarding which a judgment or a decision has entered into lawful effect.[210]

References

Balodis K (2003) Proposed regulation of commercial transactions in the commercial law of Latvia. Humanities and social sciences Latvia. current topics in Latvian law. University of Latvia, Riga

Balodis K (2005) Contractual aspects of formation and composition of commercial partnerships. Juridica Int, 10

Balodis K (2013) The Latvian law of obligations: the current situation and perspectives. Juridica Int, 1

Brizgo M, Slaidins RL, Burke JJA (2011) Latvia. In: van Gerven D (gen.ed) Cross-border mergers in Europe, vol 2. Cambridge University Press, New York

Damane L. Notariālais akts kā mantisko un nemantisko tiesību garants (Notarial deeds as guarantee of tangible and intangible rights. Dissertation) Promocijas darbs. Riga: [b.i.], 2012. p 175. Available at: https://luis.lu.lv/pls/pub/luj.fprnt?l=1&fn=F-2050448075/Linda Damane 2012.pdf

Damane L., Zīle K (2009) Mantojuma tiesību problēmjautājumu aktualizācija (Current issues of inheritance law). Jurista Vārds 2(555):7–13. Available at: http://www.juristavards.lv/?menu=doc&id=186180

Davidovičs G (2012) Lietas par tiesību dzēšanu uzaicinājuma kārtībā (Summoning procedures regarding extinguishing of rights) In: Civilprocesa likuma komentāri. II Daļa (29.-60.1) nodaļa (Commentaries to the civil procedure law. Part II, Chapters (29.-60.1)) Sagatavojis autoru kolektīvs Prof. K. Torgāna zinātniskajā redakcijā. Tiesu Namu Aģentūra

Digest I (2007) Digest of European Tort Law. Vol. I: Essential Cases on Natural Causation. In: Winiger B, Koziol H, Koch BA, Zimmermann R (eds) Contributors Andersson H., .., Torgans K. et al., Springer, Wien, NewYork

Digest II (2011) Digest of European Tort Law. Vol. II: Essential Cases on Damage. In: Winiger B, Koziol H., Koch BA, Zimmermann (eds) Contributors Andersson H., .. Torgans K. et al., De Gruyter

Grūtups A, Kalniņš E, (2002) Civillikuma komentāri. Trešā daļa. Lietu tiesības. Īpašums. Otrais papildinātais izdevums (Commentaries to the Civil Law. Part III. Property Law. Ownership. Second supplemented edition). Rīga, Tiesu Namu Agentūra, 353 p

Grūtups A, Krastiņš E (1995) Īpašuma reforma Latvijā (Ownership reform in Latvia). Redaktors J. Mozulis. Rīga, Mans Īpašums, 368 p

Digest III (2016) Digest of European Tort Law. Vol. III: Misconduct. De Gruyter. (in print)

Kārkliņš J (2003) Perspectives of contract law modernisation in latvia within the context of European contract law. Humanities and Social Sciences. University of Latvia 3(40)

[209]Osis (2012), pp. 605–614. (p. 609).

[210]Judgment of the Constitutional Court in case No 2013-08-01 on 9 January 2014. http://www.satv.tiesa.gov.lv/wp-content/uploads/2013/04/2013-08-01_Spriedums_ENG.pdf.

Karklins J (2005) Force majeure – Excluding Liability for the Breach of Contract in Latvia and Europe. Juridiske emner ved Syddansk Universitet. Jurist – og Okonomforbundets Forlag
Karklins J (2006) main modernisation directions of the latvian contract law. Summary of a doctoral thesis for the acquisition of a Doctor's degree in Jurisprudence. Riga
Kārkliņš J (2012a) Development of the general Latvian contract law after the renewal of independence and future perspectives in the context of the European Commission's solutions for developing unified European contract law. Journal of the University of Latvia "Law". Riga, Nr. 3, 2012
Kārkliņš J (2012b) Transfer of capital shares to the third persons. In: International scientific conference "The Quality of Legal Acts and its Importance in Contemporary Legal Space" 4-5 October, 2012. University of Latvia Press, Riga
Köndgen J, Borges G (2005) Commercial law. In: Reimann M, Zekoll J (eds) Introduction to German law, 2nd ed. Kluwer Law International, The Hague
Konradi F, Walter A (1935) Civillikumi ar paskaidrojumiem. Otrā grāmata. Lietu tiesības (Civil Laws with Explanations. Second book. Property Law). Sastādījuši: Likuma teksts Prof. Dr. Iur A. Būmaņa, H. Ēlersa un J. Lauvas tulkojumā. Neoficiāls izdevums. Rīga, "Grāmatrūpnieks", 399 p
Kozolchyk B (1979) The commercialization of civil law and the civilization of commercial law. Louisiana Law Rev, vol 40
Krauze R, Gencs Z (1997) Latvijas Republikas Civillikuma komentāri. Mantojuma tiesības (382.– 840. p.). (Commentaries of the Civil Law of Latvia. Inheritance Law (Art.382. – 840.)) Mans īpašums, Riga, p 392
Krūmiņa I (2008) Vai neatraidāmais mantinieks ir mantinieks? (Is a forced heir an heir?) Jurista Vārds, 1 April 2008, Nr. 13(518):1.–7. Available at: http://www.juristavards.lv/doc/173088-vai-neatraidamais-mantinieks-brir-mantinieks/
Kubilis J. (2014) Atbildības par paaugstinātas bīstamības avota radītu kaitējumu problemātika un modernizācija (Problems and modernisation of liability for damage caused by ultra-hazardous activities). Tiesību efektīvas piemērošanas problemātika. Latvijas Universitātes 72. zinātniskās konferences rakstu krājums. LU Akadēmiskais apgāds, Rīga
Kubilis J (2016a) Rīcības prettiesiskums kā civiltiesiskās atbildības priekšnoteikums Latvijas deliktu tiesībās (Unlawful Conduct as a Prerequisite for Liability under Latvian Tort Law), pp 139–147.
Kubilis J (2016b) Civiltiesiskās atbildības par nemantisko kaitējumu miesas bojājumu gadījumā pilnveidošanas iespējas. (Possibilities of Improving the Civil Liability for Non-Pecuniary Harm in Personal Injury Cases.) Jurista Vārds 37:20–26
Lange V (1937) Neatraidāmi mantinieki pēc jaunā civīllikuma (Forced heirs under the new Civil Law). Riga: [b.i.], p 23
Lībiņa-Egner I (2013) Valsts pienākums paredzēt nacionālajos tiesību aktos tādu rīcībspējas ierobežošanas regulējumu, kas atbilst tās starptautiskajām saistībām cilvēktiesību jomā. (State's responsibility to establish legal capacity regulations that are in accordance with the international law). Published: Tiesību interpretācija un tiesību jaunrade – kā rast pareizo līdzsvaru. Latvijas Universitātes 71. zinātniskās konferences rakstu krājums. LU akadēmiskais apgāds, Riga, pp 24–29. Available at: http://www.lu.lv/fileadmin/user_upload/lu_portal/apgads/PDF/Juristu-konf-71_2013_.pdf
Lošmanis A (2002) The New Commercial Code of Latvia. In book: Tiesību transformācijas problēmas sakarā ar integrāciju Eiropas Savienībā/Problems of Transformation of Law in Connection with European Integration. LU Juridiskā fakultāte, Rīga
Mantrovs V (2010) Chapter on Latvia. European Insolvency Regulations. Application of the European Regulation on Insolvency Proceedings, Directors Prof. Ph.D. Emilio Beltrán, Prof. Ph.D. Rafael Sebastián. Thomson Reuters/Aranzadi
Mantrovs V (2012) Problem Questions of Insurance Contract Regulation in Latvia. In book: Tiesību transformācijas problēmas sakarā ar integrāciju Eiropas Savienībā/Problems of Transformation of Law in Connection with European Integration. LU Juridiskā fakultāte, Rīga

Osis M (2012) Quality of the Civil Procedure Law and Legislator's Work. The Quality of Legal Acts and its Importance in Contemporary Legal Space. University of Latvia Press, Riga, p 605–614. Available: http://www.lu.lv/fileadmin/user_upload/lu_portal/apgads/PDF/Book_LU-JF_konference-2012.pdf

Pleps J (2005) Kas kavē lietas virzību (What hinders the progress of the case in the court) Jurista Vārds. 40(395), 2013, Available: http://www.juristavards.lv/doc/119617-bkas-kave-lietas-virzibub/

Rozenfelds J (2008) Valdījuma teorijas (Possession Theories). Latvijas Universitātes Zinātniskie raksti. 740. sējums. Galv. redaktors prof. J.Lazdiņš. Latvijas Universitāte, Rīga, 19 p

Rozenfelds J (2011) Aktuālas lietu tiesību problēmas. Aktuālas tiesību realizācijas problēmas (Topical problems in property law. Topical problems for exercising rights). Latvijas Universitātes 69. konferences rakstu krājums. Redkolēgija prof. J.Rozenfelds, prof. K.Torgāns, prof. I.Čepāne, prof. S.Osipova, prof. R.Balodis, prof. V.Liholaja, doc. A.Kučs. Latvijas Universitātes Akadēmiskais apgāds, Rīga, 8 p

Rozenfelds J (2013a) Reform of the property law chapter of the Civil Law of Latvia: problems and solutions. Tiesību interpretācija un tiesību jaunrade – kā rast pareizo līdzsvaru: Latvijas Universitātes 71. zinātniskās konferences rakstu krājums, Rīga, LU Akadēmiskais apgāds

Rozenfelds J (2013b) Reform of the Property Law Chapter of the Civil Law of Latvia: Problems and Solutions. Latvijas Universitātes 71. zinātniskās konferences rakstu krājums „Tiesību interpretācija un tiesību jaunrade". Redkolēgija: prof. J.Rozenfelds, prof. I.Čepāne, prof. S. Osipova, prof. J.Lazdiņš, prof. R. Balodis, prof. V.Liholaja, prof. J.Bojārs, prof. Ā.Meikališa, prof. U.Krastiņš, asoc. prof. J.Kārkliņš, asoc. prof. J.Briede, asoc. prof. A.Kučs. LU Akadēmiskais apgāds, Rīga, 17 p

Rozenfelds J (2013c) Superficies solo cedit in the Latvian law. J Univ Latvia Law 5:17 p

Rozenfelds J (2014a) Reform of Land Registration in Latvia. Juridica International. Law Review 22/2014, 8 p

Rozenfelds J (2014b) Ownership claim. J Univ Latvia Law 6:17 p

Rozenfelds J (2014c) Legal Framework of Commercial Pledge in Latvia. Latvijas Universitātes 72. zinātniskās konferences rakstu krājums „Tiesību efektīva piemērošanas problemātika". Redkolēgija: prof. J.Rozenfelds, prof. I.Čepāne, prof. S.Osipova, prof. R. Balodis, prof. J. Briede, prof. V. Liholaja, prof. U.Krastiņš, prof. Ā.Meikališa, prof. J.Bojārs, asoc. prof. J. Kārkliņš, asoc. prof. A.Kučs. LU Akadēmiskais apgāds, Rīga, 11 p

Rozenfelds J, Ose D, Osis M (2015) Evidence in Civil Law – Latvia. Maribor: Institute for Local Self-Government and Public Procurement, (Lex localis) (Book series Law & society) http://books.lex-localis.press/evidenceincivillaw/latvias

Schwartz P (2008) Das Lettländische Zivilgesetzbuch vom 28. Januar 1937 *und seine Entstehungsgeschichte* (Development of the Latvian Civil Law since 28 January 1937). Shaker Verlag Aachen, 334 p

Torgāns K (ed) (2000) Latvijas Republikas Civillikuma komentāri, Saistību tiesības. (Commentary on Civil Law of the Republic of Latvia. Obligations Law), Rīga, Mans īpašums

Torgāns K (2003) The Concept of Fault in Latvian Contract Law Requires Adjustment: Humanities and Social Sciences Latvia. University of Latvia, No. 3

Torgāns K (2008) European Initiatives (PECL, DCFR) and Modernisation of Latvian Civil Law. Juridica International, No 14

Torgāns K (2012) Civilprocesa likuma komentāri II daļa (29. 0 60.[1]nodaļa) (Commentaries of the Civil Procedure Law. Part II (chapter 29. – 60.[1]). Riga:TNA, p 1031

Torgāns K (2013) Līgumu un deliktu tiesību problēmas (Problems of Contract and Tort Law). Tiesu namu agentūra, Rīga

Torgāns K (2014a) Saistību tiesības. Mācību grāmata (Obligations Law. Text book). Tiesu namu agentūra, Rīga

Torgāns K (2014b) Atbildības par morālo kaitējumu aktualitātes (Urgent issues of liability for moral damage) - Tiesību efektīvas piemērošanas problemātika. Latvijas Universitātes 72. zinātniskās konferences rakstu krājums. LU Akadēmiskais apgāds, Rīga

Torgāns K, Bushaw A. (2002) Some comparative aspects of contract law in civil and common law systems. Problems of Transformation of Law in Connection with European Integration: International conference. (Tiesību transformācijas problēmas sakarā ar integrāciju Eiropas Savienībā: starptautiskās konferences materiāli). Latvijas Universitātes Juridiskā fakultāte, Rīga

Torgāns K, Kārkliņš J (2015) Civiltiesiskās atbildības modeļi pēc vainojamības pazīmes (Models of civil liability in respect of fault). Jurista Vārds. No 35

Zīle K (2012) Adoptēto mantošanas tiesības (Rights of Adopted Children). Published: Inovāciju juridiskais nodrošinājums. Latvijas Universitātes 70. zinātniskās konferences rakstu krājums, Riga, LU akadēmiskais apgāds, pp 117–123. Available at: http://www.lu.lv/fileadmin/user_upload/lu_portal/apgads/PDF/Juristu-konf-70_2012_.pdf

Part III

Lithuanian Law

General Frameworks of Lithuanian Law

7

Tomas Berkmanas, Marius Jonaitis, Saulė Milčiuvienė, Birutė Pranevičienė, Stasys Šedbaras, Violeta Vasiliauskienė, and Evelina Žurauskaitė

Abstract

This section of the book is devoted to the presentation of a basic temporal (diachronic) and systematic (synchronic) overview of the legal system of Lithuania. Two dimensions are covered from the diachronic perspective. The first one is a retrospective or historical overview of the historical development of Lithuanian law from the medieval period, covering the monumental Statutes of the Grand Duchy of Lithuania, to the major law-related events of contemporary Lithuania. The second diachronic perspective is a prospective overview in which the perspectives of the future development of Lithuanian law in the major legal fields (such as constitutional, labor, civil, procedural, and so forth) are presented and analyzed.

The synchronic overview of Lithuanian law also proceeds in two dimensions. The first one is devoted to the presentation of the system of law "from inside" by surveying the basic aspects of the system of Lithuanian courts and some other institutions/officials (prosecutors, attorneys, notaries, and bailiffs) that play

T. Berkmanas (✉) • S. Milčiuvienė • E. Žurauskaitė
Faculty of Law, Vytautas Magnus University, Jonavos st. 66, LT-44138 Kaunas, Lithuania
e-mail: tomas.berkmanas@vdu.lt; saule.milciuviene@vdu.lt; evelina.zurauskaite@vdu.lt

M. Jonaitis
Faculty of Law, Vytautas Magnus University, Jonavos st. 66, LT-44138 Kaunas, Lithuania

Faculty of Law, Mykolas Romeris University, Ateities st. 20, LT-08303 Vilnius, Lithuania
e-mail: marius.jonaitis@kat.lt

B. Pranevičienė • V. Vasiliauskienė
Faculty of Public Security, Mykolas Romeris University, V. Putvinskio st. 70, LT-44211 Kaunas, Lithuania
e-mail: praneviciene@mruni.eu; v.vasiliauskiene@mruni.eu

S. Šedbaras
Lithuanian Parliament (Seimas), Gedimino av. 53, LT-01109 Vilnius, Lithuania
e-mail: Stasys.Sedbaras@lrs.lt

T. Kerikmäe et al. (eds.), *The Law of the Baltic States*,
DOI 10.1007/978-3-319-54478-6_7

important roles in the implementation of justice. The second one focuses more on the influences to the system "from outside," although with a hybrid angle. First, the Lithuanian legal system is positioned in the larger domains of international law and the law of the European Union. Subsequently, specific attention is paid to the insurance of state security through/by the system of law, where not only the dangers of an internal (focus to the system of internal affairs and police) but also those of an external (focus to the system of national defense) nature are covered.

7.1 The Historical Development

Marius Jonaitis
Faculty of Law, Vytautas Magnus University, Jonavos st. 66, LT-44138 Kaunas, Lithuania

Faculty of Law, Mykolas Romeris University, Ateities st. 20, LT-08303 Vilnius, Lithuania
e-mail: marius.jonaitis@kat.lt

Compared to the other Baltic states, Lithuania has a long history of statehood that reaches substantially further back than the declaration of nation states in the Baltic region at the beginning of the twentieth century. In the history of Lithuanian sovereignty and Lithuania's legal system, one important chapter is the legal traditions of the Grand Duchy of Lithuania—a multiethnic and multiconfessional state with a great diversity of languages, religions, and cultural heritage, which in the fifteenth century was the largest state in Europe, covering the territory of present-day Belarus, Latvia, Lithuania and including large portions of the former Kievan Rus' and other Slavic lands, Estonia, Poland, Russia, and Ukraine.[1] Another important part of history of Lithuania's statehood and legal tradition is the Polish–Lithuanian Commonwealth—a state created on the basis of the Lublin Union, which was signed on July 1, 1569.

The historical development of the Lithuanian state and legal system can be divided into several periods that account for the state's changing form. These periods are the early feudal monarchy, the estate representative monarchy, the oligarchy of the nobility, the springs of constitutional monarchy, the period after a series of partitions of the Polish–Lithuanian Commonwealth between the Austrian and Russian Empires and Prussia that eliminated the sovereign states of Poland and Lithuania from the world map for 123 years, until the reinstating of Lithuania's independence in 1918; the interwar period of the First Independent Republic of Lithuania (1918–1940); the occupation and annexation of Lithuania to the Soviet

[1]Bideleux (1998), p. 122.

Union (1940–1990); and the period succeeding the reestablishment of the State of Lithuania in 1990.

The epoch of the early feudal monarchy covers approximately the thirteenth and fourteenth centuries and is marked by the formation of a centralized state. The most notable characteristic of the Lithuanian centralized feudal monarchy was the powerful authority of the grand duke that included, *inter alia*, the powers of the diplomacy chief, warlord, and supreme judge. The oldest sources of medieval Lithuanian law were oral consuetudes that regulated the relationship between the feudalists and peasants and were based on the principle that the owner of land has power over the inhabitants of this land.

Medieval Lithuanian law acquired its written form, together with the privileges passed by the grand dukes. The oldest privilege comes from 1387. Privileges regulated relationships between the grand duke and the nobility. A good example of this legal regulation is the famous principle of personal inviolability—*Neminem captivabimus nisi iure victum*. This principle was first introduced by the Polish king Władysław Jagiełło in the acts of Jedlnia (1430) and Krakow (1433) but was swiftly transferred to Lithuanian law. The privilege granted to the nobles by the grand duke Žygimantas Kęstutaitis in 1434, in addition to other important issues regarding the rights of inheritance and transfer of possessions belonging to the nobility, contained this famous rule. It comprised one of the basic rights of the nobility, meaning that the king is not granted power to punish or imprison any member of the nobility without a viable court verdict, i.e., it was required that due process be observed. Likewise, it was the basis to release anyone who had been arrested unlawfully. This principle remained in power until the partitions of the Polish–Lithuanian Commonwealth (1772–1795) showed the penetration of Western law traditions into the medieval law of Lithuania: e.g., personal inviolability was also guaranteed in the *Magna Carta* signed by King John I of England in 1215 and in the Golden Bull of 1222 signed by King Andrew II of Hungary.

Another important source of medieval Lithuanian law is the Law Code of Casimir, promulgated in Vilnius on February 29, 1468, and remaining in effect until the first Lithuanian Statute (1529). Though the original text of the code has not been preserved, copies from the late fifteenth and sixteenth centuries are available. The law code was intended mainly to protect the rights of feudal ownership and consists of 25 articles regulating issues of court procedure, resolving land disputes, assessing responsibility for theft (17 articles of the code deal with issues of theft, including sequestration of dependent persons), and cases of recompensing damages. The code gave nobles the right to try cases of dependent persons. Meanwhile, land disputes arising between the nobility were tried by special invited judges. The greatest part of the Law Code of Casimir was a source of penal law stating, *inter alia*, that legal responsibility for a crime committed begins at the age of seven and that the offender is personally responsible for the crime committed, though the institution of complicity had also been foreseen. Applying penal responsibility and the penalty imposed on the offender depended on the value of the object of the crime and on whether the crime has been committed repeatedly.

The most important sources of medieval law were the Lithuanian Statutes. The First Statute of Lithuania was prepared in 1529 on the request of nobility and passed by their legislative institution, the Seimas. The Second Statute of Lithuania, which included expanded rights for noblemen, went into effect in 1566. The third edition of the Statute, in 1588, reflects an increasing dictatorship of the nobility in governing the state and the contracted powers of the monarch. The most important sources of the Statutes were the consuetudes, land privileges, and the elements of Roman law. As was common to ancient legal acts, the Lithuanian Statutes included legal regulation from different principal branches of law. For example, the First Statute, which consisted of 13 chapters, first of all dealt with the provisions of public law—the status of the grand duke and conscription of the nobility (provisions of the first and second chapters). However, it also introduced a catalogue of the fundamental rights and liberties of the noblemen and provisions regarding the issues of private law, such as women's inheritance rights, giving them in marriage, the feudalists' land ownership and other property relations, land mortgage, etc. The Statutes were also an important source of criminal law, including provisions regarding responsibility for the murder of noblemen and dependent persons, rape, injury, and theft. Additionally, there were provisions regulating court procedure matters. In the field of civil law, the Statutes basically dealt with land ownership and introduced institutes derived from Roman law such as mortgage of possession, servitudes, and the acquiring of property by prescription. In the field of inheritance law, inheritance according to a will and on the basis of law was known. Women's and men's rights to inherit on the basis of law were unequal. The right to inherit the father's fortune belonged to the son, while the daughter could claim just a quarter of the father's inheritance as the dowry, and only if the devisor had no sons could his daughters inherit their father's fortune in equal parts. A testament could be made in a written form in the presence of three witnesses or the magistrate. But a woman's right to make a will was rendered only in case they had no offspring. A testator had the right to change his will and to withdraw the inheritance right of his children in case they wasted the family's fortune, did not render help in the senescence, or committed acts of violence toward the devisor. In the field of obligations and contract law, the Statutes most widely regulated the making of sale, lease, soak, bailment, and loan contracts. That obligations should be pursued in person and solidary obligations did not yet exist. When regulating family and marriage matters, the Statutes introduced the principle of exogamy marriage and prohibited matrimonial relations between the relatives of the first row. The marriages and children born from this relationship were considered illegal and meant penalties of a real character for the spouses. As one of the basic principles of family and marriage law, the family law provisions of the Lithuanian Statutes also implemented the principle of monogamy marriage. A double marriage was punished severely—even receiving a death sentence. Civil litigation was based on betting that witnesses will bear witness to one's truth. The party who did not agree to bet would lose the case. Criminal policy was obviously estate orientated. Punishments imposed on the noblemen for committing crimes of the same kind were substantially softer than those imposed on the rest of society. The system of criminal punishments included the death sentence (approximately 10% of all punishments given in the Statutes), banishment, and monetary fine. The responsibility for hiding a person sentenced to death, as well as for profiting from a crime, was the same as for committing that particular crime.

In attempting to define the significance of the Lithuanian Statutes for the legal system, first of all it should be noted that these legal acts written in the Ruthenian language were the most notable trait of Lithuania's autonomy during the period of union with Poland and all through the period of the Polish–Lithuanian Commonwealth. Moreover, the Statutes not only belonged to Lithuania's culture and law, but they also had a considerable impact on the development of the other states' law. For example, the Statute from 1588 served as an example for editing the Russian Sobornoye Ulozheniye in 1649.

The provisions embodied in the Statutes comprise law(s) intended for the nobility—the privileged estate of society. It also covered the clergy, which in fact did not comprise a separate estate. The Statutes did not interfere in the regulation of Canon law. At the same time, the townspeople exercised a set of privileges called the Magdeburg law. Following the Christianization of Lithuania, the grand dukes of Lithuania, aiming to encourage the spread of crafts and trade in the cities and towns, rendered the towns self-ruled based on the law of Magdeburg city. In 1387, such rights were applied to the capital city of Vilnius, and in the fifteenth century they were subsequently given to the other important cities of the country: Trakai, Kaunas, Minsk, Polock, and others. Magdeburg rights came to Lithuania from Poland, where the implemented Law of Magdeburg was different from its original German form. In Lithuania, it was augmented by the legal consuetudes of the Lithuanian cities; thus, not every case corresponded to the principal sources of Magdeburg law—the *Sachsenspiegel* (The Saxon Mirror) and the provisions of Magdeburg city. The Statutes of Lithuania were considered the superior source of law in comparison with the Magdeburg law. Additionally, neither the Statutes of Lithuania nor the Magdeburg law was applied to non-Christian communities (*basurmen*), whose interrelations were regulated by their own legal systems and confirmed by the grand duke's privileges.

Prior to the second and third partitions of the Polish–Lithuanian Commonwealth, its legal history was decorated with one more prominent monument of legal culture: the Constitution of May 3, 1791, was adopted by the Great Sejm (parliament) of the Polish–Lithuanian Commonwealth. Though it remained in force for less than 19 months, it vividly reflected fundamental ideas of Enlightenment age such as Rousseau's social contract and Montesquieu's separation and balance of the three branches of governmental powers.

After the third partition of the Polish–Lithuanian Commonwealth, which meant the complete disappearance of the state from the world map, the Lithuanian territory situated on the right bank of the Nemunas river was incorporated into the Russian Empire, while the territory on the left bank was attributed to Prussia. The loss of statehood consequently meant the decadence of the legal system. In 1840, Russia abolished the legal effect of the Third Lithuanian Statute. The main system of law that came into effect after the abolishment of the Lithuanian Statutes was the Digest of Laws of the Russian Empire, passed in 1832. The Digest consisted of 15 volumes; in 1885, it was augmented by the new 16th volume. It was never a fully completed document but a continuous, permanently revised, and supplemented incorporation of law. Newly passed laws were incorporated into the Digest but at the same time as preserving the system of their arrangement. New editions of the Digest as a whole were published in 1842, 1857, and 1893. The Digest was considered in effect in the territory of Lithuania through the newest official editions of the Digest and covering all the 16 volumes and its continuations until August 1, 1914; July 19, 1914, was when the last prewar continuation of the Digest was published. Among the abovementioned 16 volumes of the Digest, the most important are the 10th volume, which incorporated civil laws; the 15th volume, which was dedicated to criminal law, and the 16th volume, formed in 1885, which regulated court procedure.

After the restoration of statehood in 1918, the development of a national law system began. During the interwar period of the so-called First Republic, Lithuania experienced an evolution in the field of constitutional regime. This is vividly reflected in the fact that during the interwar period, three provisional constitutions, from 1918, 1919, and 1920, and three permanent constitutions, from 1922, 1928, and 1938, were in effect. This evolution reflects the essential structural changes in the government order. The provisional constitution from 1918 declared the State Council to be the legislative body, while executive power belonged to the Presidium. The provisional constitution from 1920 declared the Constituent Assembly (Steigiamasis Seimas) to have legislative power and the President and ministers to be the executive bodies. The President was elected by the Seimas. This governmental structure did not change essentially in the permanent constitution from 1922. The Seimas retained legislative powers, and the executive functions belonged to the President, elected by Seimas for the period of 3 years, and the ministers. The consequences of the takeover of December 17, 1926, when a legally elected President was deposed and authoritarian rule was established, can be seen in the constitutions from 1928 and 1938 (octroyée constitution). The President's tenure was prolonged for 7 years. The octroyée constitution from 1938 proclaimed that the President is not responsible to anyone for the act of executing his powers.

Examining the development of law in the period of Lithuania's history just discussed, one should return once again to the law that was in effect before the First World War. The reception of law that was in effect in the territory of Lithuania before the First World War was confirmed at the constitutional level. Already Article 24 of the Provisional Fundamental Principles of the Constitution of the Lithuanian State from 1918 provided the provisional retention of the laws that were in effect before the war. The prewar laws could be retained upon three conditions: first, if they were in effect in the territory of Lithuania by August 1, 1914; second, if they did not contradict the provisions of the Constitution; third, if they were not replaced by national laws. Mindaugas Maksimaitis claims that the retention was the inevitable obligation of a young state in order to escape the chaos of really existing social relations.[2] However, such constitutional provisions meant legal particularism,

[2]Maksimaitis (2012).

especially in the field of civil law. For example, though in the major part of the state the system of Russian civil law was introduced already in 1840, in the left bank of the Nemunas river (so-called Užnemunė), which was incorporated into the Russian Empire just after the defeat of Napoleon as part of Warsaw Duchy, the French Civil Code from 1804 (Napoleon's Code) remained the main source of civil law.

The most extensive reception of Russian law took place in the field of justice, in particular criminal and civil laws, law of criminal and civil litigation, and notarial law. In the period between the two world wars, Lithuania inherited the dualistic system of separate trade law, including the augmented laws of trade and commercial litigation.

In spite of the reception of foreign law, especially Russian law, legislation of new national laws that gradually replaced alien laws took place. Eventually, alien laws gained the position of the subsidiary law. In 1936, the special commission for the replacement of Russian civil laws by the national Civil Code was constituted by the State Council. At the end of 1939, the work of preparing the most important national codes—the Civil Code and the Criminal Code—was gaining speed. In the summer of 1940, the parts of the new Civil Code dedicated to the general provisions of obligations law, and family and tutelage law, were finished. Unfortunately, this work was interrupted by the Soviet occupation.

After the first Soviet occupation of Lithuania, which took place in 1940–1941, the codes of the Russian Soviet Federal Socialist Republic were brought into effect beginning on December 1, 1940. The First Soviet Occupation was interrupted by the Nazi Germany occupational rule from 1941 to 1944, when German law had to be applied. In 1944, the Second Soviet occupation began, and it continued until 1990. As it was impossible to prepare the principle codes that would reflect the essentially different social and legal reality based on socialist postulates and state property, in the short term the Presidium of the Supreme Council of the Lithuanian Soviet Socialist Republic on November 30, 1940, proclaimed a decree regarding the provisional application of civil, criminal, and labor laws of the Russian Soviet Federal Socialist Republic in the territory of the Lithuanian Soviet Socialist Republic. After the 20th Assembly of the Soviet Union's Communist Party, trends of expanding rights of soviet republics (not excluding the occupied ones) strengthened. Such tendencies are reflected as well in the field of lawmaking. On February 11, 1957, the Supreme Council of the Soviet Union passed the law "Regarding soviet republics' judicial system, legislation, delegation of passing Civil, Criminal and Procedure Codes to the soviet republics." In this way, in 1961, the Criminal Code and the Code of Criminal Procedure of the Lithuanian Soviet Socialist Republic were confirmed. In 1964, the Civil Code (which became effective in 1965), consisting of eight chapters and establishing state, cooperative property, and the Code of Civil Procedure, was confirmed. In 1969, the Code of Family and Matrimony (which became effective in 1970) was confirmed. In 1972, the Code of Labour Laws (which became effective in 1973) was confirmed. Though making its own codifications in all of the principle branches of law, Lithuania was not completely autonomous but had to follow the so-called principles of law of the Soviet Union and soviet republics, which were defined in the fields of criminal, civil, labor, family, and court procedure laws. Such principles formed the background for creating the common system of law used throughout the entire Soviet Union.

Restoration of the Independent Lithuanian Republic on March 11, 1990, again meant profound changes in the system of law. Immediately after the restoration of independence, the Provisional Basic Law of the Republic was declared. One of the most important provisions of the abovementioned law was the statement that laws and other legal acts that do not contradict the Provisional Basic Law retain their legal effect. On October 25, 1992, a referendum of citizens confirmed the Constitution that is currently in power and defines the essential principles of state functioning and society life. On December 14, 1993, the Seimas confirmed Outlines of the Legal system's reform that defined the reform of the judicial system, which facilitated the foundation of regional courts and Court of Appeal, as well as the functioning local courts and Supreme Court, and declared the fundamental restructuring of property relations, making new systematic legal acts (codes) in the fields of civil, commercial, and family relations.

The new Civil Code was confirmed on July 18, 2000, and became effective on July 1, 2001. The field of regulation of the above-mentioned Code covers civil, family, and commercial relations, which means that the conception of private law's monism was followed when codifying this part of Lithuanian law. The structure of the Code that consists of general and special parts shows the traits of the pandectist system. The special part of the Code covers chapters of private law such as family, ownership, inheritance, and obligations law. Consequently, in 2002, the new Code of Civil Procedure based on the concept of social civil procedure, meaning the active role of the judge during the litigation and particular importance of the expedition of process, was confirmed and became effective on January 1, 2003.

In the field of criminal law, Lithuania has broken with the tradition of the reception of Soviet criminal law when in 2000 the new Criminal Code was confirmed and became effective on May 1, 2003, together with the new Code of Criminal Procedure. The new criminal law distinguished the two different categories of illegal activities, crimes and misdemeanors, according to their gravity and established the criminal liability of legal persons.

Since January 1, 2003, the new Labour Code, confirmed on July 4, 2002, replaced the former Code of Labour Laws inherited from Soviet law. The Code consists of three parts (general provisions, collective labor relations, and individual labor relations). On January 1, 2017, the new Labour Code came into power. After entering the European Union on May 1, 2004, processes of harmonizing national law with the Community law have continued.

Lithuania can be considered a country that has profound legal traditions reaching back to medieval law and including famous legal monuments from this period of its development such as the Lithuanian Statutes and the Constitution of May 3, 1791. Lithuania later experienced the forced influence of the law of occupying states, and it finally created its own contemporary national law system at the end of the twentieth century and the beginning of the twenty-first century, aimed at the comprehensive implementation of the rule of law conception.

7.2 The System of the Lithuanian Judiciary

Tomas Berkmanas
Faculty of Law, Vytautas Magnus University, Jonavos st. 66, LT-44138 Kaunas, Lithuania
e-mail: tomas.berkmanas@vdu.lt

7.2.1 The Courts and Their System

The courts of Lithuania constitute a branch of the Lithuanian government that plays a certain role therein as a part of the system of checks and balances. The court system of Lithuania is made of three types of courts: courts of general jurisdiction, specialized courts (i.e., administrative courts), and the Constitutional Court. The first and the third types of courts are regulated by the Constitution. Specialized courts are established by statutory law. The main legal documents regulating the activities of the courts, apart from the Constitution, are the Law on Courts[3] and the Law on the Constitutional Court[4].

7.2.1.1 Courts of General Jurisdiction

The Law on Courts of the Republic of Lithuania (hereafter in this subsection referred to as LC)[5] is the main legal document regulating the system of the courts of general jurisdiction in Lithuania as the Constitution (namely, Chapter IX) provides only the very general outline of the courts' system. There are the following types of courts of general jurisdiction in Lithuania: district courts, regional courts, the court of appeals, and the Supreme Court. Following this system and for the purposes of determining the court's jurisdiction, the territory of Lithuania is divided into court districts and regions; the latter is the larger unit, and the former is the smaller. The proceedings in these courts are held in Lithuanian as an official state language, although the persons who do not know the language are guaranteed the services of an interpreter. As a general rule, courts of general jurisdiction solve civil and criminal cases. As a matter of exception, they also may solve some specific types of cases such as those related to the enforcement of decisions and sentences or the cases of administrative offenses. The procedure in these courts is regulated in detail in the Codes of Civil and Criminal Procedure and, in exceptional cases, in some other legal acts (for example, related to the administrative offenses/violations).

---

[3]*Law on Courts of the Republic of Lithuania*. Official Gazette, 1994, No. 46-851. The subsection relies on the updated version of the law of March 1, 2016.

[4]*Law on the Constitutional Court of the Republic of Lithuania*. Official Gazette, 1993, No. 6-120. The subsection relies on the updated version of the law of September 1, 2015.

[5]*Law on Courts of the Republic of Lithuania*. Official Gazette, 1994, No. 46-851.

District Courts There are 49 district courts in Lithuania, distributed by the principle of proportionality in relation to territory and population, and found in major towns/regions of the country. They are the first instance courts in civil, criminal, and some other specific cases (e.g., the cases related to the enforcement of decisions and sentences, the cases of the administrative offenses/violations). District courts are the only courts of general jurisdiction that do not contain internal divisions. The judges of these courts, in cases provided by law, may also carry out the functions of a pretrial or an enforcement judge. As a matter of general rule, one judge adjudicates the case in these courts, but in special instances provided by law the case may be heard by a panel of three judges (LC, Art. 36, part 1).

Regional Courts There are five judicial regions and, correspondingly, five regional courts in Lithuania: in Vilnius, Kaunas, Klaipėda, Šiauliai, and Panevėžys. Regional courts are the first instance courts for the specific and typically significant civil, criminal, and other cases that are attributed to their jurisdiction by law—for example, when the sum of the claim exceeds 43,500 euros (except for family cases, labor cases, or the cases of the compensation of immaterial damages), cases of bankruptcy or reorganization of juridical persons, cases of felonies (with some exceptions), and so on. Regional courts are also the appellate instance courts to the decisions of the district courts made as the first instance and provided that the district is located in the corresponding region. Regional courts are composed of internal divisions of civil and criminal cases. As a matter of general rule, the panel of three judges from one division adjudicates the cases in regional courts, but in special instances provided by law the case may be heard by one judge or a combined panel of three judges from two divisions (LC, Art. 36, part 2).

Court of Appeals The Lithuanian court of appeals is the one court residing in Vilnius. This court is an appellate instance court to the decisions of the regional courts made as a first instance. This court also hears specific cases related to requests for recognition and enforcement in the Republic of Lithuania of the decisions of foreign courts, international courts, and arbitration tribunals. Lastly, this court may carry out some very specific functions assigned to its jurisdiction by law (LC, Art. 21). The court of appeals is composed of internal divisions of civil and criminal cases (LC, Art. 20, part 2). As a matter of general rule, a panel of three judges from one division adjudicates the cases in this court, but in special instances provided by law the case may be heard by a combined panel of three judges from two/both divisions (LC, Art. 36, part. 4).

The Supreme Court Lithuanian Supreme Court, same as court of appeals, is the one court having its seat in Vilnius. This court is the so-called instance of cassation (or cassation review) to the decisions, judgments, rulings, resolutions, and orders of the courts of general jurisdiction that have already come into force. In other words, this court reviews the decisions of the appellate courts (i.e., of both regional courts and the court of appeals) and during the review concentrates only on the so-called issues of law with the presumption that the issues of facts are already solved in lower instances. The cassation (second) appeal and review are possible only after the appellate procedure (or first appeal) has been fully exhausted. The rule that the procedure of cassation is possible only in relation to the judicial decisions that are already in force also presumes that the decisions of the appellate instance courts come into force immediately (or conversely, the decisions of the first instance courts come into force only after the period for appeal expires). This also means that the cassation (second) appeal, in contrast to the first appeal, does not suspend the enforcement procedures of the decision of the court of the lower instance.

The Supreme Court contains the internal divisions of civil and criminal cases (LC, Art. 22, part 2). The panel of three judges, an extended panel of seven judges, a plenary session of the Court or its division, or, in special cases provided by law, a combined panel or session, hear the cases in this Court (LC, Art. 36, part 5).

The important function of the Supreme Court is the development of the uniform courts' practice of the interpretation and application of legal acts (LC, Art. 23, part 2). This rule, at least for a certain period, meant that from all the courts of general jurisdiction, only the decisions of the Lithuanian Supreme Court had the power of *de jure* judicial precedent in the Lithuanian legal system. For this purpose, the Supreme Court published and still publishes the surveys of its practice (LC, Art. 27) and corresponding recommendations. However, after the ruling of the Constitutional Court of March 28, 2006,[6] which confirmed the vertical and horizontal binding force of the judicial decisions of all Lithuanian courts, the power of the *de jure* precedent now may be attributed to any judicial decision in Lithuania.

7.2.1.2 Specialized (Administrative) Courts

After it restored its independence in 1990, Lithuania reformed its judiciary system, and the introduction of specialized courts therein was one of the major changes. However, that was a gradual process, and there were no specialized courts in the country from 1990 to 1999. Then, in 1999, the Lithuanian Parliament (*Seimas*) established administrative courts by its law. This in itself means that these courts are not constitutional institutions. The Constitution only provides that Lithuanian Parliament *may* establish specialized courts, but there is no mentioning of any kind of these courts in the main legal act of the country. After their establishment in 1999, the system of administrative courts underwent serious structural changes in 2000, but from that time until the present it remains essentially unchanged. As with the courts of general jurisdiction, the Law on Courts of the Republic of Lithuania is the main legal document regulating the structural system of administrative courts.

There are two types of Lithuanian administrative courts: regional administrative courts and the Supreme Administrative Court. There are no internal divisions in administrative courts. As a very general rule related to their jurisdiction, all these

[6] *On the compliance of item 2 of paragraph 1 of article 62, paragraph 4 (wording of 11 July 1996) of article 69 of the Republic of Lithuania's Law on the Constitutional Court and paragraph 3 (wording of 24 January 2002) of article 11, paragraph 2 (wording of 24 January 2002) of article 96 of the Republic of Lithuania's Law on Courts with the Constitution of the Republic of Lithuania.* Ruling of the Constitutional Court of the Republic of Lithuania, 2006, No. 33/03.

courts have the power to adjudicate disputes that arise from administrative legal relations (LC, Art. 12, part 4). More specifically, the decisions or actions of various institutions or officials of the second branch of government (including the municipal institutions and officials) may be appealed to these courts, making them an important instance of administrative control and part of the system of checks and balances in the country. However, there are certain exceptions to the institutions that may be appealed to these courts, also meaning that they are not the only judicial institutions participating in administrative control. For example, as a matter of exception, the acts of the Government of Lithuania (as a collegial institution) and the President of the Republic, if they may be inconsistent with the parliamentary acts or the Constitution, should be appealed not to the administrative courts but to the Constitutional Court.

The Law on the Administrative Proceedings[7] (hereafter in this subsection referred to as LAP) is the main law regulating the competence and the procedure of Lithuanian administrative courts. One of the most important provisions regulating the discretion of these courts provides that, after receiving an appeal, an administrative court does not evaluate a certain administrative act from the perspective of its political or economic purposiveness but only determines whether the legal act has not been violated in a certain case, whether an administrative institution or official has not exceeded its competence (i.e., acted *ultra vires*) or whether a certain administrative act has not infringed upon the aims and tasks upon which the institution has been established or received its powers (LAP, Art. 3, part 2).

Regional Administrative Courts Just as with the regional courts of general jurisdiction, there are five regional administrative courts in Lithuania: in Vilnius, Kaunas, Klaipėda, Šiauliai, and Panevežys. They are the first instance courts for administrative cases assigned to their jurisdiction by laws (LC, Art. 29; the main law in this case is LAP). The regional administrative court in Vilnius is distinguished by its case load and, consequently, additional jurisdiction/competence (LAP, Art. 19), which is caused by the fact that most administrative institutions are based in Vilnius. As a matter of a general rule, the panel of three judges adjudicates the cases in regional administrative courts, but in special instances provided by law the case may be heard by one judge (LC, Art. 36, part 3).

The Supreme Administrative Court Same as with the Supreme Court of general jurisdiction, the Supreme Administrative Court is the one court with its seat in Vilnius. This Court is the first and final instance for administrative cases assigned to its jurisdiction by law, an appellate instance to the decisions of the regional administrative courts made as a first instance, and also the special instance for the cases related to the renewal of court proceedings of finished administrative cases (LC, Art. 31, part 1). Notably, there is no instance of cassation in the system of

[7] *Law on the Administrative Proceedings of the Republic of Lithuania.* Official Gazette, 1999, No. 13-308. The subsection relies on the updated version of the Law of December 3, 2015.

administrative courts, and this is regarded by some as its problem. In addition, just as the Supreme Court of general jurisdiction does, the Supreme Administrative Court develops the uniform courts' practice of the interpretation and application of legal acts (LC, Art. 31, part 2). For some period, this rule meant that the decisions of the Lithuanian Supreme Administrative Court had the power of *de jure* judicial precedent in the Lithuanian legal system. For this purpose, the Supreme Administrative Court published and still publishes the surveys of its practice (LC, Art. 32) and corresponding recommendations. However, as previously mentioned, after the ruling of the Constitutional Court of March 28, 2006,[8] the power of *de jure* precedent now may be attributed to any judicial decision in Lithuania. The cases in this Court are heard by a panel of three judges, an extended panel of five judges, or a plenary session of the Court.

7.2.1.3 The Constitutional Court

Lithuania follows the model of institutionally separated constitutional review, i.e., the role of a constitutional review is delegated not to the general courts or the Supreme Court but to a separate institution—the Constitutional Court. Chapter VIII of the Lithuanian Constitution (hereafter in this subsection referred to as C) is called "The Constitutional Court" and contains all the main principles of the organization of the Court. There is a separate Law on the Constitutional Court,[9] which provides a more detailed regulation of this institution. The Constitutional Court consists of nine justices, each appointed for a single 9-year term of office, after which he/she must resign from office. The Lithuanian Parliament (*Seimas*) appoints the justices of the Constitutional Court from the candidates, which are submitted by the President of the Republic (three candidates), President of the Parliament (three candidates), and the President of the Supreme Court (three candidates) (C, Art. 103, part 1).

The Constitutional Court has two competences. The main competence is to decide whether the laws and other acts of the Parliament are (not) in conflict with the Constitution and whether the acts of the President of the Republic and the Government are (not) in conflict with the Constitution or laws (C, Art. 102, part 1). A decision on these issues is called "the Ruling." The rulings of the Constitutional Court have the power of law, are final, and are not subject to appeal. It should be noted that this Court has only the power to make *a posteriori* control by reviewing the constitutionality of enacted legal acts. If the Constitutional Court decides that some legal act violates the Constitution, this act becomes inapplicable from the day of the official promulgation of the ruling (*ex nunc*) (C, Art. 107, part 1) without the latter's retroactive validity. Nevertheless, official institutions may be obliged to

[8] *On the compliance of item 2 of paragraph 1 of article 62, paragraph 4 (wording of 11 July 1996) of article 69 of the Republic of Lithuania's Law on the Constitutional Court and paragraph 3 (wording of 24 January 2002) of article 11, paragraph 2 (wording of 24 January 2002) of article 96 of the Republic of Lithuania's Law on Courts with the Constitution of the Republic of Lithuania.* Ruling of the Constitutional Court of the Republic of Lithuania, 2006, No. 33/03.

[9] *Law on the Constitutional Court of the Republic of Lithuania.* Official Gazette, 1993, No. 6-120.

compensate the damages caused to private persons by the application of the unconstitutional act before it was invalidated by the ruling of the Constitutional Court.

The second competence of the Constitutional Court is to issue "Conclusions" on some specific constitutionally important situations such as the violation of election laws, the state of the health of the President of the Republic, possible conflicts between international treaties and the Constitution, and the possible conflicts between the actions of the Members of Parliament or state officials against whom an impeachment case has been instituted and the Constitution (C, Art. 105, part 3). The Constitutional Court may also adopt a third type of legal act, called "Decisions," which solve individual questions preventing a case from being decided in essence or by some procedural questions.

Four types of petitioners have the right to file a petition to the Constitutional Court: (1) a group of at least 1/5 of Parliament members (related to the constitutionality/legality of the laws/acts of Parliament, Government, and President); (2) the Government (related to the constitutionality of the laws of Parliament); (3) the President (related to the legality of the acts of Government); and (4) the courts of general jurisdiction or specialized (administrative) courts (related to the constitutionality/legality of the laws/acts of Parliament, Government, and President) (C, Art. 106). As private persons have no right to file a petition directly to the Constitutional Court, they may defend their constitutional rights through other courts. In the case of a possible infringement of their constitutional rights, first they should apply to any court of general or specialized jurisdiction, and then this court, if it decides that the issue raised contains constitutionally relevant element, may apply to the Constitutional Court with the corresponding request to review the issue. This approach could be criticized by putting an additional burden on private persons to defend their constitutional rights and by holding important constitutional discretion in the hands of other courts. However, such procedure functions as a *de facto* filter of petitions to the Constitutional Court, which would be instituted anyway if a private petition would be allowed. Nevertheless, the discussion about whether it would be feasible (especially taking into account monetary arguments) to give private persons the direct right to constitutional petition is constant and ongoing in Lithuania.

Lastly, it should be noted that there are two distinct theoretical approaches to the Constitutional Court as a governmental institution. First, this Court may be regarded not as a regular court but as a specific judicial institution. This approach is based on the arguments of substance—that this institution has a considerable influence on the political process in the country by its function of constitutional review and not only by the so-called "negative legislation" as such (i.e., declaring legal acts void) but also by its frequently active jurisprudence, clearly stepping into the field of what may be called "positive legislation." Opponents of this approach base their position more on the procedural arguments—that this is an ordinary court because its procedure is similar to the one in any other court, especially taking into account its adversarial nature; it may also be stated that there is no "political significance" in what this Court does as it *only* makes the higher and not the lower law valid in the case of their contradiction.

7.2.1.4 Self-Governance and Administration of Courts

In addition to the regular procedures of appeal and cassation, the other modes by which courts control, supervise, and administer their activities are (1) self-governance and (2) the administration of courts.

Self-Governance of Courts The main bodies/institutions of the self-governance of courts are (1) the General Meeting of Judges, (2) the Judicial Council, and (3) the Judicial Court of Honour. The General Meeting of Judges is the highest body of the self-governance of courts and should be attended by all judges of the country (LC, Art. 116, part 2). An ordinary session of the meeting is held on the first Friday of March at least once every 2 years, but extraordinary sessions are also possible (LC, Art. 118, parts 1 and 2). The Judicial Council is an executive body of the self-governance of courts, composed of 23 members, including the chairmen of the Supreme Court, the court of appeals, and the Supreme Administrative Court, and some other judges elected to this body in accordance with specific rules and all having a 4-year term of office in this institution (LC, Art. 119, parts 1, 2, 3, and 4). The Judicial Court of Honour is composed of 10 members, two selected by the President of the Republic, two by the Speaker of the Parliament, and six by the Judicial Council; their term of office is the same as that of the Judicial Council—namely, 4 years (LC, Art. 122, part 2). Lastly, there is also another institution—the National Courts Administration—which is funded from the budget and which has the main function of assisting the institutions of the self-governance of courts in exercising their duties (LC, Art. 114, part 3).

Administration of Courts In this field, internal and external dimensions may be distinguished. At the internal level, each Lithuanian court has its internal structure/order by which it implements the process of its administration. In this regard, specific internal judicial officers have certain important functions. They are the chairman of the court, the deputy chairman of the court, and the chairman of a division of the court (except for the district courts, which do not contain divisions), who administer court activities (LC, Art. 103, part 1). The chairman of a court has the highest discretion and powers: he/she distributes the judges into the divisions, determines the specialization of a certain judge and what cases he/she should hear, approves the structure of the court (LC, Art. 103, part 2), and performs other important functions. At the external level, the hierarchically lower courts and their activities are supervised by the highest judicial officers of hierarchically higher courts: district courts are supervised by the chairman of the relevant regional court, the regional courts by the chairman of the court of appeals, the court of appeals by the chairman of the Supreme Court, and regional administrative courts by the chairman of the Supreme Administrative Court, and the activities of all courts are supervised by the Judicial council (LC, Art. 104, part 1).

7.2.2 Other Officials Relevant to the Judiciary

7.2.2.1 Attorneys

The Constitution of the Republic of Lithuania has no separate provision on attorneys and mentions them only in one place: "A person suspected of the commission of a crime and the accused shall be guaranteed, from the moment of their detention or first interrogation, the right to defence as well as the right to an advocate" (C, Art. 31, part 6). The Law on the Bar[10] (hereafter in this subsection referred to as LB) is the main legal act regulating attorney status and their activities. As to the matter of the self-governance of attorneys, the main institution there is the Lithuanian Bar Association. This Association is comprised of the following internal organs: the General Meeting of Attorneys, the Council of Attorneys, the Honorary Court of Attorneys, and the Commission of Revisions (LB, Art. 58).

Generally, attorneys in Lithuania are regarded neither as state servants nor as law enforcement officials but as special subjects of private, noncommercial professional activity (LB, Art. 4, part 3), who do not receive compensation/salary from the state. Their special status leads to special regulation of their activities. For example, attorneys have certain restrictions in relation to the promotion of their activities—e.g., it is allowed only inasmuch as it corresponds to the principles of the attorney activities (LB, Art. 42). Attorneys may practice their profession on an individual basis and without creating a legal person (LB, Arts. 26 and 27). In civil cases and in the criminal cases containing a civil claim (and if it does not infringe upon the principles of attorney activities), attorneys may agree on an amount of compensation by tying it to the outcome of the case (LB, Art. 50, part 2). Attorneys are also obliged to have insurance in excess of 290 euros against professional civil liability for damage caused by them to natural or legal persons in the carrying out their attorney functions (LB, Art. 20, part 1). Finally, there are various specific and education requirements for persons who wish to become attorneys (LB, Art. 7), but, notably, after Lithuania's accession to the European Union, the requirements for citizens of the Member States of the EU to start an attorney practice in Lithuania have been considerably lightened (especially see LB, Art. 2, part 3).

7.2.2.2 Prosecutors

The Constitution of the Republic of Lithuania has one article—Article 118—devoted to the prosecution service. There is also the Law on the Prosecution Service[11] (hereafter in this subsection referred to as LPO), which is the main legal act regulating the activities of prosecutors in Lithuania. In Article 118 of the Constitution, it is stated that a "pre-trial investigation shall be organised and

[10] *Law on the Bar the Republic of Lithuania*. Official Gazette, 2004, No. 50-1632. The subsection relies on the updated version of the law of January 18, 2016.

[11] *Law on the Prosecution Service of the Republic of Lithuania*. Official Gazette, 1994, No. 81-1514; new version: 2003, No. 42-1919. The subsection relies on the updated version of the law of June 1, 2015.

directed, and charges on behalf of the State in criminal cases shall be upheld, by prosecutors" and that "the prosecution service of the Republic of Lithuania shall be the office of the prosecutor general and territorial prosecutorial offices." Accordingly, apart from the office of the prosecutor general, there are five regional prosecutorial regions and offices in Lithuania: in Vilnius, Kaunas, Klaipėda, Šiauliai, and Panevežys. These are parallel to the aforementioned five judicial/court regions and regional courts. Also, each of the five regional prosecutorial offices are divided internally into district prosecutorial offices and specialized offices (LPO, Art. 6, part 2); before the reform in 2011, district prosecutorial offices were separate institutions (same as district courts), but today they are considered an intrinsic institutional part of regional prosecutorial offices. The prosecutor general is appointed and released by the President of the Republic upon the assent of the Parliament (C, Art. 118). The deputies of the prosecutor general are also appointed by the President of the Republic upon the nomination of the prosecutor general (LPO, Art. 22, part 2). Other prosecutors are appointed to their posts by order of the prosecutor general, who should take into account the recommendation of the special selection commission(s) (LPO, Art. 26). Finally, there are special requirements for the persons who aim to be admitted to the prosecutorial service—for example, the requirement of a certain length of legal practice, good reputation requirement, and language and education requirements (LPO, Art. 25).

7.2.2.3 Notaries and Bailiffs

The main legal document regulating the notarial service in Lithuania is the Law on the Notarial Service[12] (hereafter in this subsection referred to as LN). Lithuania implements the Latin model of notarial service. This means that notaries in Lithuania have more powers and carry more functions than under other models and often come close in their activities to what attorneys do. For example, they may advise their clients on how to solve one or another legal issue (although, of course, they do not have the right to represent their clients in court). In general, they have not only the power to confirm the authenticity of juridical facts, but they also have the general authority/power of a state (or in the name of a state) to prevent the making of illegal transactions or documents in civil legal relationships; also, beginning in 2016, they have been granted the right to be mediators in civil disputes (LN, Art. 2). Notaries, like attorneys, are obliged to be covered by compulsory insurance in excess of 290 euros against professional civil liability for damages caused to natural or legal persons while carrying out their professional functions (LN, Art. 6^2). Also like attorneys, notaries have certain restrictions to the promotion of their activities (LN, Art. 20^1). The main institution of the self-governance of notaries is the Chamber of Notaries, to which all notaries of the country belong (LN, Art. 8). Notaries also have their Court of Honour, in which they review cases of their professional misconduct (LN, Art. 10^1).

[12] *Law on the Notarial Service of the Republic of Lithuania*. Official Gazette, 1992, No. 28-810. The subsection relies on the updated version of the law of January 1, 2016.

The activities of bailiffs in Lithuania are regulated by the Law on Bailiffs[13] (hereafter in this subsection referred to as LBs). Bailiffs in Lithuania are the main persons/officials related to the enforcement of the court decisions, having the general authority/power of a state (or in the name of a state) "to perform the functions of enforcement of writs of execution, to make findings of fact, to serve proceedings and carry out any other functions provided by law" (LBs, Art. 2). The main institution of the self-governance of bailiffs is the Chamber of Bailiffs (LBs, art. 45). Just as the other institutions discussed above, bailiffs also have their Court of honour (LBs, art. 49).

7.3 State Security and Law

Birutė Pranevičienė and Violeta Vasiliauskienė
Faculty of Public Security, Mykolas Romeris University, V. Putvinskio st. 70, LT-44211 Kaunas, Lithuania
e-mail: praneviciene@mruni.eu; v.vasiliauskiene@mruni.eu

7.3.1 The Concept of State Security in Lithuania

State security[14] is associated with the so-called traditional concept of security, in which the main subject of security is considered to be the state. "Historically, security was understood in terms of threats to state sovereignty and territory."[15] The traditional theory of security is based on the idea that all members of society or individual interests are subordinate to the interest of the state. The main aim is to protect the state from the threat of military aggression and to ensure the territorial integrity of the state.[16]

The problem with the traditional theory lies in the fact that a secure state does not necessarily mean secure citizens. It is important to secure citizens from foreign military aggression, but this action is not a sufficient condition to guarantee the security of citizens. Furthermore, the state-oriented security conception results in actions of states augmenting their military capacities, and thus they increase their security at the expense of the security of other states. Therefore, OSCE started to formulate the conception of security in the following terms: to establish state

[13] *Law on Bailiffs of the Republic of Lithuania*. Official Gazette, 2002, No. 53-2042. The subsection relies on the updated version of the law of December 22, 2015.

[14] To describe security two terms will be used—state security and national security—as they have synonymous meaning in Lithuanian legal system. For example, in the Law on the Basics of National Security both terms are used simultaneously. *Law on the Basics of National Security of the Republic of Lithuania*. Official Gazette, 1997, No. 2-16.

[15] Thomas and Tow (2002), p. 177.

[16] Pranevičienė (2011), pp. 1614–1615.

commitments not to increase their security at the expense of the security of other states.[17]

Regarding the shortcomings of the abovementioned view of state security, another theory of security orients toward the person in the first place. Only then does it orient toward the security of the whole state, which provides some answers to the problems associated with the state-oriented security conception. The conception of "human security" is relatively new but gaining acceptance. It is used to outline complex interrelated threats to contemporary society and its members.[18]

The Law on the Basis of National Security of the Republic of Lithuania outlines the main objects of national security of Lithuania: "human and citizen's rights and freedoms as well as personal security; the values cherished by the nation, its rights and conditions for a free development; independence of the State; constitutional order; integrity of the territory of the State; environment and cultural heritage; public health."[19] The wide range of the objects of security implies that Lithuania has shifted from the traditional view of security and has chosen to look at security as not only the security of the territory of Lithuania from military threats but as encompassing many varied threats to various objects of security.

7.3.2 The System of National Security in Lithuania

7.3.2.1 The Historic Development and Present Powers

The history of Lithuanian national security begins with the restoration of independence proclaimed on March 11, 1990, by the High Council of the Lithuanian Republic, which was the highest lawmaking body in the state at that moment. The state started a difficult and costly process of separation from the Soviet Union. In these difficult times, two needs were greatest: to secure the territory and the physical security of the newly created state. "From the very beginning of the independence the prevailing understanding in the public discourse was that the statehood of Lithuania is under various and great dangers and therefore the highest aims of the Lithuanian state were the protection of sovereignty and territorial integrity of Lithuania."[20]

Immediately following independence, Lithuania began to form institutions to help ensure the inner safety of the state. On April 11, 1990, the first minister of the interior was appointed to office. On May 17, 1990, the Government passed a decision "Regarding the main functions of the ministries of Lithuanian Republic"[21]

---

[17] *Helsinki Final Act.* Conference on Security and Co-operation in Europe (1975). Resolution.

[18] Greičius and Pranevičienė (2010).

[19] *Law on the Basics of National Security of the Republic of Lithuania.* Official Gazette, 1997, No. 2-16. Section I.

[20] Paulauskas (2010), pp. 15–16.

[21] *The Decision of the Government of the Republic of Lithuania of the 17th of May, 2015, No. 154, Regarding the main functions of the Ministries of the Republic of Lithuania.* Official Gazette, 1990, No. 18-476.

and charged the Ministry of the Interior with the tasks of realizing the state policy on the fight against crime, security of public order, and social tranquility. The Ministry of the Interior was also entrusted with the tasks of enacting punishments in prisons and other places and handing out passports and other documents needed for traveling abroad. The Fire and Rescue Department was established under the Ministry of the Interior.

The Law on Police was enacted December 11, 1990, and the remaining departments of the interior affairs were reorganized into police commissariats. The police as an institution was entrusted with tasks in the fields of prevention, disclosure and investigation of crimes, and other infringements of law; protection of public order, social tranquility and safety, protection of Lithuanian citizens, their rights, freedoms, and their possessions; and also the protection of the environment. The functions of the police also included the supervision of traffic safety and the provision of immediate social help to the residents in Lithuania.

The Law on Police has been changed, and the present Law on Police Activity regulates the main task of the Lithuanian police, the principles and legal grounds of its activity, the main goals of police, its organizational structure, the basics of the police communication with residents of Lithuania, nongovernmental organizations and other institutions, the powers of police officers, their rights, duties and responsibility, as well as the conditions of legality of the use of force and the questions related to financing of police institutions.[22]

Besides the functions of the fight against crime and the assurance of public security, the government of the newly restored state had to ensure the safety of its state territory. For this purpose, the Government of the Lithuanian Republic established on April 25, 1990, the Department of National Defence. Its officers started to create the system of Lithuanian military and state defense.

One of the main tasks of the newly established department was the assurance of the economic protection of the state border. The state border service was formed under the auspices of the Department of National Defence and, after a few reorganizations, was reformed and became the State Border Guard Service under the Ministry of the Interior of the Republic of Lithuania.[23] It was entrusted with the following tasks, which have not changed to date:

- to ensure the inviolability of the state border and implement the policy of state border guarding;

[22]*The Law on the Police Activity of the Republic of Lithuania*. Official Gazette, 2000, No. 90-2777, Article 1.

[23]*The Decision of the Government of the Republic of Lithuania of the 22nd of February, 2001, No. 154, Regarding the Reorganisation of the Border Police Department under the Ministry of Interior of the Republic of Lithuania and the Authorisation of the Regulation of the State Border Service under the Ministry of Interior of the Republic of Lithuania*. Official Gazette, 2001, No. 18-556.

- within the scope of its competence, to implement international agreements, laws, and other legal acts of the Republic of Lithuania, establishing the legal regime of the protection of the state border;
- within the scope of its competence, to prevent, detect, and investigate criminal activities and other violations of law, protect human rights and freedoms, and ensure public peace and security.[24]

Regarding the Department of National Defence, it was reformed by the Decision of the Government No. 435 and was liquidated, and its functions were passed over to the newly created Ministry of National Defence.[25] The Lithuanian military regiments augmented in number at the end of 1992, and the High Council of the Lithuanian Republic declared on November 19, 1992, the recreation of the Lithuanian military forces.[26] The mission of the Ministry of National Defence is to form and implement the Defence Policy of the Republic of Lithuania by training an armed forces capable of ensuring independently or together with allies the sovereignty of Lithuania, its territorial integrity, and the security of the citizens of the Republic of Lithuania and at the same time contributing to global and regional stability. The main legal act regulating the activity of the Ministry is the Law on the Organisation of the National Defence System and Military Service, which lists the responsibilities of the Ministry of National Defence.[27]

The Lithuanian Constitution states that the main issues of national defense are considered and coordinated by the State Defence Council, which consists of the President of the Republic, the Prime Minister, the Speaker of the Seimas, the Minister of National Defence, and the Commander of the Armed Forces. The State Defence Council shall be headed by the President of the Republic.[28] The procedure for its formation and activities, as well as its powers, is established by the Law on State Defence Council. The law states that the main functions of the Council are to deliberate on foreign and inner policies that guarantee the national security and territorial integrity of the Republic of Lithuania, to discuss the main political directions of Lithuanian national security and defense policy, to deliberate on and provide recommendations regarding international treaties in the defense field, to control the activity of the state institutions acting in the field of national security, and other functions.[29]

---

[24]*Ibid.*, Para. 9.

[25]*The Decision of the Government of the Republic of Lithuania of the 19th of December, 1994, No.1272 Regarding the Regulations of the Ministry of National Defence of the Republic of Lithuania.* Official Gazette, 1994, No. 99-1979.

[26]*The Act on the Restoration of the Armed Forces of the Republic of Lithuania.* Official Gazette, 1992, No. 34-1030.

[27]*The Law on the Organisation of the National Defence System and War Service of the Republic of Lithuania.* Official Gazette, 1998, No. 49-1325, Article 9.

[28]*The Constitution of the Republic of Lithuania.* Official Gazette, 1992, No, 33-1014, Article 140.

[29]*The Law on the Council of State Defence of the Republic of Lithuania.* Official Gazette, 1997, No. 41-992, Article 4.

Furthermore, the government of the restored state also had to tackle questions related to state security such as the fight against terrorism, the interception of the security services of other states, and the defense of strategical national interests. On March 26, 1990, the Government of the Republic of Lithuania declared the activity of Soviet security services stopped, and they created the State Security Department under the Government of the Lithuanian Republic,[30] which was entrusted with the functions of state security such as the fight against terrorism; the investigation of acts that can damage state security, its economic and strategic interests; the prevention of dangerous activity in objects of energetics, the main communications and other objects having strategic importance to national security; secret service; counterintelligence; etc. The legal act regulating the activity of the State Security Department was the Statute of the State Security Department; now, its activities are governed by the Law on the Basics of National Security of Lithuania. The Department conducts intelligence and counterintelligence, takes measures to protect the economic basics of Lithuania, fights terrorism and corruption, organizes the technical protection of the state connections, organizes the protection of state secrets in Lithuania and in its institutions abroad, etc.[31]

Another field is the management of crisis situations, be they natural calamities or human-caused crises. Crisis management is defined in the Lithuanian Law on the Basics of National Security as being part of all measures of national security.[32] In the Basics of National Security of Lithuania enshrined by the same law, it is established that "the principal long-term national programmes for the strengthening of national security shall be: development of the system of crisis management."[33] The institutions and structures taking part in the crisis prevention and management process in Lithuania are the Crisis Management Committee, consisting of the main ministers associated with crisis management.[34] "Where necessary, the Crisis Management Committee shall, having regard to the nature of a crisis, take a decision on establishing the Joint Co-ordination Centre consisting of representatives of appropriate ministries and other state institutions for the co-ordination of crisis management and response."[35] Crisis prevention and preparedness for crisis management are coordinated by the Office of the Prime Minister.

[30]*The Decision of the Government of the Republic of Lithuania of the 24th of May, 1991, No. 209 Regarding the Regulations of the State Security Department under the Government of the Republic of Lithuania*. Official Gazette, 1991, No. 18-479.

[31]*Law on the Basics of National Security of the Republic of Lithuania*. Official Gazette, 1997, No. 2-16.

[32]*Ibid.*

[33]*Ibid.*, Chapter 11.

[34]*The Decision of the Government of the Republic of Lithuania of the 27th of November, 200,1 No. 1427 Regarding the Composition and Regulations of the Crisis Management Committee*. Official Gazette, 2001, No. 101-3605.

[35]*Law on the Basics of National Security of the Republic of Lithuania*. Official Gazette, 1997, No. 2-16, Chapter 14.

After the formulation of the main institutions enacting state policy in public security fields such as state border protection, control of illegal migration, the prevention and control of crimes and other infringements of law, the assurance of public order, management of emergency situations, the main guidelines of the development of those institutions were drawn up by the Ministry of the Interior in the form of the strategy of the development of the public security up to 2010.[36] This set out to ensure human rights and freedoms and the safety of the persons and their belongings. The strategy stressed that the traditional tasks of the police and other jurisdictional institutions—that is, to tackle crime and ensure public safety—could not be accomplished without the evaluation of economic, social, educational, and other factors. Therefore, it is important to implement prevention programs more intensively, to include other institutions not subordinate to the Ministry of the Interior in the process of assurance of public safety, and to develop the qualities of self-preservation in citizens.

Certainly, there are many other institutions that contribute to the protection of national security in the broad sense but whose main functions are related to other fields of activity. For example, the Financial Crime Investigation Service under the Ministry of the Interior of the Republic of Lithuania implements money laundering and terrorist financing prevention measures. This helps tackle the threats to national security that arise, but it also executes many other functions not directly related to the protection of national security.

7.3.2.2 The Lithuanian Membership in International Organizations Acting in the Defense Field

Despite the successful formulation of the abovementioned institutions necessary for the safe functioning of the state, it was clear that in the case of real aggression, it would be almost impossible to defend the state only by its own military capacities. Furthermore, Lithuania acting separately would not provide it with greater influence in global economic, environmental, and other processes. Therefore, from the first days of its independence, Lithuania sought integration in international organizations acting in the fields of defense, protection of the environment, the protection of cultural heritage, and similar organizations.

The prevailing view on state security is that one of the guarantees of the safety of a particular state is its membership in international organizations. There are states that ensure their safety by their own means and that create their security components by themselves.[37] But the geopolitical situation of Lithuania determines the need to join the international collective defense organizations and collective security structures.[38] Therefore, after the international community acknowledged

---

[36]*The Decree of the Minister of the Interior of the Republic of Lithuania of the 2nd of July, 2003, Regarding the Strategy of the Development of Public Security until* 2010. Official Gazette, 2003 No.113-5092.

[37]Vareikis (2005), p. 120.

[38]*Ibid.*

its restoration of independence in 1991, Lithuania joined many international organizations.[39]

As early as June 8, 1992, the restored High Council of Lithuania, seeing the Lithuanian Republic as an inseparable part of Europe and the international community, by a Constitutional Act[40] decided to develop mutually useful relations with every state but, having been in the USSR, never and by no means to join any political, military, economical, or other state unions or cooperations that are based on the former USSR and that no Russian or other Commonwealth of Independent States or their members' military bases and military regimen can be stationed on the territory of the Lithuanian Republic.

The Lithuanian Constitution, adopted on October 25, 1992, stated that "in implementing its foreign policy, the Republic of Lithuania shall follow the universally recognised principles and norms of international law, shall seek to ensure national security and independence, the welfare of its citizens, and their basic rights and freedoms, and shall contribute to the creation of the international order based on law and justice."[41] In accordance with these constitutional provisions, Lithuania aimed to join the ranks of the international community, joined the NATO Partnership for Peace Program, and consistently sought membership in NATO.[42]

Article 136 of the Lithuanian Constitution provides that "the Republic of Lithuania shall participate in international organisations provided that this is not in conflict with the interests and independence of the State."[43] NATO, the biggest specialized organization of collective defense and security and uniting states from both the North American continent as well as from Western, Southern, and Central Europe, was an organization that Lithuania greatly wished to join. On January 4, 1994, Lithuania sent a letter to NATO asking for acceptance into the organization of military defense and political security. After the completion by the Republic of Lithuania of many preparatory steps to accession on November 21, 2002, Lithuania, together with Bulgaria, Estonia, Latvia, Romania, Slovakia, and Slovenia, was invited to begin membership negotiations. On March 10, 2004, the Seimas of the Republic of Lithuania ratified the Washington treaty[44] and became a full member of

[39]United Nations—17 September 1991; Organization of Security and Cooperation in Europe—10 September 1991; Interpol—04 November 1991, World Customs Organization—18 June 1992, North Atlantic Cooperation Council—20 December 1991; Partnership for Peace Programme—27 January 1994; International atomic energy agency—18 November 1993.

[40]*The Constitutional Act of the Republic of Lithuania on the Non-Alignment of the Republic of Lithuania to Post-Soviet Eastern Unions*. Official Gazette, 1992, No. 18-513.

[41]*The Constitution of the Republic of Lithuania*. Official Gazette, 1992, No, 33-1014, Article 135.

[42]*The Declaration of the 25th of March, 1994 of the Presidents of the Baltic States Regarding the Coordination of Actions in Development of Relationship with the European Union, NATO, Other International Structures and Regarding the Stability in Europe*. Official Gazette, 1994, No. 26-418; *The Security Agreement of 13th of June, 1994 of the Republic of Lithuania and North Atlantic Treaty Organisation*. Official Gazette, 2001, No. 73-2574.

[43]*The Constitution of the Republic of Lithuania*. Official Gazette, 1992, No, 33-1014.

[44]*The Law on the Ratification of North Atlantic Treaty*. Official Gazette, 2004, No. 40-1292.

NATO on March 29, 2004. This step helped Lithuania to ensure a sufficient level of military and political safety and allowed Lithuania to be integrated more easily in other international organizations and unions in order to enhance economic welfare and the quality of life of Lithuanian residents.

7.3.3 Present Threats to the National Security of the Republic of Lithuania

As does every state, the Republic of Lithuania creates a Strategy on National Security, which foresees the interests of national security, the premises of security policy, the policy of national security, the means and methods of implementation of the strategy of national security, risk factors, and dangers and threats to national security. Whereas the threats and dangers to national security are very dynamic, and the factors influencing security number in the tens, starting with social and economic life and ending with the political situation in the state, the Republic of Lithuania, in the formulation of the strategy of national security, not only chose to follow the narrow, traditional view of security but also enriched this view with the concept of human security and seeks to ensure military, political, and economic safety.

Globalization conditions nonmilitary risk factors, dangers, and threats to the security of nations and to their identity, which cannot be tackled by unilateral actions. Globalization as a possibility for growth and prosperity also produces powerful forces of social fragmentation, creates critical vulnerabilities, and sows the seeds of violence and conflict.[45] Transnational occurrences such as terrorism, organized crime, smuggling, illegal sale of weapons, drugs, illegal migration, and the spreading of dangerous diseases overstep the boundaries of states and become risk factors for international security. The possibility that these threats and dangers will spread is increasing, and states can conquer them only by common action.

B. Buzan identifies several key sectors affecting national security: military, political, economic, social, and environmental. If there is a security risk in these sectors, state, society, and its members are affected to some extent. The content of the notion of national security depends to a large extent on the state's ability to retain its independence, identity, and functional integrity.[46] The threats may be organized into two conditional groups. "External" threats are threats that do not depend on the will of a person (e.g., natural calamities and others) or do not depend on the will of a particular state or community (e.g., nuclear conflicts between two or more states, military intervention by foreign forces, etc.) "Internal" threats are economic and criminogenic situations in the state, social security, the situation of ethnic minorities, etc.[47]

[45]Davis (2003), p. 5.

[46]Buzan (1997), p. 161.

[47]Matulionytė (2008), p. 94.

7.3.3.1 Military Threats

According to B. Buzan, military security implies the capability of a nation to defend itself and/or to deter military aggression. Conversely, military security also implies the capability of a nation to enforce its policy choices by use of military force.[48] After the events in Ukraine in which Russia occupied the peninsula of Crimea and is involved in the civil war in the east of Ukraine, Lithuania also came into the danger zone of military action by Russia. Part of Russian territory—Kaliningrad—lies right on the border of Lithuania. "Kaliningrad in many ways has become the Russian "Gibraltar" of the Baltic wedged between Poland and Lithuania as the size of Russian forces there are greater than the entire combined forces of all three Baltic States."[49]

In the face of such threats, Lithuania has reinstated compulsory military service for men ages 19 to 26. The Law on Military Conscription was changed in April 2015 and states that persons from 19 to 26 years of age are called to serve in the compulsory initial training. Their names are chosen by a computer program.[50] In September 2015, 3,010 soldiers started their compulsory initial military service; 2,133 came on as volunteers; and 877 were from the lists having declared their will to start the military service by priority order.[51] The soldiers serve for 9 months.

In addition, the political parties signed an agreement to increase the budget allocations for national defense to 2% by 2020.[52] In 2016, the assignations for the Ministry of National Defence comprised 1.48% of the GDP.[53]

Foreign Intelligence One should not forget the serious threat that stems from the activity of foreign states' intelligence directed against the Republic of Lithuania. This activity is carried out by using traditional and nontraditional methods and new technologies and is aimed at getting the information about our state by illegal means, carrying out destructive activities, and influencing military capacities, political processes, and other spheres of social and economic life. The stealing of secret information and its illegal revelation, loss, destruction, spoiling, gathering, purchase and sale, keeping or spreading would not only be dangerous to the security of the Republic of Lithuania and its allies but would also destroy trust in the Lithuanian state. As its primary task, the State Security Department has powers in intelligence and counterintelligence fields and takes action to counter foreign intelligence activity in Lithuania.

---

[48] Buzan (1997), pp. 52–53.

[49] Howard (2016).

[50] *The Law on the Military Conscription of the Republic of Lithuania*. Official Gazette, 1996, No. 106-2427, Articles 5 and 6.

[51] Zubrutė (2016).

[52] [No, author, named] (2015). Budget statement. Appropriations for National Defence 2015.

[53] *The Law on the Establishment of the Financial Indexes of the State Budget and Municipality Budgets for the Year 2016*. TAR, 2015-12-21, No. 20134.

Cyber Threats Cyber threats arise due to two related processes: (1) the rise of the powers of international actors due to innovations in information and computer-related technologies and (2) the rising dependence on information systems, which make states more vulnerable and create new vulnerabilities.[54] This can be illustrated by recent events in Lithuania. In April 2016, unknown persons attacked the webpage of Seimas by means of DDoS attacks and twice paralyzed the work of the Internet system of the Seimas. The prosecutors started pretrial procedure regarding these attacks. The institution countering the attacks was the National Cyber Security Centre under the Ministry of National Defence,[55] which was established by the Law on Cyber Security in 2015 in order to tackle cyber security questions, especially related to strategic and secret state information.

7.3.3.2 Political Threats

Political threats are threats against the political stability of the state institutions. They can appear as threats and as pressure on the state government to enact specific policy, as attempts to overthrow the government, and as attempts to disrupt the political system of a state to make it more vulnerable to military attacks.[56] The threats may be directly disruptive acts or may involve other factors that influence the stability of the political system of the state. Lithuania has relatively stable institutions, and its democratic processes function properly. However, there are some indications that the actors in the political processes are influenced and funded by foreign states.

Foreign Propaganda The threat of foreign propaganda as a threat to the national security of the state has risen in Lithuania. In 2015, the Radio and Television Commission of Lithuania stopped the retranslation of three Russian language channels due to the spread of information encouraging discord and war.[57] The Commission acted according to the Law on the Provision of Information to the Public, which states that information instigating war or hatred, sneer, or scorn or that instigates discrimination, violence, harsh treatment of a group of people or a person belonging to it on the basis of gender, sexual orientation, race, nationality, language, origins, social status, religion, beliefs, or standpoints, cannot be published in the media.[58] In this sense, the Radio and Television Commission of Lithuania helps to protect the national security of Lithuania. It is an independent institution accountable to the Seimas, which regulates and controls the activities of

[54]Jurgelevičiūtė (2004), pp. 83–84.

[55]*The Law on Cyber Security of the Republic of Lithuania*. TAR, 2014-12-23, No. 2014-20553. Article 10 states that "The functions of the Cyber Security Centre are carried out by an institution acting under the Ministry of National Defence."

[56]Buzan (1997), p. 164.

[57][No, author, named] (2016c). The Activity Report of the Radio and Television Commission of Lithuania.

[58]*The Law on the Provision of Information to the Public of the Republic of Lithuania*. Official Gazette, 1996, No. 71-1706; Official Gazette, 2006, No. 82-3254. Article 49.

radio and television broadcasters and rebroadcasters falling under the jurisdiction of the Republic of Lithuania.[59]

7.3.3.3 Economic and Social Threats

Social threats are different from military and political threats because they appear mostly inside the state. It is not clear when social threats become threats to national security.[60] The economic safety of the state can be defined as the ability of the state and its subjects to keep the balance of the objects and systems of economy, which are sufficient for the development of the state and its subjects.[61] According to B. Buzan, dependence on external suppliers for the provision of some strategic raw material may raise dangers to the economic security of the state and therefore the national security of the state as a whole.[62]

Energetics In the energy sector, Lithuania's excessive dependence on strategic materials and energy provision from one state, the concentration of foreign capital coming from an economy that does not ensure free market or where the free market is unstable, and which is in one or several sectors that are strategically important for national security, poses a danger not only to its economic welfare but also for state security. The danger is first at the level of prices for the energy sources; second, it threatens to possibly influence state politics. Therefore, Lithuania undertakes action to lessen its dependence on one source of energy—that is, from the energy it gets from Russia and Russian companies.

To gain such independence, Lithuania has signed contracts with Norwegian and South Korean companies to build a floating storage and regasification unit named Independence, which was delivered to the Lithuanian port of Klaipėda in March 2014. The vessel can store 170,000 m^3 (6,000,000 cu ft) of natural gas and can supply all of Lithuania's needs for natural gas. From December 3, 2014, Lithuania has been able to independently meet the demand for natural gas and is no longer dependent on a single external gas supplier.[63]

Another measure that is hoped will lessen dependence on a single source of energy from one state (especially after the closure of the Ignalina nuclear power plant as part of the accession plan to the European Union) is the NordBalt project, the main aim of which is to create an electrical junction from Sweden to Lithuania, which would allow for the creation of a common electricity market between the Baltic states and the Scandinavian states.[64]

Yet another possible solution is an increase in the use of renewable sources of energy. The use of renewable sources of energy is now considered seriously not

[59] *Ibid.*, Article 47.

[60] Matulionytė (2008), p. 95.

[61] *Ibid.*, p. 96.

[62] Buzan (1997), p. 169.

[63] [No, author, named], (2016b). LNG terminal.

[64] See: www.litgrid.lt.

only as an economic, social, or environmental question but also as a matter of state security.[65] The central aim of the national strategy on renewable sources of energy is to increase the part of renewable energy in the state energy balance and to satisfy the needs of the state in such sectors as electricity, transport, and heating.[66]

Migration Uncontrolled migration, illegal migration, and the increasing emigration of Lithuanian residents is another risk factor for national security. After accession to the European Union, one of Lithuania's main tasks is the control of migration. Uncontrolled migration caused by regional conflicts has already become a destabilizing factor across Europe.

Another problem with migration in Lithuania is the emigration rate of Lithuanian residents. Lithuania's emigration rate per thousand persons is one of the highest in the European Union. Since independence, nearly 870,000 people have left Lithuania. Such high emigration numbers pose many challenges to the Lithuanian state: e.g., the demographic structure of society changes, there is a work force shortage, many gifted, talented people are leaving and have left Lithuania.[67]

7.3.3.4 Environmental Threats

Environmental security deals with environmental issues that threaten the national security of a nation in any manner. Transnational environmental problems are problems that threaten a nation's security in the most broadly defined sense. These include global environmental problems such as climate change due to global warming, deforestation, loss of biodiversity, etc.[68] The environmental threats may cause damage to the physical base of the state on such a scale as to cause a serious threat to state institutions.[69]

A worrisome project in the field of environmental security is the project to build a nuclear power plant in Astrav, Belarus. The plant is being built very close to the border of Lithuania. Lithuanian institutions and the Lithuanian population do not have adequate information about it and have not received an account of the evaluation of the environmental impact of this nuclear plant. The location for the nuclear plant was chosen without consulting with Lithuania, without having considered alternative places, and possibly in conflict with IAEA regulations. In the event of an accident in the Astrav nuclear plant, the Lithuanian capital Vilnius would face great danger, and in case of a more serious accident the entire territory of Lithuania would come under the evacuation zone.[70] Indeed, if the nuclear plant were built, it would be a threat not only to Lithuanian security but likewise to the security of the whole region.

[65]Matulionytė (2008), p. 123.

[66]Matulionytė-Jarašūnė (2010), p. 129.

[67]Europos migracijos tinklas (2016).

[68]Buzan (1997), pp. 52–53.

[69]*Ibid.*, p. 178.

[70][No, author, named], (2016a). Astrav nuclear plant.

In conclusion, even though actions against military threats still comprise a considerable part of the whole sphere of national security, the legal acts list and institutions likewise deal with other threats to national security, which are outlined in the Strategy of National Security and other related documents. The threats are interrelated, and the reaction to a threat depends both on the perception of the state of it being a threat and on the intensity of the threat in question. After the analysis carried out on the acts that form the national security policy in Lithuania and other related legal acts, it can be concluded that the dominant perception of Lithuanian national security is a broad national security conception with strong emphasis on human security issues. While at the beginning of the functioning of Lithuania as an independent state questions of military security were of paramount importance, later the situation stabilized. The Republic of Lithuania has since signed and ratified many international treaties related to human rights; therefore, the efforts to ensure national security now include both the protection of Lithuanian independence and its territorial integrity (which are important functions of the state), as well as the assurance and development of human rights.

7.4 The Impact of the European Union and International Law

Saulė Milčiuvienė and Evelina Žurauskaitė
Faculty of Law, Vytautas Magnus University, Jonavos st. 66, LT-44138 Kaunas, Lithuania
e-mail: saule.milciuviene@vdu.lt; evelina.zurauskaite@vdu.lt

The question of the influence of EU and international law on Lithuanian national law is very broad and is related to all branches of law. It is impossible to review all relevant issues in one chapter; therefore, this section is limited to (1) the implementation of international law and EU law within the Lithuanian legal system and (2) the influence of preliminary rulings of the CJEU on the judgments of national courts.

7.4.1 International Law and National Law

In Lithuania, respect for international law is the constitutional principle. As the Constitutional Court said, the constitutional principle of Lithuania is the compliance of voluntary assumed obligations and respect of universal principles of international law.[71]

[71] Ruling of the Constitutional Court of the Republic of Lithuania on the limitation on the rights of ownership in areas of particular value and in forest land (14 March 2006). http://www.lrkt.lt/en/court-acts/search/170/ta1357/content. The ruling of the Constitutional Court of the Republic of Lithuania on the prohibition for a person, who was removed from office under procedure for impeachment proceedings, to stand in elections for a Member of the Seimas. (5 September 2012) // http://www.lrkt.lt/en/court-acts/search/170/ta1055/content.

Article 135 of the Lithuanian Constitution states: "In implementing its foreign policy, the Republic of Lithuania shall follow the universally recognised principles and norms of international law..."[72] It leads to the conclusion that international general (customary) norms are applied directly in Lithuania and are one of the principles of the foreign policy of Lithuania.[73] In its ruling *On the Death Penalty Provided for by the Sanction of Article 105 of the Criminal Code*, the Constitutional Court stated that "the State of Lithuania, recognizing the principles and norms of international norms, may not apply virtually different standards to the people of this country. Holding that it is a member of the international community possessing equal rights, the State of Lithuania, of its own free will, adopts and recognizes these principles and norms, the customs of the international community, and naturally integrates itself into the world culture and becomes its natural part."[74] The Lithuanian Constitution recognizes the general (customary) norms as principles of foreign policy but does not identify them as legal sources. Article 138 of the Lithuanian Constitution explicitly states that international treaties ratified by the Seimas (Parliament) are a part of the legal system of the Republic of Lithuania.[75]

Lithuania has developed a monistic legal system.[76] The Law on International Treaties[77] declares that international treaties of the Republic of Lithuania must be executed. This means that international treaties, not from the moment of ratification but from the moment they become valid, should be executed. In its ruling *On the Convention for the Protection of Human Rights and Fundamental Freedoms*, the Constitutional Court pointed out that "upon its ratification and enforcement, the Convention will become a constituent part of the legal system of the Republic of Lithuania and will be applied in the same way as laws of the Republic of Lithuania."[78] Of course, not every international treaty is self-executing. Only these international treaties that set rights and obligations for the national legal entities are self-executing. Other international treaties, which require national implementation, are implemented by acts of Seimas or Government. If for the implementation of an international treaty national law must be adopted, the Law on International Treaties obliges the Government to initiate an adoption procedure. In this way, norms of international treaties are transformed into national law.[79]

[72]*The Constitution of the Republic of Lithuania*. Official Gazette, 1992, no, 33-1014.

[73]Vadapalas (2006), pp. 56–59.

[74]The ruling of the Constitutional Court of the Republic of Lithuania on the death penalty provided for by the sanction of Article 105 of the Criminal Code. (9 December 1998) // http://www.lrkt.lt/en/court-acts/search/170/ta1135/content.

[75]Vadapalas (2006), pp. 59–61.

[76]*Ibid.*

[77]*The Law on International Treaties*. Official Gazette, 1999, No. 60-1948. Art. 11.

[78]The ruling of the Constitutional Court of the Republic of Lithuania on the Convention for the Protection of Human Rights and Fundamental Freedoms (24 January 1995). http://www.lrkt.lt/en/court-acts/search/170/ta990/content.

[79]Vadapalas (2006), p. 69.

The Law on International Treaties[80] declares that if a ratified international treaty of the Republic of Lithuania establishes norms other than the laws of the Republic of Lithuania and other legislation in force, the provisions of the international treaty should be applied. The supremacy of international treaties, which are ratified by the Seimas (Parliament), trumps any law except the Lithuanian Constitution.

The Constitutional Court also points out that "non-ratified international treaties of the Republic of Lithuania . . . have a force which is obligatory for entities of legal relations and which is characteristic of every legal act. However, their juridical force differs from ratified treaties in that they must comply not only with the Constitution but also with laws."[81] However, this is a general rule. Some laws, for example the Civil Procedure Code,[82] establish that ratified and nonratified treaties have supremacy over the Civil Procedure Code and other laws of the Republic of Lithuania.[83] Ratified and nonratified international treaties are part of the Lithuanian legal framework and are obligatory for legal entities.

7.4.2 The Influence of European Union Law on National Law

The Lithuanian Constitution[84] was adapted by the citizens of the Republic of Lithuania in the Referendum of October 25, 1992. At that time, the EU had gone through significant development: (1) the Treaty of European Union was singed on the February, 7, 1992, and became effective on November 1, 1993; (2) a single market was created on January, 1, 1993; (3) in the period 1989–1992, Austria, Finland, Sweden, and Norway submitted membership applications and in 1995 became EU members, save Norway.

Despite the intensive process of integration in Western Europe, the referendum-approved Lithuanian Constitution had no legal provisions concerning the possible integration of the Republic of Lithuania in the European Union. Only Article 136 of the Lithuanian Constitution states that the Republic of Lithuania can participate in international organizations, if it is not in conflict with the interests and independence of the state. But systematic analysis of the Lithuanian Constitution and existence of *The Constitutional Act of the Republic of Lithuania on the Non-Alignment of the Republic of Lithuania to Post-Soviet Eastern Unions*[85] reveal that the restraint of integration is directed to the post-Soviet and Eastern Unions.

---

[80]*The Law on International Treaties*. Official Gazette, 1999, No. 60-1948, Art. 11.

[81]The ruling of the Constitutional Court of the Republic of Lithuania on the Law "On International Treaties of the Republic of Lithuania" (17 October 1995). http://www.lrkt.lt/en/court-acts/search/170/ta983/content.

[82]*Code of Civil Procedure of the Republic of Lithuania*. Official Gazette. 2002, No. 36-1340.

[83]Vadapalas (2006), p. 68.

[84]*The Constitution of the Republic of Lithuania*. Official Gazette, 1992, No, 33-1014.

[85]*The Constitutional Act of the Republic Of' Lithuania on the Non-Alignment of the Republic of Lithuania to Post-Soviet Eastern Unions*. Lietuvos aidas, 1992, No. 111-0.

For this reason, regardless of the closed nature of the Lithuanian Constitution, it was not changed essentially for the accession of Lithuania to the European Union.[86] It was mainly supplemented by The Constitutional Act on Membership in the European Union,[87] which is a constituent part of the Lithuanian Constitution[88] and obliges the passing of certain functions of the Lithuanian institutions to the EU, and reveals openness to supranational cooperation; however, it does not limit the sovereignty of the Republic of Lithuania.[89]

In the Lithuanian Constitution, for the first time the terms "European integration" and "Transatlantic integration" were mentioned by the Amendment of Lithuanian Constitution in 1996.[90] This amendment concerned the rights of foreigners to acquire land in Lithuania and became valid after entering into force in the *Europe Agreement Establishing an Association Between the European Communities and their Member States, on the One Hand, and the Republic of Lithuania, on the Other Side.*[91] Later, to avoid the possible collision of the Lithuanian Constitution and EU law, the same article was changed again in 2003.[92]

The Constitutional Act on Membership in the European Union and a supplement of Article 150 of the Lithuanian Constitution[93] established the Membership of Lithuania in the EU at the constitutional level.[94] In the case *On the Limitation on the Rights of Ownership in Areas of Particular Value and in Forest Land*, the jurisprudence of the Constitutional Court[95] confirms that *The Constitutional Act on Membership in the European Union* approves the Constitutional Membership in the European Union and removes the hypothetical collision between the Lithuanian

[86]Šileikis (1992), pp. 53–54.

[87]*The Law Supplementing the Constitution of the Republic of Lithuania with the Constitutional Act "On Membership of the Republic of Lithuania in the European Union" and Supplementing Article 150 of the Constitution of the Republic of Lithuania. Official Gazette*, 2004, No. 111-4123.

[88]*The Constitution of the Republic of Lithuania.* Official Gazette, 1992, No, 33-1014. Art 150.

[89]Žalimas (2014).

[90]*The Law of the Republic of Lithuania Supplementing 47 Article the Constitution of the Republic of Lithuania.* Official Gazette, 1996, No. 64-1501.

[91]*Europe Agreement Establishing an Association Between the European Communities and their Member States, on the One Hand, and the Republic of Lithuania, on the Other Side.* Official Gazette, 1998, No. 11-266.

[92]*The Law on Amendment of 47 Article of the Constitution of the Republic of Lithuania.* Official Gazette, 2003, No. 14-540.

[93]*The Law Supplementing the Constitution of the Republic of Lithuania with the Constitutional Act "On Membership of the Republic of Lithuania in the European Union" and Supplementing Article 150 of the Constitution of the Republic of Lithuania.* Official Gazette, 2004, No. 111-4123.

[94]Šileikis (1992), p. 58.

[95]*The ruling of the Constitutional Court of the Republic of Lithuania on the limitation on the rights of ownership in areas of particular value and in forest land. (14 March 2006).* http://www.lrkt.lt/en/court-acts/search/170/ta1357/content. *The ruling of the Constitutional Court of the Republic of Lithuania on the prohibition for a person, who was removed from office under procedure for impeachment proceedings, to stand in elections for a Member of the Seimas (5 September 2012).* http://www.lrkt.lt/en/court-acts/search/170/ta1055/content.

Constitution and *The Constitutional Act on Membership in the European Union.* The two main aspects of *The Constitutional Act on Membership in the European Union* are,[96] first, the Act establishes that the legal acts of the European Union law are constituent part of the legal system of the Republic of Lithuania,[97] and second, it establishes the supremacy of EU law over national law, stating that "in the event of the collision of legal norms, they shall have supremacy over the laws and other legal acts of the Republic of Lithuania."[98] However, it does not explicitly establish the supremacy of EU law over the Lithuanian Constitution. The relationship between EU law and the national Constitution is determined and explained by the Constitutional Court.

7.4.3 The Dialogue Between the Court of Justice of the European Union and the National Courts

Regarding the impact of EU law on the national legal systems of Member States, Article 267 of the TFEU[99] is one of the most important treaty provisions. The preliminary ruling mechanism located therein enables a dialogue between the CJEU and the national courts faced with questions concerning the application of EU law provisions. This dialogue has contributed substantially to the development and shaping of EU law but has had a considerable impact on the national legal systems of the Member States as well.

We can find an almost verbatim copy of Article 267 TFEU in relevant Lithuanian laws that set general rules on the Lithuanian judicial system[100] or regulate civil,[101] criminal,[102] and administrative[103] procedures. A special Law on the

[96] Šileikis (1992), p. 58.

[97] *The Law Supplementing the Constitution of the Republic of Lithuania with the Constitutional Act "On Membership of the Republic of Lithuania in the European Union" and Supplementing Article 150 of the Constitution of the Republic of Lithuania.* Official Gazette, 2004, No. 111-4123.

[98] *The Law Supplementing the Constitution of the Republic of Lithuania with the Constitutional Act "On Membership of the Republic of Lithuania in the European Union" and Supplementing Article 150 of the Constitution of the Republic of Lithuania.* Official Gazette, 2004, No. 111-4123.

[99] Ex Art. 234 EC, Art. 177 EEC.

[100] *Law on Courts of the Republic of Lithuania.* Official Gazette, 1994, No. 46-851. Art. 40^1 sec. 2 specifies that the Supreme Court and the Supreme Administrative Court, as well as any other court of last instance, have a duty to refer to CJEU whenever questions regarding the interpretation or validity of EU law provisions arise.

[101] *Code of Civil Procedure of the Republic of Lithuania.* Official Gazette, 2002, No. 36-1340. Art. 3 sec. 5.

[102] *Code of Criminal Procedure of the Republic of Lithuania.* Official Gazette, 2002, No. 37-1341. Articles 234 and 381 provide that the examination of the case shall be deferred when the tribunal makes a reference to competent EU judicial body regarding the interpretation or validity of EU law provisions until the competent EU judicial body gives the preliminary ruling on the matter.

[103] *Law on Administrative proceedings of the Republic of Lithuania.* Official Gazette, 1999, No. 13-308. Article 4 sec. 3, 13, 98 sec. 8.

Constitutional Court, though, expressly mentions only the possibility to make a request to the ECHR for an advisory opinion.[104] Nevertheless, the Constitutional Court was the second judicial body to refer to the CJEU back in 2007.[105] Since the accession to the EU in 2004 (and up to the present day),[106] Lithuanian judicial bodies made 42 references to the CJEU,[107] three of which were accompanied by a request for an accelerated preliminary ruling procedure (all three requests were refused)[108] and one which requested an urgent preliminary ruling procedure (the request was granted).[109] If we look at the requests for preliminary rulings made by the courts from other Member States that acceded the EU in 2004 (keeping in mind the ratio between the population[110] and the number of references to the CJEU made by the judicial bodies of that state[111]), we find that Lithuanian judicial bodies were collaborating with the CJEU just as actively as those from, e.g. Estonia or Hungary, but less actively compared to their colleagues from Latvia.[112]

From the 42 references made by Lithuanian courts, 29 cases were decided, while 13 cases are still pending before the Court of Justice. Of those 29 judgments, 12 were accompanied by the Opinion of Advocate General and one by the Advocate

[104] *Law on Constitutional Court of the Republic of Lithuania*. Official Gazette, 1993, No. 6-120. Art. 28 sec. 2, p. 3, Art. 49, sec. 1, p. 3.

[105] Case C-239/07 *Sabatauskas and others*. Judgement of the Court (Third Chamber) (9 October 2008), which concerned the EU law rules on the internal market in electricity.

[106] Until the 31st July 2016.

[107] The information regarding the references for preliminary rulings from Lithuanian judicial bodies is available at http://curia.europa.eu/.

[108] Three cases with request for an accelerated preliminary ruling procedure were: Case C-207/08 Criminal proceedings against Babanov. Order of the Court (Sixth Chamber) (11 July 2008). The only request for preliminary ruling from Lithuanian courts regarding criminal proceedings. The questions raised by the referring Lithuanian tribunal were related to the compatibility with the law of the EU of national legislation providing for criminal liability for cultivating any type of hemp. Case C-671/13 *Indėlių ir investicijų draudimas and Nemaniūnas v. AB Bankas Snoras*. Judgement of the Court (Second Chamber) (25 June 2015). Case C-688/15 *Anisimovienė and Others v. BAB Bankas Snoras* (still pending). The questions referred in the latter two cases concerned the application of the EU law provisions related to the deposit-guaranteed schemes.

[109] Case C-195/08 PPU *Rinau v. Rinau*. Judgement of the Court (Third Chamber) (11 July 2008). The questions raised concerned the application of the EU law provisions on the return of a child who has been unlawfully retained in another Member State.

[110] The statistics regarding the population of Member States are available on the Eurostat website: http://ec.europa.eu/eurostat/tgm/table.do?tab=table&init=1&language=en&pcode=tps00001&plugin=1.

[111] Court of Justice of the European Union (2016).

[112] The calculation is made by dividing the overall population of one Member State (as for 2015), indicated by Eurostat, by the number of requests for preliminary ruling made by the judicial bodies of that particular State by the end of 2015. *E.g.*, Lithuania: population—2,9 mln., references—37. Average: one request per 78,3 thousand persons. Similar, Estonia—one request per 76,4 thousand persons; Hungary—one request per 80,9 thousand persons; Latvia—one request per 41,3 thousand persons.

General's view,[113] i.e., approximately 42% of all rulings were presented with additional legal conclusions on the matter. As for the duration of the proceedings, it took approximately 16.3 months for the CJEU to deliver a judgment (the longest proceedings lasted over 23 months, the shortest were 11 months), except for the *Rinau* case, which was decided in 58 days under urgent preliminary ruling procedure, and the *Babanov* case, where the request for an accelerated preliminary ruling procedure was made but the CJEU pursuant to the Article 104 section 3 of the Rules of Procedure of the Court of Justice[114] gave its decision in less than 2 months since the answer was clearly deducible from the existing case law. Considered the average length of litigation proceedings before the national courts where, e.g., civil cases in the courts of first instance are resolved in less than 100 days and administrative cases at first instance are examined in less than 300 days,[115] the length of the preliminary ruling proceedings might act as a deterring factor.

Up to the present day, not only did the courts—both from general and special jurisdiction—make references to the CJEU requesting a preliminary ruling, but other judicial bodies as well. In 2006, the Supreme Administrative Court was the first Lithuanian judicial body to request that the CJEU clarify how certain provisions of Council directive 92/84/EEC on the harmonization of the structures of excise duties on alcohol and alcoholic beverages (the case concerned alcohol contained in chocolate products) should be interpreted in case of divergence between various language versions of the directive.[116] Up to today, the Constitutional Court has referred to the CJEU once—the Supreme Court 15 times, the Regional Court of Panevėžys one time, the District Court of Vilnius three times, the Supreme Administrative Court 15 times, the Regional Administrative Court of Vilnius four times, and the Tax Disputes Commission three times. As we can see, the two Supreme Courts, that of general jurisdiction and the administrative one, made use of the preliminary ruling mechanism more frequently than the courts of lower instance. In 2013, the year in which the highest number of references reached the CJEU from the Lithuanian judiciary, the two Supreme Courts made eight out of their 10 references.

The TDC, which according to the national law is categorized not as a "court or tribunal" but rather as a budgetary institution established under the government for

[113]Case C-195/08 PPU *Rinau v. Rinau*. Judgement of the Court (Third Chamber) (11 July 2008), decided under urgent preliminary ruling procedure.

[114]Rules of Procedure of the Court of Justice of 25 September 2012 (OJ L 265, 29.9.2012), as amended on 18 June 2013 (OJ L 173, 26.6.2013).

[115]European Commission (2016).

[116]Case C-63/06 *Profisa v. Lithuanian Customs Administration*. Judgement of the Court (Eighth Chamber) (19 April 2007).

compulsory pretrial resolution of tax disputes, has addressed the CJEU several times.[117] Upon receipt of the first reference from this institution,[118] the CJEU had to decide whether the reference for preliminary ruling from this body is admissible. The fact was questioned by the Lithuanian government itself on the ground that the TDC lacked the independence since it is a part of the organizational structure of the Ministry of Finance, to which it is required to submit annual reports and with which it is obliged to cooperate. The CJEU has pointed out that relevant provisions of the Law on Tax Administration concerning the very purpose and *modus operandi* of the Commission, the appointment of its members and the requirements that they shall meet, as well as the possibility to initiate an objection procedure in case of a conflict of interest, confer on the TDC the necessary independence for it to be regarded as a court or tribunal within the meaning of Article 267 TFEU.[119] As for the obligation to cooperate with the Ministry of Finance, the CJEU stated that there are no indications that the TDC receives any instructions or guidance from the Ministry on how one or another case should be decided. Therefore, the existence of a general obligation of cooperation is not incompatible with the independence of the Commission from the Ministry.[120] In addition, the TDC meets other criteria laid down in the settled case law of the Court of Justice when deciding whether a body making a reference is a court or tribunal for the purposes of Article 267 TFEU, such as whether the body is established by law, whether it is permanent, whether its jurisdiction is compulsory, whether its procedure is *inter partes*, and whether it applies rules of law.[121] Therefore, the first one and subsequent requests for the preliminary ruling from this judicial body were admitted by the CJEU.

Although it remains up to the referring body to decide whether the reference to the CJEU is needed, sometimes it is the higher court remanding the case back for the rehearing that recommends to the lower instance court that it consider the possibility and need to refer to the CJEU.[122] Furthermore, quite often the litigant

[117]References from the TDC: Case C-385/09 *Nidera Handelscompagnie v. State Tax Inspectorate*. Judgement of the Court (Third Chamber) (21 October 2010), Case C-250/11 *Lietuvos geležinkeliai v. Vilnius Customs Office*. Judgement of the Court (Fourth Chamber) (19 July 2012) and Case C-526/13 *Fast Bunkering Klaipėda v. State Tax Inspectorate*. Judgement of the Court (Fourth Chamber) (3 September 2015).

[118]Case C-385/09 *Nidera Handelscompagnie v. State Tax Inspectorate*. Judgement of the Court (Third Chamber) (21 October 2010).

[119]*Ibid.*, par. 36–37.

[120]*Ibid.*, par. 38.

[121]*Ibid.*, par. 35, 39.

[122]*UAB LitSpecMet v. UAB Vilniaus lokomotyvų remonto depas*. Order of the Court of Appeal of Lithuania in Case No. 2A-821-370/2015, enacted on the 14th July, 2015.

parties themselves make a request to refer to the CJEU[123] or even affirm that the court has failed to make reference when it has a duty to do so, even though the decision of the national court would have been subject to further judicial review.[124] In one case,[125] the claimant, asserting that the CJEU had not given the answers to all questions referred, insisted on referring to the CJEU for a second time during a further litigation stage in order to obtain the answers that, according to the claimant, were lacking.

In some references for the preliminary ruling from Lithuanian judicial bodies, the questions to the CJEU were not formulated correctly; therefore, they were rephrased by the CJEU[126] or redefined more precisely by the referring court itself.[127] It has also happened that the national courts asked to give an interpretation on EU legal acts that were no longer applicable to the case *ratione tempori*.[128] Despite these minor errors, on the whole none of the requests made by Lithuanian judicial bodies were refused for not conforming to the general requirements set by the case law and incorporated in the recommendations to national courts and tribunals in relation to the initiation of preliminary ruling proceedings.[129]

With respect to the two types of references, i.e., the references that concern the interpretation of the treaties (Art. 267 (1)(a)) and the references related to the validity and interpretation of acts of the institutions, bodies, offices, or agencies of the EU (Art. 267 (1)(b)), we can see that almost all references from the Lithuanian judiciary belong to the second type of cases and mostly concern the interpretation of secondary EU law. On several occasions, national courts have also raised

[123]For instance: *A.A ir kt. v. BAB bankas "Snoras"*. Order of the Supreme Court of Lithuania in Case No. 3K-3-666-706/2015, enacted on the 12th February, 2016; *BTA Insurance Company SE v. UAB Litaksa*. Order of the Supreme Court of Lithuania in Case No. 3K-7-402/2013, enacted on the 17th October, 2013; *UAB Vilniaus energija v. Vilnius Regional Department of the Lithuanian Metrology Inspectorate*. Ruling of the Supreme Administrative Court of Lithuania in Case No. A858–46/2014, enacted on the 5th January, 2015; *R.-V. and L.W. v. Municipal Administration of the City of Vilnius and Others*. Ruling of Vilnius Regional Court in Case No. 2A-1579-577/2013, enacted on the 9th October, 2013; *UAB Mechel Nemunas v. State Tax Inspectorate*. Ruling of the Supreme Administrative Court of Lithuania in Case No. A-575-22/2009, enacted on the 25th May, 2009.

[124]*UAB LitSpecMet v. UAB Vilniaus lokomotyvų remonto depas*. Order of the Court of Appeal of Lithuania in Case No. 2A-821-370/2015, enacted on the 14th July, 2015.

[125]Case C-391/09 *Runevič-Vardyn and Wardyn v. Municipal Administration of the City of Vilnius and Others*. Judgement of the Court (Second Chamber) (12 May 2011).

[126]For instance, Case C-207/08 Criminal proceedings against Babanov. Order of the Court (Sixth Chamber) (11 July 2008), Case C-385/09 *Nidera Handelscompagnie v. State Tax Inspectorate*. Judgement of the Court (Third Chamber) (21 October 2010).

[127]*Nickel & Goeldner Spedition GmbH v. UAB Kintra*. Order of the Supreme Court of Lithuania in Case No. 3K-3-150/2013, enacted on the 4th April, 2013 (Case C-157/13 *Nickel & Goeldner Spedition GmbH v. Kintra UAB*. Judgement of the Court (First Chamber) (2 September 2014).

[128]Case C-410/13 *Baltlanta UAB v. Lithuania*. Judgement of the Court (Second Chamber) (3 September 2014).

[129]Recommendations to national courts and tribunals in relation to the initiation of preliminary ruling proceedings O.J. 2012/C 338/01.

questions regarding the divergences between various language versions of applicable EU law.[130] There were only a few cases when national courts asked to give an interpretation of the treaties[131] or an interpretation of an international treaty signed by the EU[132] or in which the validity of acts adopted by EU institutions was questioned.[133]

With respect to the material scope, we can say that the Lithuanian requests for preliminary ruling are quite miscellaneous. The courts had referred to the CJEU with questions on interpretation of European law provisions related to various aspects of the application of VAT and excise duty (ten references); insurance and compensation of damages from road traffic accidents (four references); financial instruments and guarantees for investors and depositors (three references); free movement of goods and measures having equivalent effect (two references); transport and liability of air carrier for delay; competition and illegal concerted practices online; unfair commercial practices and pyramid promotional schemes; consumer protection and contract for the provision of legal services; intellectual property and supplementary protection certificate; internal market in electricity and transmission and distribution systems; principle of nondiscrimination on grounds of nationality and principle of equal treatment of persons irrespective of racial or ethnic origin, agriculture, and criminal liability; public procurement and requirements for suppliers; structural funds and obligations of the state; environment and assessment of the effects of certain plans and programs; jurisdiction and enforcement of judgments in civil and commercial matters, in matrimonial matters, and in matters of parental responsibility; actions related to insolvency proceedings;

[130] Cases: C-63/06 *Profisa v. Lithuanian Customs Administration*. Judgement of the Court (Eigth Chamber) (19 April 2007), C-250/11 *Lietuvos geležinkeliai v. Vilnius Customs Office*. Judgement of the Court (Fourth Chamber) (19 July 2012), C-515/12 *4finance UAB v. State Consumer Rights Protection Authority*. Judgement of the Court (Second Chamber) (3 April 2014), C-429/14 *Air Baltic Corporation SA v. Special Investigation Service of the Republic of Lithuania*. Judgement of the Court (Third Chamber) (17 February 2016).

[131] On art. 101 TFEU—Case C-74/14 *Eturas and Others v. Competition Council of the Republic of Lithuania*. Judgement of the Court (Fifth Chamber) (21 January 2016); on art. 34 TFEU—Case C-423/13 *Vilniaus energija v. Vilnius Regional Department of the Lithuanian Metrology Inspectorate*. Judgement of the Court (Second Chamber) (10 September 2014) and Case C-481/12 *Juvelta v. Lithuanian Assay Office*. Judgement of the Court (Second Chamber) (16 January 2014); on articles 18 and 21 TFEU—Case C-391/09 *Runevič-Vardyn and Wardyn v. Municipal Administration of the City of Vilnius and Others*. Judgement of the Court (Second Chamber) (12 May 2011).

[132] On the interpretation of the articles 19, 22 and 29 of the Convention for the Unification of Certain Rules for International Carriage by Air ("Montreal Convention")—Case C-429/14 *Air Baltic Corporation SA v. Special Investigation Service of the Republic of Lithuania*. Judgement of the Court (Third Chamber) (17 February 2016).

[133] On the conformity of Commission implementing decision and Commission working document DS/2011/14/REV 2 with the Accession Treaty and general principles of EU law—Case C-103/14 *Jakutis and Kretingalės kooperatinė ŽŪB v. National Paying Agency under the Ministry of Agriculture*. Judgement of the Court (Fourth Chamber) (12 November 2015).

recognition and enforcement of arbitral awards; and the application of restrictive measures against Belarus.

Some rulings delivered by the CJEU attracted particular attention in Lithuania because of the sensitive questions they dealt with, such as the *Rinau* case, which involved the application of EU law provisions to the return of a child born in a German-Lithuanian family, unlawfully retained by the mother, a Lithuanian national, in Lithuania. Another example is the *Vardyn* case, concerning the *vexata quaestio*—the usage of different spelling rules and diacritical marks than those of the official language in Lithuania for the surnames and forenames of persons of different nationality or citizenship, in particular, Polish surnames and forenames. Others raised wide discussion among interested groups (like lawyers or insurers) and resulted in the amendments of national legislation, administrative and private practices related to, for instance, tax administration (e.g., the *Nidera* case); differentiation of compulsory insurance premiums (e.g., the *Litaksa* case); or the content of the contract for the provision of legal services (e.g. the *Šiba* case[134]).

7.5 The Perspectives of the Lithuanian Legal System

Stasys Šedbaras
Lithuanian Parliament (Seimas), Gedimino av. 53, LT-01109 Vilnius, Lithuania
e-mail: Stasys.Sedbaras@lrs.lt

The legal foundation for the judiciary and legal framework in Lithuania was laid down in the Constitution of 1992. Over a quarter of a century, the Constitution underwent only a few amendments (nine in total), some of which were linked to the EU accession. In late 1993, the Lithuanian Parliament (the Seimas) adopted Guidelines for the reform of the national legal framework, which focused on the creation of judicial authorities and drafting of the models, codes, and other legislation to regulate various fields of social life. Upon completion of a substantial part of the work under the said Guidelines, the Seimas adopted a new set of Guidelines in 1998, envisaging not only further improvement of the institutional system but also a further course of action for drafting new legislation. These Guidelines have largely been implemented by now, and only some provisions have lost their relevance due to opting for different regulatory models. In the short term, there are no plans to draft or adopt any new guidelines for planning the general course of further development of the Lithuanian legal system. In compliance with the Constitution and as a result of the implementation of the Guidelines for the reform of the legal system, the Lithuanian judicial authorities now consist of the Constitutional Court, courts of general jurisdiction (district courts, regional courts, the Court of Appeal, and the Supreme Court), and the administrative courts (regional administrative courts and the Supreme Administrative Court).

[134] Case C-537/13 *Šiba v. Devėnas*. Judgement of the Court (Ninth Chamber) (15 January 2015).

7.5.1 The Legal Framework

The most substantial transformation in Lithuania's legal framework dates back to the period between 1998 and 2004, when the country strove for accession to the European Union (EU) and aligned its legislation with EU law. The period was marked by the drafting and adoption of the basic codes, including the Civil Code, the Code of Civil Procedure, the Criminal Code, and the Code of Criminal Procedure. Approximately a decade later, between 2008 and 2012, the aforementioned legislation was reviewed and updated in light of the experience gained in its application.

At the time, it was also planned to draft the Code of Administrative Offences, which could be referred to as the Minor Criminal Code. Because of its large scope, however, the code was not adopted until much later, with entry into force scheduled for 2016. It regulates liability for less serious offenses punishable by penalties unrelated to imprisonment. In many EU countries such offenses are generally covered by the criminal code.

In the current period, most amendments to the codes and other pieces of legislation passed by the Parliament relate to the implementation of EU directives and other EU legislation, as well as international conventions.

Constitutional Law Apart from the courts of general jurisdiction and the administrative courts, Lithuania has a Constitutional Court, which passes judgments on compliance of legislation with the Constitution and compliance of documents issued by the Government and the President with the Constitution and other laws. The court also covers a number of other constitutional matters. Access to the Constitutional Court is available to any group of Members of Parliament, the President, the Government, and the courts. The Constitutional Court receives most queries from Members of Parliament and courts. A lawyer or another litigant may seek to address the Constitutional Court by submitting a written request at any stage of the proceedings before the court of general competence or the administrative court. Such requests are generally met by the court in question. Thus, forwarding queries of individuals to the Constitutional Court is a rather straightforward process. However, there are proposals to establish an *individual complaint*, allowing all individuals to lodge their applications concerning possible infringements of their rights directly with the Constitutional Court. This requires amending the Constitution, which is considerably difficult to do. Even though the relevant constitutional amendments have already passed the drafting stage, they may only be adopted in the longer run.

There is a pending judgment of the European Court of Human Rights (ECHR) (the case of *Paksas v. Lithuania*, No. 34932/04, Grand Chamber judgment, Strasbourg, January 6, 2011), whereby Lithuania is bound to allow persons removed from office by impeachment (Heads of State, Members of Parliament, judges of the Constitutional Court or another high court) to stand as candidates in parliamentary elections, given that a certain period of time has elapsed since the impeachment. While the ECHR only refers to candidates in parliamentary elections, the Constitutional Court of Lithuania has ruled that impeached persons may not take up any official post for the performance of which taking an oath is required (including the office of the President of the Republic). Therefore, the Constitution needs to be amended in order to allow persons removed from office by impeachment to take part in parliamentary elections without running for elections of the Head of State. The Seimas made several attempts to amend the Lithuanian Constitution in order to align it with the court judgment, but final agreement has yet to be reached.

Public Law There has been a lengthy debate for several years as to the introduction of *electronic voting in all types of elections* in Lithuania. Currently under consideration are the proposals to organize electronic early voting at the polling stations. This would not be equal to online voting; instead, it would be voting in electronic voting terminals. However, there are proposals to introduce online voting for voters residing outside Lithuania. An earlier proposal for universal remote voting did not meet with approval for fear of possible cyberattacks and potential effect on the voters' will. Even if no significant amendments to the electoral procedure are made before the parliamentary elections in the autumn of 2016, substantial changes are likely to take place by the 2020 elections and maybe even earlier.

Multiple citizenship is of huge relevance to Lithuania. Lithuanian nationals and their descendants who left the country before the restoration of independence in 1990 retain Lithuanian citizenship even if they acquire the nationality of another country (countries). However, the sizeable share of citizens residing outside Lithuania who left the country in recent years raises the need to address the question of whether they and their descendants may acquire the citizenship of another country without losing that of Lithuania. The constitutional provisions are very stringent in this respect and provide for only a few limited exceptions. The problem is that the provisions in question can only be amended by a referendum. Consideration is being given to the possibility of organizing such a referendum in conjunction with the 2016 elections. However, in the absence of appropriate decisions by political parties, this matter may be postponed till a later stage, with the view to organizing a referendum during other elections, such as the presidential elections, the elections to the European Parliament, or any other elections.

In 2016, the Parliament will discuss the new *Draft Law on the Civil Service*. The regulation of the civil service in Lithuania dates back to 1995, when the Law on Civil Servants was adopted. The Law on Civil Service currently in force was adopted in 1999 and was subsequently amended on many occasions. However, even so it no longer meets the twenty-first century challenges. The new draft envisages attracting new people to the civil service and maintaining a high level of competence of the ones currently employed. It also envisages coping with the competitive pressures from the private sector and creating opportunities for young and talented people to improve their qualifications and consistently pursue their careers. The 360-degree performance assessment model, largely used by other countries and the corporate sector, is to be used for performance assessment of heads of state institutions. The draft proposes to focus greater attention on the selection, competence improvement, and performance assessment of top managerial staff. The share of top managerial staff in the public sector as against the overall number of subordinate civil servants would be in line with the practice in EU countries, where top CEOs account for 1 % of all the civil servants.

In 2016, the draft amending the *Law on Lobbying Activities* will be discussed. The draft makes the definition of lobbyists and lobbying more precise by supplementing the existing legislation with a provision that the target group of lobbying consists of public policy makers, public officials, and civil servants. In most EU countries, activities of nonprofit organizations based on the shared interests of its members and aimed at creating influence to the effect of modifying, amending, or repealing legislation and adoption or nonadoption of new legislation are considered to be lobbying. This is not the case in Lithuania; therefore, changes are proposed.

Labor Law At the moment of writing this text, there is considerable debate in the Lithuanian Parliament on the *Labour Code*, which has been valid for a number of decades, amended many times, but now fails to meet the needs of the free market. At its meeting on April 9, 2015, the Council of the Organisation for Economic Cooperation and Development (OECD) unanimously decided to invite Lithuania to open the process of accession to the OECD. One of the comments raised by the OECD is that the Lithuanian Labour Code is outdated and taxation of labor is too high. Similar comments have been made by the European Commission and the World Economic Forum. The Lithuanian legal experts have drawn up an entirely new model for regulating labor relations, which would facilitate the conclusion, amendment, and termination of contracts and create opportunities for flexible working time arrangements. This would ensure better reconciliation of work and family responsibilities and improvement of qualifications, as well as offer more flexibility to adapt to the changing conditions in the labor market.

Legislation will also be impacted by other OECD recommendations to reduce red tape and administrative burden on business, improve governance of state-owned enterprises, and combat corruption.

Civil Law The coming years will see the implementation of the *United Nations Convention on the Rights of Persons with Disabilities* (2006). The Seimas ratified the Convention and its Optional Protocol in 2010. So far, under the existing provisions of the Civil Code, it was possible to recognize persons as legally incapable by reason of mental disease and to limit the legal active capacity for persons overindulging in strong drinks, drugs, or other narcotic substances. The Convention provides for partial limitation of legal active capacity in certain areas, as determined by the court, and envisages more effective assistance to such persons. In 2015, relevant amendments to the civil laws were made. As a result, the courts will now have to meet the requirements of the Convention while passing judgments on legal active capacity. Moreover, they shall, within the period of 2 years, review all the existing decisions and decide whether or not there are cases where persons recognized as legally noncapable can, in some areas, implement their civil rights independently.

A fundamental reform of the system of foster care for children without parents and children whose parents cannot take care of them is now in progress. It promotes placing children in foster families and social families of under 12 children. Nevertheless, many children still stay in state or municipal child care institutions without proper family atmosphere. As a result, they fail to learn independent life skills. In 2015, the Parliament adopted very stringent amendments to the Civil Code, with entry into force in 2017. They provide for very limited opportunities and short deadlines for stays of children in state or municipal foster care institutions and authorize the ombudsmen for children's rights to promptly place children in foster families or social families. For example, custody in a foster care institution of children up to the age of three will only be offered in exceptional circumstances where this will be in the best interests of the child and will last no longer than 3 months, unless the competent authority agrees that the custody of the child in a foster care institution should last longer for important objective reasons.

At the end of 2015, amendments to the Code of Civil Procedure were made to facilitate and speed up the decision making on *adoption and custody of the child.* In cases of adoption, decisions shall be made within 2 months after the date of receipt of the application; a 1-month deadline will apply for cases of child custody. In the coming few years, these legislative amendments are expected to minimize the number of children under state and municipal custody, as well as facilitate and encourage adoption and raising of children in families and social families.

A similarly important issue to be addressed in the near future is the *strengthening and reform of the system of protection of the rights of the child.* At present, this is a purely municipal responsibility, while the central national authorities are obliged to provide methodological support. There is a need to return to the proposal formulated in 2010 by the Committee on Legal Affairs and Committee on Social Affairs of the Lithuanian Parliament, whereby the protection of the rights of the child lies under the remit of the Ministry of Social Security and Labour and whereby experts on the protection of the rights of the child are subordinate to it and ensure uniform protection of children's rights. Similar ideas were discussed by officials in charge of the area in early 2016 at a meeting with the Head of State and should be implemented within the coming years.

Another matter concerns the judgment of the ECHR (case *L v Lithuania* No. 27527/03 of 11 September 2007). The judgment notes that the Lithuanian Civil Code (Art. 2.27) provides for the right to *gender reassignment*, but no other legislation governing the implementation of this right exists to date. This means that in reality, it is impossible to change one's gender in Lithuania. In the opinion of the ECHR, if a country has a law providing for a certain right, it needs to adopt other acts setting out the procedure for the exercise of the said right. To date, almost a decade after the judgment, no other legislative amendments have been adopted. In the course of 2016, the parliamentary majority intends to return to the debate on gender reassignment. The debate, however, is not likely to result in any decisions on further legal regulation on gender reassignment. It is more likely that decisions will be made on amending the Civil Code itself. As 2016 is the year of parliamentary elections, political parties are unlikely to reach any agreement and the issue is likely to be postponed for the coming years.

The situation is similar as regards *assisted (artificial) fertilisation*. The Civil Code provides that "the conditions, mode and procedures of artificial fertilisation as well as matters related to the paternity (maternity) of a child born from artificial fertilisation shall be regulated by other laws" (Art. 3.154). However, the Parliament has so far failed to adopt the other laws referred to above, even though draft laws on the matter were registered in Lithuania in 2002, 2003, 2004, and 2010. As long as legal regulation is not fully in place, young families cannot expect the assisted (artificial) fertilization procedure to be fully or at least partially compensated for from the state health protection budget. In the absence of legislation on assisted fertilization in Lithuania, the European Commission initialized an infringement procedure against the country in 2014. It can be expected that adequate regulation on the matter will be adopted during the coming few years.

In 2016, there will be a debate on amendments to the law on *patient rights and compensation for damage to health*. The amendments are aimed at giving access to redress to the widest possible range of patients who suffered personal injury in health care, so they can get coverage for damages faster and easier and redirect the time and money to their own recovery. Damage to the patient's health resulting from the provision of health care services would be covered through an administrative procedure from the fund established to compensate for the material and/or nonmaterial harm to health. Instead of being focused on proving the fault of doctors, this model would be based on determining liability of patients for compensation. So far, the government is against this draft. Therefore, the debate will continue in the long term.

Law on Criminal Procedure One of the important developments in the area of criminal proceedings will be the proposal to the Parliament to amend the Code on Criminal Proceedings and the Criminal Code and discontinue the practice of *private criminal prosecution*. Criminal prosecution exists in 15 of the 28 EU Member States (based on statistics of 2014). The Lithuanian Criminal Code covers 11 offenses (e.g., causing minor bodily injury or physical pain or causing slight bodily injury, interference in freedom of action, and sexual harassment) where the burden of gathering evidence and bringing the proceedings before the court lies on the victim. For several years now, there has been a debate in the legal community on the need to abandon this practice so that the law enforcement authorities would be charged to initiate an investigation, gather evidence, and prosecute in all cases where there are elements of the crime.

In 2016, the Parliament will debate a new *Law on the Prevention and Control of Organised Crime*. The draft is aimed at prevention, i.e. prevention and more effective control, of organized crime, as well as elimination of opportunities for receipt and legalization of material gains by criminals. The draft has been designed to deter engagement in criminal activities and block opportunities for organized crime to invest the criminal money, gain profit, have the money legalized, and achieve further profit.

7.5.2 The Legal Institutional Framework

Courts At present, in Lithuania there are, *inter alia*, 49 district courts of general jurisdiction for examination of civil and criminal cases. These courts are located in nearly all districts, towns, and cities, regardless of the population size, including Vilnius with over 500,000 inhabitants and Šilalė district with a mere 25,000. Although the number of judges posted in each of the courts is dependent on the number of inhabitants, the demographic situation both in urban and rural areas is changing very fast, thus creating a considerable imbalance between the numbers of cases per judge in the lowest level of courts. This leads to differences in waiting time and duration of proceedings, while judges with equal pay are faced with unequal workload. This is why, during its last session in 2015, the Parliament adopted a resolution on the reform of the judicial system to begin in 2018. The reform will consist of cutting the number of district courts from 49 to 12 and reforming the territories covered by courts. Following the reform, the cases will be reallocated among judges in a way to equilibrate the relative workload and the deadlines for handling cases.

The reform of the lowest level of administrative courts will follow the same logic. The current five courts, characterized by substantial differences in the number of cases handled in each, will be reduced to two. One of them will be in the capital, Vilnius, and the remaining ones will be merged into a single Regional Administrative Court.

Lay Assessors (Lay Judges) Under the Russian occupation (1940–1990), there was a specific body of lay assessors in Lithuania, which was characteristic of the Soviet court system. Two lay assessors used to examine all civil and criminal cases at first instance, together with a professional judge, and had the same voting rights as the judge. The assessors, as well as the judges, were selected by the Communist Party. This was why Lithuania abandoned the system in 1992. Cases are now examined by one or three professional judges; an extended judicial panel can be established in the Supreme Court and the Supreme Administrative Court.

Sometimes proposals are made to restore the office of lay assessors. Lawyers are skeptical of this, as this is not in line with purely Lithuanian judicial tradition. There is also no clarity on assessor selection procedures, assessor rights, remuneration, ways to ensure assessor impartiality, and other matters. Clearly, the position of lay assessors will be restored sooner or later, in response to public expectations. Presently, the Ministry of Justice is home to some debate on the matter. However, it is not yet clear what model should be applied to a country with a small population.

Police Reform Year 2015 saw the adoption of a number of laws (Law on the Approval of the Statute of the Internal Service, Law on Police, etc.) to further reform the police and other authorities that perform the policing function (border guard, fire protection, etc.).

Under the aforementioned legislation, the work regulation, remuneration, and social security of law enforcement and internal security officers are completely separated from the branch of civil services (ministries, municipalities, etc.). These developments are aimed at improving the selection of officials, raising their motivation, and making it easier for them to pursue a career, obtain result-based remuneration, and ensure better protection in retirement on grounds of age or illness. The measures aim to raise the quality of statutory staff, reduce migration between the public and the private sectors, eliminate possible manifestations of corruption, as well as ensure more efficient use of budgetary resources through more efficient management of internal security and law enforcement forces. A part of the new rules will enter into force in 2016. Some remaining regulation that requires more budgetary resources is scheduled for consistent implementation over a period between 2017 and 2018.

References

[No author named] (2015) Budget statement. Appropriations for National Defence 2015. Ministry of National Defence. http://kam.lt/en/budget_1065.html

[No author named] (2016a) Astravo atominė elektrinė (Astrav nuclear plant). http://www.lzp.lt/tag/astravo-atomine-elektrine

[No author named] (2016b) Klaipėdos nafta. Suskystintų gamtinių dujų terminalas (LNG terminal). http://www.sgd.lt/index.php?id=home&L=1

[No author named] (2016c) Lietuvos radijo ir televizijos komisijos 2015 m. veiklos ataskaita (The Activity Report of the Radio and Television Commission of Lithuania for the Year 2015). http://www.rtk.lt/content/uploads/2015/09/LRTK-VEIKLOS-ATASKAITA_2015.pdf

Bideleux R (1998) A history of Eastern Europe: crisis and change. Routledge

Buzan B (1997) Žmonės, valstybės ir baimė (People, states and fear). Vilnius, Eugrimas

Court of Justice of the European Union (2016). Annual Report 2015. Judicial Activity. http://curia.europa.eu/jcms/upload/docs/application/pdf/2016-04/en_ap_jur15_provisoire2.pdf

Davis LE (2003) Globalization's security implications. Issue Paper. RAND. https://www.rand.org/content/dam/rand/pubs/issue_papers/2005/IP245.pdf

European Commission (2016) The 2015 EU Justice Scoreboard, COM (2015) 116 final. http://ec.europa.eu/justice/effective-justice/files/justice_scoreboard_2015_en.pdf

Europos migracijos tinklas (2016) Migracija: 10 metų apžvalga (Migration: the review of 10 years). http://123.emn.lt/lt/bendros-tendencijos/migracija-10-metu-apzvalga

Greičius S Pranevičienė B (2010) Asmens ir valstybės saugumo samprata, užtikrinimo poreikis ir problemos (The Concept of Personal and State Security, the Need to Ensure and Its Problems). In: Monografija 'Regnum Est. 1990 m. kovo 11-osios Nepriklausomybės Aktui – 20. Liber Amicorum Vytautui Landsbergiui'. Mykolo Romerio Universitetas, Vilnius, pp 719–739

Howard GE (2016) Lithuania's key role in countering Russian A2/AD challenge to Baltics. Delfi.lt. http://en.delfi.lt/opinion/lithuanias-key-role-in-countering-russian-a2ad-challenge-to-baltics.d?id=70576206

Jurgelevičiūtė D (2004) Informacinio saugumo ir konvencinės saugumo sampratos santykis (The Relationship between the Concept of Informational Security and the Concept Conventional Security). In: Geopolitikos akiračiai. Eugrimas, Vilnius.

Maksimaitis M (2012) Rusijos teisės šaltiniai Lietuvoje 1918-1940 m. (Sources of Russian Law in Lithuania in 1918–1940). Jurisprudence 19(2):403–418

Matulionytė E (2008) Grėsmių nacionaliniam saugumui nustatymas ir jų prevencijos galimybės (The Determination of the Threats to National Security and Possibilities of Prevention). Jurisprudencija Mokslo darbai 4(106):93–99

Matulionytė-Jarašūnė E (2010). Atsinaujinančių energijos išteklių vystymas energetinio saugumo kontekste (The Development of the Renewable Energy Sources in the Context of Energetic Security). Darnaus vystymosi strategija ir praktika/Mokslo darbai

Paulauskas K (2010) Kieno saugumas? Kuri tapatybė? Kritinės saugumo studijos ir Lietuvos užsienio politika. (Whose security? What identity? Critical studies of security and Lithuanian foreign policy). Vilniaus universiteto leidykla, Vilnius

Pranevičienė B (2011) Limiting of the right to privacy in the context of protection of national security. Jurisprudence 18(4):1609–1622

Šileikis E (1992) Lietuvos Respublikos narystė Europos Sąjungoje (The Membership of the Republic of Lithuania in the European Union). In: Švedas G (ed) Europos Sąjungos teisės įtaka Lietuvos teisinei sistemai (Lithuanian legal system under the influence of European Union law). Vilniaus universitetas Teisės fakultetas, Vilnius, pp 53–86

Thomas N, Tow W (2002) The utility of human security: sovereignty and humanitarian intervention. Security Dialogue. doi: 10.1177/0967010602033002006

Vadapalas V (2006) Tarptautinė teisė (International law). Eugrimas, Vilnius

Vareikis E (2005) Tarptautinis ir nacionalinis saugumas (International and national security). VDU leidykla, Kaunas

Žalimas D (2014) Europos Sąjungos teisės įtaka konstitucinei jurisprudencija (The influence of European Union law to the Constitutional Jurisprudence). In: Katuoka S (ed) Transnacionalinės teisinės sistemos - santykio ir sąveikos problema (Transnational legal systems - relationship and interaction problem). Mykolo Romerio universitetas, Vilnius, pp 121–152

Zubrutė L (2016) Paskelbti 2016-ųjų šauktinių sąrašai (The Lists of Conscripts of 2016 Were Published). Verslo Žinios. http://vz.lt/verslo-aplinka/politika/2016/01/11/no-title#ixzz46uWIgpTx

Lithuanian Public Law

8

Marius Bartninkas, Mindaugas Bilius, Paulius Čerka, Tomas Davulis, Edita Gruodytė, Aušra Kargaudienė, Linas Meškys, Dainius Raižys, and Tomas Veršinskas

---

M. Bartninkas
Faculty of Law, Vytautas Magnus University, Jonavos st. 66, LT-44138 Kaunas, Lithuania

Kėdainiai District Court of the Republic of Lithuania, Didžioji st. 64-2, LT-57273 Kėdainiai, Lithuania
e-mail: marius.bartninkas@vdu.lt

M. Bilius • E. Gruodytė (✉) • T. Veršinskas
Faculty of Law, Vytautas Magnus University, Jonavos st. 66, LT-44138 Kaunas, Lithuania
e-mail: mindaugas.bilius@vdu.lt; edita.gruodyte@vdu.lt; tomas.versinskas@vdu.lt

P. Čerka
Čerka & Partneriai Advocates Bureau, Vytauto pr. 43A-66, Kaunas LT-44352, Lithuania
e-mail: paulius.cerka@vdu.lt

T. Davulis
Faculty of Law, Vilnius University, Saulėtekio av. 9-I, LT-10222 Vilnius, Lithuania
e-mail: tomas.davulis@tf.vu.lt

A. Kargaudienė
Faculty of Law, Vytautas Magnus University, Jonavos st. 66, LT-44138 Kaunas, Lithuania

Law Firm "Miškinis & partners", Valančiaus str. 1A, LT-03155 Vilnius, Lithuania
e-mail: ausra.kargaudiene@3law.eu

L. Meškys
Faculty of Law, Vytautas Magnus University, Jonavos st. 66, LT-44138 Kaunas, Lithuania

KMM Law Firm, Vytauto avenue 58-11, LT-44237 Kaunas, Lithuania
e-mail: linas.meskys@vdu.lt

D. Raižys
Faculty of Law, Vytautas Magnus University, Jonavos st. 66, LT-44138 Kaunas, Lithuania

Supreme Administrative Court of the Republic of Lithuania, Žygimantų st. 2, LT-01102 Vilnius, Lithuania
e-mail: dainius.raizys@vdu.lt

T. Kerikmäe et al. (eds.), *The Law of the Baltic States*,
DOI 10.1007/978-3-319-54478-6_8

Abstract
This section of the book is devoted to the presentation of the basic institutes of Lithuanian public law: the constitutional, administrative, criminal, tax, financial, and labor law institutes. These are surveyed in two essential sections. First is the historical perspective, which provides coverage of the historical development of certain institutes. The second perspective covers the major aspects of the institutes of public law in contemporary Lithuania, concluding with expected future tendencies. Significant attention is given to the contemporary regulation of the institute, including public administration, administrative liability, and some peculiarities of administrative procedure, including an overview of the special institute of the administrative courts. In criminal law and procedure, the classification of criminal acts, the institute of diminished capacity, the criminal penal system, and stages of criminal procedure are introduced. They focus on the aspects that introduced or experienced major changes by way of the introduction of new codes. In the part of the taxes additionally to the tax regulation, the major financial instruments, including both traditional ones such as credit institutions, insurance, and pensions, and rapidly developing instruments such as markets of financial instruments and electronic money, are discussed. From the January 1, 2017, a new Labour Code will be in force, which will be discussed in the part of labor law.

8.1 Constitutional Law and Constitutional Review

Aušra Kargaudienė
Faculty of Law, Vytautas Magnus University, Jonavos st. 66, LT-44138 Kaunas, Lithuania

3 Law Miškinis & Partneriai Law Firm, Jonavos st. 66, LT-44138 Kaunas, Lithuania
e-mail: ausra.kargaudiene@vdu.lt

8.1.1 Historical Background

Each of the Constitutions that were in force in the Republic of Lithuania during the period of 1918–1940 provided that in the State of Lithuania, no law that is contrary to the Constitution had force; e.g., the third paragraph of the Constitution of 1922 provided that any law in Lithuania should be invalid if it contradicts the Constitution. Almost all of the criteria of this Constitution indicated the democratic character of this legal act; this Constitution is classified as one of the legal acts that conformed not only to the needs, requirements, demands, and concerns of the society of that time but also to the permanent values of public life and personal freedom.[1] But despite this, no special institution for constitutional review was founded during this period of time in the Lithuanian legal system. It is likely that

[1]Maksimaitis (2005), p. 385.

this feature was carried on the shoulders of other public institutions that directly applied the law and the constitutional notions. Lithuania was not an exception—during the period between World War I and World War II, the context in Europe was not very encouraging for instituting a constitutional court. However, regardless, the development of scientific assumptions and the doctrine of the Constitutional Court in Lithuania were strongly and clearly expressed.

The idea of the Constitutional Court materialized after the declaration of independence of Lithuania in 1990 and when the Constitution of the Republic of Lithuania was approved in a referendum on October 25, 1992. This legal act provides the basis for the activities of the Constitutional Court of the Republic of Lithuania. The conception of constitutional review began its historical and practical application in the Lithuanian legal system in the Constitution of 1992. Although the idea of constitutional review was known and had certain resonance in the intellectual ideas and thought of the scholars of the pre-World War II period, the main notions related to its development are related to the spectacular constitution-making process in Eastern Europe and the European constitutional review doctrine of this time.

8.1.2 The Constitution of 1992 and Its Constituent Parts

The Constitution of the Republic of Lithuania consists of 154 articles. The preamble of the Constitution reaffirms the continuity of not only the statehood of Lithuania but the Lithuanian legal system as well. The notion that the nation has created the State of Lithuania many centuries ago and based its legal foundations on the Lithuanian Statutes and the Constitutions of the Republic of Lithuania leads to the notion of a nation striving for an open, just, and harmonious civil society and "a State under the rule of law." The unanimity of constitutional norms implies that the preamble of the Constitution, its chapters, and its articles comprise the significant whole of the Constitution.

The constituent part of the Constitution is its constitutional legal acts: the Constitutional Law "On the State of Lithuania" of February 11, 1991; the Constitutional Act "On the Non-Alignment of the Republic of Lithuania to Post-Soviet Eastern Unions" of June 8, 1992; the Law "On the Procedure for Entry into Force of the Constitution of the Republic of Lithuania" of October 25, 1992; and the Constitutional Act "On Membership of the Republic of Lithuania in the European Union" of July 13, 2004.

The constitutional acts constitute the uniqueness of the Lithuanian legal system. These legal acts were not part of the legal system during the period of 1918–1940, but in the period of 1990–1991 political events formed the basis for this constitutional phenomenon. For the first time in Lithuania, a Constitutional Act (The Constitutional Law) was approved in 1991. This Constitutional Law was proclaimed by the Supreme Council of the Republic of Lithuania, taking account of the fact that during the general poll (*plebiscite*), which was held on February 9, 1991, more than three-quarters of the population of Lithuania with the active electoral right voted by secret ballot that "the State of Lithuania would be an independent democratic republic." As a result, "The State of Lithuania shall be an independent democratic republic" is a constitutional norm (Article 1) and a fundamental principle of the state. This constitutional provision has special protection. This article, according to Article 148 (the alteration of the Constitution), may be altered only by a referendum of not less than three-quarters of the citizens of Lithuania with the electoral right vote in favor thereof.

The abovementioned constitutional acts are the constituent part of the Constitution. But there are a group of constitutional acts that do not form or belong to the constituent part of the Constitution. Although the Parliament had a constitutional duty to establish the list of constitutional laws, this list was approved by the Parliament in 2012.[2] The main criteria for distinguishing these constitutional acts that do or do not constitute a part of the Constitution are their adoption procedures and their legal force.[3] However, these attitudes do not influence the main determination of the Constitution as an integral and entirely legal act.

Article 6 of the Constitution defines it as an integral and directly applicable legal act. The second part of this article guarantees that everyone may defend his personal rights and freedoms by invoking the Constitution. This notion is of decisive importance for many of the Constitutional Court's rulings. The Constitutional Court emphasizes that the integrity of the Constitution first of all implies that constitutional provisions are related as the integral formal part of the act, according to the structure of their exposition and also according to their content and their substance:

> The significance of the Constitution as integral and directly applicable act is exceptional only when evaluating constitutional provisions pertaining to human rights and freedoms. It is obvious that, while interpreting the contents of concrete constitutional provision, in many cases it is impossible to interpret it separately from other provisions of the Constitution. It is especially important to take this into account with regard to such Chapters of the Constitution as "The Human Being and the State", "Society and the State", "National Economy and Labour" and others which contain the guarantees for the implementation and means of the legal protection of constitutional rights and freedoms.[4]

[2]*Constitutional Law on the List of Constitutional Laws of the Republic of Lithuania*. Official Gazette, No. 36-1772.

[3]"The constitutional laws which are named constitutional laws by the Constitution itself and the constitutional laws that will be entered into the list of constitutional laws as well as the constitutional law whereby the list of constitutional laws is established are of lower legal power than the Constitution itself, however, the legal power of such constitutional laws is higher than ordinary laws; ordinary laws cannot be in conflict with constitutional laws" (Sinkevičius (2008)).

[4]*Conclusion of the Constitutional Court of the Republic of Lithuania in Case No. 22/94, enacted on 24 of January, 1995.*

8.1.3 The Constitutional Court, Its Tasks, Powers, and Work Procedures

The purpose of constitutional justice in Lithuania is to ensure the supremacy of the Constitution in the national legal system. The Constitution of the Republic of Lithuania provides the basis for the activities of the Constitutional Court of Lithuania (*Lietuvos Respublikos Konstitucinis Teismas*).

The Constitutional Court has repeatedly proved its unique and exclusive role in the state governmental system. In the Constitution of the Republic of Lithuania, the principle of separation of powers is not established directly. Article 5 of the Constitution, from which this principle could be derived, names the state institutions, but it does not establish that they must be separated and independent. However, in the jurisprudence of the Constitutional Court, it has been emphasized that this universal principle is derived from Article 5 of the Constitution.[5]

The Constitutional Court of the Republic of Lithuania is established by the Constitution of the Republic of Lithuania of 1992. The Constitutional Court began its activities after the adoption of the Law on the Constitutional Court of the Republic of Lithuania on February 13, 1993.[6] This law, as well as constitutional provisions, defines the tasks, functions, and powers of the court. The main procedures of the court are set also by this law's provisions. The fundamental purpose of this judicial institution is the guarantee of the supremacy of the Constitution in the legal system. But this court's role could be described more broadly because of its human rights protection process (e.g., constitutional jurisprudence is often referred to as constitutional human rights).

According to legal regulations, the court procedures can be identified this way: the Constitutional Court guarantees the supremacy of the Constitution of the Republic of Lithuania in the legal system, as well as the constitutional legality, by deciding, according to the established procedure, whether the laws and other acts adopted by the Parliament (*Seimas*) are (not) in conflict with the Constitution and whether acts of the President of the Republic and the government are (not) in conflict with the Constitution or laws.

The Constitutional Court is part of the judiciary, which has an exclusive and particular competence;[7] therefore, the principle of independence of courts and judges is applied to this court as well.

The Constitutional Court consists of nine judges. Each of them is appointed for a single 9-year term of office (Article 4).[8] One-third of the Constitutional Court's

[5]*Ruling of the Constitutional Court of the Republic of Lithuania in Case No. 24/98, enacted on 4 March, 1999.*

[6]In February and March of 1993 the Parliament (Seimas) appointed all the justices and the Chairman of the Constitutional Court.

[7]*Ruling of the Constitutional Court of the Republic of Lithuania in Case No. 12/06, enacted on 6 June, 2006.*

[8]*Law on the Constitutional Court of the Republic of Lithuania.* Official Gazette, 1993, No. 6-120.

judges are replaced (reconstituted) according to the notions of the Constitution every 3 years. The candidates are appointed by the Parliament (*Seimas*). But the candidates to the Parliament (*Seimas*) are presented by these three institutions: by the President of the Republic, the Speaker of the Parliament, and the President of the Supreme Court. In this way, during the Constitutional Court making process, all three state powers are involved: the legislature, the executive, and the judiciary. The President of the Constitutional Court is appointed by the Parliament (*Seimas*). Nomination Submission of the President of the Constitutional Court shall be made by the President of the Republic.

The functions and powers of the Constitutional Court, as a constituent part of the Lithuanian judicial system, are established in the Constitution. In Paragraph 1 of Article 102 of the Constitution, it is stated that the Constitutional Court decides whether the laws and other legal acts of the Parliament (*Seimas*) are (not) in conflict with the Constitution and whether the acts of the President of the Republic and the government are (not) in conflict with the Constitution or laws. Under the Constitution, the Constitutional Court is the institution of constitutional justice, which implements constitutional judicial control.[9]

The Constitutional Court also presents conclusions, upon request of the Parliament (*Seimas*), on (1) whether there were violations of election laws during the elections of the President of the Republic or the elections of the members of the Seimas, (2) whether the state of health of the President of the Republic allows him to continue to hold office, (3) whether the international treaties of the Republic of Lithuania are in conflict with the Constitution, (4) whether the concrete actions of the Members of the Seimas and state officials against whom an impeachment case has been instituted are in conflict with the Constitution. The President of the Republic may apply with an inquiry concerning only two issues: the election of members of the Seimas and international treaties.

The Constitutional Court adopts acts, and they are generally grouped into three types: rulings, conclusions, and decisions. All of these acts are commonly called "the decisions." But all of these legal acts have a specific and unique legal reason and specific legal consequences. The rulings and the conclusions of the Constitutional Court are called final acts because they are adopted after having considered a corresponding constitutional justice case. The specified rulings, conclusions, and decisions of the Constitutional Court are final acts of the Constitutional Court. By them a constitutional justice case is concluded. All of these final acts of the Constitutional Court are included in the general notion of "the decisions" used in Article 107 of the Constitution.

There was a problematic constitutional issue related to Article 102 of the Constitution: does the notion that the Constitutional Court shall decide whether the laws and other acts mentioned in this constitutional article are in conflict with the Constitution mean that there are some limits to constitutional review,

[9]*Ruling of the Constitutional Court of the Republic of Lithuania in Case No. 13/04-21/04-43/04, enacted on 9 May, 2006.*

concerning only the legislation that is in force? In one Constitutional Court decision, a doctrinal issue was formulated: the Constitutional Court has the power to investigate the compliance of legal acts with the Constitution if these acts are valid at the moment of investigation.[10] Otherwise, the court should refuse to consider the petition, which was, practically, what was done. This raised some theoretical and practical problems, and it was reasonably evaluated as improper.[11] However, the development of the doctrine of the Constitutional Court opened a new page,[12] and today we can state that the Constitutional Court examines the compliance not only of valid legal acts (existing legislation) with the Constitution but also of no longer valid (repealed legislation) legal acts with the Constitution, as well as the compliance of laws and other legal acts, which were adopted by the Parliament and were officially announced, with the Constitution regardless of the established date of the beginning of the application of such legal acts.

According to Article 105 of the Constitution, the Constitutional Court considers and adopts decisions concerning the conformity of laws and other legal acts adopted by the Parliament with the Constitution. Article 7 of the Constitution prescribes that only laws that are published shall be valid. These two articles were the playground of the Constitutional Court, stating that the formula "laws and other legal acts adopted by the Seimas" employed in Article 105 means that the Constitutional Court has the power to consider the compliance of the laws and other acts adopted by the Seimas and officially published with the Constitution irrespective of the established date of the commencement of the application of such laws or other parts.[13] In this way, it was confirmed that laws that are not valid but officially proclaimed are also subject to constitutional review.

The Constitutional Court gives conclusions whether international treaties of the Republic of Lithuania are (not) in conflict with the Constitution, and this conclusion

[10] *Decision of the Constitutional Court of the Republic of Lithuania in Case No. 38/94, enacted on 25 January, 1995.*

[11] Sinkevičius (2014).

[12] *Ruling of the Constitutional Court of the Republic of Lithuania in Case No. 43/01, enacted on 21 August, 2002*: "4. Under the Constitution, only the Constitutional Court shall decide whether the laws and other legal acts adopted by the Seimas are in conformity with the Constitution and whether legal acts adopted by the President of the Republic and the Government of the Republic are in conformity with the Constitution or laws (Paragraph 1 of Article 102). Paragraph 1 of Article 110 of the Constitution provides that judges may not apply laws which conflict with the Constitution. Under Paragraph 2 of the same article, in cases when there are grounds to believe that the law or other legal act applicable in a certain case conflicts with the Constitution, the judge shall suspend the investigation and shall apply to the Constitutional Court to decide whether the law or other legal act in question complies with the Constitution. These constitutional provisions mean than in cases when a court considering a case, after it questions the compliance of the law applicable in the case with the Constitution or the compliance of another act adopted by the Seimas, the President of the Republic of the Government with the Constitution or the laws, applies to the Constitutional Court, the latter has a duty to consider the petition of the said court regardless of the fact whether the impugned law or another legal act is valid or not."

[13] *Ruling of the Constitutional Court of the Republic of Lithuania in Case No. 34/2000-28/01, enacted on 19 September, 2002.*

may be requested prior to its ratification in the Parliament (Article 73).[14] On the basis of the conclusions of the Constitutional Court, Parliament makes a final decision (the ratification), as with all other issues set forth in the third paragraph of Article 105 of the Constitution (Article 107).

Article 106 names the subjects that have the right to apply to the Constitutional Court (the government, not less than 1/5 of all the members of the Seimas, the courts, and the President of the Republic), each within its powers and constitutional limits. This includes all state power institutions named in Article 5 of the Constitution.

A private person in Lithuania has no right to initiate proceedings before the Constitutional Court directly. However, a sizable number of cases go to the Constitutional Court on the basis of Article 6 of the Constitution,[15] which provides for the right of every individual to protect his personal rights on the basis of the Constitution.

The powers of the courts to suspend the consideration of an individual case and to apply to the Constitutional Court with a claim requesting investigation into the compliance of the legal act with the Constitution are explicitly stated in the Constitution. This is established in Article 110 of the Constitution. In cases where there are grounds to believe that a law or other legal acts that should be applied in a concrete individual case are in conflict with the Constitution, the judge (the court) shall suspend consideration of the case and shall apply to the Constitutional Court requesting that it decide whether the legal act in question is in compliance with the Constitution. Therefore, according to these constitutional provisions, the courts are numerous claimants to the Constitutional Court.

To raise doubts on this matter is open to any person involved in an individual case, but the final decision regarding the claim is a matter for the judge to make (i.e., of the court investigating the individual case). It is emphasized that, while suspending consideration of the case because of the application to the Constitutional Court, the court does not decide the case in essence but only creates preconditions for adopting a just court final act.[16] The grounds for the consideration of a case concerning the compliance of a legal act with the Constitution is a doubt that this legal act is in conflict with the Constitution according to the contents of the norms, the extent of regulation, the form of the procedure of its adoption, signing, publication, and entry into effect, which is established in the Constitution (Article 64).[17]

The right to raise doubts on the matter of the consideration of the law, which should be applied in the individual case, is directly related to the person's constitutional right to apply to the court (Article 30), as well as the principle of a state under

[14] *Law on the Constitutional Court of the Republic of Lithuania*. Official Gazette, 1993, No. 6-120.

[15] "Everyone may defend his rights by invoking the Constitution."

[16] *Ruling of the Constitutional Court of the Republic of Lithuania in Case No. 26/07, enacted on 24 October, 2007.*

[17] *Law on the Constitutional Court of the Republic of Lithuania*. Official Gazette, 1993, No. 6-120.

the rule of law. But the final decision depends on the court, which holds the individual case, will, or legal reasoning.

The power of courts to suspend the consideration of a case and apply to the Constitutional Court with a petition requesting an investigation into the compliance of the legal act with the Constitution is explicitly expressed in the Constitution. Article 110 of the Constitution indicates the prohibition on applying a law that is in conflict with the Constitution and a duty of a judge considering a case, if there are doubts whether the law or other legal acts applicable in the case are not in conflict with the Constitution, to suspend the consideration of the case and to apply to the Constitutional Court requesting that it decide whether the law or other legal acts in question are in compliance with the Constitution.

The terms and sequences of the consideration of applications in the Constitutional Court are determined in the notion of the Law on the Constitutional Court of the Republic of Lithuania. The consideration of each case should be finished and the final ruling issued or conclusion adopted within 4 months of the day that the petition or inquiry is received unless otherwise established by the Constitutional Court (Article 29). The rulings and the conclusions have to be adopted by a majority vote of all judges of the Constitutional Court. The justice does not have the right to disclose the opinions voiced in the deliberation room or how the justices voted (an expression of a dissenting opinion is not considered a disclosure of opinions).

8.1.4 Legal Consequences of the Constitutional Court Decisions

The Lithuanian legal system is grounded on the fundamental constitutional basis that any law or other legal act, accompanying international treaties of the Republic of Lithuania, must not contradict the Constitution; Paragraph 1 of Article 7 of the Constitution prescribes that "Any law or other statute which contradicts the Constitution shall be invalid." Article 107 provides that no act may be applied from the day of the official publication of the decision of the Constitutional Court if the act in question (or part thereof) is in conflict with the Constitution.

Therefore, under this notion, until the official promulgation of the decision of the Constitutional Court that the act in question is in conflict with the Constitution, it is presumed and it can be concluded that this legal act is in compliance with the Constitution and that the legal consequences (for instance when, under a corresponding decision of an institution, which was adopted by following the act in question, a person had acquired certain rights or a certain status or when, under a corresponding decision of an institution, a person had not been granted certain rights or a certain legal status), which have appeared on the basis of this act in question, are legitimate.[18] The power of Constitutional Court decisions as regards

[18] *Ruling of the Constitutional Court of the Republic of Lithuania in Case No. 36/2010-37/2010-38/2010-39/2010-41/2010-42/2010-43/2010-62/2010-63/2010-64/2010-65/2010-66/2010-67/2010-68/2010-69/2010-71/2010-72/2010-74/2010-75/2010-78/2010-79/2010-80/2010-91/2010-92/2010-93/2010-103/2010-104/2010-105/2010-108/2010-3/2011, enacted on 25 October, 2011.*

the conformity of legal acts with the Constitution is prospective.[19] There may be exceptions to this rule, under the Constitution; in exceptional cases, the power of decisions may be targeted also for the consequences of application of the legal act that has been recognized as being in conflict with the Constitutional notions.[20]

The evaluation of legal consequences, as well as legal reasoning, is also related to a new institution in the Lithuanian legal system: the dissenting opinion of the justice of the Constitutional Court. Article 55 of the Law on the Constitutional Court of the Republic of Lithuania concerns the procedures of the issuing of a ruling of the Constitutional Court, and it has been amended several times. The main emendations to this article are related to the institute of a dissenting opinion of a justice. A judge of the Constitutional Court who has a different opinion about an act adopted by the Constitutional Court has the right to set forth in writing the reasoned dissenting opinion. This dissenting opinion has to be pronounced within five days after the official pronouncement of the corresponding Constitutional Court's act. The dissenting opinions of the judges are published on the website of the Constitutional Court and are attached to each appropriate constitutional case. The dissenting opinion, as the constitutional institute, is related to the issue of the constitutional interpretation, and it serves for academic and scholarly debates.

Upon evaluating the changes of the national legal system, certain trends of the Constitutional Court's jurisdiction expansion can be observed. Legal and political discussions arise when the Constitutional Court allows the evaluation of issues related to the constitutionality of legal norms, even if this issue was not raised in the petition. Rule of law, separation of powers, and other constitutional principles have to be the guidelines and the limits as well for the Constitutional Court since it is the constituent part of the judicial system. The Constitutional Court ensures its position in the system by consistent and steady activity.

The Constitutional Court plays a very strong role indeed as the guarantor of the constitutional notions. This status is achieved by the Constitutional Court's activity, jurisdiction, and power. The role played by the Constitutional Court in safeguarding the main constitutional principles is one of the most strategically important roles in constitutional jurisprudence. However, it is clear that the assessment of the prospects for the effective functioning of the Constitutional Court's activity should be made not only by the jurisdiction, and the procedural novelties (e.g., the dissenting opinion of the judges in a constitutional case), but also by the consolidations of the notions of the individual constitutional complaints.

The realization of human constitutional rights idea can hardly be imagined without well-operating constitutional jurisdiction, but also without individuals' direct participation in this process. The challenge to ensure persons' constitutional

---

[19] *Ruling of the Constitutional Court of the Republic of Lithuania in Case No. 21/2003, enacted on 13 May, 2003.*

[20] *Ruling of the Constitutional Court of the Republic of Lithuania in Case No. 43/2009, enacted on 19 December, 2012.*

rights by their direct participation in the Lithuanian constitutional legal system still awaits future change and improvement.

8.2 Administrative Law and Procedure

Linas Meškys
Faculty of Law, Vytautas Magnus University, Jonavos st. 66, LT-44138 Kaunas, Lithuania

KMM Law Firm, Jonavos st. 66, LT-44138 Kaunas, Lithuania
e-mail: linas.meskys@vdu.lt

Dainius Raižys
Faculty of Law, Vytautas Magnus University, Jonavos st. 66, LT-44138 Kaunas, Lithuania

Supreme Administrative Court of the Republic of Lithuania, Jonavos st. 66, LT-44138 Kaunas, Lithuania
e-mail: dainius.raizys@vdu.lt

8.2.1 Administrative Law

8.2.1.1 Notion and Sources of Administrative Law

Just as elsewhere in the world, various definitions of administrative law can be found in Lithuania. Some authors claim that administrative law should be defined as an independent branch of law governing legal relationships in the field of state governance and the everyday activities of state agencies.[21] Others point out that administrative law encompasses legal norms created by applying general principles of law and courts' case law interpreting and clarifying legislation, and establishing (1) which subjects are given the power to perform functions of public administration and what is the extent of those powers; (2) which subjects (and to what extent do they) have the power to control whether the actors of legal relationships do not act against the law and, if necessary, to apply administrative sanctions; (3) which subjects have the power (and what kind of power) to decide on conflicts between the public administration and the citizens (administrative disputes).[22]

Administrative law is usually described as the law of governance in scientific literature because it regulates legal relationships that occur in organizing and implementing the executive, state, and public governance (administration). Being a part of public law, it is inextricably connected to public administration, and it is recognized as inescapable and the most important instrument for managing social processes and governance in the public sector. Taking that into account, one can

[21]Bakaveckas et al. (2005), p. 63.

[22]Andruškevičius (2008), p. 35.

state that public administration and administrative law are closely connected phenomena. Administrative institutions are necessary (indispensable) subjects of administrative legal relationships. Administrative law also sets out the limits of administrative subjects' activities, establishes the legal status of civil servants, and determines the forms of administrative subjects' control. It regulates relationships that occur in the process of implementing public administration, defines principles and functions of public administration, i.e., determines its content. In other words, public administration is considered the object of administrative legal regulation.[23]

Sources of Lithuanian administrative law include, first of all, the Lithuanian Constitution, wherein the main principles of public governance are established (e.g., Article 5 states that state institutions shall serve the people), as well as Constitutional laws that have a higher legal value than other laws. The list of Constitutional laws is set out in a separate piece of legislation—the Constitutional Law of the List of Constitutional Laws. Those laws are, for example, the Constitutional Law on the Official Language of the Republic of Lithuania and the Constitutional Law on the State Flag and other Flags, etc.

International treaties and agreements are another source of administrative law, which forms an integral part of the legal system of the Republic of Lithuania. If an international treaty where Lithuania is a party to establishes other rules and provisions than national laws, the provisions of international law, provisions of specific international treaties, agreements, and conventions are valid and applicable (e.g., International Covenant on Civil and Political Rights, International Covenant on Economic, Social and Cultural Rights, Convention for the Protection of Human Rights and Fundamental Freedoms, and others).[24]

Legal acts of the European Union are another source of administrative law. The Constitutional act "On Membership of the Republic of Lithuania in the European Union" establishes that the norms of European Union law shall be a constituent part of the legal system of the Republic of Lithuania. Where it concerns the founding treaties of the European Union, the norms of European Union law shall be applied directly, while in the event of the collision of legal norms, they shall have supremacy over the laws and other legal acts of the Republic of Lithuania.

An important role in the system of the administrative law sources is played by laws. The significance of these regulatory legal acts lies in the fact that they set out main administrative legal norms that can be further detailed and specified in implementing legislation. Laws set out the main principles of organizing state governance and activities; they regulate relationships in administrative political, sociocultural, and economic fields; and they also set out requirements and conditions for the implementation of the most important state tasks. One could mention the following laws as examples of laws where various administrative legal norms are set out in the abovementioned areas of legal regulation: Law on the Government, Law on Civil Service, Law on Public Administration, etc.[25]

[23]Bakaveckas (2007), p. 126.

[24]Bakaveckas (2012), p. 416.

[25]*Ibid.*, p. 420.

The government is the executive institution of the highest level of the Republic of Lithuania, which is given wide powers in all areas of public administration. For this reason, government decisions are important sources of administrative law. By its decisions, the government specifies and details laws adopted by the legislator, i.e., the Parliament of the Republic of Lithuania.

Other sources of administrative law include legal acts issued by central public administration subjects (ministries, institutions under ministries, government institutions such as orders of ministers and other subjects), regulatory legal acts adopted by municipal institutions that are valid in the territory of a particular municipality (e.g., decisions adopted by municipal councils concerning local parking tolls and others).

Administrative law sources are not only the abovementioned regulatory administrative legal acts, but they are also court decisions. Those are decisions of national courts (general competence courts, administrative courts, and the Constitutional Court), international courts (the European Court of Human Rights), and European Union courts (e.g., the Court of Justice of the European Union).

8.2.1.2 Public Administration

Public administration is considered an object of administrative legal regulation; therefore, one of the most important Lithuanian administrative legal sources is the Law on Public Administration,[26] which allows implementation of the constitutional provision that state institutions shall serve the people. This law sets out principles of public administration, fields of public administration, the system of public administration subjects, and basics of organizing administrative procedure; it also guarantees the right to appeal against acts of public administration subjects or administrative decisions, as well as objective examination of appeals and applications based on laws, and establishes other rights and duties of public administration subjects in the area of public administration.

Public administration is defined as activities of public administration subjects governed by laws and other legal acts, performed in order to implement laws and other legal acts, e.g., adoption of administrative decisions, control of the implementation of laws and administrative decisions, provision of administrative services set out in laws, administration of public services' provision, and internal administration of public administration subjects.

The system of public administration subjects in the Republic of Lithuania is composed of national administration subjects (state institutions, their civil servants and officers, state enterprises, public bodies owned or partially owned by the state, and others that are authorized to carry out public administration) and municipal administration subjects (municipal institutions, their civil servants and officers, municipal enterprises, public bodies owned or partially owned by the state, and others).

---

[26]*Law on Public Administration of the Republic of Lithuania*. Official Gazette, 1999, No. 60-1945.

In their activities, public administration subjects follow the principles established in the Law on Public Administration. First of all, that is the rule of law, which means that the powers of public administration subjects to carry out public administration must be set out in legislation, and the activities must conform to the rules established in laws. Public administration subjects must also comply with the principle of objectiveness and with the principle of proportionality. An important principle that the subjects of public administration must follow is the principle of nonabuse of power. In preparing administrative decisions, public administration subjects must, if necessary, provide the needed information or otherwise help one another, i.e., apply the principle of institutional assistance. The economic considerations are enshrined in the principle of effectiveness. Purposes set out in the Law on Public Administration are also pursued by the principle of subsidiarity and "one-stop-shop" principle. An important position in the field of public administration is taken by the principle of equality. The Law on Public Administration also imposes an obligation on the public administration subjects to respect the principle of transparency, also the principle of accountability for adopted decisions. Finally, the law also establishes the principle of innovations and openness to changes, which means that public administration subjects must look for new and effective ways to solve problems and constantly learn from examples of best practice.

Only public administration subjects have the power to adopt administrative acts in the Republic of Lithuania. Public administration subjects must consult organizations representing public interests in a certain area and in cases provided for by laws, and they must consult residents or their groups, regarding administrative decisions related to common legitimate interests of the society. A public administration subject can choose the means of consultations (meetings of interested persons, surveys, publicly announced meetings, invitations of representatives, other ways of finding out opinions), unless otherwise provided for by law. Information regarding the means of consultations, their participants, and results must be published on the website of the public administration subject that has prepared the draft of the administrative decision.

The Law on Public Administration sets out general requirements for individual administrative acts. An individual administrative act must be based on objective data (facts) and legal provisions, and the sanctions applied (withdrawal of license or permission, temporary prohibition to engage in certain activities or provide services, a fine, and others) must be well reasoned. An individual administrative act must clearly indicate the rights and duties that are established or imposed, and the procedure of appeal must be indicated, because individual administrative acts adopted by public administration subjects typically may only be appealed before administrative courts.

Every addressee of an individual administrative act or a person on whose rights and duties this individual administrative act has direct effect is informed about the adoption of this individual administrative act within three working days of its adoption, enclosing a certified (as required by law) copy of an individual administrative act, unless other laws provide otherwise. When an individual administrative act is adopted using a state IT system, an excerpt of the individual administrative act may be enclosed instead of a certified copy.

It should be noted that the Law on Public Administration also regulates the main aspects of supervision of the activities of entities (companies, institutions, organizations, and others). The law defines supervision of entities' activities as activities of public administration subjects aimed at providing methodological assistance to entities, supervising how entities comply with requirements set out in laws and other legal acts, controlling whether they properly implement those requirements, and implementing other measures that ensure proper compliance with requirements of legal acts and prevent harm to values that are protected by law.

Public administration subjects, when carrying out supervision of entities' activities, consult entities according to their competence, including performance of preventive actions aimed at preventing possible infringements of legal acts. Furthermore, public administration subjects carry out checks of entities' activities, assess received information concerning entities' activities, and apply sanctions.

It is important to note that public administration subjects carry out supervision of entities' activities according to the principles preserved in the Law on Public Administration. The essential principles of supervision of entities' activities are the principle of minimum and proportionate burden of supervision, the principle of nondiscrimination, the principle of publicity, the principle of provision of methodological assistance, and the principles of planning, division of functions, and risk assessment.

It should be noted that a system of specialized (administrative) courts was established in 1999 in Lithuania. Administrative courts decide on legal disputes in the area of public administration.

8.2.1.3 Administrative Liability

Administrative liability in Lithuania is defined as an independent type of legal liability, imposed on natural and legal persons that have committed administrative offenses, in accordance with procedures established by provisions of administrative proceedings, by imposing sanctions on them as foreseen by laws, aiming to ensure legal order and implementing state governance.[27]

Administrative liability is characterized by the fact that it is a very important legal measure in combating administrative and other offenses. The preventive role of administrative liability is extremely important in fighting malicious infringements of public order, thefts, and misuse of powers; infringements of traffic rules, environmental protection, fire safety; and other dangerous offenses.[28]

The most important legal act regulating administrative liability and the procedures of its application is the Code of Administrative Offences.[29] However,

[27]Šedbaras (2005), p. 72.

[28]Dambrauskienė et al. (2004), p. 164.

[29]*Code of Administrative Offences of the Republic of Lithuania.* TAR, 2015-07-10, No. 11216.

administrative liability is also established in other laws, e.g., the Law on Alcohol Control, the Law on Competition, and several others.

The aims of the Code of Administrative Offences are to defend human rights and freedoms and the interests of the society and the state from administrative offenses by legal measures, to ensure the implementation of the principle of justice, and to encourage peaceful coexistence of the members of society.

The Code of Administrative Offences defines which acts prohibited by law are administrative offenses; this code establishes administrative penalties and administrative measures for foreseen offenses, the basis and conditions of administrative liability, and the procedures applied in cases of administrative offenses.

It should be noted that liability can be imposed only on natural persons according to this code. Administrative liability for administrative offenses committed by legal persons is foreseen for the heads of entities or other responsible persons. However, separate laws (e.g., the Law on Competition) may establish sanctions (which are essentially administrative penalties) also to legal persons.

Administrative sanctions found in the Code of Administrative Offences are warning, fine (a fine not smaller than 10 euros and not greater than 6000 euros may be applied according to this code), and community service (which can be imposed as an alternative administrative sanction, by changing a fine or a part of it to community service). It may be mentioned that one of the types of administrative sanctions introduced in the Code of Administrative Law Infringements that was valid until the Code of Administrative Offences came into force (January 1, 2017) was administrative detention (its maximum duration was up to 30 days).

In order to implement the purpose of administrative penalty, certain other administrative measures may be imposed together with it: (1) the withdrawal of an individual's special right (e.g., a driving license); (2) confiscation of property (e.g., a vehicle); (3) obligation to participate in programs (courses) of prevention of alcoholism and drug addiction, early intervention, health care, resocialization, improvement of interaction with children, changing violent behavior, and others; (4) prohibition on attending events held in public places.

By one decision or one administrative order, only one administrative penalty and one or more administrative measure(s) can be imposed on the person who is held liable for an administrative offense.

It should be noted that the court or an extrajudicial institution that is examining an administrative offense—with respect to the personality of the person who is held liable, as well as to the nature of the administrative offense, other circumstances of the case, and whether it would help to better implement the aims of administrative penalty—has the right not to impose an administrative penalty by a reasoned decision and to impose only an administrative measure, such as an obligation to participate in programs (courses) of prevention of alcoholism and drug addiction, early intervention, health care, resocialization, improvement of interaction with children, changing violent behavior, and others.

In Lithuania, disputes concerning decisions to impose administrative sanctions are heard in general competence courts, such as district courts and regional courts (as an appellate instance).

8.2.2 Administrative Proceedings

8.2.2.1 Legal Nature and System of Administrative Proceedings

Discussions regarding administrative proceedings as an administrative law institution intensified after administrative justice reform in 1999, when the administrative courts were established. A system of quasi-courts, i.e., institutions that examine administrative disputes according to pre-court procedures, was established together with the administrative courts.

Changes of the institutional system of administrative justice were accompanied by the adoption of new legal acts that regulate the examination of administrative disputes and administrative procedures that are carried out by public administration subjects. The Law on Public Administration,[30] which establishes the order of procedures carried out by public administration subjects, as well as the Law on Administrative Proceedings,[31] and the Law on Administrative Disputes Commissions,[32] which regulates procedures of hearing administrative disputes, were adopted.

When identifying administrative process as a certain institution of law, it is important to answer the question whether administrative proceedings are a part of administrative law or if they are an independent branch of law, such as civil proceedings law or criminal proceedings law. Even though Lithuanian legal science lacks a wider discussion and exhaustive research into various aspects of administrative proceedings, certain tendencies toward the crystallization of the concept of administrative proceedings can be observed.

According to some authors, independent administrative proceedings law has undoubtedly formed in Lithuania, and it is comprised of two parts: provisions of administrative proceedings law regulating the procedures for examining and deciding on administrative cases in administrative courts and provisions regulating the resolution of administrative disputes and other questions in extrajudicial institutions.[33] Others note that changes in legislation, as well as administrative dispute resolution institutions that are actually functioning, create preconditions to raise the question regarding separation of administrative proceedings law from material administrative law.[34] However, a problematic issue that will have influence on distinguishing administrative proceedings is the complexity of procedural relationships because relationships that occur when deciding on conflicts of individuals with public authorities and their officers, and conflicts between public authorities, which are decided on by administrative courts, the Chief Administrative

[30]*Law on Public Administration of the Republic of Lithuania*. Official Gazette, 1999, No. 60-1945.

[31]*Law on Administrative Proceedings of the Republic of Lithuania*. Official Gazette, 1999, No. 13-308.

[32]*Law on Administrative Disputes Commissions of the Republic of Lithuania*. Official Gazette, 1999, No. 13-310.

[33]Laužikas et al. (2003), p. 26.

[34]Andruškevičius (2004), pp. 110–111.

Disputes Commission, and the Ombudsman, are not homogeneous in nature.[35] The third group of authors emphatically ascribes administrative proceedings to the subject of administrative law. In their opinion, provisions of (procedural) administrative law also establish procedures for pre-court dispute resolution, public (administrative) disputes, as well as the application of administrative sanctions.[36]

There is also no unanimous opinion regarding the concept of administrative proceedings. Two conceptions of the notion of administrative proceedings are forming in the Lithuanian legal science: a wide one and a narrow one. According to supporters of the wide notion of administrative proceedings, the following types of administrative proceedings can be distinguished from all procedural acts that are performed in the area of public governance: (1) adoption of administrative regulatory legal acts, (2) application of administrative liability and other administrative measures, (3) examination of administrative disputes, (4) and general (legitimate) administrative proceedings that include procedures for drafting and adopting administrative acts of positivistic nature applying law, conclusion of administrative contracts, and procedures for carrying out supervision, control, and other public administration actions by public administration institutions.[37]

Some academics criticize this conception of administrative proceedings because, in their opinion, the concept of administrative law in the wide sense is too abstract, overlaps in functions of public administration and the judiciary, and does not highlight the differences between procedural activities that are regulated by administrative procedural provisions and jurisdictional activities that are regulated by provisions of administrative proceedings. In their opinion, the concept of administrative proceedings should be connected only to the jurisdictional proceedings, i.e., the resolution of a legal dispute[38] (corresponding to the narrow conception of the notion of administrative proceedings).

8.2.2.2 Extrajudicial Examination of Administrative Disputes

Administrative disputes are examined not only by courts but also by various extrajudicial institutions in Lithuania. Pretrial dispute resolution can be mandatory or facultative. In cases when the law establishes mandatory pretrial examination of administrative cases of a certain category, the interested individual does not have the right to defend their infringed upon right or a legally protected interest in an administrative court until they use the mandatory pretrial dispute resolution procedure. In other cases, laws grant the right for the interested person to choose the means of defending their infringed upon rights or legally protected interests, i.e., the person has the right to apply directly to an administrative court or to use a pretrial dispute resolution procedure before applying to court.

[35] Andruškevičius (2001), pp. 7–15.

[36] Bakaveckas (2012), p. 20.

[37] Šedbaras (2006), p. 237.

[38] Paužaitė-Kulvinskienė (2005), pp. 35–37.

Pretrial dispute resolution institutions can be divided into two groups according to their organizational form. Institutions that are established specifically for hearing disputes of a certain category should be ascribed to the first group. Those are administrative dispute commissions (the Chief administrative dispute commission and municipal public administrative disputes commissions), tax dispute commission under the government, and the dispute commission under the Ministry of Social Security and Labour.

Another group of institutions that hears disputes according to pretrial dispute resolution procedures are public administration subjects to which the law has assigned not only public administration functions but also extrajudicial examination of administrative disputes. Decisions on disputes are usually taken by the head of the institution. Laws do not regulate in detail the procedures for examining complaints in public administration institutions. Usually the procedures for hearing complaints are established by an internal administrative act adopted by the head of the institution. A dispute in a public administration institution is usually decided on without organizing a hearing and without having directly listened to the interested persons. An appeal against a decision of a public administration institution regarding pretrial dispute resolution may be brought before the respective regional administrative court.

8.2.2.3 Administrative Courts and Their Competence

Administrative courts have been working since May 1, 1999, in Lithuania. Administrative courts are organized according to the German model of a completely independent system, separate from general competence courts. In Lithuania, there are five regional administrative courts and the Supreme Administrative Court of Lithuania. However, an organizational reform of the courts is currently underway, and after its implementation, beginning on January 1, 2018, only two administrative regional courts (Kaunas and Vilnius) will remain functioning.[39] Regional administrative courts are first instance courts, and the Supreme Administrative Court of Lithuania is the appellate instance court. Even though there is no instance of cassation in the administrative courts system, the functions of the court of cassation are carried out by the Supreme Administrative Court of Lithuania, which forms uniform case law of administrative courts in interpreting and applying legislation. Furthermore, the Supreme Administrative Court of Lithuania hears cases of certain categories as the sole and final instance (e.g., cases concerning the lawfulness of regulatory administrative acts adopted by central administration subjects or cases concerning decisions of the Central Electoral Commission).

Regional administrative courts hear cases concerning the legality of administrative acts adopted by public administration subjects that are functioning in the territory of their jurisdiction. In addition, the Vilnius regional administrative

[39] *Decision of the Parliament of the Republic of Lithuania, 22 December 2015, No. XII-2209 On reorganization of courts.* TAR, 2015-12-23, No. 20269.

court hears cases in which a party to the proceedings is a central state administration subject, and also certain other cases (e.g., tax cases, cases concerning foreigners).

The Constitutional Court has stated that the Constitution does not allow a situation in which it is not possible to check in court whether legal acts (their parts) do not contravene the Constitution or laws, when the control of compliance with the Constitution of these legal acts is not assigned to the jurisdiction of the Constitutional Court by the Constitution (those are, inter alia, acts adopted by ministers, other lower-ranking regulations, as well as acts adopted by municipal institutions).[40]

This constitutional imperative has been implemented by assigning cases concerning the lawfulness of regulatory administrative acts that establish abstract rules of conduct to the jurisdiction of administrative courts. When hearing cases concerning the lawfulness of regulatory administrative acts, administrative courts do not decide on the individual dispute concerning an infringed upon right but only assess whether a regulatory administrative act (its part) is not in breach of a law or a regulatory act adopted by the government. Only subjects, specified in the Law on Administrative Proceedings, have the right to bring a claim before an administrative court asking to examine the legality of a normative administrative act, e.g., Members of the Parliament, Ombudsmen of the Parliament, courts of general or specialized competence, if they have doubts on whether a particular regulatory administrative act, which should be applied in an individual case before the court, is compatible with a higher-ranking legal act.

If, having examined a case concerning the lawfulness of a regulatory administrative act, an administrative court finds that the challenged regulatory administrative act is in breach of a higher-ranking legal act, the court adopts a decision to annul such an administrative act (its part). When a final administrative court's decision declaring a regulatory administrative act (its part) unlawful is officially published in the Register of Legal Acts, this act becomes invalid, i.e., this regulatory administrative act is removed from the system of law.

The Supreme Administrative Court of Lithuania has noted in its case law that the legal force of a final court decision and the prohibition to apply a regulatory administrative act that has been declared invalid by a competent administrative court is binding on public administration subjects when they carry out their legislative function. The legal force of an administrative court decision cannot be overcome by repeatedly adopted regulatory administrative acts.[41]

The Supreme Administrative Court of Lithuania also delivers opinions upon request of a municipal council as to whether a member of a municipality council or a mayor, against whom a procedure of loss of mandate has been started, has breached their oath or failed to exercise their powers conferred on them by laws.

---

[40] *Decision of the Constitutional Court of the Republic of Lithuania, 5 September 2005*. Official Gazette, 2005, No. 11-4132.

[41] *Vilnius Regional Administrative Court v Ministry of Justice*. Supreme Administrative Court of Lithuania, 2007, No. I-17-11-07.

Since an independent administrative court system is created for disputes arising in the field of public administration, the question of jurisdiction delimitation between general competence courts and administrative courts is important. These questions are decided by a special judicial panel that is comprised by the chairman of the Civil Cases Division of the Supreme Court of Lithuania, deputy chairman of the Supreme Administrative Court of Lithuania, and one judge from each of those courts appointed by chairmen of those courts. Any court of general competence or an administrative court may apply to this panel if it has doubts regarding the jurisdiction that a particular case falls under.

8.2.2.4 Administrative Disputes in Judicial Proceedings

The Law on Administrative Proceedings establishes procedures for examining disputes arising from administrative legal relationships. Proceedings in administrative courts are of an investigative nature. When examining cases, an administrative court must be active both in collecting and investigating proofs and in finding out circumstances that are relevant to the case. When deciding on an administrative dispute, the court may not base its decision solely on proofs submitted by the parties to the case and the circumstances pointed out by them but must always take the initiative to establish and thoroughly, objectively investigate all circumstances relevant to the case.

If a special law does not foresee otherwise, a complaint might be submitted to the first instance court within 1 month after the day when the disputed act was published and delivered to the interested person or a notice regarding the act (inaction) was delivered to the interested person. If the applicant misses the deadline for submitting the complaint foreseen by law, the court might renew it by request of the applicant if it is established that the period for lodging a complaint has been missed for important reasons.

In any stage of the proceedings, a court can apply interim measures both on request of a party to the case or by its own initiative. Interim measures can be the following: prohibition to perform certain actions for the respondent, temporary suspension of recovery under an enforceable title, temporary suspension of the disputed individual legal act, and other measures applied by the court or the judge.

The first instance court hears cases in oral hearings. Hearings are public; however, a hearing can be held behind closed doors in order to protect the secrecy of private or family life and state, service, or commercial secrets.

Participants of court proceedings are informed about the hearing by writs of summons. During the court hearing, explanations of parties to the case are heard; witnesses, specialists, experts are interviewed; and written evidence is examined. An audio record is made to register the court hearing. A court can base its decision only on those proofs that have been investigated in the court hearing.

Decisions of the first instance administrative court may be appealed to the Supreme Administrative Court of Lithuania. All participants to the proceedings can bring an appeal. The appeal is examined in written proceedings. However, the court may decide to examine the case in oral proceedings by request of parties to the case or by its own initiative.

Proceedings that have been finished by a final court decision can be renewed on the basis foreseen in the Law on Administrative Proceedings. For example, proceedings may be renewed if the European Court of Human Rights finds that a court decision of the Republic of Lithuania is in breach of the Convention for the Protection of Human Rights and Fundamental Freedoms or when new material facts of the case come to light if they had not been known during the court proceedings.

8.2.2.5 Procedures for Applying Administrative Liability

Procedures for applying administrative liability are regulated by the Code of Administrative Offences[42] and other special laws that foresee administrative liability for infringement of provisions of these special laws.

Procedures in cases concerning offenses, the liability for which is foreseen by the Code of Administrative Offences (administrative offenses), take place according to the procedural provisions established in this code. The following stages can be distinguished in procedures concerning administrative offenses: investigation of the case, examination of the case, appeal against a decision, and compliance with a decision imposing a penalty.

In case officers, when carrying out control of compliance with legislation, or other functions established in legal acts, find that an administrative offense has possibly been committed, they start an administrative offense procedure and carry out an investigation.

When carrying out an investigation of the administrative offense, the officers may interview persons; carry out inspections of sites, premises, terrains, things, or documents; carry out identification display; require providing things or documents that are relevant to the case; or order an expert or perform other actions foreseen in the Code of Administrative Offences.

When sufficient data is gathered that an administrative offense has been committed, the officer who has carried out the investigation draws up an administrative offense report. The person who is held liable for the offense participates when the report is being drawn up and has the right to submit an explanation concerning the committed offense or remarks concerning the content of the report. An administrative order is written in the administrative offense report, i.e., an offer for the person who is held liable to voluntarily pay a fine that is equal to half of the minimum fine foreseen in the sanction or to return documents verifying a specific right to the respective institution, i.e., to agree to a withdrawal of a specific right for a fixed term. An administrative order is not subject to appeal. If a person complies with the administrative order within the set time limit, the administrative offense procedure is complete; if the order is not complied with, the proceedings continue in the usual manner.

An administrative offense report, together with the material collected during the investigation, is sent or submitted to the institution that is competent to examine the case of the administrative offense. Administrative offense cases are heard by

[42]*Code of Administrative Offences of the Republic of Lithuania*. TAR, 2015-07-10, No. 11216.

district courts and by pretrial institutions whose officers have carried out the investigation.

Participants to the proceedings may appeal to the district court against a decision that has been made in a pretrial procedure. The decision of a district court that has been taken after examining the complaint can be appealed to the regional court.

The decision of a district court, which has been made after examining the administrative offense case, can be appealed to the regional court. The decision of the regional court, made after examining the administrative offense case in appellate proceedings, comes into force on the day of its delivery and is not subject to a cassation appeal.

The procedures for applying economic sanctions to legal persons are established in specific laws that regulate certain economic activities. There is no unified legal act in the legal system of Lithuania that would establish procedures for applying economic sanctions to a legal person.

The decisions of competent authorities imposing economic or prohibitive sanctions may be appealed to the regional administrative court according to the procedures established by the Law on Administrative Proceedings.

Summarizing the abovementioned legal regulation of administrative proceedings, we can say that only clear rules of administrative proceedings can ensure legal certainty, reduce the risk of abuse, and guarantee protection of human rights. An essential issue of the administrative proceedings regulation is that certain areas of public authorities' procedural activities are not regulated in sufficient detail and clarity. Procedures for adopting individual administrative acts by public administration subjects are not established on the level of law, and procedures for pretrial administrative dispute resolution are not regulated in detail.

The Constitutional Court has noted that if certain sanctions introduced by laws amount to criminal sanctions by their severity, no matter which sort of legal liability (administrative, disciplinary, or others) they are ascribed to, and no matter how they are named in laws, the laws must establish procedural guarantees arising from the Constitution for persons that are held liable according to the respective laws. The guarantees arise, inter alia, from Article 31 of the Constitution, the provisions of which cannot be interpreted as intended only for persons that are prosecuted in criminal proceedings.[43]

Even though laws authorize the executive to impose sanctions on legal persons that may be considered punishments of a criminal nature, the legislation concerning procedures for the imposition of economic and prohibitive sanctions does not ensure all the procedural guarantees for persons that are held liable.

One viable direction for perspective improvement of administrative proceedings legislation could be preparing and adopting a code of administrative proceedings that would cover procedures of public administration, administrative dispute examination proceedings, and procedures of administrative liability application.

---

[43] *Decision of the Constitutional Court of the Republic of Lithuania, 10 November 2005*. Official Gazette, 2005, No. 134-4819.

8.3 Criminal Law and Porcedure

Edita Gruodytė and Mindaugas Bilius
Faculty of Law, Vytautas Magnus University, Jonavos st. 66, LT-44138 Kaunas, Lithuania
e-mail: edita.gruodyte@vdu.lt; mindaugas.bilius@vdu.lt

8.3.1 Criminal Law[44]

Development of the Lithuanian criminal code is directly linked to the evolution of the Lithuanian state: till the restoration of Lithuanian independence on March 11, 1990, the Soviet criminal code (enacted in 1961) was in force in Lithuania since it was part of the Soviet Union. The formation and revival of Lithuanian national criminal law was a gradual process. It began with the restoration of independence as a process of changing and supplementing the criminal code of 1961, while preparation of a national criminal code (together with the criminal procedure and penal codes) took more than 10 years, notwithstanding the fact that the working group for the drafting of the national criminal code was established in 1990.[45] The final version of the new criminal code (hereinafter in this subsection referred to as CC or Criminal Code) was enacted only in 2000,[46] postponing its entry into force until the May 1, 2003, providing the opportunity to the public, lawyers, and researchers to get acquainted with it.

The Criminal Code is a modern legal act, establishing the framework of national criminal law and policy, evaluating and reflecting relevant fundamental human rights and principles, EU legislation and international obligations, the best practices of modern democratic states in the field of criminal lawmaking, and the jurisprudence of national and international courts. During its existence, the CC has experienced a number of changes and supplements. For example, during 2015, the CC was changed and supplemented with new norms 11 times. Generally, a large part of changes are influenced by international and EU commitments; however, not all amendments are evaluated as objectively justified.[47]

[44]Some parts of this section are prepared using materials from the articles: Gruodytė (2008); Gruodytė (2011).

[45]Švedas and Prapiestis (2011), p. 21.

[46]*The Criminal Code of the Republic of Lithuania*. Official Gazette 2000, No. 89-2741.

[47]As critical examples are mentioned some norms of special part in which qualified (heavier liability) is established. One example—theft of a vehicle is established as a qualified theft which is already the second category of intentional crime for which imprisonment of up to 6 years could be provided. However, the value of the car is not important (i.e. it could be situations that theft of 200 euros (or even a cheaper one) vehicle could be punished much more strictly than theft of other property of much higher value). The next example—an organized group is defined as one of the aggravating circumstances in the general part of the CC but in few norms (Robbery and Extortion of property) it is either introduced as a feature increasing criminal liability (qualified crime) and etc. See: Švedas and Prapiestis (2011), pp. 21–22.

The CC, unlike criminal codes of the most European countries, is an integral legal act into which all international and EU obligations are transferred, i.e., no separate laws regulating criminal issues are enacted. The code has an ordinary structure and is comprised of two parts: general and special. Right now (beginning May 1, 2004) the CC is supplemented by an additional technical part: the "Implemented EU Legal acts." At the moment,[48] 30 EU acts have been implemented by the Lithuanian legislature.

In the general part of the CC, traditional issues such as basic ideas and principles of criminal law are established together with such institutes as validity of criminal law, types of criminal acts, stages and forms of criminal act, circumstances eliminating criminal liability, release from criminal liability, penalties, punishments, principles of their imposition, statute of limitations, compulsory medical treatment, etc.

In the special part of the CC, specific criminal acts and possible sanctions are established. The special part starts with crimes against humanity and state crimes, and only then are the criminal acts against human life established, which indicates that priority is given to society over the individual. In constructing the special part, the requirement of administrative punishment as a prior condition for certain criminal offenses (used in the old criminal code) were abandoned, which is evaluated by Lithuanian scholars as a positive development since the same offense due to repetition did not become more severe.[49] The special part of the CC is extended much more in comparison with the old criminal code (of 1961): there are 32 sections, while in the previous one there were only 13. The updating of the special part was determined by several factors: tendencies in the Western European countries, globalization, the evolvement of the new categories of crimes, and the aim of the legislator to make clarity more accurately distinguishing separate groups of offenses. The best example of this detailed classification is in crimes against human life and health. Here there are three separate chapters: Crimes against Human Life, Crimes against Human Health, and Crimes endangering Human Life and Health (Chapters XVII–XIX) are established.

The CC is the most important source of Lithuanian criminal law. Other sources of Lithuanian criminal law are rulings of the Constitutional Court of the Republic of Lithuania, judgments of the European Court of Human Rights, and preliminary rulings of the Court of Justice of the EU. In accordance with the doctrine of the Constitutional Court of the Republic of Lithuania,[50] continuity of jurisprudence is implied by the rule of law principle, which means that court precedents are sources

[48]According to the Criminal Code, as valid on 29th of February 2016.

[49]Abramavičius and Prapiestis (2014), pp. 161–162.

[50]Example, see: *On the compliance of item 2 of paragraph 1 of article 62, paragraph 4 (wording of 11 July 1996) of article 69 of the Republic of Lithuania's law on the Constitutional Court and paragraph 3 (wording of 24 January 2002) of article 11, paragraph 2 (wording of 24 January 2002) of article 96 of the republic of Lithuania's law on courts with the constitution of the Republic of Lithuania*. The Ruling of the Constitutional Court of the Republic of Lithuania, 2006, no. 33/03. http://www.lrkt.lt/en/court-acts/search/170/ta925/content.

of criminal law. The Constitutional Court treats the reference to the precedents as an implementation of the principle of justice and a condition for uniform court practices.[51]

Usually, because the most important achievements are enumerated,[52] the following aspects of the general part of the CC would be revealed in greater detail: classification of offenses, introduction of diminished capacity (*mens rea*), extension of corporate liability, development of factors eliminating criminal liability or discharging from criminal liability, and the reform of the penal system.

An important part of the CC due to their gravity, the classification of criminal acts is provided here. The criminal acts are classified into two sorts: misdemeanors and crimes. The first ones are petty crimes (such as intoxication of a child with alcohol (Article 161) or theft of a low value (118–188 euros) property, for which no imprisonment sanction (except the arrest penalty) can be imposed. The detailed classification is given in Scheme 8.1.

The institute of diminished capacity (Article 17 of the CC) was introduced with the enactment of the CC and is established as a result of a mental disorder, even though it is not a sufficient ground for finding a person legally incapacitated. The mental disorder must be of such a nature that a person lacks the capacity sufficient to fully appreciate the dangerous nature of the criminal act or to control his/her behavior. The court may recognize a person as being of diminished capacity only based on forensic psychiatric expert examination.[53] In Lithuania, the result for the person with established diminished capacity is dependent on the gravity of the crime, which is not typical practice in other countries.[54] In case a person has committed a less serious crime, the penalty may be commuted or he/she could be released from criminal liability (with provision of penal sanctions or compulsory medical treatment), while if a serious or grave crime is committed the penalty could be commuted only.[55] Theoretically, the institute of diminished capacity could be applied for any category of crime but it is rather seldom applied in practice. The institute is criticized for not covering other cases (such as peculiarities of social or mental maturity).[56]

In Lithuania as in most EU countries, liability for a legal person is established.[57] It could be provided only for the crimes that are indicated in the special part of the

[51]*On the Compliance of Articles 4 and 165 (Wording of 28 February 2002) of the Code of Civil Procedure of the Republic of Lithuania with the Constitution of the Republic of Lithuania.* The Ruling of the Constitutional Court of the Republic of Lithuania, 2007, no. 26/07. http://www.lrkt.lt/en/court-acts/search/170/ta1381/content.

[52]See: Gruodytė (2008); Gruodytė (2011); Švedas and Prapiestis (2011); Piesliakas (2006), pp. 37–63.

[53]The Supreme Court of Lithuania, *R.K. v State*, Case 2K-142-976, Judgment of 13 January 2015.

[54]Gruodytė and Palionienė (2014), pp. 57–76.

[55]For more details about diminished capacity in English see: Gruodytė (2008), pp. 23–24.

[56]Piesliakas (2006), p. 331.

[57]For the first time it was introduced at the end of 2002, implementing international obligations for corruption crimes.

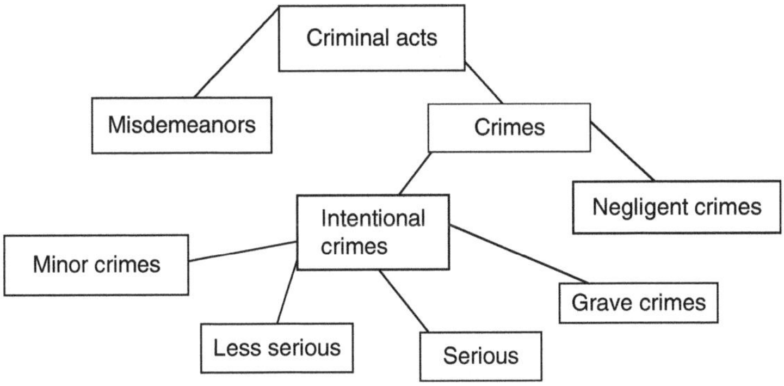

Scheme 8.1 Classification of criminal acts

CC. At the moment,[58] criminal liability for a legal entity is provided in about 50% of total crimes and is expanding.[59] The dominant categories of crimes where liability for a legal entity is established are corruption, economic, financial, environmental, intellectual crimes, and criminal acts against security of electronic data and information. However, a legal entity may also be liable for categories of crimes (for example, rape, sexual assault, sexual abuse, negligent homicide, etc.) that are traditionally treated like the ones done only by natural persons. As liability for a legal entity was not traditional to Lithuanian culture, the Constitutional Court of the Republic of Lithuania (after getting petitions from a group of Lithuanian Seimas (Parliament) and lower courts) had to evaluate if liability for a legal entity does or does not violate our Constitution. The court decided that it is in accordance with the constitutional norms.[60]

In Lithuania, as in most countries, where liability for a legal entity is introduced, liability for a legal person is derivative, i.e., a concrete natural person who committed a crime must be found, and only then should it be evaluated where liability for a juridical person could be established. Two legal theories ground corporate liability in Lithuania: the identification doctrine and vicarious liability. Three possible alternative sanctions can be imposed: a fine (from one MGL[61] (37.6 euros) up to 50 thousand MGL (1,880,000 euros)), restriction of operation of the legal entity either prohibiting the legal entity from engaging in certain activities or ordering to close certain division of the legal entity (for a period from 1 to 5 years), or liquidation of the legal entity. In practice, financial sanctions are the most

[58] According to the *Criminal Code*, as valid on 2nd March 2016.

[59] Example in 2011 liability for a legal entity was introduced for 101 crimes which constituted about 42 percent of all crimes. See: Gruodytė (2011), p. 319.

[60] The full decision of the court could be found here: http://www.lrkt.lt/en/court-acts/search/170/ta1236/content.

[61] All fines in Lithuania are defined by minimal existence level, however such a unit of measurement does not exist from 2008, as it was changed by basic size of punishments and penalties (BBN in Lithuanian). Official Gazette, 2008, No. 83-3294.

popular for a legal entity. The court is also empowered to announce the imposed penalty upon a legal entity in the media (Article 43 of the CC). Special subjects, such as the state, a municipality, a state and municipal institution and agency, as well as international public organizations, are exempt from criminal liability. As liability for a legal entity was introduced implementing international and EU obligations and making literal transposition of these acts into national law, without an assessment of the potential problems in their application there are some issues that are not regulated by the legislator. For example, the courts have full discretion in deciding which sanction and which amount of fine to provide since the legal entity as legislator provides no special criteria and the outcomes could be very uneven.[62] Other unregulated issues are conspiracy between natural and legal persons, possibility to release a legal entity from criminal liability or criminal penalty, imposition of penalty for the commission of several criminal acts, accumulation and replacement of sentences, and such and various unregulated questions of criminal procedure.[63] The Supreme Court of Lithuania has solved some unregulated issues (for example, possibility to apply release from criminal liability for a legal entity[64]); however, provision of special criminal norms would be a better decision.

Criminal policy in the CC is more balanced as there are more opportunities for releasing an offender from criminal liability or punishment and avoiding imprisonment sanction; however, such privileges are dependent on the gravity of the criminal act, the behavior of the offender (both after criminal act and his/her criminal history), and the will of the victim in certain cases.

The CC provides eight alternative circumstances eliminating criminal liability: three traditional ones, namely, self-defense (Article 28), immediate necessity (Article 31), and the detention (arrest) of a person who has committed a criminal act (Article 29), and five new ones, namely, discharge of a professional duty (Article 30), performance of an assignment of a law enforcement institution (Article 32), execution of an order (Article 33), justifiable professional or economic risk (Article 34), and scientific experiment (Article 35).

More grounds allowing the release of an offender from criminal liability are established in the CC: seven general ones and five special ones are provided in certain articles of the special part of the CC. The general grounds are the following: a case in which a person, as the result of intoxication, has committed (up to) a serious crime against his will and hence lacked capacity sufficient to fully appreciate the dangerous nature of the criminal act or to control his behavior at the time of his conduct (Article 19); a case in which a person or criminal act loses its dangerousness (Article 36); the minor relevance of a crime (Article 37);

[62]Gruodytė (2011), p. 320.

[63]See: Švedas (2011). Some Problem Aspects . . . .

[64]The court decided that a legal entity may be either released from criminal liability or provided certain criteria. See: The Supreme Court of Lithuania, *P.G., AB"B.G.I." v State*, Case 2K-7-84, Judgment of 17 April 2012.

reconciliation between the offender and the victim (Article 38); mitigating circumstances, when a person actively assisted in detecting the criminal acts committed by members of an organized group or a criminal association (Article 39); and being on bail (Article 40). Special grounds are the following: for voluntarily provision to a state institution of significant information about a *coup d'état* being prepared (Article 114); for usage of forced labor or services in case a person actively assisted in detecting the criminal acts related to trafficking in human beings (Article 147-2); for bribing or trading in influence if a person actively assisted in detecting criminal acts (Articles 226–227); for production, acquisition, or storage of narcotic drugs and psychotropic substances if a person voluntarily applies to a health institution or to a state institution (Article 259); or for illegal crossing of the state border with the intent of illegally crossing into a third state (Article 291). Some of the enumerated circumstances are conditional, i.e., the offender is released on certain conditions (for example, if a reconciliation institute is applied and the offender commits a new intentional crime within the period of one year), and in case they are infringed the release from criminal liability is revoked.

The major changes occurred in reforming the criminal penal system. With the enactment of the CC, two categories of punishments were established: six criminal penalties for crimes (for natural persons: community service, fine, restriction of liberty, arrest, fixed-term imprisonment, life imprisonment[65] (Article 42 of the CC)), four criminal penalties for misdemeanors (no imprisonment sanction), and ten penal sanctions (deprivation of special rights, deprivation of public rights, deprivation of the right to be employed in a certain position or to engage in a certain type of activities, prohibition to exercise a special right, confiscation of property, obligation to live separately from the victim's and (or) not approach the injured person closer than a prescribed distance, participation in the programs addressing violent behavior, extended confiscation of property compensation for or elimination of property damage, unpaid work, payment of a contribution to the fund of crime victims (Article 67 of the CC)). The main concept of penal sanctions is that they could be imposed on persons either released from criminal liability or from penalty or in cases of release from a custodial sentence on parole. However, the first seven penal sanctions could be applied together with the penalty imposed for a certain crime. For example, if a person committed a violent crime, programs addressing violent behavior could be imposed together with the penalty. So even though, after enactment of the CC, the principle for imposition of penalties in theory (i.e., that only one penalty may be imposed for one criminal act) is not always true, as many penal punishments could be imposed additionally along with the sanction.

[65]Up till 5th of July 2011, there were two additional penalties: deprivation of public rights and deprivation of the right to be employed in a certain position or to engage in a certain type of activities were possible for certain categories of crimes which from provided time framework were removed to the category of penal sanctions.

Special rules and regulations are established for minors (an offender under 18 years of age or in exceptional cases[66] up till 21). A life imprisonment sanction cannot be imposed on them; the maximum terminated imprisonment is 10 years (while for adult persons it is up to 20 years). As a general rule, fixed-term imprisonment for minors can be imposed only in exceptional circumstances. A minor can be conditionally released from a penalty (suspension of penalty) for any category of crime (including grave and very serious crimes) in case the imprisonment for a term not exceeding 5 years is imposed. Special reformative sanctions could be imposed on minors in cases in which he/she has been released from criminal liability or penalty or in cases of release from a custodial sentence on parole. Six alternative reformative sanctions are introduced by the legislator: warning, compensation for or elimination of property damage (only when the minor has resources that he can independently dispose of or when he is capable of eliminating the damage by his own work), unpaid reformative work (with the consent of a minor only), placement for upbringing and supervision with parents or other natural or legal persons caring for children, restriction on conduct, and placement in a special reformative facility (for a period of 6 months up to 3 years but not longer than until a minor reaches the age of 18 years) (Article 82). A court is allowed to impose not more than three mutually compatible reformative sanctions. Differently from the imposition of penal sanctions on adults, in a case in which a minor fails to comply with them, they could only be replaced with other reformative sanctions—there is no opportunity to provide criminal penalties (Article 89).

In addition to the positive tendencies reflected in the CC, at least some critical aspects can be identified. The biggest problem in Lithuania is the number of prisoners, which is increased rapidly between 2008 and January 2013, when there were 326 prisoners per 100,000 inhabitants, which is two to three times higher than the average in Europe.[67] Critical remarks are provided to the legislator regarding the quality of criminal norms: usage of evaluative, abstract, sometimes ambiguous concepts while defining criminal norms, and in the opinion of O. Fedosiukas[68] there are many norms of the CC where innocuous behavior that does not reach the gravity of a criminal level is being criminalized.[69]

[66]Where a court, having taken into consideration the nature of and reasons for the committed criminal act as well as other circumstances of the case, and, where necessary, clarifications or conclusion of a specialist, decides that such a person is equal to a minor according to his social maturity (Art. 80 of the CC).

[67]Fedosiukas (2014), p. 28.

[68]Professor of criminal law and judge in the Supreme Court of the Republic of Lithuania.

[69]Fedosiukas (2014), p. 32.

8.3.2 Criminal Procedure Law[70]

The enforcement of criminal law is influenced by criminal procedure. The main rules of criminal procedure in Lithuania are set in the Code of the Criminal Procedure[71] (hereinafter in this subsection referred to as CpC), which was enacted in 2002.

Criminal procedure in Lithuania can be conditionally divided into two parts: the pretrial investigation and the trial process. A pretrial investigation can be initiated by the victim or by the pretrial investigation officer or by the prosecutor, but the decision to begin such process can be made only by these two officials.

Lithuanian criminal procedure rules require the public prosecutor or pretrial investigation institution to automatically begin an investigation when there are signs of a crime being committed. The basis to begin an investigation is a complaint received by the public prosecutor or pretrial investigation institution or when certain findings are made by these institutions. Depending on the crime committed, some situations for beginning an investigation require a complaint by the victim.

If the complaint or information about the crime is received by the prosecutor, he has the right to begin an investigation himself and to do any investigation activity, or he may delegate it to any officer of the pretrial investigation institution. The prosecutor is responsible for all actions done in the pretrial investigation; his orders are mandatory to the pretrial investigation officers. In the pretrial investigation, the prosecutor is not a party to the case. His task is not only to collect evidence against the suspect but also to collect evidence that is in favor of the accused, that is, evidence that could result in acquittal. The prosecutor must decide for himself about the direction and extent of the investigation.

If the pretrial investigation is performed by the pretrial investigation officer, he is responsible himself for the successful investigation and has the power to decide which actions to take. Regardless, the prosecutor controls all actions by the officer (s) and can ask for their report. If there is a need, the pretrial investigation officer can impose certain coercive measures: e.g., taking the documents, obliging periodical registration at the police station, assigning a written pledge not to leave, giving a soldier to a body of troops for supervision, or giving a juvenile to the parents, guardians, or other persons responsible for taking care of the juvenile, for purposes of supervision.[72] During the investigation, the pretrial investigation officer can temporarily detain the person (for no longer than 48 h), bring a person to the court by force, and assign a prosecutor or other officers to search and inspect the person, to photograph, film, or measure the person.

Some pretrial investigation actions require involvement of the pretrial investigation judge. The pretrial investigation judge has the power to impose and sanction coercive measures, to swear and question witnesses and victims, to interrogate

[70]Some parts of this section are prepared using materials from the article: Bilius (2011).

[71]*Criminal Procedure Code of the Republic of Lithuania*, Official Gazette, 2002, No. 37-1341.

[72]Other coercive measures could be imposed only by the prosecutor or the court.

suspects, to approve decisions of the prosecutor to close the pretrial investigation, to approve decisions of the prosecutor to renew a closed pretrial investigation, and to hear complaints from the participants of the process about the actions of the pretrial investigation officers and the prosecutor. The pretrial investigation judge can only perform such actions if there is a request from the prosecutor, which he presents on his own initiative or by request from a participant in the process.

The prosecutor and pretrial investigation institutions in each case, when they find features of criminal acts, must undertake in regard to their competence all lawful measures to make an investigation in the shortest time period and to reveal any criminal acts. The CpC states that the pretrial investigation should not last more than 3 months in cases where misdemeanors are committed, not more than 6 months in cases where minor and less serious crimes are committed or for crimes committed through negligence, and not more than 9 months in cases where serious or grave crimes are committed. But all these terms can be extended by the superior prosecutor. If, after the questioning of the suspect, pretrial investigation lasts more than 6 months, the suspect or his defender can give a complaint to the pretrial investigation judge on grounds of unreasonable delay of the pretrial investigation. The pretrial investigation judge could also oblige the prosecutor to finalize the pretrial investigation by setting a time limit for this. If the pretrial investigation judge terminates the pretrial investigation, there is no possibility to renew the investigation terms on any ground. Such regulation has a direct effect on the pretrial investigation period, and, for example, in 2015 the average term of pretrial investigation was 7.1 months, and 55% of the crimes committed were revealed.[73]

The status of the victim in criminal procedure could be obtained only by the decision of the pretrial investigation officer or the prosecutor. Such status could be given only to the natural person, who suffered moral, bodily, or monetary damage. If the damage was suffered by the legal person, it can have only the status of a civil claimant in the criminal procedure.

Under Lithuanian law, every person can be a witness in the case if there is reason to believe that he knows any information that can be useful in deciding the case. The courts keep the position that testimonies of the child should be evaluated not as strict and categorically as the testimonies of adults.[74] As a witness, a person cannot be required to give testimony about the crime he possibly committed except when he agrees to do so. In this situation, the person must be questioned as a suspect. There is one exception in the law allowing for the questioning of such a person not as a suspect. A person could be questioned as a witness about the crime he possibly committed only if he agrees to be questioned and there is a decision of the prosecutor. Under these conditions, the questioned person is called a special

[73]The Report of the Prosecutor's Office of the Republic of Lithuania of the Year 2015, pp. 7, 9. http://www.prokuraturos.lt/data/public/uploads/2016/03/prokuraturos_veiklos_2015_m_ataskaita.pdf.

[74]The Court of Appeal of Lithuania, *Š. Č. v State*, Case 1A-480/2013, Judgment of 25 November 2013.

witness. Such person has the right to have an authorized representative and to ask to be declared as a suspect. For such a person, there is no legal responsibility for evasion to give testimony or for false testimony. The questioning of persons with special witness status is necessary when, under the case circumstances, it is not clear whether the person is involved in criminal activity, and this could be revealed only after the questioning or in situations when the law requires special permissions to get to question a person as a suspect. The main difference between a suspect and a special witness is that you cannot impose coercive measures on a special witness.

The pretrial investigation begins with the decision of the officials when there is information about a crime being committed. There is no need to have named a suspect in this decision. The status of a suspect can be obtained in the following situations: when he is detained (for 48 h) on suspicion that he committed a crime, when he is interrogated about the crime that he is suspected of having committed, when he is called to interrogation and there is written notice about suspicion, or when he is hiding and the status of the suspect is given by the decision of the prosecutor or pretrial investigation judge. The suspect is always provided with a written notice about suspicion. In this notice, the specifics of the crime (the place and time of the crime and other circumstances) and the criminal law that such action violates are given, as well as all rights of the suspect. When the pretrial investigation is over and the indictment is being written, the person from this moment acquires the status of an accused.

The right to defense of the suspect is enforced from the moment of the first interrogation or detention. Defense counsels in criminal procedure can only be advocates and, in some cases, advocate's assistants. During the criminal process, the suspect can refuse to have a defense counsel, but this decision is not mandatory if certain conditions are established (mostly in situations when there is an assumption that without the defense counsel the suspect will not properly exercise his rights). If the suspect asks for a defense counsel and there are no mandatory requirements for the defense to be guaranteed, there is a possibility to apply for state-guaranteed legal aid.

If a person acquires the status of a suspect, certain coercive measures can be imposed. Those are arrest, intensive observation, house arrest, the obligation to live separately from the victim or not to come closer than is established, bail, detention of documents, the obligation to check in periodically in the police station, and a written commitment not to depart. The other measures that can be imposed upon a suspect are temporary detention, placement in a medical supervisory institution, temporary removal from a position, and temporary suspension of the right to engage in certain activities. At the pretrial stage, court proceedings in which questions of imposing coercive measures are solved are not held publicly unless the court decides otherwise.

The pretrial investigation requires that all collected materials are treated as data and become evidence only when the judge declares it in his judgment. The judge at the court hears the parties, and therefore the judgment is based on evidence produced in the court. But certain evidence may be replaced sometimes by reading the record of previous statements that have been previously given in the court—for example, in the presence of a pretrial investigation judge. Which material can be considered as evidence is decided by the rules of relevance (related with the case, supports or denies a particular circumstance) and admissibility (are collected without violation of the laws). The relevant case data can also be collected by experts or specialists. They can also draw conclusions about the material that was given to them.

The pretrial investigation ends when the public prosecutor decides either to drop the charges or to write an accusation act (or to write a statement to apply the rules of summary process) or when he decides to move to the process of forced medical treatment. The charges can be dropped when the public prosecutor sees that there is not enough evidence to show that the crime was committed by that person. Grounds for the termination of the pretrial investigation are as follows: when there is not enough information to justify that a suspect is guilty of committing a crime, when the suspect or his crime becomes inoffensive because of changed circumstances, when the suspect and victim make conciliation. The pretrial investigation could also be terminated if more than one crime was committed. For such ground, there should be more than one crime committed, and some or one of these crimes should be misdemeanors, along with more serious crimes, and there should be no civil claim. To terminate pretrial investigation on these grounds is only a right; it is not the duty of the prosecutor. It is also possible to terminate pretrial investigation on the ground that the investigation has lasted too long on the basis of an unreasonable delay of the pretrial investigation.

When the pretrial process is finished, the prosecutor should write an accusation act and give the case to the court. Generally, all criminal cases can be decided in three instances of the court. At first, the case is solved in the first (or lowest) instance. Depending on the seriousness of the crime, the case could be decided in the local court (there are 49 local courts in Lithuania) or in the regional court (there are five regional courts in Lithuania). If the case was decided in the local court, the appellate instance (or the second instance) is the regional court. If the case was decided in the regional court, the appellate instance should be the Court of Appeals of Lithuania. The cassation instance (or the court of the last instance) for all decisions of the appellate instances is the Supreme Court of Lithuania (hereinafter Supreme Court). The prosecution service is similar to the court system: there is a prosecutor general's office, five regional prosecutors' offices and district prosecutors' offices. Public prosecutors are represented at each court by a hierarchical body.

The prosecutor represents the state in criminal cases. In the trial hearing, the main task of the prosecutor is to participate in analyzing and examining the evidence, to give his opinion when deciding questions that arise about the case, to give his reasoning to the court about the application of the criminal law, and for the punishment of the accused.

There are only professional judges in Lithuania. Their status is governed by the Law on Courts. The case could be solved by one, three, or seven judges, depending on the situation of the case being heard (first, appeal, or cassation). At the Supreme Court, the case could be given over for decision to the all of the judges of the court's criminal case division or even to all of the judges of the entire court (this is called a plenary session). In some cases, if there is an assumption that the case will be solved over a long period, the alternate (standby) judge could be assigned to the case. This judge should sit in the courtroom from the beginning of the hearing in the case, and when the judge who hears the case cannot participate in the hearing, the alternate judge becomes the permanent judge in the case. If this happens, the original judge cannot return to the case he was hearing.

At the court of the first instance the judge questions all witnesses, evaluates data in the case, and listens to the arguments, testimony, and questions of the parties. The case must be heard with the accused attending the hearing. The appearance of the accused is mandatory. The judgment must be based only on what has been said in the court (this includes an interrogation made by the pretrial judge during the pretrial investigation stage). When deciding the case, if the judge finds that there are grounds to believe that the law or other legal acts that should be applied in a concrete case are in conflict with the Constitution, the judge shall suspend consideration of the case and shall apply to the Constitutional Court, requesting that it decide whether the law or the other legal acts in question are in compliance with the Constitution. The judge cannot himself decide whether certain acts are unconstitutional.

A judge can in his judgment order compensation to the victim for any moral, bodily, or monetary damages. The rules of civil procedure apply in this situation. If in a criminal case it is not possible to determine the damage that the victim has suffered, then the case can be resolved in a separate civil case (except in cases where the amount of damages is an essential part of the crime).

After the decision of the court in the first instance, the appeal should be given in 20 days. An appeal process is held in the same way as a hearing at the court of the first instance. The hearing in the appellate instance could be limited to the scope of the appeal and/or to the persons who made the appeal. If the court that hears the case establishes substantial breaches of the CpC, these limitations do not apply.

There is also the possibility to bring a complaint about the verdict that was entered in the appellate instance within a limit of 3 months. The Supreme Court can hear the case only when it is a matter of (the) law (questions related with the facts are not evaluated). It should be proven that in the appellate instance, there was inappropriate use of the criminal code or material breaches of criminal procedure code occurred.

For certain offenses (for example, bodily harm, criminal damage to property, restriction of freedom of a person's actions, sexual harassment, etc.), the victim can bring a complaint directly to the court and act as a private prosecutor instead of the public prosecutor handling the case. This is known as private complaint procedure. In these cases, a pretrial investigation is not performed. If there is no suspect established or the crime effects public interest or a person for serious reasons cannot protect his lawful interests, then the pretrial investigation is performed in the usual way. The law says that all cases having to do with domestic violence are of public interest, so in these cases a pretrial investigation is always performed.

If during the pretrial investigation or in the court hearing it becomes clear that the person who committed the crime is incapable or he became (or when committing the crime was) mentally ill and cannot realize the essence of his actions and control these actions, then the process can turn to the process for applying forced medical treatment.

The CpC establishes some procedures as exception to the usual process in order to speed up the trial. For crimes in which the sentence can be any sentence stated in the CC except the cases in which, for the crime committed, only a time sentence or life sentence could be given, it is possible not to have the hearing in the court, and the sentence is imposed by court order. This process is available only when the accused agrees to such process and compensates for or eliminates the damage he did or otherwise agrees to compensate or eliminate such damage.

The CpC allows a case to be heard when the accused is in absentia. The case can be heard in absentia only when the accused is not in the territory of the Republic of Lithuania and avoids appearing in the court. The concerns of the accused are protected by a defense counsel who is assigned by the court.

The role of the pretrial investigation judge is under discussion. Lithuania chose the passive concept of such judges, so their actions are restricted by the requests made from the prosecutor, and the judges only partially ensure the rights of the process participants. The question of abolishing the autocratic powers of the prosecutor in the pretrial investigation process could be raised, and the model of a pretrial investigation judge as a supervisor of the process should be discussed.

Another problem that requires attention and could be productively raised involves the regulation of the disqualification (or self-disqualification) of the judge. The CpC does not clearly and comprehensibly regulate procedures such as those that include situations when the judge himself is deciding whether to disqualify himself from the case even when the case is decided by him alone or situations in which, if the judge decides to disqualify himself from the case, approval from the court's chairman is required, or when the case is decided in the board of judges, if the request for the disqualification for one judge is announced, then the decision is entered by the majority votes of all judges, including the judge (or judges) to whom the request for disqualification was announced. Such regulation requires reviewing because it could lead in the process to the violations of the right to an impartial trial.

The policy of the EU legislature, unique legislative measure in other EU countries, the progress of information technologies, and so forth—these all influence criminal procedure in Lithuania. The initiation of certain changes could be raised at the national or international levels. Lithuania is one of the last countries in Europe where the institute of mediation is not applied in criminal cases. It is presumed that the future of criminal procedure will focus on new methods of solving the conflict between the victim and the suspect in which the mediation will take its position among other measures of solving the conflicts in a peaceful and effective way.

8.4 Tax and Financial Law

Paulius Čerka
Čerka & Partneriai Advocates Bureau, Jonavos st. 66, LT-44138 Kaunas, Lithuania
e-mail: paulius.cerka@vdu.lt

Tomas Veršinskas
Faculty of Law, Vytautas Magnus University, Jonavos st. 66, LT-44138 Kaunas, Lithuania
e-mail: tomas.versinskas@vdu.lt

8.4.1 Development of Lithuanian Taxation System

Taxation systems vary from country to country as these systems reflect structure, national values, and priorities of the state that have been formed over centuries. In this context, Lithuania should be seen as a young state with a relatively new taxation system. Its formation has been influenced by an interesting although very challenging historical period, namely, Lithuania's evolution as a state during the twentieth century. The beginning of the development of an independent taxation system in Lithuania should be understood together with the establishment of independence in 1918. Unfortunately, this process was severely interrupted by the Soviet occupation, which lasted almost 50 years, during which time Lithuania was forced to change its trend of development toward the creation of communism and a system of central planning. Under these circumstances, cardinal changes in taxation system could not be avoided. The restoration of independence in 1990 and transformation from social planning system to market economy signified the necessity to establish an entirely new taxation system. This process was very challenging since the Soviet occupation had rerouted Lithuania from its natural development in all areas of state policy for a long time. In 1990, Lithuania was suddenly forced to familiarize itself promptly with modern trends of taxation systems that applied to a market economy context.

This stage of the establishment of the Lithuanian taxation system began in 1995, when the Law on Tax Administration of the Republic of Lithuania was accepted, which established uniform principles governing taxation and tax administration systems. This system was heavily criticized for its lack of attention toward the taxpayer, the heavy tax burden stimulation of a black economy, double taxation on some items, and the complex calculation of taxes. Consequently, the initially established system was reexamined in order to solve emerging problems.

The beginning of the stage of reform of taxation system influenced by preparation for the accession to the European Union was the year 2001, when the question of harmonization of Lithuanian taxation system with the requirements of the EU was opened in the accession to EU negotiations.[75] In this stage, provisions common to all Member States of the EU were introduced in the Lithuanian taxation system by entirely editing the Law on Tax Administration of the Republic of Lithuania and the laws on certain taxes. New principles of this taxation system were also settled, which sought to create a taxpayer-oriented system that was transparent and clear and which satisfied both the needs of citizens as taxpayers and the state.

8.4.2 Lithuanian Taxation System: General Information

Currently, Lithuania should be seen as a state that has established a taxation system frame that includes all basic taxes that are applied in developed countries; this system is still developing, however. The membership of Lithuania in the EU also influences the development of our national taxation system as Lithuania, together with other Member States, seeks common EU targets.

According to Article 127 of the Constitution of the Republic of Lithuania: "[t] axes, other payments to the budgets, and levies shall be established by the laws of the Republic of Lithuania."[76] This means that the Seimas of the Republic of Lithuania is the main institution responsible for forming the taxation system of Lithuania. Currently, the laws of the Republic of Lithuania[77] set these 24 taxes[78] in Lithuania, but 90% of total tax revenues in Lithuania come from five significant taxes: social insurance contributions, VAT, excise duties, personal income tax, and health care insurance contributions.

From the aforementioned list of taxes, one can see that the Lithuanian taxation system is not only oriented toward gathering funds for the performance of the main functions of the government; public social security and health insurance systems are also developed and funded by compulsory contributions of natural and legal persons. Special taxes are imposed for reducing negative environmental impact. Some taxes can be seen as the remuneration for services supplied by the government.

---

[75] Jukneliené (2005).

[76] *The Constitution of the Republic of Lithuania*. Official Gazette, 1992, No. 33-1014, art. 127.

[77] *Law on Tax Administration of the Republic of Lithuania* (13 April 2004, No. IX-2112, as last amended on 22 December 2009), Art. 13.

[78] Taxes in Lithuania: value added tax; personal income tax; corporate income tax; immovable property tax; inheritance tax; land tax; compulsory health insurance contributions; state social insurance contributions; contributions to the Guarantee Fund; excise duties; customs duties; state-imposed fees and charges; petroleum and gas resources tax; state natural resources tax; tax on environmental pollution; deductions from income under the Law of the Republic of Lithuania on Forestry; tax on the use of state property by the right of trust; lottery and gaming tax; fees for the registration of industrial property objects; stamp-duty; consular fees; tax on a surplus amount in the sugar sector; production charge in the sugar sector; one-off purchase tax on additional quota for white sugar production and on supplementary quota for isoglucose production; social tax (applied only in 2006 and 2007).

Taxes are usually classified according to various parameters, e.g., object of the tax, method of taxation, and type of taxpayer.[79] Various international organizations providing analysis of worldwide tax systems also use categories for the classification of taxes.[80] The presentation of taxes applied in Lithuania in the next chapter is based on classification of taxes as direct and indirect taxes.

Taxes at a glance are as follows: corporate income tax rate—5 (for small enterprises)/15%; withholding tax (%) dividends—0/15%; interest—0/10%; salaries/other income—15%; real estate tax—0.3–3% (the most common ~1%); land tax—0.1–4% (the most common ~1%); VAT rate—0%, 5%, 9%, 21% (standard).

8.4.3 Direct Taxes

8.4.3.1 Personal Income Tax

This type of tax as it is conceived today was established several centuries ago.[81] After the establishment of Lithuania's independence at the beginning of the twentieth century, some form of taxation of personal income was also applied subject to the type of income, for example, employment income tax.[82] The restoration of independence set the frame for personal income tax (hereinafter in this subsection referred to as PIT) as it is conceived today in Lithuania. Currently, the types of personal income that are taxed, payers of this tax, and other issues concerning calculation, declaration, and payment of PIT are defined in the Law on Personal Income Tax of the Republic of Lithuania (hereinafter in this subsection referred to as the Law on PIT). Lithuania imposes a flat rate of 15% on personal income for residents and the same for nonresidents. Special rules are applied for persons performing individual activities.

8.4.3.2 Corporate Income Tax

This type of tax should also be conceived as income tax. The main difference from personal income tax is its application to legal entities. Corporate income taxes in Lithuania have been applied since the establishment of independence in 1918.[83] The restoration of independence in Lithuania and the switch to a market economy led to the swift creation of private legal entities and subsequently to the new taxation system of legal persons, i.e., application of corporate income tax (hereinafter: CIT). At the beginning, the tax rate of CIT was 35%, but the tracked tendency up to today has been a clear downward trend to 15% (at least till recent recession of the economy). Current issues concerning the application of corporate income tax

[79]Marcijonas and Gudavičius (2003), pp. 18–19.

[80]For e.g. Organisation for Economic Co-operation and Development (OECD).

[81]Thuronyi (2003), p. 231.

[82]Juknelienė (2005).

[83]*Ibid.*

are governed by the Law on Corporate Income Tax of the Republic of Lithuania (hereinafter in this subsection referred to as the Law on CIT).

Payers of CIT are Lithuanian and foreign legal entities.[84] Certain legal persons are excluded from the obligation to pay CIT. These legal persons are public legal entities, the Bank of Lithuania state-owned enterprise "Deposit and Investment Insurance," and European Economic Interest Groupings.[85]

Lithuania has adopted the most common system for taxable income, where "the taxable profit is calculated on the income earned less the non–taxable income,[86] allowable deductions ... and limited allowable deductions."[87] Two well-known "ordinary and necessary" criteria are accepted since allowable deductions are all expenses actually incurred in the ordinary course of business of the entity and necessary for that entity to earn income or derive economic benefit.[88] Some types of expenses are nonallowable deductions.[89]

8.4.3.3 System of Local Taxes

Lithuanian law does not provide a definition of local taxes, though over 90% of the inflow of Lithuania's state and municipality budgets consists of tax income. According to the Constitution, only Seimas (Parliament) may establish state taxes and other compulsory payments, but municipal councils have the right, within the limits and according to the procedure provided for by law, to set local levies (local fees) and levy concessions at the expense of their own budget. Some local taxes, when attributed to a certain percentage of national tax income (with the exception of income tax), may be deemed local (regional), but municipalities have few rights to influence their rate. Thus, it is more correct to say that the competence of the municipal council is not to establish local tax but to set concession. Since real estate taxes are fully transferred into local municipal budgets, we can determine these as local taxes. We have several types of real estate taxes:

1. land tax,
2. leased land tax,
3. immovable property (real estate) tax.

---

[84]Definition of these entities is provided in Paragraphs 2 and 3 of Article 2 of the *Law on Corporate Income Tax of the Republic of Lithuania* (20 December 2001, No. IX-675, as last amended on 22 July 2009).

[85]*Law on Corporate Income Tax of the Republic of Lithuania* (20 December 2001, No. IX-675, as last amended on 22 July 2009), Art. 3.

[86]The list of non-taxable income is provided in the Article 12 of the *Law on Corporate Income Tax of the Republic of Lithuania* (20 December 2001, No. IX-675, as last amended on 22 July 2009).

[87]Their list is provided in Paragraph 2 of Article 16 of the *Law on Corporate Income Tax of the Republic of Lithuania* (20 December 2001, No. IX-675, as last amended on 22 July 2009).

[88]Law on Corporate Income Tax of the Republic of Lithuania (20 December 2001, No. IX-675), 17 article. https://www.e-tar.lt/portal/lt/legalAct/TAR.A5ACBDA529A9/BjefdQYPYs.

[89]Their list is provided in Article 31 of the *Law on Corporate Income Tax of the Republic of Lithuania* (20 December 2001, No. IX-675, as last amended on 22 July 2009).

8.4.3.4 Land Tax

In contrast to immovable property tax, land tax in Lithuania has been applied since 1992, when the Law on Land Tax of the Republic of Lithuania was adopted; it was the first object of immovable property belonging to private owners that was taxed since the restoration of independence in 1990. The object of land tax is the private land owned by natural or legal persons, with the exception of forest land and afforested agricultural land. If the tax exemption does not apply, then the person must pay land tax, which rate varies from 0.01% to 4.0% of the taxable value of the land (for example, residence land is taxed at a 0.4 rate and maximum rates (of 4%) are applied only to desolate and abandoned land; by these powers, municipalities may affect the care and maintenance of local lands). Specific tariff rates are set by municipalities as this tax is paid to the treasury of a municipality in the territory where the land is located. The municipal councils also have the right to reduce the amount of land tax or grant exemption from the payment of land tax compensating sums from their respective budgets.

The tax base is the average market value of the land, which has been established for the period of 5 years by mass appraisal. The average market value of the land is calculated according to the procedure established by the Government of the Republic of Lithuania. According to government regulations, the value reduction coefficient of 0.35 applies to agricultural land.

8.4.3.5 Immovable Property (Real Estate) Tax

There is no wealth tax in Lithuania, though one of the oldest forms of taxation is immovable property (real estate) tax.[90] Application can be tracked in Lithuania since the establishment of independence in the early twentieth century. The long period of Soviet occupation and the forcible shift toward public property ownership changed the Lithuanian society's understanding of the purpose of real estate taxation. Taxes levied on real estate in this period were generally understood as payments for the government for the use of public property (tax on immovable property employed) and paid almost exclusively by legal entities.[91]

Obligation to pay tax is assigned to both legal and natural persons for the land belonging to them by right of ownership.[92] The taxable value of land is the land price (the price of standing timber is excluded when calculating the price for forest land), "which is equal to the value of the land calculated in accordance with the Land Valuation Methodology approved by the resolution of the Government No. 205 of 24 February 1999."[93] Because of the methodology applied to calculate

[90] Carlson (2004).

[91] Aničas et al. (1987), p. 122.

[92] Tax reliefs are provided in articles 4 to 6 of the *Law on Land Tax of the Republic of Lithuania* (25 June 1992, No. I-2675, as last amended on 5 April 2007). Municipalities also may exempt natural or legal persons from or reduce the land tax rate at the expense of their own budgets.

[93] *Law on Land Tax*. http://www3.lrs.lt/pls/inter3/dokpaieska.showdoc_l?p_id=470306.

land tax, this tax is generally low for each taxpayer and not much income is generated for the municipalities' treasuries.

8.4.4 Indirect Taxes

8.4.4.1 Value Added Tax

Value added tax (hereinafter VAT) is a "consumption tax assessed on the value added to goods and services." This type of tax was introduced in the second half of the twentieth century in many countries across the world and is defined as a general and neutral tax, collected fractionally and paid by the final consumers.[94] In Lithuania, VAT as it is understood nowadays was introduced after Lithuania restored independence in 1990. Currently, the law regulating the procedure of calculation, declaration, and payment of VAT in Lithuania is the Law on Value Added Tax of the Republic of Lithuania. As Lithuania is a member of the EU, regulation of the application of this tax in Lithuania generally reflects the EU policy in this area.

8.4.5 Trends of the Lithuanian Taxation System

It is systematically established in the program of the Government of the Republic of Lithuania that personal income tax, corporate income tax, and value added tax are perceived as basic taxes forming the treasury of state and municipalities. Therefore, due to the recession of the Lithuanian economy, the tax rate of these taxes will be reviewed every year in the future draft budgets and reduced, "provided that is not in contradiction with macroeconomic stability."[95] Recent changes were, e.g., when the tax rate of value added tax was increased to 21% and the tax rate of corporate income tax was reduced to 15%; these were introduced jointly with other favorable incentives for business and to stimulate business by attracting investors to Lithuania.

Application of personal real estate tax is subject to wide discussions as to what extent and under what scheme taxation of the immovable property belonging to natural persons should be applied. It is planned gradually to tax all real estate property, starting at present from the most expensive, though unfortunately there is no clear taxation plans for immovable property belonging to natural persons in the future.

Current changes in the Lithuanian taxation system were introduced in order to ensure the macroeconomic stability of the state during an economic recession. This trend will be maintained during this recession period, causing some instability concerning tax rates of basic taxes. Although modifications concerning taxation

---

[94] European Commission (2009).

[95] *Ibid.*, item 12 of part II.

of the immovable property belonging to natural persons and progressive taxation of personal income are very desirable in the Lithuanian taxation system, there is still no clear framework for their application. Thus, the Lithuanian taxation system is still subject to development and further perfection.

In summary, it should be noticed that current changes in Lithuanian taxation system were introduced seeking to ensure macroeconomic stability of the state during the recession of economy. This trend definitely will be kept during this recession period, therefore causing some instability concerning tax rates of basic taxes. Modifications concerning taxation of the immovable property belonging to natural persons and progressive taxation of personal income, although are very desirable in Lithuanian taxation system, there is still no clear framework of their application. Thus, Lithuanian taxation system is still subject to development and perfection.

Real estate taxation issues are a source of great interest and discussion in society. None of the political parties in power is willing to enforce the full scope of real estate taxation for fear of becoming unpopular; therefore, taxation changes very gradually. Discussions after the enactment of the new Law on Real Estate Tax of the Republic of Lithuania were about the fact that natural persons had to pay this tax for the first time for property used in commercial activities or for specific property. So real estate tax raised significantly intense political and public discussions. But the expansion of the real estate tax base resulted in an increase of the incomes of municipal budgets and the autonomy of local authorities. Therefore, we can conclude that real estate tax is very significant and is an independent source of income for the local authorities, which secures freedom for their activities and lowers their dependence on the central government. This makes real estate tax an instrument of the decentralization of state.

What needs to be developed in real estate taxation? First of all, local taxes should be established by a separate law with the right of local municipalities to set such taxes and not only to set concessions at the expense of their own budget. That will establish real estate tax as the main regional tax by extending its tax base and its potential to establish its tariffs with wider limits.

8.4.6 Financial Law

Today, Lithuanian financial law provides for an advanced regulatory and supervisory system, constituting a sophisticated framework for national and international finance. Having evolved from nothing into an open system based on international standards, it is now on a quest to develop into a platform helping Lithuania to become a hub of international financial services.

Lithuanian financial law is heavily influenced by EU legislation, which often serves as a driver for modernization and standardization. Thus, it was strongly marked by the EU regulatory and supervisory reforms triggered by the recent economic downturn. In addition, in Lithuania the crisis was accompanied by a wave of important litigations and bankruptcies, leading to new developments in financial law. During the last years, important changes also resulted from Lithuania's further integration into the EU structures. Since January 1, 2015, Lithuania has been a member of the Eurozone,[96] and since January 1, 2016, it has belonged to the Single Euro Payments Area (SEPA). It participates in the European Single Supervisory Mechanism and in the Single Resolution Mechanism and contributes to the Single Resolution Fund.

The Bank of Lithuania, which is governed by the respective law,[97] remains the sole supervisory institution in charge of the financial markets since January 1, 2012.[98] The Bank of Lithuania supervises financial markets and has the power to apply administrative sanctions for violations of the respective legal acts. Its decisions may be contested in the administrative courts.[99] One of the main national legal acts designed to ensure the stability of the functioning of the financial market in Lithuania is the Law on Financial Sustainability.[100]

8.4.6.1 Credit Institutions

Under Lithuanian law, credit institutions make up part of financial institutions, which are regulated by the Law on Financial Institutions.[101] Activities of credit institutions are subject to a license delivered by the Bank of Lithuania. Credit institutions are governed by several respective laws, such as the Law on Banks,[102] the Law on Credit Unions,[103] the Law on Central Credit Union,[104] and the Law on Mortgage Bonds and Mortgage Lending.[105] In conformity with EU law, a deposit guarantee scheme governed by the Law on Insurance of Deposits and Liabilities to Investors[106] is in place and covers deposits up to the amount of 100,000 euros.[107]

The Lithuanian banking sector is marked by a strong Scandinavian presence. Some of the Scandinavian banks perform their activities in Lithuania via subsidiaries, while some act via their Lithuanian branches. The Scandinavian presence in the Lithuanian banking sector also means a Scandinavian culture on the matter, which ensures access to modern banking services. For example, the

---

[96] See: *Law on the Adoption of the Euro in the Republic of Lithuania*. TAR, 2014-04-29, No. 4875.

[97] *Law on the Bank of Lithuania*. Official Gazette, 1994, No. 99-1957.

[98] See: *Law on Reorganisation of the Supervisory System of the Financial Market*. Official Gazette, 2011-12-01, No. 145-6811.

[99] Following the procedures under the Law on Administrative Proceedings (*Law on Administrative Proceedings*. Official Gazette, 1999, No. 13-308).

[100] *Law on Financial Sustainability*. Official Gazette, 2009, No. 93-3985.

[101] *Law on Financial Institutions*. Official Gazette, 2002, No. 91-3891.

[102] *Law on Banks*. Official Gazette, 2004, No. 54-1832.

[103] *Law on Credit Unions*. Official Gazette, 1995, No. 26-578.

[104] *Law on Central Credit Union*. Official Gazette, 2000, No. 45-1288.

[105] *Law on Mortgage Bonds and Mortgage Lending*. Official Gazette, 2003, No. 97-4317.

[106] *Law on Insurance of Deposits and Liabilities to Investors*. Official Gazette, 2002, No. 65-2635.

[107] The functioning of the guarantee scheme is ensured by the State company Deposit and Investment Insurance.

largest banks provide their Lithuanian clients with multicurrency accounts, which is not the case even in some of the most financially advanced EU countries. Even if banking services in Lithuania are modern, the Lithuanian market is still waiting to see the arrival of more complex instruments, such as structured finance.

The last decade, marked by the recent economic crisis and the evolution of the Lithuanian market, was quite turbulent for the credit institutions—both in terms of a wave of litigation as well as in terms of tightening control from the supervisors. In 2011 and 2013, the Bank of Lithuania initiated the launching of bankruptcy procedures against two Lithuanian banks: *AB bankas Snoras* and *AB Ūkio bankas*, respectively. This resulted, *inter alia*, in litigations on a variety of issues between the banks under bankruptcy, their creditors, and investors.

One of the most important issues raised in the courts concerned the legal nature of certificates of deposit issued by the *AB bankas Snoras*, which was subjected to bankruptcy procedures. It was questioned if these instruments were covered by the deposit guarantee schemes. After having addressed itself to the European Court of Justice with the request of preliminary ruling, the Supreme Court of Lithuania (hereinafter SCL) ruled[108] that the certificates of deposit issued by the said bank were not transferable securities and thus were covered by the deposit guarantee schemes. Another issue raised in the courts concerned the legal status of the investors that have transferred amounts in consideration of the subscription of the bank's shares, whose issuance was never accomplished due to the commencement of the bankruptcy proceedings. Also, the issue of the responsibility of *Snoras* auditors was raised in the courts, while the litigation ended with the amicable settlement.[109] Another important issue concerned the legal regime applicable to the agreements regulated by the Law on Financial Collateral Arrangements.[110] It was questioned whether the money transferred on the basis of the financial collateral agreements had to be included in the bankruptcy estate of the bank. The SCL considered that the respective claims of the transferors had to be satisfied according to the bankruptcy laws, which impose ranking of creditors.[111]

Due to the change of market conditions resulting from the crisis, clients intensified a search for alternative nonbanking providers of credit services. Credit unions were considered one of the main alternatives. Such increased interest in their services was mirrored by a more tightened control by the Bank of Lithuania, aiding the improvement of the security of this segment of the market. Recent years have been marked by bankruptcies of several large credit unions.[112] This situation with

[108] *V. G., V. V. N. v. BAB bankas "Snoras"*. Supreme Court of Lithuania, 2015, No. 3K-7-602-684/2015.

[109] Amicable settlement agreement of 7 October 2014 was approved by the Vilnius City District Court on 5 May 2015. See: Report of the Bankruptcy Administrator to the Creditors of AB Bankas SNORAS (bankrupt) for the period ending 30 June 2015, 13 August 2015, p. 14. http://www.snoras.com/files/Ataskaita_kreditoriams_%28iki_2015-06-30%29_%28EN%29.pdf.

[110] *Law Financial Collateral Arrangements*. Official Gazette, 2004, No. 61-2183.

[111] See, for example: VšĮ Šiaulių regiono atliekų tvarkymo centras v. BAB bankas "Snoras". Supreme Court of Lithuania, 2015, No. 3K-7-301-706/2015.

[112] See, for example: cases of *Vilniaus taupomoji kasa*, *Nacionalinė kredito unija*, *Laikinosios sostinės kreditas*, *Švyturio taupomoji kasa*, *Naftininkų investicijos*.

credit unions remains noticeable, and the reforms of the entire credit union sector are being recommended. The new versions of the Law on Credit Unions and the Law on Central Credit Union are under consideration in the Seimas.

Another important forthcoming regulatory change of the Lithuanian credit market is the planned adoption of the Law on the Credit Related to the Real Property.

8.4.6.2 Markets in Financial Instruments

The Civil Code of Lithuania provides the definition of securities in general and the definitions of such securities as shares, bonds, checks, and deposit certificates.[113] The Law on Companies provides for a more detailed regulation of shares and bonds produced by companies.[114] The Law on Securities[115] is the main legal act defining the legal regime applicable to transferable securities.[116] It aims to define the rules regarding the preparation, approval, and publication of the prospectus, as well as the disclosure and storage of periodical and current information. The main legal act regulating the provision of investment services in Lithuania is the Law on Markets in Financial Instruments.[117]

In Lithuania, shares and bonds are the main financial instruments issued and traded. However, the market saw issuances of more complex financial instruments, such as deposit certificates and mortgage bonds (issued under the Law on Mortgage Bonds and Mortgage Lending[118]).

Provision of investment services is a licensed activity. Unless otherwise provided in their respective licenses, financial brokerage companies and banks may provide a full range of investment services. A limited range of investment services may also be provided by the financial advisor companies. Operation of multilateral trading facilities is also a licensed investment service. Liabilities of the providers of the investment services (banks, brokerage companies, or management companies) are subject to insurance in conformity with the Law on Insurance of Deposits and Liabilities to Investors[119] up to the amount of 22,000 euros.

Nasdaq Vilnius is the sole regulated securities market in Lithuania. It is operated by AB Nasdaq Vilnius, of which 96.34% is owned by Nasdaq. Nasdaq also owns the majority of shares in the Central Securities Depository of Lithuania (Nasdaq and Nasdaq Vilnius own 92% and 8% of the shares, respectively). Nasdaq technically integrated the three Baltic markets (Vilnius, Riga, and Tallinn) into one Nasdaq

[113]See: Articles 1.101-1.108 of the Civil Code.

[114]*Law on Companies*. Official Gazette, 2000, No. 64-1914.

[115]*Law on Securities*. Official Gazette, 2007, No. 17-626.

[116]Point 27 of Art. 3 of the Law on Markets in Financial Instruments defines what securities are considered as transferable.

[117]*Law on Markets in Financial Instruments*. Official Gazette, 2007, No. 17-627.

[118]*Law on Mortgage Bonds and Mortgage Lending*. Official Gazette, 2003, No. 97-4317.

[119]*Law on Insurance of Deposits and Liabilities to Investors*. Official Gazette, 2002, No. 65-2635.

Baltic market, with harmonized rules and the same trading system.[120] Nasdaq Vilnius also operates a nonregulated First North securities market, which is also harmonized with the respective First North markets in Latvia and Estonia.

The recent economic crisis and the bankruptcies of the two aforementioned banks caused a large number of litigations on various aspects regarding the financial instruments and the legal regime applicable thereto (see above). Recent years were also marked by litigations related to the issuance of equity-linked notes (bonds) by one of the banks. The bank not only issued equity-linked bonds that underperformed due to the economic crisis but also provided mortgage loans to, *inter alia*, its clients so that they could invest in these bonds.[121]

8.4.6.3 Consumer Credit

Consumer crediting is not a licensed activity in Lithuania. However, providers of consumer credit must be listed on an official list held by the Bank of Lithuania. The Law on Consumer Credit also regulates peer-to-peer lending platforms, which are a recent phenomenon in the Lithuanian market. Consumer credit was not governed by any specific legal act till the adoption of the law mentioned above on December 23, 2010. As the providers of consumer credit were not engaged in borrowing from nonprofessional market participants, this area of business was not supervised by the Bank of Lithuania. Eventually, the Law on Consumer Credit was adopted, and later the respective supervisory powers were transferred to the Bank of Lithuania. One could say that such regulatory and supervisory transformations caused significant tensions between the Bank of Lithuania and some consumer credit providers.[122]

8.4.6.4 Collective Investment Undertakings

The main legal act regulating collective investment undertakings (hereinafter CIUs) in Lithuania is the Law on Collective Investment Undertakings.[123] This law provides for two types of CIUs: investment funds and investment companies. An investment fund is property coowned by the respective holders of the units of the fund. Such property is managed by the management company and is held in the depository, which must be a bank. Investment companies are governed by the Law on CIUs and the Law on Companies. Both types of CIUs may be open-end CIUs or closed-end CIUs, subject to the regulations provided for in the respective laws.

---

[120]See information on the website of the Nasdaq Baltic: http://www.nasdaqbaltic.com/en/exchange-information/about-us/.

[121]See, for example: *R. B. v. AB DNB bankas*. Supreme Court of Lithuania, 2014, No. 3K-3-68/2014; *G. P. v. AB DNB bankas*. Supreme Court of Lithuania, 2014, No. 3K-3-206/2014; *S. L. v. AB DNB bankas*. Supreme Court of Lithuania, 2014, No. 3K-3-265/2014; *J. B. v. AB DNB bankas*. Supreme Court of Lithuania, 2014, No. 3K-3-517/2014.

[122]See, for example: information on the website of the Bank of Lithuania: UAB "4finance" atsiėmė skundus dėl Lietuvos banko skirtų baudų ir jas sumokėjo (UAB "4finance" Has Withdrew Its Claims Regarding the Fines Assigned by the Bank of Lithuania and Paid Them), 3rd March 2016. https://www.lb.lt/uab_4finance_atsieme_skundus_del_lietuvos_banko_skirtu_baudu_ir_jas_sumokejo.

[123]*Law on Collective Investment Undertakings*. Official Gazette, 2003, No. 74-3424.

Another legal act regulating the CUIs is the Law on Collective Investment Undertakings Intended for Informed Investors.[124] Such CIUs may be construed as companies, partnerships, or coownerships. In general terms, they are intended for professional investors, satisfying the respective legal requirements for investors investing large amounts or those who have sufficient investment knowledge, confirmed by market participants indicated in the law.

8.4.6.5 Insurance

Insurance relationships are primarily regulated by the Civil Code of Lithuania (Articles 6.987–6.1018). The code provides for the definition of insurance and establishes the general principles of insurance activities relating to, *inter alia*, the forms and types of insurance, the form and basic terms of insurance contracts, reinsurance, etc.

More specifically, insurance is regulated by the Law on Insurance.[125] This law regulates insurance and reinsurance activities, as well as insurance and reinsurance intermediation, aiming to ensure the reliability, efficiency, security, and stability of the insurance system. It defines the persons who have the right to exercise the aforementioned activities and provides for a respective legal regime applicable to such activities. It regulates, *inter alia*, aspects of the precontractual and contractual relationships between the parties to the insurance contract.

The recent economic crisis did not leave out thc Lithuanian insurance market. One of the most interesting cases was that of UAB "Būsto paskolų draudimas," whose license was suspended by the Bank of Lithuania in 2013. This company played one of the key roles in launching residential mortgage financing in Lithuania. It was created by the Government of Lithuania in 1998. Having suffered from a combination of things related to the crisis, since 2012 the company has not concluded any new insurance contracts while continuing to honor its existing contractual obligations.[126]

8.4.6.6 Pensions

Accumulation of pensions in Lithuania is regulated by the following main legal acts: (1) Law on Social Security,[127] (2) Law on Pension Accumulation,[128] (3) Law on Supplementary Voluntary Pension Accumulation,[129] (4) Law on the

[124] *Law on Collective Investment Undertakings Intended for Informed Investors*. Official Gazette, 2013, No. 68-3410.

[125] *Law on insurance*. Official Gazette, 2003, No. 94-4246.

[126] Information from the "UAB "Būsto paskolų draudimas" 2015 metų devynių mėnesių veiklos ataskaita" (UAB "Būsto paskolų draudimas" Activity Report—Nine Months of the Year 2015), 2015. http://www.bpd.lt/images/stories/statistika/2015/2015_09%20men_ataskaita.pdf.

[127] *Law on Social Security*. Lietuvos aidas, 1991, No. 107-0.

[128] *Law on Pension Accumulation*. Official Gazette, 2003, No. 75-3472.

[129] *Law on Supplementary Voluntary Pension Accumulation*. Official Gazette, 1999, No. 55-1765.

Accumulation of Occupational Pensions,[130] and (5) the Law on the Reform of the Pension System.[131]

There are three pillars of the pension system in Lithuania. The first pillar concerns pensions paid from the national social security fund, which was the sole regulated instrument for pension accumulation until the adoption of the Law on the Reform of the Pension System on December 3, 2002. This law introduced important changes in the pension system in Lithuania, which permitted, *inter alia*, pension accumulation in private pension funds. The second pillar of pension accumulation allows for assigning to private pension funds a defined part of social security charges paid. The third pillar provides for a voluntary accumulation of pensions in private pension funds independently from the social security payments to the social security fund.

As the second gear of the accumulation of pensions in private funds depends largely on the regulatory framework, one of the key issues impacting the stability and predictability of this system was the fluctuation of the percentage of the social charges paid and assigned to the private pension funds. This issue was even considered by the Constitutional Court of the Republic of Lithuania, which ultimately ruled that the reduction of the part of social charges assigned to the second gear pension funds did not contradict the Constitution.[132]

8.4.6.7 Electronic Money and Payment Services

A relatively new phenomenon in the Lithuanian financial market is electronic money. It is governed by the Law on Electronic Money and Electronic Money Institutions.[133] The first license belonging to an electronic money institution in Lithuania was delivered in 2012. As of April 27, 2016, there were three companies in Lithuania holding the license of electronic money institution and four electronic money institutions holding an electronic money institution license for restricted activity.[134]

Another comparatively new area of financial law is the regulation of payment services. Provision of payment services, which is a licensed activity, is governed by

[130] *Law on the Accumulation of Occupational Pensions*. Official Gazette, 2006, No. 82-3248.

[131] *Law on the Reform of the Pension System*. Official Gazette, 2002, No. 123-5511.

[132] See, for example: *The Ruling of the Constitutional Court of the Republic of Lithuania, 2014, No. KT50-N16/2014*.

[133] *Law on Electronic Money and Electronic Money Institutions*. Official Gazette, 2011, No. 163-7759. By the adoption of the said law Lithuania transposed into its national law the requirements of the Directive 2009/110/EC of the European Parliament and of the Council of 16 September 2009 on the taking up, pursuit and prudential supervision of the business of electronic money institutions amending Directives 2005/60/EC and 2006/48/EC and repealing Directive 2000/46/EC.

[134] Information of the Bank of Lithuania: http://www.lb.lt/electronic_money_institutions.

the Law on Payments[135] and the Law on Payment Institutions.[136] Payment initiation services is the most recent area of regulatory evolution on the matter, and work on the transposition of the Directive on Payment Services in the Internal Market[137] into national law is underway.

8.5 Labor Law

Marius Bartninkas
Faculty of Law, Vytautas Magnus University, Jonavos st. 66, LT-44138 Kaunas, Lithuania

Kėdainiai District Court of the Republic of Lithuania, Jonavos st. 66, LT-44138 Kaunas, Lithuania
e-mail: marius.bartninkas@vdu.lt

Tomas Davulis
Faculty of Law, Vilnius University, Saulėtekio av. 9-I, LT-10222 Vilnius, Lithuania
e-mail: tomas.davulis@tf.vu.lt

Though labor law was codified in 2002 by adopting the Labour Code, Lithuania is still suffering from the heritage of Soviet labor law, in which a strict and detailed statutory regulation prevailed over individual and collective agreements. Employment relations are mainly regulated by laws (the Labour Code and other laws[138]) passed by the Parliament, which may be detailed by secondary legislation passed by the government and the Ministry of Social Security and Labour. Collective agreements are not a significant source of law because they are very rare and almost exclusively concluded at the enterprise level. The role of judicial judgments is increasing since the judge-made law begins to change ineffective or disproportionate legal provisions that do not reflect the realities of the labor market. All of these

[135]*Law on Payments*. Official Gazette, 1999, No. 97-2775. This law implements the following EU legal acts: the Directive 2007/64/EC of the European Parliament and of the Council of 13 November 2007 on payment services in the internal market amending Directives 97/7/EC, 2002/65/EC, 2005/60/EC and 2006/48/EC and repealing Directive 97/5/EC; (ii) the Regulation (EC) No 924/2009 of the European Parliament and of the Council of 16 September 2009 on cross-border payments in the Community and repealing Regulation (EC) No 2560/2001; the Regulation (EU) No 260/2012 of the European Parliament and of the Council of 14 March 2012 establishing technical and business requirements for credit transfers and direct debits in euro and amending Regulation (EC) No 924/2009.

[136]*Law on Payment Institutions*. Official Gazette, 2009, No. 153-6887.

[137]Directive (EU) 2015/2366 of the European Parliament and of the Council of 25 November 2015 on payment services in the internal market, amending Directives 2002/65/EC, 2009/110/EC and 2013/36/EU and Regulation (EU) No 1093/2010, and repealing Directive 2007/64/EC.

[138]E.g., the Law on Safety and Health of Work, the Law on Trade Unions, the Law on Guarantees for Posted Workers.

sources of law are discussed in this section in order to reveal the specifics of legal regulation.

8.5.1 Collective Labor Law

Collective labor law consists of legal norms that regulate relationships related to the representation of employees and employers, the system of relationship(s) between the social partners (social partnership) with its forms (collective bargaining, information, consultation and participation, social dialogue), and disputes between social partners.

8.5.1.1 Representation of Employees

The system of employee representation has traditionally been based on the exclusive competence of trade unions for the purpose of collective representation of all employees, regardless of their will. Nevertheless, such regulation was not effective.[139] Many employees have become completely unrepresented, which means an elimination of legal possibilities to collectively bargain on wages and improve other working conditions. The introduction of the elected works council (or the workers' representative in companies with less than 20 employees) in the Labour Code strengthened employees' representation and their possibilities to negotiate. Back in 2002, because of the resistance of trade unions, implementation of this dualistic model of representation has been hampered by the introduction of different conditions and exceptions: works council has become optional and can be elected only in those enterprises where there is no trade union; if the trade union is established later than the elected works council, they must agree on a common representation. Hence, there can also be situations where there will be one or several small trade unions in large enterprises, and these unions have the right to represent all employees and the works council cannot be elected. In other enterprises, the employer will have a works council and a trade union, and employees in the general meeting choose for themselves which of them will conclude a collective agreement on their behalf.

Although unique, the Lithuanian representation model did not justify its initial hopes. Works councils covered only 15% of all enterprises, the membership of trade unions was stagnant, and the number of unionized enterprises remained low. Therefore, the new Labour Code adopted in 2016 provides new measures. In order to complete the introduction of a dualistic model, it requires that works councils become mandatory in enterprises that employ over 20 employees and would have a competence of information and consultation in local regulations and other decisions by an employer that affect all employees. Meanwhile, trade unions would have the

[139] According the research of Eurofound, trade union membership in Lithuania is quite low and since 2006 has been stable, covering up to 8-9 % of all employees.

exclusive right of collective bargaining and conclusion of collective agreements, as well as the exclusive right to strike.

Collective bargaining and collective agreements are the most significant forms of social partnership in many Western European countries. In Lithuania, the social partnership is not practically developed because of weak social partners and employers' unwillingness to collectively commit themselves. As a result, many working conditions are prescribed either by law or by individual employment contracts (in which working conditions are *de facto* established by the employer). Therefore, Lithuania is one of the world's leaders in terms of flexibility of wage determination.[140] The social partnership is mostly being developed at the enterprise and national levels. The sectorial social dialogue is struggling, and sectorial or national collective agreements are almost nonexistent. While employers' organizations decline to negotiate and to conclude sectorial and national collective agreements, the social partnership is mostly limited to mutual consultations and forums. There is also the Tripartite Council, where national organizations discuss the situation in the social sphere, consider draft legislation, and express their opinion(s) on raising the minimum wage.

8.5.1.2 Collective Agreements

The Labour Code provides for uniform procedure for collective bargaining, by determining that one party (the trade union or the employer (the employers' organization)) has to present itself to the other party and to express clearly formulated requirements. The latter has to negotiate and to provide the necessary information for negotiations. However, the Labour Code designs the procedure of conclusion of the agreement depending on levels of bargaining. The legislator regulates the conclusion and the content of a collective agreement (derogations are possible only in sectoral, territorial, and national collective agreements; such agreements must be registered with the Ministry of Social Security and Labour in order to identify the authenticity of the text). The more detailed stipulations are provided for a collective agreement at the level of workplace.

8.5.1.3 Disputes Between Social Partners

The necessary stage of procedure is hearing before the Conciliation Commission, which is comprised of an equal number of representatives of both parties. If the Conciliation Commission fails to reach an agreement on all or part of the demands, the Commission may refer to parties for hearing either to a mediator (if one party requests) or to the Labour Arbitration or to the Third Party Court (if both parties request). The latter alternative steps are not popular because they only make a longer process of a declaration of a strike. The legislator allows a trade union to initiate a strike only if the predispute settlement procedure was inefficient, the Conciliation Commission does not take a decision on the procedural obstacles or

[140] According to the Global Competitiveness Report 2015-2016 of the World Economic Forum Lithuania is in 11th place from 140 countries.

discrepancy of positions, a mediator recognizes that the dispute is not resolved, or the employer fails to comply with the decision of the Third Party Court. The employer must be given an at least five working days' written notice of the beginning of the intended strike (in activities of infrastructure or public service enterprises up to 10 working days).

During the strike, workers retain their status and the employer cannot employ other employees. In case law, the question of individual responsibility of employees (disciplinary or material) has not yet arisen because there have not been many strikes in Lithuania.[141] The law provides that in case of an unlawful strike, the trade union must compensate the losses incurred by the employer, but the funds of employees' wages cannot to be used.

The employer has the right to apply to the court to declare the strike unlawful. The court has the right to recognize a strike as unlawful if the objectives of the strike are contrary to the Constitution or other laws or if the strike was declared in breach of the procedure and requirements laid down in the Labour Code. There are cases when courts have controversially evaluated issues such as employees voting for a strike,[142] provision of minimum services,[143] the legality of the demands with respect to which the strike was called[144] or temporary suspension of the strike without motives, and intervening in the dispute in this way.

Lockouts were prohibited in Lithuania for a long time, but they were introduced in the new Labour Code as a responsive measure for employers if the trade union would declare a strike.

In general, the new Labour Code fully establishes a dualistic model, by giving the rights for collective bargaining, conclusion of collective agreements, and declaration of a strike only to the trade union, but limiting the scope of the application of collective agreements only to trade union's members. In this case, there will be a pluralism of trade unions and collective agreements, and for a strike of a collective agreement the consent of all employees (as well as all trade union members) will not be necessary. This should encourage a collective bargaining process.

8.5.1.4 Information and Consultation

Information and consultation of employees remain in the hands of the works council. The employer must inform and consult with employees' representatives in all cases[145] provided by the European Union directives, as well as before taking

---

[141]Number of strikes (warning strikes): 6 (187) in 2012, 0 in 2013; 33(45) in 2014 (Lithuanian Statistics Service data).

[142]*AB "Autrolis" v. Trade union.* Lithuanian Supreme Court, 2011, No. 3K-3-15/2011.

[143]*SP UAB "Vilniaus autobusų parkas"* v. *Trade union.* Lithuanian Supreme Court, 2001, No. 3K-3-32/2001.

[144]*UAB "Švyturys–Utenos alus" v. Trade union.* Lithuanian Supreme Court, 2012, No. 3K-3-81/2012.

[145]Directive 98/59/EC (collective redundancies), directive 2001/23/EC (transfer of undertakings), directive 2002/14/EC (information and consultation framework directive).

these decisions, which significantly affects or may affect the legal position of workers. However, even after the transfer of EU directives to Lithuania's labor law, the information and consultation culture has not improved. Employers and employees either do not know or avoid this form of cooperation, so the introduction of compulsory works councils could encourage this process. The financial sanctions to an employer for violation of collective rights is believed to improve the effectiveness of the social partnership.

8.5.2 Individual Labor Law: The Employment Contract

8.5.2.1 Parties to the Contract

The legislator defines "employee" as a natural person having reached the age of majority. Persons between the ages of 16 and 18 are permitted to do work that does not harm their health. Persons between the ages of 14 and 16 are only permitted to do light work with the consent of their parents, the school, and a doctor. The Law on Safety and Health of Work regulates their working conditions, which are put in compliance with requirements provided by directive 94/33/EC.

The legislator seeks to provide the widest possible definition of an employer by defining employer as a natural person, having reached the age of majority, as well as any organizational structure. Accordingly, the employer may be considered not only a branch and a representative office but also any other organizational division of the employer (e.g., a shop, a warehouse, or even a garage). It may cause some problems in respect of the employer's responsibilities and application of legal norms (e.g., how to calculate the size of the company or a group of employees in the case of information and consultation procedures).

The scope of the application of labor law is determined not by the definition of the subjects but by legal relationship, which is based on the employment contract. Only persons having an employment contract are considered to be in employment relation *sensu stricto*, despite the fact that some laws exceptionally classify some categories of persons as employees (e.g., civil servants, judges according to the Law on Safety and Health of Work). Other laws provide for the subsidiary application of legal norms for other relations (e.g., the working conditions of civil servants are regulated by the Labour Code for cases not stipulated by the Law on Civil Service).

National law may distinguish certain categories of persons from the scope of labor law. Even if a person actually meets the definition of an employee under the concept of free movement of workers or nondiscrimination, he/she will not necessarily be regarded as an employee in Lithuania. This applies for lawyers, notaries, civil servants, state and political officials, sportsmen, etc.

The relationship between the members of the board and the supervisory board and the company is considered to have a civil law pattern. The head of the legal person's managing body has to be related with the company by the employment contract, which leads to complex dual status. As the Supreme Court of Lithuania has ruled, where the head of the company acts in external relations representing the company, there is a civil relation, while his/her relationship with the company is considered internal, i.e., labor relations. This is important in defining the head's responsibilities toward the company and the peculiarities of termination of his contract with the company.

Quasi-employees (*Arbeitnehmeraehnliche personen* or *Quasisubordinati*) are not regulated in Lithuania's labor law. They, as well as other self-employees, fall under the scope of civil laws.

8.5.2.2 Definition of the Contract

An agreement between an employer and employee has to provide for the provision of services, subordination to the employer, and remuneration—the same features as established by the European Union Court of Justice for the cases of free movement of workers[146] or nondiscrimination.[147] Those characteristics are necessary and sufficient to consider the parties to be bound by the employment relationship, despite the fact the parties may consider it a civil contract or conclude a fictitious transaction. In accordance with the principle of "content over form," the real behavior of the parties, and not intentions or the title of a contract, is the decisive factor for assigning a relationship to employment relationship. This is especially important in determining if it is illegal employment or bogus self-employment. While hiding the employment relationship, individuals do not conclude any written contract or make other kinds of agreement that is subject to lower taxation. Both of these cases are considered illegal work.

The question of the moment of the conclusion and the entry into force of the employment contract is somewhat ambiguous in Lithuanian labor law. The employment contract shall be considered concluded when the parties reach an agreement on working conditions. Thus, it can be concluded even orally. However, the Labour Code requires that the contract must be concluded in writing. The employment contract itself must specify its effective date and the date on which the employee will start working. In addition, it is required that the employee has to start working no earlier than the day after the conclusion of the employment contract.[148] In this way, the legislator does not create legal certainty, but the written employment contract and the report of the State Social Insurance Fund are necessary; otherwise, a sanction for illegal work may be imposed.

8.5.2.3 Types of Contracts

Along with an open-ended employment contract, which is considered ordinary, the Labour Code provides for several types of employment contracts. Fixed-term contracts may be seasonal or up to 2 years. Among the types of employment contracts, the law names an employment contract on the implementation of the

[146]*Deborah Lawrie-Blum v Land Baden-Württemberg*. CJEU, 1986, No C-66/85.

[147]*Dita Danosa v LKB Līzings SIA*. CJEU, 2010, No C-232/09.

[148]This is because the controlling authorities would receive information on time and prepare for future inspection.

project, a teleworking contract (when an employee works in places other than the workplace), and employment through temporary employment agencies.

Upon concluding an employment contract, the parties may agree on a trial to assess the suitability of an employee for the agreed work, as well as the suitability of this job for the employee. A trial period shall not be longer than 3 months. During this period, both parties must decide whether they wish to continue the employment contract. Each party can terminate the employment contract with notice of three working days without paying severance pay. The employer has to prove that its decision is based on facts (complaints, reports, evidence that the employee could not cope with the work). This means that the employer has the burden of proof for an employee's inadequacy on agreed upon work.

8.5.2.4 Amendments to the Contract

If the employment contract is concluded, it can be unliterary changed for serious reasons. Changing the workplace (institutional structure), working function (position or working activity), or conditions of remuneration require the prior written consent of the employee. Other conditions may be changed without prior written consent, in the event of changes in production, its scope, technology, or labor organization, as well as in other cases of production necessity.

If an employee has not challenged the changes of the contract within 3 months, it is considered acceptance of the changes. If an employee does not agree to work under the changed working conditions, he may be dismissed from work with statutory notice and severance pay. In practice, problems arise whether the employee's refusal is considered to be itself a reason to terminate an employment contract. In this case, the court takes the position that the employer must have important reasons for the termination of a contract;[149] thus, the employee's refusal by itself is not a cause of termination of employment.

8.5.2.5 Termination of the Contract

The termination of employment contract is the most strictly regulated area of Lithuanian labor law. It is important to pay attention to the grounds of dismissal and compliance with dismissal procedure. The violation of both may be sufficient grounds to declare the dismissal unlawful.

The employment contract may be terminated upon the death or the liquidation of one of the parties, if the whereabouts of an employer (a natural person) or the representatives of an employer cannot be determined. The employment contract may also be terminated without the will of the parties, when a court judgment whereby an employee is imposed a sentence, which prevents him from continuing his work, becomes effective; when an employee is unable to perform these duties or work according to a medical conclusion; when an employee is deprived of special rights to perform certain work; and so forth.

[149] *I.T. v. UABDK "PZU Lietuva"*. Lithuanian Supreme Court, 2012, No. 3K-3-614/2012.

Another ground to be mentioned is termination of employment contract by mutual agreement, in which the parties agree on conditions of the termination of the contract (compensation, granting of unused leave, etc.).

An employee may terminate a contract by statement (resignation). The Labour Code provides for a resignation for both "important" and "unimportant" reasons. If the termination of the employment contract is justified by the employee's illness or disability restricting proper performance of work or other valid reasons set out in the collective agreement or where the employer fails to fulfill his obligations under the employment contract or violates laws or the collective agreement, the employee shall be paid severance pay. If the employee resigns for other reasons (e.g., found another job), he/she must give the employer written notice thereof at least 20 days in advance.

The employment contract may be terminated on the initiative of an employer. An employer shall be entitled to terminate an employment contract as a result of employees' breach of labor obligations (discussed in more detail in chapter *Labour Discipline*). An employment contract may also be terminated on economic, technological grounds or due to the restructuring of the workplace, as well as for other similarly valid reasons. The employer is entitled to terminate an employment contract by giving written notice in advance and by paying severance pay. An employment contract may also be terminated based on circumstances related to the qualification, professional skills, or conduct of an employee.

8.5.2.6 Working Hours and Rest Time

The need to ensure employees' rights to reasonable daily and weekly working hours, weekly rest periods, established in the European Social Charter, is implemented by 40 working hours a week (48 h, including overtime) and 8 working hours a day, a minimum of 11 h of uninterrupted rest between shifts and 35 h of uninterrupted weekly rest. At the same time, greater flexibility is created by the possibility in case of necessity to set a shift up to 24 h and to have individual working time regulation for specific activities (e.g., transport, postal, agricultural, health, and care). Although historically the right to agree on individual working time and regime is extended, existing regulation is still strict enough, provides higher standards than the minimum international requirements,[150] and is regarded as focused on the goal of protecting employees against possible abuse rather than creating a wide scope for the employee and employer to be flexible in arranging working conditions.

International commitments to set preventive measures for dangerous and unhealthy occupations, and protection of maternity and young workers, are implemented by a shorter working week for certain categories of employees (e.g., doctors, teachers, minors, persons working at night) or giving the right to claim part time work (e.g., pregnant or breastfeeding women, disabled people, minors). The Labour Code provides for four weeks of paid annual leave. Extended or additional

[150] Petrylaitė et al. (2008), p. 352.

annual leave is granted to certain categories of employees whose work involves greater nervousness, emotional and intellectual strain, and professional risk.

8.5.2.7 Remuneration

Remuneration is an essential feature distinguishing the employment relationship from similar legal relationships (e.g., voluntary work).[151] When concluding an employment contract, the parties agree on the size of salary. The salary is paid for the time actually worked, when selecting a 1-month accounting period. Parties must agree on the constant part of that which has to be paid irrespective of results of work and shall not be lower than the minimum wage. At the same time, the employer and employee may agree on a variable part of wage, clearly naming cases in which it shall be paid, and the method for how it is calculated. Legal doctrine emphasizes two types of additional benefits: bonus as an integral part of wage and bonus as a promotional tool used by the employer.[152] Bonus becomes a part of wage if parties agree on certain result-oriented conditions to be met.[153] If there is no clear formula, bonus payment is considered to be the employer's discretionary right.

The tariff wage that the parties agreed upon is paid to the employee for his actual work. For other periods (e.g., annual leave compulsory, time of mandatory medical examination, training time), an average salary is paid, calculated for the previous 3 calendar months. Implementation of provisions of the European Social Charter resulted in statutory employers' obligation to pay one and a half times higher wage for overtime work and night work and two times higher wage for working on rest days and public holidays.

8.5.2.8 Labor Discipline

One of the essential features of the employment relationship is subordination. The employer determines working conditions and practices, introduces them to an employee in advance, and has the right to require an employee to comply with the requirements laid down.

Among gross breaches of work duties that can form the basis for termination of employment contract for employee's fault are absence from work throughout the day (shift) without valid reasons, being at work under the influence of alcohol or narcotic or toxic substances, refusal to undergo a mandatory medical examination, violation of equal rights for women and men, or sexual harassment. Roughness of infringement is assessed by actual or potential adverse effects to the employer.

If the infringement is not considered to be gross, it can serve as a basis for termination of employment only if the violation is determined repeatedly within 1 year. While deciding on infringement, the employer must assess the seriousness

[151] Nekrošius (2004), pp. 45–47.

[152] Tiažkijus et al. (1999), pp. 121–123.

[153] *A.V. v UAB "Mitnija"*. Lithuanian Supreme Court, 2009, No. 3K-3-284/2009.

and consequences of breach of labor duties, employee's guilt, and his/her performance of duties before the infringement.

The law also contains procedural requirements for breach to be found. The employer must give the employee opportunity to provide an explanation. Consequences must be adapted within 1 month after the infringement has been established but no later than 6 months after the breach was committed.

8.5.2.9 Liability for Employment Related Damage

In addition to four conditions necessary for the application of the civil liability—((1) damage, (2) illegal action, (3) causal link between illegal action and damage, and (4) offender's guilt)—liability for employment-related damage is applicable where two additional conditions are met. The offender and the injured party at the time of the offense should be in employment relationships, and the occurrence of damage should be related to work activities.[154] Only if the latter two conditions are met is the legal relationship governed by labor law.[155]

Both employer and employee can become subjects of liability. The employee's damage is usually related to bodily injury or death of an employee or damage to, destruction, or loss of employee's property. Damages comprise direct losses and loss of incomes. The employee has the right to apply for nonpecuniary damages as a result of such employers' unlawful actions as failure to secure safe working conditions, employee discrimination, or other gross employee rights violations. The employee may be declared liable for loss or damage of work equipment or other property, and damage may occur in disclosure of confidential information or breach of obligation not to compete.

The principle of full compensation is applicable to the employer, while employees in general have limited liability.[156] Reasons for such limitations derive from the conclusion that the employer as the economically stronger party is responsible for the regulation of labor relations, and therefore the employer assumes at least part of the risk for possible loss of or damage to property.[157]

With direct statutory exceptions, the employer may claim damages, the amount of which does not exceed three average employee's monthly salaries. Restrictions do not apply where the employee acts deliberately or damage results from a criminal act. In addition, full liability applies in such cases of clearly abusive behavior as damage caused by an employee under the influence of alcohol or narcotic or toxic substances. Special laws may also provide for specific full liability cases.[158] Social partners may provide for additional cases of full liability in collective agreement.

---

[154] *VĮ "Šiaulių regiono veislininkystė" v G.S.* Lithuanian Supreme Court, 2008, No. 3K-3-445/2008.

[155] Nekrošius et al. (2004), pp. 356–360.

[156] *UAB "Mobili linija" v A.V.* Lithuanian Supreme Court, 2015, No. 3K-3-323-421/2015.

[157] Tiažkijus et al. (1999), pp. 146–148.

[158] E.g., full liability of manager of legal entity under Article 38 of Law on Joint Stock Companies.

8.5.3 Individual and Collective Labor Disputes for Defense of Infringed Rights

Disagreements between the subjects of labor law regarding the exercise of their rights and the fulfilment of their duties are referred to as labor disputes. As per subjects, labor disputes are classified into individual and collective labor disputes and by substance into disputes over breach or improper performance of rules of law or bilateral agreements (individual and collective labor disputes for defense of infringed rights) and disputes arising out of the regulation of mutual rights and obligations (collective labor disputes on the interest).[159] The latter are discussed in the chapter *Collective Labour Law*. Questions related to individual and collective labor disputes for defense of infringed rights' substance and nature, dispute hearing bodies and their competence, as well as the procedural peculiarities are laid down in both the Labour Code, which deals with substantial and procedural labor-law-related issues, and the Code of Civil Procedure, which sets general rules for all the civil law cases (unlike in many EU countries, there are no specialized labor courts in Lithuania;[160] labor disputes are referred to as the civil cases). It emphasizes derogations applicable to specific situations, including labor disputes. The aim of this chapter is to reveal these peculiarities.

8.5.3.1 Dispute Hearing Bodies

Courts and labor dispute commissions hear labor disputes for defense of infringed rights. The labor disputes commission is a mandatory pretrial litigation body for all labor disputes for defense of infringed rights with exemptions directly provided by law. Courts refuse to accept direct applications clarifying the obligation to apply to the commission. The purpose of such rule is to reduce the workload of courts; to enable the parties to settle the dispute in a less formalized, cheaper, and faster way; and to promote social partnership. Only the party disagreeing to the decision of the commission has the right to start an action in court. Among the main exemptions allowing direct application to the court are employee's requests to award employment-related amounts from the employer that is the subject of bankruptcy proceedings[161] and disputes between the employer and its CEO (such legal relationship is regarded to be of a civil nature since a manager shares with a company fiduciary duty).

In 2013, major amendments related to the composition and competences of the labor dispute commission as pretrial litigation body were introduced. The commission's competence has been expanded to include disputes that arise after

[159] *E.G., A.J., I.D., V.P., V.K., I.M., A.S., V.D. and H.N. v UAB "Vilniaus viešasis transportas"*. Lithuanian Supreme Court, 2015, No. 3K-7-184-313/2015.

[160] Bužinskas (2010), p. 122.

[161] All claims of creditors of a company which is the subject of bankruptcy proceedings is to be dealt with in the same case (*UAB "NCC Statyba" v BUAB "Švilda"*. Lithuanian Supreme Court, 2005, No. 3K-3-20/2005).

employment relationship has ended. This is directly related to the principles of composition of the commission and its status. Before the reform, labor dispute commissions acted at the level of the employer (enterprise) and were composed of equal employer and employee representatives, and decisions had to be unanimous. Such regulation resulted in the dependence of the body on the employer and its inefficiency. Amendments led to the formation of the commissions in territorial subdivisions of the state labor inspectorate. Commission consists of a chairman-professional lawyer employed by the state labor inspectorate, and two members-representatives of territorial workers' and employers' organizations. Decisions are taken by majority vote. Cases can be handled in absence of members other than the chairman. On one hand, such changes may result in the creation of an independent and more flexible dispute hearing body. On the other hand, only active engagement of appointed representatives of the social partners can ensure that the labor dispute commission will not operate as another (complementary) institutional stage for the settlement of disputes but will promote a social-partnership-based search for solutions.[162]

8.5.3.2 Procedural Peculiarities of Labor Disputes

The substance of the procedural peculiarities of labor disputes is determined by the social significance of legal relationship. General procedural rules that constitute the adversarial principle of the civil procedure, providing for a passive role of the judge in determining the boundaries of the proceedings and collection of evidence, should be regarded as incompatible with the fact that the employer is generally both legally and economically the stronger party in the dispute since the dispute is usually associated with the employees' social status. The goals of legal regulation are to reconcile the parties, to resolve the dispute as soon as possible, and, in case peaceful settlement is not reached, to determine the material truth in the case and to ensure the actual implementation of the principle of equality.[163]

In order to guarantee employees' right to judicial protection, they are exempt from the payment of stamp duty. An employee's request must be accepted even if it is defective, if discrepancies can be fixed during the preliminary hearing. The active role of the court provides an obligation to collect evidence on its own initiative, to go beyond the limits of request in favor of the employee, or to apply alternative means of protection of the infringed employees' rights.[164] In practice, such legal regulation means that after hearing employees' complaints, the court itself assesses what evidence is relevant, analyzes which employee's rights may have been violated, and selects an adequate remedy.

At the same time, the law contains a set of time limits for opening of proceedings and preparation and hearing of the case. A general 3-year limitation period is set for labor disputes. A procedural term of 3 months from the day when the subject

[162]Petrylaitė et al. (2013).

[163]Nekrošius (2004), pp. 283–290.

[164]Davulis (2016).

learned or ought to have learned about the violation of his rights is set for application to the commission. A procedural term of 1 month is set for the party disagreeing to the decision of the commission to start an action in court. All of the abovementioned time limits are renewable. In addition, the labor dispute commission has to resolve the dispute within 1 month (this period may be extended up to a maximum of 2 months). When the action is initiated at court, the preparations must be completed within 1 month, and another month is given to consider the case. Although such strict regulation is not always consistent with the procedural requirements, the need to collect evidence and workload of judges and labor disputes commissions, specific deadlines contribute to more rapid and thus more effective dispute resolution.

8.5.3.3 Special Remedies

The employer is responsible for proper regulation of the employment relationship. The employers' duty causes the implementation of special remedies for employees. An employer that violates the duty to pay wages and other employment-related benefits on time must pay the employee the statutory interest rate. However, in the event of late payment to workers whose employment contract has been terminated, the rate of penalty shall be calculated, linking it to the employee's average wage for the period of delay but no longer than 3 months. A similar penalty applies to an employer for illegal dismissal of an employee. If the court recognizes that the employee was dismissed illegally, average wage is awarded for a period of involuntary idle time from the day of dismissal from work until the effective date of court decision but no longer than 1 year. The court applies these penalties on its own initiative (*ex officio*), even in the absence of a worker's request. On one hand, the set of such special measures encourages employers to avoid spontaneous decisions and, in the event of a dispute, to seek for peaceful solutions. On the other hand, a literal application of sanctions could lead to disproportionate consequences for the employer, and case law stresses the need to follow the principles of reasonableness and balance of interests and formulates criteria on which the amounts awarded may be reduced.[165]

References

Abramavičius A, Prapiestis J (2014) Europos Sąjungos teisės įtaka Lietuvos baudžiamosios teisės specialiosios dalies institutams (Influence of EU to the institutes of the special part of Lithuanian criminal law). In: Bernatonis J et al (eds) Europos Sąjungos teisės įtaka Lietuvos teisinei sistemai (Influence of EU law to the Lithuanian national system). Vilniaus universiteto Teisės fakultetas, Vilnius, pp 161–190

Andruškevičius A (2001) Administracinė teisė: kai kurie metodologiniai aspektai (Administrative law: some methodological aspects). Teisė 40

[165] *A.J. v Garliava primary health care center*. Lithuanian Supreme Court, 2016, No. 3K-3-37-469/2016.

Andruškevičius A (2004) Administracinės teisės principai ir normų ribos (Administrative law principles and limits of legal norms). Teisinės informacijos centras, Vilnius

Andruškevičius A (2008) Administracinė teisė. Bendrieji teorijos klausimai. Valdymo aktų institutas. Ginčo santykių jurisprudenciniai aspektai (Administrative law. Issues of general theory. Institute of administrative acts. Jurisprudential aspects of the dispute). VĮ Registrų centro Teisinės informacijos departamentas, Vilnius

Aničas J et al (1987) Tarybų Lietuvos enciklopedija. 3 tomas (Encyclopaedia of Soviet Lithuania, vol 3). Vyriausioji enciklopedijų redakcija, Vilnius

Bakaveckas A (2007) Lietuvos vykdomoji valdžia (Lithuanian executive power). Eugrimas, Vilnius

Bakaveckas A (2012) Lietuvos administracinė teisė: teorija ir praktika. I dalis (Lithuanian administrative law: theory and practice. Part I). Leidykla MES, Vilnius

Bakaveckas A, Dziegoraitis A et al (2005) Lietuvos administracinė teise. Bendroji dalis. Vadovėlis. (Lithuanian administrative law. General section. Textbook). Mykolo Romerio universitetas, Vilnius

Bilius M (2011) Criminal procedure law. In: Szymanski C, Berkmanas T, Gruodytė E, Kiršienė J (eds) Introduction to Lithuanian Law. Justitia, Vilnius, pp 335–352

Bužinskas G (2010) Darbo ginčai: teorija ir praktika (Labour disputes: theory and practice). Mykolo Romerio universitetas, Vilnius

Carlson RH (2004) A brief history of property tax. http://www.iaao.org/uploads/A_Brief_History_of_Property_Tax.pdf

Dambrauskienė G, Marcijonas A et al (2004) Lietuvos teisės pagrindai. (Lithuanian law basics). Justitia, Vilnius

Davulis T (2016) National labour law profile: Lithuania. http://www.ilo.org/ifpdial/information-resources/national-labour-law-profiles/WCMS_158913/lang--en/index.htm

European Commission (2009) How VAT works: general overview.. http://ec.europa.eu/taxation_customs/taxation/vat/how_vat_works/index_en.htm

Fedosiukas O (2014) Lietuvos Respublikos baudžiamojo kodekso galiojimo dešimtmetis: pamąstymai apie nepasiteisinusius lūkesčius, esamą būklę ir tolesnę raidą (Ten years as the Criminal Code of the Republic of Lithuania is in force: reflections on unjustified expectations, status quo and future development). In: Švedas G et al (eds) Globalizacijos iššūkiai baudžiamajai justicijai (Impact of globalization to the criminal justice). VĮ Registrų centras, Vilnius, pp 27–42

Gruodytė E (2008) Reform of Lithuanian criminal law: tendencies and problems. Baltic J Law Polit 1:18–40

Gruodytė E (2011) Criminal law. In: Szymanski C, Berkmanas T, Gruodytė E, Kiršienė J (eds) Introduction to Lithuanian law. Justitia, Vilnius, pp 209–334

Gruodytė E, Palionienė N (2014) Riboto Pakaltinamumo Sampratos Problematika Lyginamuoju Aspektu (The issue of diminished responsibility: comparative analysis). In: Švedas G et al (eds) Globalizacijos iššūkiai baudžiamajai justicijai (Impact of globalization to the criminal justice). VĮ Registrų centras, Vilnius, pp 57–76

Jukneliené D (2005) Lietuvos mokesčių sistemos raida (The Development of Lithuania's Tax System). http://etalpykla.lituanistikadb.lt/fedora/objects/LT-LDB-0001:J.04~2005~1367153542361/datastreams/DS.002.0.01.ARTIC/content

Laužikas E, Mikelėnas V, Nekrošius V (2003) Civilinio proceso teisė. I tomas (Civil procedure law. Volume I). Justitia, Vilnius

Maksimaitis M (2005) Lietuvos valstybės konstitucijų istorija: XX a. pirmoji pusė: monografija (The history of the constitutions of the Lithuanian state: first half of the 20th century: the monograph). Justitia, Vilnius

Marcijonas A, Gudavičius B (2003) Mokesčių teisė (Tax law). Teisinės informacijos centras, Vilnius

Nekrošius V (2004) Bylų, kylančių iš darbo teisinių santykių, nagrinėjimo ypatumai civiliniame procese. Darbo teisė suvienytoje Europoje (The particularities of solving cases rising from labour legal relationships in the civil process. Labour law in the unified Europe). Vilnius, Forzacas

Nekrošius I et al (2004) Lietuvos Respublikos darbo kodekso komentaras, III dalis: Individualūs darbo santykiai (Commentary on the Lithuanian Labour Code, III Part: individual labour relationships). Justitia, Vilnius, p 2004

Paužaitė-Kulvinskienė J (2005) Administracinė justicija: teorija ir praktika (Administrative justice: theory and practice). Justitia, Vilnius

Petrylaitė D, Davulis T, Petrylaitė V (2008) Europos Sąjungos teisės aktų įgyvendinimas Lietuvos darbo teisėje (Implementation of the legal acts of the European Union in Lithuanian Labour Law). VĮ Registrų centras, Vilnius

Petrylaitė D, Blažienė I, Petrylaitė V, Zabarauskaitė R (2013) Darbo ginčų institutas Lietuvoje: teisinių mechanizmų pokyčiai, jų rezultatai ir ateities perspektyvos (Institute of Labour Disputes in Lithuania: changes in legal mechanisms, their results and future perspectives). Verslas: Teorija ir praktika 14(4):278–286

Piesliakas V (2006) Lietuvos baudžiamoji teisė. Pirmoji knyga (Lithuanian criminal law. Volume I). Justitia, Vilnius

Šedbaras S (2005) Administracinė atsakomybė (Administrative liability). Justitia, Vilnius

Šedbaras S (2006) Administracinio proceso teisinio reglamentavimo problemos Lietuvos Respublikoje (The problems of legal regulation of administrative proceedings in the Republic of Lithuania). Justitia, Vilnius

Sinkevičius V (2008) Konstitucinių įstatymų samprata: teoriniai aspektai (The concept of constitutional laws: theoretical aspects). Jurisprudencija 2(104):28–38

Sinkevičius V (2014) Kokių įstatymų ir kitų teisės aktų atitiktį Konstitucijai tiria Konstitucinis Teismas? (What are the laws and other legal acts whose compliance with the constitution is subject to review by the constitutional court). Jurisprudencija 21(3):907–923

Švedas G (2011) Kai kurie probleminiai juridinio asmens baudžiamosios atsakomybės aspektai Lietuvos konstitucinėje jurisprudencijoje ir baudžiamosios justicijos doktrinoje (Some Problem Aspects of Criminal Liability of a Legal Entity in Lithuanian Constitutional Jurisprudence and Doctrine of Criminal Justice). In: Lietuvos Respublikos baudžiamajam kodeksui – 10 metų. Recenzuotų mokslinių straipsnių, skirtų baudžiamosios politikos ir baudžiamųjų įstatymų teisėkūros, baudžiamosios teisės, baudžiamojo proceso ir nusikaltimų kvalifikavimo problematikai rinkinys (In 10 years for the Criminal Code of the Republic of Lithuania. Collection of Reviewed Scientific Articles, related to the problems of criminal policy, criminal legislation, criminal law, procedure and qualification of crimes). VĮ Registrų centras, Vilnius, pp 91–108.

Švedas G, Prapiestis J (2011) Lietuvos Respublikos baudžiamojo kodekso dešimtmetis: raidos pamokos ir perspektyvos (Ten years for the Criminal Code of the Republic of Lithuania: lessons of development and perspectives). In: Lietuvos Respublikos baudžiamajam kodeksui – 10 metų. Recenzuotų mokslinių straipsnių, skirtų baudžiamosios politikos ir baudžiamųjų įstatymų teisėkūros, baudžiamosios teisės, baudžiamojo proceso ir nusikaltimų kvalifikavimo problematikai rinkinys (In 10 years for the Criminal Code of the Republic of Lithuania. Collection of Reviewed Scientific Articles, related to the problems of criminal policy, criminal legislation, criminal law, procedure and qualification of crimes). VĮ Registrų centras, Vilnius, pp 13–30

Thuronyi V (2003) Comparative tax law. Kluwer Law International

Tiažkijus V, Petravičius R, Bužinskas G (1999) Darbo teisė (Labour law). Justitia, Vilnius

Lithuanian Private Law

9

Paulius Astromskis, Jurgita Grigienė, Julija Kiršienė, Aušrinė Pasvenskienė, Evaldas Rapolas, Siuzana Ščerbina-Dalibagienė, Jurgita Spaičienė, and Vigintas Višinskis

P. Astromskis
Faculty of Law, Vytautas Magnus University, Jonavos st. 66, LT-44138 Kaunas, Lithuania

Viliušis & Astromskis Law Firm, Jonavos st. 66, LT-44138 Kaunas, Lithuania
e-mail: paulius@astromskis.lt

J. Grigienė
Faculty of Law, Vytautas Magnus University, Jonavos st. 66, LT-44138 Kaunas, Lithuania

Čerka & Partneriai Advocates Bureau, Jonavos st. 66, LT-44138 Kaunas, Lithuania
e-mail: jurgita.grigiene@vdu.lt

J. Kiršienė • A. Pasvenskienė (✉)
Faculty of Law, Vytautas Magnus University, Jonavos st. 66, LT-44138 Kaunas, Lithuania
e-mail: julija.kirsiene@vdu.lt, ausrine.pasvenskiene@vdu.lt

E. Rapolas
Faculty of Law, Vytautas Magnus University, Jonavos st. 66, LT-44138 Kaunas, Lithuania

Magnusson Law Firm, Jonavos st. 66, LT-44138 Kaunas, Lithuania
e-mail: evaldas.rapolas@magnussonlaw.com

S. Ščerbina-Dalibagienė
Faculty of Law, Vytautas Magnus University, Jonavos st. 66, LT-44138 Kaunas, Lithuania

Ministry of Finance of the Republic of Lithuania, Jonavos st. 66, LT-44138 Kaunas, Lithuania
e-mail: siuzana.scerbina-dalibagiene@vdu.lt

J. Spaičienė
Faculty of Law, Vytautas Magnus University, Jonavos st. 66, LT-44138 Kaunas, Lithuania

Jurgita Spaičienė Advocates Bureau, Jonavos st. 66, LT-44138 Kaunas, Lithuania
e-mail: jurgita.spaiciene@vdu.lt

V. Višinskis
Faculty of Law, Mykolas Romeris University, Gedimino av. 40/1, LT-01503 Vilnius, Lithuania

Court of Appeal of Lithuania, Gedimino av. 40/1, LT-01503 Vilnius, Lithuania
e-mail: vigintas.visinskis@apeliacinis.lt

T. Kerikmäe et al. (eds.), *The Law of the Baltic States*,
DOI 10.1007/978-3-319-54478-6_9

Abstract
The section on private law covers five basic areas of Lithuanian law that are essential for understanding the basic rules of conduct that persons should follow in private relations. These are Property Law, Contract and Tort Law, Company and Insolvency Law, Family and Inheritance Law, and Civil Procedure Law. Authors provide a definition and describe the system of property rights (and their encumbrances) stipulated in Lithuanian Civil Code. Starting from a descriptive analysis of the formation of contracts, the authors continue with a review of the rules on content and interpretation of contracts and, additionally, the performance (nonperformance) and termination of them. The part on tort law describes the four elements of tort action (unlawful actions, causation, fault, and damages), then the authors continue with a review of basic defenses from tort liability and finish the tort law part with a presentation of rules on joint tortfeasors, right of recourse, and some other special rules of delictual liability. In company law, the possible types of companies in Lithuania and their main features, such as requirements for incorporation, management, and activity, are introduced. In the second subchapter, the authors provide a brief overview of the bankruptcy proceedings. In family and inheritance law, the in-depth review of the major aspects of family law and inheritance law is provided. In civil procedure, the authors explain the issues of jurisdiction in civil cases and continue with explanation of the basics of the right to apply to court.

9.1 Property Law

Julija Kiršienė
Faculty of Law, Vytautas Magnus University, Jonavos st. 66, LT-44138 Kaunas, Lithuania
e-mail: julija.kirsiene@vdu.lt

9.1.1 Regulation of Property Law

Property law is mainly regulated by Book 4, "Material Law," of the Civil Code of Lithuania (hereinafter in this subsection referred to as CC), which came into force in July of 2001. This book of CC consists of 15 sections and 262 norms. Of course, there are some laws and other legal acts that regulate some specific issues of property law, for example Constitutional Law I-1392, which regulates ownership and transfer of titles of land in Lithuania, company law, etc.

Regulation of property law has emerged under circumstances when Lithuania, after regaining independence, was in the process of building proper conditions for a free economy. However, as Prof. V. Pakalniškis notes, the "new Civil Code was largely influenced by the Russian legal doctrine, <...> after the second World

War, the Lithuanian law and doctrine of civil law were under an influence of the socialist ideology. Therefore, the application of the doctrine of property law for the new Civil Code of Lithuania was affected by stereotypical regulations established throughout the decades and due to this it was not sufficiently consistent."[1] Nevertheless, the CC was inspired and influenced by the Civil Codes of Quebec and the Netherlands, i.e., the most modern Western European doctrine of property law, but some rules and especially patterns of interpretation remained from the former (post-Soviet) civil code of Lithuania, so this regulation is a mixture of modern and common rules from Soviet times.

9.1.2 Definition of Property

According to regulation of the CC, the object of ownership right may be things and other assets.[2] Although in the legal doctrine of Lithuania there is the opinion that the things and assets are identical concepts,[3] but when interpreting norms of CC systemically, property is not only things but also securities, property rights, results of intellectual activities, information, actions and results thereof, as well as any other material and even nonmaterial values,[4] and also duties. For example, objects to succession are not only material objects (movable and immovable things) and nonmaterial objects (securities, patents, trademarks, etc.), claims of a patrimonial character and property obligations of the bequeather, intellectual property (authors' property rights to works of literature, science and art, etc.), as well as other property rights and duties stipulated by law. This opinion is confirmed by the Commentary of Book 1 of Lithuanian CC;[5] broadly, property can be described as the aggregate of rights and duties of some person. It should be noted that the best criteria for describing what can be an object of property right is the civil circulation.

9.1.3 System of Property Rights and Their Encumbrances Stipulated in the Lithuanian Civil Code

The main features of property rights are absoluteness, elasticity, stability, safety and reliability, and remedies typical for real rights.[6] The following (see Table 9.1)

[1] Pakalniškis (2004).

[2] *Civil Code of Republic of Lithuania*. Official Gazette, 2000, No. 74-2262, Art. 4.38.

[3] [No, author, named] (1997), p. 253.

[4] *Civil Code of Republic of Lithuania*. Official Gazette, 2000, No. 74-2262, Art. 1.97.

[5] Bakanas and Mikelėnas (2003), p. 213.

[6] The beginning of contemporary law of real rights are in Roman private law that have formed the system of real right (rights of possessing and using) remedies, which is different, in a sense, from the remedies typical for obligations.

Table 9.1 Property rights and their encumbrances

Property right/ encumbrance/ article of the CC	Description	Main features of the law
Possession	Factual holding of a thing can be an independent real right to thing with a purpose to have it as one's own (articles 4.22–4.36)	– Presupposition for acquiring ownership right according to acquisitive prescription – Presumption of fair acquisition of possession – Remedy for violations of possession: possessory action
Ownership	The right to manage, possess, use, and dispose of property at one's volition (articles 4.37–4.67, 4.72–4.105)	– Special rules for ownership of land and other immovable property – Two forms of common property – Special remedies: vindicative action, actio negatoria, possessory action
Trust	The right of the trustee to possess, use, and dispose of property as defined by the trustor in the interests of the beneficiary (articles 4.106–4.110, 6.953–6.968)	– The objects of the trust right may be movable and immovable things, securities or any other property – Special rules are applicable for the trust of state or municipal property; – The trustee is entitled to protect the trust right in the same ways as owner
Usufruct	The right of use and enjoyment of a thing of another, granted for a period of a person's life or for a certain period (articles 4.141–4.159)	– Right to use the thing as prescribed or as it would do a diligent owner – Fruits, products, and revenues produced by the thing while exercising the usufruct belonging to the usufructuary unless the contract or laws provide otherwise
Superficies	The right to use the land of another for constructing buildings (articles 4.160–4.164)	– May be established by the agreement of the landowner and the person becoming the superficiary or by the will of the landowner – Superficiary may be obliged to pay for this right by a lump sum or installments – Period may be fixed or indefinite
Emphyteusis	Long-term lease of immovable property as a real right (articles 4.165–4.169)	– May be established by agreement between the owner of an immovable thing and the emphyteutic lessee or by will – Lessee may be obliged to pay for this right by a lump sum or installments, but this right can be set gratuitously too – The term of emphyteusis may not be less than 10 years

(continued)

Table 9.1 (continued)

Property right/ encumbrance/ article of the CC	Description	Main features of the law
Servitute	Encumbrance of the right of the owner of immovable thing in order to ensure a proper usage of the thing in favor of which the servitude is established (articles 4.111–4. 140)	– May be established by laws, transactions, and a court judgment – Damages incurred due to the establishment of the servitude may be compensated by a lump sum or installments as stipulated by laws, contracts, court judgment, or an administrative act
Hypothec	Mortgage of an immovable thing in order to secure the performance of a present or future debt obligation (arts 4.170–4.197)	– Mortgaged thing is not transferred to the creditor – Two types of hypothec: contractual and tacit[a]; tacit hypothec may be established by law or court judgment in cases provided by the CC, for example, in order to secure state claims arising from taxation or social insurance, property claims granted by court judgment, etc. – Creditor that secured his claim with hypotec has priority right of recovery of the debt from the mortgaged thing against all other creditors
Pledge	Encumbrance of a movable thing or real rights securing the discharge of an existing or future debt obligation (arts 4.198–4.228)	– Goods in stock and things that will come into the pledgor's ownership in the future may be objects of the pledge as well
Retention	A lawful possessor of a thing of another who has the right of financial claim in respect of the owner of the thing is entitled to retain the thing until his claim is satisfied (arts 4.229–4.235)	– Despite the amount of the debt, possessor may retain the entire thing until his claim is fully satisfied – Possesor that exercises the right of retention may not lease, pledge, and otherwise encumber the thing or use it

(continued)

Table 9.1 (continued)

Property right/ encumbrance/ article of the CC	Description	Main features of the law
Property administration	Administration of the property belonging to another person if it is not administered under other titles (articles 4.236–4.252)	– Kinds of property administration: simple and full – Administration may be established by a court order, by law, by transaction, or by administrative act, for example, in case of child custody for the property of deceased in the process of inheritance

[a]The conceptually new type of pledge (hypothecs) is presented in the new CC (issued 2001)—legal or tacit pledge. Tacit pledge arises by operation of law on the debtor's property without debtor's will as it is in case of contractual mortgage. The application to register the legal (compulsory) mortgage shall be executed as a mortgage bond. If the mortgage is legal (compulsory), the mortgage bond is signed only by the creditor. The mortgage is registered in the Register of Mortgages upon the decision of the mortgage judge and upon the submission of the mortgage bond to the Mortgage Office of the locality wherein the mortgaged thing is located (*CC*, art 4.185)

presents all property rights and their encumbrances as real rights with short description and main features.

Due to limited space, we are going to present only the most relevant topics of property rights from practical and scholarly points of view.

9.1.4 Possession as Independent Real Right and Its Judicial Remedies

Possession as a property right could be treated as an independent right in rem or as a derivative—i.e., a contractual right. Possession as independent right in rem is recognized only to a person, who is the legal owner of the thing or honest and lawful possessor of the derelict (factual possessor), seeking to obtain the ownership of that thing by positive prescription. All other possessors (such as leaseholders, bailees, etc.) enjoy possession only as a derivative right. Thus, the main purpose of possession as an independent real right is to create conditions for positive prescription.

According to Pakalniškis, possession as independent real right is described by at least two criteria: (1) there is factual possession (objective element), and (2) the possessor is convinced that no one has more rights than he; thus, he possesses a thing legitimately, openly, continuously as his own, i.e., in good faith (subjective element).[7]

[7]Pakalniškis (2015), p. 34.

According to article 4.26, possession is deemed acquired in good faith until the opposite is proven. It should be noted that, in case of infringement of this right, the possessor who is not the owner of the thing has no remedy of vindication from illegal possession of the thing or right to action negatoria because those remedies can be exercised only by the owner of the thing. The factual possessor has a special remedy, described in article 4.34 of the CC, which entitles the possessor to defend his current possession and to retake the possession that has been taken away forcefully. This remedy is different from vindicative action, even if from sight they seem very similar, because vindicative action can be pursued only by the owner of the thing that lost possession. However, possessory action can be pursued by any possessor if possession was infringed, so possessory action can be pursued by the owner, leasor, or any other possessor even if he has no legal title. Moreover, the possessor in his possessory action can claim not only the return of the lost possession but also any other infringement of possession. So possessory action in some cases can also be similar to action negatoria. The main difference from this action lies also in proving the title. The plaintiff who wants to claim with action negatoria first of all shall prove his title to the thing the possession of which was violated. However, in case of possessory action, the plaintiff is not expected to prove his title to the thing—just the fact of factual possession. Thus, possessory action can be used as the alternative to vindicative action and action negatoria.

9.1.5 Content of the Right of Ownership

As a general rule, ownership right may be acquired by contract; by inheritance; by producing a new thing; by appropriating a find or a treasure; by obtaining, upon compensation, inappropriately kept public cultural values; by acquisitive prescription; and also by other ways described by law.

The owner has the right freely to manage, possess, use, and dispose of an object of ownership right. This approach to the content of the right of ownership reflects the so-called concept of "triad" enshrined in the doctrine of civil law. "In accordance with this notion the content of property includes three kinds of legally protected expectations: a right of possession (*ius possidendi*), a right of use (*ius utendi*) and a right of disposition (*ius disponendi*). This triad defining the content of property law remains in use only in Russia."[8] Indeed, contemporary codifications of civil law avoid defining the content of property by a specific right because the right to property is a natural and absolute human right; thus, scholars suggest that the laws should not provide the content of ownership right.[9]

Coownership right is the right of two or several owners to possess, use, and dispose of the property held by them in common. There are two kinds of common ownership right: (1) common partial ownership is ownership when the shares of

[8] *Ibid.*

[9] *Ibid.*, pp. 34–38.

each coowner are established in the coownership; (2) common joint ownership right is when such shares are not established, for example, property of spouses. Common ownership right shall be deemed partial, unless the laws provide otherwise.

Coownership right is the right of two or several owners to possess, use, and dispose of the object of the right of ownership held by them as common. In case of disputes, the order of possession, use, or disposal is established by a judicial procedure on the basis of a claim by one of the coowners. Each coowner has the right to transfer in possession of, lease, or otherwise alienate, mortgage, or encumber in some other way all or a part of his share held in common partial ownership. The procedure of selling the share of commonly owned property and priority right of other owners to buy it is discussed later in the section about transfer of immovable property (CC article 4.79). It should be noted that each coowner has the right to demand that his share would be separated from the common partial ownership in kind if it is possible without disproportionate damage to the property; in other cases, one or several of the coowners after separation shall receive financial compensation. Moreover, creditors of one of the coowners have the right to separate the debtor's share in order to claim debt from it.

The owner(s) shall exercise his property rights without infringing on the rights and lawful interests of other persons. For example, if damage is caused by the collapse or defect of buildings or other structures, including roads, the owner (possessor) of it shall be liable for the damage (CC article 6.266). Another example is the liability for damage caused by domestic animals or wild animals that are in somebody's custody (CC article 6.267).

A good example of how the owner can infringe public interests by improperly exercising property rights is improper maintaining of objects of cultural heritage. The CC provides that when a person improperly maintains a property that has public value due to its historic, artistic, or other properties, the public institution whose role is to protect such heritage first of all shall warn the owner about the improper keeping of such property. Then if the owner fails to fulfill the requirements, such property may be taken from him following a claim by relevant institution to state property. In other words, such property can be expropriated. The owner, in such cases, shall be compensated at market price. Due to complicated procedures, such expropriations are not frequent. But, for example, in case 2A-157/2014 at the Lithuanian appellate court,[10] improperly maintained immovable property with cultural value was not only taken from an owner, but in the same case financial compensation awarded from the state to the owner for this immovable property was significantly lower than the damages awarded to the state for improper maintenance from the owner. Moreover, for improper maintenance of property that is recognized as cultural heritage, laws provide not only civil but also administrative and criminal liability.[11]

[10]Lithuanian Court of Appeal 2014 February 14th ruling in the civil case No. 2A-157/2014.

[11]Lithuanian Republic Code of Administrative Offences article 91; Criminal Code of the Republic of Lithuania article 187, article 188; Civil Code of Republic of Lithuania article 6.245 part 1 d. clause 4; Lithuanian Republic Immovable Cultural Heritage Protection Law article 29.

As a contemporary example of new issues related to proper exercise of property rights in a technologically advanced world, the question of using drones emerges. These new unmanned aircraft technologies are more and more applicable in the agricultural industry; the transportation of parcels; entertainment; search and rescue missions; police, border protection, and military activities, as well it being useful to journalists, film companies, etc. As there are so many ways to use drones, it is expected that in a few years, the drone industry will increase dramatically, so more and more of these air vehicles will be flying over private land. Hence, the main legal issue in this regard is what the relation is between the rights of the land owner and drone owner respectively. In other words, who is the "owner" of the air space above the land plot?

As a general rule, the owner of a land parcel enjoys property rights to the space above his land parcel as much as is needed for the intended use of the parcel and so long as this activity does not contradict the law. Also, currently, the airspace of Lithuania is regulated by the Aviation Act, which provides that "The Republic of Lithuania shall have an exclusive right to the airspace above its land territory and internal and territorial waters."[12] Airspace by regulation is divided into low altitude and navigable altitude airspace; however, the airspace in between these two altitudes is not regulated by law at all. Moreover, from the abovementioned regulation, the scope of rights belonging to the airspace of landowners is far from clear.

9.1.6 Peculiarities of Property Transfers in Lithuania

As a general rule, the right of owner to transfer his title of the property to other persons is unlimited (article 4.37) because the owner has the right freely to manage, possess, use, and dispose of an object of ownership right. However, the ownership and disposition of some things can be limited due to safety, health concerns, or other public needs (for example, guns, narcotics, some drugs, etc.). Some things are even out of circulation because they are the exclusive property of the state or cannot be the object of transactions. In article 47 of the Constitution of Lithuania, it is set that the subsurface, as well as the internal waters, forests, parks, roads, and historical, archaeological, and cultural objects of state importance, as well the airspace over its territory, its continental shelf, and the economic zone in the Baltic Sea, belong to the Republic of Lithuania by right of exclusive ownership. Also, the human body, its parts, or its organs and tissues may not become objects of commercial transactions (article 2.25). In any case, things that are withdrawn from civil use or circulation must be imperatively indicated in the laws.

[12]Art. 13 Part. 1 of Aviation law.

9.1.6.1 Notarized Form of Transfer of Limited Liability Company's (LLC) Shares

As an exception, we would like to discuss the new regulation regarding transfer of LLC shares, which came into force in January of 2015. It states that the transaction of LLC share transfer shall be notarized in such cases: (1) when more than a quarter of all LLC shares are sold; (2) when the price of such transaction is higher than 14,500 eur.; and (3) when the price is paid fully or in part by immovable property. Notably, this requirement is not applicable in case of donation or exchange contracts. Previously, such contracts could be concluded in written form. This regulation was initiated by Lithuanian President Dalia Grybauskaitė. She proposed this amendment of the Civil Code with the aim of preventing the practice of fraud share transfer transactions—for example, when such contracts are concluded or changed retroactively and the moment of transfer of ownership of shares would be certain.

There is some criticism of this unique situation, especially when foreign investors want to purchase shares of Lithuanian LLC. Such contracts are usually prepared entirely in English, but the notary documents must be translated into the Lithuanian language. So translations may increase costs and take additional time. Furthermore, the notarial form requirement means that the contract must be signed by parties in front of a notary, which essentially restricts the possibilities to sign a contract at a distance.

9.1.6.2 Transfer of Immovable Property

Transactions on the transfer of immovable property, as well as transactions on the encumbrance of the immovable in Lithuania, shall be drawn up in the notarial form.

The procedure of such a transaction is as follows:

1. Verification and clarification of the property data – the notary public, at the initial stage of preparing an immovable property transaction, is required to order verification and revision of cadastral and registration data of an immovable item. The Information System for Immovable Property Transactions shall generate a certificate on the future transaction and submit it to the Registrar of Real Estate. The certificate is valid for 30 calendar days after the data revision.
2. Notarization of the immovable property transfer or encumbrance transaction—failure to comply with the requirements of the form shall render the contract invalid. The contract of purchase and sale of an immovable item may be used against third parties and have legal implications for them only in case it is registered with the public register. Among other documents that shall be submitted to notaries are the land plan, documents proving the seller's title to immovable items, and the energy performance certificate, if building is being sold, except in some cases.
3. Registration of the transfer of the property title to the real estate register—transfer of the real estate is deemed effective with respect to its parties, irrespective of its legal registration. However, only registration makes the transfer opposable to third parties. In addition to the registration, a new property

certificate is issued to the new owner of the property. Notably, notaries under request may electronically register the transaction through NETSVEP—Public Electronic Service of Transaction of Real Estate.

9.1.6.3 Transfer of Land as a Special Object of Ownership

The Constitution and other laws legally regulate the relations linked with the acquisition, possession, and transfer of land as a special object. The Constitutional Court of Lithuania in its jurisprudence states that land is an important part of the ecosystem. Moreover, it is a special natural resource in the sense that it cannot be replaced by something else or newly created or increased otherwise; thus, land is a limited resource. Proper use of land as a limited resource is a condition of the survival of the human being and society, as well as the basis of the welfare of the nation, so ensuring of rational use of land is a public interest. When legally regulating the relations linked with the use of land for business and economic activities, one must pay heed to the specificity of the nature of land as a natural resource and of land as real property. The Constitution[13] also provides that in the Republic of Lithuania, foreign subjects may acquire ownership of land, internal waters, and forests, according to a constitutional law on the implementation of article 47 of the Constitution.[14] By this law, prohibition of the acquisition of agricultural land by foreigners was set for a 7-year transition period, which ended on April 30, 2014. According to the new regulation, foreigners are entitled to purchase agricultural land in Lithuania, but there are certain safeguards. Foreign persons in this regard are differentiated by certain criteria. If we ask whether a Belorussian, Swedish, or Brazilian resident has equal conditions and opportunity for the acquisition of agricultural land in Lithuania, the answer is no.

9.1.6.4 Criteria for Differentiation of Foreign Acquirers of Land

First of all, legal regulation provides that the title to the land, inland waters, and forests of Lithuania may be acquired by foreign individuals or entities domiciled or incorporated in

- the EU Member States,
- the countries that have concluded an association agreement with the European Community and its Member States,
- the Member States of the OECD,
- NATO Member States,
- the countries that are parties to the European Economic Area Agreement.

[13]Constitution of the Republic of Lithuania, Art. 47 paragraph 3.

[14]The Constitutional Law of the Republic of Lithuania on the Implementation of Paragraph 3 of Article 47 of the Constitution of the Republic of Lithuania, 20 June 1996 No I-1392, last amended on 3 November 2011—No XI-1626; (Official Gazette, 1996, No. 64-1503; 2003, No. 34-1418).

Persons of the specified foreign countries may acquire land, inland waters, and forests on the same terms and conditions as the citizens and permanent residents and legal persons of the Republic of Lithuania. For foreign persons from other countries not specified on the list above, the ban to purchase agricultural land in Lithuania was continued.

9.1.6.5 Indirect Acquisition of Agricultural Land by Foreign Persons and Entities

Despite the prohibition of some foreign entities to purchase agricultural land in Lithuania, the latter had found ways to circumvent the imperatives of the aforementioned Constitutional Law and agricultural land in some cases was acquired indirectly, namely, through an intermediary or setting up a company as a dominant shareholder. However, in 2012, the Supreme Court of Lithuania established the case law stating that the transactions concerning the transfer of the land to the companies established in Lithuania, which are owned by the persons not eligible to acquire land in Lithuania, are in conflict with mandatory legislative provisions and are therefore to be considered null and void. In this way, the evasion of statutory prohibitions and direct acquisition of the land by the foreign persons not meeting the European and transatlantic integration criteria was prevented. This prohibition is also applicable in case of donation and even inheritance. In the case of inheritance, a foreigner-successor of agricultural land is entitled only to the amount of money retained by selling the inheritance. However, there are no restrictions on ownership of the buildings, so if such successor foreigner inherited land with buildings on it, an inheritance certificate will be issued only for buildings, and in this case the owner of the buildings and land will be different. The acquisition of agricultural land through an intermediary in court practice was also recognized as void and null.[15]

9.1.6.6 Other Special Requirements for Acquiring Agricultural Land in Lithuania

The law on acquisition of agricultural land[16] also sets general requirements for purchasers of agricultural land that are different for natural and legal persons. A natural person intending to acquire agricultural land must first prove professional skills and competence for carrying out agricultural activities. A legal person seeking to acquire ownership of agricultural land has to have engaged in agricultural activity for at least 3 years of the 10 years preceding the acquisition, he must declare land and crops, its income from agricultural activity has to exceed 50 percent of all income, and its economic viability has to be proved by a mandatory procedure. The law also limits the purchaser to a maximum of 500 hectares of

[15]Supreme Court of Lithuania 2012 February 24th ruling in the civil case No. 3K-3-57/2012.

[16]Agricultural Land Acquisition Law of the Republic of Lithuania (Official Gazette, 2003, No. 15-600; 2004, No. 124-4490; TAR, 2014-04-29, No. 2014-04860).

agricultural land with some exceptions. For the purposes of calculation of this threshold, the agricultural land held by all related parties is considered.

As a matter of rule, some persons have a priority right to acquire the land, so the landowner about the decision to sell agricultural land shall notify the selected notary or the local national land service territorial unit. Therefore, the sale/purchase of agricultural land may take more than a month.

As regards priority rights acquisition of agricultural land, first of all, article 4.79 of the CC sets the priority right of the coowner to buy the share in sale of the commonly owned land at the price at which it is sold and under the same conditions. Such information shall be given through a notary. Other persons that have a priority right to buy the plot of land are (1) the land user (for example, lessee); (2) the municipality or the state, if the land is expected to be used for public needs; and (3) owners of neighboring land plots. Written notice regarding the intention to sell the land shall indicate the price and other conditions of sale. As a general rule, the buyer must immediately pay the full price, unless the contract provides otherwise. When the other coowners or other holders of priority rights renounce their priority right to buy or fail to use such right within 1 month, from the day of receipt of such notification the seller shall have the right to sell his land to any person.

9.1.6.7 Transfer of Land with Buildings

Under the contract for purchase-sale of a building, the seller shall transfer to the buyer, together with the right of ownership to the building, the rights (ownership, lease, superficies, and others) to the land, which is occupied by the building and which is necessary for the building to be ordinarily used. As a matter of fact, even if the owners of the building and land occupied by it are different, the building can be transferred without the land owner's consent, unless it contradicts the conditions of use of the land set down by laws and (or) the contract (article 6.394 part 3).

9.1.6.8 The Moment of Property Acquisition

In some cases of property transfer, the moment of property acquisition may be particularly important. For example, if the buyer has not yet paid for a purchased car and has gone bankrupt, the question of ownership can become essential. According to general rule, the acquirer of property acquires the ownership right to the property at the moment these are transferred to him (CC article 4.49). However, it is not an imperative norm. Parties of the contract can set other moments of property acquisition.

For example, contracts when the buyer pays for purchased goods later are so-called contracts of installment (CC article 6.411). It should be noted that in accordance with the general rule, in case of installment sale agreement, the seller shall retain the right of ownership to the item that is being sold until the full sale payment is received (CC article 6.411 part 1). The title retention clause in such contracts is presumed. Retention of title means that the seller shall retain the right of ownership to the item that is being sold until the payment of the full sale price set in the contract is received. This is the general meaning of this clause.[17] The main task of reservation of title clause is that in case of the buyer's insolvency, the seller would have the right to recover the goods from the buyer until the payment of the full sale price or proceeds in cases stipulated by the contract in priority with other creditors (even secured).[18] The question in this regard is whether in the case of the buyer's bankruptcy the seller would have priority over other creditors of the buyer and would recover transferred goods (proceeds for them). According to the CC article 6.414 part 1 and article 6.349 part 2, in a case in which the buyer fails to comply with the schedule of payment of regular installments laid down in the contract, the seller may demand immediate payment of the installments due or take back the sold thing. If the buyer has paid more than half of the price of the thing, the seller shall have no right to take back the thing, unless the contract provides otherwise.

If under the purchase-sale agreement the right of ownership passes to the buyer from the moment of delivery of the thing, it shall be considered from the moment of delivery of the thing to the buyer until the payment of the full price that the thing has been pledged to the seller seeking to secure performance of obligations by the buyer (tacit pledge (hypothec)) (CC article 6.414 part 2). If within the time period indicated in the mortgage bond the debtor fails to discharge the obligation, the creditor (seller) may exercise his rights by applying to the mortgage judge with a request to sell the mortgaged thing in a public forced auction sale in order to be fully

[17]The ownership right can be resolved into different titles or rights. These titles are so real and they have such economic value that they can become an independent object of ownership right.

[18]CC, art. 2.113, stipulates such sequence of and procedure for the satisfaction of claims of a legal person's creditors:

> In the event of legal person's liquidation (bankruptcy) the following sequence of and procedure for the satisfaction of creditors' claims shall be established:
>
> 1) priority in satisfying creditors' claims shall be given to claims secured by the mortgage of property of a legal person in liquidation—from the value of the mortgaged property;
>
> 2) first in sequence for the satisfaction of claims shall be employees' claims connected with labor relations; claims of compensation for maiming or other physical injuries, occupational disease or deprivation of life resulting from an accident in the place of work as well as claims of natural persons to settle accounts for agricultural produce supplied for processing;
>
> 3) second in sequence for the satisfaction of claims shall be the claims related to taxes and other payments to the budget as well as compulsory state social insurance and health insurance contributions and foreign loans granted the State guarantee;
>
> 4) third in sequence for the satisfaction of claims shall be all other claims of creditors.
>
> 2. The claims of creditors of each successive sequence shall be fulfilled upon fully satisfying the claims of creditors of the preceding sequence. If assets are insufficient to fulfil all the claims of one sequence in full, said claims shall be satisfied in proportion to the number of claims due to each creditor.

paid the due sum from the proceeds that he is entitled to receive before other creditors, even in case of the debtor's (buyer's) insolvency.[19]

However, the moment of property acquisition can be important also in cases when the buyer paid for the goods but has not yet received them and in the process of storage or transportation they are lost or damaged because of theft, fire, or other reasons. In this case, the risk of accidental damage of a thing being transferred passes to the acquirer at the moment that he acquires the ownership rights, unless the transferor misses the deadline to transfer the thing or the acquirer misses the deadline to receive the thing; then the risk of accidental damage of the thing is upon the party that has missed the deadline (CC article 4.52).

9.1.7 Defense of Real Rights

Property rights are often defended by contractual defenses; however, the owner (among others) can exercise special proprietorial remedies, including the owner's claims directed to his property:

- action of vindication from another person's illegal possession (vindicative action, CC article 4.95),[20]
- action against violations unrelated to loss of possession (actio negatoria, CC article 4.98),[21]
- action against any infringements of possession (possesory action, CC article 4.34),[22]
- prevention of unlawful actions or prohibition to perform actions that pose reasonable threat of the occurrence of damage (preventive action, CC article 6.255),
- self-defense (CC 1.139).

9.1.7.1 Vindication of a Thing from an Acquirer in Good Faith

If a thing was gratuitously acquired from a person that had no right to transfer this property, and the acquirer could not know this (acquirer in good faith), it can be vindicated from an acquirer in good faith in all cases. If such thing was acquired upon payment, there is a different regulation for vindication of an immovable and movable thing.

---

[19] A creditor must notify a debtor in writing that if the obligation secured by a pledge within the time-period stipulated is not performed, the enforcement shall commence. If a pledge is registered in the Register of Mortgages, a written warning notice to a debtor is delivered through the Office of Mortgages.

[20] The owner shall have the right to vindicate his thing from another's illegal possession.

[21] Owner may claim elimination of all violations to his right, even if unrelated to loss of possession.

[22] Each possessor is entitled to defend his current possession and to retake the possession that has been taken away forcefully.

An immovable thing may not be vindicated from an acquirer in good faith with the exception of cases when the owner had lost this thing due to a crime committed by other persons. However, a movable thing can be vindicated from the acquirer in good faith if it was lost or stolen or the owner otherwise lost its possession against his volition. The owner in vindicating a movable or, in cases prescribed by law, an immovable thing has the right to demand

- from an illegal possessor in bad faith to restitute or recompense all income that such person received or had to receive during the entire period of possession,
- from an illegal possessor in good faith all income that such possessor received or had to receive since the time when he found out about the possession being illegal.

9.2 Contract and Tort Law

Paulius Astromskis
Faculty of Law, Vytautas Magnus University, Jonavos st. 66, LT-44138 Kaunas, Lithuania

Viliušis & Astromskis Law Firm, Jonavos st. 66, LT-44138 Kaunas, Lithuania
e-mail: paulius@astromskis.lt

9.2.1 Contract Law

9.2.1.1 The Basics of Contract Law in Lithuania

One of the main tasks in the process of drafting the new Civil Code of Lithuania (CC)[23] was to create new, modern, and effective contract law rules, which had to correspond to the changed economic situation.[24] In order to complete this task, many contract law rules had been harmonized with soft law instruments such as the UNIDROIT Principles of International Commercial Contracts (UNIDROIT Principles) and the Principles of European Contract Law (PECL).[25] As a result, the new CC, adopted on July 18, 2000, has created a comprehensive and modern regulatory system of contractual relations, where the free will of its parties is elevated above all else.[26] Most importantly, these rules have embedded the principles of paramount importance in the context of open and market-oriented economy—among other principles: the freedom of contract, *pacta sunt servanda*, good faith, and fair dealing.

[23] *Civil Code of the Republic of Lithuania*. Official Gazette, 2000, No. 74-2262.

[24] Mikelėnas (2005).

[25] Mikelėnas (2002), pp. 253–261.

[26] *Pakalniškis, V. Transcript of 2000 July 18th Parliament (Seimas) Session No. 69(504).* Stenogramos, 2000-09-01, No. 269.

Since the contract is one of the sources of obligations, most of the contract law rules are set in the sixth book of the CC, "Law of Obligations." These rules are divided into the general (articles 6.154–6.228) and the special (articles 6.305–6.1018) parts. The general part sets the general rules of obligations, principles of contract law, contract formation, interpretation, performance, and termination. The special part sets special rules for different types of the most common contracts (sales, lease, lending, etc.). Of course, special rules for certain contracts (e.g., consumer credit, public procurement, etc.) are and may be established by other special laws.

9.2.1.2 Formation of Contract

The rules on the formation of contracts (articles 6.162–6.188) basically mirrors the provisions of the UNIDROIT Principles and PECL. According to article 6.162 of the CC, a contract is concluded either by the proposal (offer) and the assent (acceptance) or by any other actions of the parties that are sufficient to show their agreement. In this regard, the concepts of offer and acceptance, as an essential tool of formation of contract, have traditionally been used to determine whether, and if so when, the parties have reached agreement.

An offer is defined by article 6.167 as a proposal for concluding a contract that is (1) sufficiently definite and (2) indicates the intention of the offeror to be bound in the case of acceptance. An offer may be addressed to a definite person or to an indeterminate number of persons (offer to public). An example of an offer to the public is the display of goods with the indicated prices on the shelves in a shop or a promise to pay for the performance of certain actions. However, price lists; prospectuses with prices; catalogues, including prices; tariff lists; and other informational materials are generally not considered to be an offer to the public (article 6.171).

The CC follows the mailbox rule and establishes in article 6.168 that an offer becomes effective when received by the offeree. Until that moment, an offer, even if it is irrevocable, may be withdrawn by the offeror if notice of withdrawal reaches the offeree before or at the same time as the offer. Expressly stating this, the article makes a clear distinction between "withdrawal" and "revocation" of an offer: before an offer becomes effective, it can always be withdrawn, whereas the question of whether or not it may be revoked arises only after that moment. According to article 6.169, an offer may be revoked if the revocation reaches the offeree before he has dispatched the acceptance. Nevertheless, an offer cannot be revoked if it is indicated therein that it is irrevocable or if there were reasonable grounds for the offeree to rely on the offer as being irrevocable and he acted accordingly. An offer loses its effect when notice of its rejection reaches the offeror or when no reply to the offer has been received within the established or reasonable time limit (article 6.170).

Acceptance is defined by article 6.173 as a statement made by the offeree or any other conduct thereof indicating assent to the offer. The requirement of "assent" to the offer means the willingness to be bound by a contract. Thus, the mere acknowledgement of receipt of the offer, or an expression of interest in it, is not sufficient.

Unless the offer imposes any particular mode of acceptance, the indication of assent may either be made by an express statement or be inferred from the conduct of the offeree. It should be noted that silence or inactivity per se does not imply acceptance of an offer. Thus, the offeree is free not only to accept or not to accept the offer but also simply to ignore it.

As in the case of offer, the acceptance also becomes effective when it reaches the mailbox of an offeror. However, if by virtue of the offer or as a result of usages or practices that the parties have established between themselves the possibility of accepting an offer without notice to the offeror (by silence or by performing concrete actions) is foreseen, the acceptance is legally effective from the moment when certain actions (or inaction) expressing the will of the offeree are performed (article 6.173). Acceptance may also be revoked if the notice of revocation reaches the offeror before or at the same time as the acceptance becomes effective.

The acceptance must be unconditional in its essence. According to article 6.178, a reply to an offer that contains additions, limitations, or other modifications of conditions set forth in the offer is considered a rejection of the offer and constitutes a counteroffer. However, a reply to an offer that purports to be an acceptance but contains additional or different conditions that do not alter the essence of the conditions of the offer constitutes acceptance if the offeror, after receiving the reply, does not immediately object to the discrepancy. If the offeror does not object, the contract is deemed concluded under the conditions of the offer with the modifications contained in the acceptance.

An offer must be accepted within the time limit fixed by the offeror—within reasonable time in view of concrete circumstances, including the capacities of the means of communication used by the parties. An oral offer must be accepted immediately unless, in consideration of concrete circumstances, a different conclusion may be reached. However, according to article 6.176, a late acceptance shall be effective if the offeror without delay informs the offeree about it or sends him a notice to that effect. Moreover, if it is possible for it to be established from a letter or any other written notice containing a late acceptance that it was sent in time, if under normal circumstances it would have reached the offeror in due time, the late acceptance shall be deemed to be effective unless the offeror without delay informs the offeree that his offer has been extinguished.

In the course of precontractual relationships, parties must conduct themselves in accordance with the principle of good faith, disclose essential information, and keep the confidentiality of negotiations. If a party acts in bad faith or breaches other precontractual duties, that party may be obliged to pay damages to the other party. These rules, set in article 6.163, firmly established the *culpa in contrahendo* doctrine in Lithuanian contract law. Besides these rules of the precontractual stage of contract formation, CC article 6.165 also sets the rules for a specific type of contract—the preliminary contract. It is an agreement to agree in the future, i.e. to conclude another, principal contract under conditions set in this preliminary contract. In case a party without due grounds avoids or refuses to enter into a principal contract, he may be bound to pay damages to the other party.

Finally, according to article 6.181, a contract is considered formed at the moment when the offeree's acceptance of conclusion of the contract reaches the offeror, unless otherwise provided for by the contract. It is a general rule, set in article 6.159, that contracts are binding solely upon consensus; thus, the form of a contract is not a necessary element of the contract, except in cases prescribed by law. When the form of a contract is a necessary element of the contract, the requirements of the form may be found in the provisions of arts 1.71–1.77 of the CC and in other articles or laws. In most of the cases, the formal requirements will be limited to a simple written form; however, some types of contracts (e.g., sale of immovable property) require verification of a notary or, in some cases, approval of the court. The CC may also require the registration of certain contracts (e.g., mortgage or sale of immovable property) in a public register.

The CC also provides special rules on the formation of public contracts, battle of forms, contracts of adhesion, and others. Of course, the grounds of invalidity or avoidance of contracts, arising from illegality, immorality, mistake, lack of capacity or free will (e.g. fraud, threat, gross disparity, etc.), are extensively regulated too. However, these rules, due to the limited scope of this coverage, will not be explained here.

9.2.1.3 Content and Interpretation of Contracts

CC article 6.196 establishes that the obligations of the parties are not necessarily limited to that which has been expressly stipulated by the parties or set in the contract. Some obligations may be implied, i.e. not expressly agreed or stated in the contract, but stem from the essence and purpose of the contract, the nature of relationships established between the parties, the principle of good faith, reasonableness, and justice.

Some rules that fill the gaps of express agreement of parties are set in the CC or other laws. Among others, there are some default rules set on the quality, price, and time for the performance of the obligations. These rules ensure the validity of contracts even in the cases where parties failed to expressly stipulate on these terms.

Where the quality of performance is determined neither by the contract nor by the law, it should be reasonable and not be lower than average in the concrete circumstances (article 6.197). Where a contract does not fix the price or establish an order for determining the price, the parties shall be considered to have made reference to the price commonly charged at the moment of the conclusion of the contract for such performance in comparable circumstances in the sphere of business concerned, or if such price does not exist, to a reasonable price (article 6.198). A contract for an indefinite period may be canceled by either party, provided the party gives notice about his intention to the other party within a reasonable time in advance (article 6.199). Additionally, the obligation which time limit of performance is not determined must be performed within 7 days from the day the creditor requested the performance unless a different time limit of performance results from laws or the essence of the contract (article 6.53).

Moreover, where the parties have left without having discussed certain conditions that are necessary for the performance of a contract, article 6.195 allows the court to fill the gaps of a contract by taking in regard nonmandatory legal norms, the intentions of the parties, the purpose and essence of the contract, the criteria of good faith, reasonableness, and justice.

Sometimes parties expressly stipulate their obligations; however, the language of such agreement is vague. In such cases, article 6.193 lays down the principle of subjective interpretation of contracts requiring, in determining the meaning to be attached to the terms of a contract, to seek for the real intentions of the parties without being limited by the literal meaning of the words. In the event where the real intentions of the parties cannot be established, the contract must be interpreted in accordance with the meaning that could be attributed in the same circumstances by reasonable persons in the corresponding position as the parties.

Of course, such interpretation of contracts should be made in good faith, taking into account their interrelation, the nature and purpose of the contract, and the circumstances under which it was formed. In interpreting a contract, regard must also be taken of the ordinary conditions, irrespective of their expression in the contract. In the event of doubt, the terms must be understood in the sense most suitable to the nature, essence, and subject matter of the contract. Regard must be paid also to the preliminary negotiations between the parties, practices that the parties have established between themselves, the conduct of the parties subsequent to the conclusion of the contract, and the existing usages. It should also be noted that article 6.193 part 4 firmly establishes the *contra proferentem* rule by saying that in the event of doubt over conditions of a contract, they shall be interpreted against the contracting party that has suggested thereof and in favor of the party that accepted those conditions. In all cases, the conditions of a contract shall be interpreted in favor of consumers and the adhering party.

9.2.1.4 Performance, Nonperformance, and Termination of Contracts

Major principles of the performance of contracts are set in article 6.200 of the CC. A contract must be performed by the parties in a proper way and in good faith. In performing a contract, each party shall be bound to contribute to and to cooperate with the other party. Of course, the parties shall be bound to use the most economical means in the performance of the contract. Moreover, where according to a contract or its nature a party in exercising certain actions is bound to make the best effort in the performance of a contract, this party shall be bound to make such effort as a reasonable person would make in the same circumstances. The parties shall be bound to perform the contract simultaneously unless otherwise provided for by laws or the contract or determined by its nature or circumstances. Many other rules on performance of contracts set in the CC include, among others, the rules on the term of performance, early and partial performance, place of performance, and distribution of payments.

Article 6.204 sets the principle of *rebus sic stantibus* and provides the possibility to modify or dissolve the contract in the event of a change of circumstances, i.e., where the performance of a contract becomes more onerous for one of the parties. The performance of a contract is considered obstructed under such circumstances that fundamentally alter the balance of the contractual obligations, i.e., either the cost of performance has essentially increased or the value thereof has essentially diminished if (1) these circumstances occur or become known to the aggrieved party after the conclusion of the contract, (2) these circumstances could not reasonably have been foreseen by the aggrieved party at the time of the conclusion of the contract, (3) these circumstances are beyond the control of the aggrieved party, (4) the risk of occurrence of these circumstances was not assumed by the aggrieved party. In such event, the aggrieved party shall have the right to make a request to the other party for the modification of the contract. Where within a reasonable time the parties fail to reach an agreement on the modification of the contractual obligations, any of them may bring an action in court. The court may either dissolve or modify the conditions of the contract with a view to restoring the balance of the contractual obligations of the parties. Other exceptions to the principle of *pacta sunt servanda* set in CC are the doctrines of impossibility of performance, force majeure, and gross disparity of the parties.

Nonperformance of a contract is described in article 6.205 as a failure to perform any of the obligations arising from the contract, including defective performance and delay of a time limit of performance. Of course, one party may not rely on the nonperformance of the other party to the extent to which such nonperformance was caused by the first party's actions or inactivity or by any other event as to which the first party bears the risk. However, as a consequence of the principle of cooperation and preservation of contract, even in the case of nonperformance, article 6.208 provides the possibility to the party failing to perform a contract at its own expense to eliminate any defects of performance if (1) he gives notice without undue delay to the other party indicating the manner and time of elimination of defects, (2) the aggrieved party has no lawful interest in refusing elimination, (3) the elimination is effective immediately, (4) and the elimination is appropriate in the concrete circumstances. The right of elimination shall not be precluded by a declaration of the other party on the dissolution of the contract. Of course, the aggrieved party may suspend performance of his obligations until the defects of performance are eliminated by the other party and may also claim compensation for damages; however, the aggrieved party shall be bound to cooperate with the other party during the entire period of the elimination of defects.

In the case of nonperformance, the aggrieved party may also establish in writing an additional period of time of a reasonable length for the performance and notify the other party about this establishment. In the event that delay in performance is not an essential violation of a contract, and the aggrieved party has established an additional period of time of reasonable length for the performance, this party may dissolve the contract upon the expiry of that period if the performance is still not cured.

In case of nonperformance, the CC allows many different remedies—among others, payment of interest or fine, demand to make or cure performance, payment of damages, and others. General rules on contractual and tortious liability are provided in Chapter XXII (Civil Liability) of Book 6, and specific rules applicable only in the case of contractual liability are provided in articles 6.256–6.262. Special rules of contractual liability applicable to specific contracts are provided by the corresponding articles for the specific contract types.

The ultimate remedy for nonperformance is the termination of contract. Of course, a contract may be dissolved unilaterally in the cases indicated in the contract, not as a remedy for nonperformance. However, according to article 6.217, a party may dissolve the contract where the failure of the other party to perform it or the defective performance thereof is considered to be an essential violation of the contract. In determining whether a violation of a contract is essential, the following conditions must be taken into account: (1) whether the aggrieved party is substantially deprived of what he was entitled to expect under the contract, except in cases when the other party did not foresee or could not have reasonably foreseen such result; (2) whether, taking into consideration the nature of the contract, strict compliance with the conditions of the obligation is of essential importance; (3) whether the nonperformance is made of malice or of great imprudence; (4) whether the nonperformance gives the aggrieved party the basis to suppose that he cannot believe in the future performance of a contract; (5) whether the nonperformed party, who was preparing for performance or was effectuating the performance of the contracts, would suffer significant damages if the contract were dissolved.

Dissolution of the contract releases both parties from the performance of the contract; however, it does not preclude the right of claim for damages for nonperformance of the contract, as well as the right of claim for penalty. Moreover, dissolution of the contract does not affect its conditions that establish the procedure of settlement of disputes or the validity of any other conditions that, taking regard to their nature, are to be in force even after dissolution. Of course, upon dissolution of the contract, each of the parties shall have the right to restitution, i.e., claim the return of whatever he has supplied the other party under the contract if this party concurrently makes the return of whatever he has received from the latter. If restitution in kind is not possible or appropriate to the parties, a compensation of value of what has been received must be made in money, provided that such compensation does not contradict the criteria of reasonableness, good faith, and justice. If the performance of a contract is successive and divisible, the party may claim restitution only of what has been received after the dissolution of the contract.

9.2.2 Tort Law

9.2.2.1 The Basics of Tort Liability in Lithuania

The Roman law concept of delict and the Civil Codes of Quebec, France, Germany, and others have served as a model[27] for the Lithuanian tort (delictual liability) law—one of the two branches of the law of obligations (the other being contracts). In the Civil Code of Lithuania (CC), the field of tort law is covered in articles

[27] Mikelėnas et al. (2001), pp. 11–12.

6.245–6.255 (general provisions for civil liability) and articles 6.263–6.291 (special provisions for noncontractual (delictual) liability).

Delictual liability is defined as a pecuniary obligation that is not related to contractual relations, except in cases where it is established by law that delictual liability shall also result from damage related to contractual relations. For the delictual liability to emerge in Lithuanian civil law jurisdiction, the claimant shall prove a total of these four elements: unlawful actions, causation, fault, and damages.

Unlawful Actions Article 6.246 part 1 of the CC generally provides that civil liability shall arise from nonperformance of a duty established by laws (unlawful refrainment from acting) or from performance of actions that are prohibited by laws (unlawful acting) or from violation of the general duty to act with care.

Duty to act with care, according to article 6.263 part 1 of the CC, means that one has the duty to obey the rules of conduct so as not to cause damage to another. Thus, in order to determine the element of unlawful actions, the plaintiff has to prove that some duty existed and analyze whether the defendant breached that duty, i.e., whether he acted with due care or whether he did what could or should have been done according to the law.

It should be noted that article 6.246 parts 2 and 3 of the CC sets two exceptions to these general rules of unlawful actions. The first one provides the rule of vicarious liability (i.e., liability for the unlawful actions of others), and the second one provides that in cases expressly stated by laws[28] the damage caused by lawful actions must also be compensated.

Causation According to article 6.247 of the CC, the defendant shall compensate only these damages that are the result of one unlawful action giving rise to civil liability. For the action to be the cause of damages, it must be a substantial factor for them to appear, although not the only one.[29]

Therefore, the factual cause inquiry is meant to determine whether the defendant's unlawful action was a substantial factor of the plaintiff's damages to appear. However, the causation analysis does not stop by the factual cause. The second part of analysis is legal cause inquiry, which is meant to determine whether, as a matter of public policy, fairness, justice, and reasonableness, the law should allow the recovery of damages from a defendant.

Fault Article 6.248 of the CC provides that civil liability shall arise only upon the fault of the defendant, except in the cases where the law expressly states that

[28]For example Article 4.100 of the CC provides the rules for expropriation of property for public needs; Article 4.129 of the CC provides the rules for compensation of damages incurred due to the establishment of a servitude and others.

[29]Mikelėnas et al. (2001), pp. 11–12; Mikelėnas et al. (2003), p. 338.

liability arises without fault (e.g., vicarious[30] and strict[31] liability cases). Under part 3 of this article, a person shall be deemed to be at fault where, taking into account the essence of the obligation and other circumstances, he failed to behave with the care and caution necessary in the corresponding conditions. Thus, the concept of fault is based on the blameworthiness of the failure to achieve the demanded level of the behavior.

Article 6.248 part 2 of the CC describes two types of fault—intentional and negligent (gross and simple).[32] The most blameworthy type of fault is the intentional one, when the defendant knows that he is committing wrongful action, foresees that his conduct will harm the plaintiff, and still acts wrongfully with the desire to harm someone. Negligence is mostly determined using the conceptual test of *bonus pater familias*. That is, if a reasonable person under similar circumstances should have acted differently, the defendant may be held liable, although he did not mean to inflict any harm or even did his best to avoid it.

It should be noted here that the type of fault is not important in determining the delictual liability per se, although it is an important factor in determining the sum of damages to be awarded, release from liability, and other issues. Moreover, the fault of a wrongdoer is presumed; therefore, it is the burden of the defendant to prove that he is innocent.

Damages Article 6.251 part 1 of the CC sets the principle of the full compensation of damages. This principle is meant, on the one hand, to place the victim in the position in which one would have been if the unlawful act would not have been committed and, on the other hand, to preclude punitive damages, i.e., precluding the victim to profit from the injury sustained.[33] Articles 6.249 and 6.250 of the CC allows the plaintiff to recover (1) the loss of property, (2) the expenses incurred, (3) the lost incomes, (4) the profit that the defendant has received from his unlawful act, and, (5) in cases provided for by law,[34] nonpecuniary damage.[35]

---

30 For example employer liability for damage caused by the fault of his employees; liability of the parents or guardians for the damage caused by minors under 14 years of age or legally incapable persons, etc.

31 For example liability for damage caused by domestic or wild animals; liability for the damage caused by operation of motor vehicles, machinery, electric or atomic energy, use of explosive or poisonous materials, activities in the sphere of construction, and exercise of other hazardous activities, etc.

32 Mikelėnas et al. (2003), p. 339.

33 *Ibid.*, p. 346.

34 For example the cases where the damages are incurred due to crime, health impairment or deprivation of life, as well as infringement of the person rights to a name, image, privacy, honour and dignity and others.

35 For example suffering, inconveniences, mental shock, emotional depression, humiliation, deterioration of reputation, deprive of social possibilities, and other, evaluated by a court in terms of money.

Even if the plaintiff cannot prove the precise amount of damages sustained, it shall be assessed by a court. The court has broad discretion in assessing the amount of damages to award. The court may reduce the amount of damages if awarding full compensation would lead to unacceptable and grave consequences, except in cases when the defendant has acted intentionally. Moreover, in assessing the amount of nonpecuniary damage, the court shall take into consideration the consequences of such damage, the gravity of the fault, the financial status of the defendant, and other circumstances, including the criteria of good faith, justice, and reasonableness. The court may order to compensate damages in kind or to pay it in money.

9.2.2.2 Defenses from Tort Liability

Article 6.253 of the CC sets the list of exceptional cases when the wrongdoer may be totally or partially exempted from liability. Despite the existence of all four elements of liability, the defendant will be released from liability if he will prove the existence of any of these events:

1. a superior force (force majeure), i.e., unavoidable events that cannot be controlled or that were not and could not have been foreseen;
2. actions of state, i.e., binding and unforeseen actions (acts) of public authorities that render the performance of a duty impossible and that could not be disputed by the parties;
3. activities of a third person, i.e., wrongful actions (or inactions) of a person for whom neither the victim nor the tortfeasor is liable;
4. actions of the victim, i.e., the wrongful actions of the victim that resulted in the appearance or increase of his damages; such actions may be the express or implied consent of the injured person to suffer the damage, assumption of the risk, the failure to act reasonably to mitigate the damages, and others;
5. state of necessity, i.e., the wrongful actions of the defendant such that he is compelled to cause damage in order to avert danger to himself, to other persons, or to their rights, as well as to the interests of the society or the state by avoiding imminent occurrence of greater damage to the person who has already sustained damage or to any other person; causing the damage in such circumstances shall be the only way of avoiding greater damage;
6. self-defense, i.e., wrongful actions of defendant with the purpose of defending himself or another person, property, inviolability of dwelling, other rights, interests of the society or the state against commenced or imminent unlawful dangerous assault; such actions shall not exceed the limits of self-defense;
7. self-help, i.e., wrongful actions of defendant by which he lawfully enforces his right in the instances where competent authorities fail to provide timely assistance and where without such actions the implementation of that right would be rendered impossible or essentially obstructed;
8. other grounds, for example, the statute of limitations, the liability of the legally incapable person, and so forth.

9.2.2.3 Joint Tortfeasors and the Right of Recourse

Article 6.279 of the CC imposes solidary liability for compensation in cases where several persons jointly cause damage. In such cases, the injured person has the right to demand damages jointly from all the tortfeasors or separately from a single tortfeasor. Despite the multiple defendants, the general principle of full compensation remains in force. That is, every cotortfeasor remains obligated until the damages are paid in full, and, on the other hand, the injured person shall not profit from his injury the same way as if only one person was liable.

In case of joint tortfeasors, the court has to determine the reciprocal claims of defendants based on the different degrees of their fault. If it is impossible to determine, the portions of damage attributable to them is considered to be equal.

Of course, any of the cotortfeasors may use against the plaintiffs' demand common and personal defenses. A cotortfeasor who paid the damages has the right to recover from other tortfeasors their respective shares of damage compensation. Notably, the right of recourse is denied in vicarious liability cases where parents, guardians, and institutions compensate damages caused by a minor or legally incapable person.

9.2.2.4 Some Other Special Rules of Delictual Liability

The Civil Code sets numerous special rules for delictual liability in cases where damages are caused by the public authority (article 6.271), in cases where damages are caused by defects of products or services (articles 6.292–6.300), in cases of damages caused by misleading advertising (articles 6.301–6.304), and others.

Damages caused by unlawful acts of institutions of public or municipal authority must be compensated by the state or municipality from the means of the state budget, irrespective of the fault of a concrete public servant or other employee of public or municipal authority institutions. The term "act" in these cases is understood as any action or inaction of a public or municipal institution or its employees that directly affects the rights of a plaintiff.

The damage resulting either from unlawful conviction, arrest, suppression, detention, or application of other enforcement measures shall also be compensated fully by the state, irrespective of the fault of the officials, prosecution, or court. The state shall also be liable to full compensation for the damage caused by unlawful actions of a judge or other court officials in a civil case. In these cases, the victim is also entitled to a nonpecuniary damage award.

In cases of damages cause by defects of products or services, the term "producer" is used in a very broad sense and includes not only the manufacturer of a finished product but also the manufacturer of component parts and raw materials or the supplier of services that marks the product (services) with his name, trademark, or any other distinctive sign. Moreover, any businessman who imports into the Republic of Lithuania a defective product with the aim of selling, leasing, or distributing it in any other way will be held liable as a producer. In cases where it is impossible to identify the producer, the law sets the presumption that any person involved in the sale of the product shall be regarded as a producer; therefore, it is the burden of the defendant to disprove that.

It should be noted that damage shall be compensated if the injured person proves defects, the occurrence of damages, or a causal link between the defects and the damages. That is, the liability of the producer or supplier for their goods or services is a no-fault liability. However, article 6.298 of the CC provides the list of specific defenses that the producer has in these cases, which due to the limited space will not be listed in detail here.

In cases of misleading advertising, article 6.301 part 1 of the CC holds that any information related to economic-commercial, financial, or professional activities that is promulgated in any form and by any means of conveyance with the aim to promote sales (supply) of goods or services, where such information in any way, including the manner of its presentation, deceives or is likely to deceive the persons to whom it is addressed or whom it reaches and which causes damage by reason of its deceptive nature, shall be seen as misleading advertising. The burden of proof also lies with the advertiser who, in case of dispute, has to prove the truthfulness of advertisements at the moment of its announcement.

Damages resulting from misleading advertising shall be compensated either by the advertiser, producer, intermediary, or publisher of advertising. Moreover, the court may also order the prohibition of further promulgation or publication of misleading advertising even if it has not yet been published but publication of which is imminent. The court may likewise order to publish an adequate denial of the misleading advertising.

9.3 Company Law and Insolvency Law

Jurgita Spaičienė
Faculty of Law, Vytautas Magnus University, Jonavos st. 66, LT-44138 Kaunas, Lithuania

Jurgita Spaičienė Advocates Bureau, Jonavos st. 66, LT-44138 Kaunas, Lithuania
c-mail: jurgita.spaicicnc@vdu.lt

Siuzana Ščerbina-Dalibagienė
Faculty of Law, Vytautas Magnus University, Jonavos st. 66, LT-44138 Kaunas, Lithuania

Ministry of Finance of the Republic of Lithuania, Jonavos st. 66, LT-44138 Kaunas, Lithuania
e-mail: siuzana.scerbina-dalibagiene@vdu.lt

The purpose of this chapter is to provide an overview of the system of company law and insolvency law in Lithuania. In order to reveal this purpose, two subchapters are presented. The first subchapter introduces the possible types of companies in Lithuania and their main features, such as requirements for incorporation, management, and activity. In the second subchapter, the reader is provided with an overview of bankruptcy proceedings. In addition, the increasingly popular restructuring procedure is reviewed and aspects of bankruptcy proceedings for natural persons are discussed. Finally, future perspectives of development in company law and insolvency law are proposed.

9.3.1 Company Law

The Civil Code primarily regulates legal persons in Lithuania. It defines the main rules of incorporation, legal capacity, bodies, termination and conversion of all legal persons, including companies. Every individual legal form of company is comprehensively regulated by a specific law. It is important to note that all companies in Lithuania are legal persons, including individual enterprises and partnerships.

The Civil Code divides all legal persons into public and private persons. Public legal persons are legal persons established by the state or municipalities, their institutions, or other nonprofit-seeking persons whose goal is to meet the public interest, while the aim of private legal persons is to meet private interests. There are only two legal forms of enterprises that are public legal persons: the state enterprise and the municipal enterprise. All remaining enterprises are private legal persons.

According to the World Bank ranking, the ease of starting a business in Lithuania takes eighth place among 189 world economies.[36] It is conditioned by specific reforms in the past few years, including a newly introduced possibility to establish a company online and the introduction of a new legal form of a company (a small partnership).[37]

Further, the types of companies that operate in Lithuania will be discussed.

9.3.1.1 Individual Enterprise (*individuali įmonė*)

The main legal act regulating individual enterprises is the Law on Individual Enterprises. An individual enterprise is a private legal entity with unlimited civil liability. The founder of an individual enterprise may be only a legally capable natural person. The owner of the individual enterprise shall not be the owner of another individual enterprise. The individual enterprise shall have a single-person management body—the manager. Unless otherwise established by the statutes of the individual enterprise, the owner shall at the same time be the manager of the enterprise.[38]

The assets shall be owned by the individual enterprise on the basis of the right of ownership. The assets of the individual enterprise shall be the assets that constitute

[36]World bank (2016).

[37]Westmore (2016).

[38]*Law on Individual Enterprises of the Republic of Lithuania*. Official Gazette, 2003, No. 112-4991, Art. 6-7.

the personal property of the owner transferred into the ownership of the individual enterprise, as well as assets acquired on behalf of the individual enterprise.[39]

9.3.1.2 General Partnership (*tikroji ūkinė bendrija*) and Limited Partnership (*komanditinė ūkinė bendrija*)

The main legal act regulating general partnerships and limited partnerships is the Law on Partnerships. A partnership is a private legal person with unlimited civil liability and can be a general partnership or a limited partnership. A general partnership is an enterprise whose entire membership consists of general partners. A limited partnership is an enterprise, the members of which include both general partners and limited partners. The general partners are jointly and severally liable for the obligations of the partnership to the extent of their ownership, while the limited partners are liable only to the extent of the property they transferred or had to transfer to the partnership. Any partnership may be formed by not less than two natural or legal persons.[40]

The agreement on partnership activities is the contract of the partnership's formation and also the document of its activity. This agreement must be made in notarial form. General partners arrange the dealings of the partnership and make decisions related to all questions of the partnership's activity.[41]

9.3.1.3 Small Partnership (*mažoji bendrija*)

The main legal act regulating the small partnerships is the Law on Small Partnerships. This law has entered into force in 2012 creating a new legal form of company—small partnership. This new legal form was introduced in order to accelerate the start-up of small and medium businesses and to reduce the costs of starting a business. The procedures of activity, management, and accountancy for the small partnership are simpler than those for the private limited liability company; furthermore, it has limited civil liability. Based on the statistical data about establishing of small partnerships, it can be alleged that this new legal form justified itself. [42]

The small partnership is a private legal entity, whose founders can only be natural persons. There can be no more than 10 members, and for establishing such a partnership there must be at least one person. There is no minimum capital requirement. In order to establish a small partnership, an incorporation contract

---

[39]*Ibid.*, Art. 8.

[40]*Law on Partnerships of the Republic of Lithuania*. Official Gazette, 2003, No. 112-4990, Art. 2-3, 8, Sec. 1.

[41]*Ibid.*, art. 3, 10, sec. 1.

[42]According to the data of the Register of Legal Entities (www.registrucentras.lt) at the end of 1st quarter 2016 the number of established small partnerships reached 7683.

shall be signed. Each member has to make a contribution, the amount of which must be discussed in the incorporation contract.[43]

The statutes of a small partnership contain the organs of the partnership and their competence, the appointment of the manager (if any), the acceptance and withdrawal of members, profit distribution rule, etc. The members of a small partnership can transfer their rights as a member or withdraw. The bodies of the small partnership can be just a members' meeting (in such a case, the representative of a company has to be appointed) or a members' meeting and a manager of a company. The profit of the company shall be divided among all the members in proportion to their contribution, unless otherwise stated in the statutes.[44]

9.3.1.4 Public Limited Liability Company (*akcinė bendrovė*) and Private Limited Liability Company (*uždaroji akcinė bendrovė*)

The main legal act regulating public and private limited liability companies is the Law on Companies. The company[45] is an enterprise whose statutory capital is divided into parts called shares. It is a private legal person with limited civil liability. The company can be a public limited liability company or a private limited liability company. The incorporator may be one natural or legal person, but in the case of a private limited liability company it must have less than 250 shareholders. The amount of the statutory capital of the public limited liability company must be not less than 40,000 €. The statutory capital of the private limited liability company must be not less than 2500 €. The shares of a private limited liability company may not be offered for sale and be traded publicly unless the laws provide otherwise.[46]

A company may be incorporated both by natural and by legal persons. Every incorporator of a company must acquire shares in the company and become its shareholder. When the company is established by two or more incorporators, a Memorandum of Association shall be drawn up. If the company is formed by only one person, an Act of Establishment shall be drawn up. The Memorandum of Association of the company or the Act of Establishment shall also be treated as the share subscription agreement. The shares of a company being incorporated must be fully paid up within the time period set in the Memorandum of Association, which may not exceed 12 months from the date of the signing of any of the above documents. The company shall be deemed incorporated from the date of its registration in the Register of Legal Entities.[47]

Shareholders are natural and legal persons that have acquired shares in the company. Each shareholder shall have rights in the company such as are incidental

[43]*Law on Small Partnerships of the Republic of Lithuania*. Official Gazette, 2012, No. 83-4333, Art. 2, Sec. 1,2, Art. 4, Sec. 1.

[44]*Ibid.*, Art. 5, 10-12, 26, Sec. 4.

[45]When the text applies both to a public and a private limited liability company, the term "company" shall be used.

[46]*Law on Companies of the Republic of Lithuania*. Official Gazette, 2003, No. 123-5574, Art. 2.

[47]*Ibid.*, Art. 6-8, 11, Sec. 1.

to the shares in the company owned by him. Under identical circumstances, all holders of shares of the same class shall have equal rights and duties.[48]

A company shall be managed by a general meeting of shareholders and a single-person management body–the company manager. A collegial supervisory body—the Supervisory Board—and a collegial management body—the Board—may be also formed in the company. A public limited liability company shall have at least one of them. The supervisory board shall be a collegial body supervising the activities of the company elected at the general meeting of shareholders for the period set forth in the statutes of the company, which shall not be longer than 4 years. The number of members of the supervisory board shall be set by the statutes of the company (at least 3 and not more than 15 members). The board is a collegial management body of the company elected by the supervisory board (if the supervisory board is not formed, by the general meeting of shareholders) for a term specified in the statutes of the company, which may not exceed 4 years. The number of the board members shall be set forth in the statutes of the company (at least three members). The manager of the company must be a natural person and shall be elected and removed from office by the board (if the board is not formed, by the supervisory board or, if the supervisory board is also not formed, by the general meeting of shareholders). The manager of the company shall organize the daily activities of the company.[49] Regarding the regulation in the Law on Companies, the diversity of corporate governance models in the companies is available. The companies apply different corporate governance models—Anglo-Saxon, Nordic, or German. It should be noted that there is not any single tradition of corporate governance model formed.[50]

The amount of statutory capital shall be equal to the aggregate amount of the nominal values of all shares subscribed for in the company. If the equity capital of a company falls below 1/2 of the amount of the statutory capital as referred to in the statutes, a general meeting of shareholders must be convened within 3 months. This general meeting of shareholders must consider a decision to restore the equity capital by shareholders' contributions, reduce the statutory capital, convert the company into another legal person, or liquidate the company.[51]

A company may issue ordinary and preference shares. Preference shares may constitute not more than 1/3 of the statutory capital. All ordinary shares shall carry a voting right. If the statutes of the company so prescribe, a company may issue ordinary shares having the status of employee shares. A company may also issue debentures and convertible debentures.[52]

A shareholder may not transfer his partly paid-up shares to other persons. A public limited liability company may not restrict the shareholders' right to dispose

[48]*Ibid.*, Art. 3.

[49]*Ibid.*, Art. 19, 31, 33, 37.

[50]Bitė and Jakuntavičiutė (2014).

[51]*Law on Companies*, Art. 38, Sec. 2,3.

[52]*Ibid.*, Art. 42–43, 55–56.

of fully paid-up shares to another person (although some exceptions exist for employee shares). In a private limited liability company, the shareholders have the right of preemption to acquire all the shares offered for sale.[53]

It should be noted that the most popular form of doing business in Lithuania is through private limited liability companies.

9.3.1.5 Cooperative Society (*kooperatinė bendrovė, kooperatyvas*)

The main legal act regulating the cooperative society is the Law on Cooperative Societies (Cooperatives). A cooperative society is a private legal person with limited civil liability, established for the purpose of meeting the economic, social, and cultural needs of its members. The members actively participate in the activity of the cooperative society. The founders of a cooperative society must be at least five natural or/and legal persons. The funds of the cooperative society shall be formed from membership fees, member shares, profit received from business activities, and other sources of income not prohibited by law. There is no set minimum capital requirement.[54]

The governing bodies of the cooperative society are the members' meeting, the board, and the manager. In a cooperative society whose membership exceeds 100, the members' meeting may be replaced by a meeting of agents. In a cooperative society whose membership does not exceed 50, the statutes may provide that it is not mandatory to form a board, in which case the manager exercises the functions of the board. The board is a collegial management body of the cooperative society elected at the members' meeting for a term not exceeding 4 years. The manager is a mandatory body of the cooperative society elected by the board (or the members' meeting, if the board is not formed). The economic financial activity of the cooperative society shall be controlled by an internal audit commission (auditor), which shall be elected at the members' meeting for a term not exceeding 4 years. The statutes may provide that economic financial activity will be controlled by the members' meeting and confirmed by an external audit company.[55]

9.3.1.6 Agricultural Company (*žemės ūkio bendrovė*)

The main legal act regulating the agricultural company is the Law on Agricultural Companies. An agricultural company is a private legal person with limited civil liability formed for the purpose of production and commercial activity, whose income over the period of an economic year for agricultural production and services rendered to agriculture comprises over 50 percent of all production income.[56] There is no set minimum capital requirement for an agricultural company.

[53] *Ibid.*, Art. 46–47.

[54] *Law on Cooperative Societies (Cooperatives) of the Republic of Lithuania*. Official Gazette, 1993, No. 20-488, 2002, No. 57-2296, Art. 2–3.

[55] *Ibid.*, Art. 15, 18, Sec. 1.

[56] *Law on Agricultural Companies of the Republic of Lithuania*. Official Gazette, 1991, No. 13-328, 2001, No. 45-1574, Art. 3.

The agricultural company may have members and member shareholders. The company must have at least two members. A company member is a natural or legal person, which has been accepted as a member by the members' meeting of the company, has a member share of the minimum amount established in the statutes, and has the right of a deciding vote. A member shareholder is a natural or a legal person that has acquired a member share in any amount, has not been accepted into company membership, and does not have a deciding vote. Member shares may not be sold or purchased publicly.[57]

The bodies of a company shall be a members' meeting, a board, and an administration. The members' meeting of the company shall be the supreme body of the company. The board and the administration are the management bodies of the company. Depending upon the decision of the members' meeting, a board may not be formed.[58]

9.3.1.7 State Enterprise (*valstybės įmonė*) and Municipal Enterprise (*savivaldybės įmonė*)

The main legal act regulating the state enterprises and municipal enterprises is the Law on State and Municipal Enterprises. A state enterprise and a municipal enterprise are enterprises formed from state/municipal property. Such property continues to be owned by the state or municipality and is administered, used, or otherwise disposed of by the enterprise acting as a trustee. They are public legal persons with limited civil liability and have special legal capacity. The aim of the state or municipal enterprise is to render public services, manufacture production, and exercise other activities for the purpose of satisfying public interests. A state or municipal enterprise cannot be a member of other legal entities.[59]

9.3.1.8 European Union Level Legal Entities: European Company SE (*Europos bendrovė*), European Cooperative Society SCE (*Europos kooperatinė bendrovė*), and European Economic Interest Grouping EEIG (*Europos ekonominių interesų grupė*)

The European Company, European Cooperative Society, and European Economic Interest Grouping are European Union level legal entities able to carry out their business on a European Community scale. Lithuania also ensured that the Council regulations concerning European Union level legal entities, such as the European Company, the European Cooperative Society, and the European Economic Interest Grouping, are all fully applicable here. The provisions of the regulations permit the creation and management of entities with a European dimension, free from the obstacles arising from the disparity and the limited territorial application of national company law. These regulations shall be binding in their entirety and directly

[57] *Ibid.*, Art. 2–3.

[58] *Ibid.*, Art. 23.

[59] *Law on State and Municipal Enterprises of the Republic of Lithuania*. Official Gazette, 1994, No. 102-2049, 2004, No. 4-24, Art. 2–3.

applicable in all Member States; however, the Member States shall make such provision as is appropriate to ensure the effective application of these regulations. The main legal acts ensuring the application of the abovementioned regulations in Lithuania are the Law on European Companies, the Law on European Cooperative Societies, and the Law on European Economic Interest Grouping.[60]

The regulation of enterprises plays a very important role in the process of improving the country's business environment. Recently, the main direction of the policy in the field of enterprise law in Lithuania concerns the simplification of applicable regulation, removal of excessive regulation, reducing the administrative burden, enhancement of corporate governance, elimination of barriers that relate to cross-border mergers and governance, and maximizing the benefits of modern technology in such a way so as to modernize corporate law—all in order to create a competitive and effective business environment.

9.3.2 Insolvency Law

9.3.2.1 Bankruptcy Law Development in the Republic of Lithuania After 1992

After the Soviet period, the first Bankruptcy Law regarding enterprises was instituted on October 20, 1992, in the Republic of Lithuania (Lithuania). The next bankruptcy act came into force as law on October 1, 1997. Gaps in this law were soon identified through law practice experience. The third Enterprise Bankruptcy Law (EBL) was enacted in 2001.[61] This law changed the existing procedure of rehabilitation in bankruptcy law. The Lithuanian Law on Bankruptcy of Natural Person (or Personal Bankruptcy) (PBL) came into force on March 1, 2013.

9.3.2.2 Legal Regulation of Bankruptcy Proceedings

Both natural and legal persons can become insolvent and incapable of paying their debts as they come due. The EBL applies to all enterprises, public establishments, commercial banks and other credit institutions registered in Lithuania.[62] More specific characteristics of bankruptcy procedure, which relate to the bankruptcy of banks, credit unions, insurance companies, agricultural enterprises, brokerage firms, investment companies, and other defined enterprises and institutions, are set forth in the special laws.

Currently, there are 2202 procedures of enterprise bankruptcy in Lithuania.[63]

---

[60] *Law on European Companies of the Republic of Lithuania*. Official Gazette, 2004, No. 78-2710; *Law on European Cooperative Societies of the Republic of Lithuania*. Official Gazette, 2006, No. 73-2764; *Law on European Economic Interest Grouping of the Republic of Lithuania*. Official Gazette, 2004, No. 4-43.

[61] *Law on Enterprise Bankruptcy*. Official Gazette, 2001, No. 31-1010.

[62] *Ibid.*, Art. 1, Sec. 2.

[63] See: http://www.bankrotodep.lt/veiklos-sritys/nemokumas-2/moni-bankrotas/vykdomos-proceduros/.

9.3.2.3 The Institution of Bankruptcy Proceedings

Bankruptcy proceedings under Lithuanian law for enterprises may commence at the initiative of a creditor or group of creditors or on the basis of an application made by the owners and the head of administration or by the liquidator of the enterprise. The aforementioned persons may apply if at least one of the following conditions is or may be present: (1) the enterprise fails to pay the remuneration and other employment-related amounts in due time; (2) the enterprise fails, in due time, to pay for the goods received and works (services) carried out, defaults on the repayment of credits, and fails to discharge other property obligations assumed under transactions; (3) the enterprise fails to pay, in due time, taxes and other compulsory contributions prescribed by law and/or the awarded amounts; (4) the enterprise has publicly announced or notified the creditors of its inability or lack of intent to discharge its obligations; (5) the enterprise has no assets or income from which debts could be recovered, and therefore the bailiff has returned the writs of execution to the creditor.

Petitions are filed in writing, in the manner set forth by the Code of Civil Procedure, in the district court that has jurisdiction over the locality in which the enterprise is situated.[64]

The enterprise must be provided with at least a 30-day grace period to fulfill its obligation before the petition in bankruptcy may be filed (compulsory pretrial procedure).[65]

The definition of an "owner" includes not only owners of unlimited liability enterprises but also shareholders (or a group of shareholders) having more than 10% of the shares in a limited liability enterprise.[66] Owners or the head of administration must file a bankruptcy petition in case the enterprise is not or will not be able to fulfill all its liabilities to the creditors and the creditors have not filed a bankruptcy petition.

Not later than 1 month from the date of the filing of the bankruptcy petition, the court must render a decision to institute bankruptcy proceedings or refuse the initiation thereof.

EBL determines that insolvency is one of the conditions for posing bankruptcy proceedings.

The definition of insolvency[67] refers to the situation where an enterprise fails to settle with creditors according to the deadline prescribed by laws or other legal acts, as well by the agreements between the creditor and the enterprise, and the aggregate value of its overdue liabilities is more than a half of the net book value of all its assets. Pending (nonoverdue) debts are not taken into account when determining the insolvency of an enterprise. If a court finds that an enterprise is insolvent and initiates bankruptcy proceedings in the case, it will appoint a bankruptcy

[64]*Civil Procedure Code*. Official Gazette, 2002, No. 36-1340, Art. 27, 135.

[65]*Law on Enterprise Bankruptcy*. Official Gazette, 2001, No. 31-1010, Art. 6, Sec. 2.

[66]*Ibid.*, Art. 2, Sec. 9.

[67]*Ibid.*, Art. 2, Sec. 8.

administrator and establish a term for the creditors to file claims. The management bodies of the enterprise lose their powers and must transfer the assets and documents to the appointed administrator.[68]

The enterprise has the right to engage in business activities only if such activities decrease the losses of the creditors incurred in relation to the enterprise's bankruptcy and to consume income for covering business-related expenses.[69]

9.3.2.4 Enterprise Bankruptcy Administrator

An appointed bankruptcy administrator may be a citizen of Lithuania or another EU Member State having the right to provide bankruptcy administration services.[70] The discharge of the administrator is possible only through a court ruling.

The bankruptcy administrator acts as an enterprise manager and the executor of court decisions and orders and/or resolutions of the creditors' committee meeting. EBL establishes broad powers on behalf of the enterprise for the administrator, including the power to manage, use, and dispose of the assets; to enter into new transactions; and to examine transactions. The administrator also has the authority to file with the court claims for the invalidation of prebankruptcy transactions and claims to declare invalid the fraudulent discharge of financial liabilities. If the court establishes the existence of a fraudulent bankruptcy, the administrator must review all contracts of the enterprise concluded within the 5-year period prior to the institution of bankruptcy proceedings and bring an action before the court for the invalidation of the contracts that are contrary to the interests of the enterprise. Creditors of the enterprise in bankruptcy have no immediate and direct means to supervise the administrator.

EBL does not establish a maximum limit for administration expenses incurred by the enterprise in bankruptcy. These expenses are paid with various types of funds (from the sale of assets of the enterprise, debts repaid to the enterprise, earnings from activities, rent for leased assets, etc.).[71] The estimate of administration costs and the procedure for payment of remuneration are established at the creditors' meeting.

9.3.2.5 Extrajudicial and Simplified Bankruptcy Procedures

Bankruptcy procedures may be applied out of court, provided that no action has been brought in a court in which claims, including claims connected with any employment relationships, have been brought against the enterprise, and also if no execution has been levied on the enterprise under the writs of execution issued by the courts or other institutions. The decision to utilize nonjudicial bankruptcy procedures is adopted at a creditors' meeting by 4/5 majority of votes. All issues

[68] *Ibid.*, Art. 10, Sec.7.
[69] *Ibid.*, Art. 10, Sec.7.
[70] *Ibid.*, Art. 11.
[71] *Ibid.*, Art. 36.

within the competence of the court may be considered and decided by the creditors' meeting.

Laws do not provide the extrajudicial procedure in the case of enterprise restructuring or personal bankruptcy.

When the administrator establishes that the enterprise has no assets or that its assets are insufficient to cover the legal and administrative expenses, the court may adopt a ruling to apply the simplified bankruptcy procedures. These procedures may last no longer than 1 year.

9.3.2.6 Protection of the Interests of Creditors

All the terms of payment of debts of the enterprise in bankruptcy shall be considered to have matured as of the day of initiation of bankruptcy proceedings. The court fixes the time period (30–45 days) within which creditors must present their financial claims. The administrator is entitled to adjust the creditors' claims according to the accounts and records of the enterprise, as well as to challenge unreasonable claims in the court.

The creditors have the power to apply to the court to challenge resolutions of the creditor's meeting, to attend the creditor's meetings, and to defend their own claims. The sole creditor is entitled to receive information on the course of bankruptcy proceedings from the bankruptcy administrator.

The most important functions of creditors' meetings are (1) making decisions related to the creditors' committee activities, (2) investigation of creditors' complaints relating to the actions of the administrator, (3) approval and revision of the estimate of administrative expenses, (4) submission of proposals to the court on the continuation and/or restrictions of the enterprise's economic activities, (5) fixing the number of employees to be employed, (6) adopting a resolution on concluding the composition with creditors.

9.3.2.7 Composition with the Creditors

The only way for an enterprise in bankruptcy to avoid liquidation may be to reach an agreement on a composition between the enterprise and the creditors.[72] The composition must be signed by at least 2/3 of the creditors whose claims have not been met in the course of bankruptcy and the administrator, after the latter has received the written consent of the enterprise owners. The court may refuse to approve the composition with the creditors if the actions provided for therein contradict the laws or infringe upon a party's rights and interests protected under law. In case of an extrajudicial bankruptcy process, the composition is subject to verification by a notary.

9.3.2.8 Liquidation of Bankrupt Enterprises

If the bankruptcy court does not enter a ruling regarding the approval of the composition within 3 months of the approval of creditors' claims by the court,

---

[72] *Ibid.*, Art. 28.

the court will declare the enterprise bankrupt and issue an order to put the enterprise into liquidation. After that, the court approves the amount of each creditor's claim (s) and the procedure of liquidation and issues other orders and directions necessary for carrying out the liquidation.[73] The administrator (liquidator) disposes of the assets and resources of the enterprise, organizes the sale or transfer of the assets, satisfies approved creditors' claims, returns the assets remaining after effecting settlement with the creditors to the owners, manages and disposes of waste hazardous to the population and the environment, etc.

9.3.2.9 Sales of Assets and Ranking of Creditors' Claims

The assets of the enterprise and receivables owed to the enterprise are appraised prior to their sale. Immovable property and mortgaged/pledged assets are sold through auction. Publicly traded securities are sold in compliance with legal acts regulating the trading of securities. The procedure for selling assets other than immovable property and pledged assets are established by the creditors. Unsold assets may be transferred to the creditors.

The claims of creditors are classified as secured or unsecured. The creditor's claims secured by pledge and/or mortgage shall be paid first of all from the proceeds obtained from the sale of the pledged assets. Unsecured creditors are creditors that have a legal claim against the bankrupt enterprise that is not linked to rights in a specific asset but that is rather an ordinary obligation of the enterprise. Unsecured creditors are ranked into categories of priority of settlement. The first rank of claims includes the claims of the employees arising from an employment relationship and claims for payment for agricultural produce purchased for processing. Claims related with employment relationships may be satisfied from the resources of the Guarantee Fund. The second rank consists of claims for payment of taxes and other payments into the state budget and also for compulsory state social insurance contributions and compulsory health insurance contributions. Lastly, the third rank are all of the claims that fall outside of those specified above.[74]

The creditors of the same rank are satisfied in proportion to the amount of their claims. Claims of the creditors of each successive sequence shall be met after full payment of the claims of the creditors of the preceding sequence. If assets are insufficient to satisfy all claims of one sequence in full, the said claims shall be paid proportionally. An important feature of the EBL is that it introduces a two-stage system for the satisfaction of creditors' claims.

9.3.2.10 The Restructuring of Enterprises

An important feature of the EBL is that it does not allow rehabilitation or similar procedures to take place after bankruptcy proceedings have been instituted against the enterprise. The Law on Restructuring Enterprises (ERL) establishes the possibility for an enterprise in temporary financial difficulties, which has not

[73] *Ibid.*, Art. 32.
[74] *Ibid.*, Art. 35.

discontinued its economic and commercial activities, to undergo restructuring.[75] Unlike the EBL, ERL applies only to enterprises and public establishments and not to other types of legal entities. Moreover, it does not apply to banks, credit unions, other credit institutions, insurance companies, variable capital investment companies, closed-end investment companies, and intermediaries of public trading in securities.

However, ERL gives a certain priority to restructuring over bankruptcy proceedings.

9.3.2.11 Long-Term Solvency of the Enterprise

An enterprise experiencing temporary financial difficulties and its creditors may agree on appropriate measures for rebuilding the long-term solvency of the enterprise. Agreements are established in a restructuring plan (Plan), which must be approved by the creditors and authorized by the courts. The plan must specify the aims and duration of restructuring, as well as the enterprise's business plan for the period of restructuring. This plan must provide for measures to insure the long-term solvency of the enterprise, the schedule for the implementation of these measures, the persons responsible for their implementation, the sources of financing, and the anticipated results.[76] The duration of the restructuring may not be longer than 4 years and may be extended by the court for a period not longer than 1 year.[77]

The court will terminate the enterprise restructuring proceedings if at least one of the following conditions exists: (1) the enterprise restructuring plan is not filed with the court within 6 months from the day when the court order to initiate restructuring proceedings becomes effective; (2) it becomes evident during the restructuring process that incorrect information about the economic situation of the enterprise has been submitted, owing to which the implementation of the restructuring plan is impossible; (3) it becomes evident that the measures provided for in the restructuring plan will not be implemented, and the enterprise fails to prove that the plan will be implemented.[78]

Currently, there are 105 procedures of an enterprise's restructuring in Lithuania.[79]

9.3.2.12 The Regulation of Personal Bankruptcy Proceedings

Lithuania was the last of the Baltic states to introduce a legal mechanism to deal with insolvency of a natural person to its legal system. By legalizing the bankruptcy of an individual, two aims are pursued: to protect the interest of creditors and to grant a fresh financial start to the debtors.[80]

---

[75] *The* ***Law on Restructuring of Enterprises.*** Official Gazette, 2001, No. 31-1012, Art. 1., Sec. 2.

[76] *Ibid.*, Art. 12, Sec. 2.

[77] *Ibid.*, Art. 12, Sec. 3.

[78] *Ibid.*, Art. 28, Sec. 1.

[79] See: http://www.bankrotodep.lt/veiklos-sritys/nemokumas-2/moni-restrukturizavimas/vykdomos-proceduros/.

[80] Ambrasaitė and Norkus (2014), pp. 176–185.

Bankruptcy of a natural person is voluntary—creditors do not have the right to initiate bankruptcy proceedings.[81] Insolvency means the condition of a natural person in which he is unable to discharge his liabilities, as they mature, exceeding 25 minimum monthly wages (PBL article 2), which amounts at present (from the July, 1, 2016) to 9500 euros.[82]

Core value and principle for personal bankruptcy proceedings is the good faith of the debtor[83] because PBL is designed to create conditions for the restoration of solvency of a natural person, farmer, or another natural person pursuing individual activity, only in case he acts in good faith. Good faith of a debtor as a precondition to personal bankruptcy proceedings should be presumed as in civil cases, and the burden of proof should rest with the creditors that claim that the debtor was dishonest.[84]

The individual will be entitled to commence bankruptcy proceedings for the second time only 10 years after the previous bankruptcy proceedings were fully finished (prohibition of repeatability).[85] The recovery of a person's solvency shall proceed in accordance to the Plan of the Solvency Recovery (Plan) and the schedule for fulfilling of the creditors' claims and reimbursement of other expenses. The court has a right to approve a Plan even it has been disapproved by the creditors. While executing the Plan, a person will be granted a monthly fixed amount for meeting his basic needs.

The term of the Plan execution shall not last for more than *three* years. The bankruptcy proceedings of natural persons are executed in the court, which must appoint a bankruptcy administrator.

Currently, there are about 985 procedures of personal bankruptcy in Lithuania.[86]

The legislators' main goal is to implement more flexible and efficient legal procedures of enterprise bankruptcy and/or restructuring, with the further goals to resolve temporary financial difficulties in their early stage(s), to avoid insolvency of enterprises, and to abolish possibilities to abuse procedures of bankruptcy and restructuring. The means to reach this goal are inducement of creditors to choose out-of-court procedures, reduction of expenses, and acceleration of processes.

[81] *Ibid.*, Art. 1, Sec. 4.

[82] *Ibid.*, Art. 2, Sec. 2.

[83] *Ibid.*, Art. 1, Sec. 1.

[84] *S.D, D.D. v. Swedbank*. Supreme court of Lithuania, 2015, No. 3K-3-342-248/2015.

[85] *Law on the Bankruptcy of Natural Persons*. Official Gazette, 2012, No. 57-2823, Art. 5., Sec. 8.

[86] See: http://www.bankrotodep.lt/veiklos-sritys/nemokumas-2/fiziniu-asmenu-bankrotas/vykdomos-proceduros/.

9.4 Family and Inheritance Law

Jurgita Grigienė
Faculty of Law, Vytautas Magnus University, Jonavos st. 66, LT-44138 Kaunas, Lithuania

Čerka & Partneriai Advocates Bureau, Jonavos st. 66, LT-44138 Kaunas, Lithuania
e-mail: jurgita.grigiene@vdu.lt

Aušrinė Pasvenskienė
Faculty of Law, Vytautas Magnus University, Jonavos st. 66, LT-44138 Kaunas, Lithuania
e-mail: ausrine.pasvenskiene@vdu.lt

9.4.1 Family Law

The state regulates in detail the conditions for marriage. "Marriage is a voluntary agreement between a man and a woman to create legal family relations executed in a legal procedure."[87] The Civil Code sets six mandatory conditions for marriage. Marriage may be contracted only with a person of the opposite sex, by a man and a woman of their own free will, by persons who by or on the date of contracting a marriage have attained the age of 18,[88] by persons who are legally capable, pursuant to the principle of monogamy and not infringing the certain affinity degree.

Lithuanian legislation does not recognize same-sex marriage. There is not even the possibility to form a same-sex partnership in Lithuania. But according to V. Mikelėnas, judges in Lithuania shall consider legal categories and institutes, even if these are not otherwise known in Lithuania.[89] So the question of whether same-sex marriages concluded abroad should be recognized in Lithuania is still not answered by Lithuanian legislation and jurisprudence.

Legislation provides the possibility for a man and a woman to form a civil partnership, but the partnership must be registered. Until now, there is only a plain declaration in Lithuanian legislation regarding such a partnership, and the law on partnership has not yet been enacted. Thus, in practice, there is no possibility to register a partnership at this point. But the Constitutional Court of Lithuania stated that "the Constitution protect families other than those founded on the basis of marriage, *inter alia* the relationship of a man and a woman living together without concluding a marriage."[90]

---

[87] *Civil Code of the Republic of Lithuania*. Official Gazette, 2000, No. 74-2269.

[88] In the cases allowed by law the court may reduce the legal age to consent to marriage.

[89] Mikelėnas (2001), p. 111.

[90] Ruling of the Constitutional Court of the Republic of Lithuania on the State Family Policy Concept in Case No. 21/2008, enacted on the 28th of September 2011.

The law allows persons to register a marriage pursuant to the procedure established by civil or church procedure. A marriage registered pursuant to the procedure established by a church (confessions) must be recorded at the Registration Office. The marriage is recognized if the marriage has been formed according to the procedures established by the canons of a religious organization registered in and recognized by the Republic of Lithuania. If the marriage was registered pursuant to a church's procedure, the dissolution of the marriage can only occur through the church's own procedure and not through the civil courts.[91]

A marriage can be terminated by operation of law. There are three bases for the termination of marriage:

1. by the mutual consent of the spouses,
2. on the application of one of the spouses (no-fault basis),
3. through the fault of a spouse (or both spouses).

The law establishes that marriage can be dissolved by the fault of the other spouse or on a no-fault basis. The Supreme Court of Lithuania has held that a person has the right to divorce. If the parties live separately and there is no possibility to renew matrimonial life, the court must dissolve the marriage.[92] In some cases, the courts do not determine who is at fault for divorce; instead, the court simply states that the parties are not living together, both parties do not perform marital duties, and therefore the marriage is dissolved due to the fault of both spouses.[93]

A marriage may be dissolved by the mutual consent of the spouses (1). By mutual consent, marriage is dissolved through a simplified court procedure. Spouses are encouraged to divorce by mutual consent and are released from stamp duty if they dissolve the marriage by mutual consent.

The Civil Code provides for the granting of a divorce on the application of one spouse (2). The Civil Code sets a few cases when a marriage may be dissolved on an application of one of the spouses, which is filed with the court, for example: "the spouses have been separated for over a year; after the formation of the marriage one of the spouses has been declared legally incapacitated by the court; one of the spouses has been declared missing by the court and one of the spouses has been serving a term of imprisonment for over a year for the commission of a nonpremeditated crime."[94] In all these cases, the question of the other spouse's fault is not raised or considered.[95] The court decides cases for divorce on the application of one spouse on the basis of a simplified procedure.

Lithuanian legislation permits a spouse to apply for divorce on the ground that the marriage has broken down through the fault of the other spouse (3). The

[91] *G.K. v. G.S*, Supreme Court of the Republic of Lithuania, 2007, No. 3K-7-6/2007.

[92] *J. K. v. A. K*, Supreme Court of the Republic of Lithuania, 2002, No. 3K-3-253/2002.

[93] *K.K. v. R.K*, Supreme Court of the Republic of Lithuania, 2005, No. 3K-3-608/2005.

[94] *Civil Code of the Republic of Lithuania*. Official Gazette, 2000, No. 74-2269.

[95] Mikelėnas and Keserauskas (2002), p. 123.

marriage is treated as a contract, and one spouse may terminate it if the other spouse has broken the conditions of marriage. Fault is defined as a serious breach of matrimonial duties, which has caused their matrimonial life to become impossible. In deciding a case of a family's dissolution, the court must resolve the questions of division of joint property, the determination of the children's residence, and maintenance questions. Where a divorce is granted on the basis of the fault of one of the spouses, the at-fault spouse shall be liable to compensate damages to the nonfault spouse, as well as compensation for nonpecuniary damage done by the divorce. The amount of nonpecuniary damages is evaluated by the court. The amount may vary from case to case because the practice of the court in determining the amount of nonpecuniary damages is still under development in Lithuania. The court could award compensation of a few thousand euros for nonpecuniary damages.[96]

Upon divorce, the court will divide the joint property of spouses. It is presumed that spouses have an equal share in joint property. But depending on the fault to divorce and depending on where the children's residence is determined, the court may depart from the presumption that the spouses have an equal share of matrimonial property. In these cases, the Supreme Court of Lithuania has established a uniform practice, that 2/3 and 1/3 of the matrimonial property is awarded for spouses, with the at-fault spouse receiving the lesser share.[97]

The law technically states that divorce can only be granted due to the fault of the other spouse. But a court practice has developed whereby divorce can be granted even without establishing the fault of the other spouse, that is, in situations where the marriage is *de facto* broken due to the fault of both spouses.

Lithuanian law provides for the possibility of separation. The institute of separation is not popular in Lithuania because it is not very difficult to obtain a divorce.

There is a special statutory and contractual legal regime applicable to the property of spouses. After concluding a marriage, spouses obtain special status and special property and nonproperty rights. The novelty in Lithuanian law is the possibility to regulate the property rights of spouses by marital contracts. Where the spouses have not made a marital contract, their property shall be subject to the statutory regime. Under the statutory rules, the property acquired by the spouses after the commencement of their marriage shall be their joint community property. Both spouses are treated as partners in acquiring the property during the marriage. Lithuania has chosen a limited form of community of property because property acquired prior to the marriage is considered as the personal property of the spouse. The law does not provide an exhaustive list of what constitutes "property"—joint community property could include any other property. Things acquired for joint property funds should be treated as joint property. Individually used weapons, motorcycles, and motorcycle helmets are treated as joint community property, but the fact that one spouse has authorization to use the weapon could be important for

[96] *R.B. v. A.B*, Supreme Court of the Republic of Lithuania, 2008, No. 3K-3-128/2008.

[97] *Z.V. v. J.V.* Supreme Court of the Republic of Lithuania, 2007, No. 3K-3-220/2007.

the division of property objects.[98] Joint coownership rights end upon the death of one spouse, upon divorce, and in other cases. The property of cohabitants who live together does not become joint community property. Lithuanian courts have stated that such persons must prove each of his "contributions" to the acquired property (for example, from whom and how much money was used to purchase a particular item). So their assets are divided by partial ownership rules. Or, in some cases, they are subject to the provisions governing joint ventures.[99]

Lithuanian legislation allows the spouses to create binding economic rights and obligations through a marital contract. A marital contract can be concluded either prior to the marriage or after marriage. A marriage contract must be entered into before a notary public. A marriage contract must also be registered in the register of marriage contracts maintained by mortgage institutions. Parties may use a marital contract in order to clarify their rights and avoid any uncertainties as to how a court may divide property at divorce. "Spouses shall have a right to stipulate in the marriage contract that: property acquired both before and during the marriage shall be the individual property of each spouse; individual property acquired by a spouse before the marriage shall become joint community property after the registration of the marriage; property acquired during the marriage shall be joint community property."[100] In a marital contract, the parties can agree only on property rights; they are not allowed to agree on nonproperty rights or establish the personal rights and duties of the spouses toward their children (that the spouse will not work, will not give birth to more children). The court can hold that a marital contract is null and void if it contradicts the mandatory legislative rules, good morality, and public order.

"The shares of the spouses in joint community property shall be presumed to be equal. Departure from the principle of the equality of the shares of the spouses in joint community property shall be permitted only in cases provided by law."[101] With regard to the interests of the minor children, the state of health or the financial position of one of the spouses, or other important circumstances, the court may depart from the principle of the equality of the spouses' shares in the community property and award one of the spouses a greater portion of the property. These criteria must also be taken into consideration by the court in deciding upon the manner of partitioning community property. In court practice, such conduct will result in the allocation of 1/3 to the negligent/at-fault spouse and 2/3 to the other spouse.[102] Particular problems may occur when spouses have only one apartment with one room. In the majority of such cases, the apartment is left to the spouse who retains custody of the children, and compensation is paid to the other spouse.[103]

[98] *A.B. v. A.B.* Supreme Court of the Republic of Lithuania No. 3k-3-14-2008.

[99] *V. P. v. V. P.* Supreme Court of the Republic of Lithuania No. 3K-3-410/2011.

[100] *Civil Code of the Republic of Lithuania.* Official Gazette, 2000, No. 74-2269.

[101] *Ibid.*

[102] *Ž.V.* v. *J. V.* Supreme Court of the Republic of Lithuania No. 3K-3-220/2007.

[103] Vitkevičius (2006), p. 160.

Financial obligations shall be satisfied from the joint common property of spouses in the event that these obligations are related to the managing of community property and transactions that were made in the interests of the family.[104] The Supreme Court of Lithuania has stated that it must first be determined whether the debt was joint or personal. Only a court can determine whether the debt was joint or personal. If the debt is considered a joint debt, it can be satisfied from the joint property of the spouses, including the salary of each spouse. But if obligation is personal, it cannot be executed from all joint property but only from the share of the indebted spouse in the joint common property.

Family law regulates relations between parents and children. The father and the mother shall have equal rights and duties in respect to their children. Parents shall have equal rights and duties by their children irrespective of whether the child was born to a married or unmarried couple, after divorce, the judicial nullity of the marriage, or separation. Parents must support their children until they reach the age of 18. The Civil Code further provides that if they continue to study at college or another higher educational institution, parents must provide maintenance until the child reaches the age of 24. However, the Constitutional Court of the Republic of Lithuania has ruled that the obligation to support children who are over 18 years old while they are studying contradicts the Constitution of Lithuania. Under the Court's ruling, such support may be granted only in exceptional cases when children have no possibility to support themselves.[105] The amount for maintenance must be commensurate with the needs of the children and the financial situation of their parents; it must also ensure the existence of conditions necessary for the child's development. If the parents (or one of the parents) fail in their duty to maintain support of their underage children, the court may issue a maintenance order. The courts stated that the average monthly financial need of a person is equal to the Lithuanian minimum monthly salary. At present, the minimum monthly salary is 380 EUR. Therefore, each parent shall provide the child maintenance in an amount equal to 195 EUR per month.[106] The maintenance is determined not on a percentage basis but on a fixed amount. The Supreme Court of Lithuania has prepared a recommendation as to how the monthly maintenance amount shall be calculated for children. For cases of a parent not paying child support, the state has established the Child Support Fund (*Vaikų išlaikymo fondas*), which pays support for children. One parent may apply to the fund for support because the other parent is not providing support. A procedure exists for the mandatory enforcement of court judgments through bailiffs. As a result, bailiffs could enforce maintenance obligations through wage deduction. If a parent continues to avoid his or her maintenance obligation, it may be imposed, with the additional possibility of the parent being subject to criminal liability.

[104] *Civil Code of the Republic of Lithuania*. Official Gazette, 2000, No. 74-2269.

[105] Ruling of the Constitutional Court of the Republic of Lithuania on Support of Childrenthuania enacted on the 6 June 2007.

[106] Ruling of the Constitutional Court of the Republic of Lithuania on the Support of Children enacted on the 6 June 2007.

"Where the parents are separated, the child's residence shall be decided by the mutual agreement of the parents."[107] In the event of a dispute over the child's residence, the child's residence shall be determined by a residence order awarded by the court in favor of one of the parents. Lithuanian law establishes the institute of the child's residence, which is similar to the institution of custody that is widespread in Western countries. The main principle in determining the residence of a child is the best interests of a child. The child's interests are the continuation of an emotional relationship between the parent and child, school/education, and economic conditions. The Supreme Court of Lithuania has provided guidance in determining the residence of a child.[108] In Lithuania, the child's residence is most often determined to be with the mother. The decision regarding the child's residence may be changed pursuant to changed conditions. The noncustodial spouse is entitled to have meetings/regular contact with the child. In practice, the parent with whom the child resides makes all major decisions with respect to the child, and the other parent maintains the right to visit the child and the duty to provide maintenance.[109] There are often violations of the noncustodial spouse's right to visit the child. There is no possibility to have shared parenting, whereby for half of the time the child resides with one parent and half of the time with the other parent. Parents shall be obliged to create conditions for the children to associate with their relatives, provided that it is consistent with the children's interests.

9.4.2 Inheritance Law

The succession law is in detail regulated mainly by the fifth book, "Law of Succession," and a number of other norms of the Civil Code of the Republic of Lithuania. After the death of a natural person (the bequeather can be only a natural person), his property rights, duties, and some other personal nonproperty rights are inherited by the heirs by operation of law (intestate) and/or by successors by the will (testate).[110] The succession arises at the moment of the death of the bequeather; it is called an opening of succession. The successors address the application on the acceptance of succession with the notary public or the district court according to the place of the opening of succession, which is the last place of domicile of the bequeather.

One of the key features of Lithuanian succession law is the principle of universal transmission, which means universal devolution of property rights and duties to one or more successors as a whole. The successors are free to decide whether to inherit

[107] *Civil Code of the Republic of Lithuania*. Official Gazette, 2000, No. 74-2269.

[108] The Decision of Supreme Court Senate No. 35 *On the application of laws in court practice, when determining the place of residence of the under-aged children, of separated parents* enacted on the 21st of June 2002.

[109] Sagatys (2006), p. 139.

[110] *Civil Code of the Republic of Lithuania*. Official Gazette, 2000, No. 74-2269, Article 5.1.

or not; however, they can exercise their freedom only in the range of succession law. That means that the successors cannot accept succession in part or according to certain conditions or exceptions.

The capacity to inherit in Lithuania belongs to natural persons, legal persons, and the state or municipalities. Natural persons who survived the bequeather, also children of the bequeather who were born after his death, have a capacity to inherit in succession by operation of law and in succession by a will. In succession pursuant to a will, natural persons named in a will before their conception also may be entitled to inherit upon their birth. A legal person can acquire a right to inherit only if the deceased expressed such intent in the testament. The state can inherit either pursuant to a will or in operation by law. In the latter case, the estate devolves to the state under the right of succession if there are neither intestate heirs nor testate successors at all or none of them accepts succession or the testator deprives the heirs of the right to inheritance.[111] In the case of testate, not only the state can inherit the property but also the municipalities.

The succession law provides the right to a person to deprive other persons of their right to inherit. Persons can also be denied their right to inherit not by the will of the testator but by law in the case of unlawful intentional actions against the bequeather or against any of his successors or against the execution of the true intentions expressed in the will of the testator when such circumstance are conducive to becoming a successor.

Under the law of succession, the right of succession by a spouse deserves special attention. The law of succession provides specific norms regarding the forfeiture of the right to inherit for a survived spouse who was by fraudulent and unfair means seeking to benefit from the death of another spouse. A survived spouse is deprived from the right to inherit if before the opening of succession the bequeather had applied to the court for the dissolution of marriage because of the fault of the surviving spouse or there was a ground for declaring the marriage null and void and the court decided that there is a ground for that.[112] If the application to the court was addressed to dissolve the marriage by the mutual consent of the spouses, the court cannot disprove expressed intent of the bequeather and ascertain that the marriage should have been dissolved because of the fault of the survived spouse.[113]

In intestate succession, the Lithuanian law of successions establishes six degrees of descendants.[114] In each degree, inheritance is divided between the persons in equal shares. First-degree descendants are the bequeather's children (including adopted children) and the bequeather's children born after his death. The second-degree descendants are the bequeather's parents (adoptive parents) and grandchildren. Second-degree heirs are entitled to inherit in the absence of heirs of the first degree, or if they do not accept or renunciate the succession, also when

[111] *Ibid.*, Article 5.62.

[112] *Ibid.*, Article 5.7.

[113] *J.M. v I.O.* Supreme Court of the Republic of Lithuania, 2009, No. 3K-3-518/2009.

[114] Civil Code of the Republic of Lithuania. Official Gazette, 2000, No. 74-2269, Article 5.11.

the first-degree descendants are deprived of the right to inherit. Third- to six-degree descendants are entitled to inherit only in the absence of a superior degree and the surviving spouse or in the case of their renunciation of succession or deprivation of the right to succession.[115] The established degrees of descendants are considered to be an exhaustive list and cannot be expanded. If there are no heirs by operation of law and/or successors by a will, the estate of the bequeather is inherited by the state.[116]

The surviving spouse is not assigned to any degree descendants and has a right to inherit alongside the first- or the second-degree descendants. With the first-degree heirs, the surviving spouse inherits one-fourth of the inheritance if not more than three heirs apart from the spouse exist; if more, then the spouse inherits with all of them in equal shares. In the absence of the first-degree heirs or under any other circumstances when the second-degree descendants inherit, the surviving spouse is entitled to a half of the inheritance. Irrespective of the number of heirs, they are entitled to the remaining half in equal shares. In the absence of first- and second-degree descendants, the surviving spouse is entitled to the whole inheritance. The amount of the inheritable estate that the surviving spouse has a right to inherit depends on the legal regime of the property of spouses. The inheritable estate consists of the individual property of the bequeather and of a share in the joint property of the spouses. First of all, it is necessary to determine the share of each spouse in the joint community property of the spouses according to the rules of law regulating the property of spouses.

The bequeather's grandchildren and great-grandchildren have a right to succeed by the right of representation. They can inherit by operation of law alongside, correspondingly, the first- and second-degree descendants if, at the time of the opening of succession, their parents, who would have been the heirs, passed away before the opening of succession. Under such circumstances, the bequeather's grandchildren and great-grandchildren can inherit in equal shares that part of the estate that would have been inherited by their deceased parent pursuant to instate succession.[117]

Another way to inherit the property is by will (testate), which must be made solely by the testator. The testator must be legally capable and able to understand the seriousness and consequences of such actions. Ordinary persuasion or requirement of interested heirs to make a will in their interests is not regarded as duress and does not influence the validity of a will. If mistakes are made in the text, however, the real intentions of the testator can be identified from the content of the will; it does not have effect on the validity of a will. In case of a disagreement between heirs regarding the content of the will, the court must determine the content according to the principles of justice, reasonableness, and good faith, with reference to the real intentions of the testator (without limiting it by the literal meaning of the

[115] *Ibid.*

[116] *O.T. v G.P.* Supreme Court of the Republic of Lithuania, 2009, No. 3K-3-539/2009.

[117] Civil Code of the Republic of Lithuania. Official Gazette, 2000, No. 74-2269, Article 5.11.

words), the actions of the testator before and after the will was made, the circumstances of the conclusion of the will and other legally meaningful conditions,[118] and also the rules of interpretation of contracts.[119] The testator has a right to oblige a testate successor to accomplish a certain assignment. It is called a testamentary reservation, and it is fulfilled in the amount of the value of inherited property after satisfying the claims of the creditors.

In certain cases, the testator's children (adoptees), spouse, parents (adoptive parents) may inherit irrespectively of the content of the will. They withhold the right to the mandatory share of inheritance if they were entitled to maintenance on the day of opening of succession. Under such circumstance, they have a right to succeed a half of the share that they would have been entitled to by operation of law.

There are two types of wills: official and private. An official will must be made in writing in two copies and attested by the notary public or an official of the Consulate of the Republic of Lithuania in the relevant state or by a person vested with such right by law.[120] The will must be signed by the testator, attested, and registered in the Notarial Register in the presence of the testator. One copy of it is given to the testator, and another copy is kept in the institution, which has attested it. In case the will of a person with hearing and speech impairment is formed, the participation of a person who understands sign language and is trusted by the testator, except when the person with hearing and speech impairment is literate and can read the text of the will and conform in writing of his awareness of the content of the will.[121] In cases when the testator because of physical disabilities, illness, or other reasons is unable to sign the will by himself, another legally capable person can sign the will upon the testator's request. It must be done in the presence of the notary (or any other person officially authorized to attest the will) and not less than two other witnesses, who must put their signatures in the will as well. The person signing the will instead of a testator cannot be a testate successor. The reason why the testator is unable to sign the will himself must be indicated in the will.

Another type of will is a private will, which must be written in the hand of the testator, may be written in any language, and must include the name and surname of the testator and the date and place of its formation, must express the true intent of the testator, and must be signed by him.[122] If the date and the place of formation are not indicated in the will, that makes it invalid only if it is impossible to identify such information in any other way. However, the will without a signature of the testator is obviously an incomplete will and is null and void. A private will written by computer or by another person's hand, although signed by the testator, is not valid.[123] In order for a private will to be valid, it must be deposited with the notary

[118] *J.K. v Č.K.* Supreme Court of the Republic of Lithuania, 2011, No. 3K-3-161/2011.

[119] *R.J. v L.Š., A.D.* Supreme Court of the Republic of Lithuania, 2013, No. 3K-3-653/2013.

[120] *Civil Code of the Republic of Lithuania.* Official Gazette, 2000, No. 74-2269, Article 5.28.

[121] *Ibid.*

[122] *Ibid.*, Article 5.30.

[123] *T.V. v Vilniaus apskrities valstybinė mokesčių inspekcija.* Supreme Court of the Republic of Lithuania, 2004, No. 3K-3-581/2004.

public or a consular official of the Republic of Lithuania in a foreign state, or it must be confirmed by the court. When a person who has written a will does not deposit it, in order to be valid, the will must be confirmed by the court within 1 year from the death of that person, which is a resolutory time limit and cannot be restored.[124] By the procedure of confirmation of the will, the court determines whether the will fulfills the aforementioned requirements of form and content and whether the true will of the testator is clearly expressed.[125]

A special attention in the Civil Code is given to the joint will of spouses, which can be only official and by which they appoint each other as the successors. The whole estate belonging to the deceased is inherited by the surviving spouse, except the mandatory share of succession.[126] The spouses may appoint the successor who will inherit the property after the death of both spouses. Until the death of one of the spouses, the will can be revoked. After the death of one of the spouses, the surviving spouse does not have a right to revise the joint will. The successor appointed by the joint will of the spouses inherits the estate that has left after the death of the surviving spouse.[127]

In order to inherit, successors must accept a succession by starting to possess the estate, by submitting the application to the district court of the place of the opening of succession for the inventory of the estate, or by applying with the notary public of the place of the opening of succession within 3 months since the opening of succession. The time limit of 3 months can be extended by the court if the successor can prove important reasons for the delay, such as that the successor had an intention to inherit but could not realize his right due to circumstances beyond his control, diligence and attentiveness of the actions of the successors, for how long and why the time limit was delayed, and other important facts that could have led to the delay.[128] The successors also have a right of renunciation of inheritance, which must also be expressed within 3 months from the opening of succession and has the same consequences as nonacceptance of succession. After the acceptance of the succession but until the issuance of the certificate, the successor has a right to transfer his rights of succession. The specific manner of purchase-sale of succession rights contract is that inheritance is devolved as a whole and a seller does not have to specify in detail the property included; he must only warrant to the buyer his status as an heir.[129] Although the courts tend to deny the possibility to transfer a certain share of the rights of succession, some scholars criticize this position and argue in favor of such a possibility.[130]

---

[124] *V.M. v V.M., R.M.* Supreme Court of the Republic of Lithuania, 2010, No. 3K-7-29/2010.

[125] *A.B. v E.B., Vilniaus miesto 9-asis notarų biuras.* Supreme Court of the Republic of Lithuania, 2015, No. 3K-3-87-248/2015.

[126] *Civil Code of the Republic of Lithuania.* Official Gazette, 2000, No. 74-2269, Article 5.43.

[127] *B.V. v V.V.* Supreme Court of the Republic of Lithuania, 2015, No. 3K-3-144-313/2015.

[128] *V.V. v L.R.* Supreme Court of the Republic of Lithuania, 2014, No. 3K-3-54/2014.

[129] *Civil Code of the Republic of Lithuania.* Official Gazette, 2000, No. 74-2269, Article 6.426.

[130] Dambrauskaitė (2010), pp. 128–129.

When successors do not actively express their acceptance of the succession but rather start to possess the property, treating it like their own, it is deemed as acceptance of the inheritance by the actual start of property possession. The successors in both ways (by starting to possess the property or by filing an application with the notary) are liable for the debts of the bequeather with his whole property. When the estate was accepted by several successors, they all are solidarily liable. In order not to be liable for the debts of the bequeather with his whole property, the successor can accept the succession in accordance with an inventory. In such case, the successor is liable only in the amount of the inherited property.

9.5 Civil Procedure Law

Evaldas Rapolas
Faculty of Law, Vytautas Magnus University, Jonavos st. 66, LT-44138 Kaunas, Lithuania

Magnusson Law Firm, Jonavos st. 66, LT-44138 Kaunas, Lithuania
e-mail: evaldas.rapolas@magnussonlaw.com

Vigintas Višinskis
Faculty of Law, Mykolas Romeris University, Gedimino av. 40/1, LT-01503 Vilnius, Lithuania

Court of Appeal of Lithuania, Gedimino av. 40/1, LT-01503 Vilnius, Lithuania
e-mail: vigintas.visinskis@apeliacinis.lt

9.5.1 Basic Provision

With the restoration of Lithuania's independence in 1990, the need for new regulation of legal relations within civil procedure arose. The existing Code of Civil Procedure[131] (hereinafter in this subsection CCP) was enforced on January 1, 2003, superseding the CCP adopted back in 1964 and amended repeatedly.

Basic provisions on administration of justice have been laid down in the Constitution[132] and Law on Courts of the Republic of Lithuania:[133] in this country, justice is administered by independent courts only (article 109 of the Constitution).

Article 117 of the Constitution establishes Lithuanian as the state language and the principle of publicity of court proceedings. Publicity of a court hearing means

[131] *Code of Civil Procedure of the Republic of Lithuania*. Official Gazette, 2002, No. 36-1340; 24/04/2002; Official Gazette, 2002, No. 42.

[132] *The Constitution of the Republic of Lithuania*. Official Gazette, 1992, No, 33-1014.

[133] *The Law on Courts of the Republic of Lithuania*. Official Gazette, 1994, No. 46-851; Official Gazette, 2002, No. 17-649.

that cases are heard in public by all courts. During a court hearing, any person of at least 16 years of age may observe the proceedings at the courtroom. However, this principle is not absolute. In certain cases, a court proceeding may be closed under a motivated ruling for the purpose of maintaining a personal and family life privacy; where a case heard in public may disclose a state, office, professional or commercial secret; or where a court has undertaken measures to reconcile the parties. Only the persons who participate in the case—and, as appropriate, witnesses, translators and experts—may be present during closed court proceedings.

Publicity of a civil case matter is an important component comprising the principle of publicity of proceedings, meaning that the material of a case heard is available for familiarization to any person interested as soon as judgment passed and the civil case has become *res judicata* and consideration of the judgment by cassation procedure is no longer allowed. The last component of publicity of proceedings is related to the publicity of judgment passed by the court, meaning that a court judgment should be made public to warrant its accessibility to all interested persons. Even where a judgment has been passed upon case hearing at a closed court session, the operative part of a judgment (except for adoption cases) must be made public. Publication of judgments has been prescribed by the Law on Courts, establishing that final acts of courts, separate decisions, and annual reviews of court practice of the Supreme Court must be published on the website of the National Court Administration in the manner established by the Judicial Council, unless provided otherwise by law.

9.5.2 Jurisdiction in Civil Cases

The Lithuanian legal system has two types of courts: general competence and specialized courts. Regional administrative courts and the Supreme Administrative Court of Lithuania are classified as specialized courts. These courts consider cases on disputes arising from an administrative legal relationship. General competence courts are district courts, regional courts, the Court of Appeal of Lithuania, and the Supreme Court of Lithuania. Consideration of civil cases is assigned to the general competence courts, unless the civil case is eligible for consideration under the Law on Administrative Proceedings of the Republic of Lithuania at a specialized court of the Republic of Lithuania due to the fact that the defendant in the civil case is a state authority.

By competence, district courts are the first instance courts considering private civil legal disputes. Meanwhile, regional courts, by competence, may be both the first instance courts in civil legal disputes and the appeal instance courts. At present, the Republic of Lithuania has 49 district courts and five regional courts of general competence. Regional courts act as the first instance to consider more complex civil legal disputes where the claimed amount exceeds EUR 4,350,000 (except for family and labor legal relationship cases and cases based on nonproperty damage claims), as well as disputes on copyright nonproperty legal relationships; civil public tender legal relationships; bankruptcy and restructuring (except cases involving natural persons' bankruptcy); other civil cases that are heard by district courts as the first instance courts following CCP and other laws. In cases other than the above, regional courts act as the appeal instance to consider disputes on legitimacy and validity of decisions adopted by district courts.

It should be noted that among all the regional courts in Lithuania, the Vilnius Regional Court holds exclusive competence for considering cases involving disputes provided for under the Law on Patents of the Republic of Lithuania and the Law on Trademarks of the Republic of Lithuania, disputes on adoption under foreign nationals' applications for adoption of a national of the Republic of Lithuania residing in the Republic of Lithuania or a foreign country, and other civil cases that, under the effective laws, are considered by the Vilnius Regional Court acting as the first instance court.

The Court of Appeal of Lithuania is exclusively the appeal instance revising civil cases decided by regional courts of first instance. The competence of the Court of Appeal of Lithuania also covers consideration of requests on recognition and enforcement of judgments of foreign courts, international courts, and courts of arbitration in Lithuania and appeals against judgments adopted by courts of arbitration in Lithuania.

The Supreme Court is the only court of the cassation reviewing *res judicata* judgments and rulings in civil cases. The Supreme Court is obligated to develop a uniform court practice of interpretation and application of statutes and other legal acts.

9.5.3 Right to Apply to Court

The Constitution of the Republic of Lithuania establishes that any person whose rights or freedoms have been violated is entitled to apply to court. A similar right to persons is guaranteed directly by the CCP, stating that each and every person concerned should have the right to appeal to court following the laws to defend their violated or contested right or interest protected by laws.

The CCP distinguishes two types of proceedings: dispute and special. The majority of civil cases are considered under the dispute proceedings, which are characterized by their applicability to consideration of mutual disputes between the parties having opposing interests. Special proceedings are the totality of exceptions of action proceedings. The aim of special proceedings is to ensure proper execution of substantive legal norms for the avoidance of any violation of subjective substantive right. Cases heard by a court under special proceedings are as follows: concerning the establishment of legally relevant facts, concerning the declaration of a natural person as dead or missing; concerning the declaration of a natural person as incapable or of a limited active capacity or declaration of a minor as emancipated, etc. Hearing a case under dispute proceedings is initiated by claim filing, and special proceedings require an application.

For the successful enforcement of a person's right of relief, the right needs to be realized in the order provided for by laws. This order involves the submission of a court document of the respective form—document of action filing or application—stating the rights or interests protected by laws that the person seeks to protect or realize. A person applying to the court should provide evidence of possession of subjective right, violation, intended violation of this right or of the right being disputed against by the defendant and indicate the substantive requirements: requested means for protection of the violated or disputed right or interest protected by laws.

The right of relief may be realized by the person both by filing an individual action to the court and by seeking collective realization of his rights and interests on the basis of class action concept. The class action concept was established in the CCP back in 2003, but the actual possibility for the application of the class action concept appeared in 2015 only after the introduction of a new section governing the procedure under class action. Class action may be filed in a regional court acting as the first instance court by a group of at least 20 natural and/or legal persons related to each other under the criterion of unity. The criterion of unity is construed as the group members' aim to defend identical or similar rights or interests protected by laws, and the requirements raised by the group members are based on the identical or similar actual circumstances, and all group members seek to defend their rights and interests protected by laws by the same method of legal protection.

The CCP also provides for the possibility of defense of a public interest. The right to defend other persons' rights and/or interests (i.e., public interest) is granted to a fairly narrow circle of entities involving the prosecutor, state and municipal authorities, and other entities definitively entitled to defend a public interest by the legal acts.

9.5.4 Summary Proceedings

The CCP provides for three forms of summary proceedings: procedure of issuance of court orders, documentary proceedings, and cases on disputes for the adjudgment of small amounts of money. Cases involving the issuance of court order are heard based on the creditor's pecuniary claims (resulting from a conflict, tort, labor relationship, adjudgment of maintenance (support), etc.).

A dispute involving pecuniary claims (resulting from a conflict, tort, labor relationship, adjudgment of maintenance (support), etc.), adjudgment of a movable item, securities, or claims arising out of immovable item tenancy agreements, in particular, on tenant's eviction, may be considered at the claimant's request under the documentary proceedings if all claims are based on the acceptable written evidence.

Cases based on disputes for the adjudgment of small amounts of money are considered to be disputes on adjudgment of amounts of money not exceeding EUR 150,000. In such cases, the court is entitled to decide on the form and procedure of case hearing.

9.5.5 Choosing a Competent Court, Court Composition

A claimant, or a special entity seeking to defend a public interest, should properly identify the district or regional court to which he is filing.

As a rule of thumb, an action should be filed in court according to the defendant's place of residence. An action against a legal person is filed according to the legal person's seat indicated in the Register of Legal Entities. Where a defendant is a state or municipality, the action should be filed according to the seat of the authority representing the state or municipality. Nevertheless, exceptions exist.

The first exception is exclusive jurisdiction of civil cases. In the event of such jurisdiction, actions on the right in rem in relation to an immovable item, on usage of an immovable item (except for claims on division of spouses' assets in marriage dissolution cases), and on annulment of an immovable item seizure are subject to the jurisdiction of the court according to the location of the immovable item or its main part. Exclusive jurisdiction also applies to actions by the testator's creditors filed during acceptance of the inheritable property by the heirs. Jurisdiction of such actions is determined according to the location of the inheritable property or its main part.

The second exception is associated with the right granted to parties of a case to change the territorial jurisdiction of the case by written agreement. It should be noted that only territorial jurisdiction of a civil case may be changed by agreement between the parties. The parties cannot agree upon the exclusive and specific jurisdiction of the civil case.

The third exception is associated with specific cases stipulated by the legislator, in particular, where a claimant may, at his own initiative, choose one of the possible courts to file the action (alternative jurisdiction). In case of alternative jurisdiction, there is the possibility to hear the case in two or more courts of general competence of the same instance; however, upon enforcement of the right of choice and filing of the action in a certain court, the claimant is no longer entitled to file the identical action in another court. Alternative jurisdiction applies where particularly significant rights and interests of the claimant are defended (paternity affiliation, damage claim, maintenance (support) cases), and the claimant is therefore subject to the certain preferences for him to enforce the constitutional right to apply in court for legal protection by choosing hearing of the case at the court that is the most acceptable to the claimant, as promptly and economically as possible.

Even if the civil case has been initiated under the effective rules of jurisdiction of civil cases, sometimes the court may pass a ruling to transfer hearing of the case to another court. For this ruling to be passed, certain objective circumstances must be present. For example, a court may pass a ruling to transfer hearing of the case to another court if it determines that hearing of the case at another court would be implemented faster and more economically, for example, based on the location of the major part of evidence. Such case transfer is also possible under the request of a defendant whose residency has been unknown initially. Upon acceptance of a case for hearing at a certain court, such court's composition should be determined for hearing of the civil case. Composition of the court hearing the civil case may be a single-person (the case is heard and judgment is passed by one judge) or a collegiate body (the case is heard and judgment is passed by three or more judges). Regardless of the number of judges actually hearing the case, the judges are deemed to act on behalf of the court they represent and to pass judgment on behalf of the Republic of Lithuania.

In a district and regional court, civil cases are usually heard under the first instance by one judge. A collegiate court is usually formed—a panel comprised of three judges—for case hearing under the appeal procedure. Cases under the cassation procedure usually are heard by a panel of three judges.

9.5.6 Averment in Civil Proceedings

Civil cases are heard under the principle of competition. The aim of the averment duty applicable to dispute parties is to provide data into the case for the court, upon analyzing and evaluating the data, to verify the existence or nonexistence of certain circumstances related to the dispute subject matter. In a civil procedure, the issue of evidence sufficiency is decided under the principle of balance of probabilities. This principle means that a court is not required to be fully convinced. Evidence is deemed sufficient for making a conclusion that the fact is more likely to exist.

Evidence in a civil case is any actual data, on the basis of which a court states that there are circumstances substantiating the parties' claims and objections and other circumstances that are significant for the correct consideration of the case, or absence of such evidence, under the procedure provided for by laws. Actual data may be determined in a case by explanations submitted by the statements of parties or third persons (in person or by representative), testimonies of witnesses, written evidence, material evidence, inspection protocols and expert reports, photo images, video and audio records obtained legally, and other means of averment. Nonetheless, the CCP provides for a rule of restriction of the above tools of averment, the essence of which is that the law provides for the cases, where averment of case circumstances may be implemented by special tools only. There are two aspects to the above restriction rule. First, case circumstances may, in certain cases, only be substantiated by certain clearly indicated tools of averment. For example, the CCP stipulates that the fact of marriage existence may be validated in a case by entry of the marriage act and the marriage certificate issued on its basis. Second, there have been cases where averment of case circumstances may be implemented by all tools of averment, except for certain tools. For example, the fact of entry into transaction without following the mandatory written form applicable to the transaction cannot be validated by testimonies of witnesses.

It should be noted that not all evidence has the same conclusive force. For example, if the written evidence submitted to the court contains corrections or other external defects or if only copies of written evidence are submitted as the original copies no longer exist for some reason, the conclusive force of such evidence is determined by the court hearing the case. Meanwhile, documents issued by state and municipal authorities, certified by other persons authorized by the state without exceeding their established competence and by following the form requirements applicable to the respective documents, are deemed to be official written evidence and possess greater conclusive force than any other evidence. Greater conclusive force means that circumstances indicated in official written evidence are considered to have been averred completely until they are invalidated by other evidence present in the case.

Evidence should be submitted to the case by dispute parties and other participants of the case. In cases where the submitted evidence is insufficient, the court may advise the parties or other participants of the case to submit additional evidence. Courts do not collect evidence at their own initiative, though there are certain exceptions to this provision. Courts collect evidence at their own initiative where required by public interest and where the person, society, or state's rights and legal interests may be violated unless such measures are assumed. A proactive role of the courts in the collection of evidence is also possible during case hearing under special proceedings, also where disputes have arisen out of family and labor legal relationships.

Nonetheless, regardless of the narrow exceptions whereby a court is authorized to collect evidence, the role of court in the averment process, in general, is limited to examination and evaluation of the evidence submitted by the parties and other participants of the proceedings.

9.5.7 Participation of a Party in Proceedings

Persons may make their cases in court in person or by representatives. Representation relationship in civil proceedings may take place on the basis of law or agreement (authorization).

Legal representation applies where a person (represented party) cannot execute his passive and active civil capacity due to certain circumstances. For example, the person is incapable and guardianship has been established for him, or the person is of limited active capacity (or is seriously ill) and care has been established for him. Thus, the persons who may participate in civil legal relationship by legal representative only should be represented accordingly in civil proceedings as well. Undoubtedly, a legal representative aiming to guarantee adequate legal assistance to the principal may authorize another representative to make the case under the contract (lawyer or associate).

The CCP provides for a finite list of entities entitled to act as representatives by authorization in hearing cases under civil proceedings. The list includes lawyers, associates (holding the written permission for representation in the certain case issued by their supervising lawyer), persons having a higher university education degree in law (where they represent their relatives or spouse, cohabiting partner), trade unions (where they represent trade union members in cases related to labor legal relationship), etc. It is important that rights of the representative by authorization (agreement) are duly executed by a document supporting the right of representation.

The rule of thumb is that arrival of a representative at a court session is considered to be proper participation by the participant of the case represented by the representative. In other words, a representative in a civil process is deemed equivalent to the person represented. Deviations from this rule are possible where the court acknowledges the necessity of participation by the person represented in the proceedings.

In case the court has not acknowledged the person's participation as necessary, the person's representative may act on behalf of the person to the full extent. In the representative's actions, procedural actions are deemed to be implemented on behalf of the represented person, with the legal consequences being imposed on the latter, of course, if the representative does not exceed the authority granted in his actions. The CCP provides that the authorization of representation in court grants the representative the right to perform absolutely all procedural actions on behalf of the represented person save for exceptions indicated in the document supporting the representation, if the represented person and the representative have provided for such exceptions.

9.5.8 Other Participants in a Proceeding

The CCP stipulates that participants in a proceeding interested in the final outcome of the case are deemed to be the persons participating in the civil case. In case of dispute proceedings, these undoubtedly are parties of the case: the claimant is the person who has initiated the civil case and submits claims in the case, and the defendant is the person seeking to object to the claimant's claims. In cases heard under special proceedings, the applicant is deemed to be a party in the civil case. Apart from the parties, third parties also have legal interest in the final outcomes of the case and file or do not file their independent claims. The third persons who file independent claims on the dispute subject matter have all the rights and duties of a claimant and may enter or be involved in the case before the beginning of final speeches. The third persons who do not file any independent claims on the dispute subject matter may enter into the case on the claimant's or defendant's side before the beginning of final speeches if the outcome of the case may influence their rights or duties.

9.5.9 Case Hearing and Adjudgment

Hearing of a civil case in court is comprised of two main stages: preparation for hearing and hearing of the civil case on the substance.

In preparation for the case hearing in court, the parties and third persons should submit all the available evidence and explanations significant for the case to the court and indicate the evidence that cannot be submitted by them to the court and the circumstances preventing from doing so and formulate their final claims and objections to the filed claims. In other words, the preparatory stage involves preparation for case hearing on the substance enabling proper hearing of the case in one court session.

There are two types of the stage of preparation for case hearing: written (in the form of preliminary documents) and oral. In each case, the preparation can be performed only in one of the two aforementioned ways.

All evidence present in the case should be examined at the court session during the case hearing on the substance. Examination of evidence starts with examination of explanations provided by the participants of the proceedings. Having heard explanations, the court moves to examination of all other evidence present in the case. In examination of written evidence, they are read aloud at the court session and submitted for familiarization to participants of the proceedings and, as appropriate, to experts and witnesses. Examination of material evidence takes place during their inspection by the court. During the investigation, the material evidence is also demonstrated to participants of proceedings and, as appropriate, to experts and witnesses.

Upon completion of examination of evidence present in the case, the court moves to hearing final speeches by the participants of the proceedings. The claimant and his representative are the first to present their final speeches, followed by the defendant and his representative. After final speeches, participants of the final speeches may speak briefly for the second time in relation to the said final speeches under the right of replication.

Having heard the final speeches, the court passes judgment on the dispute between the parties.

9.5.10 Appeal Proceedings

Judgments and rulings of the first instance court that are not *res judicata*, except the cases provided in the CCP, may be appealed.

Any case participant is entitled to file an appeal. Appeals are lodged to the first instance court, the judgment of which is appealed against. An appeal cannot be based on circumstances that have not been indicated to the first instance court. An appeal cannot involve claims not filed in case hearing at the first instance court. Claims inherently linked to the action filed are not considered to be new claims (e.g., adjudgment of penalty, interest, profits, etc.).

The CCP requires that an appeal may be lodged within 30 days upon passing of judgment by the first instance court. The term for lodging an appeal can be renewed if the court acknowledges that the term was missed due to valid reasons. A petition to renew an expired term for lodging an appeal cannot be submitted if more than 3 months have passed since the day the court judgment was pronounced.

Case hearing under appeal proceedings is limited to actual and legal basis of the appeal and verification of absolute grounds for invalidity of the judgments. An appeal instance court hears a case within the limits established in the appeal, unless required otherwise by a public interest and remaining within the appeal limits would lead to infringement of rights and legal interests of a person, the society, or the state.

An appeal is usually considered by written procedure. Nonetheless, an appeal may be considered by oral procedure if the court acknowledges the necessity of an oral hearing. Participants of proceedings may submit a motivated petition to consider the case by oral procedure; however, the petition is not binding to the court.

The appeal instance court shall pass and pronounce its judgment within 30 days from the last date of case hearing at the court session. Judgment becomes *res judicata* at the moment of its announcement.

A dispute is usually deemed to have been solved definitively as soon as the judgment has been passed. The case, however, may be finished by a ruling to dismiss the case or leave the action unheard. In considering a dispute, the first instance court also passes rulings that solve procedural issues (e.g., adjudgment of payment of stamp duties, correction of a procedural document, stay of proceeding, etc.). There are certain specific characteristic of the appeals against such rulings. The rulings may be appealed against by appeal procedure, by lodging a separate appeal to the appeal instance court separately from the court judgment only in cases provided for under the CCP or where the court ruling prevents the case from progressing further. The appeal may be lodged within 7 days from the date of the ruling. Where a court ruling under appeal pursuant to the CCP has been passed by written procedure, a separate appeal may be lodged within 7 days from the date of submission of the certified copy of ruling. The first instance court, when accepting the separate appeal (except for the cases, where a civil case was dismissed by the ruling under appeal), may dismiss the ruling under appeal and continue into case proceedings. In case the first instance court refuses to accept the separate appeal, it refers the case with the appeal to the appeal instance court.

9.5.11 Cassation Proceedings

The Supreme Court of Lithuania is the only cassation court in Lithuania.

Judgments and rulings passed by appeal instance courts may be appealed against and reviewed by cassation procedure established in the CCP. A cassation appeal may be lodged by any case participant directly with the Supreme Court of Lithuania within 3 months of the day the judgment or ruling being appealed became *res judicata*.

Cassation is impossible concerning judgments and rulings of the first instance court that have not been reviewed by appeal proceedings.

A selection panel of three judges formed by the Chairman of the Supreme Court of Lithuania or Chairman of the Civil Cases Division of the Supreme Court of Lithuania should hear a case by cassation procedure. In 2015, 2523 cassation appeals were lodged with the Supreme Court of Lithuania, of which only 574 appeals were accepted for consideration by the selection panel.[134]

A cassation court, acting within the limits of the cassation appeal, verifies the judgments and rulings appealed against only in terms of application of the law. A cassation court is bound by the circumstances determined by the first and appeal instance courts. The court, however, is entitled to act beyond the limits of the cassation appeal if required by a public interest and if remaining within the appeal limits would lead to infringement of rights and legal interests of a person, the society, or the state.

A cassation case may be heard after the expiry of the term for lodging a cassation appeal. An appeal is usually considered by written procedure. The panel of judges may determine case hearing by oral procedure if this is decided as necessary.

Ruling of the cassation court is final, not subject to appeal, and *res judicata* from the day it is passed; explanations set out in the ruling of a court of cassation are compulsory for the court rehearing the case.

9.5.12 Starting Fresh Proceedings

The starting of fresh proceedings is an option stage of civil proceedings aimed at ensuring legitimacy in the civil proceeding, i.e., at preventing any potentially incorrect and unfounded judgments from remaining *res judicata*. Fresh proceedings can be started only in the event of sufficient grounds, at the request of the parties and third persons, as well as persons not involved in the proceedings. The Prosecutor General of the Republic of Lithuania may submit petitions to start fresh proceedings in order to protect a public interest.

Fresh proceedings can be started if the following grounds exist: if the European Court of Human Rights recognizes that the decisions of the courts of the Republic of Lithuania in civil cases contradict the European Convention for the Protection of Human Rights and Fundamental Freedoms and/or its additional protocols, in which the Republic of Lithuania is a participant; where new essential circumstances in the case that were not and could not be known to the applicant during the hearing of the case are newly revealed; the knowingly false explanations of a party or third party or testimony of a witness, the knowingly false opinion of an expert, a knowingly false translation, or the falsification of documents or material evidence, due to which a wrongful or unfounded judgment was passed; if the court made a decision concerning the rights and duties of parties not involved in the hearing of the case; if an obvious error in the application of the rules of law was made in the decision of the first instance court that may have influenced the adoption of an illegal decision that was not reviewed by an appeal procedure.

[134]See: the Report for the Year 2015 by the Supreme Court of Lithuania: http://www.lat.lt/lt/naujienos/metiniai-pranesimai.html.

The petition to start fresh proceedings is impossible if it relates to *res judicata* court judgments on marriage annulment or marriage dismissal, where at least one of the parties has entered into a new marriage or registered partnership after the decision has become *res judicata*, and in bankruptcy cases.

The petition to start fresh proceedings may be lodged within 3 months from the day when the person lodging the petition has or should have learned about the circumstances forming the basis for starting the fresh proceedings. The petition cannot be lodged if more than 5 years have passed since the judgment or ruling has become *res judicata*. Repeat petition to start fresh proceedings on the same grounds is not permitted.

9.5.13 Enforcement Procedure

The CCP governs the procedure of enforcement of court judgments. Application of the enforcement procedure norms is laid down in the Judgement Enforcement Instruction approved by the Minister of Justice and other legal normative acts. The system of private judicial officers has been implemented since January 1, 2003.

The Law on Judicial Officers distinguishes[135] a judicial officer's functions and provided services in judicial officers' activities. A judicial officer enforces the enforceable documents provided for under the laws, states actual circumstances under a court order, transfers and serves documents under a court order on natural and legal persons in the Republic of Lithuania, and performs other functions prescribed by law.

An enforceable document of the special form issued by a court—writ of execution—serves as the basis for enforcement procedure.

An enforceable document is issued to a creditor that submits it for enforcement to the chosen judicial officer. If the debtor fails to enforce the judgment within the established period, the judicial officer initiates the coercive enforcement procedure. Costs of the procedure are exacted from the debtor.

In cases of pecuniary recovery, the judicial officer identifies and seizes the debtor's assets. The judicial officer has the right to receive information on the debtor and debtor's assets.

The primary method of property realization is foreclosure sale of the seized property. As of January 13, 2013, foreclosure sale is implemented in Lithuania by electronic means only. The starting price of property sold by foreclosure makes 80% of the market value of the property. In case no one has purchased the property, the property is subjected to a second foreclosure sale, where the starting price makes 60% of the market value of the property.

Upon realization of property, the recovered amounts of money, following proportionate money division system, are used to cover the enforcement costs and to pay to the creditor.

[135] *The Law on Judicial Officers of the Republic of Lithuania*. Official Gazette, 2002, No. 53-2042.

Recovery from debtor's salary or equivalent income widely applies in Lithuania. The maximum of 50% may be recovered by a judicial officer from the share of the debtor's salary, which does not exceed the minimum monthly wage established by the government, and the maximum of 70% may be recovered from another share of the debtor's salary, which exceeds the established minimum monthly wage.

In case of nonpecuniary recovery (e.g., eviction from the dwelling, transfer of the child, obligation on termination of certain actions), the court may order the paying of fines for failure to comply with the judicial officer's demands.

9.5.14 International Civil Proceedings

The CCP establishes the priority of national jurisdiction whereby if the case belongs to the jurisdiction of the courts of the Republic of Lithuania at the moment of the filing of an action, the jurisdiction remains unaffected regardless of any changes in the conditions at a later date.

If the courts of the Republic of Lithuania are competent to hear the civil cases as provided for by the rules of jurisdiction in the CCP, the competence is not dismissed if the same case is heard by a court in a foreign country. A court hearing the case has the duty to verify whether or not the case belongs to the jurisdiction of the courts of the Republic of Lithuania at its own initiative. If, after an action has already been filed, the court states that the case does not belong to the jurisdiction of courts of the Republic of Lithuania, the petition remains unheard.

In hearing family disputes, family cases belong to the jurisdiction of the courts of the Republic of Lithuania if at least one of the spouses is a national of the Republic of Lithuania or is a person without citizenship residing permanently on the territory of the Republic of Lithuania. If both spouses' (even foreign nationals) permanent place of residence is located on the territory of the Republic of Lithuania, the cases relating to their family are heard solely by courts of the Republic of Lithuania. Solely the courts of the Republic of Lithuania hear the cases related to the legal relationship between parents and children, and also adoption, if at least one of the parties is a national of the Republic of Lithuania or a person without any citizenship permanently residing on the territory of the Republic of Lithuania or if both parties' permanent place of residence is located on the territory of the Republic of Lithuania.

Judgments passed by foreign courts (arbitration courts) may be enforced in the Republic of Lithuania only after they are recognized by the Court of Appeal of Lithuania as a state authority authorized to recognize the judgment. No recognition is required for *res judicata* judgments passed by foreign courts regarding nonproperty disputes between parties who are not nationals of the Republic of Lithuania, unless such judgment is the basis for registration of a marriage act or other acts of civil state or other rights in the public register.

Judgments passed by foreign courts are recognized on the basis of international treaties. The CCP does not apply the principle of mutual recognition, and judgment of a foreign court may be recognized and enforced even if an international treaty does not exist.

References

[No author named] (1997) Civilinė teisė: vadovėlis (Civil law: manual). Vijusta, Kaunas

Ambrasaitė G, Norkus R (2014) Legal aspects of insolvency of natural persons in the Baltic states. Juridica International, 21/2014. http://dx.doi.org/10.12697/JI.2014.21.16

Bakanas A, Mikelėnas V (eds) (2003) Lietuvos Respublikos Civilinio Kodekso Komentaras. 1 leidimas (Commentary on the civil code of Republic of Lithuania), 1st edn. Justitia, Vilnius

Bitė V, Jakuntavičiutė G (2014) Types of companies' management bodies under Lithuanian law. Eur Sci J 10(16):43–64

Dambrauskaitė A (2010) Paveldėjimo teisių perleidimo sandoriai (Transfer of the rights of succession). Jurisprudencija 4(122):111–133. https://www.mruni.eu/upload/iblock/859/6_Dambrauskaite.pdf

Mikelėnas V (2001) Tarptautinės privatinės teisės įvadas (Introduction to international private law). Justitia, Vilnius

Mikelėnas V (2002) Unification and harmonisation of law at the turn of the millennium: the Lithuanian experience. Uniform Law Rev 2000/2

Mikelėnas V (2005) The main features of the new Lithuanian contract law system based on the civil code of 2000. Juridica Int 10:42–50

Mikelėnas V, Keserauskas Š (2002) Civilinio kodekso komentaras. Trečioji knyga: šeimos teisė (Commentary of civil code of the Republic of Lithuania. Third book: family law). Justitia, Vilnius

Mikelėnas V et al (2001) Lietuvos Respublikos Civilinio kodekso komentaras, Pirmoji knyga, Bendrosios nuostatos (Commentary of civil code of the Republic of Lithuania, book one, general provisions). Justitia, Vilnius

Mikelėnas V et al (2003) Lietuvos Respublikos Civilinio kodekso komentaras, Šeštoji knyga, Prievolių teisė (I) (Commentary of civil code of the Republic of Lithuania, book six, law of obligations I). Justitia, Vilnius

Pakalniškis V (2004) The doctrine of property law and the civil code of the Republic of Lithuania. Jurisprudencija 50:55–65. http://search.proquest.com/openview/5847bcb8bb5bf958cff96b34a76a6430/1?pq-origsite=gscholar

Pakalniškis V (2015) Valdymas ir valdymo gynimas Lietuvos Respublikos civiliniame kodekse (Management and Defence of Management in Lithuanian Civil Code). https://repository.mruni.eu/handle/007/14097

Sagatys G (2006) Vaiko teisė į šeimos ryšius (Child's rights to family ties). Teisinės informacijos centras, Vilnius

Vitkevičius PS (2006) Šeimos narių turtiniai teisiniai santykiai (The property relations of family members). Justitia, Vilnius

Westmore B (2016) Scaling new heights: achievements and future challenges for productivity convergence in Lithuania. Working papers, 1307. https://www.oecd.org/eco/scaling-new-heights-achievements-and-future-challenges-for-productivity-convergence-in-Lithuania.pdf

World Bank (2016) Doing business. Lithuania. http://www.doingbusiness.org/data/exploreeconomies/lithuania/

MIX
Papier aus verantwortungsvollen Quellen
Paper from responsible sources
FSC® C105338

If you have any concerns about our products,
you can contact us on
ProductSafety@springernature.com

In case Publisher is established outside the EU,
the EU authorized representative is:
Springer Nature Customer Service Center GmbH
Europaplatz 3, 69115 Heidelberg, Germany

Printed by Libri Plureos GmbH
in Hamburg, Germany